D1591081

Studies in Church History

56

(2020)

THE CHURCH AND THE LAW

THE CHURCH AND THE LAW

EDITED BY

ROSAMOND McKITTERICK
CHARLOTTE METHUEN
ANDREW SPICER

PUBLISHED FOR
THE ECCLESIASTICAL HISTORY SOCIETY
BY
CAMBRIDGE UNIVERSITY PRESS
2020

© Ecclesiastical History Society 2020

Published by Cambridge University Press
on behalf of the Ecclesiastical History Society
University Printing House, Cambridge CB2 8BS, United Kingdom

First published 2020

ISBN 9781108839631

ISSN 0424–2084

Bible quotations are taken from the Authorized (King James) Version. Rights in
the Authorized Version in the United Kingdom are vested in the Crown.
Reproduced by permission of the Crown's patentee, Cambridge University
Press.

SUBSCRIPTIONS: *Studies in Church History* is an annual subscription journal
(ISSN 0424–2084). The 2020 subscription price (excluding VAT), which
includes print and electronic access, is £116 (US $187 in the USA, Canada and
Mexico) for institutions and £64 (US $103 in the USA, Canada and Mexico) for
individuals ordering direct from the Press and certifying that the volume is for
their personal use. An electronic-only subscription is also available to institutions
at £90 (US $144 in the USA, Canada and Mexico). Special arrangements exist
for members of the Ecclesiastical History Society.

Previous volumes are available online at www.cambridge.org/StudCH

Printed in the United Kingdom by Bell & Bain Ltd
A catalogue record for this publication is available from the British Library

Contents

Contents

Contents

Preface

The theme of *Studies in Church History* 56 is 'The Church and the Law'. The volume comprises a selection of peer reviewed articles drawn from the range of communications presented at the Ecclesiastical History Society's Summer Conference at Sidney Sussex College, Cambridge in July 2018 and its Winter Meeting at the Institute for Historical Research, London in January 2019. The theme was proposed by Professor Rosamond McKitterick, who served as president of the society for 2018–19.

Professor McKitterick's theme has resulted in a rich and wide-ranging collection of papers which offer insights into the complex interactions between churches and secular law and intertwining of their interests. We should like to thank Professor McKitterick for proposing this theme and for her able presidency. Thanks are due also to all those who offered contributions and submitted their papers for consideration for the volume. We are grateful to those who reviewed the contributions, thereby helping the society to ensure that the volume is of the highest quality. A particular contribution has been made, also to this volume, by Dr Tim Grass; we thank him for the engagement he brings to his editorial work and to his involvement in the society more widely. We are grateful to the Ecclesiastical History Society for the funding which supports this post.

We are very grateful also to the society's conference secretary, Dr David Hart, whose work, planning and engagement ensured that the Summer Conference and Winter Meeting went without a hitch. He was assisted by the conference teams at Sidney Sussex College, by staff at the Institute for Historical Research, and by the society's secretary and treasurer, Dr Gareth Atkins and Simon Jenkins.

The Ecclesiastical History Society offers two annual prizes for articles accepted for publication in *Studies in Church History*. This year, the Kennedy Prize, for the best contribution by a postgraduate student, was awarded to Dan D. Cruickshank for his article 'Debating the Legal Status of the Ornaments Rubric: Ritualism and Royal Commissions in Late Nineteenth- and Early Twentieth-Century

England'. The President's Prize, for the best contribution by an early career scholar, goes to Dr Robert A. H. Evans for his article 'God's Judgement in Carolingian Law and History Writing'. These articles demonstrate excellent scholarship: we extend our congratulations to both authors.

Charlotte Methuen
University of Glasgow

Andrew Spicer
Oxford Brookes University

Contributors

Anne C. Brook
   Bradford

Paul Cavill
   Senior Lecturer in Early Modern British History, University of
   Cambridge; Fellow of Pembroke College, Cambridge

Dan D. Cruickshank
   Postgraduate student, University of Glasgow

Nicholas Dixon
   Postgraduate student, Pembroke College, Cambridge

Peter W. Edge
   Professor of Law, Oxford Brookes University

Robert A. H. Evans
   Chaplain, Christ's College Cambridge

Laura Flannigan
   Postgraduate student, Newnham College, Cambridge

Manfred Henke
   Historical Researcher, New Apostolic Church North and East
   Germany, Hamburg

Felicity Hill
   Lecturer in History, University of St Andrews

Ralph Houlbrooke
   Professor Emeritus, University of Reading

Caroline Humfress
   Professor of Mediaeval History, University of St Andrews

Marija Koprivica
   Assistant Professor, Department of History, University of
   Belgrade

Contributors

Samuel Lane
    Postgraduate student, Christ Church, Oxford

Alison K. McHardy
    Reader in Medieval English History, University of Nottingham
    (retired)

Rosamond McKitterick
    Professor Emerita of Medieval History, University of
    Cambridge; Faculty of Archaeology, History and Letters,
    British School at Rome

Chelsea Rcutcke
    Postgraduate student, University of St Andrews

Ben Rogers
    Tutor in History, University College Dublin

Jacqueline Rose
    Senior Lecturer in History, University of St Andrews

Andrew Spicer
    Professor of Early Modern European History, Oxford Brookes
    University

Catherine Sumnall
    Fellow in Geography, Sidney Sussex College, Cambridge

Tijana Surlan
    Justice, Constitutional Court of the Republic of Serbia

R. N. Swanson
    Research Fellow, Institute of Advanced Studies in Humanities
    and Social Sciences; Professor, Research Center for Social
    History of Medicine, School of History and Civilization,
    Shaanxi Normal University, China; Emeritus Professor of
    Medieval Ecclesiastical History, University of Birmingham

John W. B. Tomlinson
    Director of Studies, St John's College, Nottingham

Contributors

Martin Wellings
    Oxford

Sarah White
    Research Fellow, University of St Andrews

David L. Wykes
    Director, Dr Williams's Trust and Library, London

Tim Yung
    Postgraduate student, University of Hong Kong

Abbreviations

AJLH	*American Journal of Legal History* (1957–)
ARG	*Archiv für Reformationsgeschichte* (1903–)
BIA	Borthwick Institute for Archives
BJES	*British Journal of Educational Studies* (1952–)
BL	British Library
BN	Bibliothèque nationale de France
Bodl.	Bodleian Library
CChr	Corpus Christianorum (Turnhout, 1953–)
CChr.SL	Corpus Christianorum, series Latina (1953–)
CCR	*Calendar of the Close Rolls Preserved in the Public Record Office, 1227–1550*, 62 vols (London, 1902–55)
CCT	Corpus Christianorum in Translation (Turnhout, 2010–)
CERC	Church of England Record Centre
CERS	Church of England Record Society
ChH	*Church History* (1932–)
CICan	E. Richter and E. Friedberg, eds, *Corpus iuris canonici*, 2 vols (Leipzig, 1879–81)
CPReg	*Calendar of Entries in the Papal Registers relating to Great Britain and Ireland* (London / Dublin, 1893–)
CRL	Cadbury Research Library, University of Birmingham
CRS	Catholic Record Society
CSCO	Corpus Scriptorum Christianorum Orientalium (Paris, 1903–)
CSPD	Calendar of State Papers, Domestic
CYS	Canterbury and York Society
EHR	*English Historical Review* (1886–)
EME	*Early Medieval Europe* (1992–)
ET	English translation
HL	Huntington Library
HMC	Historical Manuscripts Commission
HistJ	*Historical Journal* (1958–)
HR	*Historical Research* (1986–)
HThR	*Harvard Theological Review* (1908–)
JBS	*Journal of British Studies* (1961–)

JECS	*Journal of Early Christian Studies* (1993–)
JEH	*Journal of Ecclesiastical History* (1950–)
JLH	*Journal of Legal History* (1980–)
JMedH	*Journal of Medieval History* (1975–)
JRS	*Journal of Roman Studies* (1911–)
JThS	*Journal of Theological Studies* (1899–)
L&P	J. S. Brewer, James Gairdner and R. H. Brodie, eds, *Letters and Papers, Foreign and Domestic, of the Reign of Henry VIII*, 21 vols in 35 pts (London, 1862–1932)
LHR	*Law and History Review* (1983–)
LMA	London Metropolitan Archive
LPL	Lambeth Palace Library
LW	*Luther's Works*, ed. J. Pelikan and H. Lehmann, 56 vols (St Louis, MO, 1955–86)
MGH	Monumenta Germaniae Historica inde ab a. c. 500 usque ad a. 1500, ed. G. H. Pertz et al. (Hanover, Berlin, etc., 1826–)
MGH Capit.	Monumenta Germaniae Historica, Capitula regum Francorum, 2 vols (1883–97)
MGH Conc.	Monumenta Germaniae Historica, Concilia (1893–)
MGH Epp.	Monumenta Germaniae Historica, Epistolae (1887–)
MGH H	Monumenta Germaniae Historica, Hilfsmittel (1975–)
MGH Poetae	Monumenta Germaniae Historica, Poetae Latinae Medii Aevi (1881–)
MGH SRG i.u.s.	Monumenta Germaniae Historica, Scriptores rerum Germanicarum in usum scholarum seperatum editi (1871–)
MGH SRM	Monumenta Germaniae Historica, Scriptores rerum Merovingicarum (1884–1951)
MGH ST	Monumenta Germaniae Historica, Studien und Texte
MidH	*Midland History* (1971–)
n.d.	no date
NF	Neue Folge ('new series')
NH	*Northern History* (1966–)
n.pl.	no place

NRS	National Records of Scotland (formerly National Archives of Scotland)
n.s.	new series
ODNB	H. C. G. Matthew and Brian Harrison, eds, *Oxford Dictionary of National Biography* (Oxford, 2004)
OHA	Rowan Strong, gen. ed., *Oxford History of Anglicanism*, 5 vols (Oxford, 2017–18)
OHCC	Oxford History of the Christian Church
OHLE	*Oxford History of the Laws of England* (Oxford, 2004–)
OMT	Oxford Medieval Texts
P&P	*Past and Present* (1952–)
PH	*Parliamentary History* (1982–)
PL	Patrologia Latina, ed. J.-P. Migne, 217 vols + 4 index vols (Paris, 1844–65)
RH	*Recusant History* (1951–)
RSEH	Records of Social and Economic History
RO	Record Office
RS	Rerum Britannicarum medii aevi scriptores, 99 vols (London, 1858–1911) = Rolls Series
s.a.	*sub anno* ('under the year')
SC	Sources Chrétiennes (Paris, 1941–)
SCH	Studies in Church History
SCJ	*Sixteenth Century Journal* (1970–)
SelS	Selden Society
SHCM	Studies in the History of Christian Missions
SHR	*Scottish Historical Review* (1903–)
s.n.	*sub nomine* ('under the name')
Speculum	*Speculum: A Journal of Medieval Studies* (1925–)
s.v.	*sub verbo* ('under the word')
THSLC	*Transactions of the Historic Society of Lancashire & Cheshire* (1849–)
TNA	The National Archives
TRHS	*Transactions of the Royal Historical Society* (1871–)
UL	University Library
TTH	Translated Texts for Historians
VCH	Victoria History of the Counties of England (London, 1900–)

VS	*Victorian Studies* (1956–)
WA	*D. Martin Luthers Werke: Kritische Gesamtausgabe*, ed. J. K. F. Knaake et al. (Weimar, 1883–)
WA.Br	*D. Martin Luthers Werke: Kritische Gesamtausgabe. Briefwechsel*, 18 vols (1930–85)

Introduction

This volume represents a collaborative but necessarily preliminary investigation of a remarkably rich and complex topic. Christian societies generally nurture a faith for which the legal terminology of judgment, law, commandments, sanctions, covenant, punishment and forgiveness is fundamental. Law and jurisdiction underpin the events recorded in the Christian Gospels and Acts of the Apostles and are especially evident in relation to the tensions and conflict between secular authorities, Jewish religious leaders and the earliest Christians. The Christian church of course has made its 'own' law since the letters of St Paul and his successors, but the degree to which this law can be distinguished from secular law has been challenged time and time again. The early history of 'canon law' and the promulgation of the codes of the Emperors Theodosius (438) and Justinian (534) exerted a very considerable influence on the development of law and of the church thereafter. The prominence of secular authorities in church matters and the formal endorsement as 'law', for example, by the Emperor Justinian in 545 of the conciliar decisions made at Nicaea (325), Constantinople (381), Ephesus (431) and Chalcedon (451) are usually taken as being of great significance. Quite what the impact was of Justinian's endorsement beyond Constantinople, or what his endorsement meant in practice, are questions that still need to be clarified, despite the wealth of scholarship expended on the decisions made by those assembled, the precedents on which they drew and the conduct of the councils themselves. Other instances can readily be found of the church in newly converted regions coming under the special protection and legislative remit of secular rulers. Yet examination of intentions voiced in legislation can only get us so far. How knowledge of such legal prescriptions was disseminated, and what people actually did with them when faced with specific and practical problems of jurisdiction, misdemeanour, organization and aspiration, not least when they clashed with aspects of their observance of their faith, their ethical standards or their understanding of the ultimate source of authority, can only be explored through evidence of cases of challenge, conflict and resolution. My own current preoccupation with the history of the early

Studies in Church History 56 (2020), 1–6
doi: 10.1017/stc.2019.1

medieval popes has inevitably involved considerations of various representations and manifestations of papal authority in Rome, Italy and the rest of early medieval Europe in the centuries immediately following the deposition in 476 of the last Roman emperor in the West. Whatever else that event precipitated, it changed the status of Roman law in the West, and created a new context and set of political and social configurations in which the law might be acknowledged or practised.

All this provides the background to my choice of the theme for the Ecclesiastical History Society's conferences for the year 2018–19. Yet the precipitating point was a contemporary matter, given a good deal of media coverage in Britain, that coincided with the invitation extended to me to become president of the society. This was the conflict between the Marriage (Same Sex Couples) Act passed by the British parliament in 2013 and the canon law of the Church of England on marriage. This was addressed at the General Synod in 2016, which refused to 'note' the Bishops' Report; it was the vicars, rectors and priests who decided that they could not continue with the current prohibition on blessing or marrying same-sex couples in church. Such a clash between a law of parliament and the law of the church is a clear indication of the reverberations of the relationship between the church and the law and the necessity for a historical understanding of that relationship. One way to achieve such an understanding is through an appeal to contextualized case studies from Late Antiquity to the present day, such as those offered in this volume.

The theme of the church and the law can, of course, be explored from a number of different perspectives. First of all, there are the legal issues and legal consequences underlying relations between secular and religious authorities in the context of the Christian church, from its earliest emergence within Roman Palestine as a persecuted minority sect through to the period when it became legally recognized within the Roman empire, its many institutional manifestations in East and West throughout the Middle Ages, the reconfigurations associated with the Reformation and Counter-Reformation, the legal and constitutional complications (such as in the German territories that introduced Luther's Reformation, Reformation England or Calvin's Geneva), and the variable consequences of so-called secularization thereafter. What were the legal consequences and implications of the Reformation, the French Wars of Religion, the French

Revolution or the political transformations of the nineteenth and twentieth centuries? All these developments might include the confiscation and restitution of property. In the English context, the reforms of 1828–32 precipitated profound reflections on the role of the church within the state. At a conceptual level, in what circumstances is heresy an offence against the state and how is heresy defined? How does secular law incorporate, or legislate for, the church? The particular complications of the introduction of Christianity to other regions and peoples in imperial and colonial contexts are not just a modern phenomenon. Tensions between local or national political jurisdictions and the membership of a worldwide religion can be observed in many areas. Numerous other questions arise. What are the constitutional peculiarities of particular churches or ecclesiastical institutions? How did missionaries (and the rulers of the regions concerned) in conversion contexts cope with the clash between what they thought of as law and required social mores, and the laws and mores they encountered in the societies into which they were introducing the Christian church and faith? Particular case studies can shed light on the many ways in which law is invoked and acted upon.

So much work is currently being done on law and history, on legal sources in historical research and on legal culture in its social and historical contexts, that reflection on the role of the church in relation to the law seems especially timely. My own interest in codification and compilation underlies a further aspect of the theme, namely, the formation of bodies of law and the degree of historical understanding brought to the use (and abuse) or study of the law by legal practitioners. The development of canon law is a case in point. There is also the problem of definition. How early, for example, can a 'code of canon law' be said to have been defined, and what are the processes by which opinion, advice on a specific problem and conciliar decision became perceived as 'law'? What light does the transmission and reception of canon law throw on such questions? Court cases, legal challenges to authority, discussions of legal culture and legal practice, legally orchestrated clashes between secular and ecclesiastical law, and legal documents of many kinds are all considered in this volume. On many occasions in recent years, as I have indicated above with just one example from the many possible, we have been confronted with contemporary discrepancies, contradictions and even rejection by religious communities of secular laws, modern social mores or social attitudes. Particular instances where church law and civil law came into conflict are considered in this volume. A further consideration is the practice of history and the evidence on which historians can draw in order to pursue these questions. What new interpretations and perspectives has recent scholarship thrown into relief? What influence does secular governance exert on ecclesiastical governance, administration and legal records, or the conduct of courts and judicial procedure? Conversely, what influence does the church exert on the conduct of legal practice and the formation of legal culture, the definition of criminal acts or the role of punishment, or such legal and social fundamentals as property ownership, inheritance, marriage practice and legitimacy?

This volume represents a selection from the papers presented in response to the theme, the questions it raises and the possible contexts in which it might be considered, at two conferences on 'The Church and the Law' organized by the Ecclesiastical History Society, in July 2018 at Sidney Sussex College in Cambridge and January 2019 at the Institute for Historical Research in London. A wonderfully diverse range of case studies was offered by scholars from Britain, continental Europe, North America, Australia and Hong Kong. Chronologically, papers ranged from Late Antiquity to the present day; geographically, topics extended from Britain and the many countries of continental Europe as far afield as Russia, China, Australia and the Americas. Constraints of space meant that not all papers offered for publication could be included, but the wealth of case studies in this volume address specific and sometimes lurid legal cases, such as the murder of papal officials in eighth-century Rome. Further considerations are of law in theory and practice, both within the church and the wider Christian community; of communities attempting compliance with, or defiance of, the law; of the problems with both the formation of bodies of church law and variable knowledge and application thereof; and of the clashes of jurisdiction between ecclesiastical or civil courts in a number of different contexts.

The articles in this volume are illustrative not only of particular contexts and specific legal problems, and instances of resistance to secular law on the part of church groups, but also of more general topics concerning the conceptualization of law, the codification of law and the principles invoked in clashes between secular law, morality and ecclesiastical regulations. A very fruitful outcome of the emphasis on case studies is the way particular, personal and individual reactions or understandings have been set within wider regional or national developments. One example is excommunication, studied in the instance of general sentences of excommunication of unknown malefactors in twelfth-century England; another concerns procedures relating to proof by witnesses. Generally, the extraordinary social and legal history that can be dug out of bishops' registers and visitation records is striking. Many case studies are of particular individuals who were instrumental in the formation or interpretation of the law of the church, and who took particular stands as a result of their understanding of the law. A number of articles throw into relief the day-to-day working of the law by administrative officials, and the role of the clergy in the maintenance of law and order, whether in the magistracy in England or more generally in local communities elsewhere. Some political crises, such as the means by which a king might be deposed, spawned new legal procedure in which the bishops, at least in the case of the deposition of the English King Edward II, played a decisive role. Personal crises of conscience in conflict with secular laws in the cases of seventeenth-century dissenting printers, legislation regarding freedom of worship in the German states of the eighteenth and nineteenth centuries, attitudes to illegitimacy in nineteenth- and twentieth-century Austria, passive resistance to the 1906 Education Act in the United Kingdom, or the complex conjunction of emotional, aesthetic and legal judgments centred on the erection of World War I memorials, for example, all yield precious evidence about the actions and thinking of many ordinary individuals. The legal records of judicial hearings in secular and ecclesiastical courts on matters of justice, moreover, reflect how difficult it was to compartmentalize faith and trust. Another striking feature of the articles selected is the number which are based on the rich resources of parish, diocesan and national archives and court records, not least those of England. Many articles, such as those discussing dispute resolution and the taking of oaths, or what might be described as the laicization of perjury in early Tudor England, have implications far beyond the ostensibly local context in which these topics are considered. Time and again, contributions show the extent to which ecclesiastical thinking fed into the formation of secular law and judgments, as well as the ways in which secular law came under scrutiny in relation to interpretations of the law of God.

Special mention should be made of the two prize-winning articles by Dan D. Cruickshank and Robert A. H. Evans. The Kennedy and President's Prizes are awarded to contributions from a postgraduate and an early career scholar respectively. Cruickshank addresses the conflict between Protestant and Ritualist Anglicans between the Royal Commissions of 1867–70, formed to investigate 'the Rubrics, Orders and Directions for Regulating the Course and Conduct of Public Worship', and that of 1904–6 on Ecclesiastical Discipline. He focuses in particular on the disputes about the use of the Prayer Book, vestments and ornaments. As with so many of the articles in this volume, the general issues, and here specifically the degree to which secular government could regulate the church's liturgy, are given life and extra significance by the precise individual examples of the impact of legislation on ordinary people's actions, in this case their formalized devotion in the churches. Evans also addresses wider concerns by looking at the degree to which thinking about God's judgement provided the theological context for formulating the practical requirements of law and justice in relation to religious, moral and theological beliefs in ninth-century western Europe. He argues that Carolingian conceptions of law and justice were informed by a belief in divine help and mercy that left room for repentance and correction.

Finally, it is a pleasure to record my thanks to all the participants in the two conferences, as well as to the contributors to this volume, who have offered such a stimulating and many-faceted set of discussions from which all of us learnt so much. I am especially grateful to my two coeditors Charlotte Methuen and Andrew Spicer and the assistant editor Tim Grass for their critical and constructive assessments and their meticulous editorial care in the preparation of all the articles in this volume for publication.

Rosamond McKitterick

The Church and the Law in the Early Middle Ages

Rosamond McKitterick*

Sidney Sussex College, Cambridge

Two case studies from eighth-century Rome, recorded in the early medieval history of the popes known as the Liber pontificalis, *serve to introduce both the problems of the relations between secular or public and ecclesiastical or canon law in early medieval Rome and the development of early medieval canon law more generally. The Synod of Rome in 769 was convened by Pope Stephen III some months after his election in order to justify the deposition of his immediate predecessor, Pope Constantine II (767–8). Stephen's successor, Pope Hadrian, subsequently presided over a murder investigation involving Stephen's supporters. The murders and the legal process they precipitated form the bulk of the discussion. The article explores the immediate implications of both the murders and the convening of the Synod of Rome, together with the references to law-making and decree-giving by the pope embedded in the historical narrative of the* Liber pontificalis, *as well as the possible role of the* Liber pontificalis *itself in bolstering the imaginative and historical understanding of papal and synodal authority. The wider legal or procedural knowledge invoked and the development of both canon law and papal authority in the early Middle Ages are addressed. The general categories within which most scholars have been working hitherto mask the questions about the complicated and still insufficiently understood status and function of early medieval manuscript compilations of secular and canon law, and about the authority and applicability of the texts they contain.*

The murders of two papal officials *c*.774 are recorded at length in two of the eighth-century papal biographies in the *Liber pontificalis*, a history of the popes written by papal officials in the early Middle

* Sidney Sussex College, Cambridge, CB2 3HU. E-mail: rdm21@cam.ac.uk.
I am very grateful to the members of the Graduate Early Medieval Seminar, University of Cambridge, as well as to Mayke de Jong, Ira Katznelson and David McKitterick for their comments on an earlier version of this article, to the anonymous peer reviewers for constructive comments, and to my fellow editors for their help in preparing this text for publication.

Studies in Church History 56 (2020), 7–35
doi: 10.1017/stc.2019.2

Ages.[1] The entire history, in the form of serial biography, was written in stages from the sixth century onwards, and covers nearly nine hundred years, from St Peter to Pope Stephen V.[2] Little reference is made at any point in the text to any interaction between ecclesiastical and secular authorities in judicial contexts, other than those which concern heresy or the martyrdom of the earliest popes. It is all the more striking, therefore, that the case of the murders of Christopher (the *primicerius* or head of the papal administration) and his son Sergius (the *sacellarius* [paymaster] and subsequently the *secundicerius*) is accorded such a disproportionate amount of space in the narrative. Of the forty-four chapters comprising the political narrative in the Life of Hadrian, thirteen are taken up with the murders and their consequences. This case and the manner in which it was dealt with by the pope raise many important questions about ecclesiastical jurisdiction, modes of punishment and knowledge of the law more generally in the early Middle Ages that are highly pertinent to the various case studies presented in this volume.

This article, therefore, first addresses the immediate implications of this case in the context of other references to law-making and decree-giving by the pope embedded in the historical narrative of the *Liber pontificalis*. I shall then discuss the wider legal or procedural knowledge implied by these references to law. Thereafter my second case study, of the Synod of Rome in 769, exposes the meagre and often ambiguous sources on the basis of which assumptions about legal resources in the early Middle Ages have been formulated, and the general categories within which most scholars have been working hitherto. The synod's context and conclusions raise further questions about the complex and still insufficiently understood development of canon law in the early Middle Ages, its relation to papal authority, the status and function of early medieval manuscript compilations of secular and canon law, and the authority and applicability of the texts they contain. Consideration of the legal issues and legal consequences underlying relations between secular and religious authorities in the

---

[1] The title is an eighteenth-century one. The text was previously known as the *Gesta pontificum romanorum* or similar titles: see my forthcoming monograph, *Rome and the Invention of the Papacy* (Cambridge, 2020); Carmela Vircillo Franklin, 'Reading the Popes: The *Liber Pontificalis* and its Editors', *Speculum* 92 (2017), 607–29.
[2] On the *Liber pontificalis*, see also Rosamond McKitterick, 'The Popes as Rulers of Rome in the Aftermath of Empire, 476–769', in Stewart J. Brown, Charlotte Methuen and Andrew Spicer, eds, *The Church and Empire*, SCH 54 (Cambridge, 2018), 71–95.

context of the early medieval popes also exposes more general questions about the church and the law. These concern not only the engagement of secular and religious authorities with the law and what that law actually comprised (Roman law, canon law, national laws and state and royal edicts) but the very formation of such bodies of law and how and why these became recognized as law and became enforceable. There is also the problem of definition. What are the processes by which opinion and conciliar decision became perceived as 'law'? How early can a 'code of canon law' be defined, and what light does the transmission and reception of 'canon law' throw on such questions?

THE MURDER OF CHRISTOPHER AND SERGIUS

The background to my first case study is as follows. The two murdered officials, Christopher and Sergius, had served Pope Stephen III (768–72). Indeed, according to the *Liber pontificalis*, Stephen owed them his very position as pope in faction-ridden Rome.[3] The biography of Stephen (Life 96) related that Christopher and Sergius had brought about the violent deposition of Stephen's predecessor, Constantine II, after the latter had been in office for thirteen months; the mutilation by blinding and death of Constantine, his three brothers and other leaders of the Roman faction supporting him; and the election of Stephen in Constantine's place in August 768. The *Liber pontificalis* reports a bewildering succession of supporters changing sides, allegations of involvement on the part of the 'perfidious Lombards', and the emergence of a new and powerful rival to Christopher and Sergius in the person of the papal *cubicularius* or chamberlain, Paul Afiarta. Paul Afiarta effected the downfall of his rivals Christopher and Sergius,[4] who were arrested and imprisoned

---

[3] All references in the *Liber pontificalis* in this article are to Louis Duchesne, ed., *Le* Liber pontificalis. *Texte, introduction et commentaire*, 2 vols (Paris, 1886; hereafter: *LP*). The English translations quoted are those of Raymond Davis, *The Lives of the Eighth-Century Popes (Liber Pontificalis)*, TTH 13, 2nd edn (Liverpool, 2007).

[4] J. T. Hallenbeck, 'Pavia and Rome: The Lombard Monarchy and the Papacy', *Transactions of the American Philosophical Society* 72/4 (1982), 1–186; Florian Hartmann, *Hadrian I. (772–795). Frühmittelalterlichs Adelspäpsttum und die Lösung Roms vom byzantinischen Kaiser* (Stuttgart, 2006); Marios Costambeys, 'The Textual Authority of the *Liber Pontificalis*: Pope Hadrian and the Life of Stephen III', in Dorine van Espelo, Michael Humphries and Giorgia Vocino, eds, *Through the Papal*

and their eyes gouged out. Christopher died of his injuries. Sergius was left to languish in a cell in the Lateran, and died under mysterious circumstances. It was subsequently established, as we shall see, that he had been murdered.

The story is taken up in the first part of the Life of Stephen's successor, Pope Hadrian I. Although Hadrian was pope from 772 to 795, the first part of his Life (chapters 1–44), is thought to have been composed in the mid-770s, probably by the same person who provided the Lives of Hadrian's immediate predecessors, Paul I and Stephen III. In other words, this contemporary author was not only responsible for the entire sequence of narratives relating to Christopher and Sergius; he was also their colleague.[5]

The *Liber pontificalis* reports the events in a far from objective manner, but nevertheless presents the narrative as a process of enquiry. In reproducing this long section of the Life of Hadrian, I have interspersed exact quotations with summaries of the lengthier passages.[6] It starts with the claim that Paul Afiarta was culpable for the death of Sergius:

> [§9] It so happened that while Paul [Afiarta] was away … it became obvious to everyone how he had brought about the death of the *secundicerius* Sergius, blind and in his prison cell.

The passage continues to explain that at this stage the pope was still loyal to Paul, and sent a message in secrecy to Leo, archbishop of Ravenna, for Leo to detain Paul Afiarta in Ravenna or Rimini. Paul was therefore imprisoned in Rimini. In the meantime, in Rome:

> [§10] [T]he blessed pontiff began a detailed inquest [*cepit curiose … inquirere*] into the *secundicerius*'s death. He called all the gaolers together and carefully questioned them on how Sergius had been removed from his cell.

It is at this point that the narrative gives a full report of everything said and done, with the gaolers' response as follows:

Lens: Shaping History and Memory in Late Antique and Early Medieval Rome, 300–900, TTH: Contexts (Liverpool, forthcoming).
[5] Life 96.5, *LP* 1: 468–9 (Davis, *Popes*, 89).
[6] Life 97.9–17, *LP* 1: 488–91 (Davis, *Popes*, 124–8).

It was in the first hour of the night that the chamberlain Calventzulus came with the priest Lunisso and the tribune Leonatus, inhabitants of the city of Anagni, and he took Sergius away; this was while the lord pope Stephen was alive, eight days before he departed this life [i.e. 16 January 772]; and he handed him over to those Campanians.

The obvious person to summon into the papal presence to answer questions is the chamberlain Calventzulus, and the *Liber pontificalis* continues:

This chamberlain [Calventzulus] was immediately brought into their midst and interrogated as to who had ordered him to remove Sergius from the cell and hand him over to these Campanians. He replied that his orders 'had been given him by the chamberlain Paul, surnamed Afiarta, by Gregory the regionary *defensor*, by the duke John, lord Pope Stephen's brother, and by the chamberlain Calvulus, in the presence of the Campanians themselves'.

The next stage of the enquiry was to send for these Campanians, Lunisso and Leonatus:

[§11] The holy prelate sent his envoys into Campania to Anagni, and had Lunisso and Leonatus brought to Rome. Taken tightly bound into the apostolic presence, they admitted that their orders to remove and kill Sergius had come from the chamberlain Paul, Gregory the regionary *defensor*, John the lord Pope Stephen's brother, and Calvulus, also a chamberlain and Paul's wicked accomplice.

Not satisfied with these confessions and allegations, the pope added a practical investigation into the scene of the crime:

The holy pontiff immediately sent his most trustworthy ministers with these Campanians to point out the place where they had killed and buried Sergius. They made their way as far as the Merulana, to the painted arch alongside the road leading to the church of God's holy mother *ad praesepe* [i.e. Santa Maria Maggiore].[7] Close to this arch here, they opened one of the tombs and displayed Sergius's body lying in it, with a rope tightened around his throat and his entire body bruised and injured; there was no doubt that he had been throttled and buried in the earth while half alive.

---

[7] H. C. Butler, 'The Roman Aqueducts as Monuments of Architecture', *American Journal of Archaeology* 5 (1901), 175–99.

The narrative now moves to a resolution of the enquiry in describing the reactions of the Roman authorities who had been part of the enquiry and of the people who also offered an opinion about the necessity for punishment:

> [§12] When all the church's chief men and judges of the militia saw this, they and the whole people went with one accord to the Lateran patriarchate and, prostrate before the apostolic feet, they earnestly begged the bountiful pontiff to order vengeance and punishment [*emendatio*] for such an unheard-of crime, in that they had presumed cruelly to murder a blind man already much tortured, for which there was no recorded precedent. They stated that if the guilt of such a disgraceful act were not atoned for [*si talis flagitii reatus non expiaretur*], his unholy presumption and rashness would mushroom in this city of Rome, and perverse men would take courage from it and try to perpetrate even worse things.

The narrative now reverts to the papal response to these demands:

> [§13] Then the holy prelate acceding to the prayers of the judges and the whole Roman people ordered the chamberlain Calvulus and the aforesaid Campanians to be handed over to the city prefect for trial before the whole people of Rome, as is done with murderers. They were taken to the public prison of the Elephantum,[8] and tried there before the whole people. The Campanians made the same confession in this trial as they had done before, but Calvulus's heart was hardened and he confessed the whole truth only with reluctance: it was by a cruel death that he gave up the ghost in that prison. In order to cut off the huge and intolerable guilt [*tantis intolerabilibus flagitii reatibus*] of the disgraceful act, these Campanians were sent into exile to Constantinople.

This was not the end of the matter. First of all, the narrative implies that the dishonourable treatment of Christopher and Sergius required some reparation, and reports:

---

[8] For the possible location of *Elefans Herbarius* in Regio VIII opposite the Theatre of Marcellus near the present church of S. Nicola in Carcere, thought to be a post-Roman prison, see Davis, *Popes*, 126 n. 21; and the illustration of its imagined appearance from Giuseppe Gatteschi's *restauro* of 1896 (complete with elephant) in Jason Moralee, *Rome's Holy Mountain: The Capitoline Hill in Late Antiquity* (Oxford, 2018), 80.

[§14] After this the blessed pope ordered the bodies of Christopher and his son Sergius to be removed and he had them honourably buried in St Peter's.

There remained Paul Afiarta's role in the affair to deal with, and this brought the archbishop of Ravenna, where Paul was in custody, into the story.

> As for the record of the trial [*gestam vero examinationis … direxit*], Hadrian sent it to Ravenna for Paul to have a complete and orderly digest of it [*ut omnia per ordinem redigerentur*]. Leo, archbishop of Ravenna, took the record [*gesta*] and without apostolic warrant immediately handed over Paul to the consularis of Ravenna. He was tried before the whole people of Ravenna and the record [*acta*] was read out to him and so he showed his guilt of the whole crime and confessed he had perpetrated the evil deed. That was how Paul was tried. But neither the archbishop nor any Ravennans informed the holy pontiff of this though he heard it through others.

Pope Hadrian's reactions are then spelt out. So far the narrative has delivered death or exile as punishments for the perpetrators, and the trial of Paul at this stage was not what Hadrian had anticipated. He had his own ideas about what might be appropriate, but so did the archbishop of Ravenna:

> [§15] Meanwhile as the distinguished pastor and outstanding pontiff wanted to save Paul's soul and prevent its eternal loss, he had a request drawn up to send to the emperors Constantine and Leo, dealing with the blind Sergius's unholy death and asking their imperial mercy for Paul, that as punishment [*ut pro emendatione*] Paul should be taken and held in exile and prison in the districts of Greece. His thrice-blessedness sent the same request to Archbishop Leo, for him to send Paul into exile to Constantinople whether by the Venetiae or another route.

Leo replied that this was 'thoroughly inexpedient' because Maurice, son of the duke of Venice, had been captured by King Desiderius and Maurice wanted to secure his son's release by exchanging Paul for him. The narrator adds a sharp comment:

> See what an opportunity the archbishop of Ravenna cunningly grasped to snuff out Paul! And so he sent the request back to the apostolic see.

[§16] The pope then instructed his *sacellarius* Gregory ... to warn archbishop Leo firmly, to make sure Paul was kept safe, and on his return from Pavia to bring him to Rome. ...

[But as soon as he had gone] the archbishop summoned the *consularis* of Ravenna and ordered him to have Paul killed.[9]

Hadrian's reaction was two-fold:

[§17] When Gregory the *sacellarius* returned from Pavia and found Paul dead ... he greatly rebuked the archbishop – why had he presumed so to deal with Paul contrary to the apostolic injunction?

When the archbishop apologized to the pope, Hadrian wrote back:

[M]y intention was to save his soul and I had decided on the penance he would have to undergo [*nam certe ego animam eius cupiens salvare, paenitentiam eum summitti decreveram*]; that was why I sent my *sacellarius* to bring him here to Rome.

This remarkable case is given striking prominence in the Life of Hadrian overall. The crimes committed by Paul Afiarta and his accomplices included the mutilation by blinding, a distinctively cruel act that recurs a number of times in eighth-century papal and Byzantine sources, as well as in ninth-century Frankish narratives. It is usually either in relation to martyrdom or as an abuse of power by a tyrannical ruler.[10] Modern scholars have argued for a transformation in the significance of blinding in the political contexts of eighth- and ninth-century Byzantium and Francia. They have suggested that such a violent act was a manifestation of legitimate power of the prince 'in majesty' defending his person and reign, in which blinding was a commutation of a death penalty; consequently it is represented as mercifulness on the part of the ruler. Yet these Roman cases, so very

---

[9] For the politics of Ravenna, see Thomas S. Brown, *Gentlemen and Officers: Imperial Administration and Aristocratic Power in Byzantine Italy A.D. 554–800* (Rome, 1984); Thomas S. Brown, 'Byzantine Italy, *c.*680–*c.*876', in Rosamond McKitterick, ed., *The New Cambridge Medieval History*, 2: *c.700–c.900* (Cambridge, 1995), 320–48; Veronica West-Harling, ed., *Three Empires, Three Cities: Identity, Material Culture and Legitimacy in Venice, Ravenna and Rome, 750–1000* (Turnhout, 2015).

[10] Geneviève Bührer-Thierry, '"Just anger" or "vengeful anger": The Punishment of Blinding in the Early Medieval West', in Barbara Rosenwein, ed., *Anger's Past: The Social Uses of an Emotion in the Middle Ages* (Ithaca, NY, 1998), 75–91, with references to the earlier literature.

different from any notion of royal or imperial compassion, have been largely overlooked, except for a recent discussion by Jeffrey Berland. Berland argues that the *Liber pontificalis* contrived to avoid making the pope specifically responsible for the blinding of so many men by representing public mutilations as if they were private acts of revenge; the perpetrators were 'Romans' or members of particular factions in the context of disputes such as that involving Christopher and Sergius.[11] It is certainly in keeping with this interpretation that Hadrian's conduct of a formal judicial process is then depicted in the narrative as reasserting papal power and Lateran disapproval of the murders associated with his predecessor as bishop of Rome.

In investigating the murders of Christopher and Sergius, the pope dealt with leading officials of the papal administration but also with lay supporters within Rome. The forensic investigation, the interrogation of the accused, the identification of the burial place of the unfortunate Sergius and his exhumation, are all directly instigated by the pope in consultation with *iudices* and the church's chief men, with vociferous encouragement from the Roman people. This reference to popular participation may of course be a rhetorical device, but popular assent was also one of the expectations of legitimate proceedings. The written reports and description of the judicial process, culminating in the exile or death of the four perpetrators brought to trial, are presented as immediate procedures.

Such speedy expedition had been normal in late Roman judicial practice, in which a short period in prison before trial was part of the criminal process, with a prompt implementation of penalties thereafter.[12] There had also been a range of possible corporal punishments, but lengthy punitive confinement in a prison was more common for lower ranks in society.[13] From the fourth century onwards, some crimes hitherto punished with exile carried the death penalty. Although the late Roman state had recognized the role of bishops as judges and punitive authorities, there is no suggestion in the Life

---

[11] Jeffrey Berland, 'Mutilations in Eighth-Century Rome' (unpublished essay, MPhil in Medieval History, University of Cambridge, 2016).
[12] On prisons, see Julia Hillner, *Prison, Punishment and Penance in Late Antiquity* (Cambridge, 2015); Guy Geltner, *The Medieval Prison: A Social History* (Princeton, NJ, 2008).
[13] Hillner, *Prison*, 119–50; see also Guy Geltner, *Flogging Others: Corporal Punishment and Cultural Identity from Antiquity to the Present* (Amsterdam, 2014).

of Hadrian that an ecclesiastical court would actually *try* the accused, as distinct from *identifying* the accused. As we have seen, having ascertained who the perpetrators were, it was the city prefect who took over in a public trial 'as was customary for murders' (*ut more homicidantium*).[14] The narrative offers no precise detail, but the death in prison of Calvulus, who had refused to confess his crime, may indicate that he was summarily executed. The forensic investigation by Hadrian and the subsequent brief incarceration of the three culprits, Calvulus, Lunisso and Leonatus, in the prison Elefantum before trial, and the speedy outcome, therefore, could all be part of a process that had changed little since Late Antiquity.

Yet the matter cannot be left there. First of all, the representation of Hadrian as morally superior and punctilious in procedure, in comparison with his predecessor Stephen, who had so unequivocally been associated with the murders of the two papal officials, and with the cavalier action of archbishop Leo of Ravenna, however much Leo may have been following the law as he understood it, highlights the strong interpretative agenda underlying all the biographies of the popes in the *Liber pontificalis*, not just that of Hadrian. The biographies up to Life 97 of Hadrian I (772–95), moreover, were widely circulated in Carolingian Francia and in Britain as well as elsewhere in Italy. The *Liber pontificalis* is part of a cluster of authoritative histories written in the later eighth and the ninth centuries that together created a very strong imaginary framework within which 'old law' associated with Roman authority, real or not, might be understood in a new context. For this reason the *Liber pontificalis* may have played a role well beyond Rome in determining perceptions of the pope and of papal authority. Whether that authority embraced a role in law-making or promoting the law of the church, and whether the *Liber pontificalis* exerted any influence in shaping perceptions of the role of the pope in relation to the 'canon law', are further questions that need to be addressed, although we shall see that this is not entirely straightforward; I can only make some preliminary observations here.[15]

---

[14] On the prefect and his functions and probable headquarters, see Carlos Machado, *Urban Space and Aristocratic Power in Late Antique Rome (AD 270–535)* (Oxford, 2019). I am very grateful to the author for allowing me to see a copy of his book in advance of publication.

[15] For the late antique legal background, see Caroline Humfress, *Orthodoxy and the Courts in Late Antiquity* (Oxford, 2007); eadem, 'Law and Legal Culture in the Age of Attila', in Michael Mass, ed., *The Cambridge Companion to the Age of Attila*

THE LAW OF THE CHURCH IN EARLY MEDIEVAL ROME

Although I have suggested that there may have been considerable continuity between late antique and eighth-century legal practice, much remains uncertain about the possible expectations of either a secular or an ecclesiastical judicial process in eighth-century Rome.[16] It is difficult to establish precisely either the legal status or the precedents for Hadrian's action. The lack of any contemporary legal texts of Roman origin or provenance for the eighth century also makes it impossible to determine which laws or set of regulations about procedure and allocation of jurisdiction may have guided the actions of the pope or the city prefect in the centuries immediately following the deposition of the last Roman emperor in the West in 476. As we noted at the beginning, whatever else that event precipitated, it changed the status of Roman law in the West, and created a new context and set of political and social configurations in which the law might be acknowledged or practised.

Let us consider procedure and the precedents in Roman law first of all. By the late fourth century, there was a considerable amount of procedural overlap between the ecclesiastical and public spheres; from Constantine's conversion onwards, Roman law had included material relating to the church. Imperial statements were widely circulated in the Theodosian Code issued in 438, and Book 16 of the code was devoted to ecclesiastical matters.[17]

(Cambridge, 2014), 140–5; eadem, 'Patristic Sources', in David Johnston, ed., *The Cambridge Companion to Roman Law* (Cambridge, 2015), 97–118; eadem, 'Bishops and Law Courts in Late Antiquity: How Not to Make Sense of the Legal Evidence', *JECS* 19 (2011), 375–400; eadem, 'The Early Church', in W. Anders and J. Wei, eds, *The Cambridge History of Medieval Canon Law* (Cambridge, forthcoming). I am grateful to Professor Humfress for sending me a copy of the last of these articles in advance of publication.

[16] Luca Loschiavo, 'Was Rome still a Centre of Legal Culture between the 6th and 8th Centuries?', *Rechtsgeschichte – Legal History* 23 (2015), 83–108.

[17] *Theodosiani Libri XVI cum Constitutionibus Sirmondianis*, ed. Theodor Mommsen and Paul M. Meyer (Berlin, 1905; hereafter: *CTh*); ET *The Theodosian Code and Novels and the Sirmondian Constitutions*, transl. Clyde Pharr et al. (Princeton, NJ, 1952); Jill Harries and Ian N. Wood, *The Theodosian Code: Studies in the Imperial Law of Late Antiquity*, 2nd edn (London, 2012); John Matthews, *Laying down the Law: A Study of the Theodosian Code* (New Haven, CT, 2000).

Heresy, for example, became a public crime in the 380s;[18] state officials, therefore, could try those charged with heresy. Conversely, both Hillner and Wiesheu have noted the evidence relating to a bishop's potential role in criminal proceedings, other than those involving charges of heresy, from Merovingian Gaul in Gregory of Tours' Lives of Martin and Germanus, and the imposition of penance as a punishment. This suggests that ecclesiastical penance, in Gaul at least, could override public punishment and that bishops also tried cases involving public crimes, especially sexual misconduct or violence against or by clerics.[19] In Frankish Gaul, Visigothic Spain and Italy, and perhaps elsewhere, imperial Roman law remained available in the Theodosian Code long after the deposition of the last emperor in the West and the emergence of the various kingdoms of western Europe.

Manuscripts of the code survive from Frankish Gaul from the sixth century onwards, for example, in a variety of forms: in its full form; in the early sixth-century abridgement, together with the interpretations of the late Roman *iurisconsults* Gaius, Hermogenianus and Paul, created by the lawyers working for King Alaric of the Visigoths and known as the Breviary of Alaric; in the apparently private compilation from the sixth century known as the *Lex Romana Burgundionum*; in a probably Frankish version of the breviary with most of the Theodosian Code's Book 16 on ecclesiastical matters appended; and in a number of other abridgements of the breviary, including the *Lex Romana Curiensis* made at the end of the eighth century and the *Epitome Aegidii*.[20] Even in the ninth century, recourse to 'Roman law' in the Carolingian world is most usually to one of these forms of the Theodosian Code, though it is almost invariably clauses from Book 16 that are cited.

Modern discussions of legal developments in relation to the church usually invoke the sixth-century Code and *Novellae* of the Byzantine Emperor Justinian as well. Although Justinian in the mid-sixth

---

[18] *CTh* 16.1.2; see also Caroline Humfress, 'A New Legal Cosmos: Late Roman Lawyers and the Early Medieval Church', in Peter Linehan, Janet L. Nelson and Marios Costambeys, eds, *The Medieval World*, 2nd edn (London 2018), 653–73.

[19] See Annette Wiesheu, 'Bischof und Gefängnis. Zur Interpretation der Kerkerbefreiungswunder in der merowingischen Hagiographie', *Historisches Jahrbuch* 121 (2001), 1–23; Hillner, *Prisons*, 261.

[20] Simon Corcoran, 'Roman Law in Ravenna', in Judith Herrin and Jinty Nelson, eds, *Ravenna: Its Role in Earlier Medieval Change and Exchange* (London, 2016), 163–98.

century had allowed bishops to conduct criminal trials as long as they collaborated with public (a preferable term to 'secular') judges regarding the imposition of penalties, it cannot be assumed that Justinian's precepts were directly relevant to eighth-century practice in the city of Rome, even if there were some knowledge of his code in early medieval Italy.[21] With the partial reconquest of Italy by Justinian's generals in the middle of the sixth century, one might have expected Justinian's Code, Digest and Institutes to have been circulated. There is so little evidence for this that it is one reason to doubt the extent and durability of Byzantine control in Italy in the sixth or early seventh centuries. The earliest extant manuscripts of the second edition (534) of Justinian's Code are a possibly Italian fragment from the sixth century now in Cologne, Historisches Archiv, Best 7050B(130), and Verona, Biblioteca Capitolare LXII (60). Each was palimpsested in Italy in the seventh and eighth centuries respectively, with new texts written on top of them. The top script of the Cologne fragment is a Latin glossary and that of the Verona palimpsest is the *Concordia canonum* of Cresconius, a 'systematic' canon law collection, arranged by topic rather than chronologically.[22] Short extracts from Justinian's Code, mostly from Book 1, all of which concerns church matters, were also incorporated into a number of ninth-century Frankish and Italian compilations of legal material.[23] In addition, half a dozen verbatim quotations by Pope Gregory I (590–604) from the code (Books 1, 7 and 9) in Letter 13.49 were recycled in various contexts during the ninth century by Hincmar of Rheims, among others.[24] Further, some key elements of the prescriptions in Justinian's *Novellae* in its original Greek were incorporated into the Latin abridgement known as the *Epitome Juliani*, which is attested in

---

[21] For discussion of some aspects of relations between Rome and Byzantium in the Early Middle Ages, see Rosamond McKitterick, 'The Papacy and Byzantium in the Seventh- and Early Eighth-Century Sections of the *Liber pontificalis*', *Papers of the British School at Rome* 84 (2016), 241–73.

[22] On the manuscripts, see E. A. Lowe, *Codices Latini Antiquiores*, 12 vols (Oxford 1935–71; hereafter: *CLA*), 8: 1167, 4: 513; Cresconius, *Concordia canonum* (*Die Concordia canonum des Cresconius. Studien und Edition*, ed. Klaus Zechiel-Eckes, 2 vols, Freiburger Beiträge zur mittelalterlichen Geschichte, Studien und Texte 5 [Frankfurt am Main, 1992]).

[23] Simon Corcoran, 'The Codex of Justinian: The Life of a Text through 1,500 years', in Bruce W. Frier, ed., *The Codex of Justinian: A New Annotated Translation with Parallel Latin and Greek Text* (Cambridge, 2016), xcvii–clxiv, at cxlviii–cxlix.

[24] Ibid. cxxi.

Italy in fragments from the eighth century and in full copies from
north of the Alps in the ninth century.[25] This in its turn was
abridged.[26] One possible general justification for the understanding
of what was 'customary' in Rome by the eighth century might be a
statement attributed to the Emperor Constantine in 333 and surviving in the informal compilation of Roman imperial laws from the
fourth and fifth centuries known as the Sirmondian Constitutions.
This allows for judicial decisions by a bishop to be upheld, while
enforcement was the responsibility of the prefect.[27] In the absence
of specific procedural regulations or any details concerning the respective punishments for clerical or secular culprits or their crimes, it may
be that older Roman law still provided the framework, if not the particular prescriptions, within which justice was administered. Thus
Roman law could have continued to provide at least judicial and

---

[25] St Gallen, Stiftsbibliothek, csg 1395, CLA VII, 986. For further information on manuscripts of the *Epitome Juliani*, see the *Bibliotheca legum* project, a database of Carolingian
secular law texts led by Karl Ubl, online at: <http://www.leges.uni-koeln.de>, accessed
30 May 2018. See also Charles Radding and Antonio Ciaralli, eds, *The* Corpus Iuris
Civilis *in the Middle Ages: Manuscripts and Transmission from the Sixth Century to the
Juristic Revival*, Brill's Studies in Intellectual History 147 (Leiden, 2007), 37; Wolfgang
Kaiser, *Die Epitome Iuliani. Beiträge zur römischen Recht im frühen Mittelalter und zum
byzantinischen Rechtsunterricht*, Studien zur europäischen Rechtsgeschichte 175
(Frankfurt am Main, 2004). On extracts from the *Epitome Iuliani* in the Carolingian
capitulary collection compiled by Ansegis, see Stefan Esders and Steffen Patzold, 'From
Justinian to Louis the Pious: Inalienability of Church Property and the Sovereignty of
a Ruler', in Rob Meens et al., eds, *Religion and Power in Early Medieval Europe: Essays
presented to Mayke de Jong on her 65th Birthday* (Manchester, 2016), 371–92; Stefan
Esders, 'Roman Law as an Identity Marker in Post-Roman Gaul (5th–9th Centuries)',
in Walter Pohl et al., eds, *Transformations of Romanness in the Early Middle Ages:
Regions and Identities*, Millennium Studien / Millennium Studies 71 (Berlin, 2018),
325–44.
[26] The *Summa de ordine ecclesiastico* in Berlin, Deutsche Staatsbibliothek, Phillipps 1735
(Burgundy, s.VIII/IX), is another instance of selections from the Epitome of Julian. It is
clearly a copy of an earlier original for it is incomplete. On St Gallen, Stiftsbibliothek, csg
722, see below, 32.
[27] *Constitutiones Sirmondiae* (*Theodosiani libri XVI cum Constitutionibus Sirmondianis et
leges novellae ad Theodosianum pertinentes*, ed. T. Mommsen and P. M. Mayer, 2 vols in 3
[Berlin, 1905]). See the discussion by A. J. B. Silks, *The Theodosian Code: A Study*
(Amsterdam, 2007); and the suggestions made by Mark Vessey, 'The Origin of the
Collectio Sirmondiana: A New Look at the Evidence', in Harries and Wood, eds,
Theodosian Code, 178–99, with reference to the earliest surviving manuscript of the full
texts of these eighteen imperial statements from Constantine to Theodosius in this collec-
tion: Deutsche Staatsbibliothek, Phillipps 1745 (Burgundy, *c*.700); *CLA* 8: 1061.

procedural guidance and the basis for a demarcation of roles (to put it no more strongly), for Pope Hadrian in the 770s.

The earliest manuscript in which the Sirmondian Constitutions survive offers a possible context for the way such a framework might have been constructed. It was produced as part of the intense conciliar and canonical activity in the archdioceses of Lyon and Vienne in the later sixth and seventh centuries, and it is generally accepted that the Sirmondian Constitutions themselves also date from this period.[28] It was, in Mark Vessey's words, 'a time and milieu in which special efforts were being made to coordinate Roman law with the law of the church and to produce, or at least to invoke, the textual warrant for both'.[29] That there may well have been similar developments in Italy, and even in Rome itself, remains to be established.[30]

Only particular cases can shed any light on how legal problems were resolved in early medieval Rome and what legal resources may have been available. Thus the procedure described in Life 97 of the *Liber pontificalis* may well indicate that some ambiguities persisted, both about jurisdiction within Rome between the bishop and the city prefect and regarding what counted as an 'ecclesiastical' matter, given that both Christopher and Sergius were papal officials. There might have been sufficient flexibility, or else uncertainty, in the procedure to be followed, for a particular practice to have been overridden, in the narrative at least, by the people of Rome begging the pope 'to order vengeance and punishment' (*ut vindictam atque emendationem fieri praecepisset*),[31] precipitating Hadrian to take charge of the initial phase of the process.

The use of the word *emendatio*, however, relates to the subsequent penalty for the offenders, not the initial procedure. It appears to signal a shift away from an earlier Roman legal understanding of swift retributive punishment, especially in relation to capital crimes, to a wish to reform an offender by punitive imprisonment or other means. By the

---

[28] Hubert Mordek, *Kirchenrecht und Reform im Frankenreich. Die* Collectio Vetus Gallica: *die älteste systematische Kanonessammlung des fränkischen Gallien. Studien und Edition*, Beiträge zur Geschichte und Quellenkunde des Mittelalters 1 (Berlin, 1975).

[29] Vessey, 'Collectio Sirmondiana', 198–9.

[30] The work to substantiate this supposition remains to be done, but the *Concordia canonum* is one indication of a similar activity undertaken in northern Italy to those evident in Frankish manuscripts: see *Cresconius*, ed. Zechiel-Eckes.

[31] *LP* 1: 490 (Davis, *Popes*, 128).

sixth century, as Julia Hillner has demonstrated, in both Justinian's *Novellae* and in various cases that appear in the letters of Pope Gregory I, exile and monastic confinement had become a relatively frequent alternative form of punishment for specific crimes, such as heresy, sexual misdemeanours by ecclesiastics or violence perpetrated against clerics.[32] By the eighth century, the rehabilitation of the criminal is an oft-voiced concern, and far more in keeping with the role of penance, remorse and an educative period of banishment, if not permanent exile to a far-away monastery.[33] *Emendatio*, usually to be translated as 'correction' or 'reform',[34] linked with the penalty of 'exile' that was invoked for the Campanians Lunisso and Leonatus as well as potentially for Paul Afiarta, could be therefore understood as reformative as well as punitive. Although exile had been a common enough fate within Roman law, in which the two principal aspects were *relegatio* and *delegatio*, the latter including a loss of property, there is no specific indication that these legal measures extended in law texts to capital crimes such as murder. We can only surmise that the way of thinking about criminals as sinners and a wish to save their souls was something with which papal thinking was imbued from the time of Pelagius I (556–61) and Gregory I onwards.[35] These two popes had dealt with a number of cases of the crimes mentioned in the Theodosian or Justinianic codes: religious dissent, violence against clerics and sexual misbehaviour. The extrapolation of such thinking to Hadrian's concern with the salvation of Paul Afiarta's soul is thus a curious extension of a Roman idea in order to punish a secular crime. It suggests that the two ideas of 'reform' of an offender, firstly by punishment and secondly by penance, were entwined in notions of justice in eighth-century Rome.[36]

When it came to the punishment of the ultimate instigator, Paul Afiarta, the pope had a clear conception of his role which echoes the

---

[32] Hillner, *Prison*, 281–2, 293–8.

[33] Mayke de Jong, 'Monastic Prisoners or opting out? Political Coercion and Honour in the Frankish Kingdoms', in eadem, Frans Theuws and Carine van Rhijn, eds, *Topographies of Power in the Early Middle Ages*, Transformation of the Roman World 6 (Leiden, 2001), 291–328.

[34] Standard Latin dictionaries such as Lewis and Short or Niermeyer cite instances from the sixth century onwards, including papal letters, for *emendatio* meaning 'reform' and 'bringing to perfection'.

[35] Hillner, *Prison*, 298–313.

[36] Ibid. 1–2.

notion implicit in the use of *emendatio* put into the mouths of the Roman people by the narrator of the Life of Hadrian. The text explains that Hadrian wished to save the souls of the murderers as well as that of Paul, the chief instigator of the crime. The pope's talk is thus of penance and penitential exile in monastic confinement. In the event, of course, matters were taken out of Hadrian's hands by Leo, archbishop of Ravenna, who appears to have had a different view of the matter: in Leo's custody, Paul was charged before the public civil authority and executed. Ultimately the *Liber pontificalis* portrays a direct clash between perceptions of how punishment should be delivered, rather than a clash of authority in conducting the trial. Yet even these different perceptions accord with the possibilities of legal judgments, not least if a bishop were presiding over the case. The only jurisdictional element articulated was Hadrian's fury that Leo as archbishop of Ravenna had disobeyed the pope's orders. Elsewhere in the *Liber pontificalis*, the concern with papal legislative activity in an ecclesiastical context is a recurring element of the narrative.

THE KNOWLEDGE AND DEVELOPMENT OF CANON LAW

Let us turn now to the second case study, also recorded in the *Liber pontificalis,* for the light it might shed on the knowledge and development of canon law, and on papal authority more generally.

The decisions taken at the Synod of Rome in April 769 appear to be a dramatic instance of the politics of legitimation in action.[37] The synod was convened by Pope Stephen III some months after his election in order to justify the deposition of his immediate predecessor Constantine II (767–8). At the end of the four days of the synod, Leontius the *scriniarius* mounted the ambo inside the basilica and announced the synod's conclusions. Then from the same ambo three bishops, Gregory of Silva Candida, Eustratius of Albano and Theodosius of Tivoli, threatened anathema for anyone transgressing

---

[37] On *damnatio memoriae* and the politics of legitimation, see, for example, Harriet I. Flower, *The Art of Forgetting: Disgrace and Oblivion in Roman Political Culture*, Studies in the History of Greece and Rome (Chapel Hill, NC, 2006); Charles W. Hedrick, *History and Silence: Purge and Rehabilitation of Memory in Late Antiquity* (Austin, TX, 2000); Mark Humphries, 'From Usurper to Emperor: The Politics of Legitimation in the Age of Constantine', *Journal of Late Antiquity* 1 (2008), 82–100.

the synod's decisions.[38] As a statement of the authority behind the new rules for papal election and the decisions formulated, this could not be clearer.

The records of the entire proceedings of the synod survive in the narrative summary incorporated into the Life 96 of Stephen III in the *Liber pontificalis*. A portion of the *Acta* for the first day is also extant in a ninth-century Verona manuscript, but only extracts from the synodal record of the third day and the new rules for papal election then agreed survive in a number of canonical collections in the tenth and eleventh centuries, such as those of Rather of Verona, Anselm of Lucca and Deusdedit.[39] In these tenth- and eleventh-century instances, the synod is referred to as providing a precedent for deposition of a bishop and action in relation to any ordinations carried out by the man deposed.

Since I have explored the case of Pope Constantine II elsewhere, neither the horrible violence meted out to him, members of his family and his loyal episcopal colleagues by Pope Stephen's faction, the question of the legal justification for Stephen's actions, nor even the subsequent record of the synod's new rules are, despite the theme of this volume, my concern here.[40] Instead, I wish to explore the wider context and implications of this synod and its personnel for our understanding of the church and the law in the early Middle Ages. The possible role of the *Liber pontificalis* in bolstering the imaginative and historical understanding of papal and synodal authority is one element of this. The fundamental questions of the wider legal or procedural knowledge and development of both canon law and papal authority, within which the new rules for papal elections were formulated and recorded, also need to be considered.

Thirteen of the bishops assembled in Rome for the synod had been summoned from Francia. Stephen had sent his legate Sergius to Francia with an invitation to Charlemagne and Carloman, the new rulers of the Frankish realm, asking them to send

---

[38] Life 96.21–4, *LP* 1: 476–7 (Davis, *Popes*, 98–9).

[39] *Epistolae Karolini aevi III*, MGH Epp. 5, 120–1.

[40] Rosamond McKitterick, 'The *damnatio memoriae* of Pope Constantine II (767–768)', in Ross Balzaretti, Julia Barrow and Patricia Skinner, eds, *Italy and Medieval Europe: Papers for Chris Wickham on the Occasion of his 65th Birthday*, P&P Book Series (Oxford, 2018), 231–48.

... some bishops, who were skilled, learned in all the divine scriptures and the teachings of the holy canons, and thoroughly expert [*ut aliquantos episcopos gnaros et in omnibus divinis Scripturis atque sanctorum canonum institutionibus eruditos*], to hold a council in this city of Rome to deal with that unholy presumption of novel error and rashness which Constantine the intruder into the holy see had dared to perpetrate.[41]

Pope Stephen subsequently received from 'the Christian kings of the regions of the Franks twelve bishops, approved men, who were very learned in the divine scriptures and the *caerimonia* of the holy canons' (*Dirigentes scilicet ipsi christianissimi reges XII episcopos ex eisdem Francorum regionibus, nimis divinis Scripturis et sanctorum canonum cirimoniis doctos ac probatissimos viros*).[42] The list of the Frankish bishops (primarily metropolitans) who were sent in answer to this summons is extant in only one manuscript, a mid-ninth-century copy of the *Liber pontificalis* written at Auxerre and now in Leiden, Universiteitsbibliotheek, VLQ 41.[43]

These Frankish bishops include one Anglo-Saxon and one Italian, and a few who had assumed office during Pippin III's reign, but half of them (marked with asterisks) had apparently been newly appointed in late 768 or 769.[44] Despite their newness in post, the text implies that the Frankish bishops, in contrast to the Italians, were chosen for their expertise in both the content of the law and the orchestration of a synod. The obvious question is what that knowledge might have

[41] '[U]t aliquantos episcopos gnaros et in omnibus divinis scripturis atque sanctorum canonum institutionibus eruditos ac peritissimos dirigerent ad faciendum in hanc Romanam urbem concilium pro eadem impia novi erroris ac temeritatis praesumptione, quam antefatus Constantinus apostolicae sedis pervasor ausus est perpetrare': Life 96.16, *LP* 1: 473 (Davis, *Popes*, 94–5).
[42] Life 96.17, *LP* I: 473 (Davis, *Popes*, 125).
[43] For analysis of the Frankish bishops, see Rosamond McKitterick, *Charlemagne: The Formation of a European Identity* (Cambridge, 2008), 299–302 (where I wrongly described Constantine II as an 'anti-pope' on p. 300), particularly Table 6. The order of names in the list is possibly significant. Given that this is the work of an Auxerre scribe, he may deliberately have given prominence to Sens, the metropolitan of Auxerre. George of Amiens had formerly been bishop of Ostia and first arrived in Francia as a papal legate in 756. Thereafter some element of ecclesiastical hierarchy is observed, for the next five bishops are all metropolitans (indicated in **bold** in Table 1), although Reims is almost at the end of the list. There are a number of Frankish ecclesiastical provinces not represented (Cologne, Arles, Trier, Rouen and Bordeaux), but this may reflect the considerable number of vacancies in sees during this decade as well as the feasibility of particular bishops being able to travel to Rome.
[44] For further comment, see McKitterick, '*Damnatio memoriae*'.

Table 1. The Frankish bishops from *Liber pontificalis*, Life 96.16 in Leiden VLQ 41 (Auxerre, s.IX^med).

Wilchar of **Sens**, archbishop of the province of the Gauls
George of Amiens (province of Reims)
Wulfram of Meaux (province of Sens)
Lull of **Mainz**
*Gaugenus of **Tours**
Ado of **Lyon**
*Hermenarius of **Bourges**
*Daniel of **Narbonne**
*Erembert of Worms, province of Mainz
Bernulf of Würzburg, province of Mainz
*Erlolf / Herulf of Langres, province of Sens
Tilpin of **Reims**
*Gislebert of Noyon, province of Reims

---

comprised in the seventh decade of the eighth century. Why should the pope have sent to Francia for learned bishops?

Such a papal appeal to the Franks for experts in divine Scripture and holy canons might seem extraordinary or even unwarranted, but it actually reflects the predominance of Frankish Gaul in terms of the surviving evidence for the creative compilation of legal material. Even to refer to 'legal material' in this general way, of course, begs the question of definition and requires an explanation, not only of what the formulation 'legal material' might cover for the early Middle Ages, but also of the role of the church in the assembly of such material. The remainder of this article, therefore, moves to a consideration of the wider questions raised by Hadrian's murder enquiry and the synod of 769.

Canon Law Compilations in the Early Middle Ages

Law in the early Middle Ages is a notoriously and fearsomely complex topic, and the legal culture and legal practice of the post-Roman polities of early medieval Europe, including the British Isles, are very diverse. Arguments have been particularly lively in relation to how we can identify law in action in relation to the surviving evidence. Modern historians currently think in terms of the broad categories of Roman law, the barbarian *leges* or law codes (from Ireland, Anglo-Saxon England, Frankish Gaul, Spain, Lombard Italy,

Burgundy, Bavaria, Alemannia and Saxony), royal edicts, especially of the Frankish rulers, ecclesiastical or 'canon' law and biblical law. There has also been a wealth of scholarship devoted to every aspect of law since at least the sixteenth century, and even now a number of web-based projects are attempting to map these categories, such as the Projet Volterra on Roman law and various data-collecting and editing projects relating to Carolingian canon law, capitularies, formulae and the vast mid-ninth-century compilations attributed to 'Benedictus Levita' and 'Pseudo-Isidore' of material from church councils and papal letters that is notorious for containing so much that is judged to be forgery.[45] Generally these projects, perhaps partly due to their having had to make a case for funding, are somewhat inclined to reinvent the same wheel, and take too little notice of a great deal of anglophone, francophone, Italian and Spanish exposition and interpretation. What these database projects have in common is their focus on the extant early medieval manuscripts of all these texts, and an enormous amount of meticulous comparative documentation and record has been achieved over the past century and a half. There are only occasional attempts to look across project boundaries.

Why might this be a problem? Essentially the manuscript compilers of 'law' in the early Middle Ages appear to have had different objectives and criteria from those that modern scholars suppose, and modern scholars, whether unwittingly or on principle, are too much influenced by eighteenth- and nineteenth-century conceptions of legal systems and too little inclined to view these texts as resources, as elaborate historical reference material, or as an arsenal of material such as comparable precedents or solutions to be invoked in arguments and decision-making, or as all of these. All the new legal text project leaders are building on earlier assemblies in print of information about texts and manuscripts, not least the classic volumes by

---

[45] See Projet Volterra, University College London, online at: <https://www.ucl.ac.uk/volterra>; *Bibliotheca legum*, online at: <www.leges.uni-koeln.de/>; the Carolingian Canon Law project, overseen by Abigail Firey in Lexington, Kentucky, online at: <http://ccl.rch.uky.edu>; *Capitularia*. Edition der fränkische Herrschererlasse, led by Karl Ubl, online at: <http://capitularia.uni-koeln.de/en/project/>; *Formulae – Litterae – Chartae*, a legal formulae project led by Philippe Depreux in Hamburg, online at: <https://www.formulae.uni-hamburg.de>; Projekt Pseudo-Isidor, online at: <http://www.pseudoisidor.mgh.de/>; Edition der falschen Capitularien des Benedictus Levita, online at: <http://www.benedictus.mgh.de/>.

Friedrich Maassen on canon law, Wasserschleben and Schmitz, Raymund Kottje and his students on penitentials, Hubert Mordek on Frankish capitularies, and the bibliographical guides and commentaries provided by Lotte Kéry, Detlev Jasper, Horst Fuhrmann and Linda Fowler-Magerl.[46]

These general categories and decisions taken long since about classification create a false impression of clearly distinct demarcation, obscure the variety within each broad category and duck the problems of definition and function of any kind of law in the new political configurations of the post-Roman world. Even deciding what can be counted as 'secular' and what as 'ecclesiastical' is not straightforward. As we have seen, Roman emperors and barbarian kings from the fourth century onwards contributed many rulings concerning the church and religion in their own legislation as well as in their statements as presidents of, or attenders at, the assemblies of clerics now known as church councils or synods.

The texts generally referred to as canon law also comprise an enormous variety of conciliar material from the first four ecumenical councils, as well as from other councils such as those of Ancyra, Gangra, Neocaesarea, Antioch and Carthage, and the provisions relating to the clergy known as the 'Apostolic canons', originally in Greek but translated into Latin in the sixth century by Dionysius Exiguus, to which Dionysius added a number of papal letters. This major Italian collection is called the *Dionysiana*, and achieved wide circulation north of the Alps from the late eighth century onwards in the

---

[46] Friedrich Maassen, *Geschichte der Quellen und der Literatur des canonischen Rechts im Abendlande bis zum Ausgang des Mittelalters*, 2 vols (Graz, 1870); F. W. H. Wasserschleben, *Die Bussordnungen der abendländischen Kirche* (Halle, 1851); Herman J. Schmitz, *Die Bußbücher und die Bußdisciplin der Kirche nach handschriftliche Quellen dargestellt* (Mainz, 1883); Raymund Kottje, *Die Bußbücher Halitgars von Cambrai und des Hrabanus Maurus. Ihre Überlieferung und ihre Quellen* (Berlin, 1980); Ludger Körntgen, Ulrike Spengler-Reffgen and Raymund Kottje, *Paenitentialia minora Franciae et Italiae saeculi VIII–IX* (Turnhout, 1994); Hubert Mordek, *Bibliotheca regum francorum manuscripta. Überlieferung und Traditionszusammenhang der fränksichen Herrschererlasse*, MGH H 15; Lotte Kéry, *Canonical Collections of the Early Middle Ages (ca.400–1140): A Bibliographical Guide to the Manuscripts and Literature* (Washington DC, 1999); Detlev Jasper and Horst Fuhrmann, *Papal Letters in the Early Middle Ages* (Washington DC, 2001); Linda Fowler-Magerl, *Clavis canonum. Selected Canon Law Collections before 1140: Access with Data Processing*, MGH H 21 (here the 'selection' is of 'virtually all the systematically arranged collections'; that is, she omits the chronologically arranged collections).

augmented form known as the *Dionysio-Hadriana*.[47] Dionysius's Latin texts of the ecumenical councils were also incorporated into many manuscript collections by independent compilers who added selections in various permutations from the synods and church councils of North Africa, Visigothic Spain, Frankish Gaul, papal Rome and Lombard Italy between the fifth and eighth centuries, and variable choices from extant papal letters, generally termed decretals, of which the earliest appears to be that of Pope Siricius (384–99).[48]

Some compilers kept the texts in chronological order. Others rearranged all the canons they chose by topic into what are known as the 'systematic' collections. All these collections are usually lumped together as canon law collections and given names according to their predominant content, the first editors, the origin of the manuscripts, the current library location or (when known) the compiler: so the *Collectio Hispana, Hibernensis, Quesnelliana, Dacheriana, Sanblasiana, Corbeiensis, Remensis, Vaticana, Parisensis, Dionysiana* and so on.[49]

This is what I think of as the 'Maassen legacy'. Pursuit of particular conciliar canons and particular configurations thereof has been a preoccupation of all those walking in Maassen's footsteps. Maassen was utterly committed to the fifth- and sixth-century origins of most of the collections he registered, and all manuscripts were described as witnesses to these hypothetical early collections. The latest text in any collection was taken to be the *terminus ad quem* rather than the compilation being related to the date of the manuscript. Any collection actually containing any texts later than the supposed original core collections was relegated to the status of an excrescence, sullying the late antique collection, rather than as indicating a later compiler assembling a variety of material for a particular place and purpose in a later context. Others besides myself have begun to see individual manuscripts as pieces of evidence in their own right, rather than

[47] Dionysius Exiguus, *Collectio canonum* (Hubert Wurm, ed., *Studien und Texte zur Dekretalensammlung des Dionysius Exiguus* [Bonn, 1939]); Latin versions did exist of some of the texts, such as 'Prisca and 'Isidore': see C. H. Turner, *Ecclesiae Occidentalis Monumenta Iuris Antiquissima*, 2 vols (Oxford, 1899, 1930).

[48] Klaus Zechiel-Eckes, *Die erste Dekretale. Der Brief Papst Siricius an Bischof Himerius von Tarragona vom Jahr 385 (JK 255), aus dem Nachlass mit Ergänzungen*, ed. Detlev Jasper, MGH ST 55.

[49] Rosamond McKitterick, *History and Memory in the Carolingian World* (Cambridge, 2004), 245–59.

merely as a means to trace a chain of copying of a particular group of canons. Of course, an extraordinary amount has been achieved in tracing the transmission of early church councils and papal decretals. More recently, the discussion of conciliar canons and collections was given a tremendous boost and extra rigour and vigour by the late Klaus Zechiel-Eckes, whose work on the pseudo-Isidorean decretals moved on from identification of late antique canonical collections to open up the possibility of active engagement with the content of these canons in contemporary debate in the eighth and ninth centuries. Even so, the emphasis of all the pseudo-Isidorean research remains the identification and dating of sources, and classification of it as genuine or false.

As indicated earlier, the status of any of these texts as 'law', on what their authority rested and how they might have been used are all problematic, as many recent studies have begun to observe. Rob Meens has commented, for example, that it is not 'easy to distinguish a canon law collection from neighbouring genres such as florilegia, penitentials or episcopal statutes'.[50] Rachel Stone has pointed out that early medievalists have long been accustomed to think of the secular laws or *leges* as the resource on which negotiation and settlement might be based, as distinct from a 'fixed body of rules systematically applied'.[51]

This seems to me to be eminently applicable to ecclesiastical law as well. In the intentions of the compilers, from those assembling the early African councils or Pope Hormisdas's commission to Dionysius Exiguus in the early sixth century onwards, there was no doubt a wish to provide a new system of rules and decisions particularly relating to the church or pertinent for church affairs (a more neutral phrase than 'ecclesiastical' or 'canon law'), and the structural models of Roman and imperial law and what Caroline Humfress has referred to as its 'substantive principles' played a role in this.[52] This is most obviously visible in the layout of the early medieval codices, with such details as rubrics and headings, tables of contents, numbering of clauses, and details of origin and date of sets of conciliar

[50] Rob Meens, Review of Fowler-Magerl, *Clavis canonum*, *EME* 17 (2009), 219.
[51] Rachel Stone, 'Canon Law before Canon Law: Using Church Canons, 400–900', paper given at the Cambridge Late Antique Network Seminar, 14 February 2014; W. Davies and P. Fouracre, eds, *The Settlement of Disputes in Early Medieval Europe* (Cambridge, 1986).
[52] Humfress, *Orthodoxy and the Courts*, 211.

and papal decisions very similar to that of the compilations of Roman law and the *leges*.

Nevertheless, for an early medievalist, verdicts such as that of Helmholz as recently as 2015, reflecting, alas, all too current a misconception, that a 'true system of canon law ... only [came] into existence in the twelfth century' are distinctly unhelpful.[53] Such a verdict elides the difference between the compilation of records of decisions and the decisions themselves, ignores how blurred supposed boundaries between 'law' and authoritative texts might have been, fails to consider how 'old' secular or ecclesiastical law with Roman authority (real or not) might have been received and understood in new contexts, and gives insufficient attention to the indications of contemporary attitudes reflected in the manuscript evidence. As far as the category of 'canon law' is concerned, moreover, the implications of the inclusion of the papal letters in compilations of conciliar canons need to be considered rather than simply taken on board as self-evidently appropriate and unproblematic additions.

Many Frankish and north Italian codices from the later eighth and the ninth centuries combine Roman law and *leges* with teaching materials about legal practice and definitions of law and justice, legal formulae and Frankish capitularies. Similarly, collections of canons from church councils appear in codices with papal letters, sermons, prayers, commentaries on the creed and historical narratives. In addition to canons from councils and papal letters, compilers often incorporated summaries and presentations of law relating to the church promulgated, or purporting to be promulgated, by Roman secular authorities.

One such text is the so-called *summa de ordine ecclesiastico* from the Berlin manuscript referred to earlier (Staatsbibliothek, Phillipps 1735). Of fifty-two promised capitula in the list of contents, it contains §§1–30 and a few words of §31. Its most recent editors suggest that it may have been produced in Frankish Gaul during the seventh or eighth centuries. In due course it provided one of the sources for the mid-ninth-century collection of 'Benedictus Levita', often associated with the corpus of canon law material known collectively as the Pseudo-Isidorean Decretals. Many other centres in the early

---

[53] R. H. Helmholz, 'Canon Law and Roman Law', in Johnston, ed., *Cambridge Companion to Roman Law*, 396–422, at 397.

Carolingian realm were actively compiling legal collections of all kinds.

Although it makes excellent sense to map the hard evidence of the surviving manuscripts, the form in which the evidence has survived has by its very complexity created a major problem of method. This is true of all the manifestations of law in the early Middle Ages. The general categories within which most scholars have been working mask the questions about the complicated and still insufficiently understood status and function of the manuscript compilations themselves, and the authority and applicability of the texts they contain. In what respect might these texts have legal status and authority? Why and by whom were they compiled? What criteria governed the selection of the material they contain? How were these books used, and by whom? Many manuscripts from the early Middle Ages, and especially from the later eighth and ninth centuries, contain what might be called legal chrestomathies, that is, they appear to be carefully designed compilations containing many different types of rules, regulations and decisions relating to political, social and religious behaviour, often together with what could be labelled supporting documents and information. Two final examples can serve briefly to illustrate the sheer variety of contents and the creativity of the compilers:

The first example is from Rhaetia, now in St Gallen, Stiftsbibliothek, csg 722, compiled *c*.800. It contains a compilation of late antique Roman law known as the *Lex romana curiensis* and dated to the late eighth century, together with a selection of clauses on ecclesiastical matters from the *Epitome Juliani*, and the episcopal statutes of Bishop Remedius of Chur (800–20) which concern both Christian observance and secular criminal topics.[54]

The second manuscript example is Paris, BN, lat 2123. Its contents are as follows:

1^r–^{v}: First Council of Ephesus §§1–4 with the declaration on original sin.

2^r–5^v: Lateran Council (649).

---

[54] Claudio Soliva, 'Zu den Capitula des Bischofs Remedius von Chur aus dem beginnenden 9. Jht.', in Clausdieter Schott and Claudio Soliva, eds, *Nit anders denn liebs und guets. Festschrift Karl. S. Bader* (Sigmaringen, 1986), 166–72; see also Reinhold Kaiser, *Churrätien im frühen Mittelalter. Ende 5. bis Mitte 10. Jahrhunderts* (Basel, 1998). A major portion of this codex comprises palimpsested leaves from a sixth-century uncial copy of Hilary of Poitiers, *In Psalmos*.

6^r–17^r: *Incipit dogma id est doctrina uel definitio de fide* (Gennadius of Marseilles, *De ecclesiasticis dogmatibus*).

17^r–24^v: commentaries on the Creed (Keefe nos 58, 254, 309, 386), often added to Pope Leo I's *Ep.* 165 as *testimonia de fide*.[55]

24^v–29^r: Leo, *Ep.* 165, and texts on the doctrine of the Incarnation attributed by the scribe to Hilary of Poitiers, Ambrose of Milan, John of Constantinople and others.

29^v–51^r: the Cononian Epitome of the *Liber pontificalis*.

52^v–54^v: Polemius Silvius, *Laterculus* (*nomina provinciarum*), with *Notitia galliarum*.

54^v–64^r: the *Canones Gregorii* version of the *Iudicia Theodori*.

64^v–104^v: the *Decreta maiorum* (= *Collectio canonum Herovalliana*), including the decree *De libris recipiendis et non recipiendis* usually attributed to Gelasius (fols 73^v–76^r).

105^r: Council of Carthage (418) §1 on original sin.

105^v–153^v: *Collectio Flaviniacensis* (a legal formulae collection).

153^v–156^v: Isidore of Seville, *Etymologiae* 16.25–6 (on weights and measures) and 2.10 (definitions of *lex*, *constitutio*, *edictum* and *mos*).

As can be seen, the diversity of this manuscript's contents includes particular statements about doctrine. The legal material includes the very distinctive 'canon law' collection known as the *Herovalliana*, which starts with a statement about the catholic faith and the Creed, defines the canon of Scripture and the biblical apocrypha, and then inserts the decree *De libris recipiendis et non recipiendis* usually (but erroneously) attributed to Gelasius (fols 73^v–76^r).[56] It is significant that the dominant theme of the abbreviated version of the *Liber pontificalis* in this codex emerges, because of the clauses selected, as the legislative activity of the popes referred to earlier.

---

[55] Susan Keefe, *A Catalogue of Works pertaining to the Explanation of the Creed in Carolingian Manuscripts* (Turnhout, 2012).

[56] E. von Dobschutz, *Das Decretum Gelasianum de libris recipiendis et non recipiendis im kritischen Text*, Texte und Untersuchungen zur Geschichte der altchristlichen Literatur 38/4 (Leipzig, 1912). For discussion, see Rosamond McKitterick, *The Carolingians and the Written Word* (Cambridge, 1989), 200–5.

The codex effectively provides the historical and specifically Roman and Western framework, within which the statements from the Eastern church councils as well as the definitions of the bishops' diverse responsibilities, and texts to assist a bishop in the discharge of these responsibilities, are to be understood.

Both these codices, like many other examples that could have been cited, appear to be independent products of late Merovingian and Carolingian ecclesiastical preoccupations and the Frankish reception of earlier Christian historical, doctrinal and legal texts. Not only is the number of compilations of early medieval 'canon law' credited to particular dioceses in Frankish Gaul far greater than for Italy, but Frankish manuscripts form the greater majority of the surviving early medieval corpus of manuscripts and fragments containing the texts designated as 'canon law' by modern scholars.[57]

The appeal for learned bishops from Francia by Stephen III in 769, therefore, accords with the clear association of many of these manuscripts with particular Frankish bishops, though some of those who can be identified occupied their sees slightly later than Stephen's request. I have already alluded to the extraordinary compilations of both canon and Roman law in Frankish Gaul. Bishops have been associated with much of this activity. Cuthbert Turner, for example, identified activity in Arles as crucial for the dissemination of 'canon law', that is, conciliar decrees and papal 'decretals' in Gaul in the sixth century.[58] Mordek's work on the compilation known as the *Vetus Gallica* (*c.*600) established that a later redaction at Autun can be associated with Bishop Leodegar (663–80).[59] Other compilations from the Frankish kingdoms in the later Merovingian and early Carolingian period are also associated with particular bishops. Thus the compilation known as *Collectio Frisingensis* (Munich, Bayerische Staatsbibliothek, Clm 6434) was produced at Freising during the

[57] Rosamond McKitterick, 'Knowledge of Canon Law in the Frankish Kingdoms before 789', *JThS* n.s. 36 (1985), 97–117, reprinted in eadem, *Books, Scribes and Learning in the Frankish Kingdoms, 6th–9th Centuries* (Aldershot, 1994), II.
[58] Turner, *Monumenta*; on decretals, see Jasper ad Fuhrmann, *Papal Letters*; Geoffrey D. Dunn, 'The Emergence of Papal Decretals: The Evidence of Zosimus of Rome', in Geoffrey Greatrex and Hugh Elton with Lucas McMahon, eds, *Shifting Genres in Late Antiquity* (Farnham, 2015), 81–92; idem, '*Collectio Corbeiensis, Collectio Pithouensis*, and the earliest Collections of Papal Letters', in Bronwen Neil and Pauline Allen, eds, *Collecting Early Christian Letters: From the Apostle Paul to Late Antiquity* (Cambridge, 2015), 175–205.
[59] Mordek, *Kirchenrecht und Reform*.

incumbency of Bishop Arbeo (764–8). Two other canon law compilations (Vienna, Österreichische Nationalbibliothek, Cod. 418, and Munich, Bayerische Staatsbibliothek, Clm 5508) are associated with Bishop Arn of Salzburg. Bishop Rachio of Strasbourg commissioned a copy of the canon law collection known as the *Collectio Hispana* in 788.[60]

CONCLUSION

This article began with a lurid murder enquiry conducted by the then reigning pope from the eighth century, and the questions it raised about procedure, punishment and legal resources in early medieval Rome. It has ended with the evidence for the compilation and commissioning of collections of legal provisions, comprising imperial, papal and conciliar decisions from Late Antiquity and the early Middle Ages on a great variety of topics, all of which had the potential to form both a body of law and a portfolio of principles and guidance. I have indicated that the role, or perceived role, of the pope, in consolidating the authority of such a portfolio needs rigorous examination. These assemblages of royal, imperial, papal and conciliar material nevertheless served as an essential resource in relation to both legal practice and conceptions of justice for secular authorities as well as for the church in the early Middle Ages.[61] How fundamental and versatile this remarkable range of resources and variety of manuscript compilations proved to be is evident in many of the case studies considered in this volume, all of which explore the legal issues and legal consequences underlying relations between secular and religious authorities throughout Christian history.

---

[60] Cologne, Dombibliothek, MS 91 is a s.VIII copy.

[61] See the articles assembled in *La Giustizia nell'alto medioevo (secoli V–VIII)*, Settimane di Studio del Centro Italiano di Studi sull'alto Medioevo 42 (Spoleto, 1995); *La Giustizia nell'alto medioevo (secoli IX–XI)*, Settimane di Studio del Centro Italiano di Studi sull'alto Medioevo 44 (Spoleto, 1997).

'Cherchez la femme!' Heresy and Law in Late Antiquity

Caroline Humfress*

University of St Andrews

In contrast with contemporary heresiological discourse, the Codex Theodosianus, *a Roman imperial law code promulgated in 438, makes no systematic gendered references to heretics or heresy. According to late Roman legislative rhetoric, heretics are demented, polluted and infected with pestilence, but they are not seductive temptresses, vulgar 'women' or weak-minded whores. This article explores the gap between the precisely marked terrain of Christian heresiologists and (Christian) legislators. The first part gives a brief overview of early Christian heresiology. The second explores late Roman legislation and the construction of the heretic as a 'legal subject' in the* Codex Theodosianus. *The third turns to the celebrated account crafted by Pope Leo I of anti-Manichaean trials at Rome in 443/4, arguing that they should be understood as part of a much broader developing regime of ecclesial power, rather than as concrete applications of existing imperial anti-heresy laws.*

INTRODUCTION: 'CHERCHEZ LA FEMME'?

In 1864, the French novelist Alexandre Dumas included the following line, spoken by a police detective, Monsieur Jackal, in the theatrical adaptation of his novel *The Mohicans of Paris*: 'There is a woman in all cases: as soon as someone brings me a report I say "look for the woman!"'[1] In popular culture, the saying '*cherchez la femme!*' is usually used to insinuate that whatever the problem is, a woman will lie behind it.[2] I am more interested, however, in the original context of

---

* School of History, University of St Andrews, 71 South St, St Andrews, KY16 9DD. E-mail: ch226@st-andrews.ac.uk.

[1] '[M Jackal] Il y a une femme dans toutes les affaires; aussitôt qu'on me fait un rapport, je dis: «Cherchez la femme!»': Alexandre Dumas, *Théâtre complet XXIV. Les Mohicans de Paris* (Paris, 1889), 103.

[2] Dumas did not, of course, invent the trope of 'bad things begin with a woman'. As Jennifer Eyl points out, '[o]ne can think of numerous literary and mythological examples: Eve in Genesis 3, Hesiod's Pandora and Helen of Troy': 'Optatus's Account of Lucilla in *Against the Donatists*, or, Women are good to undermine with', in Susan Ashbrook Harvey

Dumas' phrase: the prosecution of legal cases and the workings of criminal law. More specifically, what do we find if we 'look for the woman' in late Roman (fourth- and fifth-century) legal and heresiological writings? In an essay published in 1998, Nicola Lacey, Professor of Law, Gender and Social Policy at the London School of Economics, explores 'the unspeakable subject of sex' in relation to the present-day criminal law of England and Wales.[3] Lacey's article pivots around three fundamental issues which I shall develop as framing devices for the late Roman material being considered. First, Lacey is interested in how criminal law 'speaks' through the construction of specific legal categories and classifications;[4] in what follows, I will focus on how Roman imperial law 'spoke' through the construction of legal categories such as 'orthodoxy' and 'the heretic'. Second, Lacey is concerned with what she terms 'the relationship between sexual offences and the sexed body';[5] I am interested in how individual, sexed bodies were turned into legal subjects through late Roman trial processes. Finally, Lacey interrogates the extent to which 'shifts in cultural attitudes' influence 'coercive legal rules';[6] I am concerned here primarily with the extent to which significant shifts in early Christian heresiological discourse influenced late Roman (imperial) lawgivers.

Roman (state) legislation against heretics first appears in the fourth century. The main sources for this legislation are Book 16 of the *Codex Theodosianus*, a collection of imperial constitutions promulgated by Emperor Theodosius II in 438, and Book 1 of the *Codex Iustinianus*, first promulgated by Emperor Justinian in 529 with a second edition in 534, together with relevant *Novellae* ('new' imperial constitutions issued after 438 and 534).[7] As we shall see, the imperial

---

et al., eds, *A Most Reliable Witness: Essays in Honor of Ross Shepard Kraemer* (Providence, RI, 2015), 155–64, at 159.

[3] Nicola Lacey, 'Unspeakable Subjects, Impossible Rights: Sexuality, Integrity and Criminal Law', *Canadian Journal of Law and Jurisprudence* 11 (1998), 47–68.

[4] 'In this paper, rather than focussing on specific features of the criminal process, I shall address the question of how criminal law itself constructs the wrong of rape': ibid. 50.

[5] Ibid. 49.

[6] Ibid. 66.

[7] *Theodosiani Libri XVI cum Constitutionibus Sirmondianis*, ed. Theodor Mommsen and Paul M. Meyer (Berlin, 1905; hereafter: *CTh*; includes post-Theodosian *Novellae*); *Codex Iustinianus*, in *Corpus Iuris Civilis* (hereafter: *CICiv*), 2: *Codex Iustinianus*, ed. Paul Krüger (Berlin, 1877); Justinianic *Novellae*, in *CICiv*, 3: *Novellae*, ed. Rudolf Schöll and Wilhelm

constitutions excerpted in Book 16 of the *Theodosian Code* are over-whelmingly concerned with men and power relations between men: there are only three explicit (gendered) mentions of women in the sixty-six excerpts from imperial constitutions included in Book 16, Title 5, 'On Heretics'. Yet women feature more prominently than men in fourth- and fifth-century accounts and records of anti-heresy trials.[8] I am interested in exactly *how* and *why* women appear in these trial accounts, always in relation to the male voices of the text. My argument is that fifth-century records of heresy trials should be understood as part of a much broader developing regime of Christian ecclesial power, rather than as concrete applications of imperial anti-heresy laws.

The article divides into three main sections. The first, 'Heresy becomes a woman', gives a brief overview of early Christian heresiol-ogy and explores Virginia Burrus's argument that the 'gendered' nature of heresiological rhetoric shifted during the mid-fourth cen-tury.[9] The second explores late Roman legislation and the construc-tion of 'legal subjects' (in the sense referred to by Lacey), focusing mainly on Book 16 of the *Codex Theodosianus*.[10] Finally, the third

Kroll (Berlin, 1895). 'Imperial constitution' is the collective term for all types of author-itative communications written in the name of the emperor(s). In the extant late Roman evidence, these acts of communication usually took the (original) form of letters. For fur-ther discussion, see Simon Corcoran, 'State Correspondence in the Roman Empire: Imperial Communication from Augustus to Justinian', in Karen Radner, ed., *State Correspondence in the Ancient World from New Kingdom Egypt to the Roman Empire* (Oxford, 2014), 172–209.

[8] Comparisons could be drawn here with early modern witchcraft prosecutions: see Clive Holmes, 'Women: Witnesses and Witches', *P&P* 140 (1993), 45–78; (more broadly) Gilbert Geis, 'Lord Hale, Witches, and Rape', *British Journal of Law and Society* 5 (1978), 26–44; idem, 'Revisiting Lord Hale, Misogyny, Witchcraft and Rape', *Criminal Law Journal* 10 (1986), 319–29.

[9] Virginia Burrus, 'The Heretical Woman as Symbol in Alexander, Athanasius, Epiphanius and Jerome', *HThR* 84 (1991), 229–48. For discussion of later developments, see John Arnold, 'Heresy and Gender in the Middle Ages', in Judith Bennett and Ruth Karras, eds, *The Oxford Handbook of Women and Gender in Medieval Europe* (Oxford, 2013), 496–510.

[10] Jill Harries, *Law and Empire in Late Antiquity* (Cambridge, 1999), gives an overview of late Roman law and practice, including discussion of who made (imperial) law and an explanation of its predominantly responsive, yet at the same time proactive, nature. On the rhetorical nature of late Roman imperial law, see the classic study by Wulf Eckart Voß, *Recht und Rhetorik in den Kaisergesetzen der Spätantike. Eine Untersuchung zum nachklas-sischen Kauf- und Übereignungsrecht*, Forschungen zur byzantinischen Rechtsgeschichte (Frankfurt am Main, 1982).

part turns to the celebrated account by Pope Leo I of anti-Manichaean trials at Rome (443/4). Leo's account carefully and self-consciously draws upon and manipulates gender norms and expectations, using the Manichaeans' confessions of 'unspeakably' foul sexual acts to convict them in the legal fora of this world and the next. As we shall see, Leo did not simply seek to apply imperial law through his anti-Manichaean campaign; he sought to influence its subsequent development.

HERESY BECOMES A WOMAN

As I sat on a mountain, he who speaks these things said, I saw an animal in the air, fighting with another animal on the ground. I felt great joy because the flying one prevailed upon the earthly one. But after a while the animal on the ground turned upon the flying one, and seized it and overpowered it. The wise will understand that this story concerns every heretic who is of two minds. For it is no wonder that a pagan ['a hellene'] or a heretic who has no faith is in the church. Indeed the birds themselves are often in the church – look, there is the peacock and the Nile goose. If the heretic and the pagan spread out their hands and lift them up hypocritically, behold the birds themselves often do this, spreading their wings.[11]

Shenoute of Atripe (*c*.347–*c*.465), the leader of a large monastic community known today as the White Monastery Federation, situated across the Nile from Panopolis in Upper Egypt, addressed the words above to a church assembly, sometime during the late fourth or early to mid-fifth centuries. Using the striking imagery of two fighting creatures, Shenoute recounts a prophetic vision ('As I sat on a mountain ... I saw an animal') in order to teach the fundamental lesson that heretics and pagans are a constant danger from within. Like any expert rhetorician, Shenoute flatters his audience while expounding his message in no uncertain terms: 'The wise [that is, of course, you and me] will understand that this story refers to every heretic who is of two minds'. For Shenoute, as for late Roman legislators and (most) authors and compilers of late antique

---

[11] Shenoute, 'As I sat on a Mountain', in *Selected Discourses of Shenoute the Great: Community, Theology, and Social Conflict in Late Antique Egypt*, ed. and transl. David Brakke and Andrew Crislip (Cambridge, 2015), 39–53, at 39–40.

heresiological manuals, the heretic was the two-faced 'other' who lurked hypocritically within the church.[12] At what point, however, should we understand Shenoute's rhetorical universe as intersecting with concrete individuals and groups in early fifth-century Upper Egypt? Where the text says, 'look, there is the peacock and the Nile goose', should we imagine Shenoute pausing in his speech and pointing to real birds inside the church (or perhaps to painted images of birds on the church walls)? When he refers to the heretic and the pagan who 'spread out their hands and lift them up hypocritically', should we likewise imagine Shenoute pausing and pointing to 'real' heretics and pagans engaged in the act of prayer within the church? In other words, should we understand the birds in the church (and by analogy Shenoute's pagans and heretics) as 'real' embodied beings or as rhetorical constructs?[13]

Until twenty or so years ago, finding the heretic in late Roman texts was relatively straightforward; by which I mean that Arians, Pelagians, Nestorians and the like could exist without quotation marks around their names. To return to Shenoute, the unnamed heretics in the discourse 'As I sat on a Mountain' have tended to be identified as Origenists, a group that flourished in learned monastic environments and was subjected to 'a savage witch-hunt' (as Peter Brown termed it) by Theophilus, patriarch of Alexandria, in 400.[14] In 1992, however, Elizabeth Clark's monograph, *The Origenist Controversy* effectively challenged the idea that Origenists could be

[12] For further discussion of whether heresy always necessarily implies 'insider status' in late antique heresiological discourse, see Peter Schadler, *John of Damascus and Islam: Christian Heresiology and the Intellectual Background to Earliest Christian-Muslim Relations*, History of Christian-Muslim Relations 34 (Leiden, 2018), 20–48.

[13] For a summary of the debate over the physical presence of peacocks and Nile geese in Shenoute's church (and in Coptic churches today), see *Shenoute's Literary Corpus*, ed. Stephen Emmel, CSCO 599–600 / CSCO Subsidia 111–12, 2 vols (Louvain, 2004), 2: 611.

[14] Peter Brown, *Power and Persuasion in Late Antiquity: Towards a Christian Empire* (Madison, WI, 1992), 138. On Theophilus of Alexandria's anti-Origenist campaigns, see now Krastu Banev, *Theophilus of Alexandria and the First Origenist Controversy: Rhetoric and Power* (Oxford, 2015). On Shenoute, see further Hugo Lundhaug, 'Shenoute's Heresiological Polemics and its Context(s)', in Jörg Ulrich, Anders-Christian Jacobsen and David Brakke, eds, *Invention, Rewriting, Usurpation: Discursive Fights over Religious Traditions in Antiquity*, Early Christianity in the Context of Antiquity 11 (Frankfurt am Main, 2012), 239–61.

understood as a distinct group with a distinct theology.[15] Clark instead sought to reconstruct the polemical use of the label 'Origenist' (now to be understood within quotation marks) in theological debate and discourse. This awareness that talking about heresy necessitates a heightened rhetorical sense, alongside a subtle appreciation for processes of identity construction, is now standard in late antique studies.[16] Twenty-first-century scholars tend to approach late antique heresiological handbooks (such as Irenaeus of Lyon, *Adversus haereses*; Epiphanius of Salamis, *Panarion*; the *Refutatio omnium haeresium* attributed to Hippolytus; Theodoret of Cyrrhus, *Haereticarum fabularum compendium*; or Augustine's *De haeresibus*) as lessons in identity construction, rather than as windows onto the lived experiences of ancient Christian communities.

The 'Late Antique Cultural Turn' of the 1990s and 2000s also meant taking both women and gendered identities seriously.[17] As Judith Lieu observed in an article published in 2013: 'It has become ever more evident that the question of women belongs to the inner logic or deep grammar of the church's self-understanding.'[18] In late first-century and early second-century Christian literature,

---

[15] Elizabeth Clark, *The Origenist Controversy: The Cultural Construction of an Early Christian Debate* (Princeton, NJ, 1992).

[16] Virginia Burrus, *The Making of a Heretic: Gender, Authority and the Priscillianist Controversy* (Berkeley, CA, 1995); eadem, '"In the Theater of this Life": The Performance of Orthodoxy in Late Antiquity', in William Klingshirn and Mark Vessey, eds, *The Limits of Ancient Christianity: Essays on Late Antique Thought and Culture in Honor of R. A. Markus* (Ann Arbor, MI, 1999), 80–96; Averil Cameron. 'How to Read Heresiology', *Journal of Medieval and Early Modern Studies* 33 (2003), 471–92; Kimberley Stratton, 'The Rhetoric of "Magic" in Early Christian Discourse: Gender, Power and the Construction of "Heresy"', in Todd Penner and Caroline Vander Stichele, eds, *Mapping Gender in Ancient Religious Discourses*, Biblical Interpretation Series 84 (Leiden, 2007), 89–114; Young Richard Kim, *Epiphanius of Cyprus: Imagining an Orthodox World* (Ann Arbor, MI, 2015); Andrew Jacobs, *Epiphanius of Cyprus: A Cultural Biography of Late Antiquity* (Oakland, CA, 2016); Todd Berzon, *Classifying Christians: Ethnography, Heresiology, and the Limits of Knowledge in Late Antiquity* (Oakland, CA, 2016).

[17] As argued by Elizabeth Clark, 'The Lady vanishes: Dilemmas of a Feminist Historian after the "Linguistic Turn"', *ChH* 67 (1998), 1–31; eadem, 'Holy Women, Holy Words: Early Christian Women, Social History, and the "Linguistic Turn"', *JECS* 6 (1998), 413–30. See also Dale Martin, 'Introduction', to idem and Patricia Cox Miller, eds, *The Cultural Turn in Late Ancient Studies: Gender, Asceticism, and Historiography* (Durham, NC, 2005), 1–21.

[18] Judith Lieu, 'What did Women do for the Early Church? The Recent History of a Question', in Peter D. Clarke and Charlotte Methuen, eds, *The Church on its Past*, SCH 49 (Woodbridge, 2013), 261–81, at 280.

accusations of sexual deviance, demonic influence and promiscuity were frequently used to identify and mark out the kinds of 'false teachers' against which 2 Timothy 3: 6 warned: the *heterodidaskaloi* who worm their way into households and ensnare weak women who are weighed down with sins and led astray by diverse lusts.[19] In contrast to the weak females of 2 Timothy, Tertullian, writing in second-century Carthage, paints a picture of headstrong brazen women acting in official roles within heretical communities:

> The destruction of discipline is to them [heretics] simplicity, and attention to it they call affectation. They are in communion with everyone, everywhere. Differences of theology are of no concern to them as long as they are all agreed in attacking the truth. They are all puffed up. They all promise knowledge. Their catechumens are perfect before they are instructed. As for the women of heretics, how forward they are! They have the impudence to teach, to argue, to perform exorcisms, to promise cures, perhaps even to baptise.[20]

The heretics' way of life is a straight inversion of what Tertullian wants his readers to accept as a normative, orthodox way of life. True Christian communities, according to Tertullian, are structured hierarchically, with men on top.

Christian writings from the late first century onwards make the ideological connection between women and heresy seem 'natural', albeit in different ways and to differing effects. More specifically, Stratton comments: 'women's sexuality serves in [early Christian] discourses to locate types of Christianity on the scale of "orthodoxy" and "heresy": their sexualized bodies symbolically measure the presence of "heresy" like thermometers determining the presence of a fever'.[21] As Virginia Burrus pointed out in her classic essay of 1991, 'The Heretical Woman as Symbol in Alexander, Athanasius, Epiphanius and Jerome':

---

[19] See further Jennifer Knust, *Abandoned to Lust: Sexual Slander and Ancient Christianity* (New York, 2006), 143. Writing in the fourth century, Jerome interweaves 2 Tim. 3: 6 with his depiction of 'Manichaean orgies', during which the 'Manichaean Elect … shut themselves up alone with silly women, and between intercourse and embraces … enchant them with suggestive quotations from Virgil': Jerome, *Ep.* 22.13.3, quoted in Harry Maier, '"Manichee!": Leo the Great and the Orthodox Panopticon', *JECS* 4 (1996), 441–60, at 452.

[20] Tertullian, *De praescriptione* 41.2–8, quoted in Berzon, *Classifying Christians*, 67.

[21] Stratton, 'Rhetoric of "Magic"', 111.

[T]he historical study of women in ancient heretical movements is doubly problematic. For the heresiological sources are not only written from the point of view of a self-identified orthodoxy, but are also written by men who utilize the figure of the heretical female as a vehicle for the negative expression of their own orthodox male self-identity. Moreover, we – men and women alike – are the cultural heirs of those very orthodox men who forged the portrait of the heretical woman in the fire of their polemical rhetoric. Far from being critical and objective readers of the ancient sources, we easily resonate with the myriad of symbolic associations generated by the figure of the female heretic.[22]

The point of Burrus's article is not to unravel a series of enduring, historically static images of 'the heretical woman'. Rather, she argues convincingly for a distinct late antique development in Christian anti-heretical discourse.[23] According to Burrus, whilst the earliest Christian heresiological discourse is gendered in numerous ways (as we have seen above), 'the *topos* of heretic remains neutral as regards gender for the first three centuries'.[24] The rise of a new kind of imperial Christianity under the Emperor Constantine, however, contributed to the development of a new kind of male, orthodox, ecclesiological self-image.[25] Doctrinal and ecclesiological uses of 'the heretical woman' *topos* developed accordingly. During the course of the fourth-century, heresy literally becomes a woman.

Athanasius, bishop of Alexandria, writing in exile during the 350s against the teachings of the presbyter Arius, gives us what Burrus refers to as 'the earliest full-blown development of the figure of the heretical woman'.[26] In the opening passage of the first of his *Three Orations against the Arians*, he writes:

The so called Arian heresy, being crafty and unscrupulous, and considering that her older sisters, the other heresies, have been publicly labelled as such, pretends to wrap herself in the words of Scripture,

---

[22] Burrus, 'Heretical Woman as Symbol', 230.
[23] Ibid. 231–2; see also Nicola Denzey, *The Bone Gatherers: The Lost Worlds of Early Christian Women* (Boston, MA, 2007), 184–5.
[24] Burrus, 'Heretical Woman as Symbol', 231–2 n. 6.
[25] For a comparison with how the figure of 'the temptress' is used to construct 'exemplary male figures' in late antique rabbinic discourse, see Jordan Rosenblum, 'The Night Rabbi Aqiba slept with Two Women', in Harvey et al., eds, *Most Reliable Witness*, 67–75.
[26] Burrus, 'Heretical Woman as Symbol', 235.

> like her father the devil, and forces her way back into the Church's paradise, so that, having given herself Christian form, she might deceive someone into thinking about Christ by the most persuasive of fallacies, for she has no sound reason. And she has already misled some of the foolish, so that they are not only corrupted in what they hear, but even take and eat in the manner of Eve.[27]

According to Athanasius's rhetoric, the 'so called Arian heresy' is a daughter of the devil, to be identified with the serpent from the garden of Eden. All followers of Arius thus effectively become Eve. Athanasius's feminized idea of heresy as seductive, manipulative, deceptive, irrational and immoral may seem so natural to us today that it is easy to forget that, as Burrus argues, this was an image first developed systematically in the course of the fourth century.[28] We could multiply the examples. Epiphanius, a late fourth-century bishop in Cyprus, famously structured his catalogue of heresies, the *Panarion* or 'medicine-chest' (written 374–6), into eighty sections, one heresy for each of the eighty concubines referred to in the Song of Solomon 6: 8.[29] Heretical groups, according to Epiphanius, are adulterous concubines who have falsely taken Christ's name, in contrast to the Catholic church, which is the dove of the Song of Solomon, the perfect one, the one true virginal 'bride of Christ'.[30] As Epiphanius bluntly states: 'Do not believe a vulgar woman; for every heresy is a vulgar woman (πᾶσα γὰρ αἵρεσις φαύλη γυνή).'[31] Hence from the fourth century onwards, as Denzey suggests: 'Women emerged within church ideology not as living individuals, but as symbols of licit and illicit Christian

[27] Athanasius, *Three Orations against the Arians* 1.1–10, quoted in Burrus, 'Heretical Woman as Symbol', 236.

[28] The *systematic* development of a 'feminized' idea of heresy from the fourth century onwards was also grounded within ancient biological theories: 'The female proclivity for error is written into ancient ideas of human biology and fetal gestation: to be born female is to have ceased developing in the womb. Women are essentially "failed" or "underdeveloped" men': Eyl, 'Optatus's Account of Lucilla', 160.

[29] 'There are threescore queens, and fourscore concubines, and maidens without number. My dove, my perfect one, is only one, the darling of her mother, a chosen one to her that bore her': S. of S. 6: 8, as quoted in Epiphanius, *De Fide* 2.4 – 7.2: *The Panarion of Epiphanius of Salamis. Books II and III (Sects 47–80*, De Fide), transl. Frank Williams (Leiden, 1994), 639–44. For a detailed discussion of Epiphanius's *Panarion* and related works, see Jacobs, *Epiphanius of Cyprus*, 20–1, 176–220.

[30] Epiphanius, *De Fide* 7.1 (*Panarion*, transl. Williams, 644).

[31] Epiphanius, *Panarion* 79.8.

communities.'[32] We move now from one field of late Roman knowledge construction (the heresiological) to another (the legal).

CONSTRUCTING LEGAL SUBJECTS

This section begins with a brief note on women and Roman law, before turning to the *Codex Theodosianus* (438) and the 'unprecedented ecclesiastical Book XVI'.[33] Going beyond the question of what Book 16 of the *Codex Theodosianus* can tell us about women and (institutionalized) Christianity, I am more concerned with how religion is constructed as a distinct sphere of imperial legal discourse in Book 16 and how women are placed (or not) within that discourse. We will then narrow our focus again to Book 16, Title 5, *De haereticis*, in order to explore how exactly imperial legislators constructed heretics as legal subjects in the fourth and fifth centuries.

First, let us consider women and Roman law. As the analytical legal philosopher Leslie Green puts it 'gender is a social category superimposed upon a sexed body'.[34] The entire structure of Roman law was premised on the concept of *patria potestas*, the power of the father.[35] Recent demographic research, however, has shown that Roman fathers tended to marry late and die early. Add to this the fact that daughters and sons were usually expected to inherit equally, and in comparison with other historical legal systems we can see that elite Roman women were in a strong position relative to the Roman law

---

[32] Denzey, *Bone Gatherers*, 184.

[33] Quotation from Simon Corcoran, 'The Gregorianus and Hermogenianus assembled and shattered', *Mélanges de l'école française de Rome* 125 (2013), 285–304, at 294 (p. 10 of the edition online at: <https://journals.openedition.org/mefra/1772>, accessed 1 February 2019).

[34] Leslie Green, 'Gender and the Analytical Jurisprudential Mind', *University of Oxford, Legal Research Paper* 46 (26 August 2015), 8, online at: <https://ssrn.com/abstract=2650448>, accessed 1 February 2019. Green is here quoting the summary of 'his view' given by Joanne Conaghan, *Law and Gender* (Oxford, 2013), 18–22.

[35] John Crook, 'Patria Potestas', *Classical Quarterly* 17 (1967), 113–22, at 122, argues that the Roman legal concept of *patria potestas* needs to be divided into three distinct analytical categories: 'sacral headship; power over the persons and lives of members of the family … [what Crook terms] "gubernatorial" headship; and property headship. For the extent and intensity of each of these within the family differs from society to society.' On the late republic and early empire, see also Richard Saller, '*Patria potestas* and the Stereotype of the Roman Family', *Continuity and Change* 1 (1986), 7–22; for the later empire, see Antti Arjava, 'Paternal Power in Late Antiquity', *JRS* 88 (1998), 147–65.

of succession and property.[36] Elite late Roman women, as Clark observes, 'could, for example, retain their own property separate from their husband's, serve as guardians to their children, and [under certain scenarios] initiate divorce'.[37] The major fault line running through Roman jurisprudence was not gender but wealth and social status. In David Daube's memorable words, '[t]he have-nots, the vast majority of citizens, were right out of it.'[38] According to a constitution issued by the Emperor Constantine in 326, adultery committed by a respectable freeborn woman of high social standing reflected on society as a whole and hence should be punished; but adultery committed by a woman of low social standing reflected on no one but herself.[39] It was not worth pursuing a woman for a public crime that epitomized her lack of civil standing and respectable *mores*, if the woman in question was already deemed to have none.

As Judith Evans Grubbs has demonstrated, some (limited) fourth- and fifth-century imperial legislation was concerned with regulating both the reputations of elite Christian women and their property.[40] In the *Codex Theodosianus* there are three laws relating to Christian women and celibate lifestyles excerpted in Book 9, Title 25; two relating to widows and perpetual virgins (not necessarily Christian) in Book 13, Title 10; and one ordering that the property of 'religious' men and women who die intestate should go to their church or monastery, if they die without heirs or other claims on the inheritance.[41] Behind this legislation lie much broader shifts in patterns of elite female patronage, as Clark argues: 'The Church became a primary

[36] For further discussion, see Joëlle Beaucamp, *Le Statut de la femme à Byzance (4ᵉ–7ᵉ siècles)*, 2 vols (Paris, 1990–2); Antti Arjava, *Women and the Law in Late Antiquity* (Oxford, 1996); Caroline Humfress, 'Gift-Giving and Inheritance Strategies in Late Roman Law and Legal Practice', in Ole-Albert Rønning, Helle Sigh and Helle Vogt, eds, *Donations, Strategies and Relations in the Latin West and Nordic Countries* (London, 2017), 9–27.
[37] Elizabeth Clark, 'Ideology, History, and the Construction of "Woman" in Late Ancient Christianity', *JECS* 2 (1994), 155–84, at 171.
[38] David Daube, *Roman Law: Linguistic, Social and Philosophical Aspects* (Edinburgh, 1969), 72.
[39] *CTh* 9.7.1; *CI* 9.9.28.
[40] Judith Evans Grubbs, 'Virgins and Widows, Show-Girls and Whores: Late Roman Legislation on Women and Christianity', in Ralph Mathisen, ed., *Law, Society and Authority in Late Antiquity* (Oxford, 2001), 220–41, which also analyses the handful of laws relating to lowest-status women and Christianity.
[41] Ibid., with additional discussion of relevant imperial legislation in the post-Theodosian *Novellae* and the *Codex Iustinianus*.

outlet for female patronage, just at the moment when some older avenues of patronage were closing to aristocratic women.'[42] Under the early empire, elite women had acted as local benefactors and patrons, engaging in civic acts of euergitism alongside elite men. Under the later Roman empire, however, 'local benefaction tended to give way to the linkage between patronage and the holding of high governmental offices which were, of course, closed to women'.[43] The wealth of (some) elite women, including those such as the superrich 'aristocrat-turned-ascetic' Melanias, was redirected to charitable and religious causes, via (male) Christian ecclesiastics.[44] Hence the need for the imperial legislators to step in and regulate the extent to which the property of female ascetics and 'religious' women could – and could not – be transmitted outside their (elite) families.

As noted above, I am less concerned here with late Roman imperial legislation relating to women and the Christian church and more interested in how gender played a role in constructing the new legal category of 'the heretic' during the fourth and fifth centuries.[45] Promulgated in 438 by Emperor Theodosius II, the *Codex Theodosianus* comprises sixteen books. Each contains discrete excerpts from imperial constitutions dating back to 312, arranged chronologically under thematic rubrics (*tituli*). The fifth-century imperial commissioners who compiled and ordered it based their ordering of the material in the first fifteen books on earlier Roman legal precedents (mainly the *Praetors' Edict* and *Commentaries*, in addition to two late third-century private compilations of imperial constitutions).[46] There was no Roman law precedent, however, for how to order the legal material in Book 16. Theodosius II's editorial team thus had to come up with the eleven title headings which structure the contents

---

[42] Clark, 'Ideology, History, and the Construction of "Woman"', 179.

[43] Ibid.

[44] On Melania the Elder and her granddaughter Melania the Younger, see Catherine Chin and Caroline Schroeder, eds, *Melania: Early Christianity through the Life of one Family* (Oakland, CA, 2017). Clark, 'Ideology, History, and the Construction of "Woman"', 180, goes on to suggest that '[i]t is perhaps the Church Fathers' emotional and financial dependence on such women … coupled with their misogynistic constructions of "woman" that gives an unpleasant edge to their diatribes against rich women.'

[45] On the later fifth and sixth centuries, see Caroline Humfress, 'A New Legal Cosmos: Late Roman Lawyers and the Early Medieval Church', in Peter Linehan, Janet L. Nelson and Marios Costambeys, eds, *The Medieval World*, 2nd edn (London, 2018), 653–73.

[46] For a more detailed discussion, see Caroline Humfress, 'Ordering Divine Knowledge in Late Roman Legal Discourse', *COLLeGIUM* 20 (2016), 160–76.

of Book 16 *ex nihilo*. My argument here is that just as fourth- and fifth-century Christian theologians and ecclesiastics set about constructing a specific idea of 'the heretic', so too did fourth- and fifth-century imperial legislators. In their case, however, this was part of a much broader fifth-century reframing of the category of 'religion' itself.

Book 16 of the *Codex Theodosianus* is broadly concerned with ensuring correct relations between the human and the divine. Roman emperors had long styled themselves as responsible for overseeing and maintaining this relationship. Here, however, it is not correct human relations between humans and gods, plural, that need to be overseen and maintained, but rather relations between humans and (the Christian) God, singular. The imperial constitutions excerpted under the first and last titles of Book 16 stress that the only relationship which now matters is the one to be maintained with the supreme Christian God.[47] Titles 2 and 3 focus accordingly on the experts and specialists responsible for maintaining good relations with the Christian God: bishops and clerics of the institutional church, as well as monks.[48] Title 4 concerns those 'who argue about religion' (*De his qui super religione contendunt*) and thus threaten the safety and prosperity of the empire, as do heretics (Title 5: *De haereticis*), apostates (Title 7: *De apostatis*), Jews, Caelicolists and Samaritans (Title 8: *De Judaeis, Caelicolis, et Samaritanis*) and pagans (Title 10: *De paganis, sacrificiis, et templis*). Title 6 deals with those individuals who threaten human-divine relations by the incorrect performance of a sacred ritual.[49] Title 9 acknowledges that maintaining 'correct' relations with the Christian God also means adjusting (certain) human hierarchies, hence the rubric: 'No Jew shall have a Christian as a slave' (*ne Christianum mancipium Judaeus habeat*). An important touchstone for defining what counts as orthodox, throughout Book 16, is the male 'Catholic' episcopate. Hence *Codex Theodosianus* 16.1.2 (the famous constitution *Cunctos Populos*, issued by Theodosius I at Thessalonica on 27 February 380 and addressed to the people of Constantinople) states that

[47] *CTh* 16.1, *De fide catholica* ('On the Catholic / Universal Faith'); *CTh* 16.11, *De religione* ('Concerning "Religion"').
[48] *CTh* 16.2, *De episcopis, ecclesiis, et clericis* ('Concerning Bishops, Churches and Clerics'); *CTh* 16.3, *De monachis* ('Concerning Monks').
[49] *CTh* 16.6, *Ne sanctum baptisma iteretur* ('Holy Baptism not to be repeated').

'Catholic' Christians are to be defined as those who follow the faith of the apostle Peter as practised by Damasus, bishop of Rome and Peter, bishop of Alexandria; everyone else is to be judged 'demented and insane'.[50] This strategy of defining orthodoxy in terms of being in communion with named bishops is highlighted in later Justinianic law: the compilers of the *Codex* in 534 placed *Codex Theodosianus* 16.1.2 at the head of Book 1, so that it became *Codex Iustianus* 1.1.1.

Within the precisely marked out legal terrain of Book 16, women are referred to explicitly in only nine out of a total of two hundred and one discretely excerpted imperial texts. These nine can be loosely grouped into three categories: women, trade and employment; women and the institutional Christian church; and women and heretics. We will briefly examine each in turn.

The first category, of women, trade and employment, contains only two excerpted constitutions. *Codex Theodosianus* 16.2.10 (probably promulgated in 320) exempts clerics who engage in trade from certain extraordinary tax payments and extends the indulgence 'to their wives, children and slaves' and 'to males and females equally'. *Codex Theodosianus* 16.8.6 (issued in 339), on the other hand, refers to a specific situation where a group of Christian women had been dismissed from their jobs in an imperial weaving establishment because they had converted to Judaism. The text states that these women can be reemployed, but any Jew who leads a Christian woman astray will be subjected to capital punishment.

Our second group of constitutions from Book 16 is concerned with women in relation to ecclesiastics, ascetics and the institutional church. *Codex Theodosianus* 16.2.20 (addressed to Damasus, bishop of Rome, and read in Rome's churches on 30 July 370) states that ecclesiastics, ex-ecclesiastics and 'continents' are not to frequent the houses of widows and female wards. Clerics can receive nothing whatsoever by gift or testament from these women, unless they are related to them. A law from two years later extended this prohibition to bishops and virgins and the principle was reaffirmed by a further constitution, promulgated fifty years later at Ravenna, which adds that it is

---

[50] For a careful and nuanced discussion of this complex imperial constitution, see Neil McLynn, 'Moments of Truth: Gregory of Nazianzus and Theodosius I', in Scott McGill, Cristiana Sogno and Edward Watts, eds, *From the Tetrarchs to the Theodosians: Later Roman History and Culture, 284–450 CE* (Cambridge, 2010), 215–40, at 215–18.

not seemly for clerics to be tarnished by association with a so-called 'sister' (the broader context here is perhaps the phenomenon of 'household churches').[51] *Codex Theodosianus* 16.2.27 (given at Milan, 21 June 390) is the only constitution included in Book 16 which seems to refer to a female rank within the institutional church: 'deaconess'. According to the critical edition of Mommsen and Meyer, the text states that no woman younger than sixty years and without the requisite number of children at home can be joined to the association of deaconesses, 'according to the precept of the apostle'.[52] The woman must first arrange for the guardianship of any minor children and entrust suitable persons with the management of her property (over which she maintains certain legal rights). After she has joined the association of deaconesses, a woman is not allowed to sell any of her jewels and ornaments for the benefit of religion, but must transfer all her property, in writing, to her children, next of kin or whomever she freely chooses; she is forbidden, however, from designating any church, cleric or pauper as her heir(s).[53] The constitution ends by stating that women who shave their heads are to be kept away from the doors of churches; bishops are responsible for enforcing this.[54] Once again, two traditional Roman concerns emerge from the second group of constitutions: first, there is an attempt to prevent women from alienating family property by transferring it to extraneous persons or institutions (here, Christian clerics, churches and the poor). Second, we see a concern with maintaining social reputations: the legislators are concerned with promoting the image of male clerics as continent and chaste, in addition to reinforcing traditional Roman values concerning what counts as 'seemly' female behaviour.

---

[51] *CTh* 16.2.22 (Given at Trier, 1 December 372); 16.2.44 (Given at Ravenna, 8 May 420). For further discussion see *JECS* 15/2 (2007), special issue, 'Holy Households: Space, Property and Power', guest ed. Kristina Sessa; Kim Bowes, *Private Worship, Public Values, and Religious Change in Late Antiquity* (Cambridge, 2008).

[52] 'Nulla nisi emensis sexaginta annis, "cui votiva domi proles sit", secundum praeceptum apostoli ad diaconissarum consortium transferatur': *Codex Theodosianus*, ed. Mommsen and Meyer, 1/2: 843; cf. 1 Tim. 5: 9–10.

[53] 'Nihil de monilibus et superlectili, nihil de auro argento ceterisque clarae domus insignibus sub religionis defensione consumat, sed universa integra in liberos proximosve vel in quoscumque alios arbitrii sui existimatione transcribat ac si quando diem obierit, nullam ecclesiam, nullum clericum, nullum pauperem scribat heredes': ibid.

[54] *CTh* 16.2.27 was (partially?) repealed two months later by *CTh* 16.2.28, a result of lobbying at the imperial court.

Turning now to Book 16, Title 5, *De haereticis*, the emphasis throughout is on excluding named heretical groups from specific legal rights which, the emperors insist, have been granted to Catholic Christians and the Catholic church alone. These include rights to assemble in public; various bundles of rights relating to 'ecclesiastical' property; the right to hold ecclesiastical offices and to teach the faith; and various kinds of exemptions from taxes and other compulsory burdens. The imperial legislators refer to named heresies as pestilences, poisons and contagions and to the 'polluted minds', 'madness' and 'depraved desires' of heretics in general.[55] The Manichaeans in particular are singled out for their 'inveterate obstinacy' and 'pertinacious nature'.[56] Nonetheless, the vast bulk of imperial constitutions excerpted under Book 16, Title 5, are pragmatic: they are concerned with cutting back the capacities of heretics as legal actors. For example, a constitution issued at Rome on 22 February 407 and addressed to the prefect of the city confirms that Donatists and Manichaeans, Phyrgians and Priscillianists are to have 'no customs and no laws in common with the rest of mankind'; such heresy is to be considered a public crime, 'since whatever is committed against divine religion redounds to the detriment of all'.[57] Section two of the text orders that 'the aforesaid persons' are to have their goods confiscated; their property cannot be transmitted to any of

---

[55] *CTh* 16.5.6, 1 (given at Constantinople, 10 January 381); 16.5.15 (given at Stobi, 14 June 388); 16.5.20 (given at Rome, 19 May 391); 16.5.40, 2 (given at Rome, 22 February 407); 16.5.41, preface (given at Rome, 15 November 407); 16.5.44 (given at Ravenna, 24 November 408); 16.5.52, 5 (given at Ravenna, 30 January 412); 16.5.62, 16.5.64 (probably given at Aquileia, 6 August 425); 16.5.65, preface (given at Constantinople, 30 May 428).
[56] *CTh* 16.5.7, 1 (given at Constantinople 8 May 381); 16.5.35 (given at Milan, 17 May 399). *CTh* 16.5.65 gives a list of twenty-three named heresies and refers to the Manichaeans as 'those who have arrived at the lowest depth of wickedness'.
[57] 'Quid de Donatistis sentiremus, nuper ostendimus. Praecipue tamen Manichaeos vel Frygas sive Priscillianistas' meritissima severitate persequimur. Huic itaque hominum generi nihil ex moribus, nihil ex legibus sit commune cum ceteris. Ac primum quidem volumus esse publicum crimen, quia quod in religionem divinam conmittitur, in omnium fertur iniuriam': *CTh* 16.5.40, preface and 1 (*Codex Theodosianus*, ed. Mommsen and Meyer, 1/2: 867; *The Theodosian Code and Novels and the Sirmondian Constitutions*, transl. Clyde Pharr et al. [Princeton, NJ, 1952], 457). As noted by an anonymous reviewer, the 'Priscillianists' referred to here are probably not the followers of the Spanish ascetic Priscillian but rather 'Montanists' or 'Phrygians' and followers of Priscilla: see Theodor Mommsen et al., eds, *Les Lois religieuses des empereurs romains de Constantin à Théodose II (312—438)*, 1: *Code Théodosien XVI*, SC 497, 484.

their kin if they are also heretics; and they cannot take or receive gifts, buy or sell, or make contracts, nor can they leave a valid will. These penalties were subsequently extended to all heretics, leading to a host of legal questions and complications: What was to happen if a child had been born into a heretical sect, but subsequently became a Christian? Who was legally responsible for an orthodox daughter's dowry, if her paterfamilias was a heretic? Naturally, we also find those labelled as 'heretics' attempting to devise schemes to get around the imperial laws.[58]

Book 16, Title 5 of the *Codex Theodosianus* contains sixty-six discrete excerpts from imperial constitutions, and the female gender is explicitly mentioned in only three of these. Two constitutions from the early fifth century, both issued at Ravenna, deal with heretics who are accommodated in private urban houses or on rural estates: both male and female property owners are to be punished if the heretics have been protected with their knowledge and connivance.[59] The third instance where women are mentioned explicitly in Book 16, Title 5 concerns the Manichaean heresy. *Codex Theodosianus* 16.5.7 (given at Constantinople, 8 May 381) explicitly states that no Manichaean man *or woman* can give or receive gifts, legacies or inheritances and that Manichaeans are deprived of all right to live under Roman law; the final clause states that this law is valid not only for the future but also for the past. Taking these three constitutions together, we can see that women are only referred to explicitly in Book 16, Title 5 in connection with property rights and the diminution of legal capacity.

It is worth pausing here in order to stress what should, by now, have become obvious: heresy is not 'gendered' in the imperial legal rhetoric of the *Theodosian Code*. In accordance with what we have already seen, Curzon concludes: 'The Laws of the Theodosian Code, like the heresiologies, use the rhetoric of madness, insanity and uncontrollability to describe and denounce the heretics.'[60] In direct contrast to fourth- and fifth-century heresiologies, however, there are no gendered references to heresy or heretics in the *Codex*

---

[58] Caroline Humfress, 'Citizens and Heretics. Late Roman Lawyers on Christian Heresy', in Eduard Iricinschi and Holger Zellentin, eds, *Heresy and Identity in Late Antiquity* (Tübingen, 2008), 35–56.
[59] *CTh* 16.5.52 (given at Ravenna, 30 January 412); 16.5.54 (given at Ravenna, 17 June 414).
[60] Berzon, *Classifying Christians*, 92.

Theodosianus. Heretics are demented, polluted and infected with pestilence, but they are not seductive temptresses, vulgar 'women', or weak-minded whores.[61] This does not mean, however, that late Roman gender norms were irrelevant to the prosecution of heresy as a crime or to the construction of 'the heretic' as a legal subject. According to the legal philosopher Leslie Green, gender is not relevant to analytic jurisprudence ('what law is'), nor is gender necessarily relevant to specific problems within normative and special jurisprudence ('what the law of x says').[62] Citing H. L. A. Hart, however, Green goes on to argue that 'we cannot understand law "separately from everything else" in society … to understand law we need to understand its relations to coercive power and to social morality'.[63] Hence in order to understand the relationship between gender, law and heresy we must go beyond imperial law and begin to explore its connections with other, late Roman, coercive power regimes.

LATE ANTIQUE HERESY TRIALS: POPE LEO AND THE MANICHAEANS OF
ROME (443/4)

In the winter of 443 Leo, bishop of Rome from 440 to 461, preached two sermons concerning denunciations and legal prosecutions against Manichaeans.[64] Both these sermons have been preserved in a ninth-century manuscript, as part of a collection probably compiled by Leo himself between 440 and 445.[65] According to *Sermo* 16.5, the

---

[61] This point also stands for the anti-Manichaean rescript issued by the Emperor Diocletian to Julianus, proconsul of Africa, probably in 302: text in Salvatore Riccobono et al., eds, *Fontes iuris Romani anteiustiniani*, 2: *Auctores*, 2nd edn (Florence, 1968), 580–1.

[62] 'Gender is relevant to several problems in normative jurisprudence, and to some problems in special jurisprudence. Gender is not relevant to general jurisprudence; and that is why it gets little mention there': Green, 'Gender and the Analytical Jurisprudential Mind', 28.

[63] Ibid. 27–8.

[64] Leo, *Sermones* 9 (probably preached in 443, shortly before *Sermo* 16) and 16 (preached during the December fast of 443). On Leo's other anti-Manichaean *Sermones* (24, 34, 42, 76) and his *Ep.* 7 (to the bishops of Italy, 30 January 444), see Maier, '"Manichee!"'; *Sermons and Letters against the Manichaeans: Selected Fragments*, ed. Hendrik Schipper and Johannes van Oort, Corpus Fontium Manichaeorum Series Latina 1 (Turnhout, 2000), which also includes Leo, *Epp.* 8, 15, 15a and *Sermo* 72.

[65] For a detailed discussion of the complex manuscript transmission of Leo's sermons, see *Sancti Leonis Magni Romani Pontificis Tractatus Septem et Nonaginta*, ed. Antoine Chavasse, CChr.SL 138, L–CCI.

Caroline Humfress

surrender of Carthage to the Vandals had led to an influx of refugees into the city of Rome; hiding amongst these refugees, according to Leo, came the Manichaeans.[66] Leo had already warned his audience against the heretic lurking within and exhorted them 'to make known to your priests the Manichaeans, wherever they are hiding'.[67] Leo explains that this act of 'supreme piety' will not only 'be to your advantage before the tribunal of the Lord', but would also 'be added to the sacrifice of your alms' in the here and now.[68]

Two late fourth-century imperial constitutions, *Codex Theodosianus* 16.5.9 (given at Constantinople, 20 June 382) and 16.5.15 (given at Stobi, 14 June 388), had ordered the Praetorian Prefects of the East, Florus and Trifolius, to appoint investigators and open the courts in order to receive formal denunciations of Manichaeans and other (associated?) groups, without the 'odium' usually attached to informants.[69] Leo, however, seems to have taken this obligation upon himself. In *Sermo* 16, Leo describes how he instigated a public investigation (*inquisitio*), together with other bishops, presbyters and members of the Roman senate.[70] Manichaean leaders, both male and female (Leo specifies *electi* and *electae*), were summoned to this tribunal for questioning and 'when they had disclosed many details about the perversion of their teaching, and the customs of their festivals, they made known that crime

---

[66] For the broader history relating to Manichaeans at Rome, see Samuel Lieu, *Manichaeism in the Later Roman Empire and Medieval China: A Historical Survey* (Manchester, 1985), 164–8.

[67] Leo, *Sermo* 9.4 (*Sermons and Letters*, ed. Schipper and van Oort, 25).

[68] Ibid. See also Maier, '"Manichee!"', 450, who discusses the wider context of 'Leo's exhortations to the faithful of Rome and the bishops of Italy to enter into a campaign of denunciation and betrayal'.

[69] See also *CTh* 16.5.62 (probably issued at Aquileia, 6 August 425, addressed to the prefect of the city of Rome), which orders that Manichaeans, heretics, schismatics, astrologers and every sect that is an enemy of the Catholics are to be banished from 'the very sight of the City of Rome, in order that it may not be contaminated by the contagious presence of the criminals': *Theodosian Code*, transl. Pharr et al., 462. The touchstone for orthodoxy adopted in this constitution is communion with Pope Celestine I.

[70] Leo, *Sermo* 16.4 (*Sermons and Letters*, ed. Schipper and van Oort, 26). Bronwen Neil, translator of *Leo the Great* (Abingdon, 2009), 32, notes that Leo's tribunal 'was made up of both secular and ecclesiastical judges, and presided over by the bishop himself'. Susan Wessel stresses Leo's ability to exploit connections with Rome's senatorial aristocracy: *Leo the Great and the Spiritual Rebuilding of a Universal Rome*, Vigiliae Christianae Supplements 93 (Leiden, 2008), 121–6.

also, of which it is shameful to speak'.[71] The only concrete information that Leo includes about this crime is that it concerned a girl 'of at most ten years', who confessed to an 'unspeakable act' committed against her by an adolescent boy. We are told that corroborating confessions were secured from the two women who, according to Leo, had raised the girl expressly for this purpose; from the accused youth who had committed the act; and from the Manichaean bishop who was accused of presiding over the 'foul crime'. For the lurid details, Leo refers his audience to the *acta* of the trial itself:

> But lest we offend chaste ears by speaking of this too openly, let the records [*acta*] of the trial suffice, from which we learn most fully that in that sect no modesty, no decency, and no moral purity at all can be found. In this sect lying is the law, the devil is their religion, and dishonour their sacrifice.[72]

I am interested in two specific aspects of Leo's account. First, the dramatis personae: the accused are a girl aged ten years at most, together with the two women who raised her, an adolescent boy and a male member of the Manichaean church hierarchy. The gender cues here are, of course, crucial. The girl is specifically said to be 'at most ten years' because anything less than eleven or twelve years, the legal age at which girls could marry, would have scandalized a Roman audience. The two women are deliberately presented as perverting the archetypal female role of motherhood: they raised the girl, Leo tells us, for the sole purpose of prostituting her for the sake of religion. The Manichaean bishop, on the other hand, perverted his (male) episcopal duty of care by presiding over the 'foul crime'. Second, Leo is deliberately playing here with what can be spoken and what cannot: the girl was interrogated, she spoke in reply and her answers were recorded in the trial *acta*. Leo tells his congregation, however, that they must go and read the acts of the proceedings themselves if they wish to learn the details. The girl 'speaks' in Leo's

---

[71] 'Qui [the Manichaean Elect] cum de perversitate dogmatis sui et de festivitatum suarum consuetudine multa reserassent, illud quoque scelus, quod eloqui verecundum est, prodiderunt': Leo, *Sermo* 16.4 (*Leo the Great*, transl. Neil, 77).
[72] 'De quo ne apertius loquentes castos offendamus auditus, gestorum documenta sufficient, quibus plenissime docetur nullam in hac sectam pudicitiam, nullam honestatem, nullam reperiri penitus castitatem, in qua lex est mendacium, diabolus religio, sacrificium turpitudo': ibid. (*Leo the Great*, transl. Neil, 77).

account and yet she is silent; the crime itself, however, is literally unspeakable.

The only direct reports of late antique anti-heresy trials that I am aware of, beyond those included in the *acta* of church councils or regional synods, involve sexual crimes being committed against under-age girls. In Chapter 46 of his heresiological manual, *De haeresibus*, Augustine of Hippo refers to having read the *acta* of a trial held before an imperial tribune at Carthage in the 420s.[73] The accused include a girl named Margarite, 'not yet twelve years old', and a Manichaean 'nun' named Eusebia. Both Margarite and Eusebia claimed to have been forced to have sexual intercourse with wheat scattered beneath them, so that the ejaculated semen could be caught and baked into bread that was then to be eaten as if it was the eucharist.[74] Why this stress on 'sexual offences and the sexed body' (to borrow Nicola Lacey's phrase) in the context of early fifth-century anti-Manichaean trials, when there are no traces of sexual crimes as a marker of heretical behaviour in Book 16, Title 5 of the *Codex Theodosianus*?

The answer is probably obvious. Fourth- and early fifth-century legislation against heretics was primarily concerned with regulating legal rights and property ownership, rather than corporeal bodies. Leo, however, took on the task of discovering Manichaeans in the flesh. In *Sermo* 16.5, he singles out the women in his audience:

> [Y]ou women especially must withdraw from their acquaintance and fellowship lest you fall into the devil's snares while lending a careless ear to the delight of fabulous stories. The devil knows that man was first seduced by the mouth of a woman, and that he threw everyone out of the happiness of paradise through female gullibility; now he lies in wait for your sex with more certain cunning, so that he may strip of their faith and their honour those whom he can lure to himself through the servants of his deception.[75]

---

[73] Augustine, *De haeresibus* 46.9–10 (ed. Roel Vander Plaetse and Clemens Beukers, CChr.SL 46, 283–345, at 314–15).

[74] Ibid. Augustine includes the pun *hoc non sacramentum, sed exsecramentum*, which Leo may have borrowed: *Sermons and Letters*, ed. Schipper and van Oort, 26 n. 6, 27 n. 7.

[75] '[A]b amicitia vestra penitus abdicate, vosque praecipue, mulieres, a talium notitia et conloquiis abstinete, ne dum fabulosis narrationibus incautus delectatur auditus, in diaboli laqueos incidatis. Qui *sciens* quod primum virum mulieris ore seduxerit, perque femineam credulitatem omnes homines a paradisi felicitate deiecerit, vestro nunc quoque sexui securiore insidiatur astutia, ut eas quas sibi potuerit per ministros suae falsitatis illicere, et

The aim of exhorting women, in particular, was to encourage their denunciation of the Manichaeans in their midst:

> I offer this advice to you too, dearly beloved, begging you that if any of you know where they live, where they teach, the places where they gather, and in whose company they find protection, make it known out of faithfulness to our concern … Let those who think such people are not to be brought forward be found guilty of silence in the judgement of Christ, even if they are not stained by assent.[76]

There is a certain symmetry to Leo's argument here: As the devil seduced the first man via the mouth of a woman, so must women's mouths now denounce Manichaeans, so that women in turn are not 'found guilty of silence in the judgement of Christ'. Leo's exhortation to the women of Rome was part of a much broader ecclesial power regime: 'expressing the watchfulness of the redeemed, Leo's hearers transform themselves into subjects of the church'.[77] Leo's account of the anti-Manichaean hearings at Rome of 443 was carefully crafted so that women of true Christian faith would turn themselves into what Maier terms 'willing objects of ecclesial constraint'.[78]

In the *Codex Theodosianus* there is no trace of the highly 'gendered' anti-heresy polemic that we otherwise find in contemporary Christian writings, including those of Pope Leo I. Nonetheless, to cite Leslie Green once more, 'to understand law we need to understand its relations to coercive power and to social morality'.[79] Leo's

---

fide spoliet et pudore': Leo, *Sermo* 16.5 (*Sermons and Letters*, ed. Schipper and van Oort, 26; *Leo the Great*, transl. Neil, 77–8).
[76] 'Illud quoque vos, dilectissimi, obsecrans moneo, ut si cui vestrum innotuerit ubi habitent, ubi doceant, quos frequentent, et in quorum societate requiescant, nostrae sollicitudini fideliter indicetis … et qui tales non prodendos putant, in iudicio Christi inveniantur rei de silentio, etiam non contaminantur assensu': Leo, *Sermo* 16.5 (*Sermons and Letters*, ed. Schipper and van Oort, 28; *Leo the Great*, transl. Neil, 78).
[77] Maier, '"Manichee!"', 459. On Leo's specific 'ecclesial power regime', see also Michele Renee Salzman, 'Leo's Liturgical Topography: Contestations for Space in Fifth-Century Rome', *JRS* 103 (2013), 208–32.
[78] Maier, '"Manichee!"', 454. According to Leo, *Ep.* 7 (to the bishops of Italy, 444) and *Ep.* 16 (to Turibius, bishop of Astorga in Spain, 447), the hearings continued into 444, until the city of Rome had been cleansed of all Manichaeans. *Ep.* 7 states that those Manichaeans who refused to convert were 'made subject to the laws of the Christian Princes' and 'punished with a perpetual exile by the civil judges' (*per publicos iudices*): *Sermons and Letters*, ed. Schipper and van Oort, 47.
[79] Green, 'Gender and the Analytical Jurisprudential Mind', 28.

anti-Manichaean hearings certainly showcase his connections with
Rome's senatorial aristocracy, but they are far from being a straightforward example of procedural overlap between the ecclesiastical and
the secular legal spheres. Instead, the case of Leo and the Manichaeans
of Rome draws attention to the complex relations between imperial
law and the distinctive ecclesial power regime developed by Leo himself. Leo did not seek to apply Roman law in his anti-Manichaean
campaign of 443–4; rather, he sought to influence it.

The preamble to *Novel* 18 of Emperor Valentinian III (given at
Rome, 19 June 445, and addressed to the Praetorian Prefect
Albinus) explains:

> For what things are obscene to tell and to hear have been revealed by
> their very manifest confession in the court of the most blessed Pope
> Leo, in the presence of the most August Senate! Thus even the man
> also who was said to be their bishop both betrayed with his own
> voice and wrote out all the secrets of their crimes.[80]

Prompted by the revelations uncovered before Leo's papal tribunal,
Novel 18 goes on to confirm existing imperial legislation against the
Manichaeans, but also adds an explanatory sentence to its final enactment clause: imperial bureaucrats are to apply the full force of the law,
'for it does not appear that anything too severe can be decreed against
those persons whose unchaste perversity, in the name of religion,
commits crimes that are unknown and shameful even to brothels'.[81]
A papal ecclesiastical judgment was thus 'lent the force of an imperial
law', but the impact of Leo's anti-Manichaean tribunal went beyond
the enforcement of its sentence.[82] In *Novel* 18 Roman imperial legislation equated heretics with sexed bodies and sexual deviancy, for the
first time in (extant) imperial legislative rhetoric.

---

[80] 'Quae enim et quam dictu audituque obscena in iudicio beatissimi papae Leonis coram
senatu amplissimo manifestissima ipsorum confessione patefacta sunt? adeo ut eorum
quoque qui diceretur episcopus et voce propria proderet et omnia scelerum suorum secreta
perscriberet': Valentinian III, *Novel* 18, pr (*Codex Theodosianus*, ed. Mommsen and
Meyer, 2: 104, lines 5–8; *Theodosian Code*, transl. Pharr et al., 531). This *Novel* is transmitted as *Ep.* 8 within Leo's corpus: *Sermons and Letters*, ed. Schipper and van Oort,
48–50.
[81] 'Neque enim aliquid nimium in eos videtur posse decerni, quorum incesta perversitas
religionis nomine lupanaribus quoque ignota vel pudenda committit': Valentinian III,
Novel 18.4 (*Codex Theodosianus*, ed. Mommsen and Meyer, 2: 105, lines 25–6;
Theodosian Code, transl. Pharr et al., 531).
[82] Quotation in Wessel, *Leo the Great*, 3; see also ibid. 121–6.

The fact that reports, both written and oral,[83] of Leo's anti-Manichaean trials can be shown to have directly influenced Roman legislative rhetoric is important. But there is a broader point to be stressed here. If we want to understand the broader relationship between heresy and law in the late and post-Roman West, we need to focus on concrete individuals (such as Leo) and the specific kinds of ecclesial power regimes and socio-cultural attitudes within, and upon, which they operated, rather than relying on a grand narrative of 'the Christianization of Roman law'. As Nicola Lacey concludes with reference to modern criminal law, '[t]hough lawyers are inclined to lose sight of this obvious fact, the most important conditions for sexual equality and integrity lie in cultural attitudes rather than coercive legal rules.'[84]

[83] The imperial household may have resided in Rome from late 439/40 onwards, having relocated from Ravenna: ibid. 16. Oral reports of Leo's hearings against the Manichaeans probably reached imperial ears, in addition to written *acta* of the proceedings. We also know that the *acta* were quickly circulated beyond Italy: in 445 Leo sent *Acts on the Manichaeans*, 'which apparently meant the account of the Roman process', to Turibius of Astorga: *Sermons and Letters*, ed. Schipper and van Oort, 19.

[84] Lacey, 'Unspeakable Subjects', 66.

God's Judgement in Carolingian Law and History Writing

Robert A. H. Evans*

Christ's College, University of Cambridge

Early medieval thinkers often conceived of God in legal terms, especially when they interpreted contemporary disasters as God's 'just judgement'. Modern scholars have emphasized the importance of these ideas for motivating early medieval reform and legislation and for interpreting history itself. This article explores how these ideas were used in Carolingian legislation and history writing and argues that God's judgement was not as straightforward a theme as it first appears. God's judgement, for example, was not nearly as important for Carolingian historians as it had been for their predecessors. Similarly, in both legal and historical texts, there was great variety in how God's judgement or punishment was expressed, both in how that punishment fell and on whom (whether on the audience or on their enemies). Across these works, however, it is clear that God's judgement was almost never referred to apart from his continuing mercy and help towards to the audiences of these texts. This shows the importance of the various aspects of God's character for early medieval churches and their attitudes to law and history.

The records of the Council of Paris, held by Carolingian bishops in 829, contain numerous reflections on how Christian kings should exercise law and justice. Among these reflections, the council's delegates observed that 'because the king must … render account to the Most Equitable Judge concerning the ministry committed to him', he must enquire into the suitability of the judges he appoints, 'lest he incur divine judgement because of them'.[1] These comments illustrate

* Christ's College, Cambridge, CB2 3BU. E-mail: rae32@cam.ac.uk.
I should like to thank my doctoral supervisor, Rosamond McKitterick, and my examiners Stuart Airlie and Mayke de Jong for various invaluable conversations that prompted this article. I am also very grateful to the audience at the EHS Summer Conference in July 2018 for their helpful comments, and to the anonymous peer reviewers for many useful suggestions. Any errors are entirely my own.
[1] '[Q]uia ipse … rex aequissimo iudici … redditurus est … ne ipse pro eis iudicium incurrat divinum': Council of Paris 2.3 (MGH Conc. 2.2, 654; transl. Fraser McNair, 'Source Translation: The 829 Council of Paris on Kingship', 15 December 2017, online at:

the 'moral framework' of law in early medieval thought. As Rosamond McKitterick puts it, 'justice was a virtue'; 'worldly justice was linked to divine justice', and thereby situated 'within a framework of moral salvation'.[2] Paul Fouracre has similarly highlighted how earthly law was believed to have a heavenly counterpart.[3] The practical concerns for justice laid out by this section of the council were informed by beliefs about God and morality.

The divine judgement of which the Paris delegates warned was not only eschatological (God's judgement on the Last Day) but also historical, in that God's judgement could be, and was, discerned in contemporary events. A year before the Council of Paris, the Emperor Louis the Pious (r.813–40) wrote to his nobility in such terms. Recent disasters, including military defeats in Spain, famines and diseases, and celestial phenomena were 'driven by the just judgement of God, so that, because we fail in all things, we might be scourged both within and without'.[4] In response, Louis announced his intention to convene a series of councils to emend and correct what was amiss through further legislation. This belief in God's contemporary and immanent judgement thus provided a theological context for much thinking about law and justice in early medieval societies. Caroline Humfress and Julia Hillner have both noted the importance of theology for conceptions of law and its practice in Late Antiquity.[5] As the practicalities and dissemination of early medieval law receive

---

<https://salutemmundo.wordpress.com/2017/12/15/source-translation-the-829-council-of-paris-on-kingship/>, accessed 3 August 2018).

[2] Rosamond McKitterick, 'Perceptions of Justice in Western Europe in the Ninth and Tenth Centuries', in *La Giustizia nell'Alto Medioevo (secoli IX–XI)*, Settimane di studio del Centro italiano di studi sull'alto medioevo 44 (Spoleto, 1996), 1075–1101, at 1076, 1079–80.

[3] Paul Fouracre, 'Carolingian Justice: The Rhetoric of Improvement and Contexts of Advice', in *La Guistizia nell'Alto Medioeve (secoli V–VIII)*, Settimane di studio del Centro italiano di studi sull'alto medioevo 42 (Spoleto, 1995), 771–803.

[4] 'Agitur siquidem iusto iudicio Dei, ut, quia in cunctis delinquimus, interius simul et exterius flagellemur': *Epistola Generalis* (MGH Conc. 2/2, 600). For these texts, see Stefan Patzold, 'Redéfinir l'office episcopal. Les Évêques francs face à la crise des années 820/30', in François Bougard, Laurent Feller and Régine Le Jan, eds, *Les Élites au haut moyen âge. Crises et renouvellements*, Haut Moyen Âge 1 (Turnhout, 2006), 337–59, at 340–4; more generally, Mayke de Jong, *The Penitential State: Authority and Atonement in the Age of Louis the Pious (814–840)* (Cambridge, 2009).

[5] Caroline Humfress, *Orthodoxy and the Courts in Late Antiquity* (Oxford, 2007), 155–6; Julia Hillner, *Prison, Punishment and Penance in Late Antiquity* (Cambridge, 2015), 66–7.

increasing attention,[6] the current article will consider this aspect of its theoretical hinterland.

Many Carolingian capitularies, conciliar texts and letters shared similar concerns to those of Louis and the Council of Paris, explicitly interpreting recent events as God's judgement. In 805, for example, the Emperor Charlemagne (r.768–814) wrote to Gherbald, bishop of Liège, in response to recent disasters. These, Charlemagne wrote, were 'very notable, if we wish to consider the kind of troubles which, for our merits, we suffer each day'.[7] He continued, 'from these externals, we can learn that that we, who must tolerate such evils outwardly, are completely displeasing inwardly to the Lord'.[8] King Charles the Bald (r.840–77), similarly warned in his capitulary of Pîtres (862) that 'by our wicked deeds we have grieved and driven away the Holy Spirit … for this reason the inhabitants of the land have been killed and driven away' by the Vikings.[9] The Council of Ver in 884, meeting on the orders of Carloman II (r.879–84), realized that 'our prayers are not accepted by God, because of the shouts and wailing and the deep sighing of the poor'.[10] As a result, 'we can neither resist our enemies nor possess the kingdom of God'.[11] These texts suggest that law was strongly motivated by the belief that contemporary events portended God's judgement, vengeance or displeasure. This conviction was not confined to capitularies. Theodulf of Orléans' famous poem attacking corrupt judges (*c.*798) also warned

---

[6] Most importantly in Thomas Faulkner, *Law and Authority in the Early Middle Ages: The Frankish* leges *in the Carolingian Period* (Cambridge, 2016).

[7] '[N]otissima, si recordare volumus, qualia incommode, singulis diebus propter merita nostra, sentiamus': Charlemagne, *Ad Ghaerbaldum* (MGH Capit. 1, 244–6, at 245).

[8] '[A]b his exterioribus colligere possumus, nos per omnia Domino non placere interius, qui tanta mala compellimur tollerare exterius', ibid. (MGH Capit. 1, 245–6).

[9] 'Sed et ideo terram nostram in conspectu nostro alieni devorant, quoniam alienos a Deo diabolos effugata gratia sancti Spiritus in animas nostras recepimus': *Capitula Pistensia* 1 (MGH Capit. 2, 302–9, at 304; unpublished transl. by Simon Coupland).

[10] '[P]reces nostrae a Deo non recipiuntur, quia clamores et ploratus altaque suspiria pauperum et orphanorum, pupillorum atque viduarum praeoccupant et praeveniunt preces nostras, quae crudis carnibus fratrum nostrorum gravatae raucitudinem acceperunt nullam sonoritatem virtutum habentes': *Capitulare Vernense*, preface (MGH Capit. 2, 371–4, at 372).

[11] '[N]eque inimicis nostris poterimus resistere neque regnum Dei possidere': ibid. (MGH Capit. 2, 372).

that 'the wrath of the celestial Judge remains dreadful' against such corruption.[12]

Scholars have frequently noted how Christ himself was often depicted by early medieval writers as a judge.[13] Similarly, the importance of belief in God's judgement within history has long been recognized by modern scholarship.[14] Charlemagne's letter to Gherbald, as Yitzhak Hen puts it, showed how 'natural disasters were often interpreted as a form of divine punishment for all'.[15] Perhaps the best studied case has been that of the Viking raids, which as the above examples show were often interpreted as divine judgement by contemporaries across western Europe.[16] Beyond purely legal texts, Karl-Ferdinand Werner argued that the phrase 'by God's just judgement', which Louis' letter of 828 used, was 'the basic formula of all [early medieval] Christian historiography'.[17] For Werner, the very purpose of early medieval Christian historians was to discern God's purposes in history for the kings and their courts producing such legislation. While this could involve depicting God's help, many scholars (including Werner) have emphasized the importance of God's judgement in such histories as a warning to their audiences. Only by correctly recognizing God's punishments in history could the legislation necessary for repentance and reform be enacted.

---

[12] '[U]nde pavenda manet caelestis iudicis ira': Theodulf, *Carmina* 13 (MGH Poet. 1, 437–568, at 513; ET T. M. Andersson, *Theodulf of Orléans: The Verse* [Tempe, AZ, 2014], 103).

[13] Giles Constable, *Three Studies in Medieval Religious and Social Thought* (Cambridge, 1995), 157–65; Rachel Fulton, *From Judgement to Passion, 800–1200* (New York, 2002), 53–9.

[14] For example, Rob Meens, 'Politics, Mirrors of Princes and the Bible: Sins, Kings and the Well-being of the Realm', *EME* 7 (1998), 345–57, at 345–6.

[15] Yitzhak Hen, 'The Annals of Metz and the Merovingian Past', in idem and Matthew Innes, eds, *Uses of the Past in the Early Middle Ages* (Cambridge, 2000), 175–90, at 182.

[16] Simon Coupland, 'The Rod of God's Wrath or the People of God's Wrath? The Carolingian Theology of the Viking Invasions', *JEH* 42 (1991), 535–54; Pierre Bauduin, *Le Monde franc et les Vikings, VIIIᵉ–Xᵉ siècle* (Paris, 2009), 160–1.

[17] Karl-Ferdinand Werner, 'Gott, Herrscher und Historiograph. Der Geschichtsschreiber als Interpret des Wirken Gottes in der Welt und Ratgeber der Könige (4. bis 12. Jahrhundert)', in Ernst-Dieter Hehl, Hubertus Seibert and Franz Staab, eds, *Deus qui mutat tempora. Menschen und Institutionen im Wandel des Mittelalter. Festschrift für Alfons Becker zu seinem fünfundsechzigsten Geburtstag* (Sigmaringen, 1987), 1–31, at 12; see also idem, 'L'Historia et les rois', in Dominique Iognia-Prat and Jean-Charles Picard, eds, *Religion et culture autour de l'an Mil* (Paris, 1990), 135–42.

While this dynamic can clearly be observed in Carolingian legal material, let us compare such language with how Carolingian history writing interpreted recent events. As McKitterick and Helmut Reimitz have shown, Carolingian histories provide rich evidence for the worldviews of the Frankish elites.[18] As I have explored elsewhere, these histories reflected and informed the beliefs of those elites concerning God's agency in recent events. Since these elites were also responsible for exercising justice and implementing reform, the legal depiction of God in such historical texts deserves further exploration.[19] I shall consider the extent to which the narratives of their recent pasts depicted God in legal and judicial terms and for what purpose. Was God a 'stern and unrelenting judge', as one modern scholar has put it?[20] Were his judgements presented, as they had been by Louis the Pious and the Council of Paris, to motivate justice and legal reform? In particular, as Hillner has argued, ideas about God's forgiveness and patience led some late antique Christians to conceive of justice in terms of emendation rather than simply retribution (which would take place after death).[21] It is worth considering the extent to which God's justice could be seen as rehabilitative, or even fulfil other roles in the life of these communities.

God's Judgement in Late Antique Histories

As Werner has argued, Carolingian historians were part of a developing tradition of Christian history writing which stretched back to Late Antiquity and, ultimately, to the Bible.[22] These earlier histories were increasingly copied and read in the Carolingian empire.[23] Garry

---

[18] Rosamond McKitterick, *History and Memory in the Carolingian World* (Cambridge, 2004); Helmut Reimitz, *History, Frankish Identity, and the Framing of Western Ethnicity, 550–850* (Cambridge, 2015).
[19] For the religious messages and audience of these texts, see Robert A. H. Evans, '"Instructing Readers' Minds in Heavenly Matters": Carolingian History Writing and Christian Education', in Morwenna Ludlow, Charlotte Methuen and Andrew Spicer, eds, *Churches and Education*, SCH 55 (Cambridge, 2019), 56–71.
[20] Mayke de Jong, 'Religion', in Rosamond McKitterick, ed., *The Early Middle Ages: Europe 400–1000* (Oxford, 2001), 131–61, at 139.
[21] Hillner, *Prison, Punishment, and Penance*, 67.
[22] Werner, 'L'Historia', 137.
[23] Walter Pohl, 'Creating Cultural Resources for Carolingian Rule: Historians of the Christian Empire', in Clemens Gantner, Rosamond McKitterick and Sven Meeder, eds, *The Resources of the Past in Early Medieval Europe* (Cambridge, 2015), 15–33.

Trompf has demonstrated that many of these histories placed significant emphasis on God's judgement and retribution,[24] thereby providing Carolingian historians with various models for narrating and interpreting God's judgement in history. The phrase 'God's just judgement' can, for example, be found in the account of the death of King Antiochus, who had persecuted God's people (2 Macc. 9: 18). This phrasing was taken up with particular enthusiasm by Orosius in his *Histories*, written in the early fifth century and widely copied in the Carolingian empire.[25]

For Werner, Orosius's emphasis on God's judgement defined the tone of Christian history writing until the twelfth century.[26] A typical example, for Werner, was how the heretical Emperor Valens (r.364–78) was burned alive 'by God's just judgement' at the battle of Adrianople.[27] Valens had earlier in the narrative allowed these Goths to be converted to Arianism rather than Catholic orthodoxy. Orosius's message seems to have been clear: heresy would be punished, both in this life and the next. Valens's death, however, represented God's judgement on the opponents of the communities for which these histories were written or those who later identified with them, in this case, Catholic Christians. Valens was aligned with earlier pagan emperors who had persecuted Christians and had also suffered God's judgement.[28] As Trompf argues, emphasizing divine retribution served to encourage the audiences of these histories, since it assured them that God would vindicate their cause. Despite similarities in phrasing, this approach was different from that of Louis the Pious and the Council of Paris, who used God's judgement on their own

---

[24] Garry W. Trompf, *Early Christian Historiography: Narratives of Retributive Justice* (New York, 2000); see also Henri-Irénée Marrou, 'Saint Augustin, Orose et l'Augustinisme historique', in *La storiografia altomedievale*, Settimane di studio del Centro italiano di studi sull'alto medioevo 17 (Spoleto, 1970), 59–88, at 79–80.

[25] Orosius, *Historiae* (*Orosius. Historiarum adversum paganos libri VII accredit eiusdem liber apologeticus*, ed. Karl Zangemeister [Vienna, 1882]); ET *Orosius: Seven Books of History against the Pagans*, transl. A. T. Fear, TTH 54 (Liverpool, 2010), especially 'Introduction', 1–25. For the Carolingian reception, see discussion and references in Robert A. H. Evans and Rosamond McKitterick, 'A Carolingian Epitome of Orosius from Tours: Leiden VLQ 20', in Helmut Reimitz, Rutger Kramer and Graeme Ward, eds, *Historiographies of Identity*, 4: *Historiography and Identity towards the End of the First Millennium – A Comparative Perspective* (Vienna, forthcoming 2020).

[26] Werner, 'L'Historia', 137.

[27] '[I]usto iudicio Dei': Orosius, *Historiae* 7.33.16 (ed. Zangemeister, 519).

[28] *Orosius*, transl. Fear, 8–9.

communities to motivate reform, rather than judgement on their enemies as a cause for celebration.

A different model from Orosius was provided by the *Ten Books of
History* of Gregory of Tours, written in the 590s.[29] Like Orosius,
Gregory was widely read in the Carolingian empire and most of his
statements about God concerned judgement and vengeance.[30] In
addition to falling on those outside the community, Gregory also
often depicted divine judgement falling within his own Gallic political community. For example, Marcatrude, King Gunthram's wife,
poisoned the son of his concubine, only for her own son to die 'by
God's judgement'.[31] In the following chapter, King Charibert married Marcovefa, sister of his previous wife, and was excommunicated
by Germanus, bishop of Paris. Charibert refused to repent and
Marcovefa 'died, struck by God's judgement'; Charibert himself
died 'not long after'.[32] Gregory used God's judgement to address
questions of episcopal authority and dynastic intrigue, both with
clear moral relevance to the Christian reader.

Space forbids considering further examples, such as those offered
by Bede or the *Liber Pontificalis*, but Orosius and Gregory serve to
demonstrate that there was no single Christian way of writing
God's judgement into history. The Bible itself presented a far
wider range of approaches than that of 2 Maccabees.[33] Orosius and
Gregory also went beyond the phrasing of 'God's judgement' to
describe God's vengeance or anger, which could be depicted eschato-
logically as well as historically. The Carolingian readers of these histories would thus have noted the importance of God's judgement
from a variety of angles.

---

[29] Gregory of Tours, *Libri Historiarum X* (MGH SRM 1/1); Reimitz, *History, Identity, Ethnicity*, 27–125.

[30] Walter Goffart, *Narrators of Barbarian History (A.D. 550–800): Jordanes, Gregory of Tours, Bede, and Paul the Deacon* (Princeton, NJ, 1988), 433. On Gregory's broader language of justice, see William Monroe, '*Via Iustitiae*: The Biblical Sources of Justice in Gregory of Tours', in Kathleen Mitchell and Ian Wood, eds, *The World of Gregory of Tours* (Leiden, 2002), 99–112.

[31] '[I]udicio Dei': Gregory, *Libri Historiarum* 4.25 (MGH SRM 1/1, 158).

[32] '[P]ercussa iuditio Dei obit … ne multo post et ipse rex post eam decessit': ibid. 4.26 (MGH SRM 1/1, 158–9).

[33] Daniel Block, 'God', in Bill Arnold and H. G. M. Williamson, eds, *Dictionary of the Old Testament Historical Books* (Leicester, 2005), 337–55.

Marginalizing God's Judgement?

It is striking, therefore, that the earliest Carolingian historians significantly marginalized the importance of God's judgement in recent events. The two earliest histories were the so-called *Continuations of the Chronicle of Fredegar* and the *Royal Frankish Annals*, which both exerted a significant influence over subsequent Carolingian history writing.[34] The *Continuations* were completed between 768 and 786, possibly under the patronage of Childebrand and Nibelung, relatives of Charlemagne.[35] The first redaction of the *Royal Frankish Annals* (from 741 to 788) seems to have been written by someone associated with Charlemagne's court around 790s, who knew the *Continuations*.[36] As a result of their links to the Carolingian regime, both histories celebrated the Franks' repeated victories under Carolingian leadership.

The *Continuations* offered their readers only two examples of God's judgement. Remistianus, a rebel against King Pippin III (r.751–68) in the 760s, was captured 'through divine judgement'.[37] Earlier, in 756, Haistulf, king of the Lombards, was 'thrown from his horse by divine judgement … and cruelly lost his life and kingdom by a worthy death'.[38] The *Royal Frankish Annals* similarly reported Haistulf's death, 'struck by God's judgement', but omitted any mention of the horse.[39] The annals framed the conflict between the Franks and the Lombards in legal terms.[40] King Pippin had attacked Haistulf earlier in the narrative because Pope Stephen was 'seeking aid

---

[34] Helmut Reimitz, '*Omnes Franci:* Identifications and Identities of the Early Medieval Franks', in Ildar Garipzanov, Patrick Geary and Przemysław Urbańczyk, eds, *Franks, Northmen, and Slavs: Identities and State Formation in Early Medieval Europe* (Turnhout, 2008), 51–70, at 60.

[35] *Continuations of Fredegar* (hereafter *Cont.*; ed. and transl. J. Wallace-Hadrill, *The Fourth Book of the Chronicle of Fredegar, with its Continuations* [London, 1960]); Roger Collins, *Die Fredegar-Chroniken* (Hanover, 2007), 82–139; Reimitz, *History, Identity, Ethnicity*, 296–334.

[36] *Annales Regni Francorum* (hereafter: *RFA*; MGH SRG i.u.s. 6); McKitterick, *Charlemagne*, 32–5; Reimitz, *History, Identity, Ethnicity*, 335–45.

[37] '[P]er divino iudicio': *Cont.* 51 (ed. and transl. Wallace-Hadrill, 119).

[38] '[D]ivino iudicio de equo … proiectus utiam et regnum crudeliter digna morte ammisit': *Cont.* 39 (ed. and transl. Wallace-Hadrill, 108–9).

[39] '[P]ercussus est iudicio Dei': *RFA, s.a.* 756 (MGH SRG i.u.s. 6, 14).

[40] For this conflict, see Marios Costambeys, Matthew Innes and Simon MacLean, *The Carolingian World* (Cambridge, 2011), 59–63.

and support for the rights of St Peter'.[41] Pippin 'sought justice', while Haistulf 'refused justice', until Pippin's armies persuaded him otherwise in 755.[42] Haistulf then 'promised to respect the rights of St Peter', and bound himself to keep his promise with oaths and the exchange of hostages.[43] The author juxtaposed Haistulf's subsequent breaking of these oaths with God's judgement. In that sense, these accounts clearly connected ideas about law and justice on the international stage with God's judgement. This particular author, however, never returned to this motif.

The *Continuations* and the *Royal Frankish Annals* thus differed from the earlier histories considered above in marginalizing God's judgement within their narratives. God was, nonetheless, very important to both histories. In both the Carolingians repeatedly defeated their enemies, including the Lombards, 'with the Lord helping'.[44] The authors of the *Continuations* and the *Royal Frankish Annals* shared earlier historians' enthusiasm for divine agency in their narratives but shifted the weight from judgement and opposition to help. Both historians described God's purposes for Haistulf's death using different vocabulary from that for God's other actions within their narratives. In the *Royal Frankish Annals*, God's judgement on Haistulf and its consequences were also isolated structurally from other instances of God's agency. Most accounts of God's agency came later in the narrative, between 769 and 788. The two exceptions were Pippin's campaign against Haistulf in 755, 'with the Lord helping',[45] and then God's judgement on Haistulf. The combination of God's help to the Franks and judgement on their enemies was, in this single case, similar to Orosius's approach. Injustice occurred (and was subsequently punished by God) among those outside the community for whom this history was written. The Frankish readers of the *Royal Frankish Annals* would have been encouraged by Haistulf's death. Rather than serving to warn them to repent, it was part of the annals' wider assurance of God's favour towards the Franks.

---

[41] '[Q]uaerendo pro iustitiis sancti Petri': *RFA, s.a.* 753 (MGH SRG i.u.s. 6, 10).
[42] '[I]ustitiam … quaerendo … iustitiam vetando': *RFA, s.a.* 755 (MGH SRG i.u.s. 6, 12).
[43] '[I]ustitiam sancti Petri pollicitus est faciendi': ibid.
[44] Robert A. H. Evans, 'Christian Hermeneutics and Narratives of War in the Carolingian Empire', *Transformation: A Holistic Journal of Mission Studies* 34 (2017), 150–63.
[45] 'Domino auxiliante': *RFA, s.a.* 755 (MGH SRG i.u.s. 6, 12).

As Carolingian history writing developed, God's judgement appeared more frequently. It remained, as it had in the *Continuations* and the *Royal Frankish Annals*, primarily part of a wider discourse of divine aid. A few years after the composition of the annals, around 806, another pro-Carolingian historian wrote the *Annals of Metz*.[46] These annals covered the period from the Carolingians' rise in the late seventh century until the year 805. Hen notes that these annals were almost exactly contemporaneous with Charlemagne's letter to Gherbald and suggests that the anxieties of that letter informed the annals.[47] The author, however, consistently stressed God's help and favour towards the Carolingians throughout the narrative, with only a few references to God's judgement. In the entry for 690, Pippin II (d.714), Charlemagne's great-grandfather and ruler of the Austrasian Franks, was depicted addressing his men before the decisive battle against the Neustrian Franks at Tertry. He described his men as 'we who will submit to the Lord's judgement'.[48] In 717, Pippin's son, Charles Martel (r.715–41), faced the tyrants Chilperic and Raganfred before the battle of Vinchy. His opponents said 'that [Charles] would … undergo the judgement of divine justice'.[49] The two decisive battles which secured the rule of Pippin and Charles were therefore framed with reference to divine judgement and justice. As in the *Continuations* and the *Royal Frankish Annals*, however, God's judgement was seen as benefiting the narrative's heroes and the audience who identified with them. These examples of divine justice should be placed alongside the many expressions of divine help, inspired by the *Royal Frankish Annals*. Pippin's address to his men exhorted them to fight 'with the Lord helping'.[50] The text describes Charles Martel as winning the battle of Vinchy 'with divine mercy succouring him' and 'with God's help',[51] rather than referring to the idea of divine judgement. This reflected the dominance of the motif of God's help in

---

[46] *Annales Mettenses Priores* (hereafter: *AMP*), s.a. 745 (MGH SRG i.u.s. 10); see Paul Fouracre and Richard Gerberding, *Late Merovingian France: History and Hagiography 640–720* (Manchester, 1996), 330–49; Hen, 'Annals of Metz', 175–90.

[47] Hen, 'Annals of Metz', 182–3.

[48] '[I]udicium Domini subituri': *AMP*, s.a. 690 (MGH SRG i.u.s. 10, 8).

[49] '[U]t ibi divinae iusticiae iudicium subiret': *AMP*, s.a. 717 (MGH SRG i.u.s. 10, 24).

[50] '[I]n suum potius auxiliante Domino convertamus exitium': *AMP*, s.a. 690 (MGH SRG i.u.s. 10, 8).

[51] '[D]ivino auxilio victoria patrata': *AMP*, s.a. 717 (MGH SRG i.u.s. 10, 25).

Carolingian historians' view of the recent past, a pattern set by the *Continuations* and *Royal Frankish Annals*. There was much in this narrative to encourage the reader, but little that explicitly warned against sin or motivated repentance and reform.

GOD'S JUDGEMENT AS CORRECTION

As Mayke de Jong has shown, the idea of God's judgement became increasingly important for Carolingian political discourse in the reign of Louis the Pious.[52] Historians recounting Louis' reign certainly depicted greater misfortunes befalling the Franks than their predecessors had done. While this altered the tone in which God's agency was depicted, it did not lead to the motif of God's just judgement becoming as dominant as it had been in the writings of Orosius or Gregory.

Following a series of rebellions in the early 830s, Louis was restored in 834, and shortly after became the subject of a biography by Thegan of Trier.[53] Thegan did not mention God's help as frequently as the *Royal Frankish Annals* or the *Annals of Metz*,[54] but nor did he explicitly depict God's judgement on Louis. He described Louis' tumultuous relationship with his rebellious son, Lothar (795–855), and quoted Hebrews 12: 6: '*he whom the Lord loves, he corrects, and scourges every son whom He receives*'.[55] Thegan implicitly ascribed Louis' misfortunes at Lothar's hands to God. Rather than using the language of judgement, however, Thegan cast this as evidence of God's love for Louis. Thegan continued that 'he, who will not accept the Lord's corrections voluntarily, cannot become his son'.[56] That Louis accepted his troubles demonstrated his sonship to God, whereas Lothar's unwillingness to be corrected placed his in doubt. Thegan thus alluded to the language of God's judgement which had surrounded the Council of Paris and the later rebellions, but made a virtue out of God's apparent chastisement. In this way he invested Louis with both political and moral legitimacy rather than

---

[52] De Jong, *Penitential State*; compare the examples above.
[53] Thegan, *Gesta Hludowici imperatoris* (MGH SRG i.u.s. 64, 167–278); De Jong, *Penitential State*, 72–9.
[54] Although see Thegan, *Gesta* 15.
[55] '*Quem enim diligit Dominus* corripit; *flagellat autem omnem filium quem recipit*': ibid. 49 (MGH SRG i.u.s. 64, 242).
[56] '[Q]ui sponte correptiones Domini non suscipit, filius eius fieri non poterit': ibid.

calling for further reform, and encouraged the Frankish political community to see the troubles of the early 830s in a positive light.

Writing in the early 840s, an anonymous author known as the Astronomer also wrote a *Life of Louis*.[57] The Astronomer repeatedly emphasized God's help, and also gave a similar nuance to events which could have been interpreted as God's judgement. He mentioned God's help at numerous points, such as when Louis' men defeated the Saracens in Spain 'depending on divine help'.[58] Much later in the narrative, the Astronomer lamented how Lothar's army had been devastated by plague in Italy; it was as if Francia's 'nerves had been cut, her prudence annulled'.[59] The Astronomer continued: 'God shows how salutary, how praiseworthy, it is to observe what is represented as proceeding from his mouth, saying, *Let not the wise man boast in his wisdom, nor the strong man in his strength, nor the rich man in his riches*.'[60]

The Astronomer, whose narrative had celebrated Louis' rule, was clearly admonishing Lothar for moral failure. There was, however, no precise phrasing to confirm that God was punishing Lothar. The reader's attention was not drawn explicitly to Lothar's many sins. Instead, the author showed that Francia, all the Franks, suffered from this loss, and then addressed the reader about how to learn from this to live rightly. This was similar to the warnings pronounced by Louis and his churchmen cited above, but was altogether subtler. Lothar had opposed Louis but was also a reigning Carolingian when the Astronomer wrote. For all his faults, Lothar needed to be part of the solution to the succession crisis following Louis' death, and so part of the broader community which the Astronomer was addressing. The Astronomer appealed for greater submission to God without explicitly threatening judgement. Despite the discourse of Louis' reign, or perhaps because of its ferocity, both Thegan and the Astronomer depicted God's judgement carefully. It fell on Louis, his family and the Frankish political community very infrequently

[57] Astronomer, *Vita Hludowici imperatoris* (MGH SRG i.u.s. 64, 280–555); see also De Jong, *Penitential State*, 79–88.
[58] '[D]ivino freti auxilio' Astronomer, *Vita* 15 (MGH SRG i.u.s. 64, 328).
[59] '[Q]uasi nervis succisis ... prudentia ... adnullata': ibid. 56 (MGH SRG i.u.s. 64, 514).
[60] '[O]stendit Deus, quam salubre sit quamque sobrium observare, quod ex eius ore probatur procedere: *non glorietur,* inquiens, *sapiens in sapientia, nec fortis in fortitudine sua, nec dives in divitiis suis*': ibid.; cf. Jer. 9: 23.

and was portrayed in more rehabilitative terms than that falling on the Franks' enemies in the histories of Charlemagne's reign.

Lamenting God's Judgement

As the ninth century progressed, more historians alluded to, or engaged with questions, about God's judgement, although these remained complex and part of wider reflections on God's agency in recent history. Writing in the early 840s, the lay commander Nithard composed a history of the conflict between Louis the Pious's sons following the emperor's death in 840. The first two books were written for King Charles the Bald (r.840–77) and his court, the latter two for himself.[61] Much of Nithard's narrative depicted God's judgement as favourable to himself and Charles the Bald's supporters. Prior to the battle of Fontenoy (841), Charles's advisers told him to fight against his brother Lothar, 'relying on the justice of his case and thus on divine help'.[62] As with earlier Carolingian histories, Nithard equated God's justice with his help, and Nithard described himself as fighting at Fontenoy 'with the Lord helping'.[63] The latter two books were much clearer about God's judgement, although Nithard offered this interpretation largely through the mouths of the bishops in his narrative. They confirmed that Lothar had been 'restrained by God's judgement in this disaster',[64] and that 'God's judgement had declared His will between [the brothers]'.[65] Much like the *Annals of Metz*, Nithard depicted God's justice as a source of help.

Nithard's conclusion to his *Histories*, however, shifted to warning his readers 'how mad it is to neglect the public benefit'.[66] He asserted that this would 'offend the Creator very greatly'.[67] Nithard believed

---

[61] Nithard, *Historiarum Libri IV* (MGH SRG i.u.s. 44); Janet Nelson, 'Public Histories and Private History in the Work of Nithard', *Speculum* 60 (1985), 251–93; De Jong, *Penitential State*, 96–100.
[62] '[F]retus iustitia ac per hoc auxilio divino': Nithard, *Historiarum* 2.5 (MGH SRG i.u.s. 44, 19).
[63] 'Domino auxiliante': ibid. 2.10 (MGH SRG i.u.s. 44, 27).
[64] '[U]t iudicio Dei et hac plaga repressi': ibid. 3.1 (MGH SRG i.u.s. 44, 28).
[65] '[I]udicio Dei inter illos voluntas eius declarata sit': ibid. 3.3 (MGH SRG i.u.s. 44, 32).
[66] '[Q]ua dementia utilitatem publicam neglegat': ibid. 4.7 (MGH SRG i.u.s. 44, 49).
[67] '[D]um ex utrisque creatorem adeo offendat': ibid.

that God had indeed been offended, and proved it with examples of the natural elements making war on the once prosperous *res publica*.[68] Nithard concluded his history with the assertion that 'God's just judgement, as I said above, instilled lamentation in many'.[69] Nithard's use of the phrase 'just judgement of God' was no accident. It took a phrase that earlier historians had used to depict judgement on the enemies of their communities and focused it inwards. This concluded the history with a pessimistic call to repentance and recast the whole history as a warning of divine judgement. Although Nithard had depicted God's judgement as favourable to Charles and his men at Fontenoy, this was not a matter of straightforward triumph. Nithard had shown through Fontenoy that God's justice had significant implications for the whole political community, whether supporting Lothar or Charles. While the just could take comfort from this, it meant that those who neglected the public good risked the same fate as Lothar. There was also a strongly emotive element to Nithard's closing passage. It functioned almost as a call for readers to lament and confess their sin.

A similar pattern can be found in the *Annals of Xanten*, a set of annals covering 790 to 873, whose final redaction can be linked to the church in Cologne.[70] The later sections, especially from 863 onwards, focused on the Viking raids and ecclesiastical politics, especially the crises facing the Cologne church as a result of Lothar II's divorce case.[71] As in Nithard, the *Annals of Xanten* depicted God's judgement as favourable to their own community. When the villainous Lothar II returned from Rome, for example, the annalist wrote that 'the Lord struck him terribly with almost all his noblemen … as if the Avenger had said, *Vengeance is mine, and I will repay*'.[72] The final triumph of Archbishop Willibert's party over that of

---

[68] Ibid. (MGH SRG i.u.s. 44, 49–50).

[69] '[I]nsuper multa … maeroremque omnibus, uti praefatum est, iusto Dei iudicio incussit': ibid. (MGH SRG i.u.s. 44, 50).

[70] *Annales xantenses* (hereafter: *AX*; MGH SRG i.u.s. 12, 1–33); Heinz Löwe, 'Studien zur Annales Xantenses', *Deutsches Archiv* 8 (1951), 59–99.

[71] Stuart Airlie, 'Private Bodies and the Body Politic in the Divorce Case of Lothar II', *P&P* 161 (1998), 3–38; Karl Heidecker, *Kerk, huwelijk en politieke macht. De zaak Lotharius II, 855–869* (Amsterdam, 1997; ET *The Divorce of Lothar II: Christian Marriage and Political Power in the Carolingian World*, transl. Tanis Guest [Ithaca, NY, 2010], especially 39–40).

[72] '[E]um Dominus Roma redeuntem terribiliter percussit cum omnibus pene suis optimatibus … Quasi ultor dixisset: *Mihi vindictam, et ego retribuam*': *AX, s.a.* 870 (MGH SRG i.u.s. 12, 28); cf. Deut. 32: 35.

Lothar II's servant, Gunthar was similarly described as '*the Lord* [revealing] *His justice in the sight of the nations*'.[73] In both cases, the annalist asserted God's just intervention in history on behalf of the faithful of Cologne. Whereas earlier annals had showed God helping the empire, here God acted on the church's behalf, against the empire's own rulers.

The annalist, however, knew that God's justice placed demands on his audience. The narrative of political and military events beyond Cologne was deeply pessimistic, especially concerning the Viking raids.[74] He closed his history with a general assertion that 'the Lord continually afflicted His people with various blows, and visited *their transgressions upon them with the rod, and their sins upon them with lashes*'.[75] The annalist here alluded to Psalm 88 (Vulgate), but turned its first-person warning into a retrospective description, to depict contemporary events as expressions of God's judgement which implicitly demanded a response. As with Nithard, this concluded the history as it has survived, casting the whole work as a prompt to repentance and prayer.

Nithard and the *Annals of Xanten* were unusual in that they depicted God's judgement both for and against their own communities, in contrast to other Carolingian histories. It should be noted that both histories survived only in a single manuscript, and so did not represent the mainstream of history writing, as the *Royal Frankish Annals* or the nearly contemporary *Annals of Fulda* did. Their way of recounting the recent past aligned both histories much more closely with Carolingian reforming literature than other histories. This may, indeed, have been a direct result of lying beyond the mainstream of Carolingian history writing. Without needing to celebrate the exploits of specific Carolingian rulers on the pattern set by the *Royal Frankish Annals*, they could afford to offer a more morally complex view of contemporary events.

---

[73] 'His omnibus ita peractis *in conspectu gentium revelavit Dominus iusticiam suam*': *AX, s. a.* 871 (MGH SRG i.u.s. 12, 29); cf. Ps. 97: 2 (Vulgate). For the clash between Willibert and Gunthar, see Heidecker, *Divorce of Lothar II*, 164–8.

[74] For example, *AX, s.a.* 871 (MGH SRG i.u.s. 12, 80).

[75] '[E]t diversis plagis Dominus assidue populum suum afflixit et *visitavit in virga iniquitates eorum et in verberibus peccata eorum*': *AX, s.a.* 873 (MGH SRG i.u.s. 12, 33); cf. Ps. 88: 33 (Vulgate).

God's Help in Carolingian Law

Carolingian histories presented their readers with a subtle and complex picture of God's judgement which was often balanced with God's help and mercy. It never became a dominant feature of Carolingian history writing as it had in Orosius and Gregory. Similar complexity can be found in how Carolingian legislators depicted God's judgement. The preface to Charlemagne's greatest piece of reforming legislation, the *General Admonition*, did not mention God's judgement but his mercy.[76] Even the seemingly fearful legislative sources considered at the outset of this article found ways to bring nuance to the legal character of God which they presented. Apart from the Council of Paris and Louis' letter of 828, none of those legislative texts mentioned God's judgement explicitly. Charlemagne's letter to Gherbald mentioned displeasure (*non placere*), not judgement. The capitulary of Pîtres, similarly, made the Holy Spirit the object of human impiety, as being 'grieved', rather than the agent of judgement. Finally, the Council of Ver did not explicitly ascribe recent defeats to God, even if this was implicit, but to human impiety and immorality, which affected God's willingness to help. As with Thegan and the Astronomer, they alluded to the sense of God's displeasure without stating it directly.

Similarly, these texts all envisaged God as continuing to be favourable, even in his displeasure. Charlemagne, for example, ordered Gherbald to organize fasts so that help might be 'sought from him in whom we live, move, and have our being'.[77] Charlemagne explained to Gherbald that fasts could be completed 'with the Lord granting it, in this way', before detailing the process of litany and fasting.[78] Similarly, the Franks ought to pray 'that almighty God, who knows not only everything which happens but also everything before it happens, may convict our hearts'.[79] The means by which God's favour might be restored was itself grounded in beliefs about God's help. Louis' admonitions in 828, similarly, reported that already recent councils had met 'with God being merciful' to 'seek God

[76] 'Christi … clementiam': *Admonitio Generalis*, preface (MGH Capit. 1, 53–61, at 53).
[77] '[A]b eo, *in quo vivimus, movemur et sumus*, auxilium esse quaerendum': Charlemagne, *Ad Ghaerbaldum* (MGH Capit. 1, 245).
[78] 'Domino largiente congruenter impleta, scilicet': ibid.
[79] '[O]mnipotens Deus, qui non solum facta verum etiam antequam fiant omnia novit corda nostra compungat': ibid. (MGH Capit. 1, 246).

with all devotion so that he might be propitious to us'.[80] The capitulary of Pîtres, meanwhile, ended by saying that 'we should return to God and believe'.[81] Theodulf, similarly, enjoined corrupt judges to be merciful because Christ was merciful.[82] Each of these texts continued to envisage God as favourable, even if such favour was currently absent. The sense of divine aid which was so prevalent in Carolingian histories also informed legislative texts alongside the language of divine displeasure.

Conclusion

Carolingian historians and legislators shared a common discourse which acknowledged that God could sometimes express his displeasure through recent events, but which also pressed upon their readers the assurance of God's help and mercy. When Carolingian historians depicted God acting in recent events they consistently emphasized his help and favour to the communities for whom they wrote. Where the language of judgement did appear, such language was part of this wider discourse of divine aid. While this was similar to Orosius, who had depicted God's judgement on persecutors and heretics, the tone of Carolingian historians was altogether more positive. God was not a stern and unrelenting judge, but a source of help and comfort.

When historians did see God's judgement as falling upon aspects of Carolingian society, this view of God as a source of help persevered. God's opposition to Louis the Pious or Lothar in the works of Thegan and the Astronomer, for example, was considerably subtler than his judgement on the villains of Orosius and Gregory of Tours. It allowed space for God's mercy and for further moral lessons to be learned, rather than bringing about a decisive end to sinners. Even the histories of Nithard and the *Annals of Xanten*, with a stronger sense of lament, did not lose sight of God's help and mercy, both in bringing judgement upon their enemies and in allowing room

---

[80] 'Deumque tota devotione deposcere, ut nobis propitiari ... et ita Deo miserante fieret': *Epistola Generalis* (MGH Conc. 2/2, 599).
[81] '[A]d illum redeamus et credamus': *Capitula Pistensia* 1 (MGH Capit. 2, 305); cf. Coupland, 'Rod of God's Wrath', 539.
[82] Theodulf, *Carmina* 28 (MGH Poet. 1, 515).

for repentance. This subtlety can also be found across Carolingian legislation, even where God's displeasure was made clear.

These texts have important implications for our understanding of early medieval religion. Far from being simply being seen a wrathful judge, as modern scholars have often assumed,[83] God was conceived by early medieval thinkers as merciful and benevolent, but also as just. As well as being an important part of the language of both legal and historical sources, such language further reflected wider ideas about justice. God's mercy could be learned from the history of the recent past and, as much as his justice, could motivate human law and justice. This balance of justice and mercy was important for legal thought because it allowed space for repentance and correction, as these texts demonstrate. Such an approach is consistent with what Hillner has demonstrated about late antique Christian approaches to law as rehabilitative as much as retributive.[84] The texts considered here show the continuation of that late antique dialogue between theology and law into the medieval West. God's whole character, not just its legal aspect as judge but his mercy and favour, was relevant to conceptions of law in the early medieval church.

---

[83] For example, Fulton, *Judgement to Passion*, 53–9.
[84] Hillner, *Prison, Punishment, and Penance*, 66–7.

The Political Background to the Establishment of the Slavic Nomocanon in the Thirteenth Century

Marija Koprivica*

University of Belgrade

*The first collection of canon law translated from the Greek into the Slavic language in the ninth century supported the consolidation of Christianity among the Slav peoples. This article focuses on the nomocanon of St Sava of Serbia (*Kormchaia*), a collection which was original and specific in its content; its relationship to other contemporary legal historical documents will be considered. The article also explores the political background to the emergence of Orthodox Slav collections of ecclesiastical and civil law. The political context in which these collections originated exercised a determinative influence on their contents, the selection of texts and the interpretation of the canons contained within them. The emergence of the Slavic nomocanon is interpreted within a context in which Balkan Slav states sought to foster their independence and aspired to form autocephalous national churches.*

Due to their relatively late immigration and physical distance from political and church centres, the Slavic peoples long resisted the influence of the legal norms of the Byzantine empire and Christianity. This article focuses on the development of church law among Balkan Slavs. Their states, law and church were developed under strong influence from the empire. The Christianization of the South Slavs was a process lasting several centuries, varying in success over time. The empire's legal regulations penetrated the Slavic Orthodox world equally slowly. The penetration of Roman and Byzantine legal norms into the Balkan Slavic states was characterized, firstly, by the translation of almost all Byzantine legal collections into the Slavic language; secondly, by the acceptance of certain institutions from Roman law, albeit mediated through Greek translations; and

* Faculty of Philosophy, Department of History, University of Belgrade, Čika Ljubina 18–20, 11000 Belgrade, Serbia. E-mail: marija.koprivica@f.bg.ac.rs.

Studies in Church History 56 (2020), 78–92   © Ecclesiastical History Society 2020
doi: 10.1017/stc.2019.5

thirdly, by merging the laws with customary law and adapting this to local needs.[1]

The Slavs had already received a collection of ecclesiastical law in the period when their Christian faith was being strengthened and their ecclesiastical and liturgical life organized. The first translation of the church's law code into Old Slavic is ascribed to St Methodius, one of two brothers from Thessaloniki who played a crucial role in the Christianization of Slavic peoples, most likely between 865 and 885. The basis for the ecclesiastical legal norms is found in the *Nomocanon in Fifty Titles* of John Scholastikos. The secular part of the code, the *Zakon Sudnyi Liúdem* (*Court Law for the People*), was based on the *Ecloga*, the well-known legal code of the Byzantine emperor Leo III.[2] The first Slavic nomocanon was used in Bulgaria, which had become stronger politically in the late ninth and tenth centuries.[3] After the fall of the Bulgarian empire and the

---

[1] Paul Valliere, 'Introduction to the Modern Orthodox Tradition', in John Witte Jr and Frank S. Alexander, eds, *The Teachings of Modern Orthodox Christianity on Law, Politics, and Human Nature* (New York, 2007), 14–19; John Meyendorff, 'Contemporary Problems in Orthodox Canon Law', in idem, *Living Tradition: Orthodox Witness in the Contemporary World* (New York, 1978), 99–114; Ярослав Н. Щапов [Iaroslav N. Shchapov], 'Рецепция сборников византийского права в средневековых баканских государствах' ['Recepciia sbornikov vizantiĭskogo prava v srednevekovykh balkanskikh gosudarstvakh' / 'The Reception of Collections of Byzantine Law in Medieval States'], *Византийский временник* [*Bizantinskiy Vremennik*] 37 (1976), 123–9.

[2] For text and commentary, see М. Н.Тихомиров and Л. М. Милов [M. N. Tihomirov and L. M. Milov], *Закон судный людемъ краткой редакции* [*Zakon sudnyĭ liudem' kratkoĭ redakcii* / *Court Law for the People*] (Moscow, 1961); ET H. W. Dewey and A. M. Kleimola, eds, *Zakon Sudnyj Ljudem (Court Law for the People)* (Ann Arbor, MI, 1977). On the *Nomocanon of Methodius* and *Zakon sudnyi liudem*, see further Сергије Троицки [Sergije Troicki], 'Да ли је Закон судни људем саставио Методије или Бугарски кнез?' ['Da li je Zakon sudnyj liudem sastavio Metodije ili Bugarski knez?' / 'Was the Court Law for the People made by Methodius or the Bulgarian Prince?'], *Istorijski časopis* 14–15 (1965), 505–16; Кирил Максимович [Kiril Maksimovich], *Закон судный людем, источниковедческие и лингвистические аспекты исследования славянского юридического памятника* [*Zakon sudnyĭ liudem, istochnikovedcheskie i lingvisticheskie aspektky issledovaniia slovianskogo iuridicheskogo pamiatnika* / *Court Law for the People: The Sources and Linguistic Aspects of researching a Slavic Legal Monument*] (Moscow, 2004).

[3] Kiril Maksimovich, 'Byzantine Law in Old Slavonic Translations and the Nomocanon of Methodius', *Byzantinoslavica* 65 (2007), 9–18; Ludwig Burgmann, 'Mittelalterliche Übersetzungen byzantinischer Rechtstexte' and 'Vortrag zur slavischen Rezeption byzantinischer Kirchenrechtssammlungen', in idem, *Aufsätze zur byzantinischen Rechtsgeschichte*, Forschungen zur byzantinischen Rechtsgeschichte 36 (Frankfurt am Main, 2018), 330–2, 357–61.

establishment of Byzantine rule, the Slavic version of the code was
suppressed. However, it then found its way to Rus, where several copies of these *Kormchaias* have been found.[4] The most important manuscript representing this group is the so-called *Efremovskaia
Kormchaia* from the twelfth (or the end of the eleventh) century.[5]

The first Slavic nomocanon collections were made because of the
need to regulate the religious life of newly baptized peoples according
to ecclesiastical law. In addition, there was a need to render these peoples familiar with, and subject to, the secular laws of the empire.
Simultaneously, Balkan Slavs were working towards the establishment of their own church, with services in Old Slavic and the greatest
degree of autonomy possible. Although this first attempt at the establishment of ecclesiastical legislation among the Slavic peoples was very
important, its practical application and importance were significantly
less than those of the early thirteenth-century Slavic nomocanon.

The collection of church and civil law known as the *Nomocanon of
St Sava* shaped the legislation of medieval Slavic peoples.[6] It has been
labelled the ultimate source of *corpus juris utriusque* (civil and canon
law) for Orthodox Slavs, not only during the Middle Ages but also for
centuries afterwards.[7] It is a compilation of numerous legal documents which had emerged in the Christian East by that time.
However, in terms of its structure, size and in particular its practical

[4] *Kormchaia* (*Kormčaja Kniga, Krmčija*), according to current etymological interpretation
'the pilot's book', is a term for Slavic collections of ecclesiastical and secular law:
A. P. Kazhdan and A. M. Talbot, eds, *The Oxford Dictionary of Byzantium* (Oxford,
1991; hereafter: *ODB*), 1149.
[5] В. Н. Бенешевич [V. N. Beneshevich], *Древнеславянская кормчая XIV титулов
без толкований* [*Drevneslovı̈anskaı̈a kormchaı̈a 14 titlov bez tolkovanı̈ / Old Slavic
Kormchaia Book in 14 Titles without Interpretation*] (St Petersburg, 1906); Ярослав
Н. Щапов [İAroslav N. Shchapov], *Византийское и южнославянское правовое
наследие на Руси в XI–XIII в.* [*Vizantijskoe i juzhnoslavı̈anskoe pravovoe nasledenie na
Rusi v XI–XIII v. / Byzantine and South Slavic Legal Heritage in 11th- to 13th-Century
Russia*] (Moscow, 1978), 49–63.
[6] For a comprehensive assessment of the development and significance of the *Kormchaia*,
see Мария В. Корогодина [Marija V. Korogodina], *Кормчие книги 14 – первой
половины 17 вв. Том 1 – исследование, том 2 – описание редакций* [*Kormchie
knigi 14 – pervoj poloviny 17 veka. Tom 1: issledovanie, Tom 2: opisanie redakcii̇ /
Kormchaia Books from the 14th Century to the first half of the 17th Century*, 1: *Studies*; 2:
Description of the Redactions] (Moscow and St Petersburg, 2017).
[7] This is how the significance of the code was described by Сергије Троицки [Sergije
Troicki], *Како треба издати Светосавску крмчију, номоканон са тумачењима*
[*Kako treba izdati Svetosavsku krmčiju, nomokanon sa tumačenjima / How to publish
Saint Sava's Kormchaia, The* Nomocanon *with Interpretation*] (Belgrade, 1952), 1–2.

application, it overshadowed similar legal codes. The selection of the laws, the commentaries on them and the relationship between ecclesiastical and secular laws were all incorporated in such a way that a new legal corpus was created. Several thirteenth- and fourteenth-century manuscripts of the Serbian redaction have been preserved, and their contents are considered to be similar to the original.[8] The author, or more precisely the editor, of this version of the nomocanon was Sava Nemanjić, the Serbian prince (later a monk of Mount Athos) who became the first archbishop of the Serbian church. The emergence of the nomocanon was closely related to the establishment of the autocephalous Serbian church during the early thirteenth century.[9]

A few words about the title of the collection are in order before we consider it more closely. Slavic collections of church law are generally referred to as *Kormchaias*. However, this term was coined at a later time, most likely in Rus. The title of the oldest manuscripts is *Ова књига се зове грчким језиком Номоканон, а нашим језиком Законоправило* ('This book is called Nomocanon in the Greek

---

[8] One of the oldest manuscripts, Ilovichka Kormchaia, was published in a phototype edition: *Законоправило или Номоканон Светога Саве, Иловачки препис 1262. године* [*Zakonopravilo ili Nomokanon Svetoga Save, Ilovački prepis 1262. godine* / *The Zakonopravilo or Nomocanon of St Sava: The Ilovichka Transcription of 1262*, ed. M. Петровић [M. Petrović] (Gornji Milanovac, 1991). However, a critical edition and a translation into modern language were only provided for chapters 1–47: Миодраг Петровић and Љубица Штављанин-Ђорђевић [Miodrag Petrović and Ljubica Štavljanin-Đorđević], eds, *Законоправило Светога Саве I* [*Zakonopravilo Svetoga Save I* / *The Zakonopravilo of St Sava I*] (Belgrade, 2005). For a description of the oldest Serbian manuscripts, see Троицки [Troicki], Како треба издати [*Kako treba izdati*], 34–75; Александар Соловјев [Aleksandar Solovjev], 'Светосавски Номоканон и његови нови преписи' ['Svetosavski Nomokanon i njegovi novi prepisi' / 'The Nomocanon of Saint Sava and its Transcriptions'], *Братство* [*Bratstvo*] 24 (1932), 22–39; Vatroslav Jagić, 'Opisi i izvodi iz nekoliko južnoslovinskih rukopisa. Krmčaja Ilovička godine 1262' ['Descriptions and Extracts of a few South Slavic Manuscripts: The Kormchaia Ilovichka of 1262], *Starine Jugoslavenska akademija znanosti i umjetnosti* 6 (1874), 60–111.

[9] Миодраг Петровић [Miodrag Petrović], 'Свети Сава као састављач и преводилац Законоправила – српског Номоканона' ['Sveti Sava kao sastavljač i prevodilac Zakonopravila – srpskog Nomokanona' / 'St Sava as a Writer and Translator of Legal Rights in the Serbian Nomocanon'], *Istorijski časopis* 49 (2002), 27–47, at 29–32; Сергије Троицки [Sergije Troicki], 'Ко је превео Крмчију са тумачењима' ['Ko je preveo Krmčiju sa tumačenjima' / 'Who translated the Kormchaia with Interpretations?'], *Glas Srpske kraljevske akademije* 96 (1949), 119–42; idem, 'Da li je slovenski Nomokanon sa tumačenjima postojao pre svetog Save?' ['Did the Slavic Nomocanon with Interpretations exist before St Sava?'], *Slovo* 4–5 (1955), 111–22.

language, and in our language *Zakonopravilo*'). So the most accurate name of the thirteenth-century redaction would be *Zakonopravilo* ('Rules and Law').[10] However, the legal document in question here belongs to the category of nomocanon, available in Eastern church law. Since the term *Kormchaia* was no longer in regular use by the beginning of the thirteenth century, we will use the term nomocanon instead.

The international situation had strongly influenced the writing and composition of this legal text. It is enlightening to consider briefly the political context in which the idea of a specific Slavic corpus of ecclesiastical law developed. At the end of the twelfth century, the conduct of church politics formed the basis for state politics, within and beyond the Balkan states. In the circumstances surrounding the Fourth Crusade and the fall of Constantinople (1204), the rulers of Balkan Slavic states found an opportunity to pursue their own interests. The shadow of the Byzantine emperor, which had until then loomed over them, was now removed. They therefore undertook to improve still further the position of their states, which had already become able to exercise political independence.[11] In addition, amongst the Slavic peoples, ideas of legitimacy and legality had matured, probably as a result of the previous centuries under Byzantine law. Local rulers no longer based their power on military force alone but sought to define their positions in the light of contemporary concepts of statehood.

For Serbian and Bulgarian rulers, this implied seeking the crown from the pope and struggling for ecclesiastical independence from Constantinople. Orthodoxy recognized local, separate, autocephalous churches within a unified church community, while in the West there was only one Catholic Church, with the pope as its head. The concept of the state's political independence was also understood

[10] The Slavic compound *Zakonopravilo* corresponds closely to the original Greek, which is made up of two words: νόμος, 'law in general' (in this case state law), and κάνων, authoritative 'rules' laid down by ecclesiastical bodies: М. Петровић [M. Petrović], *О Законоправилу или Номоканону Св.Саве* [*O Zakonopravilu ili Nomokanonu Sv. Save / The Zakonopravilo or Nomocanon of St Sava*] (Belgrade, 1990), 7–39; Burgmann, 'Vortrag zur slavischen Rezeption', 361–2.

[11] John V. A. Fine, *The Late Medieval Balkans: A Critical Survey from the Late Twelfth Century to the Ottoman Conquest* (Ann Arbor, MI, 1994) 54–8, 61–4, 79–80; Stephenson, *Byzantium's Balkan Frontier*, 309–14; Snezhana Rakova, *The Fourth Crusade in the Historical Memory of the Eastern Orthodox Slavs* (Sofia, 2013), 2–6, 55–99.

differently in East and West. Byzantine emperors strove to ensure their supreme power by establishing certain formal relationships with rulers of neighbouring states. The application of high titles to Balkan rulers (*sebastokrator*, later despot) implied that they were being introduced into the ruling hierarchy within the Byzantine order, even in the cases of those states which both formally and in practice had a large degree of independence.[12] This did not fully satisfy the ambitions of the rulers of the Balkan peoples. The West, on the other hand, lacked a similar form of ruling hierarchy. Balkan Orthodox rulers therefore sought recognition of their political power and independence in the West. Skilful balancing between Rome and Constantinople brought numerous benefits to their states during the early thirteenth century.

The royal crown was a symbol that satisfied the political ambitions of Slavic Balkan rulers of that period. The unquestionable authority exercised by the papacy in providing the crown also reinforced the interests of the Catholic Church. In addition, giving the royal crown to certain rulers on the periphery of Rome's interest extended papal primacy further towards the East.[13] For Balkan rulers, the crown was not merely a matter of prestige or support for their reign, but rather a visible legitimation of their government and of the independence of their states which could be used to secure international recognition. Moreover, church affairs at the beginning of the thirteenth century were marked by the remarkable personality of Pope Innocent III (1198–1216). He focused on establishing absolute papal authority, and on asserting the role of the papacy not only in crowning, but also in selecting, kings.[14] Although the pope was concerned primarily with ecclesiastical authority, political ambition was uppermost in the minds of Balkan rulers.

The significantly strengthened Bulgarian state was therefore already a strong sphere of Roman interest at the beginning of the Fourth Crusade. The Bulgarian ruler Kalojan (1197–1207) proved

---

[12] George Ostrogorsky, 'Die *byzantinische Staatenhierarchie*', *Seminarum Kordakovianum* 8 (1936), 41–61; Günter Prinzing, 'Byzanz, Altrussland und die sogenannte "Familie der Könige"', in Martina Thomsen, ed., *Religionsgeschichtliche Studien zum östlichen Europa: Festschrift für Ludwig Steindorff zum 65. Geburtstag*, Quellen und Studien zur Geschichte des östlichen Europa 85 (Stuttgart, 2017), 43–56.

[13] Fine, *Late Medieval Balkans*, 79–81.

[14] Friedrich Kempf, 'Innocent's Claim to Power', in James M. Powell, ed., *Innocent III, Vicar of Christ or Lord of the World?*, 2nd edn (Washington DC, 1994), 173–7.

himself to be a very successful diplomat, to whom Innocent III showed great respect and on whom he bestowed a crown in 1204.[15] The correspondence between the pope and the Bulgarian ruler explicitly stresses papal supremacy and specifically points out the need to bring the Bulgarian church under Roman obedience.[16]

Serbian rulers waited rather longer for the royal crown, asking for it several times. It seems that the most serious hindrance was the interest of the kingdom of Hungary in the area. However, in 1217 Pope Honorius III sent the crown to the Serbian ruler Stefan Nemanjić, who thus became known as 'The First-Crowned'.[17] Soon after receiving the crown, Serbia also gained ecclesiastical autocephaly at Nicaea in 1219 at the hand of Emperor Theodore I Laskaris and Patriarch Manuel Sarantenos Charitopoulos. Sava was then proclaimed archbishop. The form of autocephaly granted to the Serbian church meant that in practice the council of bishops would elect a new archbishop.[18]

One of the most significant sources, Domentijan's *Life of St Sava*, testifies that Sava stayed in Thessaloniki on his return from Nicaea.[19] It is thought that he finished work on the nomocanon during his stay in Thessaloniki. However, due to the size of the collection, the number of sources and its selection of laws, the compilation must have taken many years. It is possible that Sava had earlier become

---

[15] Fine, *Late Medieval Balkans*, 31–3; Stephenson, *Byzantium's Balkan Frontier*, 309–12; Ани Данчева-Василева [Ani Dancheva-Vasileva], *България и Латинската империя (1204–1261)* [*B'lgariiā i Latinskata imperiiā (1204–1261)* / *Bulgaria and the Latin Empire (1204–1261)*] (Sofia, 1985), 40–8.

[16] *Innocentii III Romani pontificis regestorum sive epistolarum, liber septimus* (PL 215, cols 277–88).

[17] Fine, *Late Medieval Balkans*, 107; С.Ћирковић, ед. [S. Ćirković, ed.], *Историја српског народа I*, [*Istorija srpskog naroda I* / *The History of the Serbian People*] (Belgrade, 1994), 299–300.

[18] *Историја српског народа I* [*Istorija srpskog naroda I*], 317–22; Петровић [Petrović], 'Свети Сава као састављач ' ['Sveti Sava kao sastavljač'], 27–9; Zoran Milutinović, 'Legitimacy through Translation: The Miraculous Transformation of Laws and Relics', in Stephan M. Hart and Zoltan Biedermann, eds, *From the Supernatural to the Uncanny* (Cambridge, 2017), 6–20.

[19] Ђура Даничић [Đura Daničić], ed., *Живот Светога Симеуна и Светога Саве, написао Доментијан* [*Život Svetoga Simeuna i Svetoga Save, napisao Domentijan* / *The Lives of St Simeon and St Sava, written by Domentijan*] (Belgrade, 1865), 227. Domentijan's *Life of St Sava* is considered one of the most reliable sources on the life and work of the first Serbian archbishop. It was written in the second half of the thirteenth century, and its author (a monk) is thought to be one of Sava's students and associates.

acquainted with numerous works of ecclesiastical law as a monk on Mount Athos, and that he began the translation of individual segments then.[20]

Moreover, in the twelfth century the Orthodox East started to refocus on canon law. The period was marked by three excellent canon lawyers, Aristenos, Zonaras and Balsamon, who provided interpretations of the canon that remain a permanent contribution to Orthodox church law.[21] The resulting changes in Eastern church law had to be accepted by the Slavic world as well. The legal codes translated into Old Slavic in the ninth century did not include interpretations of the regulations, nor did they sufficiently reflect contemporary achievements and progress in this domain. The need for a new nomocanon was therefore very pressing. While Sava cannot compare with these great names in terms of his theological achievements, his activities are still immeasurably important for the development of Balkan Slavic spirituality. Although Sava's work does not suggest authorship or personal interpretation, his activities provided a real legislative outcome, in the form of a practically applicable legal code which would not be superseded for many centuries.

The structure of the nomocanon as a legal document does not allow for much creativity or authorial freedom. What is original is the selection and combination of texts. There are no Greek manuscripts, so far as we are aware, with the same selection of regulations in the same order, even in the canonical part of the collection, let alone in the entire code.[22] It is quite certain that this substantial work required the activity of many people and that it was compiled by combining various texts,

---

[20] Троицки [Troicki], 'Ко је превео Крмчију' ['Ko je preveo Krmčiju'], 119–42; Щапов [Shchapov], Византийское ['Vizantiĭskoe'], 120–3; Петровић [Petrović], 'Свети Сава као састављач' ['Sveti Sava kao sastavljač'], 29–32.

[21] Spyros Troianos, 'Byzantine Canon Law from the Twelfth to the Fifteenth Centuries', in Wilfried Hartmann and Kenneth Pennington, eds, *The History of Byzantine and Eastern Canon Law to 1500* (Washington DC, 2012), 170–214; М. Е. Красножен [M. E. Krasnozhen], *Толкователи канонического кодекса Восточной Церкви: Аристин, Зонара и Вальсамон: Исследование* [*Tolkovateli kanonicheskogo kodeksa Vostochnoĭ tserkvi: Aristin, Zonara i Valsamon: Issledovanie / The Commentators on the Eastern Church Canon Code, Aristenos, Zonaras and Balsamon: A Study*] (Yuryev, 1911).

[22] Suggestions of similarity with a Greek nomocanon in the Vatican Library and attempts to prove that the Slavic translation was based on a Greek model have not sustained detailed analysis; in addition to similarities, numerous differences have also been noted: Ludwig Burgmann, 'Der Codex Vaticanus graecus 1167 und der serbische Nomokanon', *Zbornik radova Vizantološkog instituta* 34 (1995), 91–106; Петровић [Petrović], 'Свети Сава као састављач' ['Sveti Sava kao sastavljač'], 32–41.

Greek and Slavic, old and new. We may also ask why older versions of the nomocanon, translated into Slavic in the ninth century, were not simply taken over and adapted. The reasons for starting afresh and organizing the legal code of the Slavic church in a completely new way lie in the fact that the older translations were no longer appropriate to the political circumstances of the thirteenth century.

The significance of this becomes clearer if we summarize briefly the contents of St Sava's nomocanon. The introduction consists of six short chapters, providing the history of ecumenical and local councils and interpretations of certain prayers. The canonical part of the collection contains forty-three chapters, classified into three groups of regulations: rules of the seven ecumenical councils, rules of local councils and rules of the holy fathers. This is a customary Orthodox approach to the organization of canonical codices. In compiling the canonical part of the volume, at least two full Greek nomocanons were used, along with several minor sources, some of which remain unknown.[23] The principal source is the *Synopsis* of Stephen of Ephesus with Aristenos's interpretation.[24] It contains an abridged text of the canon and offers an interpretation of most, but not all, regulations. The second is the *Syntagma* of Joannes Zonaras, with the full text of the canon and its interpretations. Although this source is thought to have been used to a lesser extent, it was still fundamental to about eighty canons and interpretations. As editor, Sava not only combined regulations from these sources, but in stating individual rules he also skilfully incorporated segments from both sources. Neither of these Greek ecclesiastical legal codes had previously been translated into Slavic.[25] There are also indications that Sava used the available Slavic translation of Methodius's nomocanon.

---

[23] Most of the sources for the canonical part in its original form were published in Γ. Α. Ράλλης and Μ. Ποτλής [G. A. Rhalle and M. Potle], *Σύνταγμα των Θείων και Ιερών Κανόνων των τε Αγίων και πανευφήμων Αποστόλων, και των Ιερών και Οικουμενικών και τοπικών Συνόδων, και των κατά μέρος Αγίων Πατέρων* [*Syntagma ton theion kai hieron kanonon ton te hagion kai paneuphemon apostolon, kai ton hieron oikoumenikon kai topikon synodon, kai ton kata meros hagion pateron / Constitution of the Divine and Holy Rules of the Holy and Sacred Apostles, and of the Holy and Ecumenical Local Synods, and of the Holy Fathers*], vols 2–4 (Athens, 1852–4).

[24] For a new edition, see *Alexios Aristenos, Kanonistischer Kommentar zur 'Synopsis canonum'*, ed. Eleftheria Papagianni et al., Forschungen zur byzantinischen Rechtsgeschichte NF 1 (Berlin, 2019).

[25] For an overview of the contents and sources of the Nomocanon of St Sava, see Троицки [Troicki], *Како треба издати* [*Kako treba izdati*], 77–95; Петровић

The secular part of the collection consists of selected documents concerned with civil law, of which, again, most had not been translated into the Slavic language. Two chapters of the nomocanon (45 and 47) contain parts of the substantial core of Justinian's legislation. A selection of *Novellae* on ecclesiastical constitution is first listed, and another chapter reproduces parts of the *Collectio tripartita*.[26] The secular part of the nomocanon of St Sava also contains a chapter introducing the law of Moses.[27] A specific place among civil laws in the nomocanon is given to the *Prochiron*.[28] This is a text taken over in its entirety from the ninth-century Byzantine civil code, which here appeared in Slavic translation for the first time. This code replaced the *Ecloga*, which, as a civil code, had been an integral part of older Slavic nomocanons.[29] The selection of the *Prochiron* instead of the *Ecloga* may have been a consequence of political and ideological factors. Although the *Ecloga* had already been accepted in Slavic lands, its introduction praising the imperial government and its origin during the iconoclast period met with disapproval among twelfth- and thirteenth-century lawmakers.

[Petrović], *О Законоправилу* [*O Zakonopravilu*], 125–43; Корогодина [Korogodina], *Кормчие книги II* [*Kormchie knigi II*], 14–28.

[26] *ODB*, 480; Nikolaas Van der Wal and Bernard H. Stolte, eds, *Collection Tripartita: Justinian on Religious and Ecclesiastical Affairs* (Groningen, 1994).

[27] Sven Meeder, '*Liber ex lege Moysi*: Notes and Text', *Journal of Medieval Latin* 19 (2009), 173–218.

[28] *ODB*, 1725; See K. E. Zachariæ von Lingenthal, ed., Ὁ προχειρος νομος. *Imperatorum Basilii, Constantini et Leonis Prochiron* (Heidelberg, 1837), 1–258; ET *A Manual of Eastern Roman Law: The* Procheiros Nomos *published by the Emperor Basil I at Constantinople between 867 and 879 A.D.*, transl. Edwin Hanson Freshfield (Cambridge, 1928); Ludwig Burgmann, 'Zur Entstehung des Prochiron auctum I. Das Prochiron Stephani', in idem, *Ausgewählte Aufsätze zur byzantinischen Rechtsgeschichte*, Forschungen zur byzantinischen Rechtsgeschichte 33 (Frankfurt am Main, 2015), 285–342.

[29] *ODB*, 672–3; see Ludwig Burgmann, ed., *Ecloga. Das Gesetzbuch Leons III. und Konstantinos V.*, Forschungen zur byzantinischen Rechtsgeschichte 10 (Frankfurt am Main, 1983); ET *A Manual of Roman Law: The* Ecloga, *published by the Emperors Leo III and Constantine V of Isauria*, transl. Edwin Hanson Freshfield (Cambridge, 1927). For the Slavic version of this code, see Ярослав Н. Щапов [Ĩaroslav N. Shchapov], *Византийская Эклога законов в русской письменной традиции. Исследование, издание текстов и комментарий* [*Vizantīĭskaĩa Ekloga zakonov v russkŏĭ pis'menŏĭ tradicii / The Byzantine* Ecloga *in the Russian Written Tradition: Study, Text and Comments*] (St Petersburg, 2011); Ludwig Burgmann and Jaroslav N. Ščapov, eds, *Die slavische Ecloga*, Forschungen zur byzantinischen Rechtsgeschichte 23 (Frankfurt am Main, 2011).

Although we might expect that the canonical part of the volume would provide little opportunity for pursuing political and ideological goals, such motivations may be detected even there. Indeed, several segments stand out in which political and ideological aspects are crucially important, and to which the editor of the nomocanon gave particular attention. These include his treatments of the question of caesaropapism and of the relationship between the Byzantine emperor and the patriarch of Constantinople, and his view of the Roman church.

The nomocanon is particularly noteworthy for its tendency to reject the theory of caesaropapism.[30] Although this concept was characteristic of Byzantine imperial thought, it did not serve the interests of Orthodox Slavic states. Moreover, Sava distanced himself from the regulations stressing the authority and primacy of patriarchs of Constantinople, and their pretensions toward the Slavic churches. Removal of such regulations from Slavic nomocanons was intended to facilitate the establishment of an autocephalous church and the proclamation of as much independence from Constantinople as possible, from both secular and ecclesiastical authorities.[31]

Sava made an effort to introduce into his nomocanon regulations which accentuated the balance between secular and ecclesiastical powers. The issue of the relationship between church and state, and in particular the interpretation of caesaropapism, had affected his choice of sources and interpretations significantly. Balsamon's interpretations of canonical regulations were tendentious and too supportive of the emperor and his interests. To counter this, Sava rejected Balsamon's interpretations and decided to base his nomocanon on older interpretations by Aristenos and Zonaras. The fact that Sava opted for the shortest collection with interpretations suggests that the length of the text also had a role in his decision. There was a need to regulate the daily life of the church efficiently and precisely; on the other hand, confessional and spiritual circumstances were such that the Slavs were still not ready for high-flown theological disputes.

---

[30] *ODB*, 364–5; Deno J. Geanakoplos, 'Church and State in the Byzantine Empire: A Reconsideration of the Problem of Caesaropapism', *ChH* 34 (1965), 381–403.

[31] Сергије Троицки [Sergije Troicki], 'Црквено-политичка идеологија Светосавске Крмчије и Властареве Синтагме' ['Crkveno-politička ideologija Svetosavske Krmčije i Vlastareve Sintagme' / 'Ecclesiastical-Political Ideology in the *Kormchaia* of St Sava and *Syntagma* of Blastaros'], *Glas Srpske akademije nauka* 212 (1953), 157–64.

In the second part, containing secular laws, Sava carefully selected those laws that spoke in favour of the balance between the secular and ecclesiastical authorities. Thus at the beginning of chapter 45 he included a declaration on the symphonic relationship of clergy and the empire, taken from the *Collectio in 87 Capitulorum*.[32] In addition, his insistence on certain older rules and canons regarding Roman primacy was intended to limit the influence of the patriarchs of Constantinople.[33] For this more lenient attitude to the church of Rome, circumstances from 1204 onwards were particularly important. Mount Athos was also under Latin rule, so Sava must have established contact with Latin clergy before that date.[34] In many ways they helped to form Sava as monk, priest and head of a church. Well aware of the political situation, Sava supported the coronation of his brother with the crown from Rome, and the maintenance of a relationship with the papal office. Apart from the effort to avoid regulations which emphasized the authority of the Byzantine emperor, what is noticeable is the attempt to distance the Slavic churches from the pontiffs of Constantinople. When choosing regulations for his nomocanon, Sava left out those rules and regulations present in the Byzantine church which denied Roman primacy. In this way, he sought to elevate a new autocephalous church, the heart of which was the central Balkans, above the disputes between those two ecclesiastical centres. His flexible attitude resulted in the Slavic Orthodox world remaining apart from the conflict between Rome and Constantinople.

The influence of thirteenth-century political circumstances on the structure of St Sava's nomocanon may be seen in its treatment of the topic of heresy. In the twelfth and thirteenth centuries, the Bogomil movement became very strong.[35] Realizing the religious and political importance of this problem, Sava paid specific attention to the

[32] I. B. Pitra, *Iuris ecclesiastici graecorum historia et monumenta*, 2: *A VI ad IX saeculum* (Rome, 1868), 385–405; *ODB*, 480.
[33] Троицки [Troicki], 'Црквено-политичка идеологија' ['Crkveno-politička ideologija'], 175–86.
[34] Сима Ђирковић [Sima Ćirković], 'Свети Сава између истока и запада' ['Sveti Sava između istoka i zapada' / 'St Sava between East and West'], in idem, ed, *Свети Сава у српској историји и традицији* [*Sveti Sava u srpskoj istoriji i tradiciji* / *St Sava in Serbian History and Tradition*] (Belgrade, 1995), 27–38.
[35] Bogomilism was a dualist, neo-Manichaean sect founded in tenth-century Bulgaria, which subsequently spread to the Balkans. It held that God created and ruled the spiritual part of the world, and that Satan created the material world. The movement rejected the

condemnation of heretical doctrines, dedicating several chapters to the matter and using various sources. Sava incorporated several epistles by the holy fathers dealing with the struggle against non-Christian teaching. Particular attention was paid to the Manichean heresy, whose adherents he described in the title of chapter 42, using a term familiar in the twelfth- and thirteenth-century Balkans, as 'those who now call themselves Bogomils or Babuns'.[36]

This general legal code was first accepted by the Bulgarian church, which was elevated to the level of a patriarchate and recognized as autocephalous in 1237. Very quickly, the nomocanon found its way to Rus as well. In 1262, the Russian metropolitan, Kiril III, received a copy from Bulgaria, quite certainly Sava's redaction. The need for reform resulted in a council being held in 1274 at which this version was proclaimed the official church legal code.[37]

During the following centuries this document developed only in Rus, while in Balkan lands, pressed by Ottoman attacks, interest in church legislation diminished. In time, the nomocanon (*Kormchaia*) underwent some changes.[38] Thus the first version printed in Rus (1650) differed in many respects from the oldest known manuscripts of the Serbian redaction. Reasons for these changes were numerous: whilst some were made in the process of copying, others were deliberate, motivated by political considerations. In the Russian redaction, parts of the *Epanagoge* appeared.[39] Likewise, the *Ecloga* of Emperor Leo III found its way back in. The final chapters of the collection,

---

whole organization of the Orthodox Church: *ODB*, 301; Edvard Paters, *Heresy and Authority in Medieval Europe* (Philadelphia, PA, 1980), 108–15.

[36] Иловачки препис [*Ilovački prepis*], 205–6; Законоправило [*Zakonopravilo*], ed. Петровић and Штављанин [Pertović and Štavljanin], 602–3.

[37] Елена В. Белякова and Ярослав Н. Щапов [Elena V. Beliakova and I͡Aroslav N. Shchapov], 'Традиции святого Саввы Сербского на Руси' ['Tradicii sviatogo Savvy Serbskogo na Rusi' / 'Traditions of St Sava of Serbia in Rus'], in Ћирковић [Ćirković], ed., *Свети Сава* [*Sveti Sava*], 359–68.

[38] For an overview of Russian redactions and manuscripts, see Корогодина [Korogodina], *Кормчие книги II* [*Kormchie knigi II*], 65–414.

[39] The *Epanagoge* was a book of laws of the emperors Basil I, Leo VI and Alexander, promulgated in the second half of the ninth century. Patriarch Photius took part in its composition, writing two important sections about the power of the patriarch and the emperor. Although the *Epanagoge* soon ceased to be officially circulated, it found the way into Russian law and was included in *Kormchaias*. Its provisions on the positions of the patriarch and the church contributed greatly to the strengthening of ecclesiastical authority in Rus: *ODB*, 703.

dealing with secular legislation, underwent the most changes. Of course, there had been major political and social changes between the thirteenth and seventeenth centuries, so we might expect such amendments.

As a consequence of the Ottoman invasion, Orthodox legislation ceased to develop in the late fourteenth and fifteenth centuries. The Slavic peoples became more familiar with Western legal regulations, which were often not harmonized with the tradition of laws that had applied previously. This caused some confusion: some matters, especially relating to marriage or inheritance law, were treated completely differently in various chapters of the *Kormchaia*. Contemporary Orthodox Slavic collections of church laws developed further in Rus, where they were amended, adapted, but also to a large extent copied, and regularly printed after 1650.

In conclusion, the development of Slavic church legislation was largely determined by political circumstances. During the early phases of conversion and acceptance of Christian law, in the ninth century, the direct influence of Byzantine legislation was strongest. Hence this period was marked by the prevalence of shorter collections of ecclesiastical law, which took the form of translations from Greek of complete Byzantine legal codes. However, the development of Slavic states resulted in the perception of a need to use legal codes to regulate affairs in church and state. Among Orthodox Slavic peoples, receiving Christianity and accepting its associated law resulted in a changed understanding of their own state and government: they introduced primogeniture in local dynasties, accepted the ruling hierarchy typical of the empire, and entered into vassal relations with Constantinople. Simultaneously, the idea of independent church structures developed, which would be influenced more by the rulers of these states than by Byzantine ecclesiastical and civil authorities.

The most intensive development of ecclesiastical law among Orthodox Slavs took place during the early thirteenth century, coinciding with the rise of Balkan Slavic states and their ambition to become kingdoms. The compilation of the nomocanon of St Sava was supported by the need to secure ecclesiastical and political independence. Through skilful combination of various sources and interpretations, this collection stressed the principle of conciliarity, and in particular those regulations acknowledging the autocephaly of local national churches. Politically and ideologically, the importance of the nomocanon of St Sava lies in the fact that in his selection of rules and interpretations he liberated Slavic Orthodoxy from the strong influence of the ecclesiastical and secular authority of Constantinople. In addition, he contributed to the development in which the Slavic Orthodox world stood aside during the conflict between Rome and Constantinople.

The availability of this comprehensive and reliable corpus of church law provided the independent churches in Slavic Orthodox states with the power to act. The nomocanon of St Sava was so conceived as to represent a general legal text with broad applicability. It regulated the domain of church affairs almost completely, but since the jurisdiction of church courts also included marriage law and inheritance law, this code also included regulations dealing with these areas and with some other aspects of civil law. In the Slavic Orthodox world, the code was accepted quickly and easily, since it was compiled locally, rather than imposed by Byzantine church authorities. This provided solid grounds for the subsequent growth of independent, autocephalous churches of the Serbian, Bulgarian and Russian Orthodox peoples.

Finally, the validity of a law is reflected in its applicability and longevity. The greatest evidence for the importance of this collection lies in its long use throughout the Slavic Orthodox world. Although over time numerous redactions were made and some changes introduced, the thirteenth-century *Zakonopravilo* of St Sava remained the basis of all Slavic *Kormchaias*.

General Excommunications of Unknown Malefactors: Conscience, Community and Investigations in England, *c*.1150–1350

Felicity Hill*

University of St Andrews

In high and late medieval England, general sentences of excommunication pronounced against unnamed wrongdoers were common. Responding to crimes whose perpetrators were unknown, general excommunications were a valuable tool that sought to discover and punish offenders in a number of ways. Solemn denunciations might convince the guilty to confess in order to avoid damnation, or persuade informants to volunteer information. General sentences were also, however, merely a precursor to investigations launched into those responsible. Public denunciations aided investigations conducted by clergy in the local community by publicizing and forcibly condemning the crime committed. Once discovered, suspects were summoned to the bishop's court and were either forced to make amends and do penance or excommunicated by name. This article therefore argues that general sentences were far more complex, effective and legally significant than they are often perceived to be.

In the 1160s,[1] an old man was forced by necessity to sell some wood he owned. Being old and feeble, he entrusted the business of the sale to his adolescent son. The son, however, was greedy, defrauding his father by keeping most of the sale proceeds for himself. Not suspecting his son, but certain that he had been wronged, the father asked his parish priest to bind with an anathema 'whoever had brought this loss upon him'. Three times the priest warned that he would pronounce the sentence, yet the son admitted nothing, publicly or privately. Finally the excommunication was pronounced, but

* Department of Mediaeval History, University of St Andrews, 71 South St, St Andrews, KY16 9QW. E-mail: fgh2@st-andrews.ac.uk.
I am grateful to John Arnold and John Hudson for their comments on drafts of this article, as well as to the editors and anonymous peer reviewers.
[1] 'Before the martyrdom of St Thomas'.

Studies in Church History 56 (2020), 93–113 © Ecclesiastical History Society 2020
doi: 10.1017/stc.2019.6

still the son felt no remorse, disregarding the fact that Satan now possessed his body and soul. But one night while he was fast asleep, completely naked except for a nightcap, two malignant spirits appeared. Dragging him out, the spirits cried in terrible voices, 'You are ours and you are coming with us!' In the morning, only the nightcap was found. It later transpired that the spirits had taken their (presumably still naked) prisoner to the Thames, where they had forced some sailors to ferry them across, 'for no other reason, I suspect, than that what had happened should afterwards be made known by them'.[2]

This story, related in Peter of Cornwall's *Book of Revelations* (*c*.1200) describes the excommunication of an unknown malefactor, and was intended to serve as a warning to excommunicates. Whilst the tale provides a satisfying conclusion, nonetheless a considerable problem with sentences pronounced against unnamed criminals is evident. Barring a miracle, someone excommunicated anonymously could get away with their crime. Nobody had been aware of the son's guilt; he himself had not admitted to his crime. Had the sailors not been involved, no one would have known that he had been dragged off to hell or discovered who had committed the crime. Yet such sentences, condemning unknown perpetrators after a crime, were common practice in high medieval England.

It is easy to understand why general sentences, chastising criminals whose names were not even known, might be dismissed as being of little practical value. Thus John Arnold, noting the numerous blanket excommunications in Oliver Sutton's episcopal register, has commented: 'This was not a strong form of policing, more a sign of relative impotence.'[3] There is also a recognizable connection between excommunications censuring unknown offenders and eleventh-century monastic clamours. Lester Little argued that eleventh-century maledictions were last resorts, used by those without power following the supposed collapse of Carolingian public justice. They called upon God when there was no help to be found on earth. The powerless were thus resorting to liturgy when they had no recourse to law.[4]

[2] Peter of Cornwall, *Book of Revelations*, ed. R. Easting and R. Sharpe (Toronto, ON, 2013), no. 2897.
[3] John Arnold, *Belief and Unbelief in Medieval Europe* (London, 2005), 182.
[4] Lester K. Little, *Benedictine Maledictions: Liturgical Cursing in Romanesque France* (London, 1993), 186–229.

Seen against this background, thirteenth-century general excommunications could similarly be viewed as futile shouting at the sky. However, just as Little's presentation of liturgical clamours as products of a lack of judicial authority has been criticized, the judicial procedures that accompanied general sentences in high medieval England ought also to be acknowledged.[5]

This article explores general sentences and their outcomes. Aimed at both the individuals who committed crimes and the communities around them, the ways in which general excommunications worked are both more complex and more effective than has been recognized. Most obviously, these sentences were intended to scare offenders into coming forward. Moreover, they were publicly pronounced, so that neighbours who knew the perpetrators would put pressure onto them to own up, or else report them to the authorities. The focus here, however, is on a process, probably developed during the thirteenth century, which was initiated by general sentences. Following the pronouncement of a general excommunication, an investigation (*inquisitio*) was routinely launched into who had perpetrated these offences: communal knowledge of crimes was actively sought by ecclesiastical authorities. Far from being desperate prayers, general sentences were merely the beginning of a judicial process, made possible by legal and administrative developments. Through these investigations, offenders were discovered and brought to justice. The nature of general sentences meant that it was perfectly possible for individuals to be excommunicated without anyone else knowing. Similarly, *ipso facto* sentences (*latae sententiae*) did not excommunicate named individuals, but bound anyone who had or would in future commit certain specified offences. As a result, whilst being anonymously excommunicated had serious implications for a person's soul, none of excommunication's tangible temporal consequences, such as ostracism or withdrawal of legal rights, could follow. Excommunication's consequences prior to death, particularly from a legal perspective, might be negligible.[6] Donald Logan thus

---

[5] Richard E. Barton, 'Making a Clamor to the Lord: Noise, Justice and Power in Eleventh- and Twelfth-Century France', in B. S. Tuten and T. L. Billado, eds, *Feud, Violence and Practice: Essays in Medieval Studies in Honor of Stephen D. White* (Farnham, 2010), 213–35.

[6] That the faithful might unwittingly incur *ipso facto* sentences was a cause for concern amongst medieval canonists: see Felicity Hill, 'Magna Carta, Canon Law and Pastoral Care: Excommunication and the Church's Publication of the Charter', *HR* 89 (2016),

found that even individuals known to have incurred automatic excommunication were not typically arrested by the secular arm (called upon to seize obstinate excommunicates) and Elisabeth Vodola noted that they rarely suffered withdrawal of legal rights.[7] However, investigations launched by general sentences enabled those who had incurred *ipso facto* excommunication to be denounced by name. They could subsequently be treated just like any other excommunicate. Any notion that *ipso facto* sentences did not result in the usual legal consequences is dispelled by an analysis of general sentences.

Over sixty years ago, Rosalind Hill noted that general excommunications occur frequently in the registers of Bishops Sutton and Dalderby of Lincoln and Archbishops Greenfield and Melton of York. Despite her remark that the topic deserves closer investigation, and the fact that such sentences are easily found in many more registers, these excommunications have been little studied since.[8] Certainly, in recent years a number of studies have illuminated *latae sententiae* excommunications. However, whilst deeply linked, *latae sententiae* and general excommunications are not interchangeable. The general sentences under discussion here responded to particular crimes recently perpetrated.[9] Although the ritual and penitential significance of papal and local *ipso facto* sentences has been acknowledged, attempts to seek out unknown excommunicates

---

636–50. For concerns about unknown excommunicates interacting with the faithful, see Christian Jaser, *Ecclesia maledicens. Rituelle und zeremonielle Exkommunikationsformen im Mittelalter* (Tübingen, 2013), 369–70.

[7] F. D. Logan, *Excommunication and the Secular Arm* (Toronto, ON, 1968), 139; Elisabeth Vodola, *Excommunication in the Middle Ages* (Berkeley, CA, 1986), 80, 99, 181–2.

[8] Rosalind Hill, 'The Theory and Practice of Excommunication in Medieval England', *History* 42 (1957), 1–11.

[9] The distinction is not always clear: the papal yearly excommunication is termed a 'general sentence' but corresponds better with this definition of *latae sententiae*. For *latae sententiae*, see Peter Huizing, 'The earliest Development of Excommunication *latae sententiae* by Gratian and the earliest Decretists', *Studia Gratiana* 3 (1955), 277–320; Jaser, *Ecclesia maledicens*, 359–73; Vodola, *Excommunication*, 28–35; R. H. Helmholz, *The Spirit of Classical Canon Law* (London, 1996), 383–90; Arnaud Fossier, *Le Bureau des âmes. Écritures et pratiques administratives de la Pénitencerie Apostolique (XIIIᵉ–XVIᵉ siécle)*, Bibliothèque des Écoles françaises d'Athènes et de Rome 378 (Rome, 2018), 402–6. Much of my book, *Excommunication in Thirteenth-Century England: Community, Politics and Publicity* (Oxford, forthcoming) will deal with *ipso facto* excommunications.

following a crime remain unexplored.[10] Discussions of individuals being bound by such sentences have tended to focus on petitions to the papal penitentiary for absolution. Thus Christian Jaser notes only that *ipso facto* sentences sought to induce people to turn themselves in by appealing to individual consciences.[11] R. H. Helmholz and Véronique Beaulande have both discussed cases in which those accused of incurring excommunication for assaulting clergy (*Si quis suadente*, 1139) were dealt with in court, but do not discuss the courts looking for unknown excommunicates.[12] The decree *Ad vitanda* (1418), which declared that only excommunicates who had been denounced by name ought to be avoided, not those bound by general sentences, has not prompted consideration of how someone might move from one category to the other.[13]

In theory, any offence could be punished by a general sentence, but in practice the vast majority of general sentences declared in England responded to crimes that already incurred automatic excommunication. This solved two potential problems with general sentences. The first was that excommunication required warnings. In cases where the crime incurred a *lata sententia* anyway, the perpetrator was already excommunicated and there was no need for delay before excommunication was pronounced (where no *ipso facto* sentence was

---

[10] Agostino Paravicini Bagliani has traced the development of papal general sentences pronounced annually on Maunday Thursday: 'Bonifacio VIII, la loggia di giustizia al Laterano e i processi generali di scomunica', *Rivista di storia della Chiesa in Italia* 59 (2005), 377–428, at 391–405; idem, 'Il rito pontificio di scomunica da Gregorio VII a Innocenzo III', in idem, *Il potere del papa. Corporeità, autorappresentazione, simboli*, Millennio Medievale, Strumenti e studi n.s. 21 (Florence, 2009), 215–26; Fossier, *Le Bureau des âmes*, 409–24; Christian Jaser, '*Ostensio exclusionis*. Die päpstliche Generalexkommunikation zwischen kirchenrechtlicher Innovation und zeremoniellem Handeln', in Bernd Schneidmüller et al., eds, *Die Päpste. Amt und Herrschaft in Antike, Mittelalter und Renaissance* (Regensburg, 2016), 357–83. The fourth part of Jaser, *Ecclesia Maledicens* (374–525) focuses on the Maundy Thursday papal sentence. R. H. Helmholz has also linked the growing power of the papacy to *latae sententiae*: '"Si quis suadente" (c.17 q.4 c.29): Theory and Practice', in Peter A. Linehan, ed., *Proceedings of the Seventh International Congress of Canon Law: Cambridge, 23–27 July 1984* (Vatican City, 1988), 425–38.
[11] Jaser, '*Ostensio exclusionis*', 364.
[12] Helmholz, '"Si quis suadente"', 432–7; Véronique Beaulande, *Le Malheur d'être exclu? Excommunication, réconciliation et société à la fin du Moyen Âge*, Histoire ancienne et médiévale 84 (Paris, 2006), 96–102.
[13] Jaser, *Ecclesia Maledicens*, 370–3.

involved, warnings remained necessary).[14] Additionally, it meant that the sentence was binding whoever pronounced it: the sentence was issued by the law. The one making the denunciation was merely publicizing an excommunication already incurred.[15] This solved the problem that a general sentence only bound those in the jurisdiction of the one pronouncing the sentence (as stated in the *Liber extra*).[16] The ensuing general sentence would invoke the relevant *lata sententia*, publicize the crime and launch an investigation. If the culprits were subsequently discovered, whatever offence had originally deserved the automatic excommunication would no longer be noted in other documents (for example writs ordering the capture of those excommunicated for forty days or more).[17]

The *latae sententiae* most frequently cited in general sentences were provincial *ipso facto* excommunications pronounced by Archbishop Stephen Langton in the Council of Oxford (1222), and issued by the papal legate Ottobuono in the Council of London (1268). The 'original' *lata sententia* pronounced at the Lateran Council of 1139 (*Si quis suadente*) was also often invoked. The most frequent excommunications thus punished assaulting clergymen (*Si quis suadente*), infringing the rights and liberties of churches (Council of Oxford, c.1), defamation (Council of Oxford, c.5), stealing from ecclesiastical houses, manors or lands (Council of London, c.12) and removing fugitives from sanctuary (ibid.). All these sentences were promulgated frequently in parish churches.[18] General sentences were thus typically

---

[14] For example, *The Register of Ralph of Shrewsbury, Bishop of Bath and Wells, 1329–1363*, ed. Thomas Scott Holmes, Somerset Record Society 10 ([London], 1896), 2: 470; *The Register of John Waltham, Bishop of Salisbury, 1388–1395*, ed. T. C. B. Timmins, CYS 80 (Woodbridge, 1994), no. 66.

[15] Robert of Flamborough, *Liber Poenitentialis: A Critical Edition*, ed. J. J. Francis Firth (Toronto, ON, 1971), 147; *Registrum epistolarum fratris Iohannis Peckham, archiepiscopi Cantuariensis*, ed. Charles Trice Martin, 3 vols, RS 77 (London, 1882–5), 1: 178, 392s, 180, 392t.

[16] *Liber extra* X 5.39.21 (*CICan*, 2: 896). This perhaps contradicts earlier practice: see Flamborough, *Liber Poenitentialis*, 146–7; Thomas of Chobham, *Summa Confessorum*, ed. D. Broomfield (Louvain, 1968), 210–11.

[17] These typically simply note 'manifest offences and contumacy': see Logan, *Excommunication.*

[18] Gratian, *Decretum* C.17 q.4 c.29 (*CICan*, 1: 822); F. M. Powicke and C. R. Cheney, eds, *Councils and Synods with other Documents relating to the English Church*, 2: *A.D. 1205–1313*, 2 vols (Oxford, 1964), 1: 106–7, 2: 764, 905–7. All eleven of Pecham's collected excommunications could result in general sentences, but those I have not mentioned above were less commonly cited in the process.

used in response to attacks against the church, its rights and its members. Theft was frequently cited, but it was usually theft of ecclesiastical property or from clergymen. With the exception of defamation cases, correcting private wrongs on behalf of the laity appears to have been far less common. Although Helmholz noted that *Si quis suadente* cases were treated both as criminal and civil causes in ecclesiastical courts, brought either *ex officio* or at the instance of private parties, in the cases under discussion here ecclesiastical officials seem to have been acting *ex officio,* responding to crimes that incurred automatic excommunication.[19] However, offences may well have been brought to the bishop's attention by offended parties.

Hope of divine retribution may therefore have been in the minds of some clerics who excommunicated unidentified persecutors. These clerics had often been personally injured or robbed. Nevertheless, leaving aside hopes for supernatural punishment, the intention behind general sentences was that the guilty seek absolution, make restitution and perform public penance. Such an outcome would satisfy the requirements of pastoral care, satisfy the injured party and ensure that the bishop was seen to have an effective system whereby offenders were discovered and punished. These cases are presented in the sources as self-contained, not as precursors to further proceedings elsewhere. However, further research may reveal that the process was used in this way; some of these offences would certainly have been of interest to secular authorities.[20]

The first way general sentences might work was by scaring the offender into confessing. This was linked to the idea that God would exact vengeance; convincing people that they might be struck down is the point of miracle stories such as the opening example. Perhaps more potent, however, was the fear, not that death would be hastened, but that it would be followed by an eternity in hell. General sentences were invariably pronounced with a dramatic ceremony which implied that recalcitrant excommunicates would suffer this fate. At the culmination of the ceremony bells were rung, and candles held by the clergy pronouncing the sentence were thrown

---

[19] Helmholz, "'Si quis suadente'", 432.

[20] Ian Forrest notes that violation of sanctuary, involving multiple jurisdictions, was a point of contention: *Trustworthy Men: How Inequality and Faith made the Medieval Church* (Princeton, NJ, 2018), 315–16.

to the ground, as a version of the phrase 'as these lights are extinguished, so their souls are extinguished in hell' was uttered.[21]

General sentences therefore sought to put pressure on the consciences of the guilty to bring about a confession.[22] The possibility that sinners felt anxious about being excommunicated, even if their state was not public knowledge, should be taken seriously. As Hill remarked, 'perhaps the solemnities of bell, book and candle stirred up a spark of piety even in a hardened burglar'.[23] *Latae sententie* incurred only secretly are known to have prompted petitions to the apostolic see for absolution.[24] Similarly, episcopal registers suggest that general sentences could prompt voluntary confessions from the guilty. Thus, in 1279, the bishop of Hereford received three foresters 'humbly seeking' absolution. They were afraid that they were bound (*timentes se ligari*) by an *ipso facto* excommunication promulgated against all those who maliciously prevented the bishop enjoying the liberty of his chase at Malvern.[25] In such cases, it could be argued that unacknowledged pressures (such as rumours in the parish) were behind these seemingly voluntary pleas for absolution. Certainly the formulaic language of humility used by clergy recording these confessions should be treated with caution. Any number of additional considerations could have influenced these criminals' decision to come forward.[26] Equally, however, that excommunicated criminals harboured fears about the state of their souls is perfectly credible. General excommunications could compel requests for absolution by playing upon such fears.

Nevertheless, if trying to scare sinners into confessing was the only purpose of these general sentences, it would be reasonable to view

---

[21] In formulae, 'nisi' clauses offered offenders an opportunity to avoid this fate. Much has been written about ritual excommunication. Jaser, *Ecclesia maledicens* treats it at length. For further references, see Felicity Hill, '*Damnatio eternae mortis* or *medicinalis non mortalis*: The Ambiguities of Excommunication in Thirteenth-Century England', in Andrew M. Spencer and Carl Watkins, eds, *Thirteenth-Century England XVI: Proceedings of the Cambridge Conference, 2015* (Woodbridge, 2017), 37–53, at 49–53.
[22] Jaser, '*Ostensio exclusionis*', 364; Jaser, *Ecclesia Maledicens*, 369.
[23] Hill, 'Theory and Practice', 10.
[24] See, for instance, *A Formulary of the Papal Penitentiary in the Thirteenth Century*, ed. H. C. Lea (Philadelphia, PA, 1892).
[25] *The Register of Thomas de Cantilupe, Bishop of Hereford (A.D. 1275–1282)*, ed. Robert G. Griffiths, CYS 2 ([London], 1906), 227–8.
[26] See John Arnold's discussion of the weight historians give to religious conviction as opposed to political functionalism: *Belief and Unbelief*, 7–8.

them as fairly weak. Although much of the power of general sentences derived from spiritual fears, many criminals would surely have acted like the adolescent in the opening tale, jubilantly feeling they had got away with their crime. Barring a miracle, such unidentified criminals would indeed have done so. However, the effectiveness of general sentences was not limited to appeals to criminals' consciences and fears. They were aimed at communities as much as at individuals.

General sentences were pronounced on Sundays and feast days in churches in the vicinity of the offence committed. Members of the parish, city or diocese who heard the well-publicized excommunication could report any information they had to ecclesiastical authorities, or perhaps urge the guilty to come forward. They might act out of anger or a sense of justice, or they might fear that their friend or relative would end up in hell without absolution. Often general sentences were worded dramatically; it seems that part of the intention was to persuade the audience that the offence required punishment. John of Pontoise, bishop of Winchester, described how satellites of Satan, forgetful of their salvation, with fear of God put aside, had 'with diabolic instinct' besieged a church in an armed multitude.[27] Similar language is found in many general sentences, which routinely term the unknown sinners 'sons of Belial', 'limbs of the devil' and other condemnatory titles. To ensure understanding, it was sometimes specified that these denunciations should be 'in the mother tongue understandable to all'.[28] Communities may not have always been swayed by such descriptions, but the church was certainly seeking informants. In some cases, most obviously theft, nobody might have known who was responsible. Yet if the theft described in the miracle had happened in reality, we might imagine that once it had been publicized, people would notice the son's sudden wealth and begin to suspect him. When Walter Giffard, archbishop of York, sought to find the thieves who stole a rector's horses and books, he ordered an investigation into whom the stolen goods had reached.[29] The miracle story does not mention that the priest was hoping others would turn in the thief, but probably this had long been part of the purpose of publicizing

---

[27] *Registrum Johannis de Pontissara, episcopi Wyntoniensis, A.D. 1282–1304*, ed. Cecil Deedes, 2 vols, CYS 19, 30 ([London], 1915–24), 352–3.
[28] For example, *Registrum Henrici Woodlock, Diocesis Wintoniensis, A.D. 1305–1316*, ed. Arthur Worthington Goodman, 2 vols, CYS 43–4 (Oxford, 1940–1), 352.
[29] *The Register of Walter Giffard, Lord Archbishop of York, 1266–1279*, ed. William Brown, SS 109 (Durham, 1904), 225–6.

general sentences. Some who confessed may therefore have been forced to do so by communal pressure. Conscience was certainly not the only reason to confess to a crime that incurred excommunication.

Usually, however, those who confessed did not appear of their own accord, but were cited following an investigation. This was the key development in general sentences of excommunication. General sentences had probably long sought to encourage informants, but by the end of the thirteenth century they no longer relied upon the volunteering of information. Sentences customarily launched investigations, harnessing new administrative structures and growing episcopal power to seek out communal knowledge of crimes. Vehement denunciations of unknown malefactors urged the guilty to confess, but also facilitated the ensuing investigations by publicizing the crime committed and persuasively condemning those involved.

It is difficult to be certain when investigations seeking the names of malefactors began. Evidence survives only in episcopal registers (in this period at least), which themselves begin to survive from the second half of the thirteenth century. In some form, general sentences certainly had a much longer history. The miracle story with which this article opened, set in the mid-twelfth century and recorded at the turn of the thirteenth, describes the old man's remedy as an unusual one, although this may be because he was a layman rather than because general sentences as a practice were unusual. According to his hagiography, St Hugh of Lincoln (d. 1200) issued a general sentence (the one culprit who refused to seek absolution consequently suffered terrible misfortunes).[30] Writing in the early thirteenth century, Robert of Flamborough matter-of-factly noted the practice while giving a (slightly odd) definition of excommunication by name: someone is excommunicated by name by both 'I excommunicate Peter' and 'I excommunicate he who stole that horse', if Peter stole it.[31] The earliest surviving episcopal register, of Hugh of Wells, bishop of Lincoln (1209–35), mentions numerous people bound by the general excommunication pronounced against the rebellious barons in 1215.[32] General excommunications are likely

[30] *The Life of St Hugh of Lincoln*, ed. and transl. D. L. Douie and D. H. Farmer, 2 vols (Oxford, 1961–85), 2: 197–9.
[31] Flamborough, *Liber Poenitentialis*, 153–4.
[32] *Rotuli Hugonis de Welles, episcopi Lincolniensis, A.D. MCCIX–MCCXXXV*, ed. W. P. W. Phillimore and F. N. Davis, 3 vols, CYS 1, 3, 4 ([London], 1905–9), vol. 1. It does not, however, contain general sentences of the sort under discussion.

to have become more common after 1222, when Stephen Langton ordered seven *ipso facto* excommunications to be publicized four times a year. Clergy would therefore have been increasingly aware of automatic excommunications.[33] The administrative and legal structures necessary to hold successful investigations (local clergy conducting investigations, middling clergy arranging them and the denunciations which publicized crimes, and bishops and archbishops overseeing the process and to whose court anyone discovered was sent) indicate that the the process may have developed in the mid-thirteenth century. Laymen were used from the late twelfth century to make presentments about clerical conduct in their dioceses. Reporting on fellow laypeople appears to have been the innovation of Robert Grosseteste, bishop of Lincoln, in 1238/9.[34] This process of episcopal-led investigation into unnamed excommunicates could thus have developed as diocesan authority became more centralized during the thirteenth century, although it may have earlier roots impossible to trace through the extant evidence.[35] Sampling of episcopal registers from dioceses across England indicates that general excommunications and linked investigations remained important practices into the fifteenth century. Examples towards the end of the fifteenth century are harder to find in registers. Act books of episcopal courts, which survive mostly from the fifteenth century, were beyond the scope of this study, but undoubtedly contain valuable information for later practice. The heyday of general excommunications was perhaps the two centuries from *c.*1250.

The nature of the evidence makes it difficult to know precisely how investigations initiated by general excommunications were conducted in the thirteenth and fourteenth centuries. Not all general excommunications ordered investigations, but this is probably a matter of record rather than an indication that investigations were only

---

[33] Powicke and Cheney, eds, *Councils and Synods*, 106–7, 125.

[34] L. R. Poos, ed., *Lower Ecclesiastical Jurisdiction in Late-Medieval England: The Courts of the Dean and Chapter of Lincoln, 1336–1349, and the Deanery of Wisbech, 1458–1484*, RSEH n.s. 32 (Oxford, 2001), lx–lxi; Andrew D. Brown, *Popular Piety in Late Medieval England: The Diocese of Salisbury 1250–1550* (Oxford, 1995), 77–83; Ian Forrest, 'The Transformation of Visitation in Thirteenth-Century England', *P&P* 221 (2013), 3–38.

[35] Helmholz links English canonical 'juries' to earlier Carolingian practices: 'Canonical "juries" in Medieval England', in Mario Acheri et al., eds, *'Ins Wasser geworfen und Ozeane durchquert'. Festschrift für Knut Wolfgang Nörr* (Cologne, 2003), 403–18.

sometimes launched: instructions to investigate were extremely formulaic and may often not have been enregistered as a result. Inconsistent record keeping is as likely as inconsistent procedure.[36]

Most mandates order solemn denunciations to be pronounced against the unknown miscreants, and end by instructing the recipient (usually an archdeacon or dean) to inquire 'diligently' or 'in form of law' into what had happened and into the names of those responsible. Those found were then cited to appear before the bishop. Sometimes a date and place was set for this appearance at the bishop's 'court of audience', typically wherever he happened to be in his diocese.[37] Simon of Ghent, bishop of Salisbury, thus ordered the rector of Chilton to conduct an investigation 'through people not under suspicion' (*per non suspectos*). The rector was to cite any found guilty or publicly defamed to appear before the bishop at St Mary's Church, Reading, on the third law day after Trinity Sunday (that is, about three weeks after the date of his mandate).[38] These formulaic mandates rarely provide even as much information as this, which suggests that the procedure was common. Bishops must have expected more than is usually recorded. Thus only occasionally were recipients instructed to inform the bishop of the names of those cited, but bishops would surely have expected to be told who was going to appear at their courts.[39] The investigation was intended to round up suspects, not necessarily to discover the guilty.[40] A letter in an Ely formulary (mid-fourteenth century) orders the archdeacon's official to cite those found 'culpable or stained with infamy' (*culpabiles seu infamia*

---

[36] Many registers contain general sentences, both with and without the instruction to investigate, which may have been sent as a separate mandate (e.g. *Registrum Johannis de Pontissara*, 312–13). In this case, not bothering to enregister this standard request would make sense. Investigations were conducted in cases where there is no extant mandate to conduct one, e.g. *Register of Ralph of Shrewsbury*, 2: 596–8, 694.
[37] For example, *The Rolls and Register of Bishop Oliver Sutton 1280–1299*, 4: *Memoranda, May 19, 1292 – May 18, 1294*, ed. Rosalind M. T. Hill, Lincoln Record Society 52 (Hereford, 1958), 4: 35.
[38] *Registrum Simonis de Gandavo, diocesis Saresbiriensis, A.D. 1297–1315*, ed. C. T. Flower and M. C. B. Dawes, 2 vols, CYS 40–1 (Oxford, 1934), 1: 171–3.
[39] For example, *Registrum Roberti Winchelsey, Cantuariensis Archiepiscopi, A.D. 1294–1313*, ed. Rose Graham, 2 vols, CYS 51–2 (London, 1952–6), 1: 216–17. More usually, recipients were ordered to tell the bishop what they had done.
[40] And thus might be compared to the Assize of Clarendon: Richard H. Helmholz, 'The Early History of the Grand Jury and the Canon Law', *University of Chicago Law Review* 50 (1983), 613–27, at 616–17.

respersos).[41] Ralph of Salisbury, bishop of Bath and Wells, detailed 'those you find guilty by reputation or fact' (*culpabiles fama vel facto*).[42] Similarly, archbishop Winchelsey ordered the bishop of Chichester to cause investigation to be made through local rectors, vicars and others he considered suitable, and to cite those found culpable or 'accused' (*notatos*).[43]

In many cases, the results of such investigations were not recorded. Nevertheless, we should not assume that bishops merely gave up: episcopal registers are far from exhaustive and uniform in their record-keeping practices. The register of Simon of Ghent contains comparatively more information regarding this process and successful outcomes, but this is probably down to an unusually thorough registrar rather than a more effective administration. Nor were registers designed to record what had taken place before a bishop's court.[44] What had happened following citation is generally only recorded in registers if mandates were required to carry out the bishop's judgment. Judging by the anger, shock and indignation frequently expressed in these sentences, the bishops were unlikely to leave these crimes unpunished. Moreover, they had a pastoral duty to correct sinners, as well as considerable incentive to protect the authority of their office by punishing offenders.[45] These motives were not mutually exclusive. Certainly some crimes remained unsolved: Ralph of Salisbury's register contains cases in which nobody was cited because no one had been found guilty, for instance.[46] Bishops might also have had to contend with negligent or deceitful clergy. Thus in 1280, William Wickwane, archbishop of York, was compelled to deal with the matter personally because the officials appointed failed to conduct the investigation. It is significant, however, that Wickwane ensured action was taken, personally taking on the burden. The culprits were accordingly discovered and duly denounced by name.[47]

---

[41] *Vetus Liber Archidiaconatus Eliensis*, ed. Charles Lett Feltoe and Ellis H. Minns, Cambridge Antiquarian Society 48 (Cambridge, 1917), 176–7.
[42] *Register of Ralph of Shrewsbury*, 2: 733–4.
[43] *Registrum Roberti Winchelsey*, 1: 16–18.
[44] Act books did so, but survive only rarely and in fragments before the fifteenth century.
[45] See, for example, the rationale for general sentences expressed in *Registrum Simonis de Gandavo*, 1: 8–9: failing to punish sinners was negligent.
[46] *Register of Ralph of Shrewsbury*, 2: 658–61, 694.
[47] *The Register of William Wickwane, Lord Archbishop of York 1279–1285*, ed. William Brown, SS 114 (Durham, 1907), 99–102. Several other letters relate to this case, which continued.

The process of investigation becomes clearer in cases where the results were recorded. In the York case just cited, the archbishop investigated the incident (violent occupation of a church) 'through trustworthy men'.[48] On 16 February 1308, Simon of Ghent ordered the 'truth and circumstances' of a breach of sanctuary and possible murder in New Windsor, and the names of the malefactors, to be ascertained 'through trustworthy men and more diligent jurors'.[49] There is no indication of how many trustworthy men took part or how they were selected. Ian Forrest's recent study of the role of trustworthy men might provide some answers.[50] Canon law does not help here: Helmholz's study of ecclesiastical juries in England found that they were not discussed in the canon law (neither were they unlawful under it). These juries usually consisted of about twelve jurors, who could be examined individually. In this sense they were unlike secular juries of presentment, who were treated as a group. Like secular juries, however, they were meant to report on communal knowledge, the 'public fame'.[51] The investigations associated with general excommunications must have been similar to the juries Helmholz discussed, but it is impossible to say to what extent. They appear to be perhaps a little more ad hoc than the juries he discussed.

It is clear that the investigations, however conducted, could be very fruitful, providing not only the names of the offenders but a fuller account of the offence itself. Thus it transpired in 1308 that no murder had in fact taken in place in New Windsor. In the original mandate the bishop evidently had little information; not even the victims were known. Having investigated, the official named the victims as Hugh Ide and Simon le Webbe. He had found nine men and two women, named in the letter, responsible for bloody assault and extraction of Hugh and Simon. He had warned these people to seek absolution by 12 March, but did not proceed further, waiting for further instructions from his bishop. Bishop Simon had ordered

[48] Ibid.
[49] *Registrum Simonis de Gandavo*, 1: 280–2.
[50] Forrest, *Trustworthy Men*, particularly 307–30; idem, 'Trust and Doubt: The Late Medieval Bishop and Local Knowledge', in Frances Andrews, Charlotte Methuen and Andrew Spicer, eds, *Doubting Christianity: The Church and Doubt*, SCH 52 (Cambridge, 2016), 164–85.
[51] Helmholz, 'Canonical "juries"'; cf. idem, 'Early History'.

the official to act quickly out of concern for souls; the official's reply was sent less than three weeks after the bishop's order.[52]

There were a number of possible outcomes for those found guilty or implicated during the investigation. The first was that they were cited to appear before the bishop but did not do so (or did appear, but showed no remorse or willingness to make amends). It was therefore possible for investigations to be successful, but for the guilty to remain recalcitrant. In such cases, those cited were being contumacious, even if they had not committed the original offence. They could therefore be judicially excommunicated by name, and could consequently (at least in theory) be shunned by the faithful, denied legal rights and, after forty days, arrested by the sheriff at the bishop's request. There is no knowing how many people excommunicated for contumacy had been through this process, but the assumption that general sentences had lesser practical consequences than those for contumacy should be reconsidered in light of the fact that the latter could result from the former.[53]

The second was that the accused appeared and attempted to show why they should not be denounced by name. Mandates make clear that those cited were expected to do this. In another case of a fugitive's extraction from sanctuary, the investigation revealed the names of five men who appeared and publicly confessed to wounding and dragging Adam at Wood from Fawler Chapel. A sixth man, however, had also been incriminated; the investigation 'pretended' that he was an accomplice. William de la More, the accused, 'expressly denied this', saying instead that he had been helping Adam at Wood. The bishop therefore allowed him to purge himself, with eight compurgators. He thus had to take a formal oath that he was innocent of the crime, and find eight men known to the accused and of good repute to swear that they believed he had sworn truthfully. William's ability to prove his innocence thus relied on a level of support and trust within the community.[54] If his purgation failed, he was to be dealt with along with the others, who were given public penance. It seems likely that purgation was the most common

---

[52] *Registrum Simonis de Gandavo*, 1: 280–2.
[53] Logan, *Excommunication*, 139; Vodola, *Excommunication*, 80, 99, 181–2.
[54] *Registrum Simonis de Gandavo*, 1: 24–6. For compurgation, see R. H. Helmholz, 'Crime, Compurgation and the Courts of the Medieval Church', *LHR* 1 (1983), 1–26, at 13, 17.

method of demonstrating one's innocence, but it is possible that there were other options. In 1417/18 certain men who had cut down trees in a cemetery seem to have tried their luck by claiming that 'a certain dementia' had overtaken them.[55]

In the case at New Windsor above, there is some indication that further investigation was made, this time by the 'discrete men' Peter de Periton and Robert de Worth, both of whom later held high office in the diocese.[56] Some confessed, others were legitimately convicted. The distinction here is unclear, but perhaps the former realized that the game was up and that if appearing before the bishop was inevitable it would look better to turn themselves in. Significantly, however, the names cited following the second investigation correspond only partially with those found in the first. Thus Johanna, wife of William Vigerous, appears on the first list of names but not the second, whereas her husband appears on the second but not the first. What happened in the interim is uncertain; perhaps those 'legitimately convicted' had been implicated in the first investigation and their guilt confirmed in the second. During the process, Johanna Vigerous may have been excused or purged herself.[57]

The final possible outcome was that those cited to appear did so, confessed, and humbly sought absolution. The penitents would be given public penance and would have to make restitution, returning or replacing stolen items where possible. Those involved in the violence at New Windsor were divided into five groups, given different penances according to the extent of their involvement. Twelve men were to present themselves humbly at the great doors of Salisbury Cathedral on Maundy Thursday, with uncovered heads and bare feet. There they were to receive discipline (beatings). They were also to go to New Windsor, where they had committed their offence, every solemn day and Sunday until Holy Trinity and stand outside the church throughout the mass, to show that they were excluded. They were, however, permitted to enter the church on Easter Day and the four following days. They were also to be beaten three

---

[55] *The Register of Bishop Philip Repingdon, 1405–1419, 3: Memoranda, 1414–19*, ed. Margaret Archer, Lincoln Record Society 74 ([Lincoln], 1982), 254–7. Repingdon appears not to have excused their 'avarice' on this account.

[56] John Le Neve, *Fasti Ecclesiae Anglicanae 1300–1541, 3: Salisbury Diocese*, ed. Joyce M. Horn (London, 1962), 5, 7, 21, 26, 44, 47, 100. Helmholz noted that further inquests could be ordered: 'Canonical "juries"', 414–15.

[57] *Registrum Simonis de Gandavo*, 1: 280–2.

times around the church of New Windsor, and once through the market there. The next group, of nine men, were spared going to Salisbury but were otherwise given the same penance. Six men were to offer candles and receive discipline at the doors of New Windsor church. Five women were to be beaten three times each through the market and round the church, and were to stand outside the church on three solemn days while divine services were celebrated. Finally, John Vigerous and Cecilia Coupere were to give alms worth sixpence on Good Friday. In each case, the cause of the penance was to be publicly explained to the people, who were to be encouraged to pray for the penitents. The guilty had further been obliged to take the standard oath that they would obey the church's mandates and not infringe ecclesiastical liberty. Otherwise they would automatically fall under their former sentences of excommunication.[58] The dean of Reading, put in charge of ensuring that these penances were performed, finally wrote to the bishop on 18 April confirming that all the penances had been started and some had been completed.[59]

The details of this case show how thorough the process begun by general excommunications could be. Investigations not only discovered the names of the guilty but also allowed penances to be tailored to the nature and circumstances of the offence.[60] The penances enjoined on the malefactors were of the sort typically prescribed, although penances were not necessarily performed at Easter (here the timing was probably convenient). While it could be argued that the offenders in these cases got off lightly compared the treatment of similar violence in secular courts, public penance was by no means a negligible punishment.[61] The result here was almost certainly exactly what the bishop wished. The guilty were found, forced to confess and seek absolution, and then publicly shamed. The criminals' souls were saved, and everyone in the vicinity would have been made aware of

---

[58] For example, the citizens of Beverley who obtained absolution through 'false prayers', and were re-excommunicated: *Register of Walter Giffard*, 151.

[59] *Registrum Simonis de Gandavo*, 1: 283–4. The dean's final letter is dated 1309, which may be an error: the manuscript's layout indicates it could have been added later, but why would it have taken over a year for penances to have been started?

[60] Compare Fossier, *Le Bureau des âmes*, 280–4, which discusses inquests to determine appropriate penances.

[61] For public penance, see Mary C. Mansfield, *The Humiliation of Sinners: Public Penance in Thirteenth-Century France* (London, 1995). It is conceivable that some malefactors did face secular justice; more research is required.

their crime and that the church had discovered and dealt with such sinners.

Often the records of such cases describe public confessions and humble pleas for absolution. As we have seen, however, in fact the full force of the bishop's administrative power provoked these confessions. Thus when three men 'judicially admitted' that they had bound certain people who had fled to the church of Sparsholt, they asked for absolution and were duly given penance. Walter Geffray and William de Chaulawe were to process around the church barefoot on the next three Sundays and feast days, carrying the fetters they had used in their crime. They were to receive discipline at the priest's hands, while their crimes were explained, before the church doors. John called Kyng, however, was to be beaten in the markets of Wantage and Wallingford because he was 'known to have offended more'. This detail implies a fruitful investigation rather than spontaneous confession. Penance performed in marketplaces thus appears to have been viewed as a harsher punishment. That the confession of the three men might not have been entirely voluntary is further indicated by stern instructions about what to do if they refused to carry out their penances. However, since others yet unknown were also believed to be guilty, the general sentence continued.[62]

Investigations launched by general excommunications against unknown malefactors thus often provided the names of the guilty. The process could be both effective and quick: in cases where the results of the investigations survive, names were typically discovered in weeks. At worst, this simply allowed the culprits to be denounced by name. The names of those illicitly occupying Minety Church were discovered within a month; their crimes were 'public and notorious to such an extent that there is absolutely no place for denial ... the whole people of the vicinity stands witness'. The malefactors did not give in easily, however, and the excommunications, now *nominatim* rather than *generaliter*, continued. Additionally, the names of those communicating with the unrepentant excommunicates were to be investigated.[63] Excommunication was not always a powerful sanction, but it could be coercive in various ways. The power of excommunication in general is another question entirely, but it is important that general sentences against unnamed offenders could *become* sentences against

[62] *Registrum Simonis de Gandavo*, 1: 24, 26–8.
[63] Ibid. 1: 138–40, 145–51.

110

named sinners following investigation. Then, if excommunication alone did not work, the secular power could be called upon to arrest hardened sinners. General sentences could demonstrate impotence, but hardly more so than excommunication as a whole. At best, the church was seen to deliver swift punishment of those who had violated its laws. If the guilty presented themselves as humble penitents who had been convinced of the error of their ways, ecclesiastical discipline appeared strong. Public confessions demonstrated the church's authority, while imposing absolution allowed it to appear merciful. The publicity afforded absolutions and public penances is significant; much of this was about the church being *seen* to deal with these breaches of its peace and liberties.

The ability to investigate the names of the guilty changed the nature and power of general sentences. However, one final case cautions against over-emphasizing judicial and procedural developments. The process just outlined added teeth to general sentences, but built upon and institutionalized, rather than replaced, the existing functions of this type of excommunication. In 1306, trees from the bishop of Hereford's wood at Ross were cut down and removed. The unknown malefactors were excommunicated and fourteen men duly discovered. These men were given penance to be performed around the church and marketplace of Ross (this did not involve beatings). The two ringleaders were to restore the trees taken.[64] With the culprits thus found and punished, the case was presumably closed. But nine months later, three brothers, John, Richard and Walter Irreby, appeared at the bishop's manor at Ross. They knew that the transgressions committed the previous year incurred excommunication *ipso facto*, and 'with conscience dictating' they humbly sought absolution. The bishop received them as 'penitent and contrite'. Penance was imposed on them: they were to visit the church of Hereford and offer oblations to the Virgin and St Ethelbert there, and to offer 100*s.* for the fabric of the church.[65]

The memorandum recording all this is different in form to documents following investigations; no inquiry is mentioned. The brothers appeared of their own accord, which makes sense considering that the case had, from the bishop's perspective, been wrapped up months

---

[64] *Registrum Ricardi Swinfield, episcopi Herefordensis, A.D. 1282–1307*, ed. W. W. Capes, CYS 6 (London, 1909), 407–9.
[65] Ibid. 431–2.

earlier. The language used is that of conscience and repentance. The brothers were perhaps scared for their souls. Perhaps they felt guilty for getting away with a crime for which others had been punished. Alternatively, communal pressure may have been brought to bear by neighbours who had witnessed the others' public penance, but knew of the Irrebys' guilt and deemed it unfair that they had got off scot free. Whether the Irreby brothers were driven by fear, conscience or external pressures, it seems clear that they were not forced before the bishop by the authorities. The case demonstrates the complicated, but important, interplay between authorities trying to discover the truth, communities putting pressure on the guilty through gossip and accusations, and individuals being governed by conscience. General excommunications harnessed all these mechanisms.

The case of the Irreby brothers demonstrates, nevertheless, that investigations were not infallible. The church relied on local knowledge, and needed cooperation from the community. Though the community could expect to face sanctions, usually an interdict, for being obviously uncooperative, it could nevertheless choose not to aid the church's agents or to pervert the truth. This is particularly likely when the crime incurring excommunication was merely one part of an ongoing dispute, as many were. Understanding the intricacies of events in each case would require a full examination.[66] Nevertheless, many of these problems apply equally to other medieval legal procedures, particularly juries of presentment. Both secular and ecclesiastical procedures, dependent as they were on communal accusations and suspicion, could be manipulated by the parish elites usually called upon in such situations.[67] If episcopal investigations were not infallible, they were hardly unique in this respect. Moreover, Ian Forrest has recently argued that when bishops used 'trustworthy men' to garner local knowledge, as they did here, they were willing to accept a certain level of doubt and error.[68] Provided that *somebody* was found, publicly punished and forced to make amends, whether or not all or the right people were thus dealt with may have been a

---

[66] My forthcoming book examines at greater length the general excommunications concerning the church at Thame in 1292–4.
[67] Helmholz, 'Early History'; Poos, *Lower Ecclesiastical Jurisdiction*, lx–lxiii.
[68] Forrest, *Trustworthy Men*, advances this argument throughout Part 4; see also idem, 'Trust and Doubt'.

lesser concern. Forrest's presentation of episcopal authority has much to recommend it, but it perhaps disregards any genuine concern for souls felt by bishops. It certainly did matter if people remained excommunicated. Nevertheless, through this process bishops were fulfilling their duty to do everything in their power to correct souls, even while they may be seen to be demonstrating their authority. They could not be accused of negligence. Moreover, public penance (whoever performed it) was supposed to deter others from committing similar crimes, potentially saving souls.

The practice of general excommunication was both more complex and more effective than hitherto recognized. The process initiated by sentences pronounced against unknown malefactors was not without its problems, but many issues involved were common to other contemporary legal processes. Whilst some failed cases may have shown bishops to be impotent, this was not the general impression. Instead, bishops' spiritual power was shown when they publicly imposed 'the benefit of absolution', preventing sinners from suffering in hell as they would as excommunicates. Their temporal power was shown in their ability to ascertain names of wrongdoers and bring them to justice. If there were flaws in the system, bishops had nevertheless publicly dealt with crimes against the church by named excommunication or public penance. Investigations were a crucial development, but they worked alongside, rather than replaced, general sentences. In the secular sphere, the investigation would be the first step, but the church was able, and indeed bound, to use its spiritual sanction to bolster the legal process.[69] First, public denunciations played an important part in persuading people to cooperate with the investigations. Second, investigations were not always entirely successful. The spiritual fears and possible communal pressure aroused by general sentences thus provided a fall-back, and could also lead to punishment of the guilty. General excommunication was therefore frequently an efficient and potent process, bringing about justice via a number of interconnected methods.

---

[69] Not to publicize that malefactors had incurred automatic excommunication would have been pastorally irresponsible.

The Procedure and Practice of Witness Testimony in English Ecclesiastical Courts, *c.*1193–1300

Sarah B. White*

University of St Andrews

In the twelfth century, the English church courts made considerable use of compurgation and of sworn members of the community to aid in the resolution of disputes, but by the end of the thirteenth century, academic canon law depended almost entirely on witness testimony. Romano-canonical proceduralists established rules for examining witnesses, rejecting testimonies and resolving conflicts. However, these academic ideals were not always possible or even desirable in practice. Although Roman procedure required witnesses to be eyewitnesses, English ecclesiastical practice allowed witnesses to testify to public knowledge. Furthermore, individuals who were not qualified to testify did so regardless, and their testimonies were not excluded even following exceptions. This is not to say that standard procedure was not followed; more often than not, it was. However, these differences between theory and practice indicate that practitioners (and perhaps judges) in the English ecclesiastical courts were experimenting with ways to use witness testimony beyond the confines of the academic law.

This article explores three issues relating to proof by witnesses in the English ecclesiastical courts: the admission of witnesses who legally should have been barred from testifying; the use of public reputation as proof apart from ex officio proceedings (inquisitorial proceedings initiated by the judge, not a plaintiff); and whether hearsay could constitute proof. When the church withdrew support for the ordeal at the Fourth Lateran Council in 1215, the transition to an alternative system of proof was the work of Romano-canonical proceduralists.[1]

* E-mail: sbw@st-andrews.ac.uk.
I am grateful to William Eves, John Hudson and Attilio Stella for their helpful comments on drafts of this article. Any errors or omissions are my own.

[1] Charles Donahue Jr, 'Proof by Witnesses in the Church Courts of Medieval England: An Imperfect Reception of the Learned Law', in Morris S. Arnold et al., eds, *On the Laws and Customs of England: Essays in Honor of Samuel E. Thorne* (Chapel Hill, NC, 1981), 127–58,

Studies in Church History 56 (2020), 114–130   © Ecclesiastical History Society 2020
doi: 10.1017/stc.2019.7

The procedure outlined in treatises such as the *Ordo* of Tancred of Bologna (*c.*1215) and the *Speculum iudiciale* of William Durand (*c.*1270) provided a means for examining witnesses in a manner which would elicit the truth, as well as rules for rejecting witnesses and resolving conflicts.[2] Although this procedure left some discretion to the judge, most procedural writing tended to limit the judge's discretion in the matter by providing rules by which he made decisions rather than guidance as to how he was to exercise his discretion.[3]

There were a number of forms of proof that could be used in the ecclesiastical courts, including confession, presumptions, written evidence, oaths of parties, inquests of sworn individuals and witness testimony, with the last of these being by far the most common form of proof.[4] This article discusses the use of witnesses, using the case records of the metropolitan appeal court of Canterbury. This court was chosen in part due to the large number of extant records, as diocesan court records for the twelfth and thirteenth centuries only survive in small, scattered collections, mainly consisting of correspondence rather than formal case records. The extensive collection at Canterbury allows for a broad sampling of material, especially as these records contain not only the proceedings of the court of appeal, but often also the proceedings of the lower courts from which the appeal was made.[5]

---

at 129. For further discussion of the ordeal in canon law, see also Robert Bartlett, *Trial by Fire and Water: The Medieval Judicial Ordeal* (Oxford, 1986); Finbarr McAuley, 'Canon Law and the End of the Ordeal', *Oxford Journal of Legal Studies* 26 (2006), 473–513.
[2] Tancred, *Ordo*, in F. Bergmann, ed., *Pillii, Tancredo, Gratiae, Libri de Iudiciorum Ordine* (Göttingen, 1842); Guillaume Durand, *Speculum Iuris. Cum Ioan. Andreae, Baldi, reliquorum que clarisimorum … doctorum visionibus hactenus addi solitis*, 2 vols (Lyons, 1578).
[3] Donahue, 'Proof by Witnesses', 133.
[4] For more on each of these forms of proof, see Richard H. Helmholz, *OHLE*, 1: *The Canon Law and Ecclesiastical Jurisdiction from 597 to the 1640s* (Oxford, 2004), 327–41 ('The Stage for Proof'), 604–26 ('Criminal Procedure').
[5] All the cases mentioned are available in Norma Adams and Charles Donahue Jr, eds, *Select Cases from the Ecclesiastical Courts of the Province of Canterbury, c.1200–1301*, SelS 95 (London, 1981), referenced below by case number (then case name where given), page range and specific page number. The sample set of cases from Canterbury, being mainly appeals, is not representative of the full range of cases in the period, and the absence of straightforward cases in the record does not mean they did not occur. That being said, appeals were rarely made in clear-cut cases, and the difficult or contentious issues which reached the metropolitan court are those in which procedure may have been tested more rigorously. It is also possible that this collection of cases was selected by the

Strict rules existed in Romano-canonical procedure regarding witness testimony: witnesses had to be objective, as determined by their relationship to the parties; and they had to be eyewitnesses. Proof by two eyewitnesses was not always possible in practice, but cases still had to be resolved, presenting the court with the problematic option of accepting flawed testimony or no testimony at all. Out of necessity, witnesses who were not qualified to testify did so regardless, as did those who were not eyewitnesses. Further, many witnesses in the records testified to matters about which they had no personal knowledge, referring to things that were 'commonly known', an acceptable form of proof in the inquisitorial criminal procedure of ex officio cases, but somewhat less so when establishing the substantive issues outside of ex officio proceedings.[6] There are, however, both procedural and practical arguments which could allow for the use of public reputation in a trial outside ex officio inquests. Here a distinction must be made between *fama* and hearsay: *fama* testifies to the knowledge of the community, things which are *publica et notoria,* whereas hearsay testifies to things heard from a single person, *ex relatione, ex relatu* or *per relatem.*[7]

Statistics for the forms of proof may be compiled from *Select Cases,* but a caveat must be offered regarding them. They are based on a selection of cases made for the volume, which in turn was drawn from a selection made by the prior and chapter of Canterbury.

---

prior and chapter of Canterbury to demonstrate their exercise of vacancy jurisdiction, which had been previously challenged: see ibid., Introduction, 1–119, at 35–7.

[6] Ex officio procedure was very similar to secular presentment procedure, to the extent that Richard Helmholz has suggested 'concrete connections between secular and canon law in the sphere of criminal procedure', due to parallels in the three procedural stages of both systems: public fame, use of inquests and purgation. However, there is one significant difference between the two: canonical inquests required the questioning of individuals, which differs from the practice of the self-informing secular jury: Richard H. Helmholz, 'The Early History of the Grand Jury and the Canon Law', *University of Chicago Law Review* 50 (1983), 613–27, at 616, 623, 625.

[7] See Adams and Donahue, eds, *Select Cases,* A2, Master Peter de Wilton c. Master Stephen the Scribe (*c.*1200), 3–7, at 4; A3, Master Martin, rector of Barkway c. parishioners of Nuthampstead (*c.*1199), 8–10, at 8–9; A4, William de Wrotham c. Savaric, bishop of Bath (1203x1205), 11–14, at 14; D11, Nicholas Lewyn, rector of Frankton c. Master Adam de Botingdon (1288–93), 495–503, at 500–3; D16, Master Thomas de Sutton and Oliver de Sutton, bishop of Lincoln c. Master Edward de St John (1293–4), 567–611, at 575, 585; D19, Roger de Arderne c. executors of Thomas the Linen-draper (1291–1301), 633–89, at 650.

Chosen as they were to demonstrate a range of cases, they cannot be seen as representative of the case records as a whole. That being said, they can still provide some insight into the types of evidence found in depositions. For the fifty-two cases in sections A, C and D of *Select Cases*, there are 543 individual depositions. Of these, 87 per cent refer to eyewitness testimony (exclusively or in conjunction with *fama* or hearsay), 36 per cent refer to *fama* (exclusively or in conjunction with eyewitness testimony or hearsay), and 8 per cent refer to hearsay (exclusively or in conjunction with eyewitness testimony or *fama*). Do these different levels of appeal to varying types of evidence relate simply to practical issues, or were other factors involved as well? To address this question, this article will first outline academic witness procedure, specifically with regard to suitability of witnesses, followed by an examination of the use of this procedure in practice. It will then discuss the complexities surrounding the use of local opinion as proof outside of ex officio cases, both with regard to the technical use of *fama* and the more dubious use of hearsay.

The Persons of Witnesses

In ecclesiastical procedure, parties could produce any number of witnesses at each term designated for this production. Testimony was not given publicly in court; rather, witnesses were examined in private from a list of interrogatories, that is, questions drawn up by one side or the other on the basis of the articles or points to be proven. These depositions were written down and delivered to the judge for eventual publication to the parties. In practice, the total number of witnesses could vary. Tancred states in his *Ordo* that at least two witnesses were needed to make a full proof, but a few cases in the Canterbury material have well over twenty, and the canonical limit was forty.[8] According to Tancred's *Ordo*, if a witness contradicted himself, the testimony should be rejected, and if the group of witnesses seemed to agree, their testimony should be followed. If the witnesses for one party disagreed amongst themselves, then the judge had to choose which of their statements fit the matter best and which were least suspicious. If the witnesses of the two parties disagreed, the judge was to

---

[8] Donahue, 'Proof by Witnesses', 130. In Adams and Donahue, eds, *Select Cases*, D14, Official of Lincoln c. John de Arden (1291–2), 535–48, there are forty.

reconcile their testimonies if possible, and if this were not possible, he should decide according to those which were more trustworthy, based on their social standing and relationship to the party: freeborn over freed, older over younger, a man of property over a pauper, the noble over the ignoble, a man over a woman, and a friend of the defendant over his enemy. If all the witnesses were of the same dignity and status, then the judge was to decide by number. If they were the same in number as well, the judge was to absolve the defendant.[9]

The standard restrictions regarding witnesses can be found in Tancred's *Ordo* and the Canterbury material seems to follow these exceptions quite closely.[10] Many types of people were forbidden by law from testifying: the unfree, beggars or vagabonds, the excommunicate or those accused of crime, proctors or advocates in the principal case if the case in question was an appeal, servants or relatives of the producing party, and known enemies of the party against whom they were produced. Since exceptions were not raised against witnesses until after they had testified, no one was excluded from testifying, but doubt could be cast on their testimony after the fact. Rather than delay the examination until each witness was proved to be unexceptionable, it must often have been expedient to postpone exceptions until after testimony was given, as all the exceptions could then be submitted at once. Postponing also gave the other party time to discover and consolidate further exceptions. This system also afforded an opportunity to ask for a delay, which one could argue was the most common reason for introducing anything additional to the case. In the same way, it is probable that exceptionable witnesses were introduced specifically to slow down the case and give the producing party more time to formulate their arguments, amass funds or simply frustrate their opponent.[11]

---

[9] Tancred, *Ordo* 3.6, 'De testibus'; Donahue, 'Proof by Witnesses', 131. See also Charles Donahue Jr, 'Procedure in the Courts of the *Ius commune*', in Wilfried Hartmann and Kenneth Pennington, eds, *The History of Courts and Procedure in Medieval Canon Law* (Washington DC, 2016), 74–124, at 83–94.

[10] Tancred, *Ordo* 3.11, 'De testium reprobatione'; see also Pseudo-Ulpian, *De edendo*, in Bruce Brasington, *Order in the Court: Medieval Procedural Treatises in Translation* (Leiden, 2016), 131–71, at 153–5; and the *Ordo Bambergensis*, ibid. 203–75, at 238–49. These exceptions also appear in *Glanvill*, indicating that these same restrictions may have been placed on jurors in the secular courts: *The Treatise on the Laws and Customs of the Realm of England commonly called Glanvill*, ed. G. D. G. Hall and M. T. Clanchy, OMT (Oxford, 1993), 32.

[11] Donahue, 'Proof by Witnesses', 144.

Once a witness had testified, the opposing party would not ask that the testimony be excluded; rather he would argue that no faith should be placed in the person of the witness, a phrase which suggests that the value of a testimony was left to the discretion of the judge following production.[12] Rather than the sentence depending solely on the number of unexceptionable witnesses produced by the parties, it appears that testimonies given by witnesses were evaluated in comparison with one another; the persons of the witnesses, internal consistency and details given in the testimony were all considered when deciding which party had the more convincing proof.[13]

As an example, in Master Robert de Pitchford c. Thomas de Neville (1267–72), a case which concerned the question of who the canonically instituted rector of the parish church at Houghton was, Robert's counsel argues the following series of points against Thomas's witnesses:

> Robert de Empinham gives false testimony when he says that Robert [de Pitchford] was not at the church of Houghton, because Robert [de Pitchford]'s witnesses have proved the contrary. Simon de Skeffington is a layman and cannot have knowledge of the letters of proxy. Geoffrey de Marefield is perjured because he said his co-witnesses were freemen, whereas three, Sampson, William son of Geoffrey, and Simon son of Robert, were serfs. Moreover, his testimony about the tithes was vacillating and contradictory and based on belief rather than knowledge. Walter, son of Henry, knows nothing

---

[12] Ibid. 146.

[13] The most common questions regarded the witness's status, relationship to the parties and possible prejudice or corruption, along with the necessary questions about the case: see Adams and Donahue, eds, *Select Cases*, C11, Ascelina, prioress of Higham c. Amfelicia, subprioress and the nuns of Higham 'adhering to her' (1270), 161–77, at 163; C12, Philip, rector of Guestling c. the abbot and convent of Battle (1270–1), 177–96, at 192–3; C14, The prior and monks of Stogursey c. John de Winton, rector of Over Stowey (1271–2), 207–25, at 211; C18, Master Robert de Pitchford c. Thomas de Neville (1267–72), 265–336, at 270, 291; D11, Lewyn c. Botingdon, 498; D17, Robert Dyne c. Henry Dyne (1293–4), 612–26, at 617, 626. These questions were highly specific and would often concern the weather, how the witness knew about the events, and the time of day at which something took place. When recording the depositions, the standard practice in the Canterbury cases was to record the first testimony in full, and details in the rest only when they differed from the first. Durand objected to this practice, emphasizing that all depositions were to be recorded in full: Durand, *Speculum* 1.4.[2], 'de teste', §7.8. Donahue observes that the abbreviated system of recording depositions was approved in the statutes of the Court of Canterbury in 1342: 'Introduction', to Adams and Donahue, eds, *Select Cases*, 50.

about the letters of proxy. Roger de Billesdon does not testify consistently about the proxy. Sampson ad Ecclesiam does nothing to the point. William, son of Geoffrey, was under the command of [Roger Corbet's mother] who favoured Thomas. Simon son of Robert de Skeffington proves nothing about the proctors. John de Frisby used the words *in possessione* rather than *possedit* as claimed in the article of Thomas, nor does he say for what purpose the proctors were given. The same objection goes for Roger Halden, and he does not give the reason for his information about the possession and proxy, as required by the interrogatories. Nicholas de Halstead does not give the reason for his knowledge and is a serf. Lastly, the admission of these witnesses is not legally valid because Thomas renounced his right to produce witnesses on these matters.[14]

A number of these exceptions are against the persons of the witnesses: either they are serfs and therefore not able to testify, or they are prejudiced on behalf of Thomas, like William, son of Geoffrey, who was under the command of Thomas's patrons. Some are laymen and as a result, Robert's counsel argues, they could not have understood Thomas's letter of proxy correctly. Some do not prove what they were produced to prove, like Roger Halden, who did not provide the information required in the interrogatories, and some, as was concisely said of Sampson ad Ecclesiam, did nothing to the point. What is more interesting, perhaps, is the exception against Geoffrey de Marefield, which states that the examiners found his testimony 'vacillating and contradictory'. An inconsistent or wavering testimony indicated that he might not have been be telling the truth, or that he was unsure of his story. However, Thomas later tried to argue that the case should be settled in his favour since he had a greater number of witnesses than Robert, indicating that at least at that point, Thomas's excepted witnesses had not been discounted out of hand.[15]

EYEWITNESSES AND *FAMA*

In addition to the suitability of the persons of witnesses, Romano-canonical procedure required witnesses to be eyewitnesses of an

---

[14] Adams and Donahue, eds, *Select Cases*, C18, Pitchford c. Neville, 308 (paraphrased translation is mine).
[15] Ibid. 327.

event. The limitations on who could be a witness make sense in many ways: the ideal witness would have seen the events in question first-hand and have a reputation that was beyond reproach. In reality, however, these ideal witnesses would seldom be available. Perhaps someone had observed a disputed marriage first-hand, but she was the bride's sister and therefore could be prejudiced in some way. A man might be very trustworthy and have no connections to the party whatsoever, but only have heard of the marriage, and not seen the parties exchange their vows. For these reasons, the court may in some cases have accepted testimonies from exceptionable witnesses simply because there were no other options. In cases where the judge was presented with an array of suspect witnesses and varying testimonies, public reputation was essential for corroborating accounts.[16]

In interrogatories, witnesses were often asked to testify to anything to which they knew *'si visu, auditu, sciencia, credulitate aut fama'*.[17] Often in the case of this last type of knowledge, these broader testimonies refer to whether or not someone was generally regarded to be the rector of the church in question or something similar, but they could also testify to the custom in the area (for example, regarding mortuary payments). This was not just a quirk in the way that testimonies were given; in the interrogatories prepared for the examiners, they are often told to make close inquiry concerning the source of the witness's knowledge.[18] The proof then depended on the uniformity

---

[16] Helmholz has noted that proof by notoriety, which certainly played a significant role in ex officio proceedings, played a 'distinctly minor' role in instance cases. Although witnesses often stated that something was very well known, this was rarely relied on as full proof: Helmholz, *OHLE* 1, 328.

However, 40 per cent of the depositions found in the sample set from *Select Cases* contain a combination of eyewitness account, testimony on the basis of *fama* and reports of hearsay. Adams and Donahue, eds, *Select Cases*, C18, Pitchford c. Neville, is a good example of this, as is D16, Sutton and Sutton c. St John, a dispute over the prebend of Thame. For further work on this latter case, see Felicity G. Hill, *Excommunication in Thirteenth-Century England: Community, Politics and Publicity* (forthcoming).

[17] For an example, see Adams and Donahue, eds, *Select Cases*, C18, Pitchford c. Neville, 270–1. These categories can be found in a mnemonic in the gloss on *Liber extra* X.2.20.37: *Corpus juris canonici emendatum et notis illustratum,* 4 vols (Rome, 1582), 2: 736, Additio: 'Auditus, visus, persona, scienta, causa, / fama, locus, tempus, ac certam, credulitasque, / Dum testes recipit, judex haec cuncta notabit.' Canon and civil law references are given according to the 'modern form' provided by James Brundage in *Medieval Canon Law* (London, 1995), 190–205 (Appendix 1).

[18] Adams and Donahue, eds, *Select Cases*, C18, Pitchford c. Neville, 268.

Sarah B. White

of a group's testimony concerning public knowledge. In this way, witnesses could be treated more like a trial jury than like the eyewitnesses found in the Romano-canonical tradition, and the evidence in the English ecclesiastical material suggests that witnesses were indeed being used in this unconventional way.

Another unconventional use of witness testimony is worth noting here. In canon law, exceptions that were directly contrary to the initial claim could not be brought after the publication of testimony. Perhaps to avoid this issue of timing, it appears that parties began to bring substantive exceptions by presenting them as exceptions against witnesses on the grounds that they had perjured themselves. To cite Pitchford c. Neville again, Thomas excepted that some of Robert de Pitchford's witnesses had perjured themselves when they said that his servant, also called Robert, was in possession of the church of Houghton, because on the days mentioned Robert the servant was in Northampton and therefore could not have been present.[19] While the exception was technically made against the witnesses and their supposed perjurious testimonies, the issue at stake was that Robert de Pitchford had no representative in possession of the church on the days he had said he did. An exception of absence would have been directly contradictory to the depositions on behalf of Robert de Pitchford stating that he had had a representative at the church, which had already been published, and therefore not permitted.[20] Although this exception did not mean that a new inquiry was made into Robert the servant's presence at the church, it may have resulted in the judge being slightly more sceptical of Robert de Pitchford's proofs. This manoeuvre was risky, as it could appear to be wilfully dilatory and the offending party could be liable to pay costs for the delay. It could also be that it was a last-ditch effort to shift the direction of the case. Regardless of the intent, this use of exception demonstrates that litigants and their counsel were very familiar with standard procedure, and that they were able to use it to their best advantage.[21]

[19] Ibid. 283–4.
[20] Ibid. 279.
[21] See also Adams and Donahue, eds, *Select Cases*, D5, Oliver de Brocton c. Adam Mulgars (1292–3), 387–98, at 395; D7, John St John, prior of Andover c. Executors of Edmund Paty (1293–4), 410–28, at 418; Ardern c. Executors, 670; ibid., 'Introduction', 51–2; Elham c. Alice, in Charles Donahue Jr, 'Roman Canon Law in the Medieval English Church: Stubbs vs. Maitland re-examined after 75 Years in the

To return to the issue at hand, the use of witnesses almost as a secular jury could be attributed in part to the litigants themselves, who, lacking witnesses in whom they were confident, sought to present the judge with witnesses who instead could testify to opinion in the community. Regardless of the content of the case, litigants may have been hard pressed to produce unexceptionable witnesses; those ideal witnesses who had been present at a marriage or institution might be ill, absent or deceased when it came to the litigation. It seems that litigants were also, unsurprisingly, only concerned about the suitability of the other party's witnesses. Presenting as many witnesses as possible, then trying to discredit opposing witnesses until a conclusion was achieved through sheer numbers was a reasonable tactic to try. In cases like this, a version of events agreed upon by as many people as possible, regardless of the source of their information, must have seemed like a reasonable substitute, especially keeping in mind the self-informing jury of the secular courts or the oath-helpers of compurgation procedure. In the secular courts, jurors were required to come from the locality of the case so that they could hear the case and judge the evidence presented on the basis of informed knowledge, even if they themselves had not been eyewitnesses of an event.[22] Even in cases where eyewitness testimony was requested, parties seem to have been unwilling to abandon the notion that the witness was to testify concerning not only what they themselves had seen, but what the community believed the truth to be.[23]

The main concern of the courts, on the other hand, was the conclusion of cases. In cases which could be concluded realistically by the testimony of two unexceptionable eyewitnesses, such as a marriage case, the court might be more likely to insist on adherence to these rules. In other cases, especially a benefice case like Pitchford c. Neville, it might be more expedient to allow parties the opportunity to present groups of witnesses testifying to community opinion. Mike MacNair rightly notes the ecclesiastical courts' use of 'documents, witnesses, and procedure *per notorium* on the basis of personal

---

Light of some Records from the Church Courts', *Michigan Law Review* 72 (1974), 647–716; for further discussion, see Sarah B. White, *Procedure and Legal Argument in the Thirteenth-Century English Ecclesiastical Courts* (forthcoming).
[22] Mike MacNair, 'Vicinage and the Antecedents of the Jury', *LHR* 17 (1999), 537–90, at 538.
[23] Donahue, 'Proof by Witnesses', 148.

knowledge of the ecclesiastical judge', and the acceptance of local opinion as a form of proof.[24] However, public knowledge as proof differed slightly from the canonical notion of *fama* in inquisitorial procedure, that is, ex officio procedure. Ex officio procedure was used primarily in cases of 'spiritual crimes' such as adultery, when the court itself took on the responsibility of prosecuting a case initiated by public fame and determined with an inquest similar to a secular jury.[25] Nevertheless, there is a crucial procedural difference here in that ex officio cases were meant to depend on *fama*: it was *fama* or notoriety that initiated the case in the first place, and *fama* that played the largest role in the inquiries.[26] In contrast, substantive matters in non-office cases had to be proved by witnesses testifying about direct knowledge, not that of the community.[27]

That being said, judges may have turned to *fama* to fill in the gaps when testimonies were wanting. The gloss on the *Liber extra* states that *fama* alone could not constitute a full proof except in cases of impediments to marriage.[28] However, when *fama* was added to an eyewitness account, it had the effect of corroborating that account. This corroboration would make no difference in a case with two unexceptionable witnesses, but it could make a great deal of difference in their absence.[29] In cases like this, a judge might use public reputation to determine which of two unreliable groups of witnesses was the more trustworthy. This was similar to two tactics often used by parties, the first of which was bringing as many witnesses as possible in the hope that unreliability would be outweighed by numbers,

---

[24] MacNair, 'Vicinage', 548.

[25] The preference for witnesses in Romano-canonical procedure has often been contrasted with the secular juries to suggest fundamental differences between the two systems: see primarily Frederick Pollock and F. W. Maitland, *The History of English Law before the Time of Edward I*, 2 vols (Cambridge, 1898), 2: 603–4 and n. 1. For a discussion of whether or not secular juries were truly self-informing, see Daniel Klerman, 'Was the Jury ever Self-Informing?', *Southern California Law Review* 77 (2003), 123–50.

[26] The use of *fama* and issues of due process in criminal proceedings have been discussed at length by Richard M. Fraher, 'Conviction according to Conscience: The Medieval Jurists' Debate concerning Judicial Discretion and the Law of Proof', *LHR* 23 (1989), 23–88.

[27] Ibid. 36 n. 89.

[28] 'Et ita patet, quod qualitercumque aliquid sit diuulgatum per famam, seu quasi notorium, non sufficit ad probationem ... sed cum aliis adminiculis sufficit ... sola fama sufficit ad matrimonium impediendum': *Liber extra* X.2.24.32 (*Corpus iuris canonici*, 2: 829), in the gloss on *ex fama*.

[29] Fraher, 'Conviction', 36.

and the second of which was inviting witnesses of high social standing, whose reputation might balance out any deficiencies in their testimonies. In William Smith c. Alice Dolling (1271–2), William's claim was proved by ten witnesses whilst Alice's was only proved by four; as a result, William's claim was judged to be more valid.[30] Likewise, in the case of the prior and monks of Stogursey c. John de Winton, rector of Over Stowey (1271–2), the proctor of John de Winton argued that all the opponent's witnesses had testified falsely, as shown by John's witnesses, who were greater not only in number but also in dignity, reputation and credibility.[31] This approach did not always work, however. In Pitchford c. Neville, Thomas tried to argue that his witnesses outnumbered Robert's by sixteen to five and should therefore be preferred, 'since the laws are quicker to absolve than to condemn'. He added that even had their witnesses been of equal number and dignity, the judge should favour Thomas as the defendant. In civil trials, the burden of proof was upon the plaintiff, not the defendant,[32] and Thomas seems to have been arguing here that Robert had not proved his point sufficiently. However, when the depositions are counted, Robert had twenty-two witnesses, significantly more than Thomas had claimed. Since Thomas had made exceptions to at least twelve of them earlier in the case, and presumably knew this, he may have been speaking at this point about the witnesses whose testimonies pertained to a particular article; however, if this was the case, he did not specify that it was so.[33] In these cases, therefore, the opinion of a community could assist in overcoming deficiencies in evidence, allowing the judge to conclude a case in which the proof was imperfect. Local opinion concerning an event could also be treated as a presumption, especially in marriage cases, where the knowledge of the community could be used to prove that a couple had been living together or had children. According to Ricardus Anglicus (writing in the 1190s) and a number of decretals, this is the kind of case in which *fama* alone could be proof.[34]

---

[30] Adams and Donahue, eds, *Select Cases*, C6, William Smith c. Alice Dolling (1271–2), 127–37, at 136.

[31] Ibid., C14, The prior and monks of Stogursey c. John de Winton, 221–2.

[32] Justinian, *Digest* D.22.3.2 (*Corpus Iuris Civilis* [hereafter: *CICiv*], 1: *Institutiones, Digesta*, ed. Theodore Mommsen and Paul Krüger [Berlin, 1872], 289).

[33] Adams and Donahue, eds, *Select Cases*, C18, Pitchford c. Neville, 327.

[34] 'Ratione cohabitationis, distantiae vel vicinitatis, ut supra de poen. di. I. sed et continuo, qui dixerat et cet.': Ricardus Anglicus, *Summa de ordine iudiciario*, in Ludwig

Sarah B. White

FAMA AND HEARSAY

Returning to Pitchford c. Neville, Robert and Thomas brought numerous exceptions against each other's witnesses; but witnesses who had previously been excepted against nonetheless provide additional testimonies later in the case.[35] Further, despite the large number of exceptions Thomas brought, Robert persisted in using the testimonies of these witnesses in his later arguments, indicating that despite these exceptions, his witnesses had not been entirely discounted. It is possible that all Thomas's claims were disproved, but as there is no record of this (or indeed of any replications, that is, responses to his exceptions) it is as likely that these testimonies were still considered part of Robert's proof. Additionally, the examiners in the case were specifically requested to ask witnesses what the public report of the neighbourhood was.[36] In Thomas's interrogatories, this is made even clearer: witnesses were to be asked how they knew about these matters, as was expected in inquiries about *fama*. If they said they knew who had had possession of the church by seeing, they were to be asked where, when and whether the nature of the possession was natural or civil, mental or physical, and how long and whether continuously or at intervals the church had been possessed. If they knew anything by hearing, they were to be asked where, when and from whom; if by knowledge, how; if by public report, from how many and how the report originated.[37] From these interrogatories, is it clear that testimony that related to public reputation was acceptable and even required in this case in order to resolve the disagreement. At the close of Robert's first set of exceptions, the examiners added an extra marginal note commenting that Robert's witnesses had testified to the opposite of Thomas's witnesses, and that since Robert's witnesses all knew both the litigants and each other, and because

Wahrmund, ed., *Quellen zur Geschichte des Römisch-kanonischen Prozesses im Mittelalter*, 5 vols (Innsbruck, 1905–31; repr. Aalen, 1962), 2/3: 1–114, at 62; 'Ex communi et vulgari opinione, ut ff. ad Macedonianum, 1. si quis patrem': ibid. 6; 'Verum, quia in huiusmodi dubietate fama vicinia magis debet attendi … si fama loci habet, quod vir ipsam in lecto et in mensa sicut uxorem tenuerit, quum matrimonium sit maris et feminae coniunctio': *Liber extra* X.2.23.11 (*CICan*, 2: 355). See also MacNair, 'Vicinage', 577.
[35] See Robert Wenge and Roger Woodstock, in Adams and Donahue, eds, *Select Cases*, C18, Pitchford c. Neville, 283–7, 329–30.
[36] Ibid. 268.
[37] Ibid. 269.

more of them were from the local area, they to be were deemed more trustworthy.[38] In a case like this, in which both parties produced large numbers of both witnesses and exceptions, it seems the request in the interrogatories for knowledge other than eyewitness knowledge was intended to help corroborate accounts and determine whether there was internal consistency amongst the two groups. The questions regarding public knowledge in this case also served to help prove who was generally thought to be the canonically instituted rector of the church of Houghton. Although some witnesses might not themselves have been present at the institution, they would have heard about the event from other members of the community and, being local residents, their report was taken into account.

Fama still had to be proved by witnesses, who were examined regarding the source of the reputation, and it could only be proved by those of good reputation who had reason to know about the debated question.[39] Further, proving the existence of *fama* could be difficult, due to the problematic nature of hearsay. Romano-canonical procedure limited witnesses to testifying about things which they knew directly: therefore, a witness could not attest to *fama* because he had heard it from others, but rather had to testify that a great part of the populace knew something to be true.[40] Yet even the use of hearsay might be acceptable proof in some cases. There were loopholes of sorts in procedure which allowed for proof *memoria facti* and *ab auditu*. In the *Digest*, there are two passages which suggest that the memory of things done, even when known through hearsay, could be used as proof.[41] The *Digest* specifically says that a general recollection of seeing or hearing about an event is sufficient, even if details are lacking, since most people will not remember specifics such as date and time. Ricardus Anglicus, whose work heavily influenced

---

[38] Ibid. 278.

[39] Fraher, 'Conviction', 34 n. 74. For a general discussion of *fama* in medieval Europe, see Thelma Fenster and Daniel Lord Smail, eds, *Fama: The Politics of Talk and Reputation in Medieval Europe* (Ithaca, NY, 2003).

[40] Fraher, 'Conviction', 34.

[41] '[S]ed cum omnium haec est opinio nec audisse nec vidisse, cum id opus fieret, neque ex eis audisse, qui vidissent aut audissent: et hoc infinite similiter susum versum accidet, cum memoria operis facti non exstaret': Justinian, *Digest* D.22.3.28 (*CICiv*, 1: 291); 'an memoria exstet facto opere, non diem et consulem ad liquidum exquirendum, sed sufficere, si quis sciat factum esse, hoc est, si factum esse non ambigatur: nec utique necesse esse superesse qui meminerint, verum etiam si qui audierint eos, qui memoria tenuerint': ibid., D.39.3.2.8 (*CICiv*, 1: 602).

Tancred's *Ordo*, suggested that in cases of consanguinity, witnesses could testify *de visu et auditu*.[42] Following the Fourth Lateran Council, the standards for witnesses were tightened and Tancred followed these restrictions.[43] In particular, the author of the *ordo* 'Scientiam' claimed that the decision in the decretals meant that all testimony *ab alio auditu* was prohibited, denying that the Roman sources supported it at all.[44] However, Durand allowed for *memoria facti* to be applied in cases of prescriptive title, quite possibly because witnesses would not be available for a matter so far in the past.[45] The *Ordo Bambergensis* (*c*.1182), notes that two forms of hearsay are acceptable as proof: 'we knew it from our own ears or we learned that it was so from the report of others'. This is an argument which Bruce Brasington notes as unique in the *ordines*.[46] It would appear from its use that the author of the treatise considered public reputation alone was a valid form of proof, but this affirmation is followed up with the caveat that hearsay is only acceptable 'in the aforementioned cases and especially those whose origins exceed our memory'.[47] Therefore the opinion of a community could have varying force as proof, depending on the context in which it was used.

---

[42] Richard was here citing the *Decretum*. See Gratian, *Decretum* C.35 q.6 c.5 (*CICan*, 1: 1278–9): 'quicquid inde scis aut audisti a tuis vicinis, a a tuis propinquis antiquioribus, tu per nullum ingenium'; ibid., C.35 q.6 c.8 (*CICan*, 1: 1279–80): 'sed potius, quia credant ita verum esse, et ita se a suis antecessoribus audivisse'.

[43] 'Ponit concilium duodecim, sine quibus ad probandum consanguinitatem in causa matrimoniali, non valet testimonium de auditu': *Liber extra* X.2.20.47 (*CICan*, 2: 337); also found in Tancred, *Ordo* 3.9, 'De iuramento testium', §1.

[44] 'Testimonium autem de relatione non valet … quod testimonium de auditu non valet excepta causa matrimonii secundum iura antiqua, sed illum revocatum est per Lateranense concilium. Diceret quidam, quod valet testimonium de auditu, ut si de opere antiquo quaeretur … Sed si diligenter inspiciantur duae praedictae leges, reperietur, quod ibi non requiritur testomonium de auditu, sed de facti visu': Wahrmund, ed., *Quellen*, 2/1: 51.

[45] 'Ultimo quaerit qualiter fiet probatio communic opinionis, vel etiam praescriptionis tanti temporis, cuius memoria non existit? Etc.': Durand, *Speculum* 2.2, 'De probationibus' 1.20; MacNair, 'Vicinage', 573–4 nn. 147–51.

[46] Brasington, *Order in the Court*, 242 n. 345.

[47] 'Sed notandum quia ex auditu factum testimonium dupliciter dicitur: aut quia ita esse aurium experientia didicimus et cognovimus, aut quia aliorum relatu ita fuisse didicimus. Primum improprie dicitur testimonium de auditu, proprie vero de visu de eo, quod, cum fiebat, videndo audiendo plene percipiebat … Sed proprie dicitur testimonium de auditu, nec est acceptabile, nisi in praedictis casibus et his maxime, quorum origo temporum nostrorum memoriam excedit': *Der Ordo Iudiciarius de Codex Bambergensis*, ed. Johann Friedrich von Schulte (Vienna, 1872), 309.

Conclusion

Considering these variations on the law of proof, it seems reasonable to conclude that the rule requiring two unexceptionable eyewitnesses was not adhered to very strictly.[48] Differences between academic law and practice do not mean that the former was ignored, but rather that in some cases, when strict adherence to academic law was not possible, solutions had to be found. Although exceptions were frequently brought against witnesses, their testimonies were still considered in sentencing, and public reputation was often used to support questionable testimonies. Extant records of sentences are rare, unfortunately, and those we have shed very little light on the decision-making process of the judges after the testimonies had been given. Usually, they only state that the judge had brought the sentence according to the law and with the advice of the *iuris periti*, not that he was swayed or convinced by the proofs of one party or the other, or that the proofs of one party had damaged their case.

In general, it seems as though internal consistency, not the number of unexceptionable witnesses, was to be preferred when deciding the case. Further, testimonies did not have to be eyewitness accounts, as Romano-canonical tradition would prefer it, and the English church courts accepted and even sought out testimonies that related local opinion. In this way, witnesses could be representative not only of their individual knowledge of a case, but of the alleged wider knowledge of the community. This could have been due to litigants' reluctance to abandon older forms of proof dependent on local reputation, as MacNair suggests, or a resistance to abandoning jury-like proceedings, as argued by Donahue.[49] It could also be that judges, finding themselves frequently presented with insufficient or unsuitable witnesses, had to find ways to make do with what was available. There was a possible fourth reason as well: the use of the community to enforce a sentence after the conclusion of the case. An unwelcome sentence based on the testimony of only two witnesses, eyewitness or not, may have been difficult to enforce, and the involvement of

---

[48] Indeed, of the forty-two cases from Adams and Donahue, eds, *Select Cases*, for which we have depositions, twelve of them record only a single eyewitness or none at all, and that number of cases increases once the exceptions concerning witnesses have been considered: cases A8, A10, C12, C16, C17, D5, D7, D8, D11, D17, D19.

[49] MacNair, 'Vicinage', 576–8; Donahue, 'Proof by Witnesses', 140, 150–1.

the wider community in the resolution of a dispute could ensure that the case stayed settled.

Lastly, the separation of the roles of judge and witness in canon law may have played some part. A judge was only permitted to decide a case based on the evidence presented and proved in court, not by any personal knowledge, while witnesses were to speak only from personal knowledge. This was a false division in some ways, as every judge would have to use his own discretion when deciding a case (despite the clear rules for accepting testimonies) and witnesses inevitably engaged in judgement when giving their testimonies. This contradiction can be seen even more clearly in the use of *fama*, testified to by non-eyewitnesses and speaking to the judgement of a community in a case, which may explain the proceduralists' uncomfortable relationship with this and other forms of local opinion. Public reputation as proof could also have caused some further concern in relation to the role of the judge, in that it may have been possible for a community to present an agreed-upon narrative to the court in order to validate local, unofficial adjudication.[50] Speculation aside, case records demonstrate a persistent use of *fama* and occasionally even hearsay as proof in practice, despite the development of the law of witnesses.

[50] MacNair, 'Vicinage', 589.

The Bishops and the Deposition of Edward II

Samuel Lane*

Christ Church, Oxford

The deposition of Edward II was a watershed in the legal history of later medieval England. However, the significance of the church in its accomplishment has remained controversial. This article offers a reassessment by providing a brief narrative of the episcopate's involvement in events; analysing the importance of their contribution, with particular reference to the quasi-legal aspect of proceedings; considering whether this participation reflected their own initiative or was something about which they had no choice; and questioning why so many bishops turned to oppose Edward II. It becomes evident that prelates played a key part in Edward II's downfall, and that they became involved as a consequence of the oppressive treatment which he had meted out to them, to their families and to political society more broadly.

The deposition of Edward II in January 1327 was a landmark event in the legal, political and constitutional history of later medieval England. Previous kings had certainly encountered difficulties: Stephen had fought a civil war with Matilda which saw the realm descend into chaos; John's relations with his baronage were so poor that he was forced to accede to the Magna Carta and witness the French invade with the support of many of his own subjects; and Henry III had endured a long conflict with Simon de Montfort in which he had at times been the earl's prisoner. However, all had died as kings of England.[1] The overthrow of Edward II, in which, following a successful invasion by Isabella (his queen) and Roger Mortimer (her ally and possible lover), he surrendered his authority to his fourteen-year-old son, who was then crowned Edward III, was thus an unprecedented episode in English history in the period after

* Christ Church, St Aldates, Oxford, OX1 1DP. E-mail: samuel.lane@chch.ox.ac.uk. I should like to thank Rowena E. Archer, who read an earlier version of this article, and the anonymous reviewers, for their helpful comments and suggestions.
[1] May McKisack, 'Edward III and the Historians', *History* 45 (1960), 1–15, at 5–6.

Studies in Church History 56 (2020), 131–151   © Ecclesiastical History Society 2020
doi: 10.1017/stc.2019.8

the Norman Conquest.[2] It was also an episode which lacked clear legality or established process, for there was no explicit guidance in English or canon law about the means by which a king might be deposed.[3] Correspondingly, the deposition spawned a novel legal procedure and a new legal principle: that through some combination of parliamentary decision and royal resignation, a king of England might be removed. Subsequently this was exploited as a precedent in the reign of Richard II, when the duke of Gloucester and the bishop of Ely threatened the king in 1386 by showing him an official record of Edward's deposition,[4] and doubtless set the legal backdrop for Richard's own deposition, as well as for other dramatic events of the fifteenth century, when successive parliaments declared the regimes of Henry VI, Edward IV and Richard III illegitimate.[5]

What was the role of the episcopate in this defining episode of English legal history? On the one hand, scholars such as Kathleen Edwards, Michael Prestwich and Roy Martin Haines have claimed that bishops were a major force behind Edward's downfall, with William Stubbs going so far as to call Adam Orleton, bishop of Hereford, 'the guiding spirit of the queen's party'.[6] On the other

---

[2] The question of whether Isabella and Mortimer were lovers as well as political allies at the time of their invasion and Edward's deposition remains vexed. What is more certain is that they exercised extensive royal authority on Edward III's behalf until the latter's 'coup' against Mortimer in October 1330, in an effective regency, with the consequence that the apparently direct transfer of power from Edward II to his son has been dubbed a 'legal fiction': Seymour Phillips, *Edward II* (London, 2010), 488–91, 520–1, 571–2, 611; Andrew M. Spencer, 'Dealing with Inadequate Kingship: Uncertain Reponses from Magna Carta to Deposition, 1199–1327', in idem and Carl Watkins, eds, *Thirteenth-Century England XVI: Proceedings of the Cambridge Conference, 2015* (Woodbridge, 2017), 71–88, at 85.
[3] Anthony Tuck, *Crown and Nobility, 1272–1461* (London, 1985), 93.
[4] *Knighton's Chronicle, 1337–1396*, ed. G. H. Martin, OMT (Oxford, 1995), 360–1; see also Claire Valente, 'The Deposition and Abdication of Edward II', *EHR* 113 (1998), 852–81, at 857 n. 4.
[5] Gerard Caspary, 'The Deposition of Richard II and the Canon Law', in Stephan Kuttner and J. Joseph Ryan, eds, *Proceedings of the Second International Congress of Medieval Canon Law* (Vatican City, 1965), 189–201, at 198–200; Valente, 'Deposition and Abdication', 874–6; Spencer, 'Inadequate Kingship', 86–7.
[6] William Stubbs, *The Constitutional History of England*, 3 vols (Oxford, 1874–8), 2: 361; Kathleen Edwards, 'The Political Importance of the English Bishops during the Reign of Edward II', *EHR* 59 (1944), 311–47, at 339; Michael Prestwich, *Plantagenet England, 1225–1360* (Oxford, 2005), 217; Roy Martin Haines, *King Edward II, 1283–1330* (London, 2003), 187–8; idem, 'The Episcopate during the Reign of Edward II and the Regency of Mortimer and Isabella', *JEH* 56 (2005), 657–709, at 687–92.

hand, historians such as Ian Mortimer, Paul Doherty and Seymour Phillips, whilst acknowledging that prelates played a part in developments, have suggested that they lacked real agency and influence and were instead directed and masterminded by Isabella and Mortimer.[7] This line was advanced furthest by Peter Heath, who remarked:

> Vital as was the role of prelates in Edward's deposition – so delicate a novelty could hardly have been accomplished without them – their participation was more ceremonial than formative. There is little evidence to support a view that Isabella or Mortimer embarked on invasion, conquest and dethronement under the influence, or by the counsel, of any bishop … [T]he sermons of Orleton, Stratford and finally of Reynolds were not the spontaneous initiatives of these prelates, but clearly part of an opportunist programme coordinated by Mortimer and his allies. In short, the deposition only serves to underline the limitations of ecclesiastical initiative and power in politics.[8]

This article offers a reassessment of this debate, by providing a brief account of the role of members of the episcopate in Edward's dethronement; by assessing the importance of this contribution, and whether it reflected the bishops' own initiative or was carefully extracted from them by Isabella and her cronies; and by analysing further reasons for the bishops' participation. It will become apparent that the English bishops played a crucial part in Edward's downfall, and that they did so in consequence of the legal, personal and financial oppression experienced by them, their families and political society more broadly.

The events of Edward II's deposition are well known and consequently do not require detailed rehearsal here.[9] The invasion of

---

[7] Ian Mortimer, *The Greatest Traitor: The Life of Sir Roger Mortimer* (London, 2003), 168, 170; idem, *The Perfect King: The Life of Edward III* (London, 2006), 52–6; Paul Doherty, *Isabella and the Strange Death of Edward II* (London, 2003), 108–13; Phillips, *Edward II*, 536–7; see also Natalie Fryde, *The Tyranny and Fall of Edward II, 1321–6* (Cambridge, 1979), 197.

[8] Peter Heath, *Church and Realm, 1272–1461* (London, 1988), 79.

[9] For a detailed narrative of Edward II's deposition, and a full bibliography of works on his reign, see Phillips, *Edward II*, 502–40, 614–42. For discussion of the composition of the episcopal bench in Edward II's reign, see Haines, 'Episcopate', 658–71. In January 1327, there were sixteen consecrated English bishops (the bishop-elect of Exeter, James Berkeley, only being consecrated in March 1327, after the murder of his predecessor in October 1326) and four Welsh bishops (of which only the bishop of Llandaff, John Eaglescliffe, appears to have had any involvement in events, by attending Edward III's

Isabella and Mortimer on 24 September 1326 was staggeringly successful and supported at every stage by prelates. By November, Isabella had taken control of the central administration, electing Prince Edward (the future Edward III) as keeper of the realm, with the connivance of six bishops and other earls, barons and knights; appointing John Stratford, bishop of Winchester, as acting treasurer; and making William Airmyn, bishop of Norwich, keeper of the Great Seal.[10] By December, Edward II's political defeat had been confirmed. His favourites, the Despensers, had been brutally executed; he himself had been captured and moved into custody in Kenilworth Castle; and at Christmas Isabella agreed with Walter Reynolds, archbishop of Canterbury, Airmyn, Stratford and Orleton that Edward's cruelty made it impossible for her to return to him.[11] By January 1327, the stage was set for Edward's deposition. Two bishops were sent to Kenilworth to invite him to come to parliament, but he refused.[12] On 12 January, Orleton asked parliament whether Edward should remain as king or be replaced by his son, and postponed the assembly until the next morning to allow further time for thought, deliberation and persuasion.[13] When parliament reconvened on 13 January, Orleton, Stratford and Reynolds delivered politically charged sermons which castigated Edward's kingship and invited his removal, culminating, according to the *Forma Deposicionis*, in

---

coronation). Only one Irish bishop, Alexander Bicknor, archbishop of Dublin, was to play any significant role in Edward's deposition: Haines, 'Episcopate', 692, 706; Nicholas Orme, 'Berkeley, James (c.1275–1327)', *ODNB*, 24 May 2008, online at: <https://www.oxforddnb.com/view/10.1093/ref:odnb/9780198614128.001.0001/odnb-9780198614128-e-95144>, last accessed 12 September 2019.

[10] *CCR 1323–7*, 655; R. E. Latham, ed., *Calendar of Memoranda Rolls (Exchequer), 1326–27* (London, 1968), 110–11.

[11] Haines, 'Episcopate', 688; Phillips, *Edward II*, 521.

[12] Precisely which two bishops journeyed to Kenilworth is unclear: the *Lanercost Chronicle* states it was Adam Orleton, bishop of Hereford, and John Stratford (*The Chronicle of Lanercost, 1272–1346*, ed. Herbert Maxwell [Glasgow, 1913], 254), while the *Pipewell Chronicle* prefers Orleton and Stephen Gravesend, bishop of London: Harry Rothwell, ed., *English Historical Documents, 1189–1327* (London, 1975), 278. That a delegation of two bishops was sent to Edward II at this point is confirmed by a letter from Henry Eastry, prior of Christ Church, Canterbury, to Walter Reynolds, archbishop of Canterbury, but unfortunately this does not name the bishops in question: *Literae Cantuarienses: The Letter Books of the Monastery of Christ Church, Canterbury*, ed. Joseph Brigstocke Sheppard, 3 vols, RS 85 (London, 1887–9), 2: 204–5.

[13] *Anglia Sacra*, ed. Henry Wharton, 2 vols (London, 1691), 1: 367; Phillips, *Edward II*, 525–6.

Reynolds exclaiming that 'by the unanimous consent of all the magnates the lord King Edward has been deprived of the government of the kingdom and his son put in his place, if you consent unanimously', to which the people replied 'Let it be done! Let it be done! Amen'.[14]

Thereafter, on 15 or 16 January, a delegation headed by either two or three bishops was dispatched to Kenilworth, where they arrived on 20 January.[15] According to Geoffrey le Baker, by a mixture of threats – 'that, unless he resigned the crown, the people would cease to pay royal homage to himself, would reject his sons as well and instead exalt to the kingship another who was not of the royal blood' – and promises – 'that it would be greatly to the king's credit with God if he were to reject his temporal kingdom for the peace of his subjects' – the bishops tried to induce Edward 'to resign the crown in favour of his firstborn son'. Eventually, Edward accepted their proposals, and on 21 January Sir William Trussell withdrew homage from Edward on behalf of the kingdom, and Sir Thomas Blount broke Edward's rod of office.[16] Throughout this period, a series of oaths in support of Queen Isabella and Prince Edward were sworn at the Guildhall in London by numerous influential figures, including the majority of the English bishops.[17] Finally, Edward II's removal was confirmed on 1 February 1327, with the coronation of his son. Edward III was crowned and anointed by Reynolds, assisted by Stratford and Stephen Gravesend, bishop of London, while Airmyn and Hamo Hethe, bishop of Rochester, chanted the litany.[18]

The involvement of the bishops is especially evident with regard to the legal basis for Edward's deposition. This was encapsulated in six

---

[14] Fryde, *Tyranny and Fall*, Appendix 2, 233–4.

[15] The precise composition of this embassy is unclear. The *Lancercost Chronicle* states that Adam Orleton and John Stratford headed the delegation (*Lancercost Chronicle*, ed. Maxwell, 255); the *Pipewell Chronicle* has Orleton, Stratford and Stephen Gravesend (Rothwell, ed., *English Historical Documents, 1189–1327*, 279); and Geoffrey le Baker gives Stratford, Orleton and Henry Burghersh, bishop of Lincoln: *The Chronicle of Geoffrey le Baker of Swinbrook*, ed. Richard Barber and David Preest (Woodbridge, 2012), 25–6. The *Brut*, however, suggests that only one bishop was involved in the delegation, namely John Hotham, bishop of Ely: *The Brut, or the Chronicles of England*, ed. F. W. D. Brie, 2 vols, Early English Text Society original series 131, 136 (London, 1906–8), 1: 242.

[16] *Geoffrey le Baker*, ed. Barber and Preest, 26–7.

[17] A. H. Thomas and P. E. Jones, eds, *Calendar of the Plea and Memoranda Rolls of the City of London*, 6 vols (Cambridge, 1926–61), 1: 11–13.

[18] *Chronicles of the Reigns of Edward I and Edward II*, ed. William Stubbs, 2 vols, RS 76 (London, 1882–3), 1: 324–5; Haines, 'Episcopate', 691–2.

articles of accusation, which alleged that Edward had committed a variety of heinous abuses, from breaching his coronation oath to executing members of the nobility, and resolved that in consequence 'the eldest son of the king shall have the government of the realm and shall be crowned king'.[19] According to the *French Chronicle of London*, Walter Reynolds pronounced these articles before parliament on 13 January, 'by reason whereof all the people agreed, and cried aloud, that he ought no longer to reign'.[20]

There are a number of reasons to believe that members of the episcopate were influential in the composition of this text. Firstly, there are some striking parallels between this document and the justifications for thirteenth-century depositions and abdications on the continent, namely the depositions of Emperor Frederick II and King Sancho II of Portugal by Pope Innocent IV in 1245, the abdication of Pope Celestine V in 1294, and the deposition of Adolf of Nassau by the electors of the Holy Roman Empire in 1298. Like their continental precursors, the English articles were couched in terms of the canon law theory of the *rex inutilis* ('useless king'), to the extent that Helmut Walther remarked that they 'read almost like a list of arguments from the canonistic doctrine of inutility'.[21] Just as Frederick II had been condemned for being unwilling to reform, so Edward II was accused of refusing to 'make amendment ... or to allow amendment to be made', and of having 'shown himself incorrigible without hope of amendment'.[22] Just as Sancho II of Portugal was charged with being idle and negligent, succumbing to evil counsel and failing to defend his land against Saracen incursions, so Edward II was found

---

[19] George Burton Adams and H. Morse Stephens, eds, *Select Documents of English Constitutional History* (London, 1901), 99. For the original French, see Valente, 'Deposition and Abdication', 879–81.

[20] *Chronicles of the Mayors and Sheriffs of London, A.D. 1188 to A.D. 1274 ... and The French Chronicle of London, A.D. 1259 to A.D. 1343*, ed. H. T. Riley (London, 1863), 266.

[21] Edward Peters, *The Shadow King: Rex Inutilis in Medieval Law and Literature, 751–1327* (London, 1970), 237–41; Helmut Walther, 'Depositions of Rulers in the Later Middle Ages: On Theory of the "Useless Ruler" and its Practical Utilization', *Revista da Faculdade de Ciencias Sociais e Humanas* 1 (1994), 157–68, at 162; see also J. S. Roskell, *Parliament and Politics in Late Medieval England*, 3 vols (London, 1981–3), 1: 3; Valente, 'Deposition and Abdication', 878–9.

[22] Peters, *Shadow King*, 241; David Abulafia, *Frederick II* (London, 1988), 372–3; Adams and Stephens, eds, *Select Documents*, 99.

to have 'given himself up to unseemly occupations, neglecting to satisfy the needs of his realm', to have been 'governed by others who have given him evil counsel' and to have 'lost the realm of Scotland, and other territories and lordships in Gascony and Ireland'.[23] Just as Celestine V admitted 'personal shortcomings', so Edward was found to be 'incompetent to govern in person'.[24] And just as Adolf of Nassau was alleged to have 'rejected the counsels of the wise' and permitted the mistreatment of laymen and clergymen alike, so Edward II was accused of having been unwilling 'to listen to good counsel', having imprisoned prelates and having 'put to a shameful death, imprisoned, exiled, and disinherited ... many great and noble men of his land'.[25] While there is no direct evidence that Edward's opponents drew upon the depositions of the previous century, and while there is an undeniable congruence between their allegations and Edward's own conduct, the number and nature of these similarities renders it likely that the drafters of the English articles took at least some inspiration from the precedents of Frederick, Sancho, Celestine and Adolf in establishing their legal justification for Edward's deposition.[26] If this is the case, members of the episcopate probably played a key role in drafting the articles of accusation, for as churchmen versed in canon law they were the English magnates most likely to have been aware of these precedents.[27]

Secondly, and rather less speculatively, episcopal influence in the crafting of the articles of accusation is implied by the prominence which they gave to clerical grievances: the first article complained that the king's actions had led 'to the destruction of Holy Church', and the fourth that he had 'imprisoned some of the persons of Holy Church and brought distress upon others'.[28]

Thirdly, the involvement of bishops is suggested by the context in which the articles were compiled, with the Forma recording that they were drawn up at a meeting of 'the prelates and nobles', probably in the evening of 12 January, when Jean le Bel recorded that

---

[23] Peters, *Shadow King*, 138–9; Adams and Stephens, eds, *Select Documents*, 99.

[24] Peters, *Shadow King*, 218, 240; Adams and Stephens, eds, *Select Documents*, 99.

[25] Stubbs, *Constitutional History*, 2: 364–6; Peters, *Shadow King*, 234–5; Adams and Stephens, eds, *Select Documents*, 99.

[26] Peters, *Shadow King*, 241.

[27] Ibid. 237; Haines, *Edward II*, 193; Prestwich, *Plantagenet England*, 218.

[28] Adams and Stephens, eds, *Select Documents*, 99.

[I]t was decreed that … a record should be made of all the ill-advised deeds and actions the king had committed, and of his conduct and behaviour, and how he'd ruled the country, so that it could be read in open court and the wisest in the land could debate how and by whom the kingdom should thenceforth be governed …[29]

Finally, the prelates' role in drafting the articles is revealed in Adam Orleton's remark that, while they emanated from 'the common counsel and assent of all the prelates, earls, and barons, and of the whole community of the realm', the articles were 'conceived and dictated in the presence of John [Stratford], then bishop of Winchester, now archbishop of Canterbury', before being incorporated into a public instrument by his secretary, William Mees.[30] From Isabella's invasion and initial seizure of power to the coronation of her son as king of England, and particularly with regard to the quasi-legal justification of events, it is therefore evident that members of the episcopate took a prominent part in the proceedings.

While the bishops were undoubtedly conspicuous, the question nonetheless arises of how important their role actually was. Their ceremonial role was vital, as has been conceded even by those who consider the episcopate to have lacked any practical influence behind events.[31] The bishops' place at the peak of political society is beyond doubt, and is reflected in the affirmation by John Grandisson, bishop of Exeter, in 1336 that 'the substance of the nature of the crown is principally in the person of the king as head, and in the peers of the realm as members, who hold of him by a certain homage, and especially the prelates, such that one thing cannot be severed from the crown without dividing the kingdom'.[32] Accordingly, it is perhaps unsurprising that their position in parliament, where at least some elements of Edward's deposition were effected,[33] was also widely

[29] *The True Chronicles of Jean le Bel, 1290–1360*, ed. Nigel Bryant (Woodbridge, 2011), 33; Fryde, *Tyranny*, 233 (Appendix 2).
[30] Valente, 'Deposition and Abdication', 857.
[31] For example, Heath, *Church and Realm*, 79.
[32] *The Register of John de Grandisson, Bishop of Exeter (A.D. 1327–1369), with some Account of the Episcopate of James de Berkeley (A.D. 1327)*, ed. F. C. Hingeston-Randolph, 3 vols (London, 1894–9), 2: 840; S. L. Waugh, 'England: Kingship and the Political Community, 1272–1377', in S. H. Rigby, ed., *A Companion to Britain in the Later Middle Ages* (Oxford, 2003), 208–23, at 216.
[33] For discussion of the parliament of January 1330, its questionable legality and its importance in Edward's deposition, see *The Parliament Rolls of Medieval England, 1275–1504*, ed. Chris Given-Wilson et al., 16 vols (Woodbridge, 2005), 4: 8.

recognized: in the parliament of 1341, John Stratford, by then arch-bishop of Canterbury, proclaimed that he ought to have 'the first voice after the king' in parliamentary assemblies,[34] and the *Modus Tendendi Parliamentorum*, written towards the end of Edward II's reign, explained that 'archbishops, bishops, abbots, and priors who hold by barony' constituted the second grade in parliament, after the king himself and before the 'earls, barons, and other magnates and nobility'.[35] Correspondingly, their lack of assent to major polit-ical decisions inevitably undermined these, especially if they had been taken in parliament, as in 1322, when the younger Despenser argued that his banishment by parliamentary award the previous year was invalid, because 'the award was made without the assent of the prel-ates, who are peers in parliament'.[36] The formal backing of the prel-ates for parliamentary acts which were not only important but unprecedented was thus essential.

However, the episcopate's role was not merely ceremonial. Bishops also wielded considerable moral and sacral authority as the leaders of the English church. This added weight to their decision to oppose Edward and to their criticisms of his rule, for there was an expectation that they spoke with sincerity. According to the *Historia Roffensis*, Hamo de Hethe, bishop of Rochester, told Edward II in June 1326 that it was a bishop's duty to 'tell the truth about everyone, great and small', whether in the confessional or in preaching.[37] Moreover, their involvement, with its connotation of conferring divine approval, may well have helped to legitimize an otherwise brutal *coup d'état*. This was especially so because it would have been scandalous to remove an anointed king without ecclesiastical participation, as is suggested by the significant clerical involvement in the previous depositions and abdications of the thirteenth century: Pope Innocent IV had promul-gated the depositions of Frederick II and Sancho II; Pope Celestine renounced the papacy under his own legal authority; and, while the deposition of Adolf of Nassau did not involve any appeal to the pon-tiff, Archbishop Gerhard of Mainz was prominent in events and even-tually declared Adolf deposed.[38] Similarly, only a clergyman could

---

[34] *Anglia Sacra*, ed. Wharton, 1: 39–40.
[35] Nicholas Pronay and John Taylor, eds, *Parliamentary Texts of the Later Middle Ages* (Oxford, 1980), 91.
[36] *CCR 1318–23*, 543.
[37] *Anglia Sacra*, ed. Wharton, 1: 365.
[38] Peters, *Shadow King*, 218–19; 232–7; Prestwich, *Plantagenet England*, 218.

crown Edward III as the new king. Since the 'legal fiction' of passing the crown directly to Edward III, signifying that the process of legitimate succession was merely being accelerated, was at the heart of Isabella's plans, episcopal willingness to crown Edward was key.[39]

The important role played by members of the episcopate is once again particularly apparent with regard to the legal aspects of Edward II's deposition. Naturally enough for a French princess and a magnate from the Welsh Marches, neither Isabella nor Mortimer had any formal legal training, and neither appears particularly well placed to have contrived novel legal justifications or procedures for deposing an English king.[40] It thus seems likely that they would have turned to the legal experts in their circle: men such as Henry Burghersh, bishop of Lincoln, a cousin of Mortimer's daughter-in-law, who had studied civil and canon law at the school of Angers;[41] Bishop Orleton of Hereford, whom Edward accused of being Mortimer's friend and adherent and who had acquired a doctorate in canon law by 1310;[42] and Bishop Stratford of Winchester, who had accompanied Edward and Isabella to Amiens in 1320 and who was a doctor of civil law by 1312.[43] All were early allegiants to Isabella's cause when she invaded late in September 1326, and by 26 October were with her at Bristol, giving them plenty of time to discuss, consider and plan the legal basis for Edward's downfall.[44] Indeed, Orleton and Stratford were both present at Wallingford with the queen at Christmas 1326, where it has been postulated that the decision to depose Edward was made and that the initial drafting of the justification

---

[39] Spencer, 'Inadequate Kingship', 85.

[40] R. R. Davies, 'Mortimer, Roger (1287–1330)', *ODNB*, 3 January 2008, online at: <https://www.oxforddnb.com/view/10.1093/ref:odnb/9780198614128.001.0001/odnb-9780198614128-e-19354>, last accessed 12 September 2019; John C. Parsons, 'Isabella [of France] (1295–1358)', *ODNB*, 3 January 2008, online at: <https://www.oxforddnb.com/view/10.1093/ref:odnb/9780198614128.001.0001/odnb-9780198614128-e-14484>, last accessed 12 September 2019.

[41] Nicholas Bennett, 'Burghersh, Henry (*c.*1290–1340)', *ODNB*, 23 September 2004, online at: <https://www.oxforddnb.com/view/10.1093/ref:odnb/9780198614128.001.0001/odnb-9780198614128-e-4007>, last accessed 12 September 2019; Mortimer, *Greatest Traitor*, 70.

[42] Roy Martin Haines, *The Church and Politics in Fourteenth-Century England: The Career of Adam Orleton, c.1275–1345* (Cambridge, 1978), 3, 135–6.

[43] Roy Martin Haines, 'Stratford, John (*c.*1275–1348)', *ODNB*, 28 September 2006, online at: <https://www.oxforddnb.com/view/10.1093/ref:odnb/9780198614128.001.0001/odnb-9780198614128-e-26645>, last accessed 12 September 2019.

[44] *CCR 1323–27*, 655.

for so doing was undertaken.[45] All in all, it is clear that Isabella had backing from several key bishops, and that Edward II's downfall could not have proceeded in the manner it did without episcopal support.

Did the bishops who became involved have any choice but to offer this help? Was their symbolic, practical and legal assistance willingly given? Or was it forced from them by Isabella and Mortimer? The answer to this last question appears to be emphatically not. This is suggested by Isabella's decision to reward the loyalty of supportive prelates, as is clear with regard to Stratford, Orleton and Burghersh, the three bishops whom Geoffrey le Baker thought led the embassy to Kenilworth which procured Edward's final abdication.[46] Stratford soon reaped rewards for his support of the new regime, securing on 5 February 1327 the grant of the bailiwick of Bassetlaw in Nottinghamshire to his friend Edmund de Shireford; receiving on 9 February the cancellation of the recognizances which had been demanded from him by Edward II; and gaining on 6 April a favourable response to his petition that royal custodians should not 'intermeddle' with the churches of East Meon and Hambledon in his diocese during episcopal vacancies.[47] Likewise, Orleton was given the Despenser manor of Beaumes about 9 November 1326; granted custody of the manor of Temple Guiting on 8 December; made treasurer on 28 January 1327; reimbursed for the costs associated with his diplomatic missions to the papacy (which Edward II had left unpaid) on 13 February; and granted restitution on 16 February of those of his lands, goods and chattels which had been seized by the former king.[48] Similarly Henry Burghersh was acquitted of various amercements on 10 March 1327 as 'special favour in consideration of his good service'; made treasurer of the realm (replacing Orleton) on 25 March; and given a royal licence on 12 September for receiving a messauge and two advowsons in Oxford from the convent of St Frideswide's.[49] Far from implying that episcopal support could be taken for granted, Isabella's need to show sympathetic

---

[45] Haines, *Edward II*, 187; Phillips, *Edward II*, 522–4.

[46] *Geoffrey le Baker*, ed. Barber and Preest, 25–6.

[47] *CCR 1327–30*, 24; *Calendar of Patent Rolls Preserved in the Public Record Office, 1216–1509*, 54 vols (London, 1891–1916; hereafter: *CPR*), *1327–30*, 6, 65; Roy Martin Haines, *Archbishop John Stratford* (Toronto, ON, 1986), 42, 104, 188–9.

[48] *CPR 1327–30*, 103; *CCR 1327–30*, 4, 44–5; Haines, *Church and Politics*, 167, 177.

[49] *CPR 1327–30*, 58, 166; *CCR 1327–30*, 33–4, 171–2, 188.

prelates 'special favour', and reward them handsomely at the crown's expense for their assistance, suggests that it may have been the individual bishops themselves who had decided whether they would help her, and indeed may have set the price for their services.

Still more compelling evidence that members of the episcopate acted of their own volition comes from a comparison of the events of 1326–7 with the parliamentary banishment of the Despensers in 1321. Just as Isabella's forces held military sway in the capital in 1327, so had the opposition Marcher barons who opposed the Despensers in 1321: the younger Despenser complained that they 'came in undue manner with horses and arms and all their power'; the *Anonimalle Chronicle* observed that they 'came with great forces; and they came to London completely armed'; and the *Vita Edwardi Secundi* reported that they 'came to parliament … with a very great crowd of men-at-arms', to the extent that even the royalist earl of Pembroke thought that Edward might lose his kingdom if he did not consent to their demands.[50] On both occasions Edward's opponents proved capable of forcing their chosen initiatives through parliament, the deposing of Edward II and the exile of the Despensers respectively, with the *Lanercost Chronicle* remarking that Edward's opponents in 1321 'compelled the king to hold a parliament in London and to yield to their will in all things … [so that] Sir Hugh Despenser the younger was banished for ever, with his father and son, and all their property confiscated'.[51] Although the majority of English prelates would eventually back Isabella in 1327, their support was not a given, for the episcopate as a whole had refused to support Edward II's antagonists in 1321: the *Historia Roffensis* recorded that the bishops remained outside 'in the large chamber' while the earls and barons 'sought the exile of the aforementioned Hugh and Hugh' in Westminster Hall on 14 August, before declaring the following day 'that they in no way agreed to his [Despenser's] exile'.[52] That the bishops had refused en masse to accede to procedures against Edward just six years prior to the events of 1327, in ostensibly similar

---

[50] *CCR 1318–23*, 543; *The Anonimalle Chronicle, 1307 to 1334: From Brotherton Collection MS 29*, ed. Wendy Childs and John Taylor, Yorkshire Archaeological Society Record Series 147 (Leeds, 1991), 100–1; *Vita Edwardi Secundi: The Life of Edward the Second*, ed. Wendy R. Childs, OMT (Oxford, 2005), 192–3.

[51] *Lanercost Chronicle*, ed. Maxwell, 230.

[52] Pronay and Taylor, eds, *Parliamentary Texts*, 168–9.

circumstances, suggests that those prelates who did acquiesce to Edward's deposition chose to do so.

This is confirmed by an examination of how individual bishops declined to back measures against Edward in the winter of 1326–7. At every stage of Isabella's invasion and seizure of control, certain prelates refused to support her. When she landed in September 1326, the St Paul's annalist described how Archbishop Reynolds and Bishops Stratford and Gravesend solemnly republished a seven-year-old papal bull, originally aimed against the Scots, excommunicating all invaders of the realm.[53] Initially, only a minority of prelates came to Isabella at Bristol, helped her to secure England's internal administration, or openly preached in support of her.[54] At the Westminster parliament, the *Historia Roffensis* recorded that the other magnates and bishops present swore an oath of fealty to the future Edward III, but that Archbishop Melton of York and Bishops Gravesend of London and Ross of Carlisle withheld their consent, and noted that Bishop Hethe of Rochester refused to take the oath himself, but asked Archbishop Reynolds to make his excuses.[55] Melton, Gravesend and Ross all maintained their opposition to developments as events progressed, and the *Historia Roffensis* adds that they subsequently refused to take the Guildhall oath in support of Isabella and Edward, in spite of the fact that fourteen other bishops did so.[56] Even at Edward III's coronation, although Gravesend had by then accepted his role, Melton was conspicuous by his absence.[57]

---

[53] *Chronicles*, ed. Stubbs, 1: 315.

[54] Haines, 'Episcopate', 687–8, 705–6.

[55] *Anglia Sacra*, ed. Wharton, 1: 367; Haines, 'Episcopate', 689.

[56] *Anglia Sacra*, ed. Wharton, 1: 367. The fourteen bishops were those of Dublin, Llandaff and every English see apart from Exeter (whose bishop-elect, as noted above, had not yet been consecrated) and Durham (whose bishop, Lewis Beaumont, was presumably occupied in the north): Thomas and Jones, eds, *Calendar of Plea and Memoranda Rolls*, 1: 12–13.

[57] *Anglia Sacra*, ed. Wharton, 1: 367–8; *Chronicles*, ed. Stubbs, 1: 324–5; *CCR 1327–30*, 100. Whether Ross was present at Edward III's coronation is unclear. Many historians suggest that he was absent (e.g. Phillips, *Edward II*, 539 n. 108), because he is not mentioned in the official record of the coronation or the chronicle accounts. However, R. K. Rose has suggested that he was probably present, for he is recorded as being in Westminster on 1 February to consecrate Simon Wedale as bishop of Whithorn: 'The Bishops and Diocese of Carlisle: Church and Society on the Anglo-Scottish Border, 1292–1395' (PhD thesis, University of Edinburgh, 1983), 59.

Quite why these prelates remained steadfast in their support for Edward II is unclear. Their reasons were probably various; they could have included Edward's influence in their own advancement, for Edward had been Melton's principal patron in the early stages of his ecclesiastical career;[58] a personal antipathy towards Isabella, for she had vigorously opposed Hethe's promotion to the see of Rochester in favour of her own almoner between 1317 and 1319;[59] legal objections, for Ross had many years' experience of canon law, notably as an auditor of causes in the papal palace at Avignon from 1317 to 1325, and may have had qualms about taking such as step without the approval of the pontiff;[60] and their own participation in government, for Melton had served Edward II from at least 1297, culminating in his service as treasurer between July 1325 and November 1326, which may have left him feeling some personal responsibility for the acts of the regime.[61]

It is evident, however, that while Edward II had rebuked certain of these bishops, as in April 1322, when he reprimanded Melton for inducing his clergy to grant two thousand marks to the earl of Lancaster, they had never felt the fullness of his wrath.[62] On the contrary, Edward appears to have continued to trust and respect them, as in June 1326, when he ordered Gravesend and Melton to advise those arraying troops to ward off Isabella's prospective invasion.[63] In any event, that several bishops failed to support Isabella and Mortimer, even as Edward II's fate became increasingly certain, confirms that those who opted to do so acted of their own volition. Episcopal support for the new regime was thus of both practical and symbolic significance in the deposition of Edward II, and it appears to have been the individual bishops who chose whether to offer it.

If episcopal assistance was not forcibly procured from them by Isabella and Mortimer, why did these bishops connive in the king's

[58] Rosalind Hill, 'Melton, William (d. 1340)', *ODNB*, 23 September 2004, online at: <https://www.oxforddnb.com/view/10.1093/ref:odnb/9780198614128.001.0001/odnb-9780198614128-e-18538>, last accessed 12 September 2019.
[59] Roy Martin Haines, 'Bishops and Politics in the Reign of Edward II: Hamo de Hethe, Henry Wharton, and the "Historia Roffensis"', *JEH* 44 (1993), 586–609, at 598.
[60] Rose, 'Bishops and Diocese', 11.
[61] Hill, 'Melton, William'.
[62] Kathleen Edwards, 'The Personnel and Political Activities of the English Episcopate during the Reign of Edward II' (MA thesis, University of London, 1937), 331.
[63] *CPR 1324–27*, 302–3; see also Haines, *Archbishop Stratford*, 166–70.

downfall? In particular, what had changed between 1321, when the episcopate unanimously refused to back the king's opponents, and 1327, when the majority of English bishops eventually conspired with Edward II's enemies to bring about his removal? The answer appears to lie in Edward's own response to the crisis of 1321–2. He did not meekly accept the Despensers' banishment, but instead went on the offensive. His campaigns against his domestic foes culminated his victory at the Battle of Boroughbridge on 16 March 1322, when he routed his enemies (the 'Contrariants') and captured the earl of Lancaster, whom he subsequently had executed.[64] Yet rather than taking this opportunity to conciliate his remaining opponents and rule responsibly, Edward ruthlessly exploited his newfound authority. The Statute of York of May 1322 abolished the Ordinances of 1311, a previous attempt to restrict royal abuses, and laid down that any future attempt to limit the power of the king 'shall be null and of no sort of validity or force'.[65] Thereafter, he embraced with renewed vigour the counsels of the Despensers, prompting Froissart's remark that 'Sir Hugh the younger had gained so much influence over the king, and had so moulded his opinions, that nothing was done without him, and everything was done by him'; he failed to defend English lands in France, with Sir Thomas Gray observing that the royal army in the War of St Sardos (1324) 'scarcely achieved anything, but lost much territory, for it was a disastrous period for the English'; and he acted with wanton cruelty, which underlay the comment by the author of the *Vita Edwardi Secundi* that 'the king's harshness has indeed increased so much today that no one, however great and wise, dares to cross the king's will … for whatever pleases the king, though lacking in reason, has the force of law'.[66] The government was particularly harsh in its treatment of Edward's former adversaries. In addition to Lancaster, a further twenty-six barons, knights and esquires were condemned to death without trial after Boroughbridge, with around a hundred more imprisoned.[67] Even their families were sometimes terrorized: for instance, the judgment against the younger Despenser alleged

---

[64] Christopher Given-Wilson, *Edward II* (London, 2016), 67–75.
[65] Rothwell, ed., *English Historical Documents, 1189–1327*, 547–8.
[66] *Froissart's Chronicles*, ed. John Jolliffe (London, 1967), 7; *Scalachronica*, ed. Hebert Maxwell (Glasgow, 1907), 70; *Vita Edwardi Secundi*, ed. Childs, 230–1.
[67] Given-Wilson, *Edward II*, 76–7.

that one Lady Baret, the widow of Stephen Baret (a Contrariant hanged at Swansea), 'shamefully had her arms and legs broken against the order of Chivalry and contrary to law and reason', until she was driven mad.[68] In short, as the author of the *Flores Historiarum* remarked, Edward fell into 'insane tyranny'.[69]

This had three principal ramifications. Firstly, Edward's appalling behaviour aroused discontent throughout political society, which stirred resentment of his rule, sapped his own support and spurred demands for change. Whereas bishops might well have been able to overlook Edward's unpleasant conduct in the past, even when it was directed against members of the episcopal bench, his behaviour had now deteriorated to such an extent, and affected such a considerable portion of the population, that it could no longer be ignored. Secondly, Edward's actions after 1321–2 substantially justified the charges against him in the articles of accusation, and therefore the legal basis for his deposition. Whereas prelates may earlier have baulked at opposing their monarch, or at proceeding with such a radical step as deposition, Edward had now acted in such a way that he fulfilled almost every quality of the *rex inutilis* in contemporary thought.[70] Thirdly, and perhaps most importantly, both through the text of the Statute of York, which outlawed any attempts to restrict monarchical power, and the bloody revenge he wreaked on his opponents, which made clear that anyone who spoke out against him would be at risk while he remained king, Edward had effectively precluded attempts to reform the exercise of royal authority that stopped short of deposition.[71] Whereas the prelates had previously lent their support only to more moderate schemes of reform which sought to limit royal abuses, such as the Ordinances of 1311, Edward's response to the crisis of 1321–2 essentially ruled out such initiatives. Edward's deeds after 1321 thus provoked demands for reform while ruling out any practical alternatives to his deposition and providing ideological justification for his removal. As the articles

---

[68] G. A. Holmes, 'Judgement on the Younger Despenser, 1326', *EHR* 70 (1955), 261–7, at 265; see also Fryde, *Tyranny*, 110–18. However, some doubt has been cast on this tale: Kathryn Warner, *Edward II: The Unconventional King* (Stroud, 2014), 161–2.

[69] *Flores Historiarum*, ed. H. R. Luard, 3 vols, RS 95 (London, 1890), 3: 214. For historiographical comment on Edward's 'tyranny', see, for example, Phillips, *Edward II*, 530–1; Warner, *Unconventional King*, 161; Spencer, 'Inadequate Kingship', 95.

[70] Peters, *Shadow King*, 241.

[71] Spencer, 'Inadequate Kingship', 85.

of accusation recorded, his behaviour threatened both lay society and the church, both of which prelates had a duty to defend. The sermon of Thomas Brinton, bishop of Rochester, during the Good Parliament of 1376, emphasized that it was the bishops' responsibility not only to 'stand up against or castigate' political abuses, but also to 'support the Church on their shoulders like columns and lay down their lives in defence of its liberties'.[72] Consequently, whilst the majority of bishops did not rush to join Isabella when she first landed, but waited to observe in whose direction the winds of political fortune would blow, it is hardly surprising that many prelates proved prepared to act in defence of the English church and the English realm when the time arose and Isabella's success made a change of monarch feasible.[73]

Isabella's episcopal supporters included several whom Edward had treated intolerably badly. These included the four bishops named by both Adam Murimuth and Geoffrey le Baker as Isabella's earliest adherents from the episcopal bench: Alexander Bicknor, archbishop of Dublin; Henry Burghersh, bishop of Lincoln; John Hotham, bishop of Ely; and Adam Orleton, bishop of Hereford.[74] Archbishop Bicknor had been a committed servant to both Edward I and Edward II, serving as the treasurer of the Dublin exchequer from June 1307 to April 1314, as the *custos* and justiciar of Ireland from August 1318 to March 1319, and as a diplomat, sent to Aragon in October 1324 to negotiate a marriage between Prince Edward and the king of Aragon's daughter. Yet in May 1325 Edward II turned on him, asking the pope to remove Bicknor from office on the grounds that he had accused the younger Despenser of treachery, that he had wasted the revenues of Ireland, and that as one of the diplomats present in the St Sardos War he had been responsible

[72] Siegfried Wenzel, ed., *Preaching in the Age of Chaucer: Selected Sermons in Translation*, Medieval Texts in Translation (London, 2008), 245.

[73] Haines, 'Episcopate', 697.

[74] *Adae Murimuth Continuatio Chronicarum*, ed. Edward Maunde Thompson, RS 93 (London, 1889), 46; *Geoffrey le Baker*, ed. Barber and Preest, 21. They were certainly all with Isabella in Bristol by October 1326, to witness the election of Prince Edward as *custos* of the realm: *CCR 1323–27*, 655. These were by no means the only prelates whom Edward had treated poorly who turned to support Isabella; for instance, see also J. L. Grassi, 'William Airmyn and the Bishopric of Norwich', *EHR* 70 (1955), 550–61, at 558–61 (for Airmyn, bishop of Norwich); Edwards, 'Political Importance', 340–1 (for Archbishop Reynolds); Haines, *Archbishop Stratford*, 147–9, 164.

Samuel Lane

for the loss of La Reole in September 1324.[75] Thereafter Edward pursued Bicknor through the legal system, laying criminal charges against him for errors in his accounts while he was treasurer of Ireland. This culminated in December 1325, when Bicknor was convicted of forgery. Although he escaped gaol, Edward nonetheless ordered the Dublin government to seize all Bicknor's lands and property (including those of his archbishopric) in Ireland, and the sheriffs of Gloucestershire, Shropshire and Staffordshire to do likewise in their counties in England.[76] Bicknor later complained that he had 'suffered great damages at the hands of Hugh Despenser and others in England and Ireland'.[77] Deprived of his lands and honour, it is unsurprising that Bicknor sought to ally himself with those who offered the prospect of political change. Indeed, in February 1327 the new regime pardoned him and ordered the restoration of all his confiscated property 'because of the good service' he had rendered.[78]

Edward II's ruthlessness was also exhibited against Bishop Hotham of Ely. While Hotham seems initially to have ridden high in Edward's favour, being promoted to Ely by royal request, and being appointed treasurer in 1317 and chancellor in 1318,[79] he appears to have incurred Edward's wrath following the debacle of the battle of Myton on 20 September 1319, when an English force under his joint leadership was routed by a Scottish army.[80] On 26 October 1319, Edward ordered him 'not to make execution of any mandate under the king's great seal' without the king's express consent, and in January 1320 Hotham was replaced as chancellor.[81] Thereafter, Edward's antipathy became increasingly pernicious: late in 1321,

[75] J. R. S. Phillips, 'Bicknor, Alexander (d. 1349)', *ODNB*, 23 September 2004, online at: <https://www.oxforddnb.com/view/10.1093/ref:odnb/9780198614128.001.0001/odnb-9780198614128-e-2359>, last accessed 12 September 2019.
[76] James F. Lydon, 'The Case against Alexander Bicknor, Archbishop and Peculator', in Brendan Smith, ed., *Ireland and the English World in the Late Middle Ages* (Basingstoke, 2009), 103–11, at 103–7.
[77] Philomena Connolly, 'Irish Material in the Class of Chancery Warrants Series I (C 81) in the Public Record Office, London', *Analecta Hibernica* 36 (1995), 135–61, at 145–6.
[78] Lydon, 'Bicknor', 107.
[79] M. C. Buck, 'Hotham, John (d. 1337)', *ODNB*, 3 January 2008, online at: <https://www.oxforddnb.com/view/10.1093/ref:odnb/9780198614128.001.0001/odnb-9780198614128-e-13851>, last accessed 12 September 2019.
[80] *Anonimalle Chronicle*, ed. Childs and Taylor, 98–9; Benjamin Thompson, 'The Fourteenth Century', in Peter Meadows, ed., *Ely: Bishops and Diocese, 1109–2009* (Woodbridge, 2010), 70–121, at 114.
[81] *CCR 1318–21*, 211; Buck, 'Hotham, John'.

148

the Bridlington chronicler records that Hotham was summoned to London and fined for an unknown offence; in April 1324, he was pressed for debts of more than £1,000; and in November 1324, he was forced to enter into a bond of £2,000 with the younger Despenser.[82] Yet there was also a legal element to Hotham's plight: the judgment against the younger Despenser records that he had been one of the prelates whose 'lands and possessions' the favourite had seized 'by force, against law and reason'.[83]

The fall from grace of Bishop Burghersh was even more pronounced and bloody than that of Hotham. Although Edward II appears to have been instrumental in Burghersh's elevation to the episcopate, his stock fell in June 1321 when his uncle, Bartholomew Badlesmere, joined the king's opponents.[84] After the surrender of Leeds Castle in October 1321, the bishop's brother and sister-in-law were imprisoned in the Tower of London, and following the Battle of Boroughbridge Badlesmere was taken at the bishop's manor of Stowe Park and subsequently executed at Canterbury.[85] Edward then turned against Burghersh himself, accusing him of complicity in the baronial rebellion of 1321–2; writing to the pope to demand his removal from office; confiscating his temporalities between 1322 and 1324; and permitting royal officers to encroach upon the bishop's lands. All this prompted the pope to write to the king several times in 1325 and 1326, requesting that he heed the 'bishop's demands' regarding the 'goods of the bishop and church of Lincoln detained by his [the king's] officers'.[86] It was therefore with justice that John de Schalby, the diocesan registrar of Lincoln, wrote that Burghersh had suffered 'very many persecutions' at Edward's hands.[87] With Edward's behaviour at the root of both family tragedies and personal harassment, it is hardly surprising that Burghersh chose to act against him in 1326.

The same sorry narrative of early loyalty to Edward being shattered in the face of the king's ferocity describes the career of Bishop Orleton. Orleton's initial allegiance to Edward is amply attested by his assisting

---

[82] *Chronicles*, ed. Stubbs, 2: 73; *CCR 1323–27*, 325; Buck, 'Hotham, John'.
[83] Holmes, 'Younger Despenser', 265.
[84] *Vita Edwardi Secundi*, ed. Childs, 178–181; Phillips, *Edward II*, 385.
[85] *Chronicles*, ed. Stubbs, 1: 299; *Brut*, ed. Brie, 1: 221, 224.
[86] Haines, *Church and Politics*, 137–8; Bennett, 'Burghersh, Henry'; *CPReg*, 2: 468–75.
[87] *Giraldi Cambrensis Opera*, ed. J. S. Brewer, J. F. Dimock and G. F. Warner, 8 vols (London, 1861–91), 7: 215.

the king with some of his most personal embassies to the papacy, including that of 1317, which probably aimed to absolve him from the observance of the Ordinances of 1311.[88] However, Edward's reaction to Orleton's alleged involvement in the rebellions of 1321–2 was harsh: the *Vita Edwardi Secundi* described how early in 1322 Edward 'confiscated many of his goods in revenge'; Henry de Blaneforde told of how the king allowed Orleton's goods to be ransacked, looted and thrown into the street by laymen; and the sentence against the younger Despenser alleged that the king's favourite had despoiled Orleton of his goods, horses and plate.[89] Edward's legal persecution of his bishops was particularly marked with Orleton, whom he accused of meeting with Mortimer during the latter's rebellion in the Welsh Marches in 1321–2, and of sending Mortimer reinforcements. Notwithstanding his protestations that he was a churchman, and thus could not to answer to such matters in a lay court 'without offence to God and holy church', Orleton was accused before an assize court in Hereford in January 1324, and the next month appeared before the king himself in Westminster, where he was claimed for the church by Archbishop Reynolds, but nonetheless found guilty by twelve lay jurymen, at which the sheriff of Herefordshire was instructed to seize his goods, chattels and lands.[90] The whole process was riddled with legal flaws: Orleton's indictment contained basic factual errors, and the justices held the inquisition at Westminster in his absence. In consequence, Orleton complained bitterly to the pope of 'this unjust judgment', and the parliament of 1327 annulled the decision, describing 'the record and process' as 'wholly erroneous'.[91] It is thus perhaps small wonder that Orleton referred to Edward's 'Herod-like cruelty'.[92]

While the precise punishments preferred by Edward varied, including extortion, the seizure of goods or lands and legal machinations, the bishops who first expressed their support for Isabella were united by one fact: they had all suffered enormously at the king's hands between 1322 and 1326. As John Stratford pointedly wrote

[88] Haines, *Church and Politics*, 16; John Maddicott, *Thomas of Lancaster, 1307–1322: A Study in the Reign of Edward II* (Oxford, 1970), 199.
[89] *Vita Edwardi Secundi*, ed. Childs, 202–3; *Johnannis de Trokelowe et Henrici de Blaneforde, Chronica et Annales*, ed. H. T. Riley, RS 28/3 (London, 1866), 140–2; Holmes, 'Younger Despenser', 265.
[90] *Henrici de Blaneforde*, ed. Riley, 141–2; Haines, *Church and Politics*, 144–50.
[91] *CCR 1327–30*, 44–5; Haines, *Church and Politics*, 144–6.
[92] Haines, *Church and Politics*, 51.

to Edward III in January 1341, when he appeared to be in danger of following in his father's footsteps, Edward II had

> ... caused to be taken, against the law of the land and of the great charter, the peers and other people of the land, and put some to shameful death, and of others he caused their goods to be seized and all that they had ... and what happened to him for that cause you, sire, know well ...[93]

This mattered enormously to bishops, for as Stratford warned Edward III, it was not simply a matter of personal grievances for those affected, but also a matter of spiritual concern, since such behaviour 'may be to the peril of your [the king's] soul', especially as monarchs were 'bound to keep and maintain' both 'the law of the land and ... the great charter' by their coronation oaths. Indeed, as Stratford went on to advise, such conduct was also capable of reverberating throughout English society more broadly, leading to 'the impoverishing of your land and of your estate'.[94]

Therefore, just as the deposition of Edward II was a defining moment in the history of later medieval England, so members of the episcopate were a defining influence behind his overthrow. Prelates conspired with Isabella and Mortimer at every stage of Edward's downfall: when Isabella initially seized control of the royal administration, when parliament denounced him, when embassies were dispatched to Kenilworth, and when Edward III was crowned king. They appear to have particularly shaped the quasi-legal aspect of proceedings: providing legal expertise, helping to draft the articles of accusation, and ensuring that the articles depicted Edward as a *rex inutilis*. Nonetheless, while the episcopal contribution to Edward's downfall was undoubtedly important, it was by no means obligatory. Bishops did not need compulsion from Isabella and Mortimer to conspire in the king's overthrow, for they had sufficient motivations of their own, borne not only of the violence, cruelty and legal oppression which they and members of their families had suffered at Edward's hands, but also of their duty to defend political society and the church from royal abuses.

---

[93] A. R. Myers, ed., *English Historical Documents, 1327–1485* (London, 1996), 71–2.
[94] Ibid.

Kings' Courts and Bishops' Administrations in Fourteenth-Century England: A Study in Cooperation

Alison K. McHardy*

University of Nottingham

Behind the rhetoric and theory of crown-church conflict there was much cooperation in the everyday world, where practice and pragmatism often overrode legal and theoretical rules. This article examines the ways in which fourteenth-century English bishops and their clerks responded to the demands made of them by the royal courts. Bishops were bombarded with commands from the crown, with a resulting impact on diocesan records. The crown sought historic information about finance and rights, and commanded bishops to collect clerics' debts and to enforce their attendance before the lay courts in both civil and criminal cases. Enquiries about the current status of individuals, whether professed in religious orders or legitimate, made considerable work for bishops. How enthusiastically and efficiently these orders were carried out is also evaluated and discussed.

Cooperation between the church and secular legal authority may lack the drama of church-state power contests or the intellectual excitement of theoretical conflicts of jurisdictions, yet investigation of normality and cooperation still has much to teach us, and can yield rich and surprising rewards.[1] The interaction between English royal law courts and episcopal administrations in the long fourteenth century, moreover, is a subject with abundant sources; yet it has received comparatively little attention.[2] The year 1300 is a good starting

---

* 44 Bankfield Drive, Bramcote, Nottingham, NG9 3EG. E-mail: alison.mchardy365@ gmail.com.

[1] In Lincoln, Lincolnshire Archives (hereafter: LA), register 12B, the present writer discovered a new document about John Wyclif ('John Wycliffe's Mission to Bruges: A Financial Footnote', *JThS* n.s. 24 [1973], 521–2) and an unsuspected nest of Lollards: 'Bishop Buckingham and the Lollards of Lincoln Diocese', in Derek Baker, ed., *Schism, Heresy and Religious Protest*, SCH 9 (Cambridge, 1972), 131–45.

[2] Brief exceptions are Irene Josephine Churchill, *Canterbury Administration*, 2 vols (London, 1933), 1: 520–1; R. H. Helmholz, 'Canon Law and English Common Law', in idem, *Canon Law and the Law of England* (London, 1987), 1–19, at 5–8. W. R. Jones, 'Relations of the Two Jurisdictions: Conflict and Cooperation in England during the

---

Studies in Church History 56 (2020), 152–164   © Ecclesiastical History Society 2020
doi: 10.1017/stc.2019.9

point for investigation because under Edward I there was a great leap forward in all aspects of crown record-keeping as clerks strove to make a copy of every letter they sent out, and to note every transaction they conducted. Bishops' registrars followed suit, and in the early four-teenth century some at least recorded enthusiastically and extensively the letters their bishops received from the king. Bishop Roger Martival of Salisbury (1315–30) was one whose clerks tried to make copies of every writ he received. They recorded 875 from July 1315 to February 1330,[3] an average of nearly sixty a year. The writ register of his contemporary Henry Burghersh of the huge dio-cese of Lincoln (1320–40) remains unpublished, but sampling of writs of his first six years suggests he received about 145 a year.[4] The register of their contemporary Walter Stapeldon of Exeter (1308–26) contains a similarly rich collection.[5] By contrast, Walter Reynolds at the much smaller diocese of Worcester (1308–13) aver-aged about two dozen writs annually.[6]

Writs issued by the royal courts were not, of course, the only com-mands sent to bishops by the crown; orders to attend parliament, organize prayers for national causes, provide lists of foreign bene-fice-holders, swear in local officials and even array their clergy for home defence all came to English bishops. In addition, they had to appoint the collectors of clerical taxes and to provide information about (sometimes distant) defaulters and to gather overdue sums. Those subjects lie outside the scope of this article. Writs commanded bishops to undertake many tasks on behalf of the king's courts, of

---

Thirteenth and Fourteenth Centuries', *Studies in Medieval and Renaissance History* 7 (1970), 79–210, is an overview which does not examine the evidence presented here.

[3] *The Register of Roger Martival Bishop of Salisbury 1315–1330*, 3: *Royal Writs*, ed. Susan Reynolds, CYS 59 (Torquay, 1965). On Martival's enthusiasm for recording all writs, see Kathleen Edwards, 'General Introduction to the Registers', in *The Register of Roger Martival Bishop of Salisbury 1315–1330*, 4: *The Register of Inhibitions and Acts*, ed. Dorothy M. Owen, CYS 68 (Torquay, 1975), vii-lvi, at x.

[4] LA, Reg. 5B. MCD 997 is a calendar of the first 700 writs, using Susan Reynolds's model, made by Judith Cripps, a former assistant archivist.

[5] *The Register of Walter de Stapeldon, Bishop of Exeter*, ed. F. C. Hingeston-Randolph (London and Exeter, 1892), 413–44, lists 412 writs addressed to the bishop or his vicar-general.

[6] *The Register of Walter Reynolds, Bishop of Worcester 1308–1313*, ed. Rowland A. Wilson, Dugdale Society 9 (London, 1928), 159–80.

Chancery, Exchequer, Common Pleas, King's Bench or Assize. Bishop Martival received forty-nine types of writ, not including writs of *sicut alias* or *sicut pluries*, that is, the reiterations of previous commands. By far the biggest class of business concerned debts, and came from the court of Common Pleas; these were generally writs of *venire faciatis* ordering the bishop to cause a defendant to answer one of several types of plea in cases of private debts owed by clerics. In executing these writs, bishops were, strictly speaking, violating canon law, which did not recognize lay jurisdiction over the clergy in civil matters. This, however, was widely disregarded.[7] The exchequer also issued writs of debt, but these were *fieri faciatis*, telling the bishop himself to raise money from clerics in debt to the crown, which might have resulted from their service as king's clerks.[8] The widespread use of clergy as executors also resulted in many actions for debt.[9] The King's Bench writs essentially told the bishop to make clerical defendants appear in court (*venire faciatis* and variations).[10] The pattern is similar in Burghersh's writ register: the overwhelming majority are Common Pleas writs about private debts owed by clerics. There is also an element, some ten per cent, of writs issued by the court of King's Bench concerning crimes of various kinds, including violent assault allegedly perpetrated by clerics. It looks as though the royal courts were using church administrations – accessed through the bishops – as debt collectors, gatherers of evidence and general enforcers. It should be said that using diocesan machinery for collecting money was often the courts' second choice, since

---

[7] Richard H. Helmholz, *OHLE*, 1: *The Canon Law and Ecclesiastical Jurisdiction from 597 to the 1640s* (Oxford, 2004), 315.

[8] For example, John de Berwick, keeper of the queen's gold (1285–90) and of the queen's wardrobe (1286–90), left office and died owing the crown £863 8s 4½d: *Reynolds Register*, ed. Wilson, writ nos 94, 110; T. F. Tout, *Chapters in the Administrative History of Mediaeval England*, 6 vols (Manchester, 1920–33), 2: 42 n. 2; 5: 238, 272. Adam de Wycheford, 'lately chamberlain in North Wales' and rector of Wick (Worcestershire), left office owing £211 7s 6d: Roy Martin Haines, ed., *Calendar of the Register of Simon de Montacute, Bishop of Worcester, 1334–1337*, Worcestershire Historical Society n.s. 15 (Worcester, 1996), no. 1053. In 1316, Martival was ordered to produce £10 which Master Richard Havering owed to Edward I's widow Queen Margaret: *Martival Register*, 3, ed. Reynolds, no. 64. For his career, see A. B. Emden, *A Biographical Register of the University of Oxford*, 3 vols (Oxford, 1957–9), 3: 2181–2.

[9] For example, *Stapeldon Register*, ed. Hingeston-Randolph, writ nos 55, 74.

[10] *Martival Register*, 3, ed. Reynolds, xii–xxxiv, is a formulary of all the types of writs received.

many writs included the information that a sheriff had made a return of 'no lay fee' in respect of clerical debtors.

There were, however, some questions to which only churchmen could supply an answer. A number of writs wanted information in connection with advowson disputes or disputes about the rights of, and financial burdens on, a benefice; these orders were writs of *certiorari*. These were Chancery writs, and a subgroup specifically ordered a bishop to consult registers. The wording is: *mandamus quod scrutatis registris de eo quod inde inveneritis* ('look in the registers and tell us what you find'). Variations ordered the registers of the bishop's predecessors to be consulted, and sometimes the see's other archives as well.

How far back did these enquiries want to go? Demands addressed to Bishop Buckingham of Lincoln (1363–98) furnish some interesting examples.[11] Most dramatic (or unreasonable) is a writ of 1386 concerning half the church of Milton Major and Collingtree, Northamptonshire, which wanted to know about the benefice from 'the first year of the lord king H. father of the lord John formerly king of England'. This takes us back to 1154, and the wording is so deliberate that it can hardly be an error.[12] Two other writs, one in 1372, the other in 1392, wanted information from Richard I's coronation, 3 September 1189, the limit of legal memory.[13] More realistic was the enquiry about incumbents of Marston Moretaine 'since the coronation of Henry son of King John'.[14] In the return to another writ about the same Bedfordshire benefice, dated early in 1395, the bishop reported that he had caused the registers of his predecessors to be scrutinized from the time of Hugh II, that is, Hugh of Wells (1209–35), when Gilbert de W. [*sic*] was instituted, and he sent a full list of incumbents.[15] Indeed, Gilbert de Wyville's institution can be found in the rolls of Hugh of Wells.[16] Perhaps this return

---

[11] Alison K. McHardy, ed., *Royal Writs addressed to John Buckingham, Bishop of Lincoln, 1363–1398. Lincoln Register 12B: A Calendar*, CYS 86 (Woodbridge, 1997). This register was omitted from David M. Smith, *Guide to Bishops' Registers of England and Wales* (London, 1981).

[12] McHardy, ed., *Lincoln Writs*, no. 314.

[13] Ibid., Appendix A, nos 5 (Churchill, Oxfordshire, 1372), 400 (Olney, Buckinghamshire, 1392).

[14] Ibid., nos 449, 454.

[15] Ibid., no. 455.

[16] *Rotuli Hugonis de Welles, Episcopi Lincolniensis, A.D. MCCIX–MCCXXXV*, 3, ed. F. N. Davis, CYS 4 (London, 1908), 29.

improved Chancery knowledge of Lincoln episcopal archives, because a flurry of writs, all from 1395, about several benefices, wanted information dating from the episcopate of Hugh of Wells; he was the first bishop of Lincoln to keep systematic records of his rule.[17]

No later writ wanted information from so far back, and only two asked for data from the thirteenth century. One concerned Armston hospital, Northamptonshire, and wanted to know about the form of its foundation and ordination, 'made in the time of Robert Grosseteste, it is said'. The return was: 'We made diligent search among the register of Robert Grosseteste but could not find anything about the foundation of the hospital in his time. However, we did find an *inspeximus* of two charters, one of Hugh of Wells and the other of Lady Alice de Trublevile ... and we send you their wording'. Hugh of Wells's charter remains at Boughton House, near Kettering, and the *inspeximus* of Alice's charter is in Grosseteste's rolls.[18] Clearly someone, either in Northamptonshire or in the royal Chancery, knew that Grosseteste's records would contain useful information.

The most remarkable command of this type ordered the bishop of Lincoln to send in his entire register to the royal Chancery. This came in June 1391 and was occasioned by a dispute over the archdeaconry of Buckingham.[19] Two writs in quick succession told the bishop to send 'the complete register which you have had made since your consecration, in the care of some of your staff in whom you have confidence'. The return was: 'We have scrutinized our register and send a full copy of the relevant matter, but we are not able to send our whole register'.[20] Clearly compliance with the law's demands had its limitations, which were overstepped by this order. The bishop's return is not surprising, for not only was any current register a work in

---

[17] McHardy, ed., *Lincoln Writs*, nos 463–5 (Thornton, Leicestershire), 467 (Brackley, Northamptonshire), 470–1 (three churches in Leicester, St Mary de Castro, St Leonard and St Martin).

[18] *Robert Grosseteste as Bishop of Lincoln: The Episcopal Rolls, 1235–1253*, ed. Philippa M. Hoskin, Lincoln Record Society, Kathleen Major Series 1 (Woodbridge, 2015), no. 950; see also *The Acta of Hugh of Wells Bishop of Lincoln 1209–1235*, ed. David M. Smith, Lincoln Record Society 88 (Woodbridge, 2000), no. 370, for Wells's confirmation in 1232 of the arrangement between the hospital's founders and the patron and rector of nearby Polebrook church.

[19] The archdeaconry of Buckingham was contested for much of the fourteenth century: John Le Neve, *Fasti Ecclesiae Anglicanae 1300–1541*, 1: *Lincoln Diocese*, ed. H. P. F. King (London, 1962), 15.

[20] McHardy, ed., *Lincoln Writs*, nos 390, 391.

progress, to be consulted and constantly added to, but until the epis-copate ended it was not a bound volume but remained a loose collec-tion of parchment sheets.

Some writs directed a bishop to discover the true status of an indi-vidual, subjects which only church authorities could answer. Such queries had two points in common: they arose from property disputes being held in either Common Pleas or King's Bench, and all appar-ently arose late in the proceedings. It looks as though the party which was about to lose the case made the allegation of defective legal status as a way of deferring judgment in the hope that their opponent would die, abandon the case or agree to compromise.[21] Two such enquiries are especially interesting: 'Is X a nun?', and 'Is Y legitimate or a bastard?'

It is perhaps not surprising that the question of whether a partic-ular woman was a nun should arise, for many nunneries included res-idents who were neither professed, novices or *conversae*: girls being educated, widows as paying guests or even political prisoners. The problem of identifying nuns had occupied the English church since the primacy of Archbishop Lanfranc, and during the Angevin period a series of cases before the *curia regis* concerned the disputed religious status of a number of individuals, most, but not all, of whom were women.[22] At the root of the problem was the well-established doc-trine of 'civil death', which prohibited the religious from pleading in lay courts, making wills or inheriting property, which thus passed to their next heirs as though they were already deceased.[23] The result was that the taking of religious vows became entwined with the trans-mission of property, and sometimes with the wish to remove individ-ual family members from the possibility of inheritance, and thus to benefit others. This certainly seems to have been the case with Alice de Everingham, from a landed family of Yorkshire, Nottinghamshire and Lincolnshire, who was caught up in a family

---

[21] W. Holdsworth, *A History of English Law*, 3rd edn, 3 vols (London, 1923), 3: 624–5. For this and the following two notes, thanks are due to John Hudson.

[22] For Lanfranc's pronouncement on the subject, see *The Letters of Lanfranc, Archbishop of Canterbury*, ed. and transl. Helen Glover and Margaret Gibson (Oxford, 1979), 166–7 (no. 53); Cyril T. Flower, *Introduction to the Curia Regis Rolls 1199–1230*, SelS 62 (London, 1944), 107–211.

[23] Frederick Pollock and F. W. Maitland, *The History of English Law before the Time of Edward I*, 2nd edn, 2 vols (Cambridge, 1968), 1: 433–8. Banishment and abjuring the realm were the other causes of this disqualification.

dispute and was signified as a religious apostate from Haverholme Priory (Lincolnshire) in 1366 by William Prestwold, master of the Gilbertine order.[24] The bishop's commission, convened in response to two Chancery writs the following year, examined Alice herself and the brothers and sisters of Haverholme, and reported that she was not a nun.[25] This seems to have closed the case.[26] Conversely, Maud Huntercombe apparently *was* a nun but Giles French, a king's serjeant, spotted an opportunity to gain some property from her Buckinghamshire gentry family after it suffered two key deaths in 1390 and 1391, so he abducted Maud from Burnham Abbey (Buckinghamshire). She too was signified as a religious apostate on 10 July 1391, by the abbess who described Maud as a vagabond in secular habit.[27] By then two writs had already been sent to the bishop to enquire into her status, although stay of their execution was ordered that November.[28] Soon a flurry of writs restarted the enquiry process,[29] but Bishop Buckingham had already set up a commission of enquiry in the previous July, and returned its findings on 20 April 1393. Having made diligent enquiry, 'at great trouble and expense', as he grumbled, he concluded that Maud was indeed a nun, had been so for many years, and had entered religion at the age of discretion.[30] She was to be returned to Burnham Abbey and the plaintiffs in the case, her aunts, were restored to their property.[31]

Yet more complicated was the question, 'Is X legitimate or a bastard?' This might involve not only questions of marriage but also of divorce.[32] Problems here included the fact that canon law and

---

[24] Kew, TNA, Warrants for the Great Seal: Religious Apostates, C 81/1791/2, 17 November 1366. For the order for her arrest, see *CPR 1364–67*, 369.

[25] McHardy, ed., *Lincoln Writs*, nos 43, 44; the original writ and return of no. 44 is in TNA, Certiori: Ecclesiastical, C 269/4/29.

[26] She may have been the Alice de Everingham, widow of Thomas de Normanvile, who petitioned parliament in 1395: TNA, Ancient Petitions, SC 8/312E1.

[27] TNA, C 81/1789/3, 20 April 1393. She was likely to be found in London, Buckinghamshire or elsewhere.

[28] McHardy, ed., *Lincoln Writs*, nos 416, 417; *CCR 1389–92*, 363.

[29] McHardy, ed., *Lincoln Writs*, nos 418–20, 13 November 1392, 18 January and 12 February 1393.

[30] Return to TNA, C 269/8/18, piece 1, writ of 12 February 1393.

[31] *CCR 1392–96*, 70–1. Buckingham's commission was to five doctors of law: McHardy, ed., *Lincoln Writs*, no. 417.

[32] 'The canon law proclaimed the exclusive jurisdiction of its courts over substantive matrimonial questions, and the English royal courts did not contest this claim': Helmholz, *OHLE*, 1: 522.

common law had slightly different rules for making the judgment, and that common law, being case law, tended to change its definition.[33] Whilst marriage law was church law, 'there was some skirmishing at the edges', as Helmholz puts it, over disputes about the inheritance of land.[34] In every case discovered in the writ collections, the allegation of bastardy was rejected by episcopal enquiry. All involved property, mostly of small amounts, for example 'an acre of land with appurtenances' in Gloucestershire, in a case to Reynolds of Worcester in 1310.[35] The cases coming to Martival were also comparatively modest: a messuage and two carucates of land in 1316 and an acre of land in 1327.[36] The lands in question whose heirs' status was in doubt under Stapeldon were similar. In November 1309 they concerned three messuages and four acres of land in Whitestone (Cornwall) and Nether Exe (Devon), and after some delay he reported that the plaintiff was legitimate and not a bastard.[37] In 1312 a similar enquiry arose from a dispute over two acres of land in Shillingford (Devon), to which the return gave the details that the couple in question were Adam Pynde and Rose de Holerigge whose marriage had been publicly solemnized in the face of the church, and that they had subsequently lived together as man and wife.[38]

Much higher stakes occurred in a case which came to Buckingham of Lincoln. It concerned the first marriage of Sir Bernard Brocas, soldier, courtier, friend of William of Wykeham and long-serving master of the royal buckhounds.[39] The Common Pleas writ of *inquiratis de bastardia*, dated 15 May 1385, concerned Sir Bernard's namesake and the son of his first marriage. This had taken place in 1344 or

---

[33] R. H. Helmholz, 'Bastardy Litigation in Medieval England', *AJLH* 13 (1969), 360–83, especially for changes during the fourteenth century; J. L. Barton, 'Nullity of Marriage and Illegitimacy in the England of the Middle Ages', in Dafydd Jenkins, ed., *Legal History Studies 1972* (Cardiff, 1975), 28–49.

[34] R. H. Helmholz, *Marriage Litigation in Medieval England* (Cambridge, 1974), 3.

[35] *Reynolds Register*, ed. Wilson, no. 48.

[36] *Martival Register*, 3, ed. Reynolds, nos 61, 690, 692.

[37] The common pleas writ of *inquiratis de bastardia* was dated 20 November 1309, received on 27 November, and the reply dated the following 30 April: *Stapeldon Register*, ed. Hingeston-Randolph, writ no. 64.

[38] Writ dated 24 November 1312, return 20 January 1313: ibid., no. 181.

[39] For Brocas, see Linda Clarke's biography in J. S. Roskell, Linda Clark and Carole Rawcliffe, eds, *The History of Parliament. House of Commons, 1386–1421*, 2: *Members A–D* (Stroud, 1992), 359–62.

1345, to Agnes Vavasour, heiress to five Yorkshire manors and one (Weekley) in Northamptonshire. The marriage was dissolved in 1360 but unusually both parties were given leave to remarry, which they did. Agnes married Henry Langfield, and the dispute was about her Northamptonshire land and was sparked by the felling of trees there. It looks as though Henry Langfield, following his wife's death in January 1385, was trying desperately to hold on to her Northamptonshire manor which had been inherited by his stepson, Bernard Brocas junior.[40] This was also a complicated investigation for the bishop because the Brocas family was based in Hampshire and Sir Bernard's first marriage had taken place in Berkshire, but the long and detailed enquiry was held in London. There were four witnesses: one had been born in the year of the wedding, and two only echoed the second witness. He, however, compensated by his precise and detailed recollection of the marriage, the wedding liturgy and the names of the guests.[41]

These examples showed crown-church or legal-canonical cooperation working effectively. But they were high-profile: Alice's case came before Chancery and Maud's before parliament,[42] while Brocas senior was a courtier and MP. When we ask how efficiently this cooperative mechanism usually worked, the answer is not clear-cut. In some episcopates, the rate of effective execution is impressive. Walter Reynolds at Worcester was able to execute, either wholly or in part, nearly half (sixty-five) the royal commands, although no return was recorded to a further twenty-five, while attempts to raise money were thwarted in seventeen other cases in which no buyer of the sequestered goods could be found. This was in a comparatively small diocese at a time of domestic peace. Yet the problems these writs posed are illustrated by a writ addressed to Reynolds in 1309. This exchequer *fieri faciatis de bonis ecclesiasticis* was against William de Persore, rector of Powick (Worcestershire), Reginald le Porter, rector of 'Burghton',

---

[40] *Calendar of Inquisitions Post Mortem and other Analogous Documents preserved in the Public Record Office*, 16: *7–15 Richard II* (London, 1974), no. 155, for Agnes's property. Nothing is listed for Northamptonshire.

[41] Beaurepaire and Sherborne St John (Hampshire), Clewer (Berkshire) and St Olave, Silver Street, London, on 19 June 1365. The enquiry is printed from Buckingham's *memoranda* register: LA, Lincoln Register 12, fols 306ʳ–308ᵛ; McHardy, ed., *Lincoln Writs*, nos 90–4.

[42] TNA, Ancient Petitions, SC 8/97/4804; SC 8/97/4802B; SC 8/97/4802A; SC 8/13/ 647A.

and Adam de Herewynton, executors of Reginald le Porter 'sometime sheriff of Worcestershire'. To this the return was: 'Adam de H. is not beneficed in the diocese, William le P. is dead and nothing of his goods can be found; goods of the rector of B. to the value of 40*s* have been sequestered, but no buyer for them could be found'.[43] In larger dioceses, the successful rate of return was much lower, and the answer to very many writs was that it had arrived too late for execution to take place by the date of its return to the issuing court.[44] This was not surprising, given that bishops travelled widely within their sees and further afield, and must often have been elusive. Roger Martival of Salisbury, for example, would visit his family home of Noseley, in Leicestershire,[45] as well as travelling to parliament at Lincoln in 1316,[46] while Henry Burghersh of Lincoln spent long periods near York in the summer of 1322. As well as late arrival, other common returns were that property had been seized but no buyer could be found; there was no such person in the diocese,[47] the person was unknown unless designated by his benefice,[48] the wanted man had died,[49] the debtor was not an executor of the will in question,[50] there would be no money until after harvest,[51] or the harvest had been sold and the money already dispersed.[52] An unusual reply came in January 1408 from Bishop Repingdon of Lincoln: the rector of Clipston (Northamptonshire) could not be

---

[43] *Reynolds Register*, ed. Wilson, writ no. 14. 'Boughton' is probably Bourton on the Hill, Gloucestershire.

[44] A rare example of precision is given in Burghersh's writ register where a writ of 6 July 1321 was received on 7 October: LA, MCD 997, no. 46.

[45] For details of Martival's visits to Noseley, see Edwards, 'Introduction', to *Martival Register*, 4, ed. Owen, xxxviii–xliii. Burghersh's clerks usually recorded the place and date of receipt.

[46] One writ could not be executed because he was about to set out for parliament at Lincoln: *Martival Register*, 3, ed. Reynolds, no. 25.

[47] *Stapeldon Register*, ed. Hingeston-Randolph, no. 218; McHardy, ed., *Lincoln Writs*, no. 36.

[48] LA, MCD 997, no. 106.

[49] Ibid., no. 158; *Stapeldon Register*, ed. Hingeston-Randolph, nos 126, 196, 218; McHardy, ed., *Lincoln Writs*, no. 2.

[50] LA, MCD 997, no. 27.

[51] *Reynolds Register*, ed. Wilson, no. 91; *Martival Register*, 3, ed. Reynolds, no. 52.

[52] Burghersh reported of one rector that 'before Lammas he sold to his parishioners the harvest tithes and other offerings … for which fraud and transgression we are proceeding against him in accordance with the canons': LA, MCD 997, no. 216; *Martival Register*, 3, ed. Reynolds, no. 83.

Alison K. McHardy

brought to the exchequer because he had departed for the Roman court.[53] Attempts made by the royal courts to penalize bishops by making them responsible for debts were only partly successful. Debtors were made to swear that they would save their bishop unharmed by appearing in lay courts or paying debts, but did not always keep their word, and bishops complained when they suffered for the misdeeds of their clergy. It is usually impossible to detect the dividing line between incompetence[54] (on both sides) and obstructiveness.[55] But obstructiveness on the part of bishops and their clerks there certainly was. An egregious example is the return to a Common Pleas *fieri faciatis de bonis ecclesiasticis* against Richard Ravenser for forty marks, to which the bishop of Lincoln replied: 'We have made diligent enquiry in our diocese about the ecclesiastical goods of Richard de Ravenser, but we can find none by which the 40 marks can be distrained', even though Ravenser was then archdeacon of Lincoln and prebendary of Empingham.[56] This, however, should not necessarily be seen as an example of crown-church antagonism, more as the stuff of perpetual and continuing legal sparring.[57] Responses to episcopal ineffectiveness included the issuing of writs of *sicut alias* (for the second time), *sicut pluries* (further orders), threats to the bishop[58] and sometimes professions of astonishment at a bishop's previous failures to comply, with increasing irritation at episcopal inaction.[59]

[53] This was Gryffyth Damport, formerly chancellor of Thomas (Holand), earl of Kent: LA, Register 15B (Philip Repingdon, Writs), fol. 1.
[54] For example, a series of writs to the bishop of Worcester against the rector of 'Bedyndon' elicited the return that there was no such church in the diocese. Beddington is in Winchester diocese: Roy Martin Haines, ed., *A Calendar of the Register of Wolstan de Bransford 1339–1349*, Worcestershire Historical Society 4 (London, 1966), no. 1114.
[55] Between March 1308 and midsummer 1315, the bishop of Exeter received sixty-two writs about the various debts of Nicholas de Lovetot, to one of which he made the return that 'all his ecclesiastical goods in the diocese had, long before the receipt of this writ, been sequestered by order of the Holy See', *Stapeldon Register*, ed. Hingeston-Randolph, no. 241.
[56] McHardy, ed., *Lincoln Writs*, no. 231 and n. See also Buckingham's assertion in 1363 that he could find no ecclesiastical goods of the dean of Lincoln: ibid., no. 7B.
[57] The point made by Helmholz in reviewing McHardy, ed., *Lincoln Writs*: *Legal History* 20 (1999), 137–8.
[58] McHardy, ed., *Lincoln Writs*, nos 49, 51, 75, 84.
[59] *Stapeldon Register*, ed. Hingeston-Randolph, nos 4, 5, 337; *Reynolds Register*, ed. Wilson, writ no. 91.

Another obstacle to detecting efficiency is that enthusiasm for recording the writs waned in the course of the fourteenth century, as bishops' chanceries became much more selective, and writs about private debt and crime were no longer copied. In dioceses where successive writ collections can be identified, such as Salisbury, Worcester and Lincoln, the rate of recording declined during the second half of the fourteenth century, although to some extent enthusiasm for recording writs depended upon individual bishops. Thus in Worcester diocese Adam de Ordeton's register (1327–33) contains seventeen scattered writs, or references, none arising from the types of cases discussed here, while the well-organized register of his successor Simon de Montacute (1332–7) has around fifty, with dates and places of receipt and details of returns meticulously entered. Montacute, young, aristocratic and a new-minted graduate, was a stickler for many aspects of his office.[60] The trend was generally downwards, though, and all diocesan traditions of keeping writ sections disappeared during the second quarter of the fifteenth century.[61] It is likely that practicality, rather than principle, dictated the change, for the cost in time and materials of copying every writ was surely considerable. Moreover, as the fourteenth century progressed, the impact of warfare imposed new burdens on bishops, in particular the collection of current clerical taxes and the gathering of sometimes long-standing arrears. English bishops were thus more likely to respond to immediate pressures rather than to decisions in the distant papal court.[62]

This article has examined an area of crown-church cooperation in which pragmatism, rather than principle, prevailed. It was, of course, only one part of crown-church legal interaction, and one chronological segment, albeit one which lasted over a hundred years. Previously, the two great areas of legal friction had been the jurisdiction over disputes about the rights of patronage of ecclesiastical benefices, which the crown won (and so advowsons were a lay plea), and benefit of clergy, which the church won (at least in theory). In practice, the boundaries were often blurred; both clergy and laymen sometimes

---

[60] Haines, ed., *Calendar of the Register of Simon de Montacute*; Emden, *Biographical Register*, 3: 1295–6, *s.n.* Montagu.

[61] See Smith, *Guide to Bishops' Registers*; McHardy, ed., *Lincoln Writs*, xii-xvi.

[62] In the 1370s the auditors of the *Rota* 'determined that the English custom of hearing civil cases involving clerical defendants before secular courts was a wholly invalid custom under the canon law. But nothing changed in consequence': Helmholz, *OHLE*, 1: 315.

claimed (or denied) that a case belonged to one particular jurisdiction in order to have proceedings moved from, or into, church courts, while from the early fourteenth century examples can be found of obvious laymen successfully claiming benefit of clergy. At the national level, the clergy made a series of protests and complaints from the early thirteenth century and throughout the fourteenth about infringement of their rights, usually when the crown was weak or political tension high,[63] and the laity in parliament on occasion made counter-claims.[64] At the national, international and theoretical levels, therefore, high claims might be made on both sides of the ecclesiastical-secular power divide, but at the local level cooperation was much more evident, as this article has striven to show. Also, while the crown enlisted the church to exert the authority of the royal courts, ecclesiastical authorities, for their part, turned to the secular power in order to enforce discipline by imprisoning persistent excommunicates and capturing religious runaways.[65] None of this is the stuff of heroics or drama, but in complying, however inefficiently, with commands from the crown's courts, the bishops of England during the long fourteenth century were going to considerable trouble. In acting as the crown's bailiffs, sheriffs and detective agencies they were expending time, money, ink and parchment in their cooperation with legal authority to ensure that rights were respected, fraud was unmasked and debts were paid, efforts which contributed towards making England a land where the rule of law, and laws, prevailed.

---

[63] W. R. Jones, 'Bishops, Politics and the Two Laws: The *Gravamina* of the English Clergy, 1237–1399', *Speculum* 41 (1966), 20–45; J. H. Denton, 'The Making of the "*Articuli Cleri*" of 1316', *EHR* 101 (1986), 564–89. See also Matthew Phillips, 'Bishops, Parliament and Trial by Peers: Clerical Opposition to the Confiscation of Episcopal Temporalities in the Fourteenth Century', *JEH* 67 (2016), 288–304.

[64] W. Mark Ormrod, Helen Killick and Phil Bradford, eds, *Early Common Petitions in the English Parliament, c.1290–c.1420*, Camden 5th series 52 (London, 2017), 47–8.

[65] F. D. Logan, *Excommunication and the Secular Arm in Medieval England* (Toronto, ON, 1968); idem, *Runaway Religious in Medieval England, c.1240–1540* (Cambridge, 1996).

Arbitration, Delegation, Conservation: Marginalized Mechanisms for Dispute Resolution in the Pre-Reformation English Church

R. N. Swanson*

Shaanxi Normal University

The records of diocesan and peculiar courts of late medieval England have received extensive academic scrutiny, generating a reasonably clear picture of a hierarchical pyramid ultimately headed by the papal curia. However, that picture is an incomplete depiction of the totality of the ecclesiastical mechanisms of dispute resolution. Existing scholarship largely ignores the use of arbitrated extra-curial settlements to avoid litigation (or, alternatively, a formal sentence). Concentration on the provincial court hierarchy also marginalizes the more directly papal courts of judges delegate and assorted local agents with judicial powers, which functioned within England between 1300 and the Reformation and bypassed the normal fora. Drawing on a wide range of scattered source material, this article introduces these neglected elements of the church's legal system, including the resident papal conservators appointed at the request of petitioners to exercise a general delegated papal judicial authority on their behalf, whose existence has been almost completely unnoticed. It suggests the significance of arbitration, delegation and conservation within the wider structure, and the need to give them much more attention if the practical importance of canon law in pre-Reformation England is to be properly understood and appreciated.

Among the forces which shaped and reveal the medieval English church and its place, role and influence in contemporary society, law and litigation were clearly important. Disputes were ubiquitous, repeatedly configuring and reconfiguring institutional and personal

* E-mail: r.n.swanson@bham.ac.uk. This article is an offshoot from my current research on the late medieval English parish, drawing on and continuing work supported in 2013–16 by a Leverhulme Trust Major Research Fellowship (MRF-2012-016).
I am extremely grateful to the trust for its generous support, without which this article and much other recent and anticipated work would not have been possible. The comments of the reviewers of the original version of this article were extremely valuable for its subsequent development.

Studies in Church History 56 (2020), 165–181
doi: 10.1017/stc.2019.10

ties and relationships. Seemingly congenital litigiousness makes church court records essential sources for investigation and analysis. The records of secular jurisdictions, from manors up to Westminster and Chancery, also offer massive amounts of relevant evidence and information.

The quantity and quality of the surviving court records from the diocesan and peculiar jurisdictions of pre-Reformation England has understandably, and justifiably, generated a scholarly tradition shaped as much by its concentration on those sources as by the formal structures of the church's legal system. Given the quantity, quality, accessibility and rewards of such material (the York Cause Papers or the diocesan court books from Canterbury, London and Hereford), it is perfectly understandable why scholars have not been particularly inclined or tempted to trawl less obviously promising sources.[1]

However, that failure to extend the search may result in distortion and faulty reconstructions or analyses. Potentially significant strands within the church's legal structures and procedures may not have received their due attention. Admittedly, the nature of the available sources may mean that those strands cannot realistically receive that attention; but to ignore them leaves the current view of the church and (its) law incomplete. Two major facets of these neglected or marginalized aspects are considered here. The first is the use of informal and essentially extra-curial processes of dispute resolution through arbitration, seeking either to obviate the need for (or continuance of) litigation or to avoid the ill-will which might result from a formal outcome or implementation of a sentence. The second is decidedly curial, but outside or beyond the hierarchical pattern of local, diocesan and provincial courts reflected in the usually consulted sources. Instead, it demonstrates the continuing existence across the late medieval centuries of an alternative system based on the delegation of

[1] For the church courts in late medieval England, their competence and procedures, see now R. H. Helmholz, *OHLE*, 1: *The Canon Law and Ecclesiastical Jurisdiction from 597 to the 1640s* (Oxford, 2004). Most surviving court records are surveyed in Charles Donahue Jr, ed., *The Records of the Medieval Ecclesiastical Courts*, 2: *England*, Comparative Studies in Continental and Anglo-American Legal History / Vergleichende Untersuchungen zur kontinentaleuropäischen und anglo-amerikanischen Rechtsgeschichte 7 (Berlin, 1994). The main York Cause Papers are held at York University, BIA; images are now available online at: <http://dlibcausepapers.york.ac.uk/yodl/app/home/index>, with a searchable catalogue (but incomplete set of images) at: <https://www.dhi.ac.uk/causepapers/>, both accessed 9 September 2018.

papal judicial authority to local agents, a devolution of papal justice which allowed cases to be heard in England rather than at the papal court. Admittedly, each of these strands is occasionally indicated within the standard evidence from the main church courts, but by their nature they are extraneous to them. More often they are revealed in scattered shards of evidence outside those records, their random distribution discouraging deliberate hunting and making their discovery a matter of luck more than expectation. Some of these shards survive as individual documents, obscured within family or institutional collections and deposits in record offices; others, comprising most of those so far noticed, emerge from miscellaneous entries in episcopal registers or as copies transcribed for other purposes into legal and administrative formularies or letter collections.

The goal of this discussion is not a comprehensive overview or a detailed analysis of the social forces behind the use of such mechanisms; it offers a preliminary general comment directed mainly to shaping the framework for consideration of attitudes to, and experiences of, the structures and processes of ecclesiastical law in pre-Reformation England. The narratives of the disputes and court cases which generate the evidence were individually significant to those involved; but most of the available records provide only isolated fragments of the full story. Reconstruction of specific cases therefore gives way here to the simpler and more straightforward goal of drawing attention to the practices, deploying the evidence mainly to illustrate their existence and general operation. The thrust of the argument is that the current lack of attention to arbitration and delegated papal jurisdiction distorts awareness of the mechanisms of ecclesiastical justice in pre-Reformation England, but the nature of the evidence and current state of research unavoidably make this a tentative initial assessment, an extremely sketchy sketch.

ARBITRATION

The first strand directs attention to resolution of 'ecclesiastical' disputes by extra-curial processes which produced a negotiated or mediated settlement. A case from Northamptonshire in 1458 provides a good illustration. Acting as '*arbiter, arbitrator, sive amicabilis compositor*', John Chedworth, bishop of Lincoln, concluded a case which had been long undecided before his diocesan consistory court. The churchwardens and parishioners of Lamport had sued an inhabitant of Higham Ferrers (roughly thirteen miles away) for an annual payment from a tenement in Lamport to fund the maintenance of lights within their parish church. Having examined the evidence, Chedworth found for the plaintiffs and affirmed the tenement's liability.[2]

Chedworth's mixed designation complicates analysis: formally, the three roles of arbiter, arbitrator or *amicabilis compositor* ('intermediary for a friendly agreement') differed in precise canonical understandings; but practical distinction is often unrealistic. 'Arbiter' implies decision accepting the claims of one or other party; 'arbitration' suggests mediation with an imposed settlement; while an '*amicabilis compositor*', perhaps the key term for immediate purposes, sought neither to impose a decision nor to gain grudging acceptance, but to find an equitable resolution which left both parties content. The role required (as Chedworth declared himself to be) acting 'to bring about the good of peace and concord between the parties themselves'.[3] In this context mediation and negotiation could work outside or beyond the law, or even as an explicit alternative to it, to produce an acceptable and equitable resolution which itself had legal standing for the future through documentary confirmation which could be invoked should the dispute revive.

How voluntarily the parties participated in such processes can sometimes be questioned; assertions of free will may conceal at least some degree of compulsion or coercion.[4] There are obvious

---

[2] Northampton, Northamptonshire RO, IL.730. From memory, this is the only surviving original text of such a document that I have seen, suggesting their general rarity. For an almost parallel case, see Ian Forrest, *Trustworthy Men: How Inequality and Faith made the Medieval Church* (Princeton, NJ, 2018), 57.

[3] '[P]ro bono pacis et concordie inter partes ipsos componendi' (similar phrasing regularly occurs): Linda Fowler, 'Forms of Arbitration', in Stephan Kuttner, ed., *Proceedings of the Fourth International Conference of Medieval Canon Law, Toronto, 21–25 August 1972*, Monumenta iuris canonici, Series C: Subsidia 5 (Vatican City, 1976), 133–47. See also Karl-Heinz Ziegler, 'Arbiter, arbitrator und amicabilis compositor', *Zeitschrift der Savigny-Stiftung für Rechtsgeschichte. Romanistische Abteilung* 84 (1967), 376–81; Karl S. Bader, 'Arbiter, arbitrator seu amicabilis compositor', *Zeitschrift der Savigny-Stiftung für Rechtsgeschichte. Kanonistische Abteilung* 77 (1960), 239–76.

[4] Some processes are terminated by rulings which, while declaring that the parties had agreed to submit the case to the determination of the arbiter after earlier protracted negotiations, nevertheless leave open the possibility that the ruling itself was the outcome of authoritarian intervention rather than voluntary submission: see, for example, *The Register*

similarities here with the role of arbitration and negotiated settlements in secular life, and with the search for equity which became
the preserve of Chancery. The formalized informality of arbitrated
resolutions in the secular sphere has received considerable attention
from historians of late medieval England in recent decades, in marked
contrast to the silence on its contribution to the resolution of disputes
under ecclesiastical jurisdiction. The evolution of the existing scholarship and its emphasis on processes within courts has diverted attention from processes beyond them.[5]

Once noticed, however, such settlements become noteworthy
across a range of actions, although with some disputes perhaps
excluded by the need for formal determination, such as matrimonial
issues.[6] Obviously, arbitrations which successfully pre-empted litigation would leave virtually no traces, so cannot be assessed.[7] Rejection
of a preliminary offer of negotiation could be the prelude to formal
litigation, which would also occur if discussions collapsed or an

---

of Henry Chichele, Archbishop of Canterbury, 1414–43, ed. E. F. Jacob, vol. 4, CYS 47
(London, 1947), 226–32, headed as a 'compositio', in which the parties 'se subiecerunt
et submiserunt ... ordinacioni, laudo, statuto, diffinicioni, sentencie nostris': ibid. 227.
The archbishop declares that he had been involved in working towards a solution as an
intermediary (ibid.), but the authoritarian vocabulary is used throughout, leaving it
unclear how much he was acting as *amicabilis compositor* rather than imposing his own
resolution. See also n. 19 below.

[5] Edward Powell, 'Arbitration and the Law in England in the later Middle Ages', *TRHS*
5th series 33 (1983), 49–67; idem, 'Settlement of Disputes by Arbitration in Fifteenth-
Century England', *LHR* 2 (1984), 21–43; Anthony Musson, 'Arbitration and the Legal
Profession in Late Medieval England', in Matthew Dyson and David Ibbetson, eds, *Law
and Legal Process: Substantive Law and Procedure in English Legal History* (Cambridge,
2013), 56–76, especially 62 (arbiters in a secular case identified as *amicabiles compositores*).
Arbitration receives only passing acknowledgement in Helmholz, *OHLE*, 1: 328, 446.
Forrest, *Trustworthy Men*, 53–61, pertinently incorporates ecclesiastical arbitrations into
a broader examination of trust and the mechanics of dispute resolution (this work became
available to me only after presenting the original paper).

[6] For a matrimonial case in which the ancillary financial elements were put to arbitration
but the main issue (not clarified in the record) would progress through to formal judgment, see Stafford, Staffordshire RO, B/C/1/1, Lichfield consistory court book, 1464–
71, fol. 248^r.

[7] But see ibid., fol. 62^v. Although entered in a consistory court act book, this note of an
agreement to go to arbitration is not explicitly tied to an identified court case. Nothing
indicates its motivation, but it may reflect an agreement made on the very brink of
litigation.

agreement was rejected.[8] Where litigation occurred, the costs and inconveniences of a lengthy case could provide a spur to negotiation and compromise (possibly when the personnel changed and cooler heads prevailed, or when others intervened to urge settlement).[9] Arbiters could be appointed by a court, with the proviso that failure to agree would mean continuance of the case.[10] Even at the last minute, the judges might swap hats and serve as compositors,[11] or other intervention might lead to arbitration to avoid 'ye trobble that is lyke to falle iffe ye sentence hade ben yeven'.[12] That may explain why so many suits disappear from the official records with no sentence recorded: wise counsel or pragmatism had prevailed, arbitration had been agreed in the background, without formal record, and no formal sentence was now needed. In such circumstances, the regularity of appeals to Rome and for tuition from the archiepiscopal courts of Canterbury or York may also have provided breathing space for negotiations which avoided further action.[13] That such

[8] For one collapsed set of negotiations, even though compromise had been suggested by the court (in this case actually the Council of Constance), see C. M. D. Crowder, 'Four English Cases determined in the Roman Curia during the Council of Constance, 1414–1418', *Annuarium historiae conciliorum* 12 (1980), 315–411, at 372–3, 376–80. For other litigation when one side resorted to law despite lay-engineered arbitration, see M. Dominica Legge, ed., *Anglo-Norman Letters and Petitions from All Souls MS 182*, Anglo-Norman Texts 3 (Oxford, 1941), nos 74, 327. See also Cambridge, Gonville and Caius College, MS 588/737, fol. 66^r–^{v}, in which a rector accuses his opponents (seeking funding from him for a permanent chaplain at their local chapel) of reneging on an agreement negotiated before the case was brought (but not explicitly arbitrated, and while called a *compositio*, not designated an *amicabilis compositio*).

[9] For litigation abandoned and followed by a negotiated settlement, after the chantry priest who began the process had been replaced, see Oxford, Lincoln College Archives, OAS/135–136. For an *amicabilis compositio* proposed when the litigants had already taken their dispute to the curia, see London, BL, Add. MS 32089, fols 154^r–155^v.

[10] Staffordshire RO, B/C/1/1, fol. 97^v.

[11] BL, MS Harley 2179, fols 131^r–133^v.

[12] Cambridge, UL, MS Ll.1.18, fol. 88^v.

[13] For tuition, see comments in R. H. Helmholz, 'Local Ecclesiastical Courts in England', in Wilfried Hartmann and Kenneth Pennington, eds, *The History of Courts and Procedure in Medieval Canon Law* (Washington DC, 2016), 345–91, at 353–4. The proposed leap to Rome and loss of appropriate English records usually makes it impossible to detect whether a successful appeal for tuition did actually go to the curia. Documents scattered through BL, Add. MS 32089 make it clear that tuition did not end matters, challenging the suggestion that 'a tuitorial appeal may often have been an empty gesture, from which no result was expected': Dorothy M. Owen, 'The Practising Canonist: John Lydford's Notebook', in Kuttner, ed., *Proceedings*, 45–51, at 50; repeated in eadem, ed., *John Lydford's Book*, Devon and Cornwall Record Society Publications 19 / HMC Joint

opportunities for informal 'out of court' settlements existed within the system also suggests a reality which would never be recorded, of innumerable disputes resolved by negotiation and arbitration without being brought to court.

Occasional entries in court books do reveal the integration of arbitration into the fuller and formal process of resolution, sometimes with penance being imposed for the spiritual fault, alongside the court's endorsement of negotiation of the material settlement.[14] Even when a court case did terminate in a sentence, its enforcement might be set aside for an arbitrated arrangement to clear the slate and restore amity. After a married couple from Northamptonshire lost a tithe case brought by their incumbent and the Court of Arches issued its sentence, both sides agreed to an outcome formulated by three local gentry. Setting aside the Arches decree, the incumbent was to accept 3*s* 4*d* and a token delivery of willows for all unpaid tithes, the handover presumably a performance to demonstrate compliance and reconciliation. Thereafter, the couple were to make an annual payment for tithes of willow and wood derived from the wife's dower lands from a previous marriage, and to pay equivalent tithes from other specified land, likewise in kind.[15]

Compromises and negotiated out-of-court settlements reflect an extra-judicial system of dispute resolution. Noteworthy in their own right, such settlements are also notable because, while dealing with ecclesiastical concerns, they often entailed significant lay agency, as non-clerics acted as intermediaries and shaped the eventual agreement. The extra-judicial and extra-curial evolution of the outcomes (in an abstract sense, given the frequent active involvement of ecclesiastical judges, and the links to actual court cases) does not make the process and its products extra-legal, but leaves the latter's appearance

---

Publication 22 (London, 1974), 20. For one dispute meant to be terminated by discussion and agreement following an appeal for tuition, see Christine Lutgens, 'The Case of Waghen vs. Sutton: Conflict over Burial Rights in Late Medieval England', *Medieval Studies* 38 (1976), 145–84, at 165 (especially the quotation in n. 125), 179–80. Further litigation soon followed: ibid. 149.

[14] See, for example, Staffordshire RO, B/C/1/1, with arbitrations noted at fols 62^v (see n. 7), 80^v, 97^v, 118^v, 140^v, 142^r (submission to episcopal *laudum*, with penances imposed), 248^r, 281^v, 282^v, 283^r. See also ibid., B/C/2/1, Lichfield consistory court book, 1524–6, fols 5^v, 8^v, 12^v, 103^r, 104^r, 114^v, 121^v.

[15] Northamptonshire RO, YZ.8252, 10 February 1519.

among legal records accidental rather than systematic. Compromises did not always work, or stand the test of time; they are cited in later proceedings as one or other party sought their reinforcement, or as modified (by the original arbiter or other authority) in response to changing circumstances.[16] Their existence may be attested only because the attempts to secure adherence had failed: in *fidei laesio* cases in church courts if oaths to observe the conditions had been breached, or in cases before secular courts to claim sums due by bond for similar non-observance.[17] That the arrangements were enforced is the important point; but equally important is the point that agreements were actually made, resolving disputes beyond the formal view of the courts. Many did presumably stand, without needing reinforcement by later litigation. Accordingly, assessments of the role of arbitration in secular disputes can reasonably and legitimately be transferred to the ecclesiastical arena, seeing it as

> ... an integral part of the informal machinery of dispute settlement which existed alongside the courts. [Its] ... procedures ... remained independent of court supervision in most cases, and continued to perform functions to which the courts could not aspire: they could settle feuds, make peace and restore harmonious social relations between disputing neighbors. ... [L]itigation and arbitration were not mutually exclusive processes ... but ... might complement one another and be combined in an overall strategy for the resolution of a dispute.[18]

[16] For a papal bull issued in response to an appeal from Taunton priory for modification because of the (alleged) impossibility of meeting the conditions, see *CPReg*, 6: 486. As this was confirmed in 1499, its provisions were presumably still considered relevant: *CPReg*, 17/1: 114 (no. 174). For modification by Archbishop Thomas Arundel of an earlier declaration he had issued as *arbiter, arbitrator, sive amicabilis compositor*, see London, LPL, Reg. Arundel I, fols 377ʳ–378ʳ. Bishops and other prelates perhaps normally reserved the power to amend their decrees, hoping to limit future disputes and maintain diocesan authority.

[17] For *fidei laesio*, see R. H. Helmholz, *Canon Law and the Law of England* (London, 1987), 268: all the awards cited in his n. 29 actually originated in secular disputes, but the principle holds for ecclesiastical disputes. As demonstrated in BIA, CP.E.132 (not cited by Helmholz, but invoking an ecclesiastical compromise), such cases might involve full denial by the defendant of the existence, or terms and conditions, of the earlier settlement. Aspects of this case are discussed in Forrest, *Trustworthy Men*, 45. For bonds in secular courts, see Robert C. Palmer, *Selling the Church: The English Parish in Law, Commerce, and Religion, 1350–1550* (Chapel Hill, NC, 2002), 35–6, 44 (and n. 54), 51, 132.

[18] Powell 'Settlement of Disputes', 24.

At the same time, the ostensibly voluntary and informal or extra-judicial character of arbitrated or mediated resolutions may obscure a harsher reality shaped by circumstances and institutions. The language of mutuality in the resolution contributes to creation of 'a false dichotomy between formal and informal means of resolution'; yet 'we should not be seduced into thinking that community forms of dispute resolution [which would include many of these ecclesiastical arbitrations] were intrinsically fairer and less coercive than legal judgements'.[19]

Delegation

However binding and legally enforceable their outcomes might be, arbitration and negotiation removed dispute resolution from the procedural, institutional and archival normalities and requirements of formal canon law; that extraction, and the resulting documentary lacunae, largely explains the marginalization of the processes in current mainstream scholarship. A similar line of reasoning may explain the lack of discussion of delegated papal jurisdiction which, while clearly integrated into the judicial structures of the universal church, in its local English and Welsh manifestations lay outside the standard court hierarchy of dioceses and peculiar jurisdictions linked to the provincial courts of Canterbury and York, and thence to the courts of the papal curia.

Realistic assessment of the place of the pope as universal ordinary and the papal courts as courts of first instance or appeal within England's medieval ecclesiastical history and national tradition of practical canon law or, conversely, of the integration of the English courts and litigation into the papal judicial system, remains a challenge. That England was part of that system, one which operated alongside and above the provincial arrangements, cannot be denied; but a historiographical tradition which privileges examination of the local courts within the national or provincial hierarchy, and archival losses which preclude extensive analysis of disputes dealt with at the curia, combine to discourage investigation. Limiting the present discussion to the activities within England of papal courts and judges implementing a delegated papal jurisdiction treats only one aspect

---

[19] Forrest, *Trustworthy Men*, 53 (quotations), 57–8.

of the way in which litigants sought justice from the Vicar of Christ. English cases fought at the central papal courts, whether or not they had begun in England, generated a complex and potentially extensive bureaucratic and documentary footprint, of which little trace now survives in local documents.

The actual mechanisms of papal judicial delegation varied; but the key point is that it notionally operated outside the local pyramidical norm. Delegation of papal powers to local agents was not in itself unusual, and could be considered pervasive by the fourteenth century. Beyond its integration into litigation, in England delegation is perhaps most frequently visible in the powers conferred on confessors to grant absolution and indulgences by papal authority; in the devolution to diocesan bishops of the authority to determine whether facts reported to the curia justified confirmation of dispensations granted by the papal penitentiary; and in the actions of local executors when implementing papal provisions to benefices, instituting and inducting outside the normal diocesan administrative channels.[20] Three different formats for judicial delegation to resolve disputes merit consideration here, again somewhat sketchily, because the nature of the sources makes comprehensive commentary impractical.

Of these three variants the first and most significant was the appointment of judges delegate, holding their own 'ad hoc courts' to determine specific cases.[21] They fit fairly straightforwardly into the broad pattern of a top-down structural conception of the late medieval church in which papal authority and headship was an all-pervasive given.

---

[20] For indulgences and confessors, see R. N. Swanson, *Indulgences in Late Medieval England: Passports to Paradise?* (Cambridge, 2007), 27, 45, 117–19. For dispensations, see P. D. Clarke, 'Central Authority and Local Powers: The Apostolic Penitentiary and the English Church in the Fifteenth Century', *HR* 84 (2011), 416–42, at 421–42; see also broader comment in Arnaud Fossier, *Le Bureau des âmes. Écritures et pratiques administratives de la Pénitencerie apostolique (XIIIᵉ–XIVᵉ siècle)*, Bibliothèque des écoles françaises d'Athènes et de Rome 278 (Rome, 2018), 25–8, 59–60, 280–4, 319–21, 481–3. For papal provisions, see Clarke, 'Central Authority', 441–2, drawing on Geoffrey Barraclough, 'The Executors of Papal Provisions in the Canonical Theory of the 13th and 14th Centuries', in *Acta congressus iuridicii internationalis Romae* 3 (Rome, 1936), 109–53, which I have not seen. For a range of common forms for executorial bulls which are also thereby delegations, see Michael Tangl, *Die päpstlichen Kanzleiordnungen von 1200–1500* (Innsbruck, 1894; repr. Aalen, 1959), 312–16, 335–6, 339, 340–1.
[21] Quotation from Jane E. Sayers, *Papal Judges Delegate in the Province of Canterbury, 1198–1254: A Study in Ecclesiastical Jurisdiction and Administration* (Oxford, 1971), 101.

The courts of the papal judges delegate have been described as '[t]he most fully studied, and probably the most important, institutions of ecclesiastical justice [in England] ... between 1150 and 1250';[22] but they are largely ignored in studies of the subsequent pre-Reformation centuries.[23] While the assertion that '[p]apal judges delegate became less important in the later Middle Ages' may be right,[24] that does not mean that they became unimportant. The elaboration and consolidation of England's system of church courts after 1250 doubtless reduced the need to request appointments of delegates; the expansion of diocesan and provincial court business and the greater availability and accessibility of such court archives directs attention towards them while smothering the evidence for papal delegates. That, with the ad hoc nature of the delegates' appointments and lack of centralized retention of their archives, leads to their marginalization in discussions of the church's legal system in the late medieval centuries. The current situation remains as Jane Sayers put it in the 1980s, that 'a complete picture of what records there are for the judge delegate courts between 1300 and 1500 must await detailed investigation in many places and in many collections'.[25] Arguably, until those courts are integrated into the total picture (as far as they can be) evaluation of the working and exploitation of the ecclesiastical legal system in pre-Reformation England will suffer from a real lacuna.

At this point, however, aspirations and practicalities collide. Detailed investigation of the delegated courts remains a desideratum; but the exiguous sources may make its achievement a pipe-dream. Despite that, continuity of practice is evident right through to the 1530s. How frequently judges delegate were used cannot be

---

[22] Helmholz, 'Local Ecclesiastical Courts', 349.

[23] The only extensive study of delegation in England remains Sayers, *Papal Judges Delegate*. Despite its title, Robert Brentano, *York Metropolitan Jurisdiction and Papal Judges Delegate (1239–1290)*, University of California Publications in History 8 (Berkeley, CA, 1959), does not provide a broad discussion of the system, homing in on the specific dispute over diocesan autonomy and archiepiscopal authority between York and Durham. It nevertheless offers a valuable and detailed reconstruction of that case and its convolutions: ibid. 90–2, 115–16, 125–44, 148–64.

[24] Charles Duggan, 'Judges Delegate', in Hartmann and Pennington, eds, *Courts and Procedure*, 229–43, at 243.

[25] J. Sayers, 'The Records of the Courts of the Judges Delegate in England', in Donahue, ed., *Records of the Courts*, 27–34, at 34. The comment can be extended to the early sixteenth century.

R. N. Swanson

established, and a drop is likely after 1300; but appointments were still made, and there is scattered surviving evidence of actual cases.[26] If a single case is indicative of wider practice, it is possible that judges delegate were increasingly sought so that appellants could avoid the costs of, and obstacles to, completing an appeal to Rome within the canonical year.[27]

Among the reasons for fewer appointments was the emergence of a subsidiary form of delegation, to judges identified as papal 'conservators' (*conservatores*), who form the second category of judicial delegates. Appointed in response to petitions, they received judicial powers as papal delegates to protect the interests and privileges of beneficiaries ranging from complete religious orders to individual houses and colleges, and even individual clerics. Some appointments were perpetual, others for only a few years, with petitioners sometimes

---

[26] One potential obstacle was the *praemunire* legislation of the later fourteenth century; but clear evidence of its use to obstruct judges delegate has not yet been found. Limited subject indices in the original series of *Calendar of Papal Letters*, published by HMSO, generally make the detection of matters relating to papal judges delegate (if any were registered) almost a lost cause. The 'Dublin' continuations are more rewarding; see, for example, Fuller, ed., *CPReg*, 17/1: nos 2, 8–9, 28–9, 46, 94, 197, 261, 298, 365, 405, 442, 456, 529, 661, 905–6, 924, 987–8, 990–1. For a papal judge delegate active in the mid-1520s when a long-running dispute revived, see BIA, CP.G.129,133 (image 9); for earlier stages, see Lutgens, 'Waghen vs. Sutton', 145–67, 179–84. For a court in session, see Chippenham, Wiltshire and Swindon History Centre, D5/19/1, 1531–2, fols 1ʳ–3ᵛ. For a delegation which ended in arbitration, see Staffordshire RO, B/A/1/7, fols 128ʳ–137ʳ; see also Francis Roth, *The English Austin Friars, 1249–1538*, 2 vols, Cassiciacum: Studies in St Augustine and the Augustinian Order (American Series) 6–7 (New York, 1961–6), 2: 268*–277*. Further indications of activity appear in fragments of legal processes copied into formulary or similar volumes, such as Leeds University, Brotherton Library, MS Dep.1980.1/355, fols 21ᵛ–23ʳ, 48ʳ–ᵛ, 176ʳ–179ᵛ; Gonville and Caius College, MS 588/737, fols 48ʳ–50ʳ, 53ʳ–54ᵛ, 72ʳ–ᵛ, 74ʳ–76ʳ, 79ᵛ–80ʳ, 113ʳ–ᵛ, 114ʳ–115ᵛ, 180ʳ–ᵛ, 189ʳ–ᵛ, 190ᵛ–191ʳ, 256ᵛ, 296ᵛ–298ʳ, 347ᵛ–350ʳ, 360ʳ–361ʳ, 367ʳ–ᵛ, 373ʳ–374ʳ, 375ʳ. See also the case abstracted in Dorothy M. Owen, ed., *The Making of King's Lynn: A Documentary Survey*, RSEH n.s. 9 (London, 1985), no. 127 (original record not consulted), for which further material is in BL, Add. MS 32089, fols 103ʳ–105ʳ, 122ʳ–125ʳ.

[27] BL, Add. MS 32089, fols 146ʳ–149ʳ. From the late 1380s, these documents originate in an action brought by a testamentary executor from York against changes in the provision of probate judges by Archbishop Alexander Neville of York, with Archbishop William Courtenay of Canterbury as judge. The first document (fol. 146ʳ–ᵛ) excuses non-completion of the appeal at the curia, and seeks an extension of the deadline into a second year. See also BL, MS Harley 862, fols 258ᵛ–259ʳ, a libel of c.1407 in a case before a sub-delegate which clearly substitutes for action in the curia after an appeal to Rome against a process in Arches.

seeking lengthier terms than the papacy was willing to concede.[28] Conservators attract almost no notice in the current scholarship on English church courts; indeed, their existence seems to be almost completely ignored.[29] While their jurisdictional competence may have been limited by their role, a change in the extent of their powers reflected in a standard papal bull of appointment established by Pope Clement V at the Council of Vienne greatly expanded the range of their jurisdiction, making them more assuredly equivalent to other judges delegate.[30] Their appointments doubtless diverted some of the demand for such judges.[31] Evidence of their activities is scarce, even though many of the appointees were bishops, archbishops and other prelates: their role as conservators may have evaded the structural and archival nets of diocesan administration, as the post was not technically diocesan and not exclusively episcopal. As the nominated conservators probably normally sub-delegated their duties to lesser officials, archival traces are further eradicated. As with ordinary judges delegate, a dribble of evidence attests to their continued existence and activity, but how much is concealed currently remains guesswork.[32]

---

[28] For petitions for appointments and papal responses, see *CPReg: Petitions to the Pope*, 1: *A.D. 1342–1419*, 105, 120, 135, 155, 171–2, 264, 266, 284, 335, 480 (requests for perpetual appointments cut down to six years at 172, 335; other modifications at 135, 264, 284). Repeated grants are indicated by the petition of Simon Islip as newly appointed archbishop of Canterbury for the 'usual privileges, dispensations and indults', including 'letters conservatory for five years': ibid., 189, cf. 105; see additional evidence at n. 32 below.

[29] No obviously relevant index entry was noticed in Hartmann and Pennington, eds, *Courts and Procedure*; or in Helmholz, *OHLE*, 1. There is very brief discussion of early conservators (before the Council of Vienne) in Sayers, *Papal Judges Delegate*, 108–9, cf. 265–6. For later conservators, see the brief remarks of R. W. Hunt, 'The Abbot and Convent of Merevale v. the Rector of Halsall: A Tuitorial Appeal in the Fourteenth Century before the Court of Arches', *THSLC* 101 (1949), 47–61, at 49. The regular appointment of heads of religious houses as conservators is acknowledged in Martin Heale, *The Abbots and Priors of Late Medieval and Reformation England* (Oxford, 2016), 194–5.

[30] For the main form, and a variant, see Tangl, *Die päpstlichen Kanzleiordnungen*, 321–4. Occasional petitions requesting appointment of conservators ask that they be granted 'according to the form of the Council of Vienne': *CPReg: Petitions*, 1: 15, 89, 138, 155, 264. Where the incipit of the bull of appointment is indicated in the calendared entries from the papal registers (see n. 28 above), it is generally the form in Tangl.

[31] Awareness of conservation as a variant of delegation is sometimes indicated by formal designation of judges as 'conservator and/or judge delegate', e.g. Gonville and Caius College, MS 588/737, fol. 252^r; Brotherton Library, MS Dep.1980.1/355, fol. 164^r.

[32] For sub-delegations, see A. C. Wood, ed., *Registrum Simonis Langham, Cantuariensis archiepiscopi*, CYS 53 (London, 1956), 154, 177–8, 189, 204, 213–14 (see also the

As conservators were widely sought by the exempt religious orders, it is quite possible that they provided the courts through which those orders acted as plaintiffs in disputes over matters where direct action through the normal diocesan system might have been seen as undermining their exempt status, probably (given the explicitly protective nature of the conservator's role) with an expectation, but no guarantee, of a favourable outcome.[33]

Archival eradication has also affected the third variant form of papal judicial delegation, to the legates, nuncios and other papal agents active in England during the period, which again attracts little comment.[34] The concern here is with the powers delegated to individual appointees as legates and nuncios, not the legatine judicial authority, whatever its content, which the archbishops of Canterbury and York exercised within their provinces as *legatos natos*. Despite its duration and penetration of the English church, Wolsey's early sixteenth-century legation leaves limited traces of his judicial activity. His courts certainly functioned, and attracted appeals; but any central records of their proceedings no longer survive.[35] The judicial activities of his precursors as legates and nuncios are similarly obscure. The rare evidence includes a few documents which mention courts held by Luigi Aliotti as papal collector and nuncio in first years of the fifteenth century, a combination of posts which each had their own delegated

---

disciplining of a sub-delegate at 157); *Register of Chichele*, ed. Jacob, 4: 44–51. Issue of letters is sometimes noted in papal registers, but how fully is untested: see, for example, *CPReg*, 5: 29, 115–16, 211, 290–1, 397, 425, 558, cf. 547; *CPReg*, 8: 209, 241; (for an extraordinarily generalized appointment) *CPReg*, 20: no. 360. For other indications of legal processes, in fragments of cases copied as formulary exemplars and in similar volumes, see Brotherton Library, MS Dep.1980.1/355, fols 6ʳ–8ᵛ, 102ʳ, 102ᵛ, 164ʳ–167ᵛ, 182ʳ–193ʳ (the first three citations all concern the same case, cf. BIA, CP.F.167); Gonville and Caius College, MS 588/737, fols 52ʳ–ᵛ, 81ʳ–ᵛ, 103ʳ–105ʳ, 111ʳ, 113ᵛ–114ʳ, 191ʳ–ᵛ, 252ᵛ–253ʳ, 314ʳ–ᵛ, 347ʳ–ᵛ and the following note.

[33] Documents at BL, Add. MS 32089, fols 108ᵛ–110ᵛ are from a conservatorial case of 1374 with the Carmelites as plaintiffs against obstruction by the clergy of one Norwich parish of their privilege of allowing burial to all who so choose and receiving funeral offerings. This suggests a whole class of actions involving the mendicant orders which potentially avoided the diocesan system.

[34] Legatine courts are not mentioned in Helmholz, 'Local Ecclesiastical Courts'.

[35] Peter Gwyn, *The King's Cardinal: The Rise and Fall of Thomas Wolsey* (London, 1990), 282–4. For appeals and other interventions, see, for example, Staffordshire RO, B/C/2/1, fols 2ᵛ, 8ʳ, 28ᵛ, 59ʳ–ᵛ, 84ᵛ, 92ᵛ.

judicial functions.[36] In one case, royal justices upheld a writ of prohibition against Aliotti's jurisdiction, barring further action by him. While imposing the ban, the judges nevertheless acknowledged his legitimate ex officio authority to hold courts.[37] Just over a decade later Walter Medford, whose delegated powers were solely those of papal collector, acted as judge in response to a *querela* after a proposed exchange of benefices had become contentious.[38]

Positioned outside the normal hierarchical structure of diocesan and provincial courts, the courts of these various types of papal delegate invite attention as oddities, partitioned off from the regular pattern as a separate category with little overlap. Such segregation would be misleading. Rather, their invocation must be seen as an additional strategic option for those engaged in ecclesiastical litigation in pre-Reformation England, an additional route to 'justice' which complemented and supplemented the normal structural hierarchy. As such, they added to the flexibility and potentially labyrinthine complexity of litigation, offering additional ways to defeat, obstruct or exhaust opponents. Accordingly, delegated jurisdiction is often only one element in the overall narrative of cases in which it was invoked. In the 1360s, for instance, Merevale abbey, a Cistercian house, took action before the abbot of Evesham, acting as sub-conservator of Cistercian privileges in England, when the rector of Halsall (Lancashire) took tithes from their grange at Altcar, which he claimed lay within his parish. Merevale claimed their order's exemption from such liability. The rector secured royal writs of prohibition to obstruct the conservatorial action, then initiated his own case in the matter through the hierarchy of diocesan courts, starting with those of the archdeacon of Chester, and subsequently in the provincial Court of Arches. In the intricacies of these contradictory processes, Merevale itself eventually appealed from the abbot of Evesham to Arches, seeking that court's protection

---

[36] Kew, TNA, SC 8/145/7224 (I thank Alison McHardy for drawing my attention to this document); Oxford, Queen's College, MS 54, fols 259^r–260^v; Exeter, Cathedral Archives, 1541. The encompassing case for the last two is examined in A. K. B. Evans [A. K. B. Roberts], 'Litigation for Proprietary Rights: The Case of the Obstinate Vicar', in Nigel Saul, ed., *St George's Chapel, Windsor, in the Fourteenth Century* (Woodbridge, 2005), 117–34, but she is unaware of this (and other) additional material. The dispute eventually terminated with an imposed arbitration: ibid. 131–2.

[37] Evans, 'Litigation', 125–6. The judges' discussions are recorded in Year Book, Mich. 2 Henry IV, in *Les Reports des cases*, 11 vols (London, 1678–80), 6: 9–10 (plea 45).

[38] BL, MS Harley 862, fol. 72^v.

in a process which could have taken the issue through to the papal curia but seems to have terminated in the English court.[39]

CONCLUSION

Church court archives are essential and invaluable sources for under-standing the legal culture and social functions of England's pre-Reformation church. In general, the records of diocesan and provincial courts offer sufficient evidence to extract an adequate overview of both the culture and the functions. Yet full appreciation of the place of the church and its law within the society requires attention to expand beyond the standard pyramid, to alternative or supplementary features. Arbitration and *amicabilis compositio* provided both justice without lit-igation (in a format capable of becoming legally binding), and a justice which, while generated through litigation, mitigated the partisanship of an adversarial system and made formal defeat tolerable. Continued recourse to papal delegation, in all its formats, created local courts as alternative means of access to, and exploitation of, the papacy's supreme judicial authority. These can be imagined as officially autho-rized 'pop-up' venues which facilitated litigation without the complex-ity and expense of fighting a case at the papal curia, but with the benefits of doing so.

Those are simplistic and over-optimistic characterizations, but ade-quate to summarize the aspirations. Reality was frequently different. Despite the benefits of arbitration, negotiated or arbitrated solutions could simply break down if one or other side refused to comply, in some instances generating a series of successive arbitrations which did not hold.[40] The structural and procedural intricacies of the canonical system and the loophole-hunting of those embroiled in it (not least the lawyers) often made litigation in the ecclesiastical courts a 'sophis-ticated tangle' of 'paralyzing complexity'.[41] The search for a definitive sentence (even one issued *appelatione remota*, supposedly without

---

[39] The narrative is most fully reconstructed in Hunt, 'Merevale v. the Rector of Halsall'; for proceedings in the Lichfield diocesan courts, see Annie Cottam, 'An Altcar Tithes Dispute in the Fourteenth Century', *THSLC* 82 (1930), 136–62. Other documents are in Gonville and Caius College, MS 588/737, fols 66ᵛ–67ʳ, 93ᵛ–95ᵛ, 304ʳ–ᵛ, 306ᵛ–307ᵛ.
[40] Lutgens, 'Waghen vs. Sutton', 152, 182–3 (note also 162), and n. 13 above.
[41] Brentano, *York Metropolitan Jurisdiction*, 176, 164, commenting specifically on dele-gate procedure, but the general pattern of entanglement justifies wider application.

appeal) was often frustrated. Yet the search for justice, for equitable and charitable outcomes, continued. Disputes needed resolutions, preferably ones which would last in law. The 'normal' system of church courts was the usual route to that end, but not the only one. At conceptually opposite ends of the spectrum the formalized informality of arbitration and negotiation, or the appeal to papal authority through delegation, offered alternative or supplementary mechanisms. As such, they may be marginalized in the extant sources, and in the historiography based on them. Yet their presence demands acknowledgement and appreciation as a factor in the dynamic and evolving relationships between church and law and church and people in late medieval England, and within broader examinations of the anthropology and resolution of disputes within society as a whole.

Perjury in Early Tudor England

Paul Cavill*
Pembroke College, Cambridge

The break with Rome was enforced through a nationwide programme of oath-taking. The Henrician regime resorted to oaths because they were already fundamental to the functioning of the polity. In the preceding half-century, activities as diverse as heresy prosecution, tax assessment and debt litigation depended upon oaths. Irrespective of their often mundane subject matter, oaths were held to be religious acts. Prolific oath-taking, however, led to frequent oath-breaking. Perjury was therefore a more pressing and broader concept than it is today. It was an offence against God, against oneself and against others. How this crime was prosecuted and punished sheds light on the intersection of religious doctrine, legal systems and social practice in pre-Reformation England. An analysis of perjury also draws attention to a jurisdictional shift that was underway before the Reformation. In 1485, church courts had exercised an extensive cognizance of perjury; by 1535, they no longer did. The most important factor contributing to this decline in ecclesiastical jurisdiction was the constraint imposed by common lawyers on what cases the church courts could hear. Common law defined the crime of perjury more narrowly than did canon law. Hence the contraction of the church's jurisdiction would alter how perjury was perceived.

Early Tudor England (1485–1535) was a polity and society built around the taking of oaths. Every adult from the monarch downwards swore oaths. Henry VIII took a keen interest in his coronation oath: he had it, he said, 'in remembraunce' when invoking his duty to administer justice in 1516.[1] Treaties with other princes were made binding through religious rituals of reciprocal oath-taking with foreign ambassadors, which were afterwards authenticated as transumpts at the archbishop's command by public notaries.[2] The king's subjects

* Pembroke College, Cambridge, CB2 1RF. E-mail: pc504@cam.ac.uk.
I thank Daniel Gosling, Shannon McSheffrey and Hillary Taylor for their help and two reviewers for their suggestions.
[1] San Marino, CA, HL, MS Ellesmere 2654, fols 22ᵛ–23ʳ; MS Ellesmere 2655, fol. 10ʳ–ᵛ.
[2] London, BL, MS Add. 48012, fols 24ʳ–27ᵛ.

Studies in Church History 56 (2020), 182–209   © Ecclesiastical History Society 2020
doi: 10.1017/stc.2019.11

took oaths of allegiance, to which could be added a requirement not to become the sworn retainers of anyone else.[3] Upon assumption of office, royal servants took oaths of duty. Cardinal Wolsey swore the chancellor's oath on Christmas Eve 1515 after vespers in the chapel at Eltham Palace.[4] Such oaths were tailored to the position held: the one taken by the sheriff of Cambridgeshire and Huntingdonshire added an undertaking to defend the privileges of Cambridge University.[5] It was not only the crown which exacted oaths: the practice was universal. Oaths promised the obedience of a citizen to the mayor, a tradesman to the masters of his company, a stipendiary priest to the parson and a monk to his abbot. A livery company could have sixteen different oaths.[6] Furnishing such texts stimulated record-keeping, and oaths abound in the surviving books that belonged to government departments, urban corporations and private individuals.

Oaths were categorized either as affirmations (of a fact, as in testimony to a court) or as promises (of future performance, such as payment of a debt).[7] They were an inescapable aspect of the mundane activities of buying and selling, family life, domestic and local government and law enforcement. They were a fundamental facet of the economy, essential in a commercial system that depended on trust. Alleging that someone 'woll pay no man his deutye' was thus interpreted as an accusation of habitual oath-breaking.[8] Oaths were integral to the different legal systems that operated within the kingdom too. Social and public life depended on oath-taking. A fishmonger who had 'made a vowe to make no maner Othe Duryng his lyff' (perhaps deliberately) rendered himself incapable of holding office and

---

[3] Lorraine C. Attreed, ed., *The York House Books, 1461–1490*, 2 vols (Stroud, 1991), 1: 379–82; Gordon McKelvie, 'Henry VII's Letter to Carlisle in 1498: His Concerns about Retaining in a Border Fortress', *NH* 54 (2017), 149–66, at 165–6.

[4] Kew, TNA, C54/383, m. 31[d].

[5] Rosemary Horrox and P. W. Hammond, eds, *British Library Harleian Manuscript 433*, 4 vols (Gloucester, 1979–83), 3: 173–84, at 177.

[6] T. F. Reddaway and Lorna E. M. Walker, *The Early History of the Goldsmiths' Company, 1327–1509* (London, 1975), 212–21.

[7] Andrew Chertsey, *The Floure of the Commaundementes* (London, 1510), fol. 23[r]; Barbara J. Shapiro, 'Oaths, Credibility and the Legal Process in Early Modern England: Part One', *Law and Humanities* 6 (2012), 145–78, at 148–51.

[8] London, LMA, DL/C/B/043/MS09064/011, fol. 303[v]; James Davis, *Medieval Market Morality: Life, Law and Ethics in the English Marketplace, 1200–1500* (Cambridge, 2012), 71–3.

Paul Cavill

thereby transgressed his obligations to his community.[9] Because they were sworn at major moments in an individual's life – entering service, becoming free of one's hometown, joining a guild – oaths must have constituted rites of passage. Recourse was had to oaths in informal and spontaneous contexts as well. When threatened with the stocks, a servant who had 'meddyld' with a female counterpart said that he would marry her if their master would take an oath that 'she is a good mayde save for me', which the master instantly did, swearing 'so helpe me god and halydome and by this boke'.[10]

Early Tudor England functioned the way it did because of oaths. Yet the very extensiveness of swearing routinized the practice, potentially transforming it into an act undertaken casually or even falsely. Pervasive oath-taking entailed frequent oath-breaking. Circumstance, perception and pressure must have dictated whether oaths were treated as urgent and burdensome or as formulaic and vacuous. In 1516, the government's attempted reform of sheriffs' conduct focused on getting them to implement the contents of their oaths.[11] Kings were notorious for breaking oaths made to other princes. In *Utopia*, Thomas More observed sarcastically how '[i]n Europe, of course, and especially in these regions where the Christian faith and religion prevail, the dignity of treaties is everywhere kept sacred and inviolable.'[12] Subjects sometimes behaved no better than their rulers. At the beginning of Henry VII's reign, the judges were debating how to alleviate disorder. The idea of peers taking an oath to uphold the law seemed pointless to Chief Justice Hussey, who recalled how on a previous occasion he had seen lords take a similar oath which they had then broken within the hour.[13]

But forswearing was not taken lightly. Offenders could be disgraced, punished or ostracized. In 1511, among the villagers of Littlebury in Essex, John Parkyn was 'defamed, held and reputed' to

---

[9] LMA, COL/CA/01/01/003, fol. 80ᵛ; Susan Brigden, 'Religion and Social Obligation in Early Sixteenth-Century London', *P&P* 103 (1984), 67–112, at 86–92.

[10] Hertford, Hertfordshire Archives and Local Studies (hereafter: HALS), ASA8/1, fol. 56ᵛ.

[11] *L&P* 2/1: 2579*. *L&P* is cited by document number.

[12] Thomas More, *Utopia*, ed. George M. Logan and Robert M. Adams, rev. edn (Cambridge, 2002), 83; William Tyndale, *The Practyse of Prelates* (Antwerp, 1530), sigs F7ᵛ–F8ᵛ.

[13] Year Books, Mich. 1 Hen. VII, plea 3. The Year Books are cited from the so-called 'vulgate edition': *Les Reports des Cases*, 11 vols (London, 1678–80).

184

be a perjurer because he had given false evidence under oath against the parson; as a result, some parishioners there shunned Parkyn's company.[14] To be called 'perjured' was seriously insulting; it could be a defamation worth suing over.[15] People of good conversation, credit and substance were thought unlikely to lie under oath; conversely, that a couple got so drunk that they could hardly stagger home indicated a predisposition to perjury in the mind of a neighbour.[16] In short, this was an age which saw oaths as assuring diligence, fidelity and truthfulness, yet also recognized that they were regularly broken. Perjury was thus an important concept in early Tudor England, where social practice, religious doctrine and legal structure intersected.

Early Tudor England also changed perjury. Conventionally, scholarship on early modern oath-taking and oath-breaking starts where this article stops: at the break with Rome. The succession and supremacy oaths of 1534 onwards usually constitute the point of departure and so subsequent developments are related to the Reformation.[17] The state's increasing imposition of oaths thereafter is sometimes thought to have been counterproductive, to have stimulated dissimulation and equivocation, maybe even to have assisted in a societal shift from credulity to cynicism.[18] The early modern period is also held to have exalted the autonomy of the lone conscience: 'the Reformation transformed an understanding of conscience as objective in nature, subject to the dictates of the Church, to subjective, as

---

[14] LMA, DL/C/0206, fols 35ᵛ–36ʳ.

[15] LMA, DL/C/B/043/MS09064/011, fols 50ʳ, 51ʳ, 62ᵛ–63ʳ, 105ʳ; William H. Hale, ed., *A Series of Precedents and Proceedings in Criminal Causes, extending from the Year 1475 to 1640; extracted from Act-Books of Ecclesiastical Courts in the Diocese of London* (London, 1847), no. 305; Chichester, West Sussex RO (hereafter: WSRO), Ep.I/10/1, fol. 101ʳ; Ep.I/10/4, fol. 47ʳ.

[16] TNA, STAC2/20/195; HALS, ASA8/1, fol. 20ᵛ; Alexandra Shepard, *Accounting for Oneself: Worth, Status, and the Social Order in Early Modern England* (Oxford, 2015), 133–43.

[17] The principal account is Jonathan M. Gray, *Oaths and the English Reformation* (Cambridge, 2013).

[18] These possibilities are explored in John Spurr, 'Perjury, Profanity and Politics', *Seventeenth Century* 8 (1993), 29–50; idem, 'A Profane History of Early Modern Oaths', *TRHS* 6th series 11 (2001), 37–63; Harald E. Braun and Edward Vallance, eds, *Contexts of Conscience in Early Modern Europe, 1500–1700* (Basingstoke, 2004); Edward Vallance, *Revolutionary England and the National Covenant: State Oaths, Protestantism and the Political Nation, 1553–1682* (Woodbridge, 2005); Conal Condren, *Argument and Authority in Early Modern England: The Presupposition of Oaths and Offices* (Cambridge, 2006).

individuals had to rely on their own understanding of how to behave morally ... cast adrift from an obvious institutional framework'.[19] Yet the early Tudor half-century had already altered the structure within which oaths were enforced. In 1485, church courts had exercised an extensive cognizance of perjury; by 1535, they no longer did. Obviously, the Reformation cannot explain this decline; nor, given the chronology of developments, can the break with Rome.

This article seeks to account for what had happened. To do so, it samples the records of church, common-law and conciliar courts, and it explicates the expert legal literature on the subject.[20] The article identifies two definitions of perjury, as either breaking an oath or forswearing in court. It illustrates how these interpretations were applied in the different types of court. It explores the interaction between the needs of litigants, the interests of legal practitioners and the technicalities of procedure. The article shows how perjury came increasingly under the jurisdiction of royal courts as the crime drifted out of the church's orbit. It points to the role of common lawyers in curtailing ecclesiastical jurisdiction and emphasizes their non-judicial understanding of conscience. In consequence, it is proposed, the legally enforceable definition of perjury narrowed. The post-Reformation legal system did not fully comprehend perjury in its broadest sense. This omission, it is implied, may have contributed to the elevation of individual conscience and to the growing concern about the integrity of oath-taking that scholars have identified. Thus it is suggested that early Tudor England began to laicize the crime of perjury.

I

Oaths were a doctrinal matter.[21] Taking an oath was supposed to be an act of faith, of worship even, a kind of *latria*. The theology of swearing was based on the teaching of Augustine of Hippo.[22] It

---

[19] Andrew Hadfield, *Lying in Early Modern English Culture: From the Oath of Supremacy to the Oath of Allegiance* (Oxford, 2017), 48, 308. That early modernists have underestimated the continuing influence of the medieval casuistical tradition, however, is argued in Emily Corran, *Lying and Perjury in Medieval Practical Thought: A Study in the History of Casuistry* (Oxford, 2018), 9–13, 132–42, 150–1.

[20] The seminal piece is R. H. Helmholz, 'Assumpsit and *fidei laesio*', *Law Quarterly Review* 91 (1975), 406–32.

[21] R. H. Helmholz, *The Spirit of Classical Canon Law* (Athens, GA, 1996), 146–52; Gray, *Oaths*, 17–50.

[22] Augustine, *Sermo* 180 (PL 38: 972–9); *De mendacio* (PL 40: 487–517); *Contra mendacium* (PL 40: 517–48); Corran, *Lying and Perjury*, 45–8.

embraced the gamut of swearing, encompassing vows and profanities as well as oaths. No matter what its subject was, an oath was inherently religious: the person taking it called God to witness to the sincerity and truthfulness of the matter. This spiritual character was often reinforced through swearing on a sacred object, especially the gospels.[23] Books of oaths incorporated appropriate texts on which to swear: in a volume prepared for a customs house, the gospel cursus prefaced the oath taken by shipmasters transporting wool to Calais.[24] In the Exchequer in the 1530s, royal tenants swore succession oaths upon a book containing twelfth-century gospel lessons, to the back cover of which a gilt crucifix was, and still is, nailed: a tangible reminder of the ultimate power underwriting such promises. In courts of law, the volume upon which oaths were taken was known as 'the jury book', and it too might be paired with a crucifix.[25]

Swearing too readily was, however, believed to be a slippery slope to swearing falsely. Oaths were supposed to be taken considerately rather than rashly, out of necessity for serious matters, not habitually over trifles. To swear to a moot point or to an estimate was inadvisable.[26] Profane swearing was a mortal sin, graphically imagined as crucifying Christ anew.[27] It was, however, not yet an offence that provoked society into concerted action. Maybe blaspheming was less prolific in the early Tudor period than it would become later; maybe, before the Reformation, God's vengeance was expected to alight on the individual rather than on the covenanted nation. Spiritual guides pointed to manifestations of divine punishment: twenty-five miles from London, on the highway to Cambridge, a massive haemorrhage was the fitting end for swearing by God's blood.[28] In sum, to swear

---

[23] William Lyndwood, *Provinciale* (Oxford, 1679), 108o, 110h, 110–11r.

[24] BL, MS Royal 9 A XII, fols 15ʳ–16ᵛ. The cursus excerpted the story of Christ's birth, death and resurrection. The scriptural content of oath books is discussed in Eyal Poleg, *Approaching the Bible in Medieval England* (Manchester, 2013), 84–92.

[25] BL, MS Stowe 15, fols 8ᵛ–9ʳ; Kingston upon Thames, Kingston History Centre, KD3/1/1, 45 (borough inventory, 1514); Susanne Brand, 'The Fifteenth-Century Accounts of the Undersheriffs of Middlesex: An Unlikely Source for Legal History', in David Ibbetson, Neil Jones and Nigel Ramsay, eds, *English Legal History and its Sources: Essays in Honour of Sir John Baker* (Cambridge, 2019), 159–75, at 170.

[26] Lyndwood, *Provinciale*, 116a; Chertsey, *Floure*, fol. 24ʳ; J. H. Baker, ed., *Reports of Cases by John Caryll*, 2 vols, SelS 115–16 (London, 1999–2000), 1: 27; *L&P* 4/2: 4631.

[27] Stephen Hawes, *The Conuercyon of Swerers* (London, 1509), sigs A3ʳ, A7ʳ.

[28] Richard Whitford, *A Werke for Housholders* (London, 1530), sigs C3ᵛ–C4ʳ.

wrongly was to traduce God, imperil one's soul and risk retribution. Oaths were deadly serious.

But to refuse to swear in any circumstance was an excessively literal construal of the second commandment (in the English pre-Reformation, or Catholic and Lutheran, numbering) and of the Sermon on the Mount (Matt. 5: 34–7).[29] Rejection of oath-taking was treated as heresy and associated with Lollardy. According to Alice Walker, her husband Thomas refused to seal agreements with an oath and rebuked her for wishing to swear.[30] A suspect might be asked 'whether someone ought to swear to say the truth over certain articles concerning the honour of God and the church and the health of his soul if he were ordered to by a legitimate judge'.[31] Misbelief was akin to perjury, since both traduced God. A heretic and a perjurer once performed penance together at Paul's Cross during the sermon.[32] Oath-breakers and heretics had faithlessness in common. When a member of the Shearers' Company was elected alderman in 1514, London's governors required him to transfer to a more exalted livery company. To a disgruntled shearer, his former brother was 'periured' and 'worse thene an heretyk' for breaking his oath to the Shearers' Company.[33]

As Augustine had taught, rules governing swearing constrained those seeking oaths from others. To require an oath unnecessarily when you believed someone anyway was a pardonable sin; to do so knowing that a person would forswear himself was a mortal one, the individual's sin rebounding on you.[34] When Margaret Webb produced honest female neighbours as compurgators, the judge dismissed her without taking her oath.[35] Those in positions of authority were expected to avoid giving occasion for perjury. In 1510, the Mercers'

---

[29] For the alternative numberings, see Jonathan Willis, *The Reformation of the Decalogue: Religious Identity and the Ten Commandments in England, c.1485–1625* (Cambridge, 2017), 28–36.

[30] Lyndwood, *Provinciale*, 298–9e; Dublin, Trinity College, MS 775, fol. 124ʳ (London, 1511); Shannon McSheffrey and Norman Tanner, eds, *Lollards of Coventry, 1486–1522*, Camden Society 5th series 23 (London, 2003), 95, 311.

[31] HALS, ASA7/1, fol. 42Aᵛ (John Woodward of Watford, 1527); John Foxe, *Actes and Monuments*, 2 vols (London, 1583), 2: 1102 (art. 41).

[32] Lyndwood, *Provinciale*, 55r, 56b; A. H. Thomas and I. D. Thornley, eds, *The Great Chronicle of London* (London, 1938), 262.

[33] LMA, COL/CA/01/01/002, fol. 187ʳ⁻ᵛ.

[34] Augustine, *Sermo* 180.10 (PL 38: 978); Chertsey, *Floure*, fols 23ᵛ, 208ᵛ.

[35] LMA, DL/C/B/043/MS09064/011, fol. 137ʳ.

Company of London decided that it would no longer admit as apprentice anyone who looked to be under the age of sixteen, even if he and his friends offered to swear that he was in fact old enough, for fear of encouraging perjury.[36] The same principle could be applied to criticize royal policy when it tempted people to forswear. In the later years of Henry VII's reign, preachers attacked the crown's encouragement of promoters (private individuals who prosecuted offences for a share of the statutory penalty) on this ground.[37]

II

That oaths were religious acts raised the question of how jurisdiction over perjury should be distributed between the different legal systems. In the *Provinciale*, written in the 1420s but much consulted during the early Tudor period, the canonist William Lyndwood had described perjury as a 'mixed crime' over which both ecclesiastical and secular courts exercised jurisdiction.[38] This joint competence was complicated by the fact that the two legal systems defined perjury differently. This divergence may have arisen because the offence contravened two of the Ten Commandments: the second (against taking the Lord's name in vain) and the eighth (against bearing false witness). One commandment belonged to the first table (concerning humanity's duty to God) and the other to the second table (concerning people's relations with each other). Nevertheless their import was merged: a devotional text that worked its way through the Decalogue, upon reaching the eighth commandment, rather than repeat its material referred back to the discussion of the second. Illustrations of offences against each commandment collapsed the distinction, with witnessing falsely being discussed under the second, as well as the eighth, commandment.[39]

Treating perjury as both lying under oath and violating an oath potentially conferred on the church jurisdiction over a vast number of agreements and undertakings. In fact, common lawyers had long

[36] Lætitia Lyell and Frank D. Watney, eds, *Acts of Court of the Mercers' Company, 1453–1527* (Cambridge, 1936), 382.
[37] Thomas and Thornley, eds, *Great Chronicle*, 335, 337; e.g. Guy Parsloe, ed., *Wardens' Accounts of the Worshipful Company of Founders of the City of London, 1497–1681* (London, 1964), 39–40 (a forsworn informant in 1514).
[38] Lyndwood, *Provinciale*, 315o. Other glosses, however, referred to perjury as an ecclesiastical crime that pertained to the church: ibid. 316oo, 322m. The *Provinciale* was printed in 1483, 1501, 1506 and 1525.
[39] Whitford, *Werke*, sig. E4r; Chertsey, *Floure*, fol. 22r.

feared that, if this definition were accepted, then 'every lay contract would be determined in court Christian'.[40] Not all promises were oaths, however. It was a legitimate defence before a church court to acknowledge an agreement or injunction but to deny having sworn to perform or abide by it.[41] While a simple promise might bind in the court of conscience, what made it actionable in the external forum (the church court) was solemnization through an oath.[42] The rule was no oath, no perjury. Hence Lyndwood maintained that, while the two legal systems shared jurisdiction over perjury, that of the church was superior, because it alone could resolve any doubt over the validity of an oath.[43]

Common law adopted a much narrower definition of perjury, based solely on the eighth commandment. In a reading at Gray's Inn in 1514, the bencher (or senior member) John Hales explained to his audience of students how the realm's laws were 'derived from and began with the law of God, namely the law of Moses'.[44] He then set out how responsibility for enforcing the Ten Commandments was divided between the spiritual and temporal jurisdictions. A murderer who broke the fifth commandment and a thief who broke the seventh 'would be punished by our law'; in the case of an adulterer who broke the sixth commandment, 'the punishment appertains to the spiritual law'. Secular justice enforced the eighth commandment: 'if anyone were sworn and were to bear false witness … then he would be punished by the common law through attaint'. Hales's example was limited to legal proceedings. The crime of perjury was thus distinguished from general forswearing as referring to an oath taken in a court of record.

The limitation on who swore further narrowed the scope of perjury at common law. Only jurors could commit common-law perjury, because, as the etymology implies, it was they who were

---

[40] Year Books, Mich. 2 Hen. IV, plea 45, *per* Hankford.
[41] WSRO, Ep.I/10/2, fol. 89^v; York, BIA, CP.G.306; J. T. Fowler, ed., *Acts of Chapter of the Collegiate Church of SS. Peter and Wilfrid, Ripon, A.D. 1452 to A.D. 1506*, SS 64 (Durham, 1875), 121, 185; Helmholz, 'Assumpsit', 419–20; Ian Forrest, *Trustworthy Men: How Inequality and Faith made the Medieval Church* (Princeton, NJ, 2018), 44.
[42] Lyndwood, *Provinciale*, 108q, 117a; LMA, DL/C/0206, fols 250^v–252^v; A. Percival Moore, ed., 'Proceedings of the Ecclesiastical Courts in the Archdeaconry of Leicester, 1516–1535', *Associated Architectural Societies' Reports and Papers* 28 (1905–6), 117–220, 593–662, at 159; Christopher St German, *Doctor and Student*, ed. T. F. T. Plucknett and J. L. Barton, SelS 91 (London, 1974), 232.
[43] Lyndwood, *Provinciale*, 116a, 315o.
[44] London, Gray's Inn, MS 25, fol. 290^r.

formally sworn. Witnesses did give evidence under oath, but for the information of the jury, not as matter of record.[45] In common-law theory, the jurors were the proper witnesses. In the mid-fifteenth century, Sir John Fortescue had boasted that common law was superior to civil law because it depended on *twelve* sworn men rather than on *two* (the number of witnesses required in civil, and also in canon, law).[46] The writ of attaint to which Hales referred could thus only be sued against jurors. So, when Thomas Baker gave false testimony for a plaintiff in the sheriffs' court at York in 1526, the defendant prosecuted him for perjury in the archbishop's court, producing members of the original jury as witnesses. The church court might claim jurisdiction because Baker had taken an oath upon a book of hours before testifying.[47]

III

Both secular and ecclesiastical legal systems sought to deter perjury. Royal government envisaged perjury as harming the king's subjects and displeasing God. Legislative remedies concentrated on common-law juries. In the belief that poorer jurors forswore for money, property qualifications were revised upwards, but then again downwards, once it transpired that in some places not enough people met the threshold. The procedure in attainting juries was reformed and also extended to London, whose inhabitants were thought particularly prone to perjury.[48] In June 1517, the popular preacher Rowland Phillips, vicar of Croydon, got into trouble 'for thinges vtterid in his sermon, concernynge Juries and atteyntes'.[49] The new legislation was certainly controversial: introduced in 1495, it was amended during passage so as to require renewal in the next parliament. Three times, the measure came back for renewal, on each

[45] John Fortescue, *De laudibus legum Anglie*, ed. S. B. Chrimes (Cambridge, 1942), 58–63; Christopher St German, *Salem and Bizance* (London, 1533), sigs G8ᵛ–H1ᵛ. Justices exercised discretion over whether evidence was given under oath: TNA, STAC2/18/1; J. H. Baker, ed., *Reports of Cases from the Time of King Henry VIII*, 2 vols, SelS 120–1 (London, 2003–4), 2: 317–18.
[46] Fortescue, *De laudibus legum Anglie*, ed. Chrimes, 42–3, 66–79.
[47] BIA, CP.G.181.
[48] 11 Hen. VII cc.21, 24, 26; TNA, C1/109/26; Baker, ed., *Reports of Henry VIII*, 1: 66–7; Penny Tucker, *Law Courts and Lawyers in the City of London, 1300–1550* (Cambridge, 2007), 38–9, 224–30, 345–9.
[49] HL, MS Ellesmere 2652, fol. 10ᵛ. In the month after 'Evil May Day', the king's council may have been alert to contentious preaching.

occasion having another limiting clause added, until it expired in 1512; it was revived in 1532, but again for a fixed term.[50] Perhaps the penalties in attaint seemed too draconian. After all, jury service was imposed and defeated parties could prove vindictive; it was sometimes difficult to tell what the correct verdict should have been.[51]

Attaint came to matter less over the early Tudor period, because increasingly perjury was prosecuted before the conciliar courts instead.[52] This jurisdiction extended to criminal cases and others to which the king was party. It outgrew any statutory basis to operate as an unmediated emanation of royal authority.[53] The conciliar courts dealt with common-law juries, upon referral by justices as well as upon private bill.[54] They also heard complaints against parties and witnesses.[55] Their jurisdiction extended to perjury committed in the ecclesiastical system. Compurgators who, before the ordinary, had untruthfully declared a clerk convict innocent of rape were prosecuted before the council.[56] In the 1520s, an Essex vicar complained that a neighbouring parson had hired eight men to give false evidence in the archbishop of Canterbury's court, '[t]o the gret Joperdie of the seid parsone and parjured persons yf Condinge ponysment and pennaunce should not be hade'.[57]

The conciliar courts punished perjury through public shaming in a prominent place at a busy time. Offenders wore papers on their heads announcing 'in great lettres' that '[t]hes men bene wylfully periured'. Such a penalty was described in decrees as penance.[58] As such, it resembled the sentences imposed in church courts, which on occasion also ordered perjurers to wear papers proclaiming their offence. This punishment was at the discretion of the chancellor, a prelate until

[50] 12 Hen. VII c.2; 19 Hen. VII c.3; 1 Hen. VIII c.11; 23 Hen. VIII c.3.
[51] Baker, ed., *Reports of Caryll*, 1: 120–1.
[52] John Baker, *OHLE*, 6: *1483–1558* (Oxford, 2003), 371–3.
[53] 11 Hen. VII c.25 (expired 1504); TNA, STAC1/2/124; C. B. Bayne and William H. Dunham, eds, *Select Cases in the Council of Henry VII*, SelS 75 (London, 1958), 71, 76.
[54] TNA, DL5/2, fols 103ᵛ, 104ᵛ; DL5/4, fols 122ᵛ, 135ᵛ; KB9/453/119; STAC2/20/126; BL, MS Lansdowne 639, fol. 45ʳ; HL, MS Ellesmere 2768, fol. 23ᵛ; Bayne and Dunham, eds, *Select Cases in the Council*, 62–77a.
[55] Such as TNA, STAC2/15/125–6 (defendant in Chancery); STAC2/25/74 (witnesses at assizes); STAC2/26/95 (witnesses in King's Bench).
[56] BL, MS Lansdowne 639, fol. 48ʳ.
[57] TNA, STAC2/9/159.
[58] TNA, C193/142, fol. 46ʳ–ᵛ; BL, MS Lansdowne 639, fols 47ᵛ, 48ᵛ–49ʳ; HL, MS Ellesmere 2652, fol. 10ᵛ.

1529. Apparently, it was imposed by Wolsey to such great effect that 'in his tyme' perjury 'was lesse used'.[59] According to George Gower, wearing papers would mean that he would 'no more be Reputed trewe or honest or taken In to any feloship or company', forcing him 'to fle the kings Realme neuer to be sene within the land'. Gower may not have been exaggerating much: for a member so to be punished could cause 'grete infamy ... to the hoole body' of his company.[60] The implication of being forsworn made the insult 'papirid knave' defamatory.[61] This conflation of punishment and penance reflected a general understanding of perjury as an offence against God.

Nevertheless, the rationale differed somewhat between the legal systems and between different royal courts. Like the church courts, Chancery acted out of concern for the offender's soul. Yet in describing perjury as being 'against conscience', petitioners were more concerned with an abstract sense of right and wrong. Their bills emphasized the enormity of the offence, less commonly the detrimental effect on the offender ('the losse of the lyffe eternalle').[62] In Star Chamber, an answer might reply that a bill had not shown that 'by reasoune of the othe' taken by the defendant the complainant 'is anie waise dampnyfyed'.[63] Only damage caused to others, not to oneself, by forswearing would have justified this case being heard. The Essex vicar was thus unusual in asking for penance as well as punishment. The displeasure caused to God aggravated the offence and made a punishment appropriate that was not only public but also penitential.

Church courts made greater use of oaths than did any other legal system. Every role, whether accused, party, compurgator, witness, executor, proctor, summoner or excuser of an absence, required them.[64] Such oaths were more than procedural devices: they could prove determinative where no evidence was available (such as over

[59] HALS, ASA7/1, fol. 26ᵛ; Charles L. Kingsford, ed., *Chronicles of London* (Oxford, 1905), 208; Baker, ed., *Reports of Henry VIII*, 2: 332; Henry Ellis, ed., *Hall's Chronicle* (London, 1809), 585.

[60] TNA, SP1/70, fol. 163ᵛ (*L&P* 5: 1176); Matthew Davies, ed., *The Merchant Taylors' Company of London: Court Minutes, 1486–1493* (Stamford, 2000), 237.

[61] HALS, ASA7/2, fol. 41ᵛ.

[62] TNA, C1/410/46.

[63] TNA, STAC2/22/269; STAC2/18/243; STAC2/22/203.

[64] Lyndwood, *Provinciale*, 177m, 254f, 298p; Helmholz, *Spirit*, 145, 152–61; R. H. Helmholz, *OHLE*, 1: *The Canon Law and Ecclesiastical Jurisdiction from 597 to the 1640s* (Oxford, 2004), 334–6.

a clandestine marriage contract).[65] Perjury was one of the courts' two
disciplinary terms, alongside contumacy. Refusal to swear to perform
penance was contumacy; failure to carry out the penance that you had
sworn to perform was perjury. Breaking an injunction no longer to
consort with someone with whom you were suspected of dallying
was also perjury, on account of your prior oath to comply. Perjury
in court entailed giving sworn testimony that proved false: for
instance, denial under oath of carnal knowledge when your sexual
partner confessed.[66] Judicial oaths were not necessarily taken with
especial seriousness; they might instead have prompted legalistic
responses. A perjured witness in a testamentary case had been persuaded that an oath taken before the bishop of Exeter outside his diocese 'was as noe othe before god nor cold touch him in lawe'.[67]

Church courts concerned themselves with perjury committed in
ecclesiastical contexts, such as a churchwarden's false presentment
at a visitation.[68] Religious institutions that were secular lords might
exercise a wide jurisdiction over perjury. The archdeaconry of St
Albans inquired into perjury committed in the abbey's manor courts
and inferior ecclesiastical courts. It also enforced non-judicial oaths,
in one case determining whether a defendant had sworn conditionally
(as he alleged) or absolutely.[69] Perjury committed in royal courts
arguably lay within the remit of church courts. In 1521, the commissary court of Chichester accepted a complaint from John Lee that
Richard Humfrey was perjured because he had falsely presented
Lee to secular justices for assault.[70] This case appears on one of the
last pages of the act book and so its later course is unknown, which
is disappointing because common lawyers denied the church's jurisdiction in such circumstances.[71]

[65] Lyndwood, *Provinciale*, 20–1h, 48s, 76n; WSRO, Ep.I/10/1, fols 68ᵛ, 100ᵛ; Moore, ed., 'Proceedings in Leicester', 621.
[66] Hale, ed., *Precedents*, nos 93, 131, 146; Forrest, *Trustworthy Men*, 58–9.
[67] TNA, STAC2/22/225.
[68] WSRO, Ep.I/10/2, fols 90ʳ, 93ʳ; E. M. Elvey, ed., *The Courts of the Archdeaconry of Buckingham, 1483–1523*, Buckinghamshire Record Society 19 (n.pl., 1975), 257.
[69] HALS, ASA7/1, fols 54ᵛ, 58ᵛ, 59ᵛ.
[70] WSRO, Ep.I/10/2, fol. 135ᵛ.
[71] Baker, ed., *Reports of Caryll*, 1: 382; Margaret McGlynn, ed., *The Rights and Liberties of the English Church: Readings from the Pre-Reformation Inns of Court*, SelS 129 (London, 2015), 125, 163; Anthony Fitzherbert, *La Nouel natura breuium* (London, 1534), fol. 44ʳ.

IV

The principal factor in the contraction of ecclesiastical jurisdiction was the reduction in one type of case. In 1485, one of the commonest cases in church courts was 'breach of faith' (*fidei laesio*).[72] Pledging your faith was like swearing an oath: according to Lyndwood, your faith substituted for the sacred object upon which an oath was taken. Hence breaching your faith was equivalent to breaking your oath.[73] Thus some church courts treated the terms 'breach of faith' and 'perjury' as interchangeable.[74] Any lawful undertaking was covered, including promises to observe corporate ordinances, honour pensions and abide by arbitrators' awards.[75] London's hat-makers envisaged the bishop judging violations of their ordinances; following the craft's merger with the Haberdashers' Company, however, members found themselves prosecuted in the consistory court for perjury by the larger organization.[76] Promises of service that could have been enforced under labour legislation were also broached.[77] The majority of cases concerned things owed: usually a sum of money (seldom large), and also goods and chattels, including clothing, animals, crops, even bulbs of garlic. A rural deanery could thus become the principal forum for servicing small debt claims.[78]

Most breach of faith cases were brought by private parties rather than by the court itself. Hence the church's jurisdiction over perjury was exercised more on the instance, than on the office, side.[79]

---

[72] There are complementary analyses of breach of faith, in point of law and as social practice, in Helmholz, *OHLE*, 1: 358–68; Forrest, *Trustworthy Men*, 33–62.

[73] Lyndwood, *Provinciale*, 108o, 110–11r, 315p.

[74] WSRO, Ep.I/10/1, fols 1ʳ–117ᵛ; Moore, ed., 'Proceedings in Leicester', 605, 619, 625, 645; Elvey, ed., *Courts of Buckingham*, 75–204; Forrest, *Trustworthy Men*, 44–5, 370 n. 73.

[75] Hale, ed., *Precedents*, nos 17, 68, 75; LMA, DL/C/B/043/MS09064/011, fol. 39ʳ; BIA, CP.G.189A; Helmholz, 'Assumpsit', 410–11; Forrest, *Trustworthy Men*, 39, 56–8, 60–1.

[76] London, Guildhall Library, CLC/L/HA/A/009/MS15838, fols 11ʳ–16ᵛ; LMA, DL/C/0206, fols 293ʳ–294ʳ, 301ʳ–302ʳ, 317ʳ–321ᵛ; TNA, C1/302/25.

[77] WSRO, Ep.I/10/1, fol. 3ʳ; Hale, ed., *Precedents*, no. 46; Forrest, *Trustworthy Men*, 38.

[78] L. R. Poos, ed., *Lower Ecclesiastical Jurisdiction in Late-Medieval England: The Courts of the Dean and Chapter of Lincoln, 1336–1349, and the Deanery of Wisbech, 1458–1484*, RSEH n.s. 32 (Oxford, 2001), l, liv, lvi, lxv, 300, 423, 543.

[79] Hale, ed., *Precedents*, nos 177, 238, 267; Elvey, ed., *Courts of Buckingham*, 135; Helmholz, 'Assumpsit', 411–12. Office cases could be initiated or formally promoted by individuals: Hale, ed., *Precedents*, no. 272; Moore, ed., 'Proceedings in Leicester', 619, 625.

Through breach of faith, church courts offered an effective means of enforcing a range of agreements. It was, for example, possible to sue a surety for another person's debt.[80] Some defendants confessed what they owed straight away, submitted themselves and re-promised performance on pain of excommunication (although poverty could still prevent them from satisfying the other party).[81] If not, then the standard criterion of proof was two witnesses; additionally, written evidence could be produced.[82] While judges in theory punished the breach of faith rather than the non-payment, they usually did so by requiring the defendant to honour the debt. Often, they assigned no other penance.[83] Awards could require payment in a week's time, but also by instalment, taking account of the defendant's means.[84] Summoners serving citations might collect moneys owing and payments were also made in court.[85]

Breach of faith bulked large in the business of church courts at the beginning of our period, yet by its end had almost disappeared. This trend was first detected in the diocese of Canterbury, where cases increased over the second half of the fifteenth century and then declined from the turn of the sixteenth century onwards. In the consistory court, the number of cases rose from 150 in 1454 to peak in 1491 at 684, but dwindled to a mere four in 1535.[86] A reduction has since been observed in church courts in eight other dioceses. The number of cases in Hereford's consistory court in 1509–10 was only one-fifth of what it had been in 1497–8. Even in Chichester, where church courts thrived under Bishop Sherborn (1508–36), breach of faith cases shrank.[87] The instance book of the archdeaconry

[80] WSRO, Ep.I/10/1, fol. 7ᵛ; BIA, CP.G.69; CP.G.107; Forrest, *Trustworthy Men*, 54–6.
[81] WSRO, Ep.I/10/1, fols 4ʳ, 13ᵛ, 60ᵛ, 66ʳ, 73ʳ.
[82] Lyndwood, *Provinciale*, 113d; BIA, CP.G.17; CP.G.100; WSRO, Ep.I/10/1, fol. 96ᵛ; Hale, ed., *Precedents*, no. 95; Helmholz, 'Assumpsit', 410.
[83] Helmholz, 'Assumpsit', 424–5; Forrest, *Trustworthy Men*, 36–7.
[84] Elvey, ed., *Courts of Buckingham*, 167; Fowler, ed., *Acts of Ripon*, 267.
[85] WSRO, Ep.I/10/1, fols 37ᵛ, 48ʳ.
[86] Brian L. Woodcock, *Medieval Ecclesiastical Courts in the Diocese of Canterbury* (London, 1952), 84, 89–92, 109–10.
[87] Helmholz, 'Assumpsit', 406–7, 426–8; Ralph Houlbrooke, *Church Courts and the People during the English Reformation, 1520–1570* (Oxford, 1979), 39; Richard M. Wunderli, *London Church Courts and Society on the Eve of the Reformation* (Cambridge, MA, 1981), 104–5, 108; Stephen J. Lander, 'The Diocese of Chichester 1509–1558: Episcopal Reform under Robert Sherburne and its Aftermath' (PhD thesis, University of Cambridge, 1974), 39.

of St Albans running from 1515 to 1543 contains only one such case (from 1532).[88] There does not seem to be an endogenous explanation for this decline. The interests of those staffing church courts lay in sustaining a source of income; indeed, according to a critic, perjury cases were 'only stuff to geate money for thaduocates and proctours'.[89] External factors must be considered instead.

Jurisdiction over breach of faith depended upon people choosing to bring cases before church courts. The earlier growth may have occurred because business was being transferred from manor courts, whose effectiveness was declining as seigneurial authority over tenants weakened.[90] If people were now choosing to sue elsewhere, then possible beneficiaries could have been borough courts, for it would be to these courts that much of the growing volume of debt litigation would later be directed.[91] The court books of early Tudor Ipswich, for example, reveal a jurisdiction servicing contractual and debt-related claims from the town and hinterland regularly and flexibly. There an obligor who had honoured someone else's debt could obtain redress; the central common-law courts had barely begun to offer relief in such circumstances.[92] Much of London's breach of faith business might have been absorbed by civic courts; without their records, however, it is impossible to be sure.[93] Only if it were shown that secular courts became more receptive to such cases would 'forum shopping' by litigants be a sufficient explanation for the trend.

Of greater importance may have been hostility from common lawyers. The rule that pleas of debts and chattels should be heard in the king's courts dated back to the twelfth century.[94] Common lawyers did not oppose the church's having any jurisdiction over breach of faith. Instead they identified two permissible types of case: a pure kind and a mixed kind.[95] The former was confined to correcting the sin through corporeal penance. The latter was allowable only

---

[88] HALS, ASA7/2, fols 67[v], 68[v].

[89] TNA, SP1/99, fol. 199[r] (*L&P* 9: 1071).

[90] Chris Briggs, 'The Availability of Credit in the English Countryside, 1400–1480', *Agricultural History Review* 56 (2008), 1–24, at 19–24.

[91] Craig Muldrew, *The Economy of Obligation: The Culture of Credit and Social Relations in Early Modern England* (Basingstoke, 1998), 199–271.

[92] BL, MS Add. 24435, fol. 2[v]; Baker, *OHLE*, 6: 855.

[93] Wunderli, *London Church Courts*, 105; Tucker, *Law Courts*, 116–21, 333.

[94] Constitutions of Clarendon, c.15.

[95] McGlynn, ed., *Rights and Liberties*, 125; Anthony Fitzherbert, *La Graunde Abridgement* (London, 1577), fol. 194[r] ('Consultacion', plea 5, *per* Solyard).

where the thing in question was spiritual. Although the church's office jurisdiction was more tolerable, its instance jurisdiction was not rejected outright. What was unacceptable was compelling a party to perform a 'temporal act', such as paying a debt, which pertained to the king's courts.[96] The crown had long offered subjects the writ of prohibition as a means of preventing church courts from hearing improper cases. Lyndwood had, however, advised only technical compliance. He recommended the careful drafting of the libel (or bill of complaint to a church court) as a way of eluding the writ. Common lawyers remarked upon the uninformative nature of libels.[97] The issue was therefore whether the rule could now be enforced more effectively than in the past.

The statutory offence of *praemunire* provided the solution by allowing the common-law courts to decide the real issue. *Praemunire* referred in an open-ended way to any activity that infringed the crown's jurisdiction. Over the fifteenth century, it had come to be applied to church courts within the realm, as well as to those outside it.[98] Hence a husbandman who sued in Norwich's consistory court for breach of a monetary obligation could be prosecuted by the other party, who alleged that 'the matiere shulde be determyned at the Commen Lawe acordyng to the said statute and not in the spirituell courte'.[99] The number of *praemunire* actions brought in the court of King's Bench picked up from the mid-1490s, just as breach of faith cases peaked. *Praemunire* actions for hearing pleas involving debts and chattels (which would have comprised most breach of faith cases) were concentrated in the first decade of the sixteenth century.[100] They covered church courts in nine dioceses: Canterbury, Durham, Exeter, Hereford, Lincoln, London, Norwich, Salisbury and York. Joining litigants as defendants were judges, proctors, registrars and summoners. They included the

---

[96] Year Books, Pasch. 38 Hen. VI, plea 11; Mich. 20 Edw. IV, plea 9; Trin. 12 Hen. VII, plea 2; Baker, ed., *Reports of Henry VIII*, 1: 235; Fitzherbert, *Nouel natura breuium*, fol. 45^r–^{v}.

[97] Lyndwood, *Provinciale*, 315o; Year Books, Trin. 22 Edw. IV, plea 47; J. H. Baker, ed., *The Notebook of Sir John Port*, SelS 102 (London, 1986), 18.

[98] Daniel F. Gosling, 'Church, State, and Reformation: The Use and Interpretation of *Praemunire* from its Creation to the English Break with Rome' (PhD thesis, University of Leeds, 2016), 120–57.

[99] TNA, C1/124/70 (1486x1493).

[100] Gosling, 'Church, State, and Reformation', 162–5, 213–16.

chancellors of Lincoln and Norwich dioceses, the commissary of St Paul's Cathedral and the official of the archdeacon of Wiltshire.[101] At the Huntingdonshire quarter sessions in 1506, the commissary of Ramsey Abbey was indicted simply for asking a defendant to swear that she did not owe anything.[102]

Praemunire actions presumably deterred parties from bringing breach of faith cases and church courts from hearing them. Even though actions almost never resulted in convictions, the expense, inconvenience and worry must have been considerable. Whether a church court would still compel payment of a debt may also have influenced potential litigants. From 1500, Canterbury's consistory court stopped ordering payment of debts and instead awarded penance. So doing brought the court's practice into conformity with common law, just as *praemunire* actions intensified, but made it less attractive. The volume of cases in 1511 was one-third of what it had been in 1499. Then, in 1511, the consistory court resumed ordering payment of debts; perhaps litigants had by then found other forums, for the number of cases did not recover.[103] Nevertheless breach of faith cases continued to be heard into the 1530s.[104] Descriptions are often too brief to tell what was being sought. A libel of 1534 insisted that it sought nothing but canonical correction.[105] In 1532, the consistory court of Durham dismissed a case brought by the city's tailors on account of its civil character, but heard another concerning payment for a horse three years later.[106] Still, breach of faith was by then only a vestige of what it had been a half-century before.

---

[101] TNA, KB27/973, rotulet 35[d]; P. R. Cavill, '"The Enemy of God and His Church": James Hobart, Praemunire, and the Clergy of Norwich Diocese', *JLH* 32 (2011), 127–50, at 136–43; TNA, KB27/960, rotulet 77; KB27/994, rex rotulet 3.

[102] TNA, KB9/442/112–14.

[103] Woodcock, *Medieval Ecclesiastical Courts*, 90–1; Helmholz, 'Assumpsit', 424; Wunderli, *London Church Courts*, 105–7.

[104] BIA, CP.G.252; CP.G.293; TNA, C1/632/20; Alice M. Cooke, ed., *Act Book of the Ecclesiastical Court of Whalley, 1510–1538*, Chetham Society n.s. 44 (Manchester, 1901), 182, 184.

[105] BIA, CP.G.239. Perhaps this statement was made because the plaintiff had a common-law remedy in the action of account.

[106] James Raine, ed., *Depositions and other Ecclesiastical Proceedings from the Courts of Durham, extending from 1311 to the Reign of Elizabeth*, SS 21 (London, 1845), nos 39, 45.

V

The curtailment of ecclesiastical jurisdiction was based on common-law principles, but these were not secular ones. For John Hales, a vision of divine law infusing all present-day legal systems rationalized restricting what cases church courts could hear. In his reading at Gray's Inn in 1514, Hales explained why churchmen should not hear many breach of faith cases:

> In this realm there are two manners of jurisdiction, namely spiritual jurisdiction, which is derived from the pope and the spirituality, and the temporal jurisdiction, which is given to the king and the temporality. And the two jurisdictions resemble two swords (*deux espes scilicet swordes*) and each ought to aid the other. The jurisdictions have a certain determination, over which matters they have authority. Each of them ought to keep to its own and not meddle with the jurisdiction of the other. The spiritual jurisdiction commences with the spiritual commands such as matrimony, bastardy, bigamy, etc. And other matters do not appertain to those men who do not have knowledge of the division of things, so no more debt, covenant or contract with oath. These do not appertain to such men because they do not know when a contract is good and when it is not, which could be through a nude pact (*ex nudo pacto*) with an oath and still it is not a contract in our law, and therefore they ought not to meddle with that.[107]

Hales barred ecclesiastical jurisdiction because churchmen regarded an oath as validating an agreement. For common lawyers, however, it was the reciprocal benefit, or quid pro quo (what would come to be called the 'consideration'), that did so. Hence a nude pact, or promise without mutual benefit, was not enforceable.[108]

Unlike civil law (from which the term came), canon law did enforce a nude pact. While few breach of faith cases seem likely to have concerned nude pacts, the existence of a reciprocal inducement was, strictly speaking, irrelevant to church courts in determining the validity of a promise.[109] Significantly, common lawyers maintained that a nude pact was not actionable, rather than that it was in no

---

[107] Gray's Inn, MS 25, fol. 292^r.

[108] Baker, ed., *Reports of Caryll*, 2: 514; D. J. Ibbetson, *A Historical Introduction to the Law of Obligations* (Oxford, 1999), 80–3; Baker, *OHLE*, 6: 813–17, 862–8.

[109] Helmholz, 'Assumpsit', 414–16; Helmholz, *Spirit*, 161–4. A plaintiff's interest in the contract being performed could be stated explicitly: Cooke, ed., *Act Book of Whalley*, 48.

way binding. In his *Doctor and Student* of 1528 and 1530, Christopher St German explained why. With a quid pro quo, it was reasonable to infer an intention to be bound; with a nude pact, only its maker could know what his or her intention had been. A nude pact could be binding in the internal forum of conscience, over which, however, neither legal system should exercise cognizance.[110] This was a bold attempt to dictate to the church the partition between the 'penitential' and the 'contentious' forums.[111]

Breach of faith in church courts could be remedied as breach of contract at common law. But rules restricted what kinds of contract would be enforced. An action of covenant redressed failure to perform a promise, but only when the agreement was in writing. An action of debt did not require written documentation, but permitted defendants to wage their law (that is, deny by swearing alongside oath-helpers).[112] Wager relied on litigants' consciences preventing them from forswearing; though church courts were barred for trying false wager as perjury, Chancery might provide relief.[113] A new remedy for verbal agreements was, however, emerging: the action of *assumpsit*. As a species of trespass, *assumpsit* did not permit wager, and it allowed agreements to be proved orally. By 1400, *assumpsit* was available for *mis*feasance (partial or inadequate performance), for which no other remedy existed. Over the fifteenth century, *assumpsit* remained unacceptable for *non*feasance, because it would have duplicated existing actions.[114] This position began to change around the turn of the sixteenth century. By 1532, the majority opinion in King's Bench favoured *assumpsit* lying for nonfeasance as well.[115] Now it could be alleged against the church's jurisdiction

[110] St German, *Doctor and Student*, ed. Plucknett and Barton, 227–33; A. W. B. Simpson, *A History of the Common Law of Contract: The Rise of the Action of Assumpsit*, rev. edn (Oxford, 1987), 376–96.
[111] Lyndwood, *Provinciale*, 327r, 337g.
[112] Simpson, *History of Contract*, 3–196; Ibbetson, *Introduction to Obligations*, 24–38; Baker, *OHLE*, 6: 819–32, 835–7.
[113] TNA, C1/369/92; C1/410/46; C1/713/22; St German, *Doctor and Student*, ed. Plucknett and Barton, 108–9, 232–3; McGlynn, ed., *Rights and Liberties*, 163; Norman Doe, *Fundamental Authority in Late Medieval English Law* (Cambridge, 1990), 150–3.
[114] Year Books, Mich. 21 Hen. VII, plea 5; Simpson, *History of Contract*, 199–315; Ibbetson, *Introduction to Obligations*, 126–51; Baker, *OHLE*, 6: 757–60, 839–62.
[115] Baker, ed., *Reports of Caryll*, 2: 417; J. H. Baker, ed., *The Reports of Sir John Spelman*, 2 vols, SelS 93–4 (London, 1977–8), 1: 4–6.

that '[a]ctions upon … breking of promisez lye at the kinges cort.'[116] Thereafter *assumpsit* became the principal action for breach of contract.

The action of *assumpsit* expanded as breach of faith declined in church courts. The one did not directly supplant the other: *assumpsit* was uncommon before the mid-sixteenth century, and most breach of faith cases concerned sums below the forty-shilling minimum in the central royal courts.[117] Nevertheless the coincidence suggests some cross-fertilization. Common lawyers would not have acknowledged any connection. In their perspective, lack of relief at common law did not legitimate the exercise of ecclesiastical jurisdiction: hence confining church courts within their proper (and historic) bounds did not oblige the profession to devise compensatory remedies.[118] Yet in the first decade of the sixteenth century the common law borrowed ecclesiastical models in order to develop a rival jurisdiction over defamation and used the same form of trespass action as *assumpsit* to do so.[119] Up to a point, an action of *assumpsit* resembled breach of faith.[120] *Assumpsit* was an action for breach of promise, for which it awarded compensation. A stress on the promise (as opposed to the contract) mirrored the priority of the faithful promise in breach of faith cases.[121] The faithful element in *assumpsit* was, however, superfluous: it did not substantively affect the pleading, nor did it turn the promise into a sacred obligation. Defendants opposed on the grounds of not having made a simple promise, rather than not having pledged their faith.[122] Chancery's burgeoning jurisdiction over unsworn agreements thus seems equally likely to have spurred the development of *assumpsit*.[123]

[116] McGlynn, ed., *Rights and Liberties*, 162.
[117] Helmholz, 'Assumpsit', 409–10; Wunderli, *London Church Courts*, 107, 153.
[118] St German, *Doctor and Student*, ed. Plucknett and Barton, 76–7, 144–5, 232–3.
[119] R. H. Helmholz, ed., *Select Cases on Defamation to 1600*, SelS 101 (London, 1985), lxxii, 42; Ibbetson, *Introduction to Obligations*, 112–25.
[120] Helmholz, 'Assumpsit', 413–28; Ibbetson, *Introduction to Obligations*, 135–40.
[121] Baker, ed., *Reports of Spelman*, 1: 5; Cooke, ed., *Act Book of Whalley*, 47–8.
[122] Lyndwood, *Provinciale*, 108o, 271dd; Simpson, *History of Contract*, 214, 574–9. King's Bench and Common Pleas later diverged over whether a promise could be implied or had to be expressed: Baker, *OHLE*, 6: 869–74.
[123] Fitzherbert, *Graunde Abridgement*, fol. 12ʳ ('Accion sur le case', plea 45); Year Books, Pasch. 8 Edw. IV, plea 11; Pasch. 7 Hen. VII, plea 2; Simpson, *History of Contract*, 275–80.

To take stock, a conjectural explanation of the decline of breach of faith cases might go something like this. Most litigants were not really seeking canonical correction, but rather payment and performance, which were, however, the remedies that church courts reluctantly felt less able to offer. Put off by the possibility of *praemunire* actions, most litigants turned instead to local courts and later to the central common-law courts as well. Common lawyers thus circumscribed the remit of breach of faith in a way that rendered it significantly less appealing. The church's office jurisdiction over perjury may have been too reliant upon its instance jurisdiction to thrive separately. In 1540, it was alleged that London's diocesan courts 'durst not' prosecute even perjury committed in front of them 'for feare and drede of A preminire'.[124] Common lawyers provided the impetus behind this development, not only because they wished to take a slice of the church courts' business, but also because they objected to the perceived usurpation of royal jurisdiction and had developed an effective instrument to do something about it. Intriguingly, the same trend occurred a little earlier in France, where civil lawyers adopted a jealously royalist perspective: a peak in the church's cognizance of debt in the mid-fifteenth century, followed by a decrease that became pronounced after the turn of the century.[125] By contrast, in contemporary Scotland, where a lay legal profession was only beginning to develop, the church's jurisdiction continued to be exercised unchecked.[126]

VI

The decline of breach of faith occurred before the break with Rome. The pressure applied to the church in the years immediately preceding did, however, prompt attacks on a facet of ecclesiastical procedure connected to perjury. As well as enforcing oaths, church courts took oaths from those appearing before them. The preliminary oath entailed an open-ended commitment to answer truthfully and to comply with judgments; hence some individuals resisted taking it, at least before knowing the articles against them. Refusal could result in either

---

[124] TNA, STAC2/32/151.
[125] Tyler Lange, *Excommunication for Debt in Late Medieval France: The Business of Salvation* (Cambridge, 2016), 76–219.
[126] Simon Ollivant, *The Court of the Official in Pre-Reformation Scotland: Based on the surviving Records of the Officials of St. Andrews and Edinburgh*, Stair Society 34 (Edinburgh, 1982), 65–6, 86–7, 163.

conviction or excommunication; acceptance could lead to self-incrimination or perjury.[127] The early evangelical William Tyndale expounded oath-taking in an orthodox manner, adopting Augustine's defence of needful swearing.[128] Nevertheless he accused judges in church courts of coercing suspects into taking oaths: 'Yf they desyre to knowe their accusers, naye say they, the mater is knowen well ynough and to moare then ye are ware of. Come laye youre hande on the boke, yf ye forswere your selfe, we shall bringe proves.'[129] Tyndale's caricature captured the perception that defendants were disadvantaged in comparison with those at common law. These criticisms were ventilated in the early 1530s, both in the Commons' Supplication against the Ordinaries (1532) and in the treatises of Christopher St German, to which Thomas More replied.[130]

There were two main dimensions of this criticism. The first was that people did not know the charges against them or their source. In instance cases, defendants had a statutory right to obtain a copy of the libel; in office cases, they could receive a summary of the charges, if they knew to ask for it.[131] A consultation upon a writ of prohibition in 1527 confirmed that the statute did not apply to ex officio proceedings.[132] The second element was the oath to tell the truth. It was a canonical principle that 'no one is obliged to betray themselves'; this did not, however, confer an unqualified privilege against self-incrimination, but only protection from being required to reveal hidden faults. The oath could be demanded where a probable cause, grounded in 'public fame', existed.[133] The two criticisms coalesced because the rationale for imposing an oath might not be apparent

[127] Margaret Bowker, ed., *An Episcopal Court Book for the Diocese of Lincoln, 1514–1520*, Lincoln Record Society 61 (Lincoln, 1967), 62, 67; Elvey, ed., *Courts of Buckingham*, 40; Hale, ed., *Precedents*, nos 253, 294, 321, 332.
[128] William Tyndale, *An Exposicion vppon the .V.VI.VII. Chapters of Mathew* ([Antwerp, 1533]?), fols 46ᵛ–49ʳ; Hadfield, *Lying*, 115–17.
[129] William Tyndale, *The Obedience of a Christen Man* (Antwerp, 1528), fol. 77ᵛ.
[130] Gerald Bray, ed., *Documents of the English Reformation, 1526–1701*, rev. edn (Cambridge, 2004), 53–5; John Guy, 'Thomas More and Christopher St German: The Battle of the Books', in Alistair Fox and John Guy, *Reassessing the Henrician Age: Humanism, Politics and Reform, 1500–1550* (Oxford, 1986), 95–120.
[131] 2 Hen. V st.1 c.3; Francis Douce, ed., *The Customs of London, otherwise called Arnold's Chronicle* (London, 1811), 192; TNA, C269/11/17.
[132] BL, MS Add. 48012, fols 50ʳ–51ᵛ.
[133] Lyndwood, *Provinciale*, 109p, 109r, 312i–k; Thomas More, *A Dyaloge [concerning Heresies]* (London, 1529), fols 78ʳ–79ᵛ; Foxe, *Actes and Monuments*, 2: 1102, 1118–19; R. H. Helmholz, 'The Privilege and the *Ius Commune*: The Middle Ages to

to the individual concerned. Hence an examinee might be taken by surprise. A debtor to his parish church was interrogated about non-payment of personal tithes, perjury in the manor court and usury as well.[134] George Gower complained that he was deemed to have committed perjury merely for interpreting the subjective term 'famyliar-ite' differently from the judge.[135] Put under oath, without knowing their accusers or the evidence against them, and forced to answer 'subtle interrogatories', examinees incriminated themselves, forswore or did both.

Heresy cases proceeded ex officio.[136] During the prosecutions in the diocese of London in 1528, the requirement to take the preliminary oath produced several refusals: one suspect had to be asked twice, another acceded upon receiving 'wiser counsel', a third agreed once he had heard the articles against him and a fourth only complied after being imprisoned in the stocks in Lollards' Tower.[137] Interrogation under oath could, in fact, assist a suspect: in 1533, Thomas White of Rye swore that he had never read the books found in his possession nor believed the heresies contained within them, whereupon the judge, 'because he could have no proofs, at least not true ones, against him', admitted White at his request to purgation.[138] Such examinations tempted people to forswear, as perhaps White did; for that reason, defendants and their witnesses in capital cases at common law did not testify under oath. Examination under oath entrapped others who were seeking to avoid perjury, perhaps 'some simple silly soul precisely standing to the clear testimony of his own well-known conscience'. It was the fear of perjuring oneself that made ex officio prosecution so effective.[139]

---

the Seventeenth Century', in idem et al., *The Privilege against Self-Incrimination: Its Origins and Development* (Chicago, IL, 1997), 17–46, at 32–5.

[134] HALS, ASA7/1, fol. 54ᵛ; Hale, ed., *Precedents*, nos 277, 315.

[135] TNA, SP1/70, fol. 163ʳ⁻ᵛ (*L&P* 5: 1176).

[136] Ian Forrest, *The Detection of Heresy in Late Medieval England* (Oxford, 2005), 68–76, 171–206; Gray, *Oaths*, 170–85.

[137] BL, MS Harley 421, fols 19ᵛ–20ᵛ.

[138] WSRO, Ep.I/10/5, fol. 9ʳ⁻ᵛ.

[139] Bray, ed., *Documents*, 55; Jason Powell, ed., *The Complete Works of Sir Thomas Wyatt the Elder*, 1: *Prose* (Oxford, 2016), 303; Shapiro, 'Oaths: Part One', 154–9; R. H. Helmholz, 'Introduction', to idem et al., *Privilege against Self-Incrimination*, 1–16, at 8–9, 14–15.

Paul Cavill

What connected St German's criticism of heresy proceedings to his earlier jurisprudential work was a standard of proof. He wished to prevent church courts from reaching within the forum of conscience to discover hidden faults.[140] Evidence from witnesses, and not that from suspects themselves, should form the basis of prosecution. A particular bugbear of his, therefore, was that, contrary to the normal canon-law bar, in heresy cases the testimony of perjured witnesses was admissible.[141] From a different religious position, Tyndale agreed: present-day judges compel people 'ether to forswere them selves by the allmightie God and by the holy Gospell ... or to testifie agenst them selves', whereas truly Christian judges would rely on witnesses and leave what could not be proven by their evidence to God.[142] Such criticism could seem hypocritical. As Thomas More pointed out, interrogation under oath was not confined to heresy trials or even to church courts: it was practised in the conciliar courts and also at common law, for example, by justices of the peace examining suspects.[143] In 1534, a statute restricted the grounds on which someone might be cited before an ecclesiastical judge on suspicion of heresy, by requiring a presentment, indictment or accusation. But the legislation said very little about the conduct of a trial and so seems to have left the oath itself unaltered.[144]

The efficacy of examination under oath was thus acknowledged. That is perhaps explicable in the light of the contribution of oath-taking to an undoubted achievement of early Tudor government: reforming the system of taxation. The fixed quotas of fifteenths and tenths were replaced with subsidies whose yields depended on individuals' sworn self-valuations. The requirement for the assessment of

[140] St German, *Salem and Bizance*, sigs F4ᵛ, F8ᵛ.
[141] Ibid., sig. G6ᵛ, citing VI 5.2.8 (*CICan*, 2: 1072); Lyndwood, *Provinciale*, 114f; E. D. Stone and B. Cozens-Hardy, eds, *Norwich Consistory Court Depositions, 1499–1512 and 1518–1530*, Norfolk Record Society 10 (n.pl., 1938), no. 228; Henry A. Kelly, 'Inquisition, Public Fame and Confession: General Rules and English Practice', in Mary C. Flannery and Katie L. Walter, eds, *The Culture of Inquisition in Medieval England* (Cambridge, 2013), 8–29, at 15.
[142] Tyndale, *Obedience*, fol. 52ʳ⁻ᵛ.
[143] Thomas More, *The Debellacyon of Salem and Bizance* (London, 1533), sig. H4ʳ⁻ᵛ; BL, MS Lansdowne 639, fols 46ʳ, 56ʳ; HL, MS Ellesmere 2652, fol. 10ᵛ; MS Ellesmere 2655, fol. 16ᵛ; Bayne and Dunham, eds, *Select Cases in the Council*, 33.
[144] 25 Hen. VIII c.14; Stanford E. Lehmberg, *The Reformation Parliament, 1529–1536* (Cambridge, 1970), 186–7; Henry A. Kelly, 'Thomas More on Inquisitorial Due Process', *EHR* 123 (2008), 847–94, at 882–9.

one's wealth to be given under oath was introduced in the subsidy act of 1514, which John Hales drafted in the same year that he read at Gray's Inn.[145] The orchestration of oath-taking reached a new pitch in the general proscription of 1522.[146] Of this military and fiscal survey and similar expedients William Tyndale demanded, 'How many thousandes forsware them selfes?'[147] Tyndale was not complaining about the revenue lost through underassessment, but rather about the occasion given to so many people to commit perjury. In fact, this levy, when combined with a forced loan the following year, raised about £200,000. Presumably, sworn self-valuation worked because many, in order to avoid perjuring themselves, assessed their wealth accurately.[148] The survey involved a nationwide organization of commissioners, instructions on how oaths should be imposed and the tailoring of texts to different groups. Perhaps it became a model for the succession and supremacy oaths that the crown would demand in the next decade.[149] This resort to oaths to enforce the break with Rome was a significant, but logical, extension of early Tudor policy.

VII

There is thus an irony that as oaths became more important to public life after the break with Rome, so the circumference of perjury contracted. The revision of canon law drafted in the mid-1530s restated the traditional view and hence did not clarify the extent of the church's effective jurisdiction over perjury.[150] In 1541, Edward Hall (the chronicler) gave a reading at Gray's Inn in which he sought to integrate ecclesiastical law into contemporary common law. Hall's eighth lecture considered the church courts' claim to punish usury, perjury and defamation.[151] Each was a crime over which the church had exercised fuller jurisdiction in 1485 than it did by 1541 on

---

[145] 5 Hen. VIII c.17; Roger Schofield, *Taxation under the Early Tudors, 1485–1547* (Oxford, 2004), 19, 88, 90.

[146] J. J. Goring, 'The General Proscription of 1522', *EHR* 86 (1971), 681–705.

[147] Tyndale, *Obedience*, fol. 39ʳ; Tyndale, *Practyse*, sigs G3ᵛ–G4ʳ.

[148] As is suggested in a letter of 1528 from Archbishop Warham: Henry Ellis, ed., *Original Letters, illustrative of English History: Third Series*, 4 vols (London, 1846), 2: 31–2 (*L&P* 4/2: 4631).

[149] *L&P* 3/2: 2484–5; *L&P, Addenda*, 1/1: 410; Gray, *Oaths*, 51–115.

[150] Gerald Bray, ed., *Tudor Church Reform: The Henrician Canons of 1535 and the Reformatio legum ecclesiarum*, CERS 8 (Woodbridge, 2000), 24–5.

[151] McGlynn, ed., *Rights and Liberties*, xlv–xlix, 176–9.

account of inroads by secular law.[152] The lecture gave examples of broken oaths that were perjury in one law, in both or in neither. Hall seems to have been trying to assimilate the canon- and common-law definitions of perjury, the former relating to any legitimate oath and the latter to an oath sworn before a court. This endeavour may explain Hall's category of perjuries committed at common law, but not punishable by it. Although the text breaks off here, it does not look as though Hall envisaged the church courts stepping in under these circumstances. Hall's lecture thus shows the challenge of reflecting society's broad understanding of perjury within a narrower legal framework.

In retrospect, the church's quondam jurisdiction over breach of faith has seemed an unnatural intrusion into the secular sphere that would inevitably disappear. Objectively, ecclesiastical cognizance of spiritual actions, as oaths were, appeared perfectly fitting; the problem was that, taken to its logical conclusion in a society where oath-taking was so widely practised, this jurisdiction had encompassed too much. Perjury in early Tudor England thus provides a small, local manifestation of a vast, transhistorical issue: the appropriate manner through which the church (as institution, personnel and abstraction) should relate to the law, whether through independent codes and courts, through co-option into the activities of other legal systems or through spiritual guidance for participants in the legal process. Over the early Tudor period, the crown assumed greater responsibility for the supervision of justice within its domain. More concertedly than in the past, it overrode different legal systems and subjugated autonomous jurisdictions. Royal authority enabled greater coordination and orchestration between ecclesiastical and secular law, albeit not necessarily on the church's terms. Ideas derived from canon law influenced proceedings in the conciliar courts, where perjury was increasingly being prosecuted. Yet, in consequence, a concern with the spiritual condition of the individual receded, and perjury thus became more like other crimes in royal courts: an offence against God, the king and his subjects, rather more than against oneself. Early Tudor England hardly secularized perjury, but perhaps did begin to laicize the concept.

In a pattern observable with certain other offences, after a mid-century hiatus the common law expanded to fill the gap left by the curbing of ecclesiastical jurisdiction during the early Tudor period.

[152] Baker, *OHLE*, 6: 781–99, 832–5; Helmholz, *OHLE*, 1: 379–82, 593–6.

It did so in part by naturalizing aspects of canon and civil law. The statute of 1563 that extended the definition of perjury to include witnesses possibly drew upon the revision of canon law undertaken in the previous decade.[153] Had this revision been adopted and also implemented, ecclesiastical jurisdiction over perjury would once more have been considerable. Instead, it dwindled to perjury committed before church courts, over which the clergy were even denied exclusive cognizance.[154] While a staunch defender of the ecclesiastical system could insist that the broader jurisdiction was merely in abeyance, it never revived.[155] Other types of litigation drove the recovery of business in church courts.[156] In 1581, jurors convicted of perjury in Star Chamber were ordered to wear papers at the assizes and there listen to a sermon, so that 'by the preacher they mighte be towched in conscience'.[157] What endured was the church's extralegal role of exhortation and instruction, or perhaps we should rather say its capacity to appeal to the individual's internal forum. Thus our modern, attenuated definition of perjury, as an offence confined to the courts, may be traced back ultimately to early Tudor England.

[153] Bray, ed., *Tudor Church Reform*, 548–55; 5 Eliz. I c.9; Michael D. Gordon, 'The Perjury Statute of 1563: A Case History of Confusion', *Proceedings of the American Philosophical Society* 124 (1980), 438–54, at 448–52.
[154] Francis Clerke, *Praxis* (London, 1684), 178–9; Helmholz, ed., *Select Cases on Defamation*, 82; James Dyer, *Les Reports* (London, 1688), fol. 302ᵛ; BL, MS Lansdowne 639, fol. 75ʳ; Michael D. Gordon, 'The Invention of a Common Law Crime: Perjury and the Elizabethan Courts', *AJLH* 24 (1980), 145–70, at 158–60.
[155] Richard Cosin, *An Apologie for Sundrie Proceedings by Iurisdiction Ecclesiasticall* (London, 1593), pt 1, 47–52.
[156] R. B. Outhwaite, *The Rise and Fall of the English Ecclesiastical Courts, 1500–1860* (Cambridge, 2006), especially 15–22, 64–70.
[157] HL, MS Ellesmere 2768, fol. 46ʳ; Barbara J. Shapiro, 'Oaths, Credibility and the Legal Process in Early Modern England: Part Two', *Law and Humanities* 7 (2013), 19–54, at 39–48.

Conscience and the King's Household Clergy in the Early Tudor Court of Requests

Laura Flannigan*

Newnham College, Cambridge

The early Tudor Court of Requests was closely attached to the king's person and his duty to provide 'indifferent' justice. In practice, however, it was staffed by members of the attendant royal household and council. Utilizing the little-studied but extensive records of the court, this article traces the rising dominance of the dean of the Chapel Royal and the royal almoner as administrators and judges there from the 1490s to the 1520s. It examines the relationship between supposedly 'secular' and 'spiritual' activities within the central administration and between the formal and informal structures and ideologies of the church, the law and the royal household. It explores the politics of proximity and the ad hoc nature of early Tudor governance which made the conscience-based jurisdiction in Requests especially convenient to the king and desperate litigants alike. Overall the article argues that although the influence of clergymen in the court waned towards the end of the sixteenth century in favour of common-law judges, its enduring association with 'poor men's causes' and 'conscience' grew directly from these early clerical underpinnings.

In the late fifteenth and early sixteenth centuries, litigants without remedy at the rigid English common law could increasingly sue to the king's extraordinary justice. This justice was executed within an expanding range of distinct central tribunals, including the courts of Chancery and Star Chamber as well as the little-studied Court of Requests, which emerged as the judicial arm of the attendant royal council in the late fifteenth century. In Requests, petitioners from across England, Wales, Ireland, Calais and the Channel Islands presented cases ranging from breaches of faith and trust to accusations of armed riot and serious assault. Their bills of complaint appealed directly to the mercy, pity and charity of the king on the basis of their poverty and other disadvantages relative to powerful local

* Newnham College, Cambridge, CB3 9DF; E-mail: laura.flannigan17@gmail.com.

Studies in Church History 56 (2020), 210–226   © Ecclesiastical History Society 2020
doi: 10.1017/stc.2019.12

opponents. By the late sixteenth century, Requests had come to be known as 'the poore mannes Courte' and 'the courte of conscience'.[1]

Of all the discretionary justice courts of the early Tudor period, Requests was most closely associated with the king. Unlike the Westminster-based Chancery and Star Chamber, Requests was attendant on the royal person; its petitions were invariably addressed to the 'king our sovereign lord'; and its commissions might be authorized under the king's signet seal and sign manual. In this sense, Requests best fulfilled the ideal that the administration of 'indifferent' justice to all subjects was the 'chief charge' of the king himself, as Henry VII's minister Edmund Dudley expressed it in 1509.[2] A hands-on role for the king in judicial administration could never be expected to work in practice, however, 'since he is not able to do it by himself in all places'.[3] Dudley and many of his contemporaries felt a workable compromise to be the appointment of particularly 'well lernyd men' of 'good consciens' to 'pass without delay a just judgment on anyone requesting it'.[4] In Requests, the application of justice at the king's discretion was often delegated not to common lawyers or officers of state, as with the chancellor in Chancery and Star Chamber, but to certain clergymen employed within the royal household. Requests therefore serves as a valuable case study for the prominent role of churchmen in early Tudor centralized justice.

This article charts when and how these clergymen handled business in the early Court of Requests. It is based on a full survey of the 3,293 catalogued Henrician-era pleadings files and the six order and decree books surviving in the court's archives dating from the period between the earliest records in 1493 and 1535.[5] Although these records show that many churchmen, including bishops, abbots and priors, served as judges in Requests in the early Tudor period, this article focuses on the dean of the Chapel Royal and the royal almoner. From 1493 to the 1520s, the individuals holding these offices most consistently received, managed and determined cases

---

[1] As in the 'Description of the Cortes of Justice in England', written by the MP Alexander Fisher of Gray's Inn in 1576: Kew, TNA, SP12/110, fol. 44ʳ.
[2] Edmund Dudley, *Tree of Commonwealth*, ed. D. M. Brodie (Cambridge, 1948), 34.
[3] Stephen Baron, *De regimine principum (1509)*, transl. P. J. Mroczkowski (New York, 1990), 79.
[4] Dudley, *Tree of Commonwealth*, 34; Baron, *De regimine principum*, 79.
[5] TNA, Pleadings series, REQ2, bundles 1–13; Order Books series, REQ1/1–5, 104–5, plus fragments in REQ 3/22, 29, 30.

presented to Requests. Indeed, by the late 1510s they were the two primary judges in the court, virtually to the exclusion of all others.

This research contributes to scholarship over the last thirty years on the innovative discretionary justice courts of fifteenth- and sixteenth-century England.[6] Particularly influential is Gwilym Dodd's recent study of the role of late medieval 'bishop-councillors' in parliament, Chancery, and the king's council, and their blurring of the boundaries between activities typically seen (anachronistically) to pertain to either the church or the state.[7] Indeed, the involvement of churchmen was a 'vital prerequisite' for an emerging form of justice that technically represented the 'secular law' of central government but which operated on the basis of canon- and civil-law notions of reason and conscience, as Dodd argued. Tracing this trend towards the practical and theoretical influence of churchmen in discretionary justice into the sixteenth century, it is contended here that the dean and the almoner played a similarly central role in the Court of Requests. By the late 1510s they were integral to the ability of Requests to offer the conscience-based remedies requested by petitioners in cases which otherwise concerned temporal matters. Moreover, owing to their proximity to the king they were ideally placed to facilitate and embody his personal oversight of indifferent justice.

It has been argued that the early sixteenth century was a period of 'popularisation' and growth for both new and existing central courts under the prerogative of the strong early Tudor kings.[8] Focus on ecclesiastical personnel and their contributions to innovative, centralized forms of governance aids in de-laicizing traditional administrative histories of this period, beyond the prolonged concentration in the late twentieth century on its two most prominent ministerial figures, Thomas Cromwell and Thomas Wolsey.[9] The Court of

[6] Including John A. Guy, 'Wolsey, the Council, and the Council Courts', *EHR* 91 (1976), 481–505; Timothy S. Haskett, 'Conscience, Justice and Authority in the Late Medieval English Court of Chancery', in Anthony Musson, ed., *Expectations of the Law in the Middle Ages* (Woodbridge, 2001), 151–64.
[7] Gwilym Dodd, 'Reason, Conscience and Equity: Bishops as the King's Judges in Later Medieval England', *History* 99 (2014), 213–40, at 215.
[8] John A. Guy, *The Court of Star Chamber and its Records to the Reign of Elizabeth I* (London, 1985), 6; S. J. Gunn, *Early Tudor Government 1485–1558* (Basingstoke, 1995), 77.
[9] Most famously in G. R. Elton, *The Tudor Revolution in Government: Administrative Changes in the Reign of Henry VIII* (Cambridge, 1953); John Guy restored the balance in Wolsey's favour: 'The Privy Council: Revolution or Evolution?', in Christopher

Requests records make it possible to gain a fuller account of the men at the heart of a burgeoning central institution, and provide the means for looking beyond formalized structures to those more ad hoc patterns of judicial activity around the monarch. A thorough analysis of the records permits a fresh examination of the nature of the household clergy's role in the principle and practice of the court in its formative years.

As various historians of sixteenth-century England have acknowledged, the Requests records, from the bills of complaints to the final decrees, are kept in one relatively coherent archive and are undoubtedly valuable for early Tudor political and legal history.[10] Nevertheless, they have remained little studied since I. S. Leadam's Selden Society volume was published in 1898.[11] Notable exceptions include D. A. Knox's 1974 thesis on the Edwardian Requests, featuring a detailed examination of the court's 'bench', and Tim Stretton's extensive work on the experience of women suing at the Elizabethan Requests.[12] More recently, Hannes Kleineke has emphasized the origins of the court in the conciliar function for receiving 'Requests' under Richard III, although the relationship between the clerk appointed for the same in 1483 (the civil lawyer John Harrington) and the tribunal of judges represented by the surviving Court of Requests archive is yet to be elucidated.[13] After tracing the growing influence of the dean and the almoner through the pleadings and order books for the early Court of Requests, this article examines the significance of these offices to the administration of royal, conscience-based justice. It will be argued that these clergymen

Coleman and David Starkey, eds, *Revolution Reassessed: Revisions in the History of Tudor Government and Administration* (Oxford, 1986), 59–86.

[10] G. R. Elton, 'Why the History of the early Tudor Council remains unwritten', in idem, ed., *Studies in Tudor and Stuart Politics and Government: Papers and Reviews 1946–1972* (Cambridge, 1974), 308–38, at 328; John Baker, *OHLE, 6: 1483–1558* (Oxford, 2003), 203–4.

[11] I. S. Leadam, ed., *Select Cases in the Court of Requests, A.D. 1496–1569*, SelS 12 (London, 1898).

[12] D. A. Knox, 'The Court of Requests in the Reign of Edward VI 1547–1553' (PhD thesis, Cambridge University, 1974); Tim Stretton, *Women waging Law in Elizabethan England* (Cambridge, 1998).

[13] Hannes Kleineke, 'Richard III and the Origins of the Court of Requests', *The Ricardian* 11 (2007), 22–32.

played a key role in defining the jurisdiction and authority of Requests as it operated for the rest of the Tudor period and beyond.

There are three key pieces of evidence for the staffing of the Court of Requests found routinely within its archives, representing three distinct aspects of activity. The first comprises the lists of attendant judges that are noted most frequently in the earliest order and decree books, alongside entries recording the appearances of accused parties, interlocutory court orders and final decrees. Typically, the names of individuals with spiritual and ecclesiastical offices are listed on the left-hand side, separate from the holders of temporal offices, such as knights and lawyers, who appear in the right margin. On occasion, the lists are supplemented by the signatures of the same judges below the entries, apparently in authorization of the decisions made. The lists and the signatures together represent the actual presence of the judges, wherever the royal court might be situated, for hearings of evidence from the principal parties, as well as their contribution to the decision-making process which led to the court's decrees and awards.

Secondly, signatures on the surviving petitions processed by the court in this period show the more day-to-day work of individual judges outside formal hearings. Various accounts discovered in the Requests archive show that prospective petitioners approached the royal court in person to exhibit their written bills of complaint. A list of costs written up by Joan and Thomas Strachey in 1518 referred to the 'tyme as we were at London to compleyne', indicating that they may have attended Requests at Westminster.[14] However, from the early 1490s through to the 1530s petitioners also sought access to Requests as it moved around with the royal progress, especially where this was more convenient for them than a journey to London. In 1511, Roger Dyner presumably submitted his petition concerning the withholding of lands in Mountsorrel in Leicestershire while the royal entourage was nearby on progress, as a writ for commission was subsequently issued from 'or monastery besides oure town of Lestre'.[15] Later on during the same progress, Cecile Arden, a widow from Chester, 'sued by byll of peticion' to the king 'at [the] Castell of Nottyngham'.[16] The reverse side of petitions was usually signed by one of the Requests judges, endorsing the issuing of

---

[14] TNA, REQ2/13/100.
[15] TNA, REQ2/4/366.
[16] TNA, REQ2/12/198.

privy seal summonses or the committal of a case to local examiners. On occasions when the petition endorsements are ascribed a clear date, they do not usually align with the dates provided in the court's books for formal sittings. These signatures therefore probably reflect the more impromptu administrative capacity of the judges, who were conveniently present at the itinerant royal court each day, for receiving exhibited petitions and for providing immediate remedy in the form of sanctioned process.

Thirdly, some of the judges also acted as counter-signatories on writs for commission formally issued from the court under the signet seal. These writs, declaring themselves to be 'By the King', addressed commissioners directly and called upon them to fulfil the king's intention for 'Justice [to] be equaly ministred unto every of our sub-giettes'.[17] Here the judges appear to have acted in an administrative capacity alongside the king, who might lend either his own sign manual or, in the case of Henry VIII after 1510, a stamped signature to the top of the document. The locations from which these writs were issued include the palaces of Westminster, Greenwich and Richmond, as well as the royal manor of Woodstock and more private houses such as Langley, set within acres of royal forest.[18] Such writs and their counter-signatures therefore indicate not only the judges' habitual proximity to the king as he progressed around the country, but also their direct facilitation of the administration of the king's outwardly personal justice.

Examining the attendance lists, petition endorsements and writ counter-signatures together reveals three distinct but concentric circles of activity in Requests: the first and largest contained those sitting at arranged hearings to judge cases; second represented those receiving and handling petitions in a more ad hoc fashion; and the third and smallest, most private circle included those facilitating the process by which the king personally authorized the court's writs. If the personnel in each of these circles are examined for years in which all three evidence types are extant, then the changing nature of the Requests judiciary during the early sixteenth century in favour of the household clergy can be observed.

---

[17] TNA, REQ2/1/1 and countless other examples throughout REQ2 and REQ3.
[18] Simon Thurley, *Houses of Power: The Palaces that shaped the Tudor World* (London, 2017), 105, 310–11.

In the years 1496–7 the Requests order book yields seventeen attendance lists, featuring fifteen different named judges.[19] The largest group of sitting judges in this period included six men, observed on just one occasion in March 1496. More commonly three judges sat together, and throughout April and May 1496 Thomas Savage signed several entries off alone. Savage, initially as bishop of Rochester and subsequently as bishop of London, was the most regular attender, appearing in thirteen lists.[20] He seems to have been the presiding judge in the court from early 1495, probably in connection with his capacity as 'president of the [king's] council'.[21] Thomas Jan, dean of the Chapel Royal, had been a judge since late 1493, and appeared in eleven lists during these years. Other clergymen, such as Robert Sherborne, archdeacon of Huntingdon and Buckingham and secretary to Henry VII, appeared only once or twice during the same period.

Like the main royal council of which it was a committee, the Court of Requests of the 1490s was characterized by a fluid composition and a balance of professions amongst the judges.[22] The fifteen listed individuals include members of the household clergy, such as the dean and the almoner; high-ranking ecclesiastical figures, such as the bishops of London and Rochester and the prior of St John of Jerusalem; men with temporal offices, including the household knight Charles Somerset (identified usually as *miles*); and peers related to the royal family, such as Viscount Welles and the earl of Derby, Thomas Stanley. They also include three doctors of civil law, Robert Middleton, Edmund Martyn and Richard Hatton; both Martyn and Hatton served as masters in chancery, but additionally all three each held various vicarages, rectories, canonries and

---

[19] TNA, REQ1/1, fols 3ʳ, 21ʳ, 23ʳ, 23ᵛ, 30ᵛ, 156ᵛ, 160ᵛ, 165ʳ, 165ᵛ, 166ʳ, 166ᵛ, 167ʳ, 168ᵛ, 171ᵛ, 178ʳ. The figures, in order of frequency of appearance, are Thomas Savage, Thomas Jan, Dr Robert Middleton, John Viscount Welles, Sir John Digby, William Greville, Dr Edmund Martyn, Charles Somerset, Richard Fitzjames, Robert Rydon, Robert Sherborne, the earl of Derby, the prior of St Johns, Richard Mayhew and Dr Richard Hatton; for their biographies, see Leadam, ed., *Select Cases*, cx–cxiv.

[20] Savage was first recorded as bishop of London in the court records in April 1497, following his appointment to that office late in 1496: TNA, REQ1/1, fol. 23ʳ. In 1501 he was appointed archbishop of York. At that point his engagement in Requests appears to have ceased, his last attendance being recorded in March 1501: REQ1/2, fol. 128ᵛ.

[21] A title ascribed to him in the Requests books in December 1497: TNA, REQ1/1, fol. 45ᵛ; S. B. Chrimes, *Henry VII* (London, 1972), 103.

[22] Ibid. 98–103.

deanships across the country and Hatton was also one of the king's chaplains.[23] Some common-law influence is also evident from the inclusion on at least two occasions of William Greville of the Inner Temple, the recorder of Bristol who would become a serjeant-at-law in 1503.[24]

Overall, then, the Requests judges of the mid-1490s were men with diverse backgrounds, positions and expertise, united by their service to the king. Yet apart from Savage, only the dean, Jan, additionally undertook the more administrative responsibility of receiving petitions and providing immediate direction for litigants.[25] Furthermore, the only surviving commission writ from around this time was signed by Henry VII and counter-signed by Jan, at Woodstock.[26] As well as helping to underpin the court's conscience-based judgments in these early years, the household clergy were conveniently placed to ensure that the court's process moved smoothly day by day.

Collating the same information for the years 1520–1 gives a different picture. Attendance registers were, by that time, written into the order books very infrequently, but where they do exist it can be seen that the circle of judges hearing Requests cases comprised a maximum of three men. In all instances this included the dean of the Chapel Royal (John Clerk) and the almoner (with John Stokesley replacing Richard Rawlins in that role some time in 1521) with one additional person.[27] The involvement of an extra sitting judge was occasional and irregular. John Gilbert (or 'Gylberd', referred to only as an *armiger*) and Roger Lupton, the provost of Eton, appear in just one attendance list each.[28] In the absence of more frequent lists, other evidence beyond the Requests books corroborates the dominance (and perhaps the isolation) of the dean and almoner as judges by the late 1510s. From at least 1504, pleas at King's Bench and Common Pleas described hearings before the dean and then, from 1510, before the

---

[23] A. B. Emden, ed., *A Biographical Register of the University of Cambridge to 1500* (Cambridge, 1963), 293, 1277; Leadam, ed., *Select Cases*, cx, cxiii.

[24] John Baker, *The Men of Court 1440 to 1550: A Prosopography of the Inns of Court and Chancery and the Courts of Law*, SelS supplementary series 18 (London, 2012), 783.

[25] TNA, REQ2/2/90; REQ2/10/8; REQ2/5/319; Richard Mayhew, the almoner, also signed a petition which might be dated to this period: REQ2/4/345.

[26] TNA, REQ2/2/145.

[27] TNA, REQ1/4, fol. 3^r; REQ1/105, fol. 1^v.

[28] TNA, REQ1/105, fol. 1^v.

dean and almoner together.[29] By the mid-1510s, petitioners to Requests referred to the dean as the 'Presydent of the Kyngs Court of Requests', and might ask for hearings before him specifically.[30] The earlier fluidity of the Requests tribunal had given way to the more routinized practice of retaining just two specific officers to pass judgment, either alone or as a pair. Furthermore, in 1520–1 only the dean of the Chapel Royal and the almoner endorsed petitions and counter-signed commission writs. The extant records suggest that no-one else was involved in overseeing the court's process in this period, so that what had earlier been relatively distinct circles of activity had become almost indistinct from one another.

Conversely, as the dean and the almoner came to the fore, the formal input of bishops, abbots and priors, common lawyers, knights and peers of the realm to the court's business appears to have declined significantly. This was notwithstanding the continuing role of the bishops of Durham, Winchester, Norwich and Hereford alongside the justices of the common-law benches, knights and noblemen, in the judicial business of the main royal council throughout the 1510s.[31] Temporary committees founded to expedite cases from Star Chamber in 1518, 1519 and 1520 also featured prominent ecclesiastical councillors as their leading members, including the 'Lorde of Westminster', 'Deane of Paules', and 'Lorde of Sainte Johnes'.[32] Senior churchmen and other councillors did not withdraw from conciliar justice entirely at this time, then, but only from Requests. This perhaps reflects the increasing separation of Requests from the main royal council during the institutional reforms at Westminster under Wolsey and the growing volume of business in the larger conciliar courts based there, where such leading ecclesiastical figures were routinely employed. By 1520–1, these developments had left the dean and the almoner almost exclusively responsible for the management and provision of judgments in Requests. This reduction in the number of active judges was despite the fact that the volume

---

[29] See Baker's summary of these cases: John Baker, *The Reinvention of Magna Carta 1216–1616* (Cambridge, 2017), 459–60.

[30] TNA, REQ2/6/207; REQ2/1/1; REQ2/2/74; REQ2/3/126, 183; REQ2/4/160; REQ2/6/182; REQ2/12/77.

[31] The business of the main council was distinct from the Requests tribunal in that it handled disputes between peers of the realm and those matters touching the king directly, such as instances of seditious speech: San Marino, CA, HL, MS Ellesmere 2655, fols 1ʳ–18ᵛ.

[32] TNA, SP1/19, fol. 142ʳ; HL, MS Ellesmere 2655, fols 12ʳ, 16ʳ.

of business coming before Requests was also increasing, with the number of cases heard there in 1520–1 more than double that for 1496–7.[33]

The association between Requests and these two offices and their incumbents by the late 1510s has not gone entirely unnoticed, but the reasons for, and implications of, their dominance (or isolation) there are yet to be fully explained.[34] From the court's earliest surviving records in 1493 to the 1530s, seven successive deans of the Chapel Royal and six successive almoners acted in Requests. Of the deans, the majority were doctors in canon law or civil law (or both), although Geoffrey Symeon (1501–8) and William Atwater (1508–14) were theologians. In comparison, the almoners were all doctors of theology, with the single exception of Wolsey (1509–14), for whom there is no evidence of a doctorate. Few of these deans or almoners had any previous experience of legal practice, and none possessed any formal common-law qualifications that might fill the gap left by the absence of routine common-law input in the court by the mid-1510s. They may well have gained experience of administering that law through suits conducted in the context of their private or official business, however, and it is probable that some had engaged in matters of common law as royal councillors. For example, while operating as the presiding figure in Requests, Dean Veisy also led a series of enclosure commissions in various counties across England.[35]

Additionally, most of the deans and almoners were ordained and had risen to prominence in the king's inner circle as royal confessors or chaplains. As part of his office, the dean had oversight of all the clergy who made up the peripatetic Chapel Royal, responsible for supporting the king's spiritual needs, and would himself frequently have conducted divine service and administered the sacraments to the king and queen.[36] The almoner was frequently depicted in accounts of the royal household and chronicles of this period at the

---

[33] TNA, REQ1/1 gives 244 entries for 1496–7, whilst REQ1/104, 105, and the fragments in REQ3/22, 29 and 30 together give 511 entries for 1520–1.

[34] Guy, 'Wolsey', 495–6.

[35] I. S. Leadam, ed., *The Domesday of Inclosures 1517–1518, being the extant Returns to Chancery for Berks, Bucks, Cheshire, Essex, Leicestershire, Lincolnshire, Northants, Oxon, Warwickshire by the Commissioners of Inclosures in 1517 and for Bedfordshire in 1518*, 2 vols (London, 1897), 1: 81, 83–6.

[36] David Baldwin, *The Chapel Royal: Ancient and Modern* (London, 1990), 231.

Laura Flannigan

king's right-hand side, proffering advice and wisdom while also being central to courtly processions and rituals, including the distribution of royal alms.[37] Both offices would therefore have required attendance upon the king and his court, and the dean at least was often also sworn in as a member of the main royal council.

Yet all the known occupants of both these posts in the early Tudor period simultaneously held various non-resident ecclesiastical posts, from vicarages and rectories to archdeaconries, across the country. As dean, Symeon was very active in handling Requests petitions in the later years of Henry VII's reign, whilst also serving as dean of Chichester from 1504 and Lincoln from 1506. Closer to the royal court, the deans of the Chapel Royal were often also canons and deans at St George's Chapel at Windsor or St Stephen's Chapel at Westminster. All these more minor ecclesiastical positions, as well as the deanship or almonership, would have been surrendered on appointment as a bishop. This was a career path followed by almost all the deans and almoners active in this period, whether immediately, as in the case of Wolsey (who moved from being almoner to being bishop of Lincoln and then archbishop of York, all in 1514), or sometime later in their careers (as was the case for almoner Stokesley, who was appointed bishop of London in 1530, seven years after leaving the almonership, during which time he served as archdeacon of Dorset).

With a stint judging the interpersonal disputes of supplicants to the king as a stepping-stone in an otherwise largely ecclesiastical career, it is tempting to perceive these men merely as 'state functionaries' seeking preferment through service to the crown.[38] Yet it was not simply that the dean and the almoner happened incidentally to take upon themselves seemingly 'secular' state duties at the royal court. Their involvement in Requests had come by the 1510s to be part and parcel of their numerous duties within the king's household clergy. The work associated with Requests – hearing cases, directing petitions and signing writs – stayed with these offices, and did not

[37] C. M. Woolgar, *The Great Household in Late Medieval England* (New Haven, CT, 1999), 163; James Gairdner, ed., *Letters and Papers illustrative of the Reigns of Richard III and Henry VII* (London, 1861), 392; Edward Hall, *Hall's Chronicle; containing the History of England during the Reign of Henry the Fourth and the succeeding Monarchs, to the End of the Reign of Henry the Eighth* (London, 1809), 540, 565, 674, 730.
[38] A viewpoint discussed, and dismissed, by Dodd: 'Reason, Conscience, and Equity', 222.

move with their incumbents. So, where Richard Halswell's suit to the court in 1519 was examined before 'the reverent fader yn god Doctor John Veyse … then Dene of yor Chapell', once Veisy had been created bishop, 'Mr Doctor Clerk [was] ordeyned by yor grace Deane of yor Chapell', and he took over the management of the case.[39] The duties in Requests belonged to the office, a reversal of the situation in the 1490s, when individuals such as Thomas Savage (as bishop of Rochester and bishop of London) might attend Requests hearings in numerous successive roles. Just as Dodd argued of the fifteenth-century clerical chancellors (who, he suggested, officialized the earlier ad hoc engagement of clerics in conciliar tribunals and royal commissions) the dean and almoner came routinely to personify the 'indivisibility of church and state' through the 'ideological bridge' of equitable discretionary justice, despite their relatively junior place in the ecclesiastical hierarchy.[40]

In the first instance, the growing connection between the offices of dean and almoner and Requests from 1493 to the 1520s evolved as a result of the continuing day-to-day attendance of both dean and almoner at court. Here, in the public spaces of the royal residences and at moments of religious ritual, they might be on hand to receive and direct petitions and available to sit with other judges to hear cases. Additionally, owing to their spiritual counselling of the king, these men also had the most direct access to the monarch's person and thus to those faculties for royal mercy and pity that petitioners explicitly sought. These fell under the broader conceptual aegis of conscience, which had several potential facets when expressed as a legal principle in Requests. It was occasionally evoked in reference to the conscience of the defendant and the need to save them from dishonesty or sin, a concept found also in Chancery. Far more often, however, conscience in Requests meant the personal conscience of the king himself, and the more universal notions of fairness and reason that he was expected to exemplify and inculcate in his justice system. The offices of the dean and the almoner lay at the intersection between the formal structures of the royal household and the ecclesiastical hierarchy, within which the majority of the holders of these offices quickly rose, and the more informal arrangements resulting from the politics of proximity.

---

[39] TNA, REQ2/3/134.
[40] Dodd, 'Reason, Conscience, and Equity', 226–39.

Seeing the dean and the almoner as thus integral to the very nature of Requests business, how did they apply these notions of conscience? The early Requests dealt with a wide range of case types, testing the reason and legal expertise of its judges, including typically common-law cases of debt and title to land as well as more unusual matters, such as an alleged riot against a Derbyshire rent collector in 1496, the potentially deliberate fire at a London inn in 1513, and the attempt to force William Cartwright's servant 'to have eten all yor seid prevy seal with the wex' in 1517.[41] Yet, regardless of specific case type, the court was generally appealed to when litigants had been otherwise prevented from accessing the common law, due as much to the petitioner allegedly being 'not of substance' or a general fear of powerful opponents as to issues relating to technical jurisdictional boundaries between equity or conscience and civil or common law.

Although Requests cases concerned purely temporal matters of real property and money rather than issues of sin or personal impropriety typical of the ecclesiastical courts, petitioners nevertheless framed their suits in moralistic terms. The unconscionable behaviour of accused parties was described as an affront to 'right and good con-science' and a 'perilous example' to others. It was in this sense that Requests was both a court for 'poor men's causes' and a court of conscience and reason. The king's duty to provide indifferent justice for all, combined with the acknowledged limitations of the common-law courts and the relative flexibility of the extraordinary equitable jurisdictions in both process and remedy, meant that Requests could be a particularly productive avenue for vulnerable litigants. The judgments provided at the discretion of the dean and the almo-ner and recorded in the order books weighed up the evidence and individual circumstances of both parties and compelled them to reach a friendly reconciliation. This was typically to be achieved through the restoration of property or money to the petitioner and the threat of a fine for obstinate defendants. Like the fifteenth-century 'bishop-councillors' of the council and Chancery, the judges in Requests benefited from the favour of the king and the prestige of exercising justice at his discretion, and from the rewards that fol-lowed. Yet in the course of their work in the court, conducted along-side their clerical duties within the royal household, they were also

[41] TNA, REQ2/2/81, 192; REQ2/4/337.

able to cultivate their spiritual vocation. The creative jurisdiction of Requests, unbound by the customs, maxims and statutes of English law, allowed them to put their administrative experience and learning in natural law to use in the care of vulnerable litigants.[42]

Perhaps the firmest evidence of the discretion of the dean and the almoner at work within the Requests process is to be found in the provisions for the admission of destitute litigants to the court *in forma pauperis*. A statute of 1495 had stipulated that 'poor' litigants might have their fees for counsel and process entirely waived in the king's 'Courtes of Recorde', although this was a category probably not including Requests, as equity courts were typically held to operate beyond the law of the land and without setting legal precedent.[43] Such provisions had a much longer heritage in Roman civil law and canon law and had been offered in English church courts throughout the late medieval period, to the extent that the church was perceived to specialize in poor people's litigation.[44] The survey of the Henrician Requests pleadings archive has uncovered only twenty-eight visible admissions *in forma pauperis*. Twenty-three date to between 1517 and 1523, roughly coinciding with the period in which the dean and the almoner were most predominant; indeed, most were signed off by the Deans Veisy (trained in the civil law) and Clerk (a canonist), or the Almoner Stokesley (a doctor of divinity).[45] It might be speculated that the dominance of these clergymen and the relative absence of common-law input allowed canon- and civil-law decretals concerning the care of destitute litigants to come to the fore in the court's practice.[46]

---

[42] Dodd, 'Reason, Conscience, and Equity', 221–3, 225–6.

[43] 'An Acte to admytt such persons as are poore to sue in forma pauperis' (1495), 11 Hen. VII c.12; it is probable that several bishops helped formulate this statute: C. G. Bayne and William Huse Dunham, *Select Cases in the Council of Henry VII*, SelS 75 (London, 1958), 28.

[44] R. H. Helmholz, *Canon Law and the Law of England* (London, 1987), 47; James A. Brundage, 'Legal Aid for the Poor and the Professionalization of Law in the Middle Ages', *JLH* 9 (1988), 169–79, at 171.

[45] TNA, REQ2/1/2; REQ2/2/54, 66; REQ2/3/140, 165; REQ2/4/50, 52; REQ2/5/58, 323; REQ2/6/34; REQ2/7/40, 122, 127, 130; REQ2/8/339; REQ2/12/126, 155, 159; REQ3/6 Tolby v Knighte; REQ3/9 Cause v Abbot of Furness; REQ3/10 Pante v Knight, Symmes v Bekford.

[46] There are just 'two dozen' identified in Chancery for 1515–29: Franz Metzger, 'The Last Phase of the Medieval Chancery', in Alan Harding, ed., *Law-Making and Law-Makers in British History: Papers presented to the Edinburgh Legal History Conference, 1977* (London, 1980), 79–89, at 82; and only two admissions in Star Chamber for the

Otherwise, the influence of the dean and the almoner was most strongly felt in the continuing involvement of the king himself in Requests throughout the 1510s. Their spiritual vocation, understanding of theology and canon law and proximity to the king's person meant that they were best placed to interpret his conscience in practice. Their obtaining of the signatures of both Henry VII and Henry VIII successively on the writs for commission is especially indicative of the notion of royal care for justice put into action through the encouragement of his continually attendant spiritual counsellors. That this practice reached a peak in the early years of Henry VIII's reign and that no such role for the king is observable in the other conciliar courts would appear to confirm that it was the dean and the almoner specifically who helped to foster the perception of Requests as a court overseen by the 'king our soverain lorde' directly. This principle of personal royal involvement in Requests remained enshrined in its petitioning protocol, its position in the household and the authorization of its process under the royal sign manual throughout the late fifteenth and early sixteenth centuries, even when the hands-on Henry VII was succeeded in 1509 by a young king who admitted to finding all writing 'tedius and paynefull'.[47]

Thereafter, although Requests would continue to be seen as the monarch's own court through to its demise in 1643, from the mid-1520s onwards it settled increasingly at Westminster, severing its physical connection with the king. It also experienced a period of general decline in its business, and in the presence of the dean and the almoner as its judges. Richard Sampson and Edward Lee, the dean and the almoner respectively from c.1523, were relatively inactive in Requests in comparison to some of their predecessors, though this was probably a result of their being on diplomatic embassies rather than a deliberate effort to reallocate Requests business to non-ecclesiastical figures. Indeed, in January 1529, a list of 'Counsaillours as be appointed ... in the kynges Courte of Requestes' entered into the order book (on an otherwise blank page, distinct from any recorded court business) nominated the 'dean of the kinges chapel', the bishops of Lincoln and of

---

same period: Guy, *Court of Star Chamber*, 62; one better known example of such decretals is William Lyndwood, *Provinciale seu constitutions Angliae* (Oxford, 1679), 68c.
[47] *L&P* 3: 1.

St Asaph, the abbot of Westminster, the prior of St John's and the vicar of Croydon, as well as various members of the royal household and council and the common lawyers Thomas Nevill and William Sulyard.[48]

Amongst these names, at the bottom of the list, was Christopher 'St Jermyne', the author of the legal treatise *Doctor and Student* (1528), which examined the place of conscience as a juridical principle alongside the maxims, customs and statutes of English common law.[49] St German's inclusion despite his advanced age (in 1529 he was nearly seventy) and the fact that he had not practised law since 1511 indicates that the list probably did not truly reflect the present judges in Requests in the same way that the 1490s lists and accompanying signatures generally did.

Nevertheless, a strong clerical presence in the Requests judiciary was sustained throughout the reign of Edward VI, with Thomas Thirlby (dean of the Chapel Royal and later bishop of Westminster, Norwich and Ely) particularly active in endorsing petitions.[50] Requests would never again see the same domination of its business by the royal household clergy specifically, however. By the Elizabethan period it was staffed by lay masters of Requests, who were invariably formally appointed officials and politicians trained at the common-law inns of court.

In contrast, as this article has shown, the late fifteenth-century Court of Requests had reflected the trend, identified by Dodd, for the increasing centrality of 'bishop-councillors' to the enactment of discretionary justice. Later, in the distinctive context of the early sixteenth-century attendant Court of Requests, this form of discretionary justice came to be dominated by the lesser ecclesiastics of the household clergy, who in turn became integral to the conscience-based remedies offered there. The engagement of the dean of the Chapel Royal and the almoner in Requests was a result in the first instance of the need to have some practical and convenient means to serve petitioners arriving at the royal court. Indeed, facilitating petitioners' claims to conscience in Requests would, for the men holding these offices, have aligned with their duties in almsgiving and

---

[48] TNA, REQ1/5, fol. 43[v].

[49] Christopher St German, *Doctor and Student*, ed. T. F. T. Plucknett and J. L. Barton, SelS 91 (London, 1974).

[50] Knox, 'Court of Requests', 70–3.

leading divine service. As such, there was no true divide between the judges' spiritual and secular duties, or between those they owed to the church and to the state. In Requests, more than in any other early Tudor court, the care for the king's soul and his delegated duties as justice-giver converged.

As the earlier ad hoc administrative fluidity of Requests evolved into settled formality, and as jurisdictional boundaries became increasingly blurred, the sway held by these clergymen over its management was increasingly controversial and their presence undoubtedly declined. Yet in 1580 the politician and antiquarian William Lambard still observed that 'within these 40 yeares' the Court of Requests had predominantly served 'very poore men, not able to sue at the Common Law', and its association with 'conscionable Cases' presented through supplication to the monarch's mercy was sustained into the following century.[51] The principles and processes inherent in the Court of Requests were thus permanently shaped by the early Tudor clergymen who had once been on hand to administer and determine causes there.

---

[51] William Lambarde, *Archeion or, a Discourse upon the High Courts of Justice in England*, ed. Charles H. McIlwain and Paul L. Ward (Cambridge, 1957), 118; Thomas Blount, *Nomo-Lexikon, a Law-Dictionary, interpreting such Difficult and Obscure Words and Terms, as are found either in our Common or Statute, Ancient or Modern Lawes* ([London], 1670), *s.v.* 'Court of Requests'.

Restoration of Deprived Clergy during the 1559 Royal Visitation of the Eastern Dioceses

Ralph Houlbrooke*

University of Reading

It is well known that many of the English clergy took advantage of the statutory authorization of clerical marriage under Edward VI, but then suffered deprivation when that authorization was rescinded in Mary's reign. Less familiar are the proceedings that enabled incumbents who had lost their livings as a penalty for marriage to recover them after Elizabeth I's accession. This article focuses on a neglected source, an act book kept during the royal visitation of the eastern dioceses (London, Norwich and Ely) in 1559. It seems likely that this document records a large majority of the suits undertaken by deprived married clergy for the recovery of their livings in those dioceses. Most claimants were successful, but some suits failed, for a variety of reasons. Other sources, and the work of previous scholars in the field, shed some light on the recovery of their livings by men who do not appear in the act book. Probably rather more than a quarter of the men deprived for marriage under Mary in these dioceses recovered their livings in or after 1559. Many others had died or for various reasons did not seek restoration to the benefices of which they had been deprived.

The advent of clerical marriage during the English Reformation, which ultimately transformed the social position of the clergy, was at first a highly controversial issue.[1] After it had been embraced by many clergy in the second half of Edward VI's reign, its eradication became a high priority for Mary's Counter-Reformation. The Elizabethan settlement in turn enabled clergy deprived on account of their marriages under Mary to recover their former livings. As we shall see, the legal bases of both the Marian deprivations and

* Department of History, School of Humanities, University of Reading, Whiteknights, Reading, RG6 6AH. E-mail: r.a.houlbrooke@reading.ac.uk.
I should like to thank Felicity Heal, Peter Marshall and the anonymous peer reviewers for their comments on earlier drafts of this article.
[1] The most recent study is Helen L. Parish, *Clerical Marriage and the English Reformation: Precedent, Policy and Practice* (Aldershot, 2000).

Studies in Church History 56 (2020), 227–245 © Ecclesiastical History Society 2020
doi: 10.1017/stc.2019.13

the Elizabethan restorations were contested. The Marian proceedings are better documented than the Elizabethan restorations, and have also received more attention from historians. It has long been clear that under Mary many more men lost their livings because of marriage than did so on account of their religious nonconformity: the proportion was between a quarter and a third of all incumbents in those parts of the country where clerical marriage had been most widespread. The impact of this disruptive change was, however, offset by the fact that many of these men agreed to be separated from their wives and were placed in new livings.[2]

Deprivations of clergy for religious nonconformity have bulked larger in accounts of the Elizabethan settlement than the restoration of married men removed from their livings under Mary. Until recently, most historians were inclined to base their approximate estimates of the number of deprivations for nonconformity on the work of Henry Gee, published in 1898. He concluded that not many more than two hundred were deprived for non-compliance during the years 1558–64. Between 1564 and 1570 (he believed) 'nonconformity appeared to be due to Puritan rather than to Roman sympathies'.[3] Some Roman Catholic historians questioned Gee's estimates. H. N. Birt's history of the Elizabethan settlement, published in 1907, includes his finding that seven hundred parochial incumbents were deprived before 1565, but in the absence of detailed supporting evidence, this figure failed to gain widespread acceptance.[4] Many writers of subsequent general accounts have cautiously given rather higher figures than Gee's, but in somewhat vague terms, or for a different time span.[5] Peter Marshall and John Morgan have

---

[2] Hilda E. P. Grieve, 'The Deprived Married Clergy in Essex, 1553–1561', *TRHS* 4th series 22 (1940), 141–69; Geoffrey Baskerville, 'Married Clergy and Pensioned Religious in Norwich Diocese, 1555', *EHR* 48 (1933), 43–64; E. L. C. Mullins, 'The Effects of the Marian and Elizabethan Religious Settlements upon the Clergy of London, 1553–1564' (MA thesis, London University, 1948), 122.

[3] Henry Gee, *The Elizabethan Clergy and the Settlement of Religion 1558–1564* (Oxford, 1898), viii, 251.

[4] Henry N. Birt, *The Elizabethan Settlement of Religion: A Study of Contemporary Documents* (London, 1907), 197.

[5] For an extensive list of references, see Peter Marshall and John Morgan, 'Clerical Conformity and the Elizabethan Settlement revisited', *HistJ* 59 (2016), 1–22, at 2 nn. 5–8. The works there cited include G. R. Elton, *England under the Tudors*, 3rd edn (London, 1991), 276 ('240–300 beneficed clergy … in the years 1560–6'); Christopher Haigh, *English Reformations: Religion, Politics, and Society under the Tudors*

recently challenged Gee's estimates more thoroughly. They suggest that nearly 560 conservative clergy probably lost their parish livings as a result of the Elizabethan settlement in the province of Canterbury alone.[6]

The extent to which the restoration of clergy deprived for marriage contributed to overall changes in clerical ranks after Elizabeth's accession has been largely ignored in general discussions of the effects of the settlement. This article seeks to remedy that neglect. It focuses on the Elizabethan restorations in the English dioceses where the adoption of clerical marriage had been most widespread under Edward VI. It explores the process of recovery through the prism of a neglected source: the act book of the royal visitation of the eastern dioceses in 1559. It examines the legal basis of the restorations and the operation of judicial procedures before presenting an approximate estimate of the number of clergy of these dioceses who took advantage of the opportunity presented in 1559. As will be seen, a relatively small proportion of those deprived for marriage sought restoration in and after 1559. Reasons for this outcome will be suggested. The overall numbers were nevertheless quite large. This article does not attempt to trace the subsequent careers of those displaced during the process of restoration. It will, however, emphasize the importance of distinguishing between them and those men deprived of their livings on religious grounds.

In 1559, Queen Elizabeth's first parliament restored the royal supremacy over the church in England together with Protestant worship, set out in a revised version of the Edwardian Prayer Book of 1552. The queen appointed commissioners to enforce the new religious settlement throughout England and Wales. Six sets of commissioners were each entrusted with the visitation of a group of dioceses and the execution of all aspects of ecclesiastical jurisdiction within them. Their responsibilities, specified in letters patent of 24 June, included enquiry into the state of churches and the behaviour of clergy and people; the punishment of criminous clergy and those who refused to subscribe the received religion; the exercise of probate

---

(Oxford, 1993), 244 ('probably about 300 lost their benefices in the first two years of the reign'); Felicity Heal, *Reformation in Britain and Ireland*, OHCC (Oxford, 2003), 211 ('after 1559 ... all but between 200 and 400 of the beneficed men remained in place').
[6] Marshall and Morgan, 'Clerical Conformity', 10.

jurisdiction; the issue of injunctions; institution and induction to vacant livings; and restoration in cases of unlawful deprivation.[7] The visitors travelled through each diocese in their circuits, stopping at cathedrals and several major parish churches. At each centre the churchwardens made their presentments, and the clergy were required to subscribe a declaration acknowledging the restoration of the royal supremacy and the doctrinal validity of the Book of Common Prayer and royal injunctions. The commissioners dealt with testamentary business and cases between parties as the visitation proceeded.

This article focuses on cases concerning the restoration of deprived clergy heard by the visitors of the eastern dioceses of London, Norwich and Ely. Most of the commissioners for the visitation were peers or knights, but nearly all the work fell on the shoulders of three men: Robert Horne, a Marian exile, who was to be nominated bishop of Winchester in 1560; Thomas Huyck, LL D, future chancellor of the diocese of London (1561–74) and John Salvyn, a common lawyer.[8] Their first recorded session took place in the London consistory court at St Paul's Cathedral on 9 August. They then sat at various churches in London before setting out on or about 27 August on their journey round the three dioceses. Between 12 October and early December they once again sat at St Paul's.[9]

The six teams of visitors kept no uniform corpus of documents. A variety of partial records survives, including act books for the northern province and the eastern dioceses. The extant act book for the eastern dioceses (TNA, PROB 34/1) is a very different record from the neatly written and well-organized act book of the

---

[7] Only the letters patent for the northern province survive. The instructions in all six commissions were almost certainly identical. The universities and Eton College were visited separately. See Gee, *Elizabethan Clergy*, 89–93, 130–6; C. G. Bayne, 'The Visitation of the Province of Canterbury, 1559', *EHR* 28 (1913), 636–77, at 645–6.

[8] Gee, *Elizabethan Clergy*, 94–5; R. Houlbrooke, 'Horne, Robert (1513x15–1579)', *ODNB*, 3 January 2008, online at: <https://www.oxforddnb.com/view/10.1093/ref:odnb/9780198614128.001.0001/odnb-9780198614128-e-13792>, accessed 3 August 2019; Joseph Foster, ed., *Alumni Oxonienses 1500–1714*, 4 vols (Oxford, 1891–2), 2: 780. Huyck had graduated DCL at Oxford in 1554, and had probably not been a Genevan exile: *pace* Patrick Collinson, *Archbishop Grindal 1519–1583: The Struggle for a Reformed Church* (London, 1979), 101.

[9] Gee, *Elizabethan Clergy*, 95–7; Kew, TNA, PROB 34/1, fols 1r, 61r–v, 121r, 160r, 163r (isolated act of 19 January 1559/60).

northern visitation.[10] Suits by clergy deprived of their livings under Mary are the largest and best recorded category of business in PROB 34/1. The heading on the first folio refers particularly to inter-party cases of restitution of ecclesiastical benefices.[11] These cases are the subject of this article. No provision was made for the recovery of their places by the considerable number of stipendiary clergy dismissed from their cures because of their marriages.[12] The book also contains scattered entries relating to several miscellaneous ex officio matters. Some of these were connected with the enforcement of the settlement, such as measures taken to deal with the concealment of images, orders to produce inventories of church goods, and action taken against a few clergy who were reluctant to conform. Others concerned breaches of matrimonial law or clerical misbehaviour.[13] The visitors also heard many matrimonial and testamentary suits. This volume is clearly not a complete record of the visitors' proceedings. John Strype drew on a since lost record of the commissioners' enforcement of the settlement at St Paul's Cathedral.[14] There is a separate will register (PROB 34/2/1), and the surviving subscriptions of the clergy of these and some other southern dioceses are kept at Lambeth Palace.[15]

The first scholar to use PROB 34/1 to study the effects of the Elizabethan settlement appears to have been Edward Mullins, in his MA thesis of 1948 on the London clergy.[16] Mullins identified several London incumbents deprived under Mary who were restored in 1559. In over seventy years since 1948 the volume seems to have remained almost completely neglected. Very few historians have

[10] *The Royal Visitation of 1559: Act Book for the Northern Province,* ed. C. J. Kitching, SS 187 (Durham, 1975).

[11] 'Causis Beneficialibus siue Restitucionis beneficiorum ecclesiasticorum &c inter partes inferius descriptas'.

[12] For an exceptional listing of unbeneficed men, see Baskerville, 'Married Clergy', 44, 53, 57, 60–2, 64.

[13] For example, TNA, PROB 34/1, fols 51^v, 53^v, 55^r, 76^v, 83^r, 96^r, 107^r, 112^v.

[14] John Strype, *Annals of the Reformation and Establishment of Religion ... in the Church of England during Queen Elizabeth's Happy Reign,* 4 vols (Oxford, 1824), 1/1: 248–55; Gee, *Elizabethan Clergy,* 143.

[15] London, LPL, clerical subscriptions in CM XIII/2/57, 58.

[16] Mullins acknowledged the volume's discovery at Somerset House by Dr L. Hotson of Arlington, USA: 'Effects', 172–3.

mentioned it or drawn on it, let alone analysed it thoroughly.[17] Meticulously repaired and handsomely bound since Mullins consulted it in a somewhat dilapidated state, the volume may comprise more than one original act book.[18] However, there seem to be no good grounds for thinking that there are gaps in its record of cases during the period that it covers: all the dates assigned to hear sentence in these cases refer to sessions actually recorded in the act book. Thereafter cases may have been dealt with by the more permanent body of commissaries in ecclesiastical causes in London established on 19 July 1559.[19]

The three dioceses of London, Norwich and Ely whose visitation was partially recorded in PROB 34/1 included the region where clerical marriage had been most widespread after it had been made lawful by statutes of 1549 and 1552. The legal basis of the process of restoration and the judicial procedures employed present questions of considerable interest. The visitors of the northern province, and no doubt those responsible for the other five groups of dioceses, were empowered by commission issued on 24 June 1559 to restore all those deprived contrary to the statutes and ordinances of the kingdom of England and the order of ecclesiastical law.[20] On 19 July, the letters patent naming the commissioners or commissaries for ecclesiastical causes based in London authorized them to hear and determine by the laws of the realm

> … all causes and complaints of all them which in respect of religion or for lawful matrimony contracted and allowed by the same were injuriously deprived, defrauded or spoiled of their lands, goods, possessions, rights, dignities, livings, offices spiritual or temporal; and them so deprived as before, to restore into their said livings and put them

---

[17] But see the brief references in Felicity Heal, 'The Parish Clergy and the Reformation in the Diocese of Ely', *Proceedings of the Cambridge Antiquarian Society* 66 (1976), 141–64, at 157; Parish, *Clerical Marriage*, 227.

[18] The act book used by Mullins, frayed and damp stained in some places, consisted of five unequal gatherings of unnumbered paper sheets, and fourteen loose ones. The folios have been numbered, although fols 77–92 are out of chronological sequence: see Mullins, 'Effects', 172; and the heading on fol. 93ʳ: 'Liber actorum iudicialium in negotio restitucionum Clericorum ob matrimonii causam depriuatorum'.

[19] Gee, *Elizabethan Clergy*, 137–42. The visitors of the northern province referred two cases to the London commissioners: *Royal Visitation of 1559*, ed. Kitching, 50, 55. I have found no such referrals in TNA, PROB 34/1.

[20] Gee, *Elizabethan Clergy*, 92.

into possession, amoving the usurpers in convenient speed, as it shall seem to your discretions good …[21]

It seems likely that all or nearly all those restored to their livings early in Elizabeth's reign had been deprived for marriage, whatever their religious sympathies may have been. The twenty-ninth of the royal injunctions that the clergy were required to subscribe during the visitation observed that the marriage of priests and ministers of the church had not been prohibited by the word of God or any example of the primitive church. It had been made lawful by act of parliament during Edward VI's reign, 'whereupon a great number of the clergy of this realm were then married, and so yet continue'.[22]

In making this assertion, the commissions and the injunction seemingly ignored the fact that the Edwardian statutes authorizing marriage had been repealed in Mary's first parliament and never re-enacted. Two bills, one for the restoration of clergy deprived for marriage or heresy, and another to authorize the queen to restore deprived clergy, failed in the parliament of 1559.[23] The restoration of the married clergy thus rested on the royal prerogative, exercised by a queen who had notorious reservations concerning clerical marriages. Most of the injunction concerned the regulation of such marriages. It is by no means clear how the authors of the Elizabethan commissions of 1559 and those who implemented them might have justified the description of the deprivation of the married clergy as being contrary to the laws of England, given the repeal in 1553 of the relevant Edwardian statutes. Mary, using the authority she still possessed as supreme head of the church, had issued on 4 March 1554 an injunction ordering bishops and their officers to remove from their benefices all those who had married and used women as their wives 'contrary to the state of their order and the laudable custom of the Church'.[24]

The eastern visitation act book records or refers to some 120 claims for restoration to benefices, over four times as many as the twenty-eight entered in its northern counterpart. A few appear only in the form of scribbled notes of the parties' names and livings, but the great majority were the subject of formal entries. The benefices

---

[21] Ibid. 149.
[22] Gerald Bray, ed., *Documents of the English Reformation* (Cambridge, 1994), 342.
[23] Grieve, 'Deprived Married Clergy', 161–2.
[24] Bray, ed., *Documents*, 315–16, 342.

concerned included four prebends, two canonries, one cathedral deanery and an archdeaconry.[25] The rest were parish livings.[26]

Procedure in these cases was summary, and most were speedily despatched. The record normally begins with the certification of the citation of the defendant, followed by the parties' appearance in court, either personally or by means of their proctors. Defendants frequently failed to appear at the due time, but their absence was seldom allowed to delay proceedings for very long. Some claimants had evidently been unable to identify the present incumbent of their former benefices. Their cases were therefore undertaken *contra omnes contradictores*.[27] (Some of the 'usurpers' were not the men instituted to the benefices in question on the plaintiffs' deprivation, but their successors.) The plaintiff's case was presented, according to the eastern act book, by means of a 'rescript in place of a summary petition'. Plaintiffs or their proctors then usually produced supporting evidence of their institution and induction, and the whole process and sentence of their 'pretended' deprivation. This normally sufficed to secure their restoration. Plaintiffs' personal statements were not usually recorded. However, one claimant, John Walsyngham, alleged that he had been instituted to the vicarage of Fressingfield in Suffolk in 1541–2. After he had occupied it peacefully for no short period of time, he had been deprived and spoiled of it in the first year of Queen Mary, contrary to the order of law and the statutes of the realm, that is, the Edwardian legislation legalizing priests' marriages, by a judge incompetent in this regard. The language of this complaint was entirely in line with official rhetoric.[28]

Plaintiffs were successful in eighty-four out of 120 suits.[29] A further seventeen livings are known from other evidence to have been

[25] *Royal Visitation of 1559*, ed. Kitching, 41–56; TNA, PROB 34/1, fols 2ᵛ, 10ᵛ, 74ʳ⁻ᵛ, 110ᵛ (prebends of St Paul's, Norwich and Ely), 27ʳ, 45ᵛ (canonries of St Paul's), 25ʳ (deanery of Norwich), 23ʳ (archdeaconry of Ely). The two canonries are described as prebends in the act book, but neither the claimants nor the 'usurpers' appear in the lists of Marian and Elizabethan prebendaries in Cambridge, Corpus Christi College, MS 122, 6–8, 12–13, 17. John Leeke, who claimed the 'fifth prebend', appears as a 'pettycannon in Poules churche': ibid. 46.
[26] For restorations to places in the fraternity within the hospital of St Katharine's by the Tower, not counted as benefices here, see TNA, PROB 34/1, fols 51ʳ, 53ᵛ.
[27] For example, ibid., fols 16ᵛ, 55ᵛ, 63ʳ.
[28] Ibid., fol. 71ʳ; cf. Bayne, 'Visitation', 671–2 (judgment of the south-western commissioners in a case concerning the benefice of Burscot).
[29] Some undertook more than one suit.

occupied by act book claimants during the period immediately following. Any court records that might have thrown further light on their recovery of these benefices have perished. The London Commission probably dealt with several unfinished suits. Another possibility is that some disputes were settled extra-judicially, as appears from one entry in the visitation book. When John Copsheaf sought to recover the rectory of St Lawrence (Essex), both he and the Marian incumbent Thomas Hinde appeared in court. Then, however, the parties entered into a peaceful agreement, as Copsheaf alleged. The case was dismissed. Copsheaf was later reported to have been instituted to the rectory in 1560, perhaps as a precaution.[30]

The procedure seemed loaded against the Marian 'usurpers'. Defendants were described as 'pretended' incumbents. Some of them nevertheless questioned the validity of the proceedings.[31] Ralph Birche, rector of Wickford (Essex), not only alleged that Christopher Eton had been legitimately deprived, but pointed out that Eton had not appealed against the sentence, which had thus become *res judicata*, and three *fatalia* or legal deadlines had since elapsed. However, it seems that Birche soon realized the futility of these objections. He gave up the fight and renounced his title.[32] Some other defendants challenged the legal basis of the process of restitution. The proctor acting for Thomas Darbyshire, rector of Hackney and later a famous Jesuit, and Thomas Collyer, prebendary of Finsbury in St Paul's Cathedral, pointed out that the acts of Edward VI authorizing the marriage of the clergy had been repealed by Mary's statute. The delicts for which the claimant John Spendlove had been deprived had been committed after that statute. The commissioners nevertheless delivered their sentences for Spendlove.[33] Humphrey Busbie faced a claim to the London living of St Stephen Walbrook by the redoubtable Protestant Thomas Becon. Busbie not only challenged the contents of Becon's summary petition

---

[30] TNA, PROB 34/1, fol. 62^r; Corpus Christi College, MS 122, 38. However, Hilda Grieve could find no record of any such institution: 'Deprived Married Clergy', 166.

[31] Cf. *Royal Visitation of 1559*, ed. Kitching, 42, 43, 45, for defendants' belief that claimants had been justly or lawfully deprived.

[32] TNA, PROB 34/1, fols 12^v, 35^r.

[33] Ibid., fols 48^{r-v}, 91^v; cf. P. Arblaster, 'Darbyshire, Thomas (1518–1604)', *ODNB*, 23 September 2004, online at: <https://www.oxforddnb.com/view/10.1093/ref:odnb/9780198614128.001.0001/odnb-9780198614128-e-7142>, accessed 14 May 2019.

but recused Robert Horne as a judge partial to Becon in this case. Given Horne's known sympathies, Busbie's objection may seem quite reasonable, but it nonetheless proved irrelevant to the conduct of the suit.[34]

Only a small minority of defendants managed to hang on to their livings. The visitors gave an exceptional sentence in favour of William Maddock, rector of Wiveton (Norfolk), when the claimant Thomas Brigges admitted that he had held it for two years as a deacon, without dispensation. He renounced his title. Thomas Norley seems to have abandoned his claim to the rectory of Swanton Morley, also in Norfolk, after the proctor for the defendant, Charles Parker, alleged that Norley had obtained the benefice by simony and had held various benefices with cure of souls without dispensation. Parker still held the benefice in 1561, although he was then said to be living overseas.[35] Thomas Parkynson, 'usurper' of the rectory of Willingham (Cambridgeshire) also seems to have kept that benefice. He produced witnesses and documents, including of letters of acquittance signed by the claimant Lancelot Rydley, and the case was submitted to arbitration.[36] William Latymer, biographer of Anne Boleyn and her former chaplain, failed to recover the rectory of Witnesham (Suffolk). He had allegedly not only obtained one or two other benefices after Witnesham without any dispensation but also freely resigned Witnesham for an annual pension. He was presented to other parish livings in 1559 and was appointed dean of Peterborough in December. The case record ended with the note *concordia facta*.[37] In some other cases, plaintiffs' failure to pursue their claims probably allowed 'usurpers' to retain the benefices they occupied.

As the visitation proceeded, and the futility of opposing the great majority of claims to restitution became increasingly apparent, large numbers of defendants simply failed to appear to hear sentence or

[34] TNA, PROB 34/1, fols 44[r], 78[r].

[35] Ibid., fols 94[v], 95[r]; Corpus Christi College, MS 97, fol. 207[r].

[36] TNA, PROB 34/1, fols 111[v], 143[r]; Corpus Christi College, MS 580B, fol. 16[r].

[37] TNA, PROB 34/1, fols 105[r] 132[v]; Corpus Christi College, MS 97, fol. 235[r]; A. Hope, 'Latymer [Latimer], William (1498/9–1583), dean of Peterborough and biographer of Anne Boleyn', *ODNB*, 3 January 2008, online at: <https://www.oxforddnb.com/view/10.1093/ref:odnb/9780198614128.001.0001/odnb-9780198614128-e-47142>, accessed 3 August 2019. Besides Witnesham, he had had Speldhurst, Kent (1538–53) and St Mary Abchurch, London (1553–4). Grieve, 'Deprived Married Clergy', 146–7, mentions precautionary resignations by married clergy. Latymer is nevertheless listed in the Norwich 'Deprivation Book': Baskerville, 'Married Clergy', 58.

even to attend the commencement of suit. Proceedings went ahead in their absence and as a penalty of their contumacy. A few defendants or their proctors protested when sentence was delivered, but there is no clear evidence that any of these protests resulted in an actual appeal. There is nothing in the record to show that ousted incumbents actively resisted the visitors' decisions. At Hardwick (Cambridgeshire), however, the sequestration of the benefice, presumably a common, albeit seldom mentioned, consequence of these suits for restitution, was allegedly obstructed by one George Castell. Not the incumbent, he may have been the farmer of the rectory. He had, so the claimant Nicholas Stannett reported, threatened to stick his dagger in anyone who came on his ground to sequester or take his goods.[38]

Several incumbents – although many fewer than those who 'contumaciously' absented themselves from all or some stages of the proceedings – renounced their title, right and interest in the benefice in dispute. The motive for such renunciations on the part of some incumbents was simply that they were able to return to the benefices of which they had been deprived under Mary. These were clergy who had made themselves capable of institution to another benefice by renouncing their wives. One Essex case amounted to a straightforward exchange: Anthony Redferne recovered Little Chesterford, freely given up by Adam Richardson, and Richardson recovered Panfield, given up by Redferne.[39]

Priests' wives who had been separated from their husbands either compulsorily (in the case of the ex-religious clergy) or by mutual consent (in the case of secular clergy) were left in a precarious position. A few men had been punished for continuing to consort with their 'women'. A systematic study of the wills made by deprived married clergy of the diocese of Norwich shows that several made provision for their wives and children, despite the uncertainty of their wives' legal status. This uncertainty persisted even after Elizabeth's accession, though more men then referred to the women concerned as their wives. The wife of Peter Stancliff, deprived of West Rudham (Norfolk), allegedly married another man, from whom she was

---

[38] TNA, PROB 34/1, fol. 56^r.
[39] Grieve, 'Deprived Married Clergy', 156; TNA, PROB 34/1, fol. 66^r.

reclaimed by Stancliff after Elizabeth's accession.[40] One wife of a deprived priest appears in the act book of the eastern visitation. Rose Hunt sued John Hunt, described as rector of Bulmer (Essex), for restitution of conjugal rights, alleging that he had divorced himself from her for no legitimate cause. John confessed that he had married Rose and lived with her for two years in marital affection. However, their marriage had been dissolved by Nicholas Harpsfield, presumably in his capacity as vicar general of the diocese of London, who had declared that the marriage had been solemnized to the dishonour of the clerical order. (John, a former canon of St Osyth, would have had no choice in the matter.) The visitors told Rose to hear sentence at a later session, but no sentence was recorded.[41]

The act book of the visitation of the eastern dioceses in 1559 provides an incomplete picture of the process of restoration of clergy deprived for marriage under Mary. Other sources show that seventeen act book claimants recovered their benefices, even though the outcomes of their cases are not clear from the *acta* themselves. Some deprived incumbents recovered their old benefices either before or after the period covered by the act book. Fortunately there are two local studies, already mentioned, that between them deal with much of the diocese of London: Mullins's thesis on the clergy of London and Grieve's pioneering investigation of the deprived married clergy of Essex, based on a meticulous analysis of a wide range of sources.[42] For the diocese of Norwich, a uniquely comprehensive list of deprived clergy survives, extensively annotated by Geoffrey Baskerville.[43]

Much additional evidence concerning the mid-sixteenth-century deprivations and restorations of the clergy has been published since 1970. The Clergy of the Church of England Database, launched in 1999, is still far from complete in its coverage of the dioceses of

---

[40] J. F. Williams, 'The Married Clergy of the Marian Period', *Norfolk Archaeology* 32 (1959), 85–95, at 86, 90–2, 94; cf. Parish, *Clerical Marriage*, 205, 212, 214–15, 222.

[41] TNA, PROB 34/1, fol. 71ʳ; Grieve, 'Deprived Married Clergy', 151, where the incumbent (vicar) appears as 'John Sherman'. For the will of John Hunt alias Sherman of Herringfleet (Suffolk), clerk, proved in 1572, see Norwich, Norfolk RO, Norwich Consistory Court will register Brygge, fol. 463.

[42] Mullins, 'Effects', 177–8, 199–200; Grieve, 'Deprived Married Clergy', 141–69.

[43] Baskerville, 'Married Clergy', 43–64.

London and Norwich.[44] Peter Marshall and John Morgan recently drew attention to a substantial but 'hitherto almost completely neglected resource': C. W. Field's *The Province of Canterbury and the Elizabethan Settlement of Religion*, privately produced in a small number of typescript copies in 1973. Field supplied a detailed list of all the deprivations, ejections and resignations of clergy that he could find between 1558 and the early 1570s. He also included a good many such events from before that period.[45] The great majority of the men deprived under Queen Mary and restored in or after 1559 were not reinstituted, so that the main evidence of their restoration in episcopal registers (Field's principal source) lies in references to their deaths or resignations in the entries of their successors' institutions. Field distinguished between 'ejections' of incumbents replaced by their restored predecessors and 'deprivations', mostly on account of nonconformity. He supplied such details of the predecessors of the 'ejected' men as he had been able to find. The great majority of the men restored had been deprived on account of their marriages. Field does not seem to have consulted the eastern visitation act book, although he correctly identified as 'recoverers' many of the successful plaintiffs who appear in it. Field nevertheless made mistakes, especially in identifying as 'ejected' several of the first men instituted to the living in question in or after 1554 rather than the 'pretended incumbent' actually sued in 1559.[46]

A source that is very helpful in establishing whether a man already known to have been deprived actually recovered his living after Elizabeth's accession is the set of diocesan lists of clergy returned in answer to enquiries by Archbishop Matthew Parker in 1560 and 1561, which have survived among the Parker manuscripts in the library of Corpus Christi College, Cambridge. Hilda Grieve and Edward Mullins made systematic use of these returns, and their

---

[44] Clergy of the Church of England Database (CCEd), 28 March 2017, online at: <http://theclergydatabase.org.uk/>, last accessed 21 August 2018.

[45] C. W. Field, *The Province of Canterbury and the Elizabethan Settlement of Religion* (n. pl., 1973). I owe my introduction to Field's work to Marshall and Morgan, 'Clerical Conformity', 9. I am grateful to Peter Marshall for sending me a draft of this article in advance of publication.

[46] See, for example, the suit between George Smyth and Robert Ashton for Coveney (Cambridgeshire): TNA, PROB 34/1, fol. 114[r]. Field, *Province of Canterbury*, 96, assumed that Richard Moke was the ejected 'usurper'. Another caveat concerning Field's conclusions is that 'ejection' seems too strong a term to use in some cases of willing resignation.

recent transcription by Fiona McCall has made them much more easily searchable.[47]

Mullins's thesis covers 113 London parishes, most of which lay within the city walls, and some just outside. He found that sixteen London parish clergy and two prebendaries recovered benefices after Elizabeth's accession. Thirteen of those parish clergy and the two prebendaries appear in the act book of the eastern visitation, along with two minor canons and one incumbent whom Mullins did not include.[48] Grieve concluded that at least twenty-eight out of eighty-eight clergy deprived for marriage in Essex had recovered benefices in the county by the time lists of the clergy of the diocese of London were returned to Archbishop Parker during the winter of 1560–1. She identified twenty-three of the twenty-eight by name.[49] Twenty-five men appear as successful claimants in the act book of the eastern visitation, including four not named by Grieve.[50] Field correctly listed two further restorations.[51]

The extensive diocese of Norwich contained well over half the parishes covered by the eastern circuit of 1559. The surviving list of both beneficed and unbeneficed clergy recently removed from their livings or cures in the diocese was probably compiled in the spring of 1555. The eighteenth-century antiquary and churchman Thomas Tanner added a few names to it. In 1933 Baskerville published this 'Deprivation Book', which records the names of 236 beneficed clergy, with separate references of his own to some fourteen additional men, bringing the total number of deprived incumbents to 250.[52]

---

[47] These returns are in Corpus Christi College, MSS 97, 122, 580 A–C. They are being prepared for publication under the direction of Helen Parish of the University of Reading.
[48] Mullins, 'Effects', 177–8, 199, 426 (William Tolwyn of St Antholin's, for whom see TNA, PROB 34/1, fol. 149ᵛ).
[49] Grieve, 'Deprived Married Clergy', 143, 148, 150–1, 153, 156, 160–1, 163–5, 166–7. These men recovered twenty-seven livings between them.
[50] James Bilney (Chigwell), Edmund Beane (Stanway), William Smyth (Wanstead) and Christopher Eton (Wickford): TNA, PROB 34/1, fols 35ʳ, 41ʳ, 68ʳ, 144ᵛ.
[51] John Thomas (Prittlewell) and Roger Cotton (Wakering Magna): Field, *Province of Canterbury*, 197, 199; confirmed by Richard Newcourt, *Repertorium ecclesiasticum parochiale Londinense: An Ecclesiastical Parochial History of the Diocese of London*, 2 vols (London, 1708–10), 2: 474, 574.
[52] Baskerville, 'Married Clergy'. The list of beneficed clergy contains 243 entries. Six pluralists appear twice in the 'Deprivation Book', and one man was twice recorded at the same benefice under different archdeaconries. For Baskerville's additions, see ibid. 45 (nn. 1, 3), 47.

Baskerville stated that no more than twenty-five of those so deprived in the diocese of Norwich could certainly be identified as having 'got back to their former parishes'. This seems to be the result of a simple slip, because his own annotations of the 'Deprivation Book' entries refer to the restorations of at least thirty-four men.[53] Thirty-nine men who appeared before the visitors in 1559 succeeded in recovering their livings. Both the visitation act book and Baskerville's annotations name some men not included in the other source. If we add to the thirty-nine claimants named in the eastern visitation book fourteen men whose names are not recorded there but annotated by Baskerville, the resulting total is fifty-three. Three men in the 'Deprivation Book' but not recorded by Baskerville as restored appear in the diocesan return for the winter of 1561–2.[54] One more incumbent, though not mentioned in the 'Deprivation Book', left or lost his living *c*.1554 and had returned to it by the winter of 1561–2.[55] If these four men are added, the provisional number of incumbents restored in the diocese of Norwich comes to fifty-seven, or nearly a quarter of those deprived under Mary.

Baskerville noted that the episcopal registers contain references to five men restored to their livings between 1559 and 1561. Two of the five were reinstituted in the spring of 1559: John Browne, rector of Wreningham, on 18 April, and John Chadwick, rector of Litcham, on 25 May. Both livings had been vacant, so no Marian incumbent was ejected to make way for them,[56] but the restoration of the married clergy had not yet been officially authorized. This helps to explain why Browne subsequently took the precaution of asserting his claim to the benefice before the visitors against *omnes contradictores*. The other three men, who appeared in the register only in 1561, were described as restored to the livings of which they had previously been deprived.[57]

---

[53] John Bemonde, who recovered Oxwick (Norfolk) only after the death of his 'supplanter' in 1563, has not been included: ibid. 51.

[54] Including John Hede of Houghton (Norfolk). Baskerville notes that he 'Resigned 1559'; should this have read 'Restored'? See ibid. 55.

[55] This was Jeffrey Emerson, the married incumbent of Haddiscoe (Norfolk): Francis Blomefield and Charles Parkin, *An Essay towards a Topographical History of the County of Norfolk*, 11 vols (London, 1805–10), 8: 16; Corpus Christi College, MS 97, fol. 226[r].

[56] Field nonetheless assumed that Richard Russell, instituted to Litcham (Norfolk) in 1554, had been ejected: *Province of Canterbury*, 215.

[57] Baskerville, 'Married Clergy', 46, n. 7; TNA, PROB 34/1, fol. 94[r]; Norfolk RO, DN/REG 12, book 18, fols 219[v], 221[v]; DN/REG 13, book 19, fols 50[v], 53[v], 61[r].

In the small diocese of Ely, at least thirty-four clergy were deprived of livings under Mary I.[58] Nine Ely clergy who lodged claims before the visitors recovered livings, and at least one more deprived incumbent appears from other evidence to have succeeded in doing so.[59] In Middlesex and the part of Hertfordshire within the London diocese, seven act book claimants succeeded in their suits, and other sources enable us to identify a further two clergy restored to their former benefices.[60]

Overall, some ninety-three clergy who had been deprived of livings in Mary's reign recovered benefices after commencing suits before the visitors of the south-eastern dioceses. Some of these men recovered more than one benefice. Other sources of information indicate that a further twenty-nine former incumbents regained benefices. This is probably a minimum figure, though it seems unlikely that many more restorations of deprived clergy have yet to be discovered. Broadly speaking, it appears that over a quarter of the clergy deprived for marriage under Mary in the eastern dioceses recovered livings after Elizabeth's accession. No doubt many of the deprived had died in the interval, especially during the period of heavy mortality in the later 1550s. But many of the survivors did not pursue claims. Some were presumably content to remain in the benefices to which they had been inducted after putting away their wives under Mary. No doubt the possibility of another reversal of religious policy influenced many clergy. If they took their old livings from 'usurpers', they faced the possibility of being summarily turned out of them once again if Catholicism were to be restored once more. As we have seen, a proctor acting for two prominent Marian incumbents had pointed out before Elizabeth's visitors that the married clergy had been deprived of their livings under Mary only after the repeal of the Edwardian legislation that sanctioned their marriages. Elizabeth's first parliament had passed no new laws on the subject, so that the restoration of the married clergy depended on the exercise of royal prerogative. It would hardly be surprising, then, if many men ousted under Mary chose not to seek restoration to their former livings, or if some decided to move as soon as possible to another benefice that offered

---

[58] Heal, 'Parish Clergy', 154.

[59] The benefices concerned were a prebend and nine parochial livings: see n. 62 below.

[60] Robert Best (St Martin in the Fields) and Thomas Banester (Broxbourne, Hertfordshire): Newcourt, *Repertorium*, 1: 692; Field, *Province of Canterbury*, 192.

them a more secure tenure. In one case, a claimant had only just had
sentence passed in his favour when he renounced his title. This was
Thomas Whitby, who had sued for the recovery of his former bene-
fice of Aylsham (Norfolk) against all gainsayers. In 1561 he reportedly
held two livings not far from Aylsham, Elsing and Sharrington.[61]
Baldwin Derham spontaneously resigned his right to the rectory of
Downham Market (Norfolk), which he had claimed against *omnes
contradictores*, even before sentence had been given. He, like
Whitby, held two other benefices in Norwich diocese in 1561.[62]
There was no shortage of vacant benefices during the early years of
Elizabeth's reign.

Marriage by itself provided no strong evidence of Protestant convictions. Nor (as Grieve long ago emphasized) did a man's status as a
'usurper' ejected from a benefice on the restoration of a previous
incumbent in 1559 give a reliable indication of his disaffection
towards the Elizabethan settlement. Some of these 'usurpers' had
themselves been married men whose formal repudiation of their
wives had enabled them to take a new living under Mary. Many of
those ejected in 1559 soon found other livings. Nearly two-thirds
of the Essex 'usurpers' did so 'almost immediately', according to
Grieve. This evidence undermined Birt's assumption, which Grieve
noticed in passing, that such 'usurpers' were sound Catholics whose
claim to be ranked among the deprived Marian priests had been
unfairly ignored by Protestant writers.[63] Marshall and Morgan cited
Grieve's findings, and recognized that incumbents who had to make
way for men restored in or after 1559 'were not necessarily sympa-
thisers with the old order'. Their figure of 101 parishes in the diocese
of London 'deprived of their priests' nevertheless includes about forty
parishes whose incumbents were 'ejected' to make way for men
deprived under Mary. Field correctly identified some of those men
as conservative nonconformists. There is however nothing to show
that the majority belong in this category. Over half of the parishes
affected lay in the county of Essex, which Grieve studied so thoroughly. Several of the 'ejected' priests listed by Field had been
deprived for marriage themselves; some recovered their livings in

[61] TNA, PROB 34/1, fol. 95ᵛ; Corpus Christi College, MS 97, fols 202ʳ, 204ʳ.
[62] TNA, PROB 34/1, fols 63ʳ, 64ᵛ; Corpus Christi College, MS 97, fol. 248ʳ.
[63] Grieve, 'Deprived Married Clergy', 167–8.

1559.[64] Marshall and Morgan also cited Field's findings for the diocese of Ely, including nearly all his 'ejections', in the total number of deprivations. Those findings illustrate very clearly the need for care in using Field's work. He listed ten ejections in this diocese. He correctly identified three incumbents ejected in 1559. In three cases, however, he seems to have been mistaken in believing that an Elizabethan ejection took place, while in four others his identification of the individual ejected in 1559 was incorrect.[65] In the diocese of Norwich, at least half the named 'usurpers' removed by the visitors in 1559 to make way for men deprived under Mary had obtained other benefices within the diocese before the winter of 1561–2.[66] The total numbers of deprivations 'for conservative sympathies' provisionally given by Marshall and Morgan, on the basis of Field's research,[67] will certainly need to be adjusted downwards, although by what margin only further investigation can determine.

The act book of the eastern visitation of 1559 has been a neglected asset. This investigation points to four main conclusions. First, the act book is an invaluable source for understanding the process of restoration of the clergy deprived under Mary, a process that was by no means always smooth, tidy or uncontested. Second, although the act book is certainly not a complete record of the restorations in the eastern dioceses, we can be reasonably confident that a substantial

[64] Marshall and Morgan, 'Clerical Conformity', 10 (incumbents identified as clear conformists by Field already subtracted); Field, *Province of Canterbury*, 191–200; Grieve, 'Deprived Married Clergy', 148, 156, 165–6, 168. Although Field distinguished in individual parish entries between the 'deprived' and the 'ejected', he did not do so in the summary lists of deprived incumbents at the end of each diocesan section.
[65] Correctly identified: Caldecote, Gamlingay, Little Eversden; no evidence of Elizabethan ejection: Boxworth, Swaffham Prior (where Field confused two separate benefices), Westley Waterless; incorrect identification of the 'ejected' incumbent: Bottisham, Coveney, Hardwick, Linton. He did not find evidence of the restoration by the visitors of the incumbents of Dullingham and Over. The succession at Cherry Hinton *probably* indicates Marian deprivation and Elizabethan restoration there too. See Field, *Province of Canterbury*, 96–9; TNA, PROB 34/1, fols 112^r, 114^{r-v}, 115^{r-v}, 116^r, 149^v; CCEd, Ely diocese, location IDs 861, 888, 962, 1002–3, 1015.
[66] Of those ejected by the visitors and listed by Field in *Province of Canterbury*, 220–1, John Cotton (Richard in Field), Robert Dixon, Hugh Evans, Richard Gatefould ('Patefield' in Field), Robert Pierson, John Simpson, Henry Symonds, John Toller, Robert Walton or Waltham, Anthony Wilkinson and Edward Williamson all appear in Corpus Christi College, MS 97, fols 199^r, 204^r, 205^r, 208^r, 211^r, 230^r, 234^r, 236^r, 248^r. Field noted, however, that an Anthony Wilkinson had fled overseas by 1577.
[67] Marshall and Morgan, 'Clerical Conformity', 10.

majority of the restored clergy appear in it. Third, only a minority of the clergy deprived of their livings under Mary sought to recover them in or after 1559. This finding broadly confirms the results of local studies by previous investigators. Three main explanations for this state of affairs may be suggested. Many of the men concerned had no doubt fallen victim to the terrible mortality of the intervening years. Some were content to remain in the parishes to which they had moved after separation from their wives. This article has particularly emphasized a third explanation: the potentially precarious nature of restorations based solely on the exercise of the supreme governor's prerogative, in the event of the reversal of the settlement by a Catholic successor. Finally, we have seen the diversity of the reactions to the Elizabethan settlement of 'usurpers' ousted to make way for victims of the Marian purge of the married clergy. Some became Catholic nonconformists, either in 1559 or later, but they were probably outnumbered by those who accepted benefices in the Elizabethan church and ended their careers as conformists or firm supporters of the settlement.

Adiaphora, Luther and the Material Culture of Worship

Andrew Spicer*

Oxford Brookes University

The celebration of the late medieval mass and other religious ceremonies was carefully delineated through the ecclesiastical regulations of the Catholic Church. This legalistic approach to worship was strongly criticized by both Desiderius Erasmus and Martin Luther before 1517. With the subsequent Reformation, Luther reacted against Catholic legalism which, he argued, ensnared the faithful and threatened Christian freedom. He was therefore particularly reluctant to specify what he considered to be the appropriate form, place and setting for his German mass. Luther utilized the concept of adiaphora *to argue that such issues were matters of indifference as they were not fundamental for salvation. However, this stance was tempered by his realization that such Christian freedom actually did require direction to ensure that the Reformation message was not confused or lost.*

During the seventeenth and eighteenth century, English merchants and travellers to Germany and the Baltic were surprised by the pre-Reformation furnishings that remained in the Lutheran churches they visited, particularly commenting on the altarpieces, organs and statues.[1] The survival of these aspects of late medieval worship has been attributed to the so-called 'preserving power' of Lutheranism. Significant quantities of ecclesiastical plate and vestments, together with images and altarpieces, remain to this day through having

* School of History, Philosophy and Culture, Oxford Brookes University, Oxford. OX3 0BP. E-mail: aspicer@brookes.ac.uk.

An earlier version of this article was delivered in September 2017 at 'Indifferent Things? Material and Ceremonial Church Practices in the 16th and 17th Centuries in the Baltic Region', at the Niguliste Museum: Art Museum of Estonia, Tallinn. I am grateful to the audiences at this conference and the Ecclesiastical History Society's Winter Meeting, as well as the anonymous peer reviewers, for their comments and feedback.
[1] Andrew Spicer, 'Lutheran Churches and Confessional Identity', in idem, ed., *Lutheran Churches in Early Modern Europe* (Farnham, 2012), 1–15, at 3–5; Margaret Aston, *Broken Idols of the English Reformation* (Cambridge, 2016), 994.

Studies in Church History 56 (2020), 246–272   © Ecclesiastical History Society 2020
doi: 10.1017/stc.2019.14

been retained by Lutheran congregations.[2] Recent scholarship, however, has acknowledged that this material culture has not always survived without some adaptation to accord with the needs of Lutheran
worship.[3] Furthermore, it has been questioned whether 'preservation'
or 'survival' are the appropriate terms to refer to these items associated
with pre-Reformation worship but with which the Lutheran faithful
continued to engage.[4]

Adiaphora has become a convenient term to explain the retention
of this ecclesiastical material culture, particularly in relation to religious art and images, within the Lutheran tradition.[5] *Adiaphora*, a
Greek term, had its origins in classical philosophy but had been
adopted by the some of the Church Fathers. The meaning of the concept gradually evolved so that by the late Middle Ages, it had come to
refer to things that were permitted because they had neither been
divinely commanded nor prohibited, as determined by the New
Testament. These were matters which were not regarded as necessary
for salvation. It was this understanding of the term that was applied
by the Reformers in the early sixteenth century. A distinction was
drawn between those ceremonies and rituals which had been divinely

[2] Bridget Heal, 'Sacred Image and Sacred Space in Lutheran Germany', in Will Coster
and Andrew Spicer, eds, *Sacred Space in Early Modern Europe* (Cambridge, 2005), 39–59;
eadem, '"Better Papist than Calvinist": Art and Identity in Later Lutheran Germany',
German History 29 (2011), 584–609, at 588–90; eadem, *A Magnificent Faith: Art and
Identity in Lutheran Germany* (Oxford, 2017), 45–50; Caroline Bynum, 'Are things
"Indifferent"? How Objects change our Understanding of Religious History', *German
History* 34 (2016), 88–112; *Martin Luther: Treasures of the Reformation. Catalogue*
(Dresden, 2016), 360–3. See also Martin Wangsgaard Jürgensen, *Ritual and Art across
the Danish Reformation: Changing Interiors of Village Churches, 1450–1600* (Turnhout,
2018); Evelin Wetter, '"On Sundays for the laity … we allow mass vestments, altars
and candles to remain": The Role of Pre-Reformation Ecclesiastical Vestments in the
Formation of Confessional and Corporate National Identities', in Spicer, ed., *Lutheran
Churches*, 165–95.
[3] *Martin Luther: Treasures of the Reformation*, 199; Maria Crăciun, 'Iconoclasm and
Theology in Reformation Transylvania: The Iconography of the Polyptych of the
Church at Biertan', *ARG* 95 (2004), 61–97; eadem, 'Marian Imagery and its Function
in the Lutheran Churches of Early Modern Transylvania', in Spicer, ed., *Lutheran
Churches*, 133–64. See also Andrew Spicer, 'The Material Culture of Early Modern
Churches', in Catherine Richardson, Tara Hamling and David Gaimster, eds, *The
Routledge Handbook of Material Culture in Early Modern Europe* (Abingdon, 2017), 82–97.
[4] Bynum, 'Are things "Indifferent"?'
[5] Ibid. 91–2; Joseph Leo Koerner, *The Reformation of the Image* (London, 2004), 157–8.

ordained and those which had been established by the Catholic Church.[6]

The late medieval church had been criticized by men such as John Wyclif, Jan Hus and Jean Gerson for the proliferation of ecclesiastical laws which imposed these human, rather than divinely ordained, practices on the Christian faithful.[7] Erasmus explained that his purpose in writing the *Enchiridion militis Christiani* (1503) was 'to counteract the error of those who make religion in general consist in rituals and observances of an almost more than Jewish formality, but who are astonishingly indifferent to matters that have to do with true goodness'.[8] He criticized the ecclesiastical establishment for the superstitious manner in which 'they observe silly little ceremonies, instituted by men'.[9] Erasmus also attacked the blind observance of certain religious devotions such as 'being an assiduous churchgoer, prostrating yourself before the statues of the saints, lighting candles, and repeating a certain number of prayers'. He concluded: 'God has no need of this'.[10] These rituals were indifferent matters because they were not 'ends' in themselves.[11] Martin Luther reacted against the legalism of the Catholic Church

---

[6] For aspects of this subject, see Jason A. Fite, 'Adiaphora: Theological War in Elizabethan England', *Puritan Reformed Journal* 9 (2017), 113–140; Daniel R. Hyde, 'Lutheran Puritanism?: Adiaphora in Lutheran Orthodoxy and Possible Commonalities in Reformed Orthodoxy', *American Theological Inquiry* 2 (2009), 61–83; Joyce Irwin, 'Music and the Doctrine of Adiaphora in Orthodox Lutheran Theology', *SCJ* 14 (1983), 157–72; Wade Johnston, *The Devil behind the Surplice: Matthias Flacius and John Hooper on* Adiaphora (Eugene, OR, 2018); John T. Pless, 'The Relationship of Adiaphora and Liturgy in the Lutheran Confessions', in Gerald S. Krispin and Jon D. Vieker, eds, *And every Tongue confess: Essays in Honor of Norman Nagel on the Occasion of his Sixty-Fifth Birthday* (Dearborn, MI, 1990), 195–210; Bryan D. Spinks, 'Adiaphora: Marriage and Funeral Liturgies', *Concordia Theological Quarterly* 62 (1998), 7–23; Bernard J. Verkamp, 'The Limits upon Adiaphoristic Freedom: Luther and Melanchthon', *Theological Studies* 36 (1975), 52–76; idem, *The Indifferent Mean: Adiaphorism in the English Reformation to 1554* (Athens, OH, 1977).

[7] Verkamp, *Indifferent Mean*, 10–11.

[8] Erasmus to John Colet, December 1504, in *Collected Works of Erasmus: The Correspondence of Erasmus*, ed. R. A. B. Mynors et al. (Toronto, ON, 1974–), 2: 85–9, at 87.

[9] *Collected Works of Erasmus: Spiritualia*, ed. John O'Malley, 3 vols (Toronto, ON, 1988–99), 1: 74.

[10] Ibid, 79.

[11] Ibid. 79–83; Verkamp, *Indifferent Mean*, 36–7.

by arguing that it was an issue of Christian freedom whether or not matters that had neither been forbidden nor ordained by God were observed.[12]

Luther's attack on canon law and the legal impact of his theology have been the focus for several studies.[13] This article will focus more specifically on his theological response to the ecclesiastical laws and requirements relating to late medieval worship. Firstly, it will discuss Luther's criticism of the careful delineation by the Catholic Church of the liturgical requirements for the mass and their implications. He made a distinction between aspects of religious practice that had been divinely ordained or condemned, and those which were to be regarded as indifferent matters. This also had significant ramifications for Luther's stance on the liturgy and the material culture of worship. Some of Luther's most trenchant comments concerning *adiaphora*, particularly with regard to images, were made following the liturgical changes at Wittenberg and a new church order promulgated in January 1522 that ordered the removal of altars and images. In the subsequent decades other German princes and magistrates introduced church orders that defined a number of aspects of religious practice.[14] Although recent research has discussed *adiaphora* in relation to images and religious art,[15] this article will consider more broadly Luther's understanding of the concept in connection with the material culture and setting for services. It will also explore the extent to which Luther considered that there were limits to the application of the principle of *adiaphora*.

---

[12] Verkamp, 'Limits upon Adiaphoristic Freedom'.

[13] See John Witte Jr, *Law and Protestantism: The Legal Teachings of the Lutheran Reformation* (Cambridge, 2002); Harold Berman, *Law and Revolution, 2: The Impact of the Protestant Reformations on the Law* (Cambridge, 2004); Virpi Mäkinen, ed., *Lutheran Reformation and the Law* (Leiden, 2006).

[14] Volker Leppin, 'Kirchenausstattungen in territorialen Kirchenordnungen bis 1548', in Sabine Arend and Gerald Dörner, eds, *Ordnungen für die Kirche – Wirkungen auf die Welt. Evangelische Kirchenordnungen des 16. Jahrhunderts*, Spätmittelalter, Humanismus, Reformation 84 (Tübingen, 2015), 137–55.

[15] Koerner, *Reformation of the Image*, 157–61; Sergiusz Michalski, *The Reformation and the Visual Arts: The Protestant Image Question in Western and Eastern Europe* (London, 1993), 14–15, 191; Reimond B. Sdzuj, *Adiaphorie und Kunst. Studien zur Genealogie ästhetischen Denkens*, Frühe Neuzeit 107 (Tübingen, 2005); Bridget Heal, 'Kirchenordnungen und das Weiterbestehen religiöser Kunstwerke in lutherischen Kirchen', in Arend and Dörner, eds, *Ordnungen – Wirkungen*, 157–74.

I

During the summer of 1516, Martin Luther lectured on St Paul's epistle to the Romans. In his lectures, the Reformer discussed how the law of Moses, with its restrictions on diet and other religious obligations, had been surpassed with the coming of Christ. Luther drew parallels with the restrictions of Mosaic law and criticized the ecclesiastical laws and ceremonies of the Catholic Church. In particular, he challenged the regulations relating to the liturgy and requirements for worship, which he regarded as being at odds with the new law instituted by Christ:

> Nor does it belong to the new law that we build this or that church or that we ornament them in such and such a way, or that singing be of a certain kind or the organ or the altar decorations, the chalices, the statues and all of the other paraphernalia which are contained in our temples. Finally, it is not necessary that the priests and other religious wear the tonsure or go about in distinctive garb as they did under the old law. For all these things are shadows and signs of the real thing and thus are childish.[16]

Luther argued that this did not mean that 'all churches, their ornamentation, all offices in them, all sacred places, all fast days, all feast days, all the distinctions between the priests, bishops, and religious in rank, garb' should be abolished, but he pointed out that 'none of them are necessary for salvation'.[17] Four years later in *The Freedom of a Christian* (1520), Luther similarly criticized 'those numberless mandates and precepts of pope, bishops, monasteries, churches, princes, and magistrates upon which some ignorant pastors insist as if they were necessary to righteousness and salvation'.[18]

The standard authority on liturgical practice and worship on the eve of the Reformation was the *Rationale divinorum officiorum*. Compiled in the thirteenth century by Guillaume Durande (William Durand), bishop of Mende, this collection of ecclesiastical laws became one of the most circulated liturgical treatises, with over two hundred Latin manuscripts and further vernacular translations.[19]

---

[16] *WA*, 56: 493–4; *LW*, 25: 487.
[17] *WA*, 56: 494; *LW*, 25: 487–8.
[18] *WA*, 7: 37, 68; *LW*, 31: 370.
[19] *The Rationale divinorum officiorum of William Durand of Mende*, ed. Timothy M. Thibodeau, Records of Western Civilization (New York, 2007); M. Albaric,

It addressed a range of ecclesiastical matters such as church buildings, altars and vestments, as well as rituals such as consecration, dedication and reconciliation. In some cases, there are extensive descriptions of the liturgical items required for the celebration of the mass as well as their allegorical significance. For example, the material from which a chalice could be made was carefully delineated:

> [T]he Council of Rheims decreed that the sacrifice be offered in vessels of silver or gold; or on account of poverty, out of tin, since it does not rust, but not out of wood or copper. The vessels should not be made of glass on account of the danger of spilling the wine; neither should it [*sic*] be made of wood since it is a porous and spongy material that will absorb the Lord's Blood; neither should it be made of brass or copper, since the strength of the wine mixed with rust would induce vomiting when drunk.[20]

The chalice was consecrated for liturgical use and during the mass it became 'a new sepulchre for the body and blood of Christ'.[21] The exposition on the mass included a section on altar linen, specifically the corporal which was placed on the altar beneath the chalice during the mass. According to canonical decree:

> [N]o one should presume to celebrate the sacrifice of the altar on a silk cloth, or on a cloth that had been dyed, but on pure linen that has been consecrated by a bishop; namely a linen that comes from the earth, that is born and woven from the earth, just as the Body of our Lord Jesus Christ was buried in a linen shroud.[22]

The section included further descriptions regarding the symbolism and use of these altar linens, with the final clause noting that a papal decree ordered that 'consecrated women or nuns must not touch the sacred vessels, such as the chalice or paten, or the sacred linens, that is the corporals'.[23] As these examples illustrate, the

'Les Éditions imprimées du *Rationale Divinorum Officiorum* de Guillaume Durand de Mende', in P.-M. Gy, ed., *Guillaume Durand, Evêque de Mende (v.1230–1296). Canoniste, Liturgiste et homme politique* (Paris, 1992), 183–205.
[20] *Rationale divinorum officiorum*, ed. Thibodeau, 46.
[21] Ibid. 98.
[22] William Durand, *Rationale IV. On the Mass and each Action pertaining to it*, ed. Timothy M. Thibodeau, CCT 14, 241.
[23] Ibid. 243.

material culture relating to the celebration of the medieval mass was not only closely outlined but the purpose and symbolism of each item was carefully explained.

Luther attacked this highly legalistic and prescriptive approach towards worship and dismissed the 'despotic' demands of these canonists and liturgical writers. In *The Babylonian Captivity of the Church* (1520), he compared the *Rationale divinorum officiorum* with the *Ecclesiastical Hierarchy*, a text attributed to Pseudo-Dionysius the Areopagite, who lived in the late fifth or early sixth century. According to Luther, the latter merely described 'certain churchly rites and amuse[d] himself with allegories without proving anything'; he made a similar accusation regarding Durande's work, concluding that 'such allegorical studies are for idle men'. For Luther, theologians should not devote their attention to allegories until they have 'exhausted the legitimate and simple meaning of the Scripture'.[24] He also questioned the authority of these liturgical injunctions. While Luther did not object to the composition of such rites and ceremonies by churchmen, he rejected 'the right to turn their opinions into articles of faith', asserting: 'we refuse to be bound by such things as if they were necessary to salvation, which they are not'.[25]

A similar stance can also be seen in *The Misuse of the Mass*, written in 1521 and published the following January. Luther criticized the Catholic Church for imposing ceremonial laws in matters that had not been instituted by Christ, such as in the celebration of the mass: 'We do not condemn the practice of conducting the sacrament with chasubles and other ceremonies, but we do condemn the idea that they are necessary and are made a matter of conscience, whereas all things Christ did not institute are optional, voluntary and unnecessary, and therefore also harmless.' Luther continued by arguing that by making 'a sacrifice of the sacrament', the church had gone beyond mere ceremonies to change its character completely. The church had acted 'contrary to the word and example of Christ – something which even Christian freedom cannot excuse, since it is the most damnable idolatry and blasphemy'.[26]

In his later works, Luther continued to express his hostility towards the church's prescriptive approach towards religious

---

[24] *WA*, 6: 562; *LW*, 36: 110.
[25] *WA*, 6: 563; *LW*, 36: 111.
[26] *WA*, 8: 511; *LW*, 36: 168.

practices, together with the rules and regulations surrounding the conduct of rituals and the material culture of worship. In his commentary on Psalm 2 (1532), he criticized 'legalistic worship' and the focus on external ceremonies and matters, when 'the form and nature of true religion is simple'.[27] Luther considered that 'when [Catholics] teach about the worship of God, they only mean services chosen by themselves'.[28] The burgeoning demands and exponential growth of canon law was condemned in *On the Councils and the Church* (1539). Reflecting on external matters, such as the time and place of services, Luther observed: 'The pope, to be sure, has scribbled the whole world full of books about these things and fashioned them into bonds, laws, rights, articles of faith, sin, and holiness so that his decretal really deserves ... to be consigned to the fire'.[29] Luther compared the external aspects of public worship with a christening robe worn by a child for baptism; the robe was necessary but it did not sanctify or baptize the child. Furthermore, there needed to be moderation, so that the child was not smothered by these swaddling clothes. He concluded that 'similarly, moderation should also be observed in the use of ceremonies, lest they become a burden and a chore. They must remain so light that they are not felt.'[30]

The volume of ecclesiastical laws and the penalties imposed on those who failed to heed these regulations also raised concern. Luther believed that this legal accumulation of restrictions could have a crushing effect on the Christian faithful. In his commentary on John's gospel, Luther condemned the papacy for the proliferation of ecclesiastical law:

> They establish one ordinance after the other – countless ordinances, as we experienced to our sorrow at the time. Every year we had a new theologian, and these fools only plague the conscience. It was a serious offense, for example, merely to touch the corporal or the chalice. They made everything a mortal sin ... This was the necessary consequence of the legalistic rule of these teachers. Thus one law gave rise to many others; for individual cases are infinite, and each law grew into a hundred interpretations.[31]

27 *WA*, 40/2: 301, 303; *LW*, 12: 85, 86.
28 *WA*, 40/2: 305; *LW*, 12: 88.
29 *WA*, 50: 650; *LW*, 41: 174.
30 *WA*, 50: 651; *LW*, 41: 175.
31 *WA*, 33: 434–5; *LW*, 23: 273.

Not only had the Catholic Church created this vast array of laws relating to conduct of worship, it was compounded in Luther's eyes by the definition of breaches of these regulations as a mortal sin. A decade earlier in *On the Babylonian Captivity of the Church*, as part of his attack upon the conception of ordination as a sacrament and the priesthood as a separate estate, Luther had criticized the 'superstition [which] counts it a great crime if the laity touch either the bare chalice or the corporal'.[32]

It was a matter of Christian freedom that the faithful should not be constrained by ecclesiastical laws, but they were free to make their own decisions regarding matters which had neither been commanded nor forbidden by God. Luther therefore condemned those who forbade aspects of religious practice which in his reading had been left to individual free choice by God. In his Lenten sermons preached in 1522, Luther asserted that 'things are matters of choice and must not be forbidden by anyone, and if they are forbidden, the forbidding is wrong, since it is contrary to God's ordinance'.[33] The following month, in his tract *Receiving both Kinds in the Sacrament*, Luther further developed this concept of the freedom of the Christian in relation to the rituals and material culture of worship:

> [L]et the old practice continue. Let the mass be celebrated with consecrated vestments, with chants and all the usual ceremonies, in Latin, recognizing the fact that these are merely external matters which do not endanger the consciences of men. But besides that, through the sermon keep the consciences free, so the common man may learn that these things are done not because they have to be done that way or because it would be heresy to do them differently, as the nonsensical laws of the pope insist. For one must attack rigorously and roughly those tyrants who would ensnare and coerce by means of laws, in order that Christian freedom may remain intact.[34]

For Luther, the faithful should not be subjected to ecclesiastical laws that imposed upon them religious practices or forms of worship that were indifferent matters.

Luther's antipathy to the legalism of the late medieval church focused, like that of earlier critics, on the proliferation of ecclesiastical

---

[32] *WA* 6: 566; *LW*, 36: 115–16.
[33] *WA* 10/3: 21–2; *LW*, 51: 79.
[34] *WA*, 10/2: 29; *LW*, 36: 254.

laws but also on the exceptional burden that this imposed on the faithful, which far exceeded the expectations placed on them by divine law. The ecclesiastical laws relating to the setting and material culture of worship conflicted with the freedom of Christians to reach their own decisions regarding indifferent matters.

II

On 24 January 1522, the town council in Wittenberg published a church order which introduced liturgical changes to the celebration of the mass and outlawed begging, reassigning ecclesiastical revenues to a common chest to assist the poor. These regulations had been compiled by the magistrates in consultation with the university professors, especially Andreas Karlstadt and Philip Melanchthon. The liturgy of the mass was simplified, the words of consecration now being delivered in German and communion being administered in both kinds. The measure required the removal of altars and religious images from the churches to prevent idolatry.[35]

The magistrates had introduced the church order in spite of Elector Frederick the Wise's decree, issued the previous month, against religious innovation and for the continuance of traditional forms of worship.[36] The church order was a response to increasing religious agitation and unrest in Wittenberg. During Luther's absence, following his abduction after the Diet of Worms, Karlstadt and Gabriel Zwilling assumed a leading role in the town's religious affairs. Hostility towards the celebration of the mass and religious images in particular escalated in the university town. Although Luther had strongly criticized the Latin mass in *On the Babylonian Captivity*, he had only proposed limited modifications to the liturgy. Practical changes to the mass were introduced during his absence

---

[35] *Die Wittenberger und Leisniger Kastenordnung, 1522, 1523*, ed. Hans Lietzmann (Bonn, 1907), 4–6; Leppin, 'Kirchenausstattungen in territorialen Kirchenordnungen', 138–43; Martin Brecht, *Martin Luther*, 2: *Shaping and Defining the Reformation, 1521–1532* (Minneapolis, MN, 1990), 38–40; Amy Nelson Burnett, *Karlstadt and the Origins of the Eucharistic Controversy: A Study in the Circulation of Ideas* (New York, 2011), 29; Thomas H. Schattauer, 'From Sacrifice to Supper: Eucharistic Practice in the Lutheran Reformation', in Lee Palmer Wandel, ed., *A Companion to the Eucharist in the Reformation*, Brill's Companions to the Christian Tradition 46 (Leiden, 2013), 205–30, at 212–13.
[36] Burnett, *Karlstadt*, 27, 29.

from Wittenberg. These reforms began in late September 1521 with communicating in both kinds and culminated in the development of an evangelical mass, celebrated by Karlstadt on Christmas Day. After a short sermon, he administered communion without vestments, just reciting the words of consecration in German rather than Latin, omitting the remainder of the canon, and placing the host and the cup into the hands of the communicants.[37] It was in this context that the Wittenberg magistrates issued their church order making liturgical changes, which included the removal of altars and images, and establishing a common chest for poor relief. Karlstadt's treatise *On the Removal of Images and that there should be no more Beggars among Christians* was also published at the end of January or early February 1522.[38] These reforms angered the elector but also divided the Wittenberg reformers, some of whom adopted a more conservative stance on images than Karlstadt.[39]

Luther returned to Wittenberg in early March 1522 and later that month preached the Lenten or Invocavit sermons. In this series of eight sermons delivered on consecutive days, Luther responded to the recent events in the town. The sermons were published the following year and as their title indicates they dealt 'briefly with the masses, images, both kinds in the sacrament, eating [of meats], and private confession, etc.'. Undoubtedly the sermon which has received the most attention related to the use of images; it had been published separately soon after the sermons were delivered and went through seven further editions that year.[40] Nonetheless, across all the sermons we see Luther explaining his position with regard to ceremonies and

[37] Irmgard Pahl, ed., *Coena Domini*, 1: *Die Abendmahlsliturgie der Reformationskirchen im 16. / 17. Jahrhundert* (Freiburg, 1983), 7–8, 13; Burnett, *Karlstadt*, 15, 26–9; Schattauer, 'Sacrifice to Supper', 212–13; Natalie Krentz, 'The Making of the Reformation: The Early Urban Reformation between Continuity and Change', *Reformation & Renaissance Review* 19 (2017), 30–49, at 41–2.
[38] *Die Wittenberger und Leisniger Kastenordnung*, 4–6; Andreas Karlstadt, *Von abtuhung der bilder und das Keyn bedtler vnther den Christen seyn sollen, 1522, und die Wittenberger beutelordnung*, ed. Hans Lietzmann (Bonn, 1911); Andreas Karlstadt, 'On the Removal of Images and that there should be no more Beggars among Christians', in *The Essential Carlstadt: Fifteen Tracts by Andreas Bodenstein (Carlstadt) from Karlstadt*, transl. and ed. E. J. Furcha (Waterloo, ON, 1995), 100–28; Neil R. Leroux, '"In the Christian City of Wittenberg": Karlstadt's Tract on Images and Begging', *SCJ* 34 (2003), 73–105; Michalski, *Reformation and the Visual Arts*, 9–11.
[39] Burnett, *Karlstadt*, 27, 29–30.
[40] Michalski, *Reformation and the Visual Arts*, 13.

the material culture of worship, which he regarded as being *adiaphora* or indifferent matters. Furthermore, the sermons stressed that the importance of not imposing particular positions on what were indifferent matters; they should 'not make liberty a law'.[41]

In the Invocavit sermons, Luther was obliged to adopt a position which attacked the extremism of Karlstadt while upholding the distinction between the evangelical faith and Catholicism. Although Luther also regarded such religious practices and aspects of liturgical material culture as indifferent matters or *adiaphora*, this did not mean he was uninterested in these issues; he felt obliged to respond to what he regarded as Karlstadt's fanaticism.[42] Luther identified 'the things which are "musts", which are necessary and must be done, things which must be so and not otherwise … For all works and things, which are either commanded or forbidden by God and thus have been instituted by the supreme Majesty, are "musts".'[43] Besides those matters ordered by God, Luther argued that there were also 'things which are not necessary, but are left to our free choice by God and which we may keep or not, such as whether a person should marry or not, or whether monks and nuns should leave the cloisters. These things are matters of choice and must not be forbidden by any one.'[44] Luther distinguished between these categories, emphasizing that in considering such matters 'you should take this attitude: if you can keep to it without burdensomeness, then keep it; but it must not be made a general law; everyone must be free'.[45] There were certain aspects of worship that were commanded by God but other matters relating to ceremonies and ecclesiastical material culture were not divinely ordained.

Images fell within this category of indifferent matters or *adiaphora*. Luther preached in the Lenten sermons that images 'are unnecessary, and we are free to have them or not, although it would be much better if we did not have them at all. I am not partial to them.'[46] The following day, he argued that 'images are neither here nor there, neither

[41] *WA*, 10/3: 24; *LW*, 51: 81.
[42] Burnett, *Karlstadt*, 30; Bryan Spinks, *Luther's Liturgical Criteria and his Reform of the Canon of the Mass*, Grove Liturgical Study 30 (Bramcote, 1982), 13.
[43] *WA*, 10/3: 21; *LW*, 51: 79.
[44] *WA*, 10/3: 22; *LW*, 51: 79.
[45] *WA*, 10/3: 21; *LW*, 51: 79.
[46] *WA*, 10/3: 26; *LW*, 51: 81.

evil nor good, we may have them or not, as we please'.[47] Pointing to the eighth-century Byzantine controversy over images, Luther claimed that this related to a desire 'to make a "must" out of that which is free', that is, to establish particular rules relating to the use of images when it is a matter of Christian freedom as to whether or not they should be permitted. He deployed a series of biblical examples to illustrate to the congregation that images per se were not wrong but it was the worship of images that was condemned by the Scriptures.[48] Luther summarized this in his next sermon: 'on the subject of images in particular, we saw that they ought to be abolished when they are worshipped; otherwise not, – although because of the abuses they give rise to, I wish they were everywhere abolished'.[49]

Despite favouring the removal of images, Luther condemned those who 'rush, create an uproar, break down altars and overthrow images'. Iconoclasm not only usurped the role of the authorities, it was also regarded as counterproductive. Violent actions only served to entrench opinions about images. Rather, 'it should have been preached that images were nothing and that no service is done to God by erecting them; then they would have fallen all by themselves'.[50] Images are not therefore deserving of attention, they should be ignored; ultimately they will be overthrown not by human actions but through the preaching of the Word of God.

Three years later, in *Against the Heavenly Prophets in the Matter of Images and Sacraments* (1525), Luther developed this argument further: 'I approached the task of destroying images by first tearing them out of the heart through God's Word and making them worthless and despised … For when they are no longer in the heart, they can do no harm when seen with the eyes.'[51] For Luther, 'the matter of images is a minor and an external thing';[52] they are *adiaphora*. Responding to Karlstadt's hostility towards them, he argued: 'according to the law of Moses no other images are forbidden than an image of God which one worships. A crucifix, on the other hand, or any other holy image is not forbidden'.[53]

[47] *WA*, 10/3, 35; *LW*, 51: 86.
[48] *WA*, 10/3: 27; *LW*, 51: 82.
[49] *WA*, 10/3: 30–1; *LW*, 51: 84.
[50] *WA*, 10/3: 29; *LW*, 51: 83.
[51] *WA*, 18: 67; *LW*, 40: 84.
[52] *WA*, 18: 73; *LW*, 40: 90.
[53] *WA*, 18: 68; *LW*, 40: 85–6.

While reiterating that images should continue to be tolerated in places of worship because their presence was not contrary to God's commandments, Luther was also concerned to ensure that a new Protestant form of legalism did not emerge to determine the material culture of worship. In *Against the Heavenly Prophets*, Luther particularly attacked 'the murderous spirits' who portrayed the retention of images as sinful, ensnaring the conscience with laws in matters of *adiaphora*. Karlstadt was portrayed as being no better than the papacy, for seeking to 'capture' souls and consciences 'with laws and burden them with sin without good cause'.[54] In particular, Luther proclaimed:

> I say and declare that no one is obligated to break violently images even of God, but everything is free, and one does not sin if he does not break them without violence. One is obliged, however, to destroy them with the Word of God, that is not with the law in a Karlstadtian manner, but with the Gospel. This means to instruct and enlighten the conscience that it is idolatry to worship them, or to trust in them, since one is to trust alone in Christ. Beyond this let the external matters take their course. God grant that they may be destroyed, become dilapidated or that they remain. It is all the same and makes no difference, just as when the poison has been removed from the snake.
>
> Now I say this to keep the conscience free from mischievous laws and fictitious sins, and not because I would defend images.[55]

Through arguing that certain aspects of ecclesiastical material culture and ceremonies were *adiaphora*, Luther sought to challenge the views of Karlstadt, Zwingli and other radical reformers. In the Lenten sermons and *Against the Heavenly Prophets*, Luther argued that he was not defending the use of images and rituals, as he personally did not consider they were an important aspect of the setting for worship. However, as their presence was not contrary to God's commandments, he opposed efforts to define them as sinful. Through the true preaching of the Word of God, their role in worship would diminish and ultimately disappear.[56]

---

[54] *WA*, 18: 68, 73; *LW*, 40: 85, 90–1.
[55] *WA*, 18:73–4; *LW*, 40: 91.
[56] Ibid.

Towards the end of his life, Luther discussed another aspect of worship that he regarded as *adiaphora* but on which he had resisted the attacks and challenges of Karlstadt and others to outlaw the practice. This concerned the elevation of the host.[57] Luther responded to the objections of the 'blustering and jolting' of Karlstadt to retaining the elevation of the host in the following terms:

> Now when I saw such a mad spirit raving against us without cause and saw that he wanted to make a sin for us – and such an abominable sin – even though it was no sin nor could it be, I decided that in opposition to, in defiance of, and to the chagrin of this same devil I would retain the elevation which I was nonetheless inclined to drop in opposition to the papists. For I did not want to permit, and still will not permit, the devil to teach me how to arrange or determine something in our church.[58]

Luther went on to argue:

> I wanted to have it regarded as a free choice (even as it is a free matter and must be that), in which no sin could take place, whether one upheld it or dropped it … For whatever is free, that is, neither commanded nor prohibited, by which one can neither sin nor gain merit, this should be in our control as something subject to our reason so that we might employ it or not employ it, uphold it or drop it, according to our pleasure and need, without sinning and endangering our conscience …[59]

The elevation was therefore *adiaphora* and not 'such a grave, great and horrible sin, as Karlstadt's spirit wanted it to be'.[60] It was a matter of Christian freedom as to whether this ritual was employed but, just as importantly, Luther opposed the new legalism of Karlstadt's approach that sought to compel the abolition of something indifferent.

III

Luther had criticized the material culture of worship in 1516 and, writing to the faithful at Halle in 1527, he condemned the abuses

[57] Burnett, *Karlstadt*, 15, 18–19, 29, 31, 33.
[58] *WA*, 54: 164; *LW*, 38: 315.
[59] *WA*, 54: 165; *LW*, 38: 316.
[60] Ibid.

of the papacy. Masses which once 'may have been right and proper' had become 'a blasphemous circus to the detriment of faith'. He asked, given that 'all the churchly ornaments and religious customs in the service may once have been good, but now since they have been so shamefully and openly misused and made into a disgrace to God, why should we continue with them any longer?'[61] Three years later, in his *Admonition concerning the Sacrament of the Body and Blood of our Lord* (1530), Luther decried how Catholics

> ... have pretended to bestow great honour upon the sacrament by placing it in a golden, exquisite monstrance, by saying that it should be handled in golden chalices and patens and by especially anointing the fingers of the priests with ointment; you have used costly corporals, eucharistic vestments, and altar cloths, a tablet, candles, and flags along with various processions and songs, as if much depended on these.[62]

In this tract, Luther did not denounce the material culture of the mass per se but he regarded it as symptomatic of how the meaning of Christ's institution had been altered by the church so that the mass had come to be seen as a sacrifice. Luther concluded: 'How they do everything in excess in quite an intolerable and repulsive way!' However, he did not condemn the use of the liturgical plate.

The German reformer considered that there were sound pastoral reasons for keeping certain ceremonies and aspects of the material culture of worship. As these had neither been commanded nor condemned by God, it was a matter of Christian freedom as to whether or not they were retained. In the Lenten sermons, while discussing the Catholic Church's rules on fasting, Luther had explained the importance of maintaining such religious practices:

> [T]here are some who are still weak in faith, who ought to be instructed, and who would gladly believe as we do. But their ignorance prevents them ... Towards such well-meaning people we must assume an entirely different attitude from that which we assume toward the stubborn. We must bear patiently with these people and not use our liberty; since it brings no peril or harm to body or soul; in fact, it is rather salutary, and we are doing our brothers and sisters a great disservice besides. But if we use our liberty unnecessarily, and deliberately

[61] *WA*, 23: 419–21; *LW*, 43: 159.
[62] *WA*, 30/2: 608; *LW*, 38: 114.

cause offense to our neighbour, we drive away the very one who in time would come to our faith.[63]

Luther was arguing that although the freedom of individual Christians meant that they could repudiate and remove ceremonies and objects considered to be *adiaphora*, there was the risk that in doing so they might alienate others who might be brought in time to the true faith.

The tolerance of indifferent matters for the benefit of those who were less inclined to accept the religious reforms was taken further by Luther when he discussed the material culture of worship in his liturgical reforms. Two weeks after his return to Wittenberg, on 17 March 1522, Luther advised his friend Nicholas Hausmann, the pastor at Zwickau, not to 'permit any innovations either on the basis of a common resolution or by force. Only with the Word are those things to be fought ... with the Word they are to be overthrown, with the Word they are to be destroyed'.[64] At the end of that month, Luther commented that he had advised Duke John Frederick of Saxony not to 'introduce anything new if this could not be done without giving offense to those weak in faith'.[65]

The following year, Luther expressed anxiety about making innovations to the setting of worship in his *An Order of Mass and Communion for the Church at Wittenberg* (1523): 'I have been hesitant and fearful, partly because the weak in faith, who cannot suddenly exchange an old and accustomed order of worship for a new and unusual one'; he admitted that 'I must bear with them, unless I want to let the gospel itself be denied to the people'.[66] In this new liturgical form for Wittenberg's parish church, Luther's intention was not 'to abolish the liturgical service of God' completely but 'to purify the one that is now in use from the wretched accretions which corrupt it and to point out an evangelical use'.[67] This liturgy retained 'the external additions of vestments, vessels, candles, and palls, of organs and all the music, and of images'.[68] On matters such as vestments, Luther again reasserted the importance of

[63] *WA*, 10/3: 38; *LW*, 51: 87.
[64] *WA*.Br 2: 474; *LW*, 48: 401.
[65] *WA*.Br 2: 489–90; *LW*, 49: 3–4.
[66] *WA*, 12: 205; *LW*, 53: 19.
[67] *WA*, 12: 206; *LW*, 53: 20.
[68] *WA*, 12: 208; *LW*, 53: 22.

Christian freedom when it came to *adiaphora*: 'We permit them to be used in freedom, as long as people refrain from ostentation and pomp. For you are not more acceptable for consecrating in vestments. Nor are you less acceptable for consecrating without vestments'.[69] Three years later in his *German Mass*, Luther commented that on Sundays, 'we retain the vestments, altar, and candles until they are used up or we are pleased to make a change. But we do not oppose anyone who would do otherwise.'[70]

The continuation of existing practices rather than adapting to the new order of things had been considered by Luther in his sermons on St Paul's epistle to the Galatians published in 1519. In his introduction, Luther discussed the subject of the epistle, which was the preservation of some of the Jewish ceremonial laws in the churches of Judaea.

> The apostles observed these practices, not as being necessary but as being permissible and as doing no harm to those who place their trust for salvation, not in these things themselves but Jesus Christ. For to those who believe in Christ whatever things are enjoined or forbidden in the way of external ceremonies and bodily righteousness are all pure, *adiaphora*, and are permissible, except insofar as the believers are willing to subject themselves to these things of their own accord or for the sake of love.[71]

Luther's commentary pointed out that while some of the apostles continued the old ceremonies with the Jews, Paul and Barnabas 'sometimes did them, and sometimes they did not do them – in order to show that these deeds were simply *adiaphora*'.[72] Luther revisited Galatians in 1535 when he took a slightly more nuanced view, that it remained a matter of indifference if the apostles continued to follow Jewish laws, such as those that applied to diet. However, if this was done 'for the sake of conscience [it] is a denial of Christ and the destruction of the Gospel'.[73] Although Luther did not draw any parallels between the continued acceptance of Jewish religious practice by the apostles and surviving traditional Catholic ceremonies which had not been proscribed, it might be regarded as providing some biblical legitimacy for them.

---

[69] *WA*, 12: 214–15; *LW*, 53: 31.
[70] *WA*, 19: 80; *LW*, 53: 69.
[71] *WA*, 2: 451; *LW*, 27: 161–2.
[72] *WA*, 2: 478; *LW*, 27: 202.
[73] *WA*, 40/1: 211; *LW*, 26: 118.

IV

Luther had challenged the radical changes to the ritual of the mass in his Lenten sermons, he nonetheless sought to reform the existing liturgy.[74] When, in late October 1523, he informed Hausmann, who had made several requests for a form of worship, of his intention to publish a liturgy for the celebration of the mass, revising the canon and 'some of the ungodly prayers'. He emphasized that it was unnecessary 'to alter the rest of the ritual, together with the vestments, altars and holy vessels, since they can be used in a godly way and since one cannot live in the church of God without ceremonies'.[75]

Luther also wanted to keep some liturgical music, observing that 'the chants in the Sunday masses and vespers [should] be retained; they are quite good and are taken from Scripture', although some other elements, such as the antiphons and responsories, should not be sung until they could be cleansed of the 'filth' that they contained.[76] However, music was not *adiaphora*, according to Luther, it was created as a gift from God to mankind; it was not a human invention. True worship included the vocal singing of praises to God, but he acknowledged the development of instrumental music.[77] In 1523, Luther also wished that there were 'as many songs as possible in the vernacular which the people could sing during mass'.[78] The following year, writing to Hausmann, Luther lamented that he 'lacked a talent for music' which was required to write a German mass.[79] In spite of the inclusion of vernacular hymns within the *German Mass*, there appears to have been limited enthusiasm for congregational singing in Wittenberg.[80]

In reforming the liturgy, Luther did not want to replace the legalistic approach of Catholicism by prescribing a new form of worship

---

[74] *WA*, 12: 206; LW, 53: 20.

[75] *WA*.Br 3: 184; *LW*, 49: 55–6.

[76] *WA*, 12: 37; *LW*, 53: 13–14.

[77] Robin A. Leaver, *Luther's Liturgical Music: Principles and Implications* (Grand Rapids, MI, 2007), 69–70; Irwin, 'Music and the Doctrine of Adiaphora', 158–9; Joyce Irwin, *Neither Voice nor Heart alone: German Lutheran Theology of Music in the Age of the Baroque* (New York, 1993), 11–12.

[78] *WA*, 12: 218; *LW*, 53: 36.

[79] *WA*.Br 3: 373; *LW*, 49: 90.

[80] Joseph Herl, *Worship Wars in Early Lutheranism: Choir, Congregation, and Conflict* (Oxford, 2004), 14–15; see also Robin A. Leaver, *The Whole Church Sings: Congregational Singing in Luther's Wittenberg* (Grand Rapids, MI, 2017).

for evangelical use. This reticence and concern can be seen in his comments in *An Order of Mass and Communion for the Church at Wittenberg* in 1523 and his *German Mass* three years later. In the final section of the Latin *Order of Mass*, Luther emphasized that this form was not to be imposed on other communities:

> This much, excellent Nicholas [Hausmann], I have for you in writing about the rites and ceremonies which we either already have instituted in our Wittenberg church or expect to introduce, Christ willing, at an early date. If this example pleases you and others, you may imitate it. If not, we will gladly yield to your inspiration and are prepared to accept corrections from you or from others.[81]

The following year, Luther wrote to Hausmann ruling out calling 'a council of our party for establishing unity in the ceremonies' due to the political situation as well as his scepticism about the effectiveness of church councils. Furthermore, Luther argued that congregations should not be compelled to follow a certain order 'by decrees of councils, which are soon converted into laws and snares for souls'. In external matters, congregations could either follow one another voluntarily or be permitted their own customs.[82] Similar sentiments were expressed in the opening lines of Luther's preface to the German mass in 1526:

> I would kindly and for God's sake request all those who see this order of service or desire to follow it: Do not make it a rigid law to bind or entangle anyone's conscience, but use it in Christian liberty as long, when, where, and how you find it to be practical and useful. For this is being published not as though we meant to lord it over anyone else, or to legislate for him, but because of the widespread demands for German masses and services.[83]

Luther acknowledged that there were other acceptable liturgies and clearly stated: 'I do not propose that all of Germany should uniformly follow our Wittenberg order'.[84] His German mass was not to be imposed on the people; the ceremonies and material culture of worship remained *adiaphora*, in which there remained the Christian freedom to choose what was appropriate.

---

[81] *WA*, 12: 219–20; *LW*, 53: 39.
[82] *WA*.Br 3: 373–4; *LW*, 49: 90–1.
[83] *WA*, 19: 72; *LW*, 53: 61.
[84] *WA*, 19: 73; *LW*, 53: 62.

V

In spite of arguing that the ceremonies and material culture of worship should not be prescribed, there was an inherent danger in allowing some the freedom to determine their own forms of worship. Luther had warned in *The Freedom of a Christian* against those extremists who wanted 'to show that they are free men and Christians only by despising and finding fault with ceremonies, traditions and human laws' but neglected 'the weightier things which are necessary to salvation'.[85] Luther had condemned the liturgical changes that Karlstadt had implemented in Wittenberg during his absence and referred to his 'monstrosities' at Orlamünde, which included the destruction of images and abolition of ecclesiastical vestments, accusing him of 'an untamed desire for glory'.[86] There had been a proliferation of German masses and services during the early 1520s, for which Luther acknowledged that there was a widespread demand, but he was cautious about 'the great variety of new masses, for everyone makes his own order of service'. In the preface to his own German mass, Luther condemned those who have

> ... no more than an itch to produce something novel so that they might shine before men as leading lights, rather than being ordinary teachers – as is always the case with Christian liberty: very few use it for the glory of God and the good of their neighbour; most use it for their own advantage and pleasure.[87]

Christian freedom was permissible in relation to *adiaphora*, but only up to a point.

Luther's concern with regard to indifferent matters was not limited to the possible innovations of religious radicals, but extended to the challenges that diversity of religious practice might pose for the confused or those who were still to be converted to the true faith. The deregulation of worship that stemmed from the concept of the freedom of a Christian had caused anxiety about the correct liturgical forms during the 1520s.[88] Luther expressed his reluctance, in 1524, about coercing communities to adopt a single form of wor-

---

[85] *WA*, 7: 69; *LW*, 31: 372.
[86] See above, 255–6; *WA*.Br 3: 254; *LW*, 49: 72–3.
[87] *WA*, 19: 72; *LW*, 53: 61.
[88] Witte, *Law and Protestantism*, 65.

ship.[89] Nonetheless, writing the following year to the Livonian ministers at Tartu, he argued that some uniformity in doctrine and religious practice was necessary to avoid confusion amongst the faithful. There needed to be a middle way between the restriction of Christian freedom through imposing laws and not having any restrictions:

> [T]hose who devise and ordain universal customs and orders get so wrapped up in them that they make them into dictatorial laws opposed to the freedom of faith. But those who ordain and establish nothing succeed only in creating as many factions as there are heads to the detriment of … Christian harmony and unity.[90]

Luther therefore called upon these ministers to reach 'a common decision about these external matters, so that there will be one uniform practice throughout your district instead of disorder – one thing being done here and another there – lest the common people get confused and discouraged'.[91]

As well as avoiding confusion, some uniformity relating to the ritual and material culture of worship was also regarded as being helpful for encouraging 'those who are still becoming Christians or need to be strengthened'. In his first commentary on Galatians, Luther observed that Paul and Barnabas had continued to observe Jewish ceremonies, even though they were not enjoined to do so, 'in order to win the Jews'.[92] Even in Wittenberg, the service needed to be for all the townspeople, 'among whom are many who do not believe and are not yet Christians'.[93] Rather than leaving the shape and form of worship in each church to Christian freedom, Luther argued that 'it would be well if the service in every principality would be held in the same manner and of the order observed in a given city would also be followed by the surrounding towns and villages'. He regarded this a being 'essential especially for the immature and the young who must be trained and educated in Scripture and God's Word daily'. Luther added: 'And if it would help matters along, I would have all the bells pealing, and all the organs playing, and have everything ring that could make a sound'.[94]

---

[89] *WA.Br* 3: 373–4; *LW*, 49: 90–1. See above, 254.
[90] *WA*, 18: 417–18; *LW*, 53: 46.
[91] *WA*, 18: 419; *LW*, 53: 47.
[92] *WA*, 2: 478; *LW*, 27: 202.
[93] *WA*, 19: 74; *LW*, 53: 63.
[94] *WA*, 19: 73; *LW*, 53: 62.

Luther's concern for visual conformity in religious practice led him in the 1540s to drop the elevation of the host from the German mass. He explained:

> [T]he sole reason why we are discontinuing the elevation is because nearly all of the churches have given it up for a long time already. Consequently, we wanted to agree with them and not practise something distinctive in a matter that in itself was open and could be retained or discontinued without endangering the conscience.[95]

Although the ritual was considered to be *adiaphora*, Luther compromised on Christian freedom for the sake of regional uniformity. Nonetheless, he went on to argue:

> If you come to a place where they still observe the elevation, you should not be offended nor should you condemn them, but accept it because it is taking place without sinning and without endangering the conscience. Perhaps they are as yet not able to change it. Nevertheless, it is of course desirable and makes a better impression if one agrees about this matter in all churches.[96]

Luther acknowledged that there were also practical considerations that made it appropriate to regulate some aspects of worship, even with regard to indifferent matters. Preaching at the inauguration of the new chapel at Torgau in 1544, Luther considered the significance of the sabbath being Sunday or gathering in a particular building for services. He concluded that Christians were not bound to external matters, such as which day was the sabbath, but had the freedom to make their own decisions.[97] Nonetheless, this should not be applied in the interests of the individual but for the whole congregation:

> [I]f everyone were to start something new as he pleased, changing days, hours and places this would not be right … Rather everyone should agree in these things, make themselves ready, and come together to hear God's Word and to respond to him by calling upon him together, praying for every kind of need, and thanking him for benefits received.

[95] *WA*, 54: 165; *LW*, 38: 316–17.
[96] *WA*, 54: 166; *LW*, 38: 319.
[97] *WA*, 49: 591–2; *LW*, 51: 335–6.

If this cannot be done under [one] roof or in the church, then let it be done outdoors or wherever there is room.[98]

In *On the Councils and the Church* (1539), Luther had been more specific about the need for certain ceremonies and church furnishings for worship, even though they were to be regarded as *adiaphora*.

[T]he church has other externals that do not sanctify it either in body or soul, nor were they instituted or commanded by God; but ... they are outwardly necessary or useful, proper and good – for instance certain holidays and certain hours, forenoon or afternoon, set aside for preaching and praying, or the use of a church building or house, altar, pulpit, baptismal font, candlesticks, candles, bells, priestly vestments, and the like. These things have no more than their natural effects ... To be sure, Christians could be and remain sanctified even without these items, even if they were to preach on the street, outside a building, without a pulpit, if absolution were pronounced and the sacrament administered without an altar, and if baptism were performed without a font – as happens daily that for special reasons sermons are preached and baptisms and sacraments administered in the home. But for the sake of children and simple folk, it is a fine thing and conducive to good order to have a definite time, place, and hour to which people can adapt themselves and where they may assemble.[99]

Nonetheless, Luther argued that there should be a balance between established religious practice and Christian freedom regarding indifferent matters, which meant that a legalistic approach to worship similar to that of the Catholic Church should not be adopted:

And no one should (as no Christian does) ignore such order without a cause, out of mere pride or just to create disorder, but one should join in observing such order for the sake of the multitude, or at least not disrupt or hinder it, for that would be acting contrary to love and friendliness.

Nevertheless, there should be freedom here: for instance if we are unable, because of an emergency or another significant reason, to preach at six or seven, at twelve or one o'clock, on Sunday or Monday, in the choir of St Peter's, one may preach at a different

---

[98] *WA*, 49: 592; *LW*, 51: 336.
[99] *WA*, 50: 649; *LW*, 41: 173.

hour, day or place, just as long as one does not confuse the people, but properly apprises them of such a change. These matters are purely external (as far as time, place and persons are concerned) and may be regulated entirely by reason to which they are altogether subject.[100]

He concluded that: 'everything must be conducted peacefully and in order, and yet there must be freedom if time, person or other reasons demand a change'.[101]

VI

From this close reading of what Luther actually said regarding the ceremonies and material culture of worship, the survival of aspects of pre-Reformation worship appears to have been purely due his perception of them as indifferent matters, *adiaphora*. In reality, the situation was far more nuanced and represented Luther's attempt to focus on what he believed to be the essential issues surrounding worship. He opposed the ecclesiastical laws that determined the character and form of late medieval piety and worship, but also sought to ensure that they were not replaced by a new, Protestant form of legalism, something which he accused Karlstadt of introducing with his liturgical reforms. Luther therefore avoided providing clear instructions for the faithful regarding the appropriate appearance of a place of worship and the performance of services. He did not seek to impose on others the forms of worship devised for Wittenberg. It was a matter of Christian freedom, whether or not past religious practices that had neither been ordained nor condemned by God were still employed by congregations. Although the retention of images and the elevation of the host certainly did not accord with Luther's own position on such matters, they were regarded as *adiaphora*. As such practices had not been prescribed or proscribed by God, it did not matter whether or not they continued. Their retention meant that those less committed to religious change were not alienated by dramatic alterations to the form and setting of worship. It was anticipated and hoped that preaching the Word of God would bring about the conversion of those less convinced of Luther's teaching and that eventually such religious practices would fade away. Yet in spite of

[100] *WA*, 50: 649–50; *LW*, 41: 173–4.
[101] *WA*, 50: 650; *LW*, 41: 174.

advocating religious freedom with respect to *adiaphora*, Luther recognized that some limit or regulation was necessary, for example, in organizing weekly services.

That these aspects of late medieval piety did not disappear but remained to be witnessed by the English merchants and travellers in the seventeenth and eighteenth centuries was not solely due to Luther's position on indifferent matters. It was also related to the disputes over *adiaphora* that erupted during the 1550s and 1560s. After the defeat of the Lutheran princes at the battle of Muhlberg in 1547, the imposition of the Interim of Augsburg limited evangelical religious practice and divided the movement. The compromises made by Philipp Melanchthon and the Wittenberg theologians to preserve what they could of the Lutheran evangelical programme were opposed by Matthias Flaccius Illyricus and the Gnesio-Lutherans, who claimed that Luther's teachings had been abandoned. At the heart of these disputes was the claim to Lutheran orthodoxy and what could or could not be regarded as *adiaphora*.[102] The arguments and disputes of the Adiaphorist controversy ushered in a change from the way Luther had regarded indifferent matters. For Luther, there is a sense that the need for *adiaphora* in worship was transitory; the pre-Reformation ceremonies and material culture of worship would diminish over the years. It was necessary only until such time as those who were uncertain could be brought to the true faith.

The fractures in the Lutheran movement after 1548 were visible in the material culture and setting for worship. The Interim of Augsburg had instructed that altars, paintings and images be retained in places of worship. In the regions that opposed it, churches were stripped of their surviving altarpieces and religious statues to demonstrate that they remained true to Luther's legacy rather to Catholicism. Furthermore, the removal of altarpieces meant that the minister

---

[102] See Heal, *Magnificent Faith*, 50–2; Irene Dingel, 'The Culture of Conflict in the Controversies leading to the Formula of Concord (1548–1580)', in Robert Kolb, ed., *Lutheran Ecclesiastical Culture, 1550–1675*, Brill's Companions to the Christian Tradition 11 (Leiden, 2008), 15–64, at 34–9; eadem, Jan Martin Lies and Hans-Otto Schneider, eds, *Der Adiaphoristische Streit (1548–1560)*, Controversia et Confessio 2 (Göttingen, 2012); Markus Friedrich, 'Orthodoxy and Variation: The Role of Adiaphorism in Early Modern Protestantism', in Randolph C. Head and Daniel Christenssen, eds, *Orthodoxies and Heterodoxies in Early Modern German Culture: Order and Creativity, 1550–1750*, Studies in Central European Histories 42 (Leiden, 2007), 45–68; Sdzuji, *Adiaphorie und Kunst*, 127–71.

Andrew Spicer

could face the congregation during the German mass as the Reformer had intended. Elsewhere the retention of altarpieces and images, even some new commissions, indicated a more moderate response from those who argued that such matters were *adiaphora* and did not compromise their worshipping God.[103] With the rise of the Reformed faith within the empire in the later sixteenth century, the material culture of worship distinguished Lutheran from Reformed places of worship. The principle of *adiaphora* had come to be a marker of confessional identity.[104] The increasing confessional importance of the visual appearance of church interiors represented a more nuanced stance on indifferent matters. It raises the question whether, after 1548, *adiaphora* ceased to be a matter of indifference.

[103] Heal, *Magnificent Faith*, 52, 55–7.
[104] Heal, "'Better Papist than Calvinist'"; Wetter, "'On Sundays for the laity'", 165–95.

A Godly Law? Bulstrode Whitelocke, Puritanism and the Common Law in Seventeenth-Century England

Jacqueline Rose*

University of St Andrews

Debates surrounding both the church and the law played an important role in the conflicts that marked seventeenth-century England. Calls for reform of the law in the Civil Wars and Interregnum complicated the apparent relationship between puritanism and the common law, as the first fragmented and the second came under attack in the 1640s and 1650s. This article first analyses the common lawyer Bulstrode Whitelocke's historical and constitutional writings that defended the common law against demands for its reform and argued that its legitimacy derived from its origins in, and resemblances to, the law of Moses. Refraining from the radical application of this model employed by some contemporaries, Whitelocke instead turned to British history to make his case. This article then examines Whitelocke's views of the relationship between common law and ecclesiastical jurisdiction in his own day, show-ing how, both as a lawyer and as a puritan, he navigated laws demanding religious conformity. Whitelocke's career therefore demonstrates how lawyers could negotiate the fraught relationship between the church and the law in the aftermath of the reconfigurations provoked by the Civil Wars and Restoration.

This article explores the relationship between puritanism and the common law in mid-seventeenth-century England, as both were re-forged in the crucible of the Civil Wars. In that conflict, puritan-ism fragmented into its competing elements of godly discipline and individual spirituality, as institutional and theological norms broke down. This political and religious chaos also disrupted the common law, which came under attack from various demands for reform

* School of History, St Katharine's Lodge, The Scores, St Andrews, KY16 9BA. E-mail: jer9@st-andrews.ac.uk

Versions of this article were presented to the EHS Summer Conference in Cambridge and the Comparative Legal History workshop at St Andrews in 2018. Quotations in it from the Whitelocke Papers at Longleat House are included by permission of the Marquess of Bath, Longleat House, Warminster, Wiltshire.

Studies in Church History 56 (2020), 273–287   © Ecclesiastical History Society 2020
doi: 10.1017/stc.2019.15

Jacqueline Rose

ranging from procedural improvement, through claims that it was an instrument of oppression, to demands that it be reduced to the law of God.[1] In this period, old assumptions about the superiority of the common law had to be re-examined and newly defended. The arguments that resulted prompt a reconsideration of the relationship between puritanism and the common law. The predominant stress in previous accounts of this relationship has been on how they were associated (or at least allied) against claims to authority made by monarchs and the Church of England in the late sixteenth and early seventeenth centuries. An older whiggish approach would interpret such behaviour as a search for religious and political liberty, fought along the twin fronts of 'puritanism' against 'Anglicanism' and 'constitutionalism' against 'absolutism'. While these simplistic binary divisions have been removed, the emphasis on puritan-common law associations survives. In challenging the jurisdictional claims of High Commission and its ex officio process, aggressively using prohibitions to restrict ecclesiastical courts and claiming that *praemunire* could apply to courts within England, men such as James Morice, Robert Beale, Nicholas Fuller and Edward Bagshaw represented the partnership of godly religion and common law practice.[2]

Yet, as Christopher Brooks has noted, 'while the history of English law had come to be inscribed in parallel with the history of the English church', there were many different ways to represent and interpret the details of their relationship.[3] This article explores how one puritan common lawyer, Bulstrode Whitelocke, envisaged that relationship in a career that spanned the period from the 1620s to

[1] For surveys, see Donald Veall, *The Popular Movement for Law Reform, 1640–1660* (Oxford, 1970); Blair Worden, *The Rump Parliament, 1648–1653* (Cambridge, 1974), 105–18; and n. 13 below.
[2] For a nuanced account of Elizabethan and early Stuart lawyers and ecclesiastical law, see Christopher W. Brooks, *Law, Politics and Society in Early Modern England* (Cambridge, 2008), 93–123; see also Ethan Shagan, 'The English Inquisition: Constitutional Conflict and Ecclesiastical Law in the 1590s', *HistJ* 47 (2004), 541–65; John Guy, 'The "Imperial Crown" and the Liberty of the Subject: The English Constitution from Magna Carta to the Bill of Rights', in Bonnelyn Young Kunze and Dwight D. Brautigam, eds, *Court, Country and Culture: Essays on Early Modern British History in Honor of Perez Zagorin* (Rochester, NY, 1992), 65–88. For older views relating to Weberian or Marxian frameworks, see David Little, *Religion, Order, and Law: A Study in Pre-Revolutionary England* (Oxford, 1970); Christopher Hill, *Society and Puritanism in Pre-Revolutionary England* (Harmondsworth, 1964).
[3] Brooks, *Law, Politics and Society*, 123.

the 1670s; that is, one that saw the breakdown and reconstitution of both puritanism and the common law. Whitelocke provides an excellent case study of a legal practitioner who also wrote about law, history and the constitution, who was concerned about the relationship between temporal and ecclesiastical jurisdiction, and whose own puritanism was multifaceted. This article will explore how he sought out 'resemblances' to the common law in the ancient British past and sacred history in order to affirm its status and how he, compared to others, dealt with its perceived relationship to the law of Moses, setting this in the context of his spiritual commitments. In so doing, it encourages reflection on the ways in which periods of crisis may provoke new ways of thinking about religion, law and the relationship between them, and highlights how the same examples of this relationship could be deployed in radical or moderate ways, depending on the legal, religious and historical preconceptions and circumstances of the person using them.

Until 1640 Whitelocke's legal career took a standard path. During the 1620s, he followed some of the judges on circuit, and 'took notes of the most remarkable things and passages'. Even at this stage his wide-ranging interests were as much chorographical as legal; holy wells jostle assizes.[4] He wrote reports on the prerogative court of Star Chamber in the 1630s, and his account of his experience in putting cases in the vacations of the Inns included 'the imitation of Starrechamber proceedings'. As Whitelocke's career developed, so too did his legal knowledge broaden: to the law of justices of the peace and forest law.[5] A moderate parliamentarian and peace negotiator in the 1640s, Whitelocke's legal skills remained in demand. He chaired the committee on the impeachment of Charles I's leading minister, the earl of Strafford. He drafted the bill against dissolving parliament without its own consent and gave legal counsel, and he drafted ordinances (laws passed by parliament's authority without the royal assent). Nonetheless, he saw his promotion to be one of the commissioners of parliament's seal in 1648 as being 'as badde newes as ever came' and skilfully sidestepped involvement in drawing

---

[4] *The Diary of Bulstrode Whitelocke, 1605–1675*, ed. Ruth Spalding, RSEH n.s. 13 (Oxford, 1990), 56, 51. On this, see Blair Worden, 'The "Diary" of Bulstrode Whitelocke', *EHR* 108 (1993), 122–34; Jonathan Fitzgibbons, 'Rethinking the English Revolution of 1649', *HistJ* 60 (2017), 889–914.
[5] *Diary*, ed. Spalding, 58, 70, 98; BL, Add. MS 37343, fol. 131ʳ.

up the articles of treason against Charles I.[6] After the regicide, Whitelocke was appointed one of the three Commissioners of the Great Seal, who acted as the judges in the Court of Chancery. He avoided exemption from the Act of Indemnity at the Restoration, but failed to regain a position. Instead he turned to writing, composing (*inter alia*) an account of the writ of summons to parliament, a history of Britain, and that favoured genre of failed politicians, his memoirs.[7]

Godly Law

A new godly republic provided both motivation and opportunity for a new godly common law. Those who sought such an object might think they had a prominent contemporary example of a legal system directly employing a scriptural model, the Massachusetts law code of 1648. 'About nine years since', this explains, 'wee used the help of some of the Elders of our Churches to compose a modell of the Iudiciall lawes of Moses with such other cases as might be referred to them.'[8] Even this, however, was not a pure application of a biblical code. The following guide, arranged alphabetically, with internal cross-referencing, focused on legislation from the 1640s. Only one section, on capital crimes, cited the Bible in support of the death penalty for idolatry, witchcraft, blasphemy, murder, rebellion and being a rebellious son.[9] The mixture of case and statute law with a cluster of biblical authorities in this document both drew on and contrasted with John Cotton's *Abstract* of the law, dubbed by one contemporary 'Moses his Judicials', arranged thematically, which only ever cited the Bible.[10] Still, as Bernard Capp has shown, Fifth Monarchists and other radicals turned to the colony for detailed accounts of how to

[6] *Diary*, ed. Spalding, 207.
[7] For his biography, see Ruth Spalding, *The Improbable Puritan: A Life of Bulstrode Whitelocke, 1605–1675* (London, 1975). This says little about Whitelocke's Restoration career and ideas, for which see my article, 'Bulstrode Whitelocke and the Limits of Puritan Politics in Restoration England', in Justin Champion et al., eds, *Politics, Religion, and Ideas in Seventeenth- and Eighteenth-Century Britain* (Woodbridge, 2019), 81–99.
[8] *The Book of the General Lauues and Libertyes concerning the Inhabitants of the Massachusets [sic]* (Cambridge, MA, 1648), sig. A2r.
[9] Ibid.; George Lee Haskins, *Law and Authority in Early Massachusetts* (New York, 1960).
[10] [John Cotton], *An Abstract of the Lawes of New England* (London, 1641); for the title, see Haskins, *Law and Authority*, 124.

implement the judicial law of the Old Testament in their own day. To at least one member of the Barebones parliament of 1653, the lay preacher Samuel Highland, Massachusetts provided the model for a new law based on that of God.[11]

Such hopes never came to fruition in England, despite the chances for law reform that had seemingly existed after the regicide and the establishment of England's new republican government. Some contemporaries saw Whitelocke as a potential sponsor of reform. Peter Ball wrote to him in December 1649, enclosing proposals for 'remagnifying the Law, & rendering it perfectly intelligible to the professors and acceptable to the people'. Ball planned to maintain the substance of the law, but to translate it into English and organize it into 'one … scientificall method' of definitions, divisions, principles and exceptions, combining it into one volume and funding a public reader of the resulting 'Pandected' law. He saw Whitelocke as the man who could make this vision reality.[12] Whitelocke sat on the committee that appointed the Hale commission to reform the law, and was jointly responsible for receiving the commission's recommendations.[13] His papers include a copy of a letter nominating commissioners, previously cited for its suggestion of moderate rather than radical reformers,[14] but noteworthy too for its proposing certain nominees on the basis of their knowledge of other legal systems. As late as April 1654, there were complaints about the lack of Whitelocke's presence (he was on an embassy to Sweden) when chancery reform was mooted.[15] Yet when this was proposed in April 1655, Whitelocke refused to implement it and was dismissed as Lord Commissioner, although he did not totally lose Cromwell's favour.[16]

---

[11] Austin Woolrych, *Commonwealth to Protectorate* (Oxford, 1982), 271–3; Bernard Capp, *The Fifth Monarchy Men* (London, 1972), 157–71, especially 164, 170–1; William Aspinwall, *The Legislative Power* (London, 1656), 30–1; Hugh Peters, *Good Work for a Good Magistrate* (London, 1651), 32.

[12] Longleat House, Whitelocke Papers, vol. 10, fol. 80ʳ; Wilfred Prest, 'Law Reform and Legal Education in Interregnum England', *HR* 75 (2002), 112–22.

[13] On the Hale commission, see Mary Cotterell, 'Interregnum Law Reform: The Hale Commission of 1652', *EHR* 83 (1968), 689–704; Alan Cromartie, *Sir Matthew Hale, 1609–1676: Law, Religion, and Natural Philosophy* (Cambridge, 1995), 58–73; and items in n. 1 above.

[14] Worden, *Rump Parliament*, 272; see also ibid. 111 on Ball.

[15] Whitelocke Papers, vol. 10, fols 159ʳ–160ʳ; vol. 15, fol. 138ᵛ.

[16] For his representation of this episode, see Bulstrode Whitelocke, *Memorials of the English Affairs: Or, an Historical Account of what passed from the Beginning of the Reign*

Donald Veall argues that Whitelocke was the one person who might have reformed the law, and it was decisive that he did nothing.[17] Why not? Even if J. G. A. Pocock's claims about a parochially insular common law mind have been challenged, many common lawyers, supporters of a mixed polity and a significant role for parliament in the seventeenth century, used the history of the 'ancient constitution' to back up their claims, albeit their arguments about Anglo-Saxon parliaments and the inclusion of the commons therein, and the lack of fundamental change in 1066, were of dubious historical accuracy, as contemporary royalists and tories increasingly pointed out.[18] Whitelocke did discuss medieval history and was concerned about possible points of discontinuity in the common law. But he also saw, and employed, many 'usable pasts', not least early British and sacred history, in defending the common law. His claims about England's legal and constitutional 'resemblances' to ancient Israel included an emphasis on one particular historical moment: when the early British king Lucius had taken the law from the Old and New Testaments. For Whitelocke, however, taking a law 'out of *Moses' Law*' was something done a millennium before, not something to start again from scratch. Analysis of his arguments underlines the religious dimensions of historical cases for the legitimacy and superiority of the common law. The crucial question was not whether to have a godly law or not, but whether one already existed or needed constructing.

At times, Whitelocke offered the sort of defences of the common law that might be expected, especially regarding 1066. In November 1649 he told the House of Commons that the multiplicity of suits and consequent delays were due to England's flourishing trade, not to the law itself.[19] A year later, he temperately endorsed the idea

---

of *King Charles the First, to King Charles the Second his Happy Restauration* (London, 1682), 606; Stuart E. Prall, 'Chancery Reform and the Puritan Revolution', *AJLH* 6 (1962), 28–44.

[17] Veall, *Popular Movement*, 122–3.

[18] J. G. A. Pocock, *The Ancient Constitution and the Feudal Law … A Reissue with a Retrospect* (Cambridge, 1987); Janelle Greenberg, 'The Confessor's Laws and the Radical Face of the Ancient Constitution', *EHR* 104 (1989), 611–37; Brooks, *Law, Politics and Society*, 83–7, 121–3; Paul Christianson, 'Young John Selden and the Ancient Constitution, *c.*1610–1618', *Proceedings of the American Philosophical Society* 128 (1984), 271–315; Mark Goldie, 'The Ancient Constitution and the Languages of Political Thought', *HistJ* 62 (2019), 1–32.

[19] Whitelocke, *Memorials*, 415–17; BL, Add. MS 37345, fol. 24ʳ–ᵛ.

that law French (and court hand) be abolished, as he thought this would do no harm, but he argued against the idea that it was a relic of Norman tyranny. William I had vanquished Harold, but never conquered England, being admitted on condition that he maintain the laws. Here Whitelocke made a classic case for common law continuity: 'our laws appear in many particulars to have bin the same before the Norman invasion, as they are att this day'.[20] He made the same point a decade later, in the *Notes* on the writ of summons to parliament that he dedicated to the restored monarch Charles II. Here he argued that William had called a body of representatives from each county to show him what the English customs were and that English laws had been applied to Normandy, not vice versa. For Whitelocke, the Normans were just one of many examples of how a change in governors might have altered or added a few things, but left the body of the law intact. '[The] antient home borne native lawes … [are] the same that they were att the first being of any commonweale in this island, and … little or nothing altered by the incursions of conquerors.' Even the Saxons, those heroes of freeborn, pre-Norman-yoke law to some Civil War radicals,[21] had not introduced the law, for they were uncivilized pagans, and the common law was for civilized Christians. The *merchenlage* and *westsaxonlage* were, Whitelocke claimed, older British laws, deriving from the second century, when 'Lucius the first brittish king' founded the laws 'upon the holy scriptures, divers of them continuing to this day'. These Britons ultimately came 'from Japhet and his posterity', giving the seventeenth-century common law the status of the least changed and most original law there was.[22]

In defending the common law, Whitelocke had a favoured strategy and favoured word: 'resemblances'. These resemblances pointed back to the pre-Saxon era and to the religious underpinning of the common law. In his *Notes upon the Kings Writt*, Whitelocke compared the division between unwritten common law and statute to the position of the Israelites before and after the Ten Commandments. He thought there were 'some resemblances' between the judges

[20] BL, Add. MS 37343, fol. 236ᵛ.
[21] Most famously described by Christopher Hill, 'The Norman Yoke', in John Saville, ed., *Democracy and the Labour Movement, Essays in Honour of Dona Torr* (London, 1954), 11–67.
[22] *Whitelockes Notes upon the Kings Writt for choosing Members of Parlement*, ed. Charles Morton, 2 vols (London, 1768), 1: 408, 424, 427–8, 430–1.

pronouncing common law and Moses giving judgment, although he
said these had been inherited elsewhere too, for example among the
Swedes and the Goths. The word is found again in his two-volume
history of Britain from Brutus to the end of Roman government: at
the end of the first volume, in chapter 81, resemblances to British
government; and in chapter 29 of volume 2, resemblances to
Jewish laws and government, in which Whitelocke worked through
the Bible, book by book, finding similarities. Chapter 78 explored
resemblances to British manners, chapter 79 those to Roman government, although Whitelocke firmly rejected any idea that English law
derived from Roman law. While admitting that the names of legal
entities derived from Latin, he gave a number of reasons why
Roman law would not have been imposed: it was not Roman policy
to do this (even when, eventually, Britain was made a province,
because it was too uncivilized for the Romans to bother doing so);
Roman law was not settled at the time the Romans governed
Britain; and no trace of it seemed to be extant. Citing the fifteenth-century common lawyer Sir John Fortescue, Whitelocke
firmly associated Roman law with absolute and arbitrary government,
and so deemed it ill suited to the English 'mixed, not absolute, government'. Common law was 'much more free', much more appropriate.[23]
Quoting John Selden (perhaps the most historically sophisticated early
Stuart lawyer), Whitelocke insisted that 'all laws in generall are originally equally ancient' as they all derived from natural law; in England,
the common law came from King Lucius and the Scriptures, and its
model was not the law of Rome but that of Moses.[24]

It was not unusual to deny the influence of Roman law on
England, but it is intriguing that Whitelocke buttressed this position
by twisting an example usually cited to show the English church's
autonomy into one deployed to defend legal autochthony. King
Lucius was a figure whom sixteenth-century Protestants frequently
referenced. According to them, when he converted to Christianity
he had asked the bishop of Rome, Eleutherius, for guidance.
Eleutherius had supposedly replied that papal authority was not
necessary, for 'you be God's vicar in your kingdom'; a brilliant,

[23] *Writt*, ed. Morton, 1: 412; BL, Add. MS 37342, fol. 151ʳ⁻ᵛ.
[24] *Writt*, ed. Morton, 1: 430, 413; BL, Add. MS 37342, fol. 152ʳ (ch. 28). Selden's comment comes on p. 17 of his 'Notes on Fortescue', in John Fortescue, *De laudibus legem
Angliae* (London, 1616).

if historically dubious, early endorsement of royal ecclesiastical supremacy. As Felicity Heal has shown, Lucius was an extremely pliable figure in the sixteenth century, cited by Catholics as well as Protestants.[25] Yet the role that Lucius could play in *legal* arguments has been less often noticed. Whitelocke's account brings it to the fore, as when he argued:

> [That] the Roman laws were not then in use here, appears by the letter sent from the king, to Eleutherius Bishop of Rome desiring to have the Roman lawes, sent into Britaine, that the people might be governed by them … by the Answear of Eleutherius, the Roman & civil laws wee may alwayes reject, out of the Testaments by the Councell of your Realme, take a law, &c. … Lucius & his State, did accordingly consulte & consider to supply and take lawes out of <u>Moses' lawe</u> for it is very apparent (as may be more particularly showed elsewhere) that many of our positive & written lawes are grounded upon Moses lawe, & at this time was the most generall & certaine ground layd both of our positive & written lawes that continue yet …[26]

Here, godly monarchy was used to demonstrate how neither canon nor civil law was admissible if it ran against the common law, although these might be useful (Whitelocke said vaguely) if the municipal law failed. The manuscript in which this account was given formed the opening to Whitelocke's quasi-autobiographical, quasi-historical 'Annales'. In the preface to them, dated July 1664, Whitelocke told his intended audience, his children, that he had included 'some (though weake) vindications, of the antiquity, iustice, and honour of the English lawes, & people Custumes & gouernment'. To say that laws and rights were introduced by heathens and conquerors was a great blot on them; despite some alterations and additions, they were still very near the laws of the Hebrews.[27]

For Whitelocke, attention to early British history and the Old Testament served to legitimize more than revolutionize common law. His position on the constitution was similar. Although he rejected absolute monarchy as illegitimate on the basis of his

---

[25] Felicity Heal, 'What can King Lucius do for you? The Reformation and the Early British Church', *EHR* 120 (2005), 593–614, quotation at 598.
[26] BL, Add. MS 37342, fols 147^r–153^v, especially 149^v, 151^v–152^v. Brooks, *Law, Politics and Society*, 107, notes that Beale and Morice cited Lucius when arguing about ex officio jurisdiction and incorporated consultation with lawyers into the narrative.
[27] BL, Add. MS 4992, fols 5^r, 7^r.

interpretation of the warnings to the Israelites who demanded an earthly king in 1 Samuel 8, this was a far cry from the exclusivist republican claim that all kingship was illegitimate because it was idolatrous.[28] In arguing that the three estates of the realm were king, lords and commons (a contentious position associated with Civil War parliamentarianism, for it reduced the king to an estate and omitted the bishops) he drew on a range of comparisons, and again cited the Hebrew constitution as the crucial explanatory model: 'This mixture of three estates, in supreame councells, we find amongst the Hebrewes, and most other nations in imitation of them.'[29] That King Lucius and his public council had taken the laws of the kingdom from the Old and New Testaments[30] was, for Whitelocke, the exemplification of how to blend the ancient constitution, British history and scriptural models. It also meant that radical reconstitution of the common law was unnecessary: it was, at root, a godly law already.

COMMON LAW, ECCLESIASTICAL JURISDICTION AND THE PROSECUTION OF NONCONFORMITY

What did this vague origin in sacred history mean, in Whitelocke's eyes, for the relationship between common law and ecclesiastical law? This was particularly contentious during this period both in theory and in practice, given its implications for the prosecution of Protestant Nonconformity. Whitelocke emphasized how important it was 'that the true religion established may be mainteyned' when giving a charge to the grand jury of Abingdon in the 1630s. This duty, their 'speciall care', would involve enforcing sober morality, detecting Jesuits and seeking out 'conceited Sectaries'.[31] But Whitelocke himself might have felt some sympathy towards the last group, as he refused to enforce statutes governing conformity to the Church of England in 1634. According to the modern edition of his

---

[28] Republican exclusivists (like Milton) read rabbinical commentaries on the book of Samuel as suggesting that all kingship was idolatrous: Eric Nelson, *The Hebrew Republic* (Cambridge, MA, 2010), 23–56. For more on Whitelocke's view on this, see my 'Whitelocke and the Limits of Puritan Politics'.

[29] *Writt*, ed. Morton, 2: 57; Michael Mendle, *Dangerous Positions: Mixed Government, the Estates of the Realm, and the Making of the Answer to the XIX Propositions* (University, AL, 1985).

[30] BL, Add. MS 37342, fols 57ʳ–58ᵛ.

[31] Whitelocke Papers, vol. 5, fol. 230ᵛ.

Diary, when summoned to the privy council to explain himself, he told the earl of Holland, the high steward of Abingdon, that 'he might have bin censured to incroach uppon the jurisdiction & rights of the Church, if as a Justice of peace he should have taken cognisance of them'. Yet this tones down the more expansive manuscript, which includes him being accused of complying with (as well as countenancing) the puritans, and depicts Whitelocke as explaining that he 'knew no common Lawe, nor Statute, in force, for the punishment of them, especially by Justices of the peace, & that the complainers did not preferre any Indictment against them. & privately, I acknowledged … that I was not convinced of their crimes'.[32]

Respect for the boundaries of ecclesiastical jurisdiction (not something for which common lawyers were famed) was exposed as a mere excuse when, several months later, Whitelocke gave a charge to the Oxford Quarter Sessions on the power of temporal courts in ecclesiastical questions '& the antiquity thereof'.[33] While the text of this charge is not extant, his later essays argued that all ecclesiastical jurisdiction derived from monarchs (citing Lucius in support), that there had been mixed ecclesiastical / temporal courts before 1066, that fathers of families had once exercised ecclesiastical jurisdiction, and that both they and kings were priests who could and should preach.[34] Forms of ecclesiastical usurpation of royal authority should be prosecuted, but Dissenters should not be punished. This radical collapsing of the distinction between ecclesiastical and temporal authority would be a fixture of Restoration anticlerical writing, occasionally coupled with demands (not spelled out by Whitelocke, but a necessary feature of 1650s law reform debates due to the collapse of the ecclesiastical courts) for temporal courts to judge marriage and probate. Such arguments were sometimes deployed in church courts seeking to prosecute Nonconformity, including claims that no ecclesiastical process should be recognized if it did not run in the king's name (as per a defunct statute of the 1540s), that the canons were not valid because not ratified by parliament, that the entire Anglican system was therefore guilty of *praemunire* and that it should be taken over and governed by a lay viceregent.[35]

---

[32] *Diary*, ed. Spalding, 90–1, 92–3; BL, Add. MS 37343, fols 5ʳ–7ʳ.
[33] BL, Add. MS 37343, fol. 131ʳ.
[34] Bulstrode Whitelocke, *Essays Ecclesiastical and Civil* (London, 1706); BL, Add. MS 21099.
[35] Jacqueline Rose, *Godly Kingship in Restoration England* (Cambridge, 2011), 194–202.

Most Dissenters probably contented themselves with less explosive (but more effective) strategies of finding technical errors in the process summoning them. Whitelocke gave free legal advice to Baptists and 'fanatics' (his term), and to the French church in London (unspecified, but probably in the wake of demands that it conform to Anglican ritual).[36] Unfortunately, none of the content of this advice seems to survive, leaving historians with just one example of Whitelocke's argument on a case of religious Dissent, and that not a typical one. The case was that of the Quaker James Nayler, tried by parliament in 1656 for re-enacting, in Bristol, Christ's entry into Jerusalem. Whitelocke thought Nayler's views 'strange'. He asserted that magistrates and Christians had a duty to 'bear ... testimony against these abominable crimes'. The 'wicked fellow ... deserves all punishment'. But he opposed the death penalty on several grounds. The commonwealth's survival was not dependent on executing Nayler, so death was not justified under natural law. By divine law, a blasphemer should die. Here Whitelocke turned to the stoning demanded in Leviticus 24, just as Massachusetts did. Where the colonists cited verses 15 to 16 to insist on the death penalty, however, Whitelocke referred instead to verse 12 ('they put him in ward, that the mind of the Lord might be shewed them') to argue that one should wait on God in a doubtful case. Moreover, this case *was* doubtful. Nayler's behaviour was not heresy according to the first four general councils of the church. What counted as blasphemy under human law changed. In the course of showing this, Whitelocke cited the Bible, Gregory of Tours, the royalist John Spelman, the Calvinist political theorist David Paraeus, a case from Bordeaux, the 1648 Blasphemy Ordinance, *De haeretico comburendo* and the cases of Strafford and Laud. Most importantly, to try Nayler would be to create a retrospective law, a dangerous proceeding. A Catholic government might have punished the Quaker, but that was no precedent for Protestants to follow.[37]

---

[36] *Diary*, ed. Spalding, 743, 753, 754, 832, 682; Larry J. Kreitzer, 'William Kiffin and the Nonconformist Response to the Conventicle Act of 1670', in idem, *William Kiffin and his World*, part 2 (Oxford, 2012), 173–204, at 169, 173, hints at the emphasis on procedural errors; for other Dissenters' strategies, see Craig W. Horle, *The Quakers and the English Legal System, 1660–1688* (Philadelphia, PA, 1988).
[37] *Cobbett's Complete Collection of State Trials and Proceedings for High Treason and other Crimes and Misdemeanors*, 5 [1650–61] (London, 1810), cols 821–8 (Lev. 24: 12 for waiting on God); *The Diary of Thomas Burton*, ed. John Towill Rutt, 4 vols (London, 1828), 1: 32, 57–8; cf. *Book of the General Lauues*, 5.

Whitelocke's position on Nayler was somewhat ironic given his later life. If we turn from the legal to the spiritual dimensions of that life, we find evidence of puritanism in transition from what is sometimes termed church-type to sect-type behaviour: from a national reformed church to individual gathered congregations. Whitelocke exhibited what might be deemed some traditional puritan characteristics. His writings repeatedly praise models of sober living, such as Job, and condemn drunken excess. He partly attributed William I's victory in 1066 to Harold's army spending the night before the battle drinking and debauching rather than praying. He was also a firm believer in the action of Providence in his own life as well as on this macro-historical canvas, filling his diary with accounts of how God blew the tiles off a new building when Whitelocke was grumpy, and eased his bowel movements when godly clergy joined him in prayer.[38] While ill in 1670, he wrote a 'History of Persecution', in large part an abridgement (albeit running to over two hundred double-column folios) of John Foxe's *Acts and Monuments*. Deeply indebted to Foxe though this narrative was, it diverged from the Tudor martyrologist in its employment of the language of 'liberty of conscience' to describe the Israelites' desire to follow their religion in Egypt. Tellingly, Whitelocke used the term used to denote temporary toleration in the Restoration in stating that Pharaoh would not grant this 'indulgence'.[39]

It may be no coincidence that Whitelocke turned to this specific project months after the passage of the viciously intolerant Second Conventicles Act, for he firmly rejected the strict uniformity of the Restoration church. While still attending his parish church, he sheltered ejected Presbyterians, met the leading Independent John Owen and had increasing contact with the Quaker William Penn. He took out a licence under the Indulgence of 1672 to allow Nonconformist meetings at his house and continued to host gatherings of over a hundred people even after the Indulgence was withdrawn in 1673.[40] Furthermore, Whitelocke would himself preach or 'speak' to his household with increasing regularity from the late 1660s, or have

---

[38] *Writt*, ed. Morton, 1: 324–8; BL, Add. MS 37342, fols 129ʳ–130ᵛ, 37ᵛ, 9ʳ; BL, Add. MS 37341, fol. 28ᵛ; *Diary*, ed. Spalding, 762, 804.
[39] Whitelocke Papers, vol. 27, fols 10ᵛ, 9ʳ; for more on this work, see my 'Whitelocke and the Limits of Puritan Politics'.
[40] The licences were not recalled until 1675. The legal limit was five attendees from outside the household.

his son read out his sermons if he was ill.[41] Here was the changing nature of puritanism embodied: while Whitelocke reinscribed Foxe, some of his own sermons were posthumously published by Penn.[42]

CONCLUSION

The crisis of the Civil Wars exposed the tensions within both puritanism and the common law, and placed their apparent partnership under severe strain. Different visions of that relationship had existed before, but were now multiplied as a campaign to reform the common law sometimes took the form of demands for a new godly law. Even those puritans and parliamentarians who were willing to work for the new republic, however, could defend the common law as sufficiently rooted in godliness already. This was more than a reflexive or insular common-law mind. If Whitelocke's praise of common law partly represented a predictable pride in its antiquity, it was framed in historical terms that went beyond pre-Norman and Saxon history to the ancient British past and a moderate interpretation of a Hebrew model. The context of the Civil Wars and their aftermath rendered these historical bases for the common law particularly contentious. For Whitelocke, the law of Moses granted legitimacy to seventeenth-century common law, but was not a model by which to replace it, just as the Hebrew constitution pointed in the direction of moderate mixed monarchy, not of republican exclusivism.

The plurality of puritanism is now a familiar refrain in early modern historiography. Much has been written, too, about common law in the Elizabethan and early Stuart period, but its nature and the intellectual milieu of its practitioners during the Civil Wars, Interregnum and Restoration remain relatively uncharted territory. Educated in the golden age of the early Stuart Inns of Court, but practising law and writing its history into the Restoration, Whitelocke bridges this division. His combination of common law practice, historical writings and disgust at religious intolerance suggests a new avenue for exploration: how the relationship between religion and the common law developed in the mid-to-late

[41] For details, see the Restoration years of the *Diary* and my 'Whitelocke and the Limits of Puritan Politics'.
[42] Bulstrode Whitelocke, *Quench not the Spirit*, [ed. W. Penn] (London, 1711). Penn also edited the 1709 edition of the *Memorials*.

seventeenth century, as both lawyers and puritans reconstituted their beliefs in the aftermath of the puritan revolution. From this, we may learn not only about different visions of the connections between the church and the law, but also about how an established pattern of associations changes into a new relationship between them.

'Very Knaves Besides': Catholic Print and the Enforcers of the 1662 Licensing Act in Restoration England

Chelsea Reutcke*

University of St Andrews

This article explores the motivations of three enforcers of the Licensing Act of 1662 in regard to their treatment of the illicit Catholic book trade in London during the Restoration. As censors, the Stationers' Company, the Surveyor of the Press, Roger L'Estrange, and the bishop of London, Henry Compton, were intended to unite the concerns of the book trade, the state and the church. However, each used the Licensing Act to pursue their own interests. Contemporaries and historians have both viewed the act as being unsuccessfully enforced; this article explores whether full enforcement was ever the goal. Using the case of Catholic print, it posits that it was precisely the act's flexibility that encouraged its repeated renewals. Moreover, exploring the print of the Catholic minority in London highlights the differences between the written law and the enforced law. Finally, this article suggests that at times there existed an informal toleration for the printers and booksellers engaged in Catholic book production that enabled books to escape detection and the Catholic book trade to continue despite the Licensing Act.

In July 1676, wardens of the Stationers' Company seized Anthony Lawrence for printing a Catholic book, *The Great Sacrifice of the New Law*.[1] Upon delivering Lawrence to the Privy Council, one of the wardens, Samuel Mearne, informed the printer that 'if he had not behaved saucily to him and the other officers of the Company,

---

* School of History, University of St Andrews, 71 South St, St Andrews, Fife, KY16 9QW. E-mail: creutcke@gmail.com.

[1] Donald F. McKenzie and Maureen Bell, *A Chronology and Calendar of Documents relating to the London Book Trade 1641–1700*, 3 vols (Oxford, 2005; hereafter: *CCLBT*), 2: 21 July 1676 (references are presented using the dates given in these volumes); James Dymock, *The Great Sacrifice of the New Law* ([London], 1676). Dymock's work was an English translation of the Roman mass; Wing gives the place of publication of the 1676 edition as Antwerp (Wing D2972), but the *CSPD* (cited in *CCLBT*) clearly describes it as being printed in London. There may have been a separate, unlisted edition, part of it may have been printed abroad, or Wing may have been incorrect about the location.

Studies in Church History 56 (2020), 288–305   © Ecclesiastical History Society 2020
doi: 10.1017/stc.2019.16

they would not have brought him before the King and Council'.[2] Mearne had every right to apprehend Lawrence under the terms of the Licensing Act of 1662, which required that all pamphlets and books receive an official licence in order to prevent the spread of 'seditious and heretical' material. *The Great Sacrifice*, clearly, had no such licence; promoting a faith outside the Church of England automatically rendered it seditious. Lawrence, a bookseller and registered recusant since 1674, provided an easy target.[3] The act enabled random searches to be carried out on any printing house or bookshop. However, Mearne's motives in arresting Lawrence were neither legally nor ethically based; less than a year later Mearne was censured for reselling *The Great Sacrifice* on the Oxford black market for a tidy profit.[4] Instead, his comment indicates a more complex relationship between the written law and the enforced law, one framed around personal motivations and relationships.

This article explores how the enforcers of Restoration censorship viewed Catholic texts printed in London by examining how the enforcers' personal interests were reflected in the ways they prosecuted those texts.[5] Their varied interests provide insight into when

[2] *CCLBT*, 2: 20 December 1676.
[3] John Cordy Jeaffreson, ed., *Middlesex County Records*, 4: *1667–88* (London, 1892), British History Online, December 2014, online at: <http://www.british-history.ac.uk/middx-county-records/vol4/pp45-57>, accessed 15 May 2018.
[4] *CCLBT*, 2: 7 March 1677.
[5] London operated as the centre of the English book trade and surpassed the Scottish and Irish markets. The comparatively small number of presses operating in the English provinces and in Edinburgh, Aberdeen and Dublin resulted in far less centralized organization or regulation. The Stationers' Company attempted to regulate the Scottish and Irish presses throughout the late seventeenth century, with limited success. Outside London during the latter half of the seventeenth century, the king, local bishops or privy and town councils carried out ad hoc censorship. Meanwhile, the university presses of Oxford and Cambridge largely regulated themselves, although they could not grant their own licenses without royal permission. Attempts to increase this regulation occurred after the Restoration, usually involving the appointment of London-based stationers or censors. For instance, after 1670, the crown attempted to increase regulation in Ireland by forming a printing guild constituted by members of the Stationers' Company. Most books available in Wales came from London or Oxford, and Wales did not have a specific regulatory or censorship system: see Alastair Mann, 'The Anatomy of the Printed Book in Early Modern Scotland', *SHR* 80 (2001), 181–200, at 193–6; John Barnard, 'The English Provinces', in idem and D. F. McKenzie, eds, *The Cambridge History of the Book in Britain*, 4: *1557–1695* (Cambridge, 2002; hereafter: *CHBB*), 665–86, at 665–6; Robert Welch, 'The Book in Ireland from the Tudor Re-conquest to the Battle of the Boyne, ibid. 701–18, at 716–17; Philip Johnes, 'Wales', ibid. 719–34, at 721, 729–30; Michael Treadwell, 'Lists of Master Printers: The Size of the London Printing

Catholic books were prosecuted, when and why authorities chose to enforce the law, and when (if ever) Catholic print was permissible. Exploring these interests is critical not only to understanding when and why certain works were prosecuted but also to recognizing how books could escape detection. The Licensing Act, or the 'Act for preventing the frequent abuses in printing seditious treasonable and unlicensed Books', provides the lens through which these topics are viewed.[6] The article analyses the three main London enforcing bodies from 1662 to 1678: the Stationers' Company, the Surveyor of the Press and the bishop of London. It then turns to the period from 1679 to 1684, when the main censorship law lapsed, to show how press regulation changed when these interests disappeared, leaving it governed only by the king's preferences.

Renewed every few years from 1662 until it lapsed in 1679, and reinstated in 1685 and again renewed regularly until 1695, the Licensing Act was the dominant censorship law during the Restoration.[7] It represented the fulfilment of earlier Stuart press regulation and established the rules for licensing, importation and prosecution.[8] Although the act ostensibly forbade 'offensive' print in England or 'any other His Majesties Dominions or in the parts beyond the Seas', it dealt principally with the London book trade, as London was by far the largest centre of book production in Britain.[9] To ensure the book trade's conformity to the act, in 1663 Charles II officially named Roger L'Estrange as Surveyor of the Press.[10] To enforce the act, L'Estrange and the Stationers' Company wardens were to conduct searches, the secretary of state

---

Trade, 1637–1723', in Robin Myers and Michael Harris, eds, *Aspects of Printing from 1600* (Oxford, 1987), 141–70, at 142–8.

[6] 'Act for preventing the frequent abuses in printing seditious treasonable and unlicensed Books', 14 Car. II c.33, in John Raithby, ed., *Statutes of the Realm*, 5: *1628–80* (London, 1819), 428–35.

[7] Parliament failed to renew the Licensing Act in 1679 amidst debates over the exclusion crisis. It was revived at James II's accession (1 Jac. II c.17 §15) before lapsing permanently in 1695: Raymond Astbury, 'The Renewal of the Licensing Act in 1693 and its Lapse in 1695', *The Library* 5th series 33 (1978), 296–322.

[8] Timothy Crist, 'Government Control of the Press after the Expiration of the Printing Act in 1679', *Publishing History* 5 (1979), 219–38, at 220–1. This included the Star Chamber decrees of 1586 and 1637 restricting trade to London, Cambridge, Oxford and York.

[9] See n. 5 above.

[10] *CCLBT*, 1: 15 August 1663.

to issue warrants, and the bishop of London and the archbishop of Canterbury to evaluate and dispose of seized writings.[11] Each had their vision of censorship shaped by financial, political or ecclesiastical motives, to which were added the interests of the king. The new act expanded the distribution of responsibility between the book trade, the state and the church, and augmented the king's influence by empowering his messengers to conduct searches alongside representatives of the Stationers' Company.[12]

Whilst the act was about licensing, its stated purpose was to guard against anything 'contrary to ... the Church or the Government or Governors of the Church State or Common wealth', and the dangers of 'seditious and heretical pamphlets'.[13] Although religious concerns were at its core, to meet this challenge the act targeted all unlicensed print. Proving a lack of a licence was far simpler and faster than proving sedition or heresy or the comparable crime of *scandalum magnatum*. This afforded the state a great deal of flexibility. It could apply the act against any unlicensed work and then tailor the punishment to the transgressor.[14] For instance, in 1666, unlicensed texts were discovered at the shops of Thomas Leach, John Darby and Thomas Milburn. Stationers' Company wardens arrested Darby and Milburn for printing a Quaker and a Catholic book respectively, and seized their presses, but they took no action against Leach for his pamphlet on the Great Fire of London.[15] The language of the Licensing Act left plenty of room for manoeuvre for state or personal agendas to shape how it was actually enforced.

Until now, most appraisals of Restoration censorship have focused on its persecution or its inefficiency. However, Catholic print had a varied and ever-changing relationship with the censors. At times royally endorsed and rarely targeted with the same vigour as Dissenting print, Catholic books continued to be produced. While enforcers

[11] While the act established a detailed pre-publication licensing system, this article focuses on its provisions for unlicensed works that escaped this system.
[12] Michael Treadwell, 'The Stationers and the Printing Acts at the End of the Seventeenth Century', in Barnard and McKenzie, eds, *CHBB*, 4: 755–76, at 765.
[13] 14 Car. II c.33 §1.
[14] Ibid. The act stipulated fines, seizure and destruction of goods and presses, and imprisonment as punishments but did not provide further specification.
[15] *CCLBT*, 1: [undated] 1666. The text Darby printed was unnamed, but Milburn was charged with printing Roger Castlemaine's *English Catholicke Apologie*, and *London's Flames* was found at Leach's shop.

opposed the threat of popery and policy makers legislated against it, it was not always practicable to pursue every case, particularly against those who did not embody the stereotypical traits of hidden, foreign or proselytizing Catholicism. As the following will show, the institutionalized intolerance of the written statute was paired with flexibility of enforcement, thus providing a parallel to the rigid penal laws and daily coexistence described by historians of Catholicism and toleration.[16] The flexibility derived from the differing interests of the Stationers' Company, secretary of state and church, who all played distinct roles in enforcement. Awareness of that flexibility also enabled these parties to serve their unique interests. Regulation of the press should be viewed by scholars as a necessary formal position (helpfully) mitigated by different interests and the actual experience of toleration.

By evaluating the interests of the enforcers of the Licensing Act in terms of their relationships to Catholic print, this article offers a new method of viewing the censorship law in practice and raises the profile of Restoration Catholic print culture. Control of the press has received significant attention from book historians, who focus on the enforcers of censorship and the continual circulation of unlicensed print.[17] Although the resulting studies address the causes of unlicensed print, almost always blaming the Stationers' Company for infringements of the laws, they do not consider fully whether this ineffectiveness was bad or resulted in a necessary balance to the market.

---

[16] Alexandra Walsham, *Charitable Hatred: Tolerance and Intolerance in England, 1500–1700* (Manchester, 2006); William J. Shiels, '"Getting on" and "getting along" in Parish and Town: Catholics and their Neighbours in England', in Benjamin Kaplan et al., eds, *Catholic Communities in Protestant States: Britain and the Netherlands* c.*1570–1720*, Studies in Early Modern European History (Manchester, 2009), 67–83; Gabriel Glickman, 'The Church and the Catholic Community 1660–1714', in Grant Tapsell, ed., *The Later Stuart Church, 1660–1714: Politics, Culture and Society in Early Modern Britain* (Manchester, 2012), 217–42.

[17] J. Walker, 'The Censorship of the Press during the Reign of Charles II', *History* 35 (1950), 219–38; Philip Hamburger, 'The Development of the Law of Seditious Libel and the Control of the Press', *Stanford Law Review* 37 (1985), 661–765; Treadwell, 'Stationers and Printing Acts'; Robin Myers and Michael Harris, eds, *Aspects of Printing from 1600* (Oxford, 1987); Anne Dunan-Page and Beth Lynch, eds, *Roger L'Estrange and the Making of Restoration Culture* (Burlington, VT, 2008); Maureen Bell, 'Offensive Behaviour in the English Book Trade 1641–1700', in Robin Myers, Michael Harris and G. Mandelbrote, eds, *Against the Law: Crime, Sharp Practice and the Control of Print* (London, 2004), 61–79.

Moreover, censorship studies tend to focus on case studies of Dissenting or radical presses. These case studies demonstrate a severe state censorship programme.[18] However, a focus on Catholic books and bookmen complicates this view; the level of persecution of Catholic print was continually changing during the reign of Charles II. This focus reveals that while there continued to be anxieties over the illegal importation of Catholic books printed abroad, Catholicism also had a strong presence in the capital,[19] and this extended beyond the traditional elite and clerical circles.[20] Moreover, Catholic books were not just overseas products; they were also domestically produced, mostly in London, by Protestants and Catholics alike.[21] This is important given London's position as a visible centre of anti-popish sentiments, particularly in the house of Commons, which frequently brought forth proposals to limit the 'growth of popery'.[22]

While persecution of Catholic print networks occurred, this persecution needs to be placed within the context of a wider censorship system that often chose not to pursue these networks. In line with the evidence of recent studies calling into question the strength of anti-popery or the enforcement of the penal code, personal tolerance was often apparent.[23] While maintaining social control required the

[18] Stephen Bardle, *The Literary Underground in the 1660s: Andrew Marvell, George Wither, Ralph Wallis, and the World of Restoration Satire and Pamphleteering* (Oxford, 2012); Kate Peters, *Print Culture and the Early Quakers* (Cambridge, 2005).
[19] The Licensing Act also regulated imports.
[20] For 'elite' Catholics, see Gabriel Glickman, *The English Catholic Community, 1688–1745: Politics, Culture and Ideology*, Studies in Early Modern Cultural, Political and Social History 7 (Woodbridge, 2009); Geoff Baker, *Reading and Politics in Early Modern England: The Mental World of a Seventeenth-Century Catholic Gentleman* (Manchester, 2010). For lay metropolitan Catholics, see Francis Dolan, *Whores of Babylon: Catholicism, Gender, and Seventeenth-Century Print Culture* (Notre Dame, 2005); Penny Richards, 'A Life in Writing: Elizabeth Cellier and Print Culture', *Women's Writing* 7 (2000), 411–25.
[21] For examples of cross-confessional book production, see *CCLBT*, 1: 8 June 1669; 2: 27 October 1678.
[22] See Roger Flexman, ed., *A General Index to the Eighth, Ninth, Tenth, and Eleventh Volumes of the Journals of the House of Commons* (London, 1780), 49–50, for a list of speeches given against recusants.
[23] Scott Sowerby, 'Opposition to Anti-Popery in Restoration England', *JBS* 51 (2012), 26–49; Peter Walker, 'Leicestershire and the Three Questions: James II's Canvass of the Gentry on the Question of Repeal of the Test Acts and Penal Laws in 1688', *Transactions of the Leicestershire Archaeological and Historical Society* 87 (2013), 207–24; Walsham, *Charitable Hatred*, 300–6.

existence of harsh laws on the books, people could view the crimes of their neighbours more leniently, especially if it served their own interests or the harmony of the whole. I shall investigate how religious beliefs affected the enforcement of secular laws and how they interacted with other values and interests.

Keith Wrightson described seventeenth-century English laws governing moral behaviour as 'a conflict between the concept of order … embodied in legislation and the somewhat broader area of behaviour permitted', that is, in practice by the law enforcers.[24] This observation also pertains to the Licensing Act. Every party empowered by the act looked to their own interests and interpreted their role as an enforcer in the light of them. These interests were often in conflict and as a result the act failed to prevent the circulation of unlicensed print throughout London and beyond.[25] Simply put, 'licensing as a system … was certainly not successfully enforced', as Treadwell recognizes,[26] but that did not mean that all enforcers would have seen it as failing, or regarded it as failing in the same way.

<h2 style="text-align:center">THE STATIONERS' COMPANY</h2>

The first of the groups tasked with regulating the print industry, the Stationers' Company, bore principal responsibility for hunting down unlicensed books. However, they were reluctant to act unless doing so benefited themselves. Few possessed the time, means or desire to seek out seditious or heretical texts. They focused on works that infringed their own patents, namely foreign English-language imports and pirated editions.[27] For instance, John Hetet's study of the accounts of the Stationers' Company found that in 1663 they 'only hounded printers of pirated primers' for which the company held the official monopoly.[28] When the company did pursue seditious works, they

[24] Keith Wrightson, 'Two Concepts of Order: Justices, Constables and Jurymen in Seventeenth-Century England', in John Brewer and John Styles, eds, *An Ungovernable People: The English and their Law in the Seventeenth and Eighteenth Centuries* (London, 1980), 21–46, at 21.
[25] Crist, 'Government Control', 224.
[26] Treadwell, 'Stationers and Printing Acts', 765.
[27] Bell, 'Offensive Behaviour', 68.
[28] John Hetet, 'The Wardens' Accounts of the Stationers' Company, 1663–79', in Robin Myers and Michael Harris, eds, *Economics of the British Book Trade 1605–1939* (Cambridge, 1985), 32–59, at 36.

often resold the books and loose sheets seized during raids, which meant that they were not actually removed from circulation.[29] In addition, the high prices commanded by illicit Catholic works prompted many stationers to engage in the black market trade. This was the case for Mearne, as described in the introduction, who was nevertheless remembered as a 'zealous seeker-out of illegal presses'.[30]

The Stationers' Company was unable to overcome the financial incentives of illicit print. One printer described works 'treasonable and seditious, and most profitable for sale'.[31] In his autobiography, the Carmelite Walter Joseph Travers recalls that whilst publishing an English translation of the life of St Teresa of Avila, 'the bill for printing was very heavy, owing to the risk the printer, a Protestant, ran in publishing a forbidden book'.[32] On top of this, unlicensed printers (those operating outside the company) continued to set up printing houses, and this opened the market for the publication of illicit and difficult-to-trace work.[33] The Catholic queen, Catherine of Braganza, employed an unlicensed master printer, John Winter, to produce a devotional work, *A Liturgical Discourse of the Holy Sacrifice of the Masse*, despite having legal permission to acquire books for her chapel.[34] If members of the Stationers Company could not resist printing unlicensed books for profit, they could hardly be expected to curb the practice.

The other branches of press regulation were well aware of the shortcomings of the Stationers' Company, which Bishop Compton of London referred to as 'a Company of malicious persons and of very knaves besides'.[35] In a bid to increase his own control over the press, L'Estrange explained the failure of censorship based on the

---

[29] *CCLBT*, 2: 20 December 1676.

[30] Howard M. Nixon, *English Restoration Bookbindings: Samuel Mearne and his Contemporaries* (London, 1974), 10.

[31] Anon., *The London Printers Lamentation, or, the Press opprest, and overprest* (London, 1660), 4.

[32] Walter Joseph Travers, 'Autobiography of Father Bede of St. Simon Stock (Walter Joseph Travers)', in Benedict Zimmerman, ed., *Carmel in England: A History of the English Mission of the Discalced Carmelites, 1615 to 1849* (London, 1899), 171–307, at 243.

[33] Walker, 'Censorship', 220–2.

[34] Angelus à Sancto Francisco [Richard Mason], *A Liturgical Discourse of the Holy Sacrifice of the Mass*, 2 parts ([London], 1669–70); *CCLBT*, 1: 15 October 1669.

[35] *CCLBT*, 2: 27 March 1677.

actions of the Stationers' Company: 'They are both *Parties* and *Iudges* ... they are Entrusted (effectually) to search for their own Copies; to Destroy their own Interests; to Prosecute their own Agents, and to Punish Themselves: for they are the Principal Authors of those Mischiefs which they pretend now to Redress.'[36]

L'Estrange wrote from a highly biased position, hoping to commandeer the company's role in enforcing censorship, but, as already observed, his complaint had merit. Many stationers operated as both booksellers and printers and relied upon the networks of bookmen and intermediaries. They often lacked the motivation to prosecute their own. Even the king's appointee, Richard Royston, used his position to forewarn John Crook to remove copies of *Fiat Lux*, a Catholic text, before the wardens could conduct a search of Crook's shop.[37] Business relations between colleagues frequently trumped adherence to the law.

Those who assisted the stationers in these searches could also be swayed. In 1669, Barden, a constable, was apprehended for refusing to seize popish books from Johnson, a printer and bookseller.[38] Another report describes a constable, probably the same one, acquiring and returning these same books to Johnson.[39] Several years later, a 'government official' caught a Protestant in the act of printing the new translation of the life of St Teresa for Abraham Woodhead and Walter Joseph Travers. Travers recorded: 'we were in danger of losing everything that had already been done, and being heavily fined besides', but after a few weeks the official returned the confiscated sheets.[40] No report of the discovery was submitted by any party. Although in neither case were the searchers' motivations clear, Barden's semi-public actions must have jeopardized his career.

On other occasions when the company took action against Catholic print, their efforts were thwarted not by their own men, but by the royal family. In 1669, the company used the crime of printing a Catholic book to harass John Winter.[41] Over the course

---

[36] Roger L'Estrange, *Considerations and Proposals in Order to the Regulation of the Press together with Diverse Instances of Treasonous, and Seditious Pamphlets, proving the Necessity thereof* (London, 1663), 24.

[37] Hetet, 'Warden's Accounts', 43.

[38] *CCLBT*, 1: 5 June 1669.

[39] Ibid.: [June 1669?].

[40] Travers, 'Autobiography', 243.

[41] *CCLBT*, 1: 7 June 1669, 4 October 1669.

of the previous six years, the company had endeavoured to annexe Winter's printing house; this Catholic book provided the justification for seizing his presses.[42] However, the queen declared that she had commissioned the work from Winter and demanded his release, to which the company grudgingly acceded.[43] A similar situation occurred seven years later, when the king halted the prosecution of Anthony Lawrence for printing *The Great Sacrifice*.[44] Hindrances to enforcement of the act thus came both from within and from above the company.

In the print trade, economics, family ties and business relationships, as much as religion, motivated action. The company's fierce protection of its privileged status guaranteed its intervention whenever its various patents were threatened, but the bonds among stationers, the importance of the patrons and the financial gains of illicit print similarly ensured that its policing of the book trade could never be complete. As a result, the Stationers' Company earned a reputation for being unreliable. Nevertheless, its influence and the authority it traditionally exercised over the presses ensured that it remained the authority best situated to police printers without overhauling the book trade.

THE SURVEYOR OF THE PRESS

With the half-hearted efforts of the Stationers' Company, regulation of the press next fell to the secretary of state. However, the majority of the secretary of state's duties relating to the press, including the licensing of books, passed via warrant to the Surveyor of the Press, a post held by Roger L'Estrange from 1663 until 1679 and again from 1685 to 1688.[45] As surveyor, L'Estrange received assistance from Messengers of the Press, appointed by the crown with approval from the Stationers' Company.[46] He viewed himself as the supervisor

---

[42] Treadwell, 'Lists of Master Printers', 145–50.
[43] *CCLBT*, 1: 15 October 1669, 7 March 1670.
[44] Ibid. 2: 13 September 1676.
[45] Ibid. 1: 15 August 1663; Tim Harris, *Revolution: The Great Crisis of the British Monarchy, 1685–1720* (London, 2006), 72. This post derived its powers from the Licensing Act; when that lapsed in 1679, the position lapsed with it. In 1685, the renewal of the act prompted a new warrant from James II restoring L'Estrange's former powers.
[46] Leona Rostenberg, 'Robert Stephens, Messenger of the Press: An Episode in 17th-Century Censorship', *Papers of the Bibliographical Society of America* 49 (1955), 131–52.

of the company, leading to friction between it and himself.[47] Like his patron, the earl of Arlington, L'Estrange was a firm royalist working to suppress any work that insulted the royal family or defended the regicide of Charles I.

As the Restoration took shape, L'Estrange released several vitriolic pamphlets against Presbyterians and in support of the old royalists.[48] On his appointment as Surveyor of the Press, L'Estrange compiled a list of seditious pamphlets to be suppressed.[49] He sorted these titles by category, including works proposing that 'the Duty of the Subjects [is] but Conditional' or that 'The King has no Power to Impose in Ecclesiastical Affairs'.[50] While the inclusion of a large number of non-conformist works is unsurprising, it is striking that none of the titles or categories in L'Estrange's catalogue referred to Catholicism. L'Estrange's focus on Dissenting works, and his lack of concern with Catholic printing, continued throughout his career.[51]

Neither the crown nor the secretary of state attempted to diminish or restrict L'Estrange's powers, giving little indication that they might have disapproved of his priorities. However, he was not invulnerable. In 1663, L'Estrange licensed and advertised a book by a Catholic, *Philanax Anglicus*, which claimed that the nature of Protestant ideology had resulted in Charles I's execution by his Protestant subjects.[52] In response, the Nonconformist pamphleteer Ralph Wallis warned that Catholic interests had corrupted licensing regulation.[53] Despite L'Estrange's express opposition to legal toleration, his informal tolerance of Catholicism opened him up to accusations that he was a crypto-Catholic,[54] and this suspicion increased in 1679, when L'Estrange supported the duke of York's claim to the succession

---

[47] *CCLBT*, 2: [before 20 February 1677].

[48] Roger L'Estrange, *A Caveat to the Cavaliers* (London, 1661); idem, *Interest Mistaken, or, The Holy Cheat* (London, 1662).

[49] Idem, *Considerations and Proposals*.

[50] Ibid. 19, 21.

[51] Peter Hinds, *'The Horrid Popish Plot': Roger L'Estrange and the Circulation of Political Discourse in Late Seventeenth-Century London* (Oxford, 2010), 34–5.

[52] Sir Henry Janson, *Philanax Anglicus* (London, 1663); Bardle, *Literary Underground*, 54; Martin Dzelzainis, 'Milton's *Of True Religion* and the Earl of Castlemaine', *Seventeenth Century* 7 (1992), 53–69, at 57–8. *Philanax Anglicus* was sold by the queen's bookseller in ordinary, Thomas Sadler.

[53] Bardle, *Literary Underground*, 54.

[54] Hinds, *Horrid Popish Plot*, 163–6.

against those who sought his exclusion.[55] Resentment of his practices forced L'Estrange to flee during the Popish Plot of 1678. However, L'Estrange never openly converted, nor did he describe himself as a Catholic, even under James II when it became popular to do so. L'Estrange seems to have been an Anglican who placed loyalty to the crown and royal prerogative above religious persecution.

There can be little doubt that L'Estrange's actions closely aligned with the desires of the crown or that he permitted Catholic books when the king desired it. In the first decade of the Restoration, with the memory of the Interregnum still fresh, the government's focus was primarily on the suppression of Nonconformist and anti-monarchical print.[56] Quaker printers were frequent targets during these years, which saw the arrests of leading figures such as Anna Brewster, Francis Smith and Susannah Calvert.[57] In comparison, English Catholics, many of whom had demonstrated their loyalty on the battlefield or at the exile courts, were viewed as a lesser threat. Indeed, in the early years of the Restoration, Catholic loyalist works such as Thomas Blount's *Boscobel*, which described how Catholics had aided Charles II's escape after the Battle of Worcester in 1651, circulated freely.[58] In addition, L'Estrange's persecution of Dissenting authors and printers had the potential to aid Catholics by hampering their chief counter-polemicists. However, L'Estrange's toleration went beyond the tenuous position adopted by Charles II's government.

Later, while serving under James II, L'Estrange recorded in his history that 'the Scandal is not to be Born; not to be Defended; and never to be Forgiven, to Charge Roman Catholicks with Vndutifullness to their Sovereign'.[59] The 'dutifulness' and loyalty of Catholics distinguished them from other nonconforming groups in L'Estrange's mind. His stance was to protect the reputation of the crown, and, for the most part, he did not view Catholic works as damaging to either church or state, especially when compared to those of Dissenters and parliamentarians. When they were discovered, unlicensed Catholic works were still often prosecuted.

[55] Roger L'Estrange, *The Case put, concerning the Succession* (London, 1679).
[56] Walker, 'Censorship', 230.
[57] Ibid. 227–35.
[58] Thomas Blount, *Boscobel: Or, the History of His Sacred Majesties Most Miraculous Preservation after the Battle of Worcester* (London, 1660).
[59] Roger L'Estrange, *A Brief History of the Times* (London, 1687), 14.

However, to L'Estrange, (English) Catholicism was not the main source of the 'seditious and heretical pamphlets' against which he had been commissioned to guard. He held a more ideological stance, less affected by the economic imperatives of the Stationers' Company but driven by concern about radical Protestant sedition.

THE BISHOP OF LONDON

The priorities of the Stationers' Company and of L'Estrange as Surveyor of the Press often (perhaps unintentionally) enabled the continuation of Catholic printing. In contrast, the ecclesiastical authorities were not as permissive. They were tasked with assessing the content of printed works. The Licensing Act called for most genres of books to pass through the hands of the bishop of London or the archbishop of Canterbury to receive a licence. Moreover, these two men often determined the fate of any seized unlicensed religious texts. The bishop of London exerted this control in the capital, where the vast majority of works were printed. Unlike the Stationers' Company, and even (to an extent) L'Estrange, the bishop's income did not derive from the book trade, and he did not have its functioning interests in mind. His task was to defend the church and ensure conformity in print, and this separated him from the ecosystem of the marketplace.

While Humphrey Henchman, bishop of London from 1663 to 1675, had taken a moderate approach to his role in overseeing the press, his successor, Henry Compton, reached beyond his mandate to target, prosecute and destroy Catholic works. In this case it is apparent that the rigour of censorship depended on personal convictions, rather than just on institutionally determined interests. A known opponent of the Roman Catholic Church, Compton viewed Catholicism, foreign and domestic, as the greatest threat facing England.[60] In the 1660s, he had twice anonymously published anti-popish and anti-Jesuit tracts.[61] Compton thus represented a counterbalance to L'Estrange, advocating a somewhat accommodating stance

---

[60] Andrew M. Coleby, 'Compton, Henry (1631/2–1713)', *ODNB*, 3 January 2008, online at: <http://www.oxforddnb.com/view/10.1093/ref:odnb/9780198614128.001.0001/odnb-9780198614128-e-6032>, accessed 15 August 2018.
[61] Edward Carpenter, *The Protestant Bishop: Being the Life of Henry Compton, 1632–1713, Bishop of London* (London, 1956), 60, 67–9.

towards Dissenters while believing that the full force of church and state was required to stamp out the growing Catholic threat.[62]

However, Compton's view of censorship required him to act beyond the remit of the Licensing Act. In theory, the bishop's role in punishing publishers of unlicensed print only came into play after L'Estrange and the Stationers' Company had fulfilled their parts and delivered seized books to him.[63] However, Compton demanded search warrants from the secretary of state or Privy Council following any rumour of a Catholic book. It was Compton who drew attention to *The Great Sacrifice*, and he ordered the wardens of the Stationers Company to confiscate the work.[64] In 1676, he called for a search of the queen's residence, Somerset House, after hearing that 'Popish and unlicensed Books were lodged in three warehouses over the stables'; this was carried out.[65] He bullied and frustrated those around him, especially the royal family, as he sought to impose what he understood to be appropriate levels of censorship. However, he also tried to bypass the proper authorities. In 1679, he ordered the Customs House to seize all copies of the pro-Catholic *The Increase and Growth of the Popish Religion*, without first informing the Privy Council.[66] Compton was the instigator of a number of similar investigations and initiatives, and the political and religious climate of the mid- to late 1670s made it expedient for the government to comply.

However, Compton could not bypass the king or the judiciary. As in the case of the Stationers' Company, the king and the courts proved able to prevent, or at least reduce, punishment inflicted on printers or booksellers found in Compton's searches. As indicated above, the king forbore to prosecute Lawrence. Likewise, none of the men suspected of hiding books at Somerset House, Moor, Turner and Dod, appear in the London Sessions Records.[67] Whilst Compton was able to seize many Catholic books, he had less success in obtaining severe punishments against Catholic booksellers.

---

[62] Coleby, 'Compton'.
[63] It should be noted that the bishop and archbishop were responsible for issuing licences for texts outside the fields of common law, history, affairs of the state and heraldry or books produced by the university presses: 14 Car. II c.33 §2.
[64] Carpenter, *Compton*, 67.
[65] Ibid.; *CCLBT*, 2: 9 September 1676.
[66] *CCLBT*, 2: 3 January 1679.
[67] Hugh Bowler, ed., *London Sessions Records, 1605–1685*, CRS 34 (London, 1934).

It is important to give Compton credit for his role in press regulation. Anti-popery had increased since Charles II's Declaration of
Indulgence in 1672 and the revelation the following year of the
duke of York's conversion to Catholicism. However, it was not
until Compton's appointment in 1675 that confiscations of popish
print markedly increased. He influenced all the major prosecutions
of Catholic bookmen in the late 1670s.[68] Similarly, under
Compton, more pamphlets underwent the process of damasking,
or defacing in such a way as to render the text unreadable.
Damasking may well have signalled 'a concern to see that proscribed
print work did indeed get cancelled', as Juliet Fleming suggests; however, state-ordered damasking was rare and over half of the orders for
it came from Compton.[69] He enacted more destructive punishments
as well. During the Popish Plot, Compton ordered the books and
papers of the Catholic publisher James Thompson 'to be publicly
burnt at the Old Exchange'.[70] For contemporaries, this would have
been a counterpart to the bonfires lit in the context of mock papal
processions, which aimed to stir up anti-popish sentiments by
reminding the public of the secretive and scheming nature of
Catholics.[71] These actions went far beyond what was expected of
Compton in fulfilling his role as the bishop responsible for censorship
in London. The fervour with which he attacked Catholic print seems
to have stemmed from his own hatred of the religion.

Like L'Estrange, Compton lost his influence over the regulation of
the press when the Licensing Act lapsed in 1679. As a result, prosecutions against Catholic printers and booksellers also ceased, though
the bishop continued to hold book burnings for texts previously
seized under the act. Compton represented the extreme end of censorship against Catholicism. He pushed against, or went beyond, the
boundaries of his role as stated in the Licensing Act, to the frustration
of the royal family and many tories. However, in the late 1670s he
had public fear of popery on his side. Given that Compton's position

[68] My doctoral work on late Restoration English Catholic print culture will show this in
more detail.
[69] Juliet Fleming, 'Damask Papers', in Andy Kesson and Emma Smith, eds, *The
Elizabethan Top Ten: Defining Print Popularity in Early Modern England* (London,
2013), 179–91, at 182.
[70] *CCLBT*, 2: 28 October 1678.
[71] Odai Johnson, 'Pope-Burning Pageants: Performing the Exclusion Crisis', *Theatre
Survey* 37 (1996), 35–57.

was considered extreme, it follows that the standard approach to censorship was more lenient.

The role of individual interests under the Licensing Act becomes clear by looking at what happened when it expired and the king took a more direct role in censorship. When the act lapsed in 1679, the archbishop of Canterbury and bishop of London, the Stationers' Company and the secretary of state the (and therefore the Surveyor of the Press) all lost their mandate to intervene. Charles II turned to older sedition laws to make cases against Dissenting printers, then pressured the judges in those trials to extend his own prerogative in their sentences. After the third trial, he achieved a court ruling that 'permitted the Crown to prohibit unlicensed publications of news without a statute'.[72] This also led to a change in the types of Catholic books that were prosecuted. During the previous two decades, those appearing in the records had been educational or devotional in content. These were mass books or manuals of daily prayers, which served to maintain an established community without access to priests. However, after 1679, the prosecuted Catholic works all related to the Popish Plot, its resulting trials and the various plots that followed. The most infamous of these books was the earl of Castlemaine's *Compendium,* which attacked the state for arresting Catholic lords and executing priests.[73] Content that criticized the government, rather than sympathy shown for Catholics, made books like these targets.

Reports of seized Catholic books are sparse during the final years of Charles II's reign, but non-political Catholic books did not vanish. In 1684 the Catholic bookseller Matthew Turner advertised books of contemplation and devotion.[74] That same year the tory printer Nathaniel Thompson included three Catholic ballads published during the Popish Plot (which could be categorized as news) in his collection of loyalist ballads.[75] The government did not attempt to categorize these as seditious or damaging to the crown, as it had done with Dissenting works in three trials in the preceding years.

[72] Hamburger, 'Seditious Libel', 684–8.
[73] Roger Palmer, *The Compendium, or, A Short View of the Late Tryals in relation to the present Plot against His Majesty and Government* (London, 1679); *CCLBT,* 2: 26 September 1679 n. 24, quoting from the *Domestic Intelligence.*
[74] Le sieur Combes, *An Historical Explication of what there is most remarkable in that Wonder of the World, the French King's Royal House at Versailles* (London, 1684), 141–4.
[75] Nathaniel Thompson, *A Choice Collection of 120 Loyal Songs* (London, 1684), 139–41, 148–55, 248–50.

Moreover, Thompson's inclusion of the ballads embedded them in royalist rhetoric. They served both tory and Catholic audiences, blaming whigs and Dissenters for the late troubles while offering sympathy for the sufferings of Catholics. The ballads embodied the alignment between pro-tory and pro-Catholic print brought on by the exclusion crisis which emphasized loyalty to the crown above all else.

The strongest demonstration of the alignment between tory and pro-Catholic stances emerged in 1680 with a new edition of Thomas Blount's *Boscobel*, that same Catholic book that had openly circulated in 1660.[76] Henry Brome, principal royalist bookseller and ally of L'Estrange, sold both the first and the new edition. The new edition followed the indictment of the duke of York as a recusant and offered a royalist show of support for coexistence with Catholics.[77] The political climate and the interests of the king now actively endorsed a Catholic book. In the king's mind, there were good and bad Catholics, and the defining feature of the former was absolute loyalty to the crown. Catholic books that fitted this message could receive an official licence.

CONCLUSION

In Restoration England, religion was one of many motivations that drove the enforcers of censorship. Economics, political affiliations and business relations all played their role. The empowering of a trade guild, a private citizen and ecclesiastical leaders to regulate the London press produced this fracturing diversity. Yet parliament continued to renew the Licensing Act without alteration until it lapsed in 1679, a victim of the exclusion crisis. Something about this 'inefficient' system clearly met the needs of censorship. This article posits that, like the penal codes, the Licensing Act could not be, and was not meant to be, regularly enforced. What might be seen as corruption by personal interests provided room for the type of discretion needed to maintain ties within a community. Meanwhile, the simplicity of proving a lack of licence made it an ideal tool to harass Dissenting and Catholic printers during moments of political tension. These

---

[76] Thomas Blount, *Boscobel: or The compleat History of His Sacred Majesties Most Miraculous Preservation after the Battle of Worcester, 3 Sept. 1651* (London, 1680).
[77] Dorothy Turner, 'Royalism, Romance, and History in Boscobel: or, The History of His Sacred Majesties Most Miraculous Preservation', *Prose Studies* 22 (1999), 59–70, at 67.

tensions were embodied most significantly in the actions of
L'Estrange against Nonconformists and Compton against papists.
Their influence waxed when the public or king agreed with them
and waned when this support evaporated.

Regulatory authorities permitted or restricted Catholic works
according to their political and economic interests. By and large,
Catholic books did not affect Stationers' Company monopolies,
but they did provide useful avenues of illegal revenue. When
Catholic books promoted a much-desired call for loyalism, press regulators pursuing the king's interests saw them as advantageous, or at
least non-threatening. When the Popish Plot unfolded, informal
toleration vanished, and more informers reported on Catholic book
activity to the enforcers.[78] These years also demonstrate the numerous social levels at which grudging acceptance had been the rule, from
the court to the bookmen's neighbours who now reported them.
Popish anxieties again gained precedence. However, it should be
noted that Compton was the only one of the three main regulators
actively to target Catholic print.

Imperfect regulation and irregular enforcement of laws were not
unique to the book trade; indeed, these were common themes in
the early modern period. However, exploring the enforcement of
the Licensing Act demonstrates the restraints and allowances under
which Catholic bookmen operated in late Restoration London.
This new understanding of how the state attempted to regulate
England's book trade alters our perspective on whether censorship
succeeded or failed and helps us assess how Catholics negotiated
these regulations. As with the penal laws, official intolerance sat
alongside practical coexistence. In both cases, religion was not the
only interest when it came to enforcing laws; however, it was always
a factor.

[78] *CCLBT*, 2: 11 November, 4, 28 December 1678.

Protestant Dissent and the Law: Enforcement and Persecution, 1662–72

David L. Wykes*

Dr Williams's Library, London

Religious Dissent was shaped by the law. The Act of Uniformity (1662) set out the terms of conformity, and those who could not accept those terms risked prosecution. A great many were convicted under the earlier Elizabethan and Jacobean recusancy statutes, but new laws, such as the Conventicle Acts (1664, 1670) and the Five Mile Act (1665), were also passed. Anthony Fletcher's essay, published in 1984, remains almost the only study of enforcement, in which he argued that the impact of the penal laws on Dissent has been exaggerated because the Conventicle Acts were not systematically enforced. A range of contemporary accounts will be used to suggest that their impact was greater than has been appreciated because of the enforcement of other statutes and the harassment of ejected ministers and their supporters.

Protestant Dissent in England and Wales dates from the Restoration of Charles II in 1660. In many ways it was shaped by the law. The Act of Uniformity (1662) formed the basis of the Restoration religious settlement. Deliberately uncompromising, the act established an exclusive episcopal state church requiring conformity to a prescribed doctrine and liturgy. A substantial body of ministers who belonged to the Church of England and believed in a national church were forced out as a consequence, with the loss of their livelihoods. In all, just over two thousand ministers and teachers refused to submit between 1660 and 1662. Many of these ministers became active Dissenters, preaching and gathering congregations despite the laws and the threat of prosecution.[1] They were joined by an important minority of their former parishioners who sought a godly ministry and therefore failed to conform or to conform fully. In addition, Baptists, Independents

---

* Dr Williams's Library, 14 Gordon Sq, London, WC1H 0AR. E-mail: director@dwl.ac.uk.

[1] A. G. Matthews, *Calamy Revised; being a Revision of Edmund Calamy's Account of the Ministers and others Ejected and Silenced, 1660–2* (London, 1934).

Studies in Church History 56 (2020), 306–319
doi: 10.1017/stc.2019.17
© Ecclesiastical History Society 2020

and Quakers would have nothing to do with the Church of England and had already formed their own separatist churches before 1660.

Even before the Act of Uniformity, the existing Elizabethan and Jacobean recusancy statutes could be enforced against all who failed to attend their parish church for worship or to receive communion. A great many Dissenters who refused to attend church and conform outwardly continued to be convicted after 1662 by these statutes, which had originally been passed against Catholics. In addition, those who failed to take the oaths of allegiance, most notably Quakers, suffered imprisonment. New laws were also passed to prevent ejected ministers from preaching to their former parishioners and Dissenters from assembling for worship. The first Conventicle Act (1664) prohibited meetings of five persons or more, aged 16 or over, for worship outside the Church of England. A second Act (1670) introduced greater fines against the preacher and those who provided the meeting place, and allowed for only one justice rather than two to convict. It also encouraged the use of informers by rewarding them with a third of the fines. The Five Mile Act (1665) prevented ministers who refused to take the oaths prescribed from coming within five miles of a borough which returned MPs or a parish where they had preached since the Act of Oblivion. Those convicted were subject to a £40 fine or six months' imprisonment. There has been a long tradition among historians of Dissent, from Edmund Calamy's account of the ejected ministers in the early eighteenth century to the modern period, which has emphasized the sacrifice the ejected ministers made in giving up their livings and their subsequent sufferings because of their Nonconformity.[2] Recent historians have tended to downplay the sufferings and sacrifice by Dissenters and their supporters and stress the easy accommodation reached with the authorities, particularly at the parish level.[3]

This study examines the practical consequences of the enforcement of the laws against Dissenters after 1662. It returns to a question that Anthony Fletcher proposed at the Summer Conference of the

[2] Edmund Calamy, *An Abridgment of Mr Baxter's History of his Life and Times* (London, 1702); Gerald R. Cragg, *Puritanism in the Period of the Great Persecution 1660–1688* (Cambridge, 1957); Lee Gatiss, *The Tragedy of 1662: The Ejection and Persecution of the Puritans* (London, 2007); Alan P. F. Sell, ed., *The Great Ejectment of 1662: Its Antecedents, Aftermath, and Ecumenical Significance* (Eugene, OR, 2012).
[3] For example, Samuel S. Thomas, *Creating Communities in Restoration England: Parish and Congregation in Oliver Heywood's Halifax* (Leiden, 2013).

David L. Wykes

Ecclesiastical History Society in 1983.[4] He argued that historians
have been too ready to accept that 'the decades between the
Restoration and the Toleration Act can be represented as the period
of the "Great Persecution"'. He asked: 'how far were these acts actually enforced? How easy were they to enforce?'[5] Fletcher focused on
the two Conventicle Acts, examining the Quarter Session order books
and related records for eight counties taken from the north, the
Midlands and the south of England. As a result of his analysis, he concluded that the impact of the penal laws has been exaggerated because
the Conventicle Acts were not systematically applied. He found only
a handful of justices in each county active in enforcing them.[6] His
discussion remains almost the only detailed study of the enforcement
of the penal laws against Protestant Dissenters using archival
evidence.

This article argues that Fletcher's approach was too narrow. The
number of prosecutions and successful convictions is not the only
measure of the effectiveness of a law. The threat of prosecution
undoubtedly encouraged many to conform outwardly. Even those
willing to hazard the law took steps to evade its penalties: for example,
by meeting secretly at night, or in small groups to avoid exceeding the
limit on the numbers attending a meeting set by the Conventicle
Acts. These acts, whilst they inflicted harsh penalties, were not the
only means by which Dissenters were harassed and persecuted.
Dissenters were more likely to be presented under the recusancy
laws for not attending church or receiving the sacrament, and for
other offences, such as refusing the oaths of allegiance.[7] It was an

[4] Anthony Fletcher, 'The Enforcement of the Conventicle Acts 1664–1679', in
W. J. Sheils, ed., *Persecution and Toleration*, SCH 21 (Oxford, 1984), 235–46.
[5] Ibid. 235.
[6] Ibid. 237–44.
[7] The conclusion that a large numbers of Dissenters were presented for recusancy offences
at the quarter sessions and correction courts is derived from an extensive study of the original court records: for example, Cambridge, UL, EDR/B/2/54, 56, Archdeacon of Ely
Visitation Book, 1662, 1663; Nottingham, Nottinghamshire Archives, A50,
Archdeaconry of Nottingham Act Books, 1661–3, 1665–6, 1668–78; Northampton,
Northamptonshire RO, X637.1, Archdeaconry of Northampton Court Book, 1662,
1663; QSR1/28–34, Northamptonshire Quarter Sessions, 1662–1664; Wigston, RO
for Leicestershire, Leicester and Rutland, 1 D 41/13/68, 71–76, 78, Correction Courts
following Archdeacon's visitations, July 1661 – October 1673; Leeds, West Yorkshire
Archive Service, RD/C/6, Archdeaconry of Richmond, Visitation and Correction
Courts, 1668; Chelmsford, Essex RO, D/AEV/8, Archdeaconry of Essex, April 1665 –
March 1670/1; D/AMV/1, 2, Archdeaconry of Middlesex, 1662–3, 1663/4–1665;

easier task for the churchwardens to present those who were absent from the parish church on Sundays than to surprise and then to identify who was present at a conventicle. The penalty for not attending church under the Act of Uniformity of 1558 (1 Eliz. c.2) was a fine of a shilling for each Sunday, collected for the benefit of the poor by the churchwardens. The churchwardens also had to make a presentment twice a year at the archdeacon's visitation of the names of those not attending church or receiving the sacrament. The threat of the church courts for Dissenters was real. Roger Lowe, an apprentice shopkeeper in Lancashire who was active in attending meetings and hearing Nonconformist ministers, was tricked by a friend at dinner into believing that he 'was cited to Bishop's Court for Nonconfformitie to Common Prayer'. After this, he wrote, 'I eate no more, but went to Town Heath and prayd to God to deliver me and consulted with my selfe how to doe [it].' When he discovered the truth, he was clearly very relieved.[8] Those presented were required to appear in person before the correction court, and their case was often put off from one court to another. Failure to attend court, or non-payment of fees and fines, resulted in excommunication. This was not perhaps much of a penalty for a sectary, but serious for a moderate Dissenter who did not wish to separate from the world. The church courts also had a host of petty procedures to weary the Dissenter.

This study examines the experience of the Dissenters themselves to consider the reality of the laws against Nonconformity. Evidence will be used from diaries, autobiographical accounts, church books and other contemporary sources to suggest that the impact of the laws was greater than Fletcher argued. The Conventicle Acts were only one aspect of the statutes enforced against Dissenters, and not

Anon., 'Lancashire Recusants and Quakers', *THSLC* 64 (1912), 309–19, at 309, 310–15; John Rogan, 'Episcopal Visitations in the Diocese of Durham, 1662–71', *Archaeologia Aeliana* 4th series 34 (1956), 92–109, at 98, 100. David L. Wykes, 'Early Religious Dissent in Surrey after the Restoration', *Southern History* 33 (2011), 54–77, at 58, is based on an analysis of the *Surrey Quarter Sessions Records: The Order-Book for 1659–1661, and the Sessions Rolls for Easter and Midsummer, 1661*, ed. D. L. Powell and H. Jenkinson, Surrey Record Society 13 (Guildford, 1934); *Surrey Quarter Sessions Records: The Order-Book for 1661–1663, and the Sessions Rolls from Michaelmas, 1661, to Epiphany, 1663*, ed. D. L. Powell and H. Jenkinson, Surrey Record Society 14 (Guildford, 1935).
8 *The Diary of Roger Lowe, of Ashton-in-Makerfield, Lancashire, 1663–74*, ed. William L. Sachse (London, 1938), 58–9 (17 April 1664).

necessarily the most significant. Moreover, the harassment of Dissenters by the authorities did not inevitably lead to indictment and conviction. This study will examine the first decade of Dissent between the Act of Uniformity and Charles II's Declaration of Indulgence, the period both shortly before and after the passing of the two Conventicle Acts. For reasons of space, it will largely exclude Baptists and Quakers, who formed only a small minority of Dissenters in this period. The latter have been well studied, particularly with regard to their use of the law to frustrate indictments and to overturn convictions.[9]

Although Dissenters had to endure three decades of persecution, it was never continuous. There were periods of more intense persecution, for example the early 1660s and 1680s, which were generally related to times of political uncertainty. In the early 1660s, there were still concerns about the threat to the recently restored monarchy from armed uprisings and plots. In the 1680s there was a severe reaction against Dissenters because of their support for the exclusion from the succession of the Catholic duke of York, later James II. There were also denominational differences. Because of the Civil War and the Interregnum, the radical sects (the Quakers and Baptists) and the separatists or Independents were the particular focus in the 1660s. In the 1680s many Presbyterians were presented for the first time, because of their political alliance with the Whigs. In addition persecution could depend upon the animus of a local justice or official.

Even before the Restoration settlement became law and the Church of England was restored, Dissenters were under pressure to conform. It is clear that those opposed to the Anglican settlement did not have to wait until the Act of Uniformity to be pressed or even harassed. Parish constables were already presenting individuals for not attending church or for holding unlawful religious meetings under the Elizabethan and Jacobean recusancy statutes. At the Easter 1661 Quarter Sessions for Surrey, over seventy individuals were presented for not attending their parish church.[10] The Book of Common Prayer was the focus of much of the effort by the bishops and church

---

[9] Craig W. Horle, *The Quakers and the English Legal System, 1660–1688* (Philadelphia, PA, 1988).

[10] Wykes, 'Early Religious Dissent in Surrey', 58. See also Nottinghamshire Archives, Archdeaconry of Nottingham Act Books, 1661–3; RO for Leicestershire, Leicester and Rutland, 1 D 41/13/68, Archdeacon's Correction Courts, July 1661 – April 1664.

officials against ministers, but its use also had gentry and popular support. As early as September 1660, before the church was legally restored, Philip Henry, minister at Worthenbury, Flintshire, and his friends, Robert Fogg and Richard Steele, were presented at the Flint Assizes for not using the Prayer Book, less than four months after the return of the king and two years before it was required by law. Henry and Steele were presented at the spring assizes, and Steele again in October 1661.[11] A group of eight puritan ministers in Surrey were likewise presented at the sessions in October 1661. The same eight were presented again at the next sessions in January 1662, and one minister a third time in April 1662. These presentments were all before the Act of Uniformity was passed on 19 May 1662, enforcing the use of the new Prayer Book.[12]

Ministers were also under pressure to use the Prayer Book in their parishes. It was pressed upon Henry in April by Leonard Perkins, one of the churchwardens. The following Sunday, Edward David, the other churchwarden, offered the Prayer Book, and this was the pattern for much of the rest of the summer.[13] Henry's dislike of the Prayer Book gave his opponents in the parish a rod with which to beat him. Oliver Heywood, minister at Coley, a township in the vast parish of Halifax, by midsummer 1661 perceived 'a black cloud [that] thickens up on us in this congregation, my old adversarys haue now got that advantage ag[ains]ᵗ me they haue been long seeking'. He feared that the bishop and his officials would soon 'urge us to a conformity' and that 'we must comply to humane ceremonys or haue our mouths stopt'.[14] In August 1661 he was offered the Prayer Book when he went into the pulpit by the churchwarden, at the instigation of his old adversary Stephen Ellis. Heywood demanded to know with what authority it was offered: 'he gaue me no answ. but when I would not take it he laid it upon the cushion, I took it down and laid in the lower pulpit'.[15] Heywood did not escape for long. On 13 September,

---

[11] *Diaries and Letters of Philip Henry, M. A. of Broad Oak, Flintshire, A. D. 1631–1696*, ed. Matthew Henry Lee (London, 1882), 72, 81, 82, 97.

[12] Wykes, 'Early Religious Dissent in Surrey', 59–60.

[13] *Diaries of Philip Henry*, ed. Lee, 83, 84, 89, 93 (11, 14 April, 16 June, 25 August 1661).

[14] 'Rev. O. Heywood's Autobiography', ed. J. Horsfall Turner, in *The Rev. Oliver Heywood, B.A. 1630–1702; His Autobiography, Diaries, Anecdote and Event Books*, 4 vols (Brighouse, 1882), 1: 178–9.

[15] Ibid. 178, 179 (25 August 1661).

he was cited to appear at the consistory court in York. He was advised to appear, but on doing so the officials would not tell him the charge and he was told to return in three weeks. Until restored by parliament, the court had no authority and 'therefore they cannot bite', as Heywood noted,[16] although clearly the officials still sought to harass Nonconformist ministers and their supporters.

Although Nonconformist ministers, both before and after the Act of Uniformity became law, were the focus of much of the official effort, the Independents or Congregationalists as separatists were also the subject of considerable attention. For the Independents at Cockermouth, their difficulties appear to have begun almost immediately following the Restoration. 'In this yeare began the afflictions of the churches to tumble in upon them, heapes upon heapes.'[17] As early as 1661 the church at Cockermouth appears to have experienced serious opposition. Several of the meetings for worship had to be held 'in parts & parcells here and there, as they could, because of the great violence of evill men'. By the Act of Uniformity, 'which stops the mouths of all that will not abjure, ... all publike liberty is denyed'.[18] Care is necessary in interpreting these early references, since they were almost certainly written up retrospectively. The Cockermouth Church Book was compiled by the minister George Larkham, curate of Cockermouth until he was displaced by the return of the sequestrated incumbent in 1660. Larkham left Cockermouth with his family and sought shelter at Broughton Tower in Lancashire with Roger Sawrey, a former parliamentarian colonel. Sawrey, however, was arrested for his support of Nonconformist meetings, and Larkham was forced to take refuge at Gomersal in West Yorkshire.[19]

In Larkham's absence, the years 1663 to 1667 are very sparsely recorded in the Church book. Nevertheless it is clear that its members suffered '[t]he Vexations pillings & finings of many or most of the Church by the power of the justices for non-conformity.' Inevitably they also experienced 'the sad Apostacy & backsliding' of some of the weaker members. Even those who remained loyal often

[16] Ibid. 179–80.
[17] *The Cockermouth Congregational Church Book (1651–c.1765)*, ed. R. B. Wordsworth, Cumberland and Westmorland Antiquarian and Archaeological Society Record Series 21 (Kendal 2012), 21.
[18] Ibid. 22.
[19] Richard L. Greaves, *Deliver us from Evil: The Radical Underground in Britain, 1660–63* (New York and Oxford, 1986), 189; *Cockermouth Church Book*, ed. Wordsworth, xxxi.

compromised with the authorities in upholding their testimonies. 'Besides those (in the pastors absence departed & turned aside) many of the church staggered & miscarried, through weaknes it is hoped, some of which since have given satisfaction to their brethren.'[20] Persecution and the threat of persecution led to the falling away of members. The Church of England clergy certainly believed stricter enforcement of the statutes would lead to greater conformity. The archdeacon of Northampton, John Palmer, told his bishop in 1669 that those who supported Dissent would 'return apace to the Church' if the justices held monthly sessions in the main towns and executed the statute of 1 Eliz. c.2 against recusants. They had come in fast in 1662 and 1664 '& we then baptized children of some years'. These were older children whose parents had not had them baptized earlier or as infants, in many cases because they were Quakers or Baptists.[21] The Cockermouth Church Book makes clear that persecution of the church and its members intensified. They were forced to meet secretly, often at night, and in small numbers. In July 1671 it was agreed they would meet for the sacrament in two parts. In the case of the part meeting at Hemshill, 'all are to be in before sun-rising because of the difficulty of the day'.[22]

Heywood's ministry as a Nonconformist quickly brought him to the attention of the authorities. Following his refusal to conform in August 1662, he took his leave of 'my dear congregation at Coley'. He was soon 'further cast out of [the] church assembly' when he was excommunicated on 2 November. He was excommunicated again in January 1663 for preaching a funeral sermon at Bolton, although in fact another had preached in his place, and again on 6 December that year.[23] Being excommunicated was a serious matter for Heywood, who like most ejected ministers believed in a national

---

[20] *Cockermouth Church Book*, ed. Wordsworth, 23–4.
[21] Northamptonshire RO, Fermor Hesketh (Baker) MS 708, 'An Account of the Conventicles held in the 7 Western Deaneryes of the Diocese of Peterborough', 76 (11 August 1669).
[22] *Cockermouth Church Book*, ed. Wordsworth, 37–8, 135 (10 February, 9 March, 1670/1, 26 March, 16 April, 14 July 1671).
[23] 'Heywood's Autobiography', ed. Turner, 1: 182, 184. Once the excommunication had been published Heywood would have remained under its sentence until he purged himself. Yet he makes clear that another excommunication was published against him in January 1663 and a third in December that year. There is no evidence to suggest he had purged the earlier offences; indeed all the evidence is that he remained a contumacious person.

church, although he could not accept the terms of the Act of Uniformity. When he went to hear the minister at Coley Chapel on 21 December, the churchwarden 'came in fury to me before the minister took his text and would have taken me out', but Heywood refused to leave. The churchwarden then 'charged the minister to forbear preaching to an excommunicate person'. Heywood replied that 'if he would not preach I would'. After a little time the minister took his text and gave his sermon.[24] Those who attended Heywood's meetings were also threatened. The churchwarden, Heywood's enemy Stephen Ellis, 'belched out grievous threatenings how he would punish the fanaticks in the place, ... went to several houses to charge them to come to the common-prayers, or he would fetch away some cows'.[25] Ellis then demanded four shillings from Heywood's servant for Heywood's absence from church for four Sundays. As Heywood recounted in his diary, his servant said to Ellis that 'if I came he would put me out of church, yes, s[ai]th he, and so I will too, for the law must be executed, both to keep me away and punish my absence'.[26] Heywood favoured the appointment of John Hoole, 'a very late conformist', but he noted that he could not 'peaceably goe to my owne chappel to hear him'.[27] Because he had 'a great desire to wait upon god in publick ordinances', he asked a friend to consult the dean of York. The answer was somewhat ambivalent. An excommunicate was not permitted to be present at prayers or sermon, but privately the dean wondered if a churchman would be so malicious to hinder any from hearing the word.[28]

Heywood was also subjected to unofficial harassment. He found his house was regularly watched, and he and his hearers threatened. 'Many wondered at my safety and liberty', especially considering 'the rage of mine enemys'.[29] Threatened with arrest, Heywood left home and was absent for about a month. Heywood and his supporters also suffered from informers. The first Conventicle Act came into force on 1 July 1664 and greatly increased the risks in attending Nonconformist meetings. On Sunday, 2 October, 'Nathan Whitley's man, and one Widow Bancroft watcht under the gates in

[24] Ibid. 184–5.
[25] Ibid. 185.
[26] Ibid. 190.
[27] Ibid. 192.
[28] Ibid. 193.
[29] Ibid. 185.

the fore-noone while I both prayed and preacht, and gave out many bitter threatening words', both to Heywood's servants and to those attending the meeting. Nonetheless, they were left undisturbed.[30] Subsequently Heywood heard that 'there are several persons suborned to watch my house', to see who attended his meetings for the purpose of informing Sir John Armitage, a justice.[31]

Furthermore, under the Conventicle Act a constable could enter a suspect's house without a warrant, providing all sorts of opportunities to harass Dissenters. In September 1665, Heywood was at prayer when the constable and two other men 'came furiously in, searcht the house', but fortunately found only four other persons besides the family, within the limit set by the law. It was, Heywood admitted, 'much different from other times'.[32] He faced further difficulties when his landlord insisted that he gave up his house.[33] Those who wanted to worship outside the Church of England found their attempts compromised by the need for secrecy. The joy that Heywood expressed when he found somewhere more remote is evident: 'we have a more private place then ever before, where I can sing and speake as loud as I please without feares of being overheard'.[34]

For many ministers the Five Mile Act of 1665 added to their troubles. This act prohibited ministers who refused to take the oaths prescribed from coming within five miles of a borough which returned MPs or a parish where they had preached since the Act of Oblivion. Richard Baxter in his autobiographical account wrote of the particular difficulties the act caused: 'In many Countries, it was hard to find many places which were not within five Miles of some Corporation, or of some place where we had Preached before (for some Ministers preached in a great number of Parishes at several times).'[35] Having been driven first from their parishes by the Act of Uniformity, the Five Mile Act then forced them further away from their friends who supported them.[36]

---

[30] Ibid. 192.
[31] Ibid., cf. 196.
[32] Ibid. 198 (17 September 1665).
[33] Ibid. 201 (14 February 1665/6).
[34] Ibid. 232 (November 1666).
[35] *Reliquiae Baxterianae, or, Mr. Richard Baxters Narrative of the most Memorable Passages of his Life and Times* (London, 1696), part 3, 3–4, §10.
[36] David L. Wykes, 'Dissent and Charity, 1660–1720', in Clyde Binfield, G. M. Ditchfield and David L. Wykes, eds, *Protestant Dissent and Philanthropy in Britain, 1660–c.1920* (Woodbridge, 2019), 28.

To Heywood the day the Act came into force was 'a day of great scattering, hundreds of ministers being by act of Parl. banished fiue miles from the places where they haue formerly preacht, if they take not an oath, which they generally refuse'. He retired to Denton 'to live in exile'.[37] John Earl, when he was ejected, moved to Lewes, Sussex, and preached as far afield as Chichester in the extreme west of the county, Maidstone in Kent, and London, often travelling on foot. He was frequently arrested and fined. According to Edmund Calamy in his account of Earl, '[n]o part of his Sufferings went nearer his Heart, than those occasion'd by the *Five Mile Act*, which made Ministers hide like the worst of Criminals.'[38] Nevertheless, one consequence of the act was to force ministers to travel more widely, thereby reaching audiences who had not previously heard regular preaching. Earl said later that 'he knew some Ministers, who had it not been for the Act, had wanted Bread for their Families. Being scatter'd about, they fed many, who fed them and theirs.'[39] At least 215 ejected ministers were imprisoned for preaching or for contravening the Five Mile Act.[40]

By the fact of their refusal to conform, Nonconformist ministers and their supporters were vulnerable to accusations of disloyalty and plotting. In addition, the futile insurrection in London by the Fifth Monarchist Thomas Venner in January 1661, whilst easily suppressed, caused the authorities to make the link between religious resistance and political subversion. In the early years after the Act of Uniformity, Nonconformist ministers were often caught up in rumours of plots. Philip Henry heard in February 1663, at the time of the Farley Wood Plot, of the imprisonment of Robert Yates, who had been ejected from Warrington. Yates had been imprisoned 'upon the malicious information of a person of small credit, who swore, hee mov'd him to take up Arms ag^t ye King for ye Presbyterians & promis'd him 40s p. week pay'.[41] Henry was aware that he and other Nonconformist ministers faced similar risks: 'Tis only from Gods Providence holding ye Chayn that tis not every ones case … considering our own impotency to gainsay & the ene-

[37] 'Heywood's Autobiography', ed. Turner, 1: 201 (24 March 1665/6).
[38] Edmund Calamy, *An Account of the Ministers … who were Ejected or Silenced after the Restoration in 1660*, 2 vols (London, 1713), 2: 672 [*sic* 687].
[39] Ibid.
[40] Mathews, *Calamy Revised*, lix.
[41] *Diaries of Philip Henry*, ed. Lee, 129 (14 February 1662/3).

myes malice to accuse.'[42] In fact, Henry and his friends did not escape. Nine months later, in October, Henry was arrested and examined by two justices out of sessions. He was told he had been arrested on reports of a plot, but Henry was also charged with frequenting conventicles, particularly during the previous month. This Henry strongly denied. The authorities clearly saw a link between Nonconformist meetings and plotting. Henry and his friends were released on providing recognizances. They were comparatively fortunate. John Taylor, the former curate of Holt, Flintshire, was caught at a private meeting or conventicle near Wrexham with many others. They were bound over to appear at the next Quarter Sessions at Llanrwst. At the Quarter Sessions, the justices swore and used much foul language towards them and bound them over to the assizes. Most were then released on taking the oath of allegiance, but some of those present were not so lucky. Because of the remoteness of Llanrwst, they were not known and could not obtain sureties, and so remained in prison.[43]

Even when Dissenters were spared harassment or overt pressure to conform, their religious activities were still affected by the statutes in force. Roger Lowe of Ashton-in-Makerfield in Lancashire kept a diary for nearly four years from January 1663 to October 1667, in which he recorded his religious activities. In April 1663, his minister, James Woods, who had been the curate of Ashton until silenced by the Act of Uniformity in 1662, left the parish to live in Thelwall, near Warrington in Cheshire.[44] The reasons were not given by Lowe in his diary, although presumably Woods was under pressure for his Nonconformity. Woods was to visit his former parish on a number of occasions, but his appearances were infrequent, and on average he only returned to Ashton once every two months.[45] Without a regular minister, the godly had to maintain their own religious meetings. The Sunday after Woods's departure, Lowe, his friend Thomas Smith, 'and severall young women … assembled together in [the] feilds' where Lowe repeated a sermon.[46] More commonly, the meetings were held at the houses of two supporters, either that of Robert

[42] Ibid.
[43] Ibid. 157, 159 (14 July, 14 August 1663)
[44] *Diary of Roger Lowe*, ed. Sachse, 18, 19 (23, 26 April 1663).
[45] Analysis of Lowe's diary undertaken by the author.
[46] *Diary of Roger Lowe*, ed. Sachse, 20 (3May 1663).

Rosbothom or John Robinson. Until his death in February 1667, Woods was the only Nonconformist minister to visit Ashton, and it is clear from Lowe's diary there was very little godly preaching in the parish as a consequence. Woods's death reduced those occasions still further. Opportunities to receive the Lord's Supper were even more infrequent. Lowe, who travelled widely, only recorded three occasions in nearly four years.[47]

Like many Dissenters in other parishes, Lowe had to seek his religion outside Ashton. He visited a wide area on business, and he took the opportunity to travel, often with friends, to hear sermons. His master lived in Leigh, where Woods's son, James junior, who also refused to conform, lived and to whom Lowe made frequent reference. On two occasions Lowe visited Woods senior in Thelwall.[48] In his extant diary, Lowe named at least seven other Nonconformist ministers whom he heard preach, although rarely more than once. On one occasion he travelled nearly forty miles to hear Thomas Gregg preach at Broad Oak.[49] Lowe was also aware of a small number of conformist ministers who failed to conform fully, such as John Tilsley and John Angier at Dean Church, and Richard Grimshay at Lymm, some of whom he went to hear. Other ministers, such as Thomas Gregg and James Woods junior, although they refused to conform, were able to preach openly in the early years because their chapel was not consecrated.[50] Yet despite all these efforts Lowe did not hear sermons on a regular basis.

Anthony Fletcher found few prosecutions under the Conventicle Acts, and he concluded that the persecution of Dissenters had been exaggerated. But the situation was rather more complicated than the study of the enforcement of the Conventicle Act alone would suggest. The effectiveness of a law is not judged by the number of convictions but by its success in discouraging individuals from committing an offence. It is impossible to say how many were dissuaded from attending Nonconformist meetings by the Conventicle Acts. Nonetheless the threat of prosecution clearly encouraged even those individuals determined to ignore the injunction against illegal meetings to take

[47] Ibid. 44, 78, 90–1.
[48] Ibid. 25, 57.
[49] Ibid. 120 (7 February 1667/8).
[50] Matthews, *Calamy Revised*, 12, 234–5, 486, 540–1; *Diary of Roger Lowe*, ed. Sachse, 57, 63.

steps either to avoid discovery or to remain within the law, for example by meeting secretly at night or in small groups. Fletcher did not take account of the widespread use of the earlier recusancy statutes against Dissenters, nor did he examine the Dissenters themselves to identify the threats and harassment they experienced. The use of informers and the actions of their enemies locally greatly increased the difficulties Dissenters faced. The experience of Roger Lowe demonstrates that even in parishes where Dissenters were not subject to regular harassment their religious activities were still limited by the laws against Nonconformity. After his minister Woods had left Ashton there was very little godly preaching in the parish, and almost no access to the sacraments. Lowe, because of his business as an apprentice shopkeeper, had greater opportunities than most Dissenters to hear Nonconformist ministers on his travels, but even he and his friends were unable to hear sermons regularly. Once the evidence for the large-scale presentment of Dissenters under the recusancy laws, together with the threats and harassment they experienced, is taken into account, it is no longer possible to accept Fletcher's conclusions that Dissenters suffered little persecution or that the impact of the penal laws has been exaggerated.

Dissenters not only suffered from the enforcement of the law, but clearly it created and shaped Dissent as well. The Restoration religious settlement forced those ministers who refused to conform out of the church, imposing the Book of Common Prayer and making all other forms of religious worship illegal. Dissenters were forced to modify the way they met and worshipped by how the law was enforced. Moreover, a direct consequence of the threats and persecution was the falling away of the weaker members, leaving a remnant whose faith was often intensified by persecution, which in some cases seems to have encouraged a more sectarian strain among previously moderate Dissenters.[51] The destructive nature of religious intolerance on its victims is now better understood. Historians perhaps need to recognize the consequences for Dissenters in the period after 1662 of the abuse, bigotry and intolerance they experienced.

[51] C. G. Bolam et al., *The English Presbyterians: From Elizabethan Puritanism to Modern Unitarianism* (London, 1968), 87, 98–9.

The House of Lords and Religious Toleration in Scotland: James Greenshields's Appeal, 1709–11

Ben Rogers*

University College Dublin

This article examines how the House of Lords, as the ultimate appellate authority of the new kingdom of Great Britain, formed after the union of 1707, provided a degree of religious toleration for Scotland's episcopalian minority when they supported James Greenshields's appeal on 1 March 1711. Greenshields was a Scottish episcopalian minister who appealed to the Lords in February 1710 after he was imprisoned by the Edinburgh magistrates for using the English Book of Common Prayer to conduct a service for a private episcopalian congregation. The Lords' decision confirmed that no law in Scotland proscribed the Prayer Book liturgy and provided a degree of legal recognition to the episcopalians who used it. This article examines the arguments that Greenshields and his supporters used to advance his appeal. In doing so, it sheds new light on the relationship between Scotland's established church, the nation's episcopalian minority and the new British state.

On 30 December 1710, Narcissus Marsh, archbishop of Armagh, wrote to Thomas Tenison, archbishop of Canterbury, to provide a reference for a Scottish episcopalian minister named James Greenshields. Greenshields had recently returned to his native Scotland after ministering in Ireland. Marsh testified that Greenshields's time in Ireland had been uncontroversial, but submitted that 'what his Behaviour has been in Scotland, I will not undertake to give you any account of, He being best able to do it himself'.[1] Greenshields had been imprisoned in Edinburgh's tolbooth in September 1709 after he was caught using the English Book of Common Prayer to conduct a service for a private episcopalian congregation. He was cited before the presbytery of Edinburgh and the

---

* E-mail: rogersb@ucd.ie.

The author would like to thank Alasdair Raffe and the anonymous peer reviewers for their comments on this article.

[1] London, LPL, Correspondence of Thomas Tenison, MS 1029, fol. 110, Narcissus Marsh to Tenison, 30 December 1710.

Studies in Church History 56 (2020), 320–337   © Ecclesiastical History Society 2020
doi: 10.1017/stc.2019.18

city's magistrates, and his sentence was confirmed by the Court of Session, which was Scotland's highest civil court. In February 1710 Greenshields appealed to the House of Lords, which, after Scotland and England had united under the Treaty of Union in May 1707, was the ultimate appellate authority of the new kingdom of Great Britain, with power to overturn decisions of the Court of Session despite the securities that Scotland's legal system held under the union.[2]

On 1 March 1711, the Lords decided in favour of Greenshields. Their decision had four consequences for Scotland's religious affairs. First, it confirmed that there was no law in Scotland that allowed the nation's episcopalian minority to be prosecuted for using the English Book of Common Prayer of 1662, even though this constituted a form of Nonconformist worship in Scotland. Second, it provided a degree of legal toleration to the ministers who continued to use the Prayer Book. Third, it challenged the authority of the Church of Scotland and its established presbyterian standard of polity, and the Calvinism expressed by its doctrinal standard, the Westminster Confession of Faith. These two standards had been re-established in the church by the Scottish parliament in June 1690 after the epis-copal structure that had existed since 1662 was abolished during the revolution of 1688–9.[3] Both standards had also been reaffirmed by this parliament in November 1706 when it passed the 'Act for Securing of the Protestant Religion and Presbyterian Church Government'.[4] Fourth, the Lords' decision confirmed the upper house of the Westminster parliament as the leading legal authority in the kingdom of Great Britain and hence as the ultimate arbiter of Scotland's religious divisions. It thus highlighted the issue of par-liamentary sovereignty, which would ultimately be demonstrated by

[2] *Records of the Parliaments of Scotland to 1707*, 1706/10/315, 'Act ratifying and approv-ing the Treaty of Union of the Two Kingdoms of Scotland and England', 16 January 1707, online at: <http://www.rps.ac.uk>, accessed 2 September 2019; Christopher A. Whatley with Derek J. Patrick, *The Scots and the Union* (Edinburgh, 2006), 306–7.
[3] Alasdair Raffe, *Scotland in Revolution, 1685–1690* (Edinburgh, 2018), 140–4; Tim Harris, *Revolution: The Great Crisis of the British Monarchy, 1685–1720* (London, 2006), 378–88.
[4] *Records of the Parliament of Scotland*, 1706/10/251, 'Act for Securing of the Protestant Religion and Presbyterian Church Government', 12 November 1706, online at: <http://www.rps.ac.uk>, accessed 2 September 2019; Derek J. Patrick, 'The Kirk, Parliament and the Union, 1706–7', in Stewart J. Brown and Christopher A. Whatley, eds, *The Union of 1707: New Dimensions* (Edinburgh, 2008), 94–115.

the British parliament when it passed the Toleration Act for the episcopalians on 3 March 1712.[5]

Previous historians have provided similar interpretations of the Greenshields controversy. Legal scholars such as Brian Levack and John Cairns have shown that the appeal demonstrated the Lords' ability to overturn the decisions of the Court of Session.[6] Tristram Clarke, in his doctoral thesis on the Scottish episcopalians, offers a detailed investigation into the Greenshields controversy and the political machinations that lay behind it.[7] Articles about the appeal by Richard Tompson and Jeffrey Stephen have taken different approaches. Tompson was less concerned to discuss the appeal's legal implications for the episcopalians, but provides a thorough outline of how it progressed.[8] Stephen also outlines the controversy, and offers interesting insights on the role of the English Book of Common Prayer in the appeal, but similarly does not focus on how the Lords' decision equated to a degree of legal recognition being given in Scotland to this English liturgical standard.[9] Both historians show that the Lords' decision led to the passage of the Toleration Act in March 1712, but neither of them has shown how that decision helped to form the basis of this statute.

The controversy that surrounded Greenshields's appeal provides an insight into the relationship between the Church of Scotland, the nation's episcopalian minority and the legal authority of the new British state. This article will explore this relationship to show how the appeal was used by an episcopalian tolerationist movement in Scotland to secure full legal toleration for their co-religionists by virtue of the statute in 1712. To do this, it will focus on three issues.

[5] *The Statutes of the Realm: Printed by the Command of His Majesty King George the Third*, 2nd edn, 11 vols (London, 1963; first published 1810–28), 9: 557–9.
[6] Brian P. Levack, *The Formation of the British State: England, Scotland, and the Union 1603–1707* (Oxford, 1987), 98; John W. Cairns, 'Scottish Law, Scottish Lawyers and the Status of the Union', in John Robertson, ed., *A Union for Empire: Political Thought and the British Union of 1707* (Cambridge, 1995), 243–68.
[7] Tristram Clarke, 'The Scottish Episcopalians, 1689–1720' (PhD Thesis, University of Edinburgh, 1987), 200–50.
[8] Richard S. Tompson, 'James Greenshields and the House of Lords: A Reappraisal', in W. M. Gordon and T. D. Fergus, eds, *Legal History in the Making: Proceedings of the Ninth British Legal History Conference Glasgow 1989* (London, 1991), 109–24.
[9] Jeffrey Stephen, 'English Liturgy and Scottish Identity: The Case of James Greenshields', in Allan I. Macinnes and Douglas J. Hamilton, eds, *Jacobitism, Enlightenment and Empire, 1680–1720* (Cambridge, 2014), 59–74.

First, it will provide some brief background to the events of the Greenshields controversy. Second, it will examine the progress of the appeal and how it was understood by contemporaries. Third, it will address the appeal's legal implications for the Church of Scotland and the episcopalians. To conclude, the article will assess what the Lords' decision meant for the future legal regulation of religious divisions in Scottish society.

THE BACKGROUND

The episcopalians were Scotland's largest Nonconformist group by the time of the Greenshields controversy. Their Nonconformity stemmed from their reluctance either to accept the Church's presbyterian structure or to subscribe to orthodox Calvinism as defined by the Westminster Confession, after they were re-established in June 1690. During the Restoration period, the episcopalians had grown distant from Calvinism as articulated by the confession and many started to favour an Arminian understanding of predestination.[10] This became apparent after 1690 when many episcopalians refused to subscribe the confession, despite being required by law to do so, and were deprived by ecclesiastical visitation commissions.[11] The group was also compromised by its members' Jacobite sympathies. Many had been reluctant to accept William and Mary after they were offered the Scottish crown in 1689, and maintained their allegiance to James II / VII and his successors. Although more episcopalians were willing to accept Anne after she acceded in 1702, many of these ministers continued to harbour Jacobite sympathies.[12]

Although the episcopalians' Nonconformity originated at the revolution of 1688–9, during the 1690s there were no widespread calls either for them to be legally tolerated as a separate church or for their

[10] Alasdair Raffe, 'Presbyterians and Episcopalians: The Formation of Confessional Cultures in Scotland, 1660–1715', *EHR* 125 (2010), 570–98; idem, *The Culture of Controversy: Religious Arguments in Scotland, 1660–1714* (Woodbridge, 2012), 48–50.
[11] Ben Rogers, 'Religious Comprehension and Toleration in Scotland, 1689–1712' (PhD Thesis, University of Edinburgh, 2019), 116–29.
[12] Bruce Lenman, 'The Scottish Episcopal Clergy and the Ideology of Jacobitism', in Eveline Cruickshanks, ed., *Ideology and Conspiracy: Aspects of Jacobitism, 1689–1759* (Edinburgh, 1982), 36–48; Tristram Clarke, '"Nurseries of Sedition"?: The Episcopal Congregations after the Revolution of 1689', in James Porter, ed., *After Columba, after Calvin: Religious Community in North-East Scotland* (Aberdeen, 1999), 61–9.

suppression. Instead, the Scottish authorities promoted comprehension throughout the 1690s, seeking to receive episcopalians into the church under a series of settlements. However, as the government's approach to comprehension became associated with the strict terms that the presbyterians desired, which involved ministers having to accept presbyterianism as the only government of the church and subscribe the Westminster Confession as the confession of their faith, the many episcopalians who would have conformed under a flexible comprehension settlement became alienated. By 1703 many episcopalians were practising Nonconformity and an organized tolerationist movement of ministers, politicians and pamphleteers had emerged to call for the legal protection of their co-religionists as a separate church. A toleration act to this effect was proposed to the Scottish parliament in May 1703.[13] The act failed but episcopalian toleration became a recurrent presbyterian fear in the years that followed.

During the debates over the union treaty late in 1706, many presbyterians feared that a British parliament could impose toleration of the episcopalians on Scotland. Writing to Lord Godolphin, the English lord treasurer, on 22 September, John Erskine, earl of Mar and secretary of state for Scotland, stated that Sir James Steuart of Goodtrees, who was Scotland's lord advocate or chief public prosecutor, opposed the union treaty because of 'the loosing of our soverainity & [a fear] that a toleration will ruin Presbitrie'.[14] In a series of addresses to the Scottish parliament during its debates over the treaty in November, the commission of the General Assembly, which was the standing committee of the Church of Scotland's main legislative body, presented a variety of arguments to outline the dangers of a British parliament. The commission's first address against the union asked that the church's presbyterian structure and the Westminster Confession be reaffirmed and 'that this Provision should be held and observed in all time coming as a fundamentall article and Essential Condition of any Treaty or Union'.[15]

This address was influential because its demands formed the basis of the Act for Securing of the Protestant Religion and Presbyterian

[13] *An Act for the Toleration of the Episcopal Church in Scotland which was thrown out by the Scotch Parliament An. 1703* (Edinburgh, 1703); Clarke, 'Scottish Episcopalians', 135–8.
[14] London, BL, Add. MS 28055, fol. 388^r–^{v}.
[15] Karin Bowie, ed., *Addresses against Incorporating Union, 1706–1707*, Scottish History Society 6th series 13 (Woodbridge, 2018), 40–1.

324

Church Government that Anne's Scottish administration proposed on 4 November 1706 to address presbyterian concerns. This act resolved most of the issues that the commission had raised in its address of 27 October. It reaffirmed the act of 1690 that had re-established presbyterian government and the Westminster Confession, and asserted that these standards would remain secured under a union with England. Anne's government hoped that the act would encourage the Church of Scotland to support the union, but the commission raised further issues in its second address to parliament on 8 November. This asked whether the Church of Scotland would be treated as a Nonconformist church by its English counterpart or whether it would be treated equally in a bi-confessional British state. It also pointed out that presbyterians could not accept that churchmen held civil power and that in the British parliament 'tuenty six prelates are to be Constituent members and Legislators'.[16] A draft of the second address stated that this dangerous parliamentary situation meant that episcopalian toleration 'shall be Judged in point of civil policy in a parliament of Brittain necessary and inavoidable'.[17]

Sir James Ogilvy, earl of Seafield and lord chancellor of Scotland, argued that these hostile presbyterian sentiments motivated parliament to pass the Act for Securing of the Protestant Religion. He informed Godolphin when the act was first read on 11 November that its purpose was 'to exclude the power of the Parl[i]ament of Britain to grant a toleration within Scotland'.[18] John Dalrymple, earl of Stair, who was one of the Scottish commissioners who negotiated the treaty, had a different view. He informed Robert Harley, the English secretary for the northern department, on 12 November that the act provided no 'distinct exemption from the power of the Parliament of Britain'.[19] Stair's interpretation reflected the widespread belief, after this act was ratified together with the Treaty of Union on 16 January 1707, that the British parliament's sovereignty was unlimited and could not be restricted by previous Scottish statutes.[20]

---

[16] Bowie, ed., *Addresses*, 48–9; Alasdair Raffe, 'Petitioning in Scottish Church Courts, 1638–1707', *Parliaments, Estates & Representation* 38 (2018), 323–36.

[17] Bowie, ed., *Addresses*, 55.

[18] BL, Add. MS 28055, fol. 338ʳ.

[19] *Report of the Manuscripts of the late Allan George Finch, Esq., of Burley-on-the-Hill, Rutland*, vol. 3, HMC 71 (London, 1957), 348.

[20] Colin Kidd, *Union and Unionisms: Political Thought in Scotland, 1500–2000* (Cambridge, 2008), 101–15.

The issue of parliamentary sovereignty worried some presbyterians, such as John Stirling, principal of the University of Glasgow, who feared that it allowed the Westminster parliament in its capacity as the British parliament to overrule the Act for Securing of the Protestant Religion. John Barrington Shute, a leading English Nonconformist and a correspondent of Stirling, addressed the principal's concerns in a letter of 13 March. Shute disagreed with the widespread notion that parliament's sovereignty was unlimited and offered two reasons why the union had provided the church with an 'Indefeasible Security'. First, he argued that the act's authority 'in Law cou[l]d not be defeated or destroy[e]d & cou[l]d only be broke by violence & force'. Second, since the union treaty had been negotiated by Scotland and England, 'nothing can destroy this Contract by [th]e consent of [th]e Partys contracting'. Once the government was united, there was 'no way nor method in Law of defeating [th]e Security the Church ... gain[ed] by the Union'.[21]

This approach was not shared by the many presbyterians who feared that the sovereignty of the British parliament meant that it could still introduce legal toleration of episcopalianism in Scotland. This is evident in the work of James Webster, an anti-union presbyterian, in his pamphlet *Lawful Prejudices against an Incorporating Union with England* (1707). Webster rejected the idea that the act of 1706 prevented a British parliament from acting against the church. A British parliament, he argued, could 'overturn our Church constitution, when they shall think it convenient'. He felt that 'a Toleration will certainly follow the Union' and 'open the Sluice, and let in a Deluge of Errours and Heresy'.[22]

THE APPEAL

The Greenshields appeal exacerbated presbyterian fears about the prospect of legal toleration being imposed upon them. It began at a time when many presbyterians questioned the legal security that they held under the union. The failed Jacobite invasion in February 1708 and the resulting crackdown on episcopalian worship by Steuart of Goodtrees in the following months revealed how extensive

[21] Glasgow, Glasgow UL, Murray MS 651, unpaginated.
[22] [James Webster], *Lawful Prejudices against an Incorporating Union with England* (Edinburgh, 1707), 9–11; Raffe, *Culture of Controversy*, 79.

episcopalian Nonconformity had become. In March 1708 seventeen episcopalian ministers were prosecuted by Edinburgh magistrates for keeping illegal meeting houses.[23] Furthermore, the abolition of the Scottish privy council the following May forced the Scottish religious authorities to rely on the Scottish courts to prosecute episcopalian Nonconformists.[24]

The church's precarious position after the union was behind the commission of the General Assembly's decision to issue the 'Act against Innovations in the Worship of God' on 5 August 1709. The act asserted that the Act for Securing of the Protestant Religion had been 'violated by Persons of known Disaffection to the present Establishment'. These ministers had introduced 'Set Forms, Rites and Ceremonies … contrary to the foresaid Purity and Uniformity'.[25] This act formed the basis of the presbytery of Edinburgh's case against Greenshields when he was cited before them later that year. However, the act was not supported by parliamentary legislation and this would be highlighted by Greenshields and his allies when the controversy grew.

The main issue of the controversy was the claim by Greenshields that there was no civil law in Scotland that proscribed private episcopalian worship and the use of the English Book of Common Prayer, and that he had not violated an earlier Scottish 'Act anent Intrusion into Churches' from 1695 that prohibited ministers intruding on vacant parishes. This claim, as Stephen has shown, was asserted from the beginning of the controversy. In the published account of his appearance before the presbytery in September 1709, Greenshields stated that he had been asked to minister 'by some English Gentlemen, who then attended Her Majesty's Service in Edinburgh, and others of the Communion of the Church of England'. He argued that he had qualified in Ireland by taking the required oath abjuring the Stuart Pretender and insisted that there was 'no Law, which prohibited or restrained the Exercise of the Worship of the Church of England in Scotland, in a private manner'.[26] By 'a private manner' Greenshields meant the private

---

[23] *A Narrative of the late Treatment of the Episcopal Ministers within the City of Edinburgh since March last 1708* (London, 1708), i–iii, 4–8; Clarke, 'Scottish Episcopalians', 190–2.
[24] P. W. J. Riley, *The English Ministers and Scotland, 1707–1727* (London, 1964), 92–5.
[25] *Acts of the General Assembly of the Church of Scotland, 1638–1842* (Edinburgh, 1843), 418–19.
[26] *The Appellant's Case* ([London?], 1710).

household to which he ministered. However, his acknowledgement that he had taken the abjuration oath was important because many episcopalians feared that it could be imposed on Scotland. The oath, which had been enacted by the English and Irish parliaments in 1702, required ministers to swear allegiance to Anne, abjure the Jacobite pretender and promise to support the Hanoverian succession.[27] These requirements challenged the episcopalians' Jacobite sympathies and set Greenshields apart from his co-religionists.

Greenshields expanded on these points in the bill of suspension that he presented to the Court of Session in November 1709 challenging the magistrates' decision. He insisted that the statute of 1695 against intrusion did not apply to him because he had not intruded upon a vacant parish and had only privately ministered 'to those of the same Communion with himself'.[28] When the session ruled against him, Greenshields maintained that he had never 'invaded the Sacred Office of the Ministry' and that using the Book of Common Prayer did not 'clash with any Law, establishing Uniformity of worship, or the Act of Union'. These reasons, he argued, proved that his confinement had 'no foundation in Law' and 'in a United Kingdom, should be far less used than formerly'.[29]

When Greenshields made this argument, he presented himself as an atypical episcopalian who stood out from the stereotyped image that the authorities feared. He was not a Jacobite, he had qualified himself by taking the required oaths, and he only wanted to provide the religious services that his congregation desired. This view, as Clarke has demonstrated, was promoted by tolerationist supporters of Greenshields to convince tory and high church groups in England to support legal toleration for the episcopalians.[30] These groups eventually gained the ascendency after Anne invited Harley to form a tory ministry in May 1710 and the tories, who now included numerous Scottish MPs from the largely pro-episcopalian shires, won a majority in that year's general election. Goodtrees, whose removal the tories had long desired, was replaced as lord

---

[27] *Statutes*, 7: 747–50; Raffe, *Culture of Controversy*, 90–1.

[28] Tompson, 'Greenshields', 114.

[29] *To the Right Honourable Lords of the Council and Session: The Petition of Mr James Greenshields Minister of the Gospel* ([Edinburgh?], 1709), 3–5.

[30] Clarke, 'Scottish Episcopalians', 254–7.

advocate by Sir David Dalrymple who, despite his sympathy for the episcopalians, did not support their legal toleration.[31]

One anonymous account of the controversy emphasized Greenshields's atypicality and insisted that his co-religionists had always possessed the right to use the English Book of Common Prayer. The author claimed that episcopalians had been prosecuted in the 1690s because 'they were not Qualified to the Government', but that they had never been cited before the authorities for preaching a heterodox religious message. The author thus argued that the authorities were hypocrites for prosecuting Greenshields for using the Book of Common Prayer even though he had qualified himself by taking the oaths of allegiance and abjuration.[32]

There were many conflicting opinions as to how the Lords would interpret the appeal. Writing in February 1710, Mar asserted that if the Lords had immediately considered the appeal 'it would have been reversed & that would have given an absolat toleration in Scotland without any restriction'. However, the whig majority in the Lords had initially considered the appeal as a local dispute, and they did not issue a decision on it. Mar also discussed the possibility that the controversy could be used as a pretext to introduce legal toleration through statute. He argued that if the church was 'so wise not to oppose a legall limited toleration it would be the greatest security they ever had'. He believed that if the presbyterians continued with persecutory activities 'a toleration as is here [in England] must cure it'.[33] Mar was referring to a Scottish version of England's Act for exempting their Majestyes Protestant Subjects dissenting from the Church of England from the Penalties of certaine Lawes (1689), which had granted legal protection to Nonconformist ministers if they took the oath of allegiance and subscribed thirty-six of the

---

[31] Daniel Szechi, 'The Politics of Persecution: Scots Episcopalian Toleration and the Harley Ministry, 1710–12', in W. J. Shiels, ed., *Persecution and Toleration*, SCH 21 (Oxford, 1984), 275–87; David Wilkinson, 'Dalrymple, Hon. Sir David (*c*.1665–1721)', in D. W. Hayton, E. Cruickshanks and S. Handley, eds, *The History of Parliament: The House of Commons 1690–1715*, 5 vols (Woodbridge, 2002), online at: <https://www.historyofparliamentonline.org/volume/1690-1715/member/dalrymple-hon-sir-david-1665-1721>, accessed 2 September 2019.

[32] *A True State of the Case of the Reverend Mr. Greenshields, now Prisoner in the Tolbooth in Edinburgh* (London, 1710), 5–6.

[33] Edinburgh, NRS, Correspondence of Lord Grange, GD124/15/975, 1.

Thirty-Nine Articles of the Church of England.[34] To satisfy the Church of Scotland, it is likely that a Scottish version of this act would have used the Westminster Confession as a doctrinal test, under which most episcopalians would not qualify due to their reluctance to accept its particular definition of orthodox Calvinism.[35]

Many episcopalians came out in favour of the use of the English Book of Common Prayer and used arguments like those of Greenshields to defend it in response to a wider crackdown on their worship. In May 1709, the northern circuit court indicted forty episcopalians from Banff and Aberdeen for charges that included intrusion, the erection of illegal meeting houses and using the Book of Common Prayer. The prosecutions were based on the Act for Securing of the Protestant Religion and earlier legislation that had been passed by the Scottish parliament, which the court believed required all ministers to adhere to the uniformity of worship that was prescribed by law.[36] In a petition to the queen, the following year, the episcopalian ministers and laity of Banff complained of the court's actions and of the 'usurpation of the presbyterian party over our persons and Consciences'.[37]

Despite the growth in demand for the prayer book liturgy, Daniel Defoe urged the episcopalians not to push for toleration. In his pamphlet, *Greenshields out of Prison and Toleration settled in Scotland*, written shortly after Greenshields was released from the tolbooth in 1710, Defoe argued that the Act for Securing of the Protestant Religion meant that the English should not expect the 'People of Scotland should Admit, Receive, or Tolerate, the English Liturgy among them'.[38] He was of the opinion that Scotland's long history of hostility towards the Book of Common Prayer, combined with its lack of official recognition in Scotland (with the exception of Charles I's ill-fated attempt to introduce a Scottish Book in 1637), meant that the Scots would not accept it. It is unclear whether this was Defoe's own view, or why he denied the obvious fact that the

---

[34] *Statutes*, 6: 74–9; Ralph Stevens, *Protestant Pluralism: The Reception of the Toleration Act, 1689–1720* (Woodbridge, 2018), 13–18.

[35] Rogers, 'Religious Comprehension', 212–26.

[36] NRS, Mar and Kellie Judicial Papers, GD124/6/171, 1; Stephen, 'English Liturgy and Scottish Identity', 69–74.

[37] NRS, Episcopal Chest Manuscripts, CH12/12/1855.

[38] [Daniel Defoe], *Greenshields out of Prison and Toleration settled in Scotland, or the Case of Mr. Greenshields farther examined* (London, 1710), 6.

Book of Common Prayer was being used in Scotland. Robert Harley, Defoe's former patron, may have employed him to produce this pamphlet to discourage the episcopalians, and their tory allies in his own party, from offending the Church of Scotland by using the controversy to push for toleration.[39] To this end, Defoe outlined two arguments against legal toleration if it should be enacted by parliament in response to the controversy. First, if legal toleration should be introduced, then Defoe argued that it would not be given 'without the Incumbrance of Oaths'. The episcopalians who would take such oaths would be abandoned by their congregations and it would create a 'worse Confusion than there is now'. Second, any toleration settlement would be rejected by the nonjurors because it would be 'clog'd with Oaths, Abjurations, praying for the queen, and submitting to the Presbyterian Church in Discipline'.[40] The Greenshields controversy, Defoe argued, did not justify tolerating the use of the Book of Common Prayer in Scotland or, indeed, the episcopalians in general.

Defoe's arguments were shared by some of the Scottish bishops. On 2 November, Bishop Alexander Rose of Edinburgh wrote to Archibald Campbell, who would later be consecrated as a nonjuring Scottish bishop, to distance himself from Greenshields. He acknowledged that Greenshields had initially approached him after being asked by Edinburgh's English residents 'to perform divin[e] office by the English liturgy'. Rose reported that he had asked Greenshields to consider 'who ar[e] to be constituents of y [ou]r meeting house', but refused to let his answer be considered as a licence. He felt that his actions 'cannot infer anything like an allowance or licence to Mr Greenshields'.[41] John Sage, who had been consecrated in 1705, made a similar point to Campbell on 18 November, but he felt that the imprisonment of Greenshields should not be used by the tolerationists.[42] Although Sage had supported toleration in 1703, he now insisted that the episcopalians 'do not want a Toleration'. 'No law', he argued, 'obliges us to be of the presbyterian communion, no law forbids Meeting houses, nay no law obliges those

---

[39] J. A. Downie, *Robert Harley and the Press: Propaganda and Public Opinion in the Age of Swift and Defoe* (Cambridge, 1979), 62.
[40] [Defoe], *Greenshields*, 9–11.
[41] NRS, Episcopal Chest, CH12/12/1815.
[42] Clarke, 'Scottish Episcopalians', 148.

who officiate in Meeting houses to Qualify'. Instead, the episcopalians wanted an 'Equitable Connivance' and should be allowed 'to enjoy what the Law allows us'. This allowance meant that 'no hot alarms shall be given to the Dominant Kirk … so warm as those which must necessarily result from a formal Toleration'.[43] In short, Sage was happy with the de facto toleration that was permitted to episcopalians if they kept their heads down and did not provoke the authorities to implement the laws against intrusion.

Despite these arguments, the image of Greenshields as an atypical episcopalian was used effectively by his supporters to convince the Lords to back the appeal. Bishop William Nicolson of Carlisle, who was one of his English supporters, in a testimonial that he wrote for Greenshields to present to Archbishop Tenison when he arrived in London in September 1710 to further his appeal, wrote that the character of Greenshields was 'widely different from that of a daring and seditious incendiary'.[44] Although Nicolson was a low church bishop, the positive image of Greenshields that he and others of his churchmanship portrayed built on a pre-existing sympathy towards the Scottish episcopalians within the Church of England that was shared by low and high church clerics. This sympathy was demonstrated when the bishops voted in favour of Greenshields when the Lords considered his appeal on 1 March 1711. Despite assertions from some influential Scottish peers, such as John Campbell, duke of Argyll, and his brother Archibald, earl of Ilay, that Greenshields's appeal violated the Act for Securing of the Protestant Religion, there was widespread agreement that it was legal.[45] Nicolson noted in his diary on 1 March that there 'was little or no Debate on the main Subject' and the Court of Session's verdict was 'unanimously reversed'.[46]

George Lockhart of Carnwath, MP for Midlothian and a committed Jacobite, outlined in a pamphlet two reasons why the Lords favoured Greenshields. First, they viewed the appeal as 'a Civil Cause, arising from the Nature Rights of Mankind, to worship God after any manner not expressly prohibited by the Laws of the

---

[43] NRS, Episcopal Chest, CH12/12/1980.

[44] Clyve Jones and Geoffrey Holmes, eds, *The London Diaries of William Nicolson, Bishop of Carlisle, 1702–18* (Cambridge, 1983), 551.

[45] Clarke, 'Scottish Episcopalians', 245–7; Tompson, 'Greenshields', 114–15.

[46] Holmes and Jones, eds, *London Diaries*, 553.

Land'. The presbytery of Edinburgh's reliance on the city's magistrates and the Court of Session to prosecute Greenshields 'pla[i]nly shew[e]d the case is of Civil, and not Ecclesiastical' concern. Second, the Lords questioned whether any laws in Scotland prohibited publicly accessible episcopalian meeting houses. They acknowledged that the basis of the prosecution had been Greenshields's alleged violation of the statute against intrusion but decided that this charge was false because the act did not cover episcopalians who preached in private meeting houses. Since Greenshields had not intruded into a vacant parish, there was no legal basis for the presbytery to act against him.[47]

According to Lockhart, these reasons motivated one unnamed Scottish peer to argue that the Lords should favour Greenshields because if they did not it would 'encourage the Presbyterian Faction to continue, nay, encrease their persecuting Temper'. The whig lords, in Lockhart's mind, were trying to appease Scotland's presbyterian establishment at the expense of the episcopalians. In an address that he claimed to have given to the Lords during the debate, he assured them that the presbyterians' strength was 'nothing but a Bugbear to frighten Children and Strangers'. This address was challenged by an unnamed English lord who stated that if Greenshields's appeal was dropped the queen would issue instructions to prevent the Scottish authorities from acting against episcopalian meeting houses. This was in turn countered by the Scottish lord, who insisted that there was no law in Scotland upon which such instructions could be based and that any claim that such a law existed was an 'Old Weather-beaten Argument'.[48] This view was supported by most of the house when they voted by 68 to 32 in favour of Greenshields. However, Argyll and Ilay were outraged by the decision and walked out of the chamber after their attempt to call for an adjournment failed.[49]

---

[47] [George Lockhart], *The Present State of Mr. Greenshields Case, now before the Right Honourable the House of Lords: In a Letter from a Commoner of North-Britain* (London, 1711), 5–7; Daniel Szechi, 'Lockhart, George (1681?–1731)', *ODNB*, 23 September 2004, online at: <http://www.oxforddnb.com>, accessed 2 September 2019.
[48] [Lockhart], *Present State*, 13.
[49] Tompson, 'Greenshields', 113–14.

The Legal Implications

The Lords' decision sparked a debate on whether episcopalians now enjoyed legal protection to erect meeting houses and use the English Book of Common Prayer. John Anderson, the minister of Dumbarton, told Principal Stirling on 18 March that the 'hinge of the controversie' rested on whether to allow the episcopalians 'liberty' to use the English liturgy and to plant their own ministers.[50] Writing after the Lords' decision, Ilay stated that 'there stands at present a toleration in Scotland, decreed by a sentence and unlimited either in point of faith, or qualifications whatsoever'.[51]

One proposal, prepared for Archbishop Tenison just after the Lords' decision and which Clarke attributes to Greenshields, argued that the 'Decree of the Lords of Parliam[en]t is not sufficient to protect the Clergy in the use of the English Liturgy'. Instead, the proposal argued that meeting houses and the Book of Common Prayer should be protected by an act of parliament. It asserted that Edinburgh should have six meeting houses and that the towns, shires and former episcopal seats should have one each. This would lead to a total of forty houses, that would be supported by private collections and the former bishops' rents that would be granted to them by parliament. The religious qualification, the proposal suggested, should 'be the same as here in Engl[an]d', but it did not clarify whether episcopalians would qualify by accepting the Thirty-Nine Articles or the Westminster Confession. The proposal's civil qualifications were more stringent and challenged the episcopalians' Jacobite sympathies by requiring them to take the oath of abjuration.[52]

From March 1711 onwards there was an increased local demand for episcopalian worship and the Book of Common Prayer in their traditional areas of strength. An undated episcopalian petition to Anne by unnamed episcopalian heritors in the north-east asked her to protect their meeting houses against the presbyterian judicatories and stated that their request was supported by many parishes that

---

[50] Glasgow UL, Murray MS 650, unpaginated.
[51] Joseph McCormick, ed., *State Papers and Letters addressed to William Carstares, Confidential Secretary to King William during the whole of his Reign* (Edinburgh, 1776), 791.
[52] LPL, Papers of Thomas Tenison, MS 954(32), 'Some proper Methods to circulate the English Liturgy in Scotland', n.d.; Clarke, 'Scottish Episcopalians', 328–30.

'have already the English worship [settled] amongst [the]m, as in Old Aberd[ee]n Peterhead & Fraserburgh'. The petitioners insisted that they would not disturb 'her Maj[esties] Governm[en]t or the national Setlement of this Church'.[53]

The growth in demand for episcopalian worship and the liturgy alarmed the presbyterian authorities. Their concerns were allayed briefly when Steuart of Goodtrees was brought back as lord advocate in 1711. This caused the supporters of episcopalian toleration, such as Lockhart of Carnwath, to argue that a new wave of persecution was imminent, but the Lords' decision prevented the Scottish authorities from prosecuting episcopalians as they had done before.[54]

After the decision, many episcopalians started to argue that the Church of Scotland had no jurisdiction over them. On 12 November 1711, Henry Murray, an episcopalian in Dunkeld, was cited before the presbytery of Perth for intruding upon the parish, having his communicants kneel during communion, and introducing 'a Liturgy, and set Form, in the Publick Worship of God'. Murray, in his protestation against this citation on 21 November, reiterated the arguments that Greenshields had used. He denied the presbytery's authority to cite him and insisted that the statute against intrusion did not apply to him since he preached 'in a Meeting-House, and to a willing People'. Murray told the presbytery that if his actions were a crime it was 'purely Civil', and that the liturgy of the Book of Common Prayer was 'agreeable to the Word of God'. He reminded the presbytery that the Lords' decision in favour of Greenshields proved that 'where there is no Law there can be no Transgression'. Despite this, the presbytery deposed him on 10 January 1712.[55]

CONCLUSION

On 3 March 1712, the British parliament passed the Act to prevent the disturbing of those of the Episcopal Communion in that part of Great Britain called Scotland in the Exercise of their Religious

---

[53] NRS, Episcopal Chest, CH12/12/1855.
[54] [George Lockhart], *A Letter from a Scots Gentleman residing in London, to his Friend in Edenborough* ([London?], 1711), 11–15; Clarke, 'Scottish Episcopalians', 287–8.
[55] *The Church of England still Persecuted, or the Case of Mr Murray, depos'd by the Presbytery of Perth, on the Tenth of January, for reading the English Service* ([Edinburgh?], 1712), 2–3.

Worship and in the use of the Liturgy of the Church of England.[56] The act resolved most of the legal ambiguities that the Lords' decision had revealed. Episcopalian ministers could erect meeting houses and use the liturgy if they qualified by swearing the oath of allegiance to Anne. However, the act's effectiveness was limited when Ilay and the whig lords inserted a clause requiring the swearing of the abjuration oath, effectively restricting the number of episcopalians who would qualify under it by requiring them to abjure the Stuart pretender. Despite this, the act ensured that a separate episcopalian church would be legally protected, and thus effectively ensured that the exclusive national status of the established Church of Scotland had ended.

The MPs who supported the act, such as Lockhart of Carnwath, had been some of the most ardent supporters of Greenshields, and their ability to argue that the episcopalians were being persecuted by a presbyterian established church convinced the tories to support the legislation. The act confirmed the British parliament's legal authority as the ultimate arbiter of Scotland's religious affairs, but this authority had already been demonstrated by the Lords' decision to support Greenshields's appeal in March 1711. The Lords' decision had three legal implications for Scotland's religious affairs. First, it redefined 'intrusion', as it was classified under the Scottish statute of 1695, to mean a minister who was trying to take control of a vacant parish church, not one setting up a meeting house. Second, it affirmed that there was nothing to prevent episcopalians from using the English Book of Common Prayer. Third, since the liturgy was not proscribed by any civil law, it laid down that the Scottish courts were not allowed to act on behalf of the courts of the Church of Scotland. The kirk's discipline was restricted to its own members and this would be confirmed by the Toleration Act of 1712.

The Greenshields appeal reveals the legal complexities that surrounded the relationship between the emerging British state, the Church of Scotland and the nation's episcopalian minority. It showed that that the British parliament was now the ultimate arbiter of Scotland's religious affairs, and that groups existing outside the established Church of Scotland could seek the state's recognition. The Lords' decision also provided a basis for the state's parliamentary sovereignty to be exercised decisively in 1712, when the Toleration Act

[56] *Statutes*, 9: 557–9.

was ratified despite widespread protests that it violated the union. Above all, the appeal demonstrates that the British state's authority to grant legal legitimation was a crucial factor in the recognition of religious pluralism in Scotland. This authority became more pronounced during the eighteenth century as parliament intervened more frequently in Scotland's religious affairs. The penal statutes that were introduced against the episcopalians after the Jacobite rebellions in 1715 and 1745, and their eventual loosening under the Episcopal Relief Act of 1792, show how the British state's legal authority normalized religious relations in eighteenth-century Scottish society.

Toleration and Repression: German States, the Law and the 'Sects' in the Long Nineteenth Century

Manfred Henke*

Groß Grönau

At the beginning of the period, the Prussian General Law Code did not provide for equal rights for members of 'churches' and those of 'sects'. However, the French Revolution decreed the separation of church and state and the principle of equal rights for all citizens. Between the Congress of Vienna (1815) and the revolution of 1848, Prussian monarchs pressed for the church union of Lutheran and Reformed and advocated the piety of the Evangelical Revival. The Old Lutherans felt obliged to leave the united church, thus eventually forming a 'sect' favoured by the king. Rationalists, who objected to biblicism and orthodoxy, were encouraged to leave, too. As Baptists, Catholic Apostolics and Methodists arrived from Britain and America, the number of 'sects' increased. New ways of curtailing their influence were devised, especially in Prussia and Saxony.

This article sheds light on a period of transition in Germany between the late absolutist General Law Code of 1794 and the provisions on religion in the republican constitution of Weimar passed in 1919. During that period the rise of free churches was eased by gradual changes in the legal system. What changes were made? How did they relate to long established concepts of the states' legal prerogatives in matters of religion? What was the legal content of the term 'sect'? And why could the nineteenth-century jurist Hermann Fürstenau observe that if a German state wanted to introduce 'complete religious liberty' it would have 'to treat all religious societies as sects'?[1]

Various aspects of this subject have been discussed from a denominational perspective, but without asking what policies the states

* Hauptstraße 53B, 23627 Groß Grönau, Germany. E-mail: Manfred.henke@nac-history.com.
[1] Hermann Fürstenau, *Das Grundrecht der Religionsfreiheit nach seiner geschichtlichen Entwickelung und heutigen Geltung in Deutschland* (Glashütten im Taunus, 1975; first published 1891), 257–8.

Studies in Church History 56 (2020), 338–361   © Ecclesiastical History Society 2020
doi: 10.1017/stc.2019.19

pursued when dealing with 'sects'. The rather deficient state of scholarship is reflected in a slim volume summing up the results of a joint research project undertaken by members of established and free churches initiated in the course of preparations for the five hundredth anniversary of the Lutheran Reformation. Its title, *Heilung der Erinnerungen. Freikirchen und Landeskirchen im 19. Jahrhundert*, suggests that relations between established and free churches have been bitterly antagonistic, so that a healing of memories is still needed.[2] A voluminous study of dissent in nineteenth-century Germany refers to state action against sects, insinuating that the authorities aimed to suppress religious dissent but lacked the necessary legal instruments to do so effectively.[3] In an ambitious attempt to find precursors of the free churches in deviant religious groups since the Reformation, Karl Heinz Voigt, a noted historian of German Methodism, points to the need for further research on their relations with the secular and ecclesiastical authorities.[4]

My own research on apostolic congregations in Germany has raised questions about the legal framework regulating the formation and functioning of religious societies outside the established church. These can only be answered by looking at the treatment other 'sects' received at the hands of the state, or rather states, for there were still twenty-five of them, even after Prussia annexed several in the wake of the Austro-Prussian War of 1866. Each state had at least one established church and power to legislate in matters of religion. Prussia set standards against which the laws of some of the smaller states will be discussed. An overview of legal approaches will emerge that answers some questions but raises many more. This is a report of work in progress.

LAW AND LEGAL PRACTICE REGARDING RELIGION BEFORE 1830

In the Peace of Augsburg (1555) it had been agreed that two 'religious parties' within a church still deemed universal should coexist within

---

[2] Walter Fleischmann-Bisten, Ulrich Möller and Barbara Rudolph, eds, *Heilung der Erinnerungen: Freikirchen und Landeskirchen im 19. Jahrhundert* (Leipzig, 2018).
[3] Herbert Strahm, *Dissentertum im Deutschland des 19. Jahrhunderts. Freikirchen und religiöse Sondergemeinschaften im Beziehungs- und Spannungsfeld von Staat und protestantischen Landeskirchen*, Münchener kirchenhistorische Studien NF 5 (Stuttgart, 2016), 64–72, 566–73.
[4] Karl Heinz Voigt, *Kirchliche Minderheiten im Schatten der lutherischen Reformation vor 1517 bis nach 2017* (Göttingen, 2018), 15–16.

the Holy Roman Empire: the Catholic party and the party of the Augsburg Confession (1530), that is, the Lutherans. Secular princes were given the power to determine the religion to which their subjects were expected to adhere. If they did not grant the adherents of the opposing 'religious party' permission to engage in domestic worship without a minister (*devotio domestica simplex*), they had to give them permission to emigrate. The Peace of Westphalia (1648) extended this system to include Calvinists by defining their teachings as 'essentially' in accordance with the Augsburg Confession. 'Sects' were in theory not tolerated,[5] but a number of princes did tolerate them for sound economic reasons. Like the Jews, 'sectaries' usually lived in their own settlements, segregated from the rest of society.[6]

The Prussian kingdom had a long history of toleration.[7] There were Mennonites in the formerly Polish territory acquired in the first partition of Poland (1772) and in the city of Krefeld, which the Hohenzollerns had inherited from the house of Orange in 1702.[8] They were subjected to a number of civil disabilities in return for not having to bear arms.[9] Moravians in Silesia had been granted a number of privileges in 1742, 1746 and 1763 that gave them a position akin to that of the established churches, as they were deemed to be close to them by virtue of their adherence to principles laid down in the Augsburg Confession. Their registers of births, marriages and deaths were legally valid documents, whereas Mennonites and others had to hand in transcripts of their registers to the local incumbent,

---

[5] Martin Heckel, *Vom Religionskonflikt zur Ausgleichsordnung. Der Sonderweg des deutschen Staatskirchenrechts vom Augsburger Religionsfrieden 1555 bis zur Gegenwart*, Bayerische Akademie de Wissenschaften. Philosophisch- historische Klasse, Abhandlungen NF 130 (München, 2007), 10, 15–16, 18–19, 25–6; Joachim Whaley, *Germany and the Holy Roman Empire*, 2 vols (Oxford, 2012), 1: 333–4, 623–6.

[6] Cf. ibid. 2: 263–9; Voigt, *Kirchliche Minderheiten*, 113–32; Erwin Freytag, 'Nichtlutherische Religionsgemeinschaften unter dem landesherrlichen Kirchenregiment', in Walter Göbell and Lorenz Hein, eds, *Schleswig-Holsteinische Kirchengeschichte*, 4: *Orthodoxie und Pietismus*, Schriften des Vereins für Schleswig-Holsteinische Kirchengeschichte 1st series 29 (Neumünster, 1984), 233–67.

[7] Christopher Clark, *Iron Kingdom: The Rise and Downfall of Prussia 1600–1947* (London, 2007), 115–24, 236–7; H. F. Jacobson, 'Ueber die Arten der Religionsgesellschaften und die religiösen Rechtsverhältnisse der Dissidenten in Preussen', *Zeitschrift für Kirchenrecht* 1 (1861), 393–443, at 392–3.

[8] Mark Jantzen, *Mennonite German Soldiers: Nation, Religion, and Family in the Prussian East, 1772–1880* (Notre Dame, IN, 2010), 23–6, 108–11.

[9] Ibid. 27–33, 35–42, 54–70, 102–6.

who would then enter them into the registers he kept.[10] To their dismay, however, even the Moravians were classed as a 'sect' in an edict on religion of 9 July 1788, as were the Mennonites and the Jews.[11] In contemporary parlance, a 'Christian' was usually identified as a member of one of the three 'approved' confessions, Catholic, Lutheran and Reformed.[12]

In 1794 a General Law Code was published as *Allgemeines Landrecht für die Preußischen Staaten*. Using terms coined by Enlightenment thought, the three 'churches' defined in 1788 were classed as 'publicly approved religious societies' and the 'sects' as 'tolerated religious societies'. Only the former could call their buildings 'churches' or use bells.[13] Those terms, together with the dichotomy of 'church' and 'sect' as defined in the edict of 1788, continued to be legal terminology.[14] All religious societies were obliged to 'instil into their members awe towards the Godhead, obedience to the laws, loyalty to the state and morally good intentions towards their fellow-citizens'. Failure to do so would lead to their dissolution.[15]

The *Allgemeines Landrecht* granted liberty of conscience but imposed tight restrictions, even on domestic worship. It provided that 'each head of a household can arrange his domestic worship as

---

[10] Dietrich Meyer, 'Zinzendorf und Herrnhut', in Martin Brecht et al., eds, *Geschichte des Pietismus*, 2: *Der Pietismus im achtzehnten Jahrhundert* (Göttingen, 1995), 3–106, at 45–6; Jacobson, 'Ueber die Arten der Religionsgesellschaften', 395–6; R. W. Dove, 'Die rechtliche Stellung der evangelischen Brüdergemeinden in Preussen', *Zeitschrift für Kirchenrecht* 3 (1863), 460–8. The full texts of their privileges can be found in Berlin, Geheimes Staatsarchiv Preußischer Kulturbesitz (hereafter: GStA PK) I, HA Rep 76 III Sekt. 1 Abt. XIIIa, Nr. 3 Bd. 2 (unfoliated).

[11] K[arl] Goßner, *Preußisches evangelisches Kirchenrecht*, 1: *Führer durch das Recht der Landeskirche der neun älteren Provinzen insbesondere für Geistliche und Selbstverwaltungs-Organe, Verwaltungsbeamte und Juristen*, 2nd edn (Berlin, 1914), 25–6. For the background, see Clark, *Iron Kingdom*, 267–72.

[12] See, for example, Jantzen, *Mennonite German Soldiers*, 41.

[13] *Allgemeines Landrecht für die Preußischen Staaten* (Berlin, 1794), part 2, title 11, §§10, 11, 13. For the intellectual background of the term *Religionsgesellschaft* ('religious society'), see Heckel, *Vom Religionskonflikt zur Ausgleichsordnung*, 79–80.

[14] For examples, see Jantzen, *Mennonite German Soldiers*, 166, 254. Gerhard Anschütz, *Die Verfassungs-Urkunde für den Preußischen Staat* (Berlin, 1912), 216–17, explains the legal situation in 1912.

[15] 'Jede Kirchengesellschaft ist verpflichtet, ihren Mitgliedern Ehrfurcht gegen die Gottheit, Gehorsam gegen die Gesetze, Treue gegen den Staat, und sittlich gute Gesinnungen gegen ihre Mitbürger einzuflößen': *Allgemeines Landrecht*, part 2, title 11, §13.

he pleases',[16] but a cabinet order (*Kabinettsordre*) of 9 March 1834 explicitly excluded ministers of religion from this provision and restricted attendance at house prayers to 'the head of the house's family and the persons living with him and integrated into his household.[17] 'Secret meetings under the pretext of domestic worship' were expressly forbidden.[18] New religious societies could be formed subject to state approval and meet for worship in private homes or 'in certain buildings dedicated to that purpose'. They were not necessarily granted corporate rights, and they could not purchase the buildings they used for their meetings.[19] In the eyes of the law, a religious society was a local group, never a nationwide association of believers with a common creed.[20]

In an important draft for the Civil Code, Carl Gottlieb Svarez had classed Jews and 'merely tolerated religious parties' together because neither of them were authorized to register or certify births, marriages and deaths.[21] Generally speaking, both groups lacked full civic rights, and the registry of the *Ministerium für geistliche, Unterrichts- und Medicinalangelegenheiten* ('Ministry of Religious, Educational and Medical Affairs'; short title *Kultusministerium*) reflected this view: 'Affairs of sects and Jews' were classed together, whereas they seem to have been kept apart in the *Ministerium des Innern und der Polizei* ('Ministry of the Interior and Police'), whose department of religion and public education was upgraded to constitute the *Kultusministerium* in 1817.[22] As one author put it, individuals were

---

[16] 'Jeder Hausvater kann seinen häuslichen Gottesdienst nach Gutfinden anordnen': ibid., §7.

[17] '[D]aß zu dem häuslichen Gottesdienste nur den Mitgliedern der Familie das Hausvaters und den bei ihm wohnenden, seiner Hauszucht unterworfenen Personen der Zutritt gestattet [wird]': Ernst Rudolf Huber and Wolfgang Huber, eds, *Staat und Kirche im 19. und 20. Jahrhundert. Dokumente zur Geschichte des deutschen Staatskirchenrechts*, 5 vols (Darmstadt, 2014; first published Berlin, 1973–95), 1: 607. This order was issued against Old Lutherans, as discussed below.

[18] *Allgemeines Landrecht*, part 2, title 11, §9.

[19] Ibid., §§10, 13, 24.

[20] Ibid., §36.

[21] Jacobson, 'Ueber die Arten der Religionsgesellschaften', 399–400.

[22] GStA PK, unpublished 'Findbuch' for I. HA Rep. 76 Kultusministerium, III Evangelisch-geistliche Angelegenheiten Bd. 1, Sektion 1 Generalia, Abt. XIIIa, typewritten entry 'Sekten- und Judensachen'; Christina Rathgeber, 'Strukturelle Vorgeschichte und Gründung des Kultusministeriums', in Wolfgang Neugebauer, ed., *Das preußische Kultusministerium als Staatsbehörde und gesellschaftliche Agentur (1817–1934)*, 1/1: *Die Behörde und ihr höheres Personal – Darstellung*, Acta Borussica, NF Series 2 (Berlin, 2009),

free to believe whatever they pleased, but once they made their conviction public by joining a religious society outside the establishment,
they had to put up with the inferior legal status accorded to members
of that group.[23]

Napoleon Bonaparte's rise to power put an end to the Holy
Roman Empire in 1806. In 1803, the German territories west of
the Rhine had been annexed by France, ecclesiastical princes and
lesser secular rulers deposed, their territories redistributed and a
Rhenish Confederation of middling powers formed. The injunction
against sects ended without anybody taking much notice. In the
newly created Kingdom of Westphalia, ruled by Jérome Bonaparte,
the constitution of 1807 granted complete religious liberty and full
equality in the eyes of the law.[24] In contrast, in Bavaria an edict of
24 March 1809, in terms directly influenced by the Prussian Civil
Code, permitted 'private religious services' to new religious societies
only if the monarch granted them a charter; it also defined the conditions attached to those services.[25]

Napoleon's interference in German affairs brought about a 'geopo-
litical revolution' which reduced the number of German states from
over three hundred to thirty-nine, and the Congress of Vienna made
of Prussia 'a colossus that stretched across the north of Germany'.[26]
The German Confederation founded in 1815 was made up of sovereign princes. In their Articles of Confederation (*Bundesakte*) they
guaranteed equal rights for all 'Christian co-religionists', but the context shows that this referred only to Catholics, Lutherans and
Calvinists. Even then, Catholics could not everywhere expect to
enjoy equal rights with Protestants. As to the Jews, the princes
declared their intention to improve and equalize their legal status

---

4–19, at 4–5; Bärbel Holtz, 'Zuständigkeiten, Tätigkeitsgebiete und Organisationsstruktur:
Die Jahre von 1817–1866', ibid. 20–31, at 20–1; Jürgen Kloosterhuis, *Archivarbeit für
Preußen* (Berlin, 2000), 68–9, 433. My conclusion is based on a survey of registry notes
in GStA PK I, HA Rep 76 III Sekt. 1 Abt. XIIIa, Nr. 1, Bd. 1 to Bd. 4 (Jewish affairs)
and ibid., Nr. 3, Bd. 1 to Bd. 4 (Moravians).

[23] Anke Breitenborn, 'Die Minderheitenproblematik in den preußischen Staaten und das
ALR', in Günter Birtsch and Dietmar Willoweit, eds, *Reformabsolutismus und ständische
Gesellschaft* (Berlin, 1998), 321–40, at 331.

[24] Fürstenau, *Religionsfreiheit*, 85, 95–6.

[25] Ibid. 91–2, (text) 306–8.

[26] Clark, *Iron Kingdom*, 295, 389.

all over Germany without loss of those rights which they had already been granted in some. 'Sects' were not taken into consideration.[27]

Under French rule, legal reforms had been introduced in parts of Germany.[28] In the Prussian territories formerly belonging to the Kingdom of Westphalia, the constitution of 1807 with its provisions on religious liberty and civic equality remained 'fully valid',[29] although the modern *code civil* had been replaced by the more restrictive *Allgemeines Landrecht* of 1794.[30] In those parts of the Prussian Rhine province that had been under direct French rule, the *code civil* remained in force, and with it the civil registration of births, marriages and deaths, which was also retained in Baden, Bremen and Lübeck, but abolished in Braunschweig and Hamburg.[31] After some hesitation the Prussian government decided in 1818 to tolerate the differences in the legal system until the 'revision of the complete Prussian legal and judicial system', which had been envisaged in 1817, had been completed.[32] Eventually, a civil code (*Bürgerliches Gesetzbuch*) for the whole of the newly united German empire took effect on 1 January 1900.

The rise of new 'Sects' before the Prussian Toleration Edict of 1847

Frederick William III of Prussia inadvertently produced a new 'sect' by his project of a church union of Lutheran and Reformed parishes.

[27] Bundesakte, Article 16 (drafts and final text in Huber and Huber, eds, *Dokumente*, 1: 113–15); Ernst Rudolf Huber, *Deutsche Verfassungsgeschichte seit 1789*, 8 vols (Stuttgart, 1957–91), 1: 414–15; Joseph Freisen, *Verfassungsgeschichte der katholischen Kirche Deutschlands in der Neuzeit auf Grund des katholischen Kirchen- und Staatskirchenrechts* (Leipzig and Berlin, 1916), 79; Fürstenau, *Religionsfreiheit*, 99–126.
[28] The classic study is Elisabeth Fehrenbach, *Traditionale Gesellschaft und revolutionäres Recht* (Göttingen, 1974; 3rd edn 1983).
[29] [Kultusministerium], *Mittheilungen aus der Verwaltung der geistlichen, Unterrichts- und Medicinal-Angelegenheiten in Preußen* (Berlin, 1847), 217.
[30] Gerhard Deter, 'Das preußische Allgemeine Landrecht in der Provinz Westfalen – Rezeption und Wirkung', in Karl Teppe and Michael Epkenhans, eds, *Westfalen und Preußen. Integration und Regionalismus* (Paderborn, 1991), 82–97.
[31] Karl Stiefel, *Baden 1648–1952*, 2 vols (Karlsruhe, 1977), 2: 1219–24; Antjekathrin Graßmann, ed., *Lübeckische Geschichte*, 2nd edn (Lübeck, 1989), 556–7; Kurt G. A. Jeserich, Hans Pohl and Christoph von Unruh, *Deutsche Verwaltungsgeschichte*, 6 vols (Stuttgart, 1983–8), 2: 744, 795, 805.
[32] Ilja Mieck, 'Preußen von 1807 bis 1850. Reformen, Restauration und Revolution', in Otto Büsch, ed., *Handbuch der preußischen Geschichte*, 2: *Das 19. Jahrhundert und große Themen der Geschichte Preußens* (Berlin and New York, 1992), 3–292, at 99.

He initiated this on the three hundredth anniversary of the Lutheran Reformation in 1817, and produced a new liturgy in 1821 to bring about unity of worship. When the king ordered the adoption of that liturgy in Silesia in 1830, a vigorous opposition movement came into existence. For about four years the Prussian government tried to contain the 'Old Lutherans' by depriving the popular movement of its leaders.[33] The conflict escalated when a village preacher in Hönigern, in the Wrocław (Breslau) district, was removed from his incumbency in September 1834. When the villagers refused to hand the church over to his successor, a detachment of four hundred infantry and a hundred cavalry dispersed the crowd guarding the church and installed the new incumbent in time for the Christmas service.[34] The movement spread throughout Prussia. In 1837 and 1838, about two thousand Old Lutherans emigrated to Australia and North America after the government had illegally obstructed that move for several months.[35]

From the outset, the Old Lutherans aimed at being recognized as a tolerated religious society outside the established church.[36] In December 1835, the minister of religious affairs argued that they could not be recognized as a 'sect' because their doctrine did not significantly differ from that of the 'church', echoing a sentiment earlier expressed by Frederick William III. Thus, they were 'separatists' who ought to be forced back into the church to which they properly belonged.[37] Unimpressed, the Old Lutherans continued to have the sacraments administered by their own ministers in separate assemblies. On 9 March 1834 Frederick William III issued a cabinet order

---

[33] Christina Rathgeber, *Herausforderung für den Staat. Die Altlutheraner und die preußische Religionspolitik (1830 bis 1847)*, Acta Borussica NF 2 (Berlin and Boston, MA, 2017), 4–15 (the work is a collection of sources printed from the manuscripts in GStA PK, preceded by a summary of events); cf. Christopher Clark, 'The Politics of Revival: Pietists, Aristocrats, and the State Church in Early Nineteenth-Century Prussia', in Larry Eugene Jones and James Retallack, eds, *Between Reform, Reaction, and Resistance* (Providence, RI, and Oxford, 1992), 31–61; idem, *The Politics of Conversion* (Oxford, 1995), 213–19, 225–36; idem, 'Confessional Policy and the Limits of State Action: Frederick William III and the Prussian Church Union, 1817–1840', *HistJ* 39 (1996), 985–1004.
[34] Rathgeber, *Altlutheraner*, 17, 95–114.
[35] Ibid. 17–19; documents ibid. 134–48, 160–1, 166–7, 176–8; Clark, 'Confessional Policy', 998.
[36] Rathgeber, *Altlutheraner*, 7.
[37] Ibid. 7, 124–7.

forbidding all separatist assemblies except in family worship without a minister[38] and a declaration against the carrying out of ministerial acts by non-ministers, punishable by a fine of fifty talers or six weeks in prison.[39] The Old Lutherans also ignored those orders. Both the minister of justice and the Provincial Supreme Court (*Oberlandesgericht*) in Frankfurt an der Oder questioned the legality of the king's orders. Moreover, whereas the king assumed that only ordinations performed in the established church had the force of law, the lawyers declared that there was no law against the validity of Old Lutheran ordinations. Various courts refused to act against offenders; nevertheless, the king continued on a course that seemed increasingly unlikely to succeed.[40]

Frederick William III was succeeded by his son Frederick William IV in 1840. Like his father, the new king became deeply involved in church affairs, but unlike his father he was at pains to resolve the conflict with the Old Lutherans, and also a further conflict with the Catholics in the Rhine Province.[41] Whereas the old king had insisted that the Old Lutheran leaders had 'with criminal intent used the intellectual limitations of their parishioners, falsely claiming they were denied liberty of conscience … to confirm them in their disobedience',[42] his son, who was deeply committed to the Evangelical Awakening, sympathized with the Old Lutherans' piety.[43] Frederick William IV ordered the release of imprisoned ministers and permitted assemblies, even a general synod, hoping to persuade Old Lutherans to remain within the established church and suggesting they might assemble as private religious associations within the church.[44] When this failed, he issued a 'General Concession' (*Generalkonzession*) in July 1845. By its terms, the Old Lutherans were not allowed to call

[38] Compare n. 17 above.

[39] Rathgeber, *Altlutheraner*, 14–15; both texts in Huber and Huber, eds, *Dokumente*, 607–8. In their introduction, the compilers state as objective fact that sacraments were performed by laymen, as the government argued, whereas the law courts upheld the validity of Old Lutheran ordinations, as shown below: ibid. 605–6.

[40] Rathgeber, *Altlutheraner*, 21–4, 27–8, 120–2, 139–55, 157–74, 185–7.

[41] Ibid. 36–7.

[42] '[W]elche in verbrecherischer Absicht sich der Beschränktheit der Gemeindeglieder bedienen, um sie mit Vorspiegelung beschränkter Gewissensfreiheit … in ihrem Ungehorsam zu bestärken': ibid. 155–7, quotation at 156, cf. 20, 29.

[43] Ibid. 30–3. On the king's religion, see David E. Barclay, *Frederick William IV and the Prussian Monarchy 1840–1861* (Oxford, 1995), 75–92.

[44] Rathgeber, *Altlutheraner*, 30, 189–235.

themselves a 'church', but they could assemble as separate congregations and were further allowed to form 'an association of these congregations under a common executive not answerable to the evangelical church of the land'. They did not have to contribute financially to the parish system (as the Mennonites did) and they received corporate rights and permission to own property.[45] Unlike the Mennonites and others,[46] they did not have to hand in notices of their baptisms, marriages and funerals to the incumbents for registration, but reported them directly to the civil courts as the parish ministers did; like the parish ministers, Old Lutheran ministers could issue legally valid certificates of baptisms, marriages and deaths.[47]

The Baptists came to the notice of the central Prussian authorities only after the accession of Frederick William IV. In 1840 there were Baptist congregations in three Prussian cities: Memel (Klaipeda), Bitterfeld and Berlin. The new minister of religious affairs attempted a policy of suppression in the provinces while at the same time trying to accommodate the Baptists in the capital.[48] In Memel, the consistory applied to the local law court (*Land- und Stadtgericht*) to have recourse to a royal order to the consistories of 23 February 1802. This was directed against parents who neglected their duty to have their children baptized within six weeks after birth, particularly those who wanted 'to excel before others as enlightened persons'. In such cases, the parish ministers were to admonish the parents. If the parents failed to comply, the children were to have temporary guardians appointed who would have them baptized.[49] However, the judges refused to grant the order because the parents declared that they had severed all connection with the established church, and the local prefect (*Landrat*) agreed with the lawyers and refused to give his support to further measures.[50]

Outside Prussia, Baptists in the Kingdom of Hannover and the Duchy of Brunswick were not so fortunate. In Hannover, the constitution of 26 September 1833 decreed that the king had the right to 'approve other Christian confessions and sects' besides the Protestant

[45] Ibid. 30–2.
[46] *Allgemeines Landrecht*, part 2, title 11, §498; cf. Jantzen, *Mennonite German Soldiers*, 65.
[47] *Allgemeines Landrecht*, part 2, title 11, §503; Fürstenau, *Religionsfreiheit*, 140–1.
[48] GStA PK I, HA Rep. 77, Sekt. 1, Abt. XIIIa, Nr. 17 Bd. 1.
[49] Ibid., HA Rep. 84 a 1040, unfoliated, documents 7c.
[50] Ibid., HA Rep. 77, Sekt. 1, Abt. XIIIa, Nr. 17 Bd. 1, fols 68–9.

and Catholic churches,[51] but when Baptists arrived in his dominions, the ecclesiastical authorities insisted that their children must be baptized, and parents were told there were no legal provisions to release them from church membership. The authorities referred to what they called the 'Prussian law' and had ten children baptized between 1843 and 1847 after appointing temporary guardians for them.[52] In Brunswick, there were five such cases between 1852 and 1856, even though a judge had ruled against the practice.[53]

A second attempt at suppressing Baptists in Prussia was made in Bitterfeld in the province of Saxony. In July 1842, the minister of religious affairs ordered the regional government to indict the local Baptist minister, Werner, for violating the declaration of 9 March 1834 against the performing of ministerial acts by non-ministers.[54] However, in a judgment dated 20 June 1843, the local court (*Land- und Stadtgericht*) of Delitzsch dismissed the case against Werner, arguing that 'the actions are not performed according to the rite of the established Catholic or Reformed churches, consequently they cannot be regarded as interference with the rights of the preachers of those confessions'. In addition, they accepted Werner's plea that he was an ordained minister of a sect whose assemblies and rites were tolerated in Berlin.[55] On 28 February 1844, the provincial court (*Oberlandesgericht*) in Naumburg reversed that judgment, arguing that it did not matter what kind of rite was used. Werner was to go to prison for eight days because in performing baptisms he had ignored the magistrates' prohibition. In addition, his ordination was declared invalid on the basis that it lacked state approval.[56] This judgment was subsequently quashed by the supreme court of appeal in Naumburg in September 1844, which restored the original judgment.[57]

[51] *Grundgesetz des Königreiches Hannover nebst dem Königlichen Patente, die Publication desselben betreffend* (Hannover, 1833), 27 (§30).
[52] Peter Muttersbach and Gotthard Wefel, *Die Anfänge des Baptismus zwischen Harz und Heide* (Norderstedt, 2015), 81–4, 91–5.
[53] Peter Muttersbach, 'Rechtslage und Rechtspraxis zum Kirchenaustritt und Taufzwang im Herzogtum Braunschweig', in Fleischmann-Bisten, Möller and Rudolph, eds, *Heilung der Erinnerungen*, 92–109.
[54] GStA PK I, HA Rep. 77, Sekt. 1, Abt. XIIIa, Nr. 17 Bd. 1, fol. 268.
[55] Ibid., Bd. 2, fols 113–15.
[56] Ibid., fols 290–3.
[57] Ibid., Bd. 3, fols 64–8; cf. Reinhard Assmann, 'Kirchlicher Widerstand gegen die Duldung der ersten Baptistengemeinden in der preußischen Provinz Sachsen 1840 bis

In the meantime, the minister of religious affairs had decided on a course of action for the Baptists in Berlin which was to become regular practice under the toleration edict of 1847. Originally, the minister of the interior and police, von Rochow, had argued that Baptists should be accepted as a tolerated sect under the terms of the Civil Code. Von Rochow recognized that like the Mennonites they rejected infant baptism and baptized believers. However, unlike the Mennonites, Baptists did not refuse oaths, public office or military service; moreover, they were well established in Britain and America.[58] He incurred the displeasure of the king, who alleged that the police should have taken stricter measures against Baptists. Von Rochow argued that the law did not allow him to order such measures and reiterated his view that Baptists should be recognized as a tolerated religious society in the terms of the Civil Code. Any other course of action might cause gaps in the registration of births, marriages and deaths, which might make military recruitment more difficult.[59]

In June 1842 von Eichhorn, the minister of religious affairs, delegated negotiations with the Baptists of Berlin, represented by their minister Gottfried Wilhelm Lehmann (1799–1882), to a commission.[60] Together they found a solution the king was willing to accept. The Baptists were not to be hindered in their activities, provided these remained inconspicuous. They were to be tolerated 'in fact', but not officially acknowledged as a sect. A cabinet order of 30 March 1842 against baptisms in rivers or lakes[61] was to be upheld: This would deprive the Baptists of a means of propagating their views. However, Eichhorn (the minister of religious affairs) suggested that 'if the Baptists manage to perform their baptisms in secret, such an act remains per se unnoticed and unpunished by the authorities'.[62]

1847', in Fleischmann-Bisten, Möller and Rudolph, eds, *Heilung der Erinnerungen*, 74–91, at 82, 84–5.
[58] GStA PK I, HA Rep. 77, Sekt. 1, Abt. XIIIa, Nr. 17 Bd. 1, fols 38–9.
[59] Ibid., fols 196–8.
[60] Ibid., fols 230–45, 256–8, 270–3.
[61] Ibid., fol. 199.
[62] 'Gelingt es den Baptisten, ihre Taufen im Verborgenen zu vollziehen, so entzieht sich ein solcher Akt von selbst der öffentlichen Kenntnißnahme und Ahndung': ibid., Bd. 2, fols 22–5, quotation at 24.

Manfred Henke

Paradoxically, anybody who wanted to join the legally non-existent sect was to declare this at a police station and get a certificate that he had done so.[63] It seemed important to uphold the fiction that the sect would disappear if one did not acknowledge it.[64] In a cabinet order of 17 March 1843, the king agreed that Baptists were not to be acknowledged as 'a tolerated religious party', but that they were to be permitted to proceed with their activities.[65]

Baptist theology reflected that of the Evangelical Awakening. However, the kind of state church promoted by the king and his awakened entourage was also challenged from the rationalist side. Theologians at the University of Halle had for generations taught in the tradition of the Enlightenment. Against the opposition of the faculty, the Prussian government had in 1825 appointed Friedrich August Tholuck (1799–1877), a proponent of the Evangelical Awakening, to a chair of theology there. From 1841 assemblies of rationalist Protestant ministers and laymen openly confronted the conservatives favoured by the government. Several rationalist ministers were deposed and from 1846 'free Protestant' congregations, popularly dubbed 'friends of the light', formed around deposed ministers such as Gustav Adolf Wislicenus of Halle and Leberecht Uhlig of Magdeburg. They soon found themselves in league with rationalist Catholics who, from 1844 formed so-called 'German Catholic' or 'Christ Catholic' congregations. Their best-known leader was Johannes Ronge of Silesia. Quite a high percentage of the leaders of these congregations were not only religious but also political radicals and held prominent positions in the abortive revolution of 1848–9. Robert Blum, a 'German Catholic', became a martyr of the radical revolutionaries.[66]

---

[63] Ibid., fols 24ᵛ–25ᵛ.
[64] Cf. ibid., fol. 22.
[65] Ibid., fol. 105.
[66] Helmut Obst, 'Lichtfreunde, Deutschkatholiken und Katholisch-apostolische Gemeinden', in J. F. Gerhard Goeters and Rudolf Mau, eds, *Die Geschichte der Evangelischen Kirche der Union*, 1: *Die Anfänge der Union unter landesherrlichem Kirchenregiment (1817–1850)* (Berlin, 1992), 317–32, at 319–27; Mathias Tullner, *Geschichte des Landes Sachsen-Anhalt*, 3rd edn (Magdeburg, 2001), 100–8; Jörn Brederlow, *'Lichtfreunde' und 'Freie Gemeinden'. Religiöser Protest und Freiheitsbewegung im Vormärz und in der Revolution von 1848/49*, Studien zur modernen Geschichte 20 (Munich and Vienna, 1976), 82–96; Martin Friedrich, *Die preußische Landeskirche im Vormärz* (Waltrop, 1994), 110–36, 208–33, 295–7.

1847 TO 1850: TOLERATION, REVOLUTION, CONSTITUTIONS AND TWO
NEW 'FOREIGN SECTS'

On 30 March 1847, Frederick William IV issued a *Patent, die Bildung neuer Religionsgesellschaften betreffend* ('Patent concerning the Formation of new Religious societies').[67] It was his answer to the rationalists who, in his view, disturbed the peace of the church. He had initiated the proceedings that led up to the patent in 1844, before the rationalists had actually formed any congregations of their own, wanting to ease their way out of the established church. Recognizing that in order to pass a new law he would have needed the consent of the council of state, which he was unlikely to achieve, he and his advisers had agreed at an early stage that there would be no new law, but rather an affirmation of the General Law Code.[68] Its regulations were referred to in a way that amounted to a reinterpretation, if not a negation, of its intent.[69]

To ward off rationalist claims to equal rights with Moravians and Old Lutherans, the king insisted on a novel interpretation of the Civil Code, according to which there were two kinds of tolerated religious societies. Those that were 'in basic agreement with the Augsburg Confession' (1530) might expect to be granted a better status than those that were not.[70] A novel interpretation of the privileges granted to the religious societies mentioned in the legislation of 1788 and 1794 declared, against the actual wording of those laws, that whereas the established churches were 'privileged publicly received religious societies', Moravians and Old Lutherans were also 'publicly received religious societies', albeit 'unprivileged'. Only the Mennonites and some minor groups such as the Quakers were

---

[67] *Gesetz-Sammlung für die Königlichen Preußischen Staaten 1847* (Berlin, 1847), 121–8. The *Gesetzessammlungen* of nearly all German states have been digitized and can be accessed online at: <https://de.wikisource.org/wiki/Gesetzblätter>.
[68] Friedrich, *Die preußische Landeskirche*, 389–400.
[69] Fürstenau, *Religionsfreiheit*, 143.
[70] 'Materialien, betreffend die rechtliche Entwicklung der Religions-Verfassung in Preußen', in [Kultusministerium], *Mittheilungen*, 12–35, especially 33–5; Friedrich, *Die preußische Landeskirche*, 399. Hattenhauer, 'Das preußische Religionspatent', 121, 131–2, relying on the official statement, wrongly attributes the threefold classification of religious societies to the General Law Code. Goßner, *Preußisches evangelisches Kirchenrecht*, 25–6 n. 4, presents evidence that a threefold division is a later construct alien to the *Allgemeines Landesrecht*.

classed as 'tolerated religious societies'.[71] As to the rationalists, Ludwig von Gerlach, one of a group of brothers close to the king, argued on 14 December 1846 that the 'free congregations' of Protestants and Catholics, together with liberal Jewish groups, ought to be prohibited since their doctrine was contrary to the General Law Code because it undermined awe towards the Godhead and obedience towards the higher powers.[72] He particularly objected to the original plan to tolerate them formally and then grant them civil registration.[73]

In practice, whereas formal toleration had originally been envisaged and was still possible, the new religious societies, with very few exceptions, came to occupy a different position from all the older ones in being only tolerated 'in fact'. The king asserted that anybody could leave the church and join another religious association without loss of civic rights. However, there would be a period of time in which new associations were in the process of formation, and during that period they would be 'tolerated in fact', but not yet recognized as a new religious society or corporation.[74] They first had to prove that they would not cease to exist within a short time. The authorities simply permitted subjects to join together for 'religious exercises', provided these did not pose a threat to public order. In this capacity, such associations were subject to the regulations laid down for any kind of private assembly. Initially, those regulations were fixed in the General Law Code, and from 11 March 1850 in a law relating to public assemblies, which decreed that an association must have a chairperson (*Vorsteher*), keep and submit lists of members and statutes, and report when and where it intended to meet. The police had the right to attend a meeting, provided they came in uniform.[75] An important stipulation was hidden in paragraph 2 of the collection of references to the Civil Code. Until the new associations were recognized as new religious societies, their members were still held to belong legally to their former churches. They had to pay parish dues but could not claim the privileges of

---

[71] Jacobson, 'Ueber die Arten der Religionsgesellschaften', 394–7; GStA PK I, HA Rep. 89.E.VII.19, fols 68, 118–19.
[72] Ibid., fol. 81.
[73] Ibid., fol. 80ᵛ; cf. Barclay, *Frederick William IV*, 40–2, on the Gerlach brothers. Their influence on the king's decisions is discussed throughout the book.
[74] Jacobson, 'Ueber die Arten der Religionsgesellschaften', 418–20.
[75] *Gesetz-Sammlung für die Königlich-Preußischen Staaten 1850* (Berlin, 1850), 277–83.

'real' parishioners.[76] Initially, they did not even enjoy equal civic rights, because their legal status was as yet undefined.[77] It is little wonder that nobody considered this an attractive option. Soon there were complaints that there were persons who 'took up a position inimical to the church' by joining rationalist 'free congregations' without giving up their church membership.[78]

In 1848 the revolution parliament assembled in the *Paulskirche* in Frankfurt am Main passed the *Grundrechte des deutschen Volkes* ('Fundamental Rights of the German People'), which, in article 5, decreed full liberty of religious belief and practice. The articles were incorporated into the Prussian constitution of the same year and the revised constitution of 1850. Article 12 of the revised constitution guaranteed equal civic rights regardless of religious creed, but this also involved equal duties. It stipulated that 'the performance of civic duties must not be impeded by the exercise of liberty of conscience'. In other words, the nation state propagated by liberal thought claimed precedence over religious conviction.[79] Mennonites who insisted on their traditional objection to warfare had a hard time. In the past they had had to accept civil disabilities in return for being exempted from military service. Now they pleaded in vain to be allowed to remain second-class citizens, but exempted from conscription. The Mennonite community was rent by a conflict between traditionalists, who often chose to emigrate rather than profit from the king's offer to do ambulance service in times of war, and 'progressives', who sought better integration into German society, shared its nationalist variety of liberalism and were proud to perform military service.[80]

During the middle of the century two new religious societies – the Catholic Apostolic Church (or Irvingites) and the Methodists – began to propagate their teachings in Germany. Their opponents liked to

[76] *Gesetz-Sammlung 1847*, 123, Fürstenau, *Religionsfreiheit*, 144.
[77] GStA PK I, HA Rep. 89.E.VII.19, fol. 94.
[78] Berlin, Evangelisches Zentralarchiv, EZA 7/6976, fols 8–9, circular issued by the Evangelischer Oberkirchenrat, 25 February 1852.
[79] Anschütz, *Die Verfassungs-Urkunde*, 183, 233. The full text of *Die Grundrechte des deutschen Volkes* is available online at: <http://www.verfassungen.de/de06-66/grundrechte48.htm>. This document was incorporated as 'Abschnitt VI' into the constitution passed by the revolutionary Parliament on 28 March 1849.
[80] Mark Jantzen, 'Equal and Conscripted: Liberal Rights confront Mennonite Conceptions of Freedom in Nineteenth-Century Germany', *Journal of Mennonite Studies* 32 (2014), 65–80; idem, *Mennonite German Soldiers*, 137–59.

characterize them as foreign influences. The leaders of the Catholic Apostolic Church were British, while Methodism was propagated by Germans who had emigrated to the USA and later decided to return to Germany to spread the new faith they had adopted while abroad. The Catholic Apostolic Church first took root in Prussia; the Methodists had their first successes in Württemberg, Saxony and parts of Thuringia. They were relative latecomers in Prussia.[81]

In the midst of the revolution of 1848, the first Catholic Apostolic congregation was established in Berlin by Thomas Carlyle (1803–55), a Scottish advocate and the church's apostle for northern Germany.[82] Their religious and social teachings were conservative and they claimed that they did not want to separate from existing churches but rather to testify to what was lacking in them, inviting the leaders in church and state to acknowledge the spiritual authority of a re-established apostle ministry. They refused to declare their dissent from the established church, but profited from the patent of March 1847 because they could be considered a new religious society in process of formation. The king, evidently sympathizing with their views, made it known in June 1852 that he did not deem it proper to exclude Catholic Apostolic believers from the communion of the national church, especially since they wanted to remain within it. As he saw it, '[T]he Irvingites agree with the creeds of the evangelical church in essentials and only deviate in matters of church organization and liturgy.'[83]

Catholic Apostolics had their banns published and their marriages performed in the local parish church. They therefore did not have to register as dissenters or 'dissidents' from the established churches. Occasionally, ministers refused to perform such marriages, thus forcing an unwilling Catholic Apostolic to register as a dissident in order to qualify for a civil marriage.[84] Catholic Apostolic ministers did,

---

[81] Karl Heinz Voigt, 'Die Methodistenkirche in Deutschland', in Karl Steckel and C. Ernst Sommer, eds, *Geschichte der Evangelisch-methodistischen Kirche* (Stuttgart, 1982), 85–107, at 85–93.

[82] Tim Grass, *The Lord's Work: A History of the Catholic Apostolic Church* (Eugene, OR, 2017), 98–103.

[83] '[D]ie Irvingianer der Hauptsache nach im Bekenntnisse mit der Evangelischen Kirche einig seien und nur in Verfassungssachen und in der Liturgie von ihm abweichen': Evangelisches Zentralarchiv, EZA 7/3458 Irvingianer 1, fol. 276.

[84] Ibid., fols 190–212; GStA PK I, HA Rep 76 III Sekt. 1 Abt. XIIIa Nr. 25 Bd. 1, fols 230–8; cf. Grass, *Lord's Work*, 101.

however, perform baptisms and were sometimes proceeded against. In 1853, Carlyle reported that several priests under his jurisdiction had been punished for baptizing, 'although recently a priest accused of baptizing has been acquitted by the Supreme Court'.[85] He added: 'By a recent edict of the Government, the public prosecutors have been forbidden to take up any more accusations against the ministers or members of dissenting bodies for celebrating religious rites.'[86] When some Protestant clergy tried to refuse to enter Catholic Apostolic baptisms into their registers they were told that apart from their spiritual functions they were also state functionaries entrusted with the registration of births, marriages and deaths.[87]

THE STRUGGLE FOR CIVIL REGISTRATION AND CORPORATE RIGHTS

In article 19, the Prussian Constitution of 1850 envisaged the introduction of civil registration, and in particular of compulsory civil marriage, which was required to precede any church wedding. For years, a decision on how to enact this reform in law was delayed by conservative Protestants and Catholics,[88] while the 'free congregations', whether Protestant or Catholic, petitioned frequently in favour of civil registration.[89] Compulsory civil registration was eventually introduced in Prussia in 1874, and in the whole German Reich in 1875. By that time Frederick William IV had died and Germany had been united under Prussian leadership. In addition, in May 1873, as part of a palette of laws directed primarily against Roman Catholics, it became possible for a person to leave their former church without having to continue paying church dues.[90]

---

[85] *Apostles' Reports: July 1853* (n.pl., 1853), 18.

[86] Ibid. 21.

[87] GStA PK I, HA Rep 76 III Sekt. 1 Abt. XIIIa Nr. 25 Bd. 1, fols 278–382.

[88] Freisen, *Verfassungsgeschichte*, 106; Stephan Buchholz, *Eherecht zwischen Staat und Kirche. Preußische Reformversuche in den Jahren 1854 bis 1861* (Frankfurt am Main, 1981), 106–7; [Kultusministerium], *Aktenstücke aus der Verwaltung der Abtheilung des Ministeriums der geistlichen Angelegenheiten für die inneren evangelischen Kirchensachen vom 26. Januar 1849 bis 11. Juni 1850: Amtlicher Abdruck* (Berlin, 1850), 66–75.

[89] See, for example, GStA PK I, HA Rep. 76 III Sekt. 1 Abt. XIV Nr. 162 Bd. 2, fols 157–9; Bd. 3, fols 23–43, 81–4, 151, 159, 167ᵛ–169ʳ, 181–9, 343; Bd. 4 (unfoliated), petitions and reports 1860–1; Bd. 5, petitions and reports 1862; Bd. 6, petitions and reports 1862–5; Bd. 7, identical printed petitions sent in by 44 free religious congregations in 1865 and a summary of proceedings.

[90] *Gesetz-Sammlung für die Königlichen Preußischen Staaten 1873* (Berlin, 1873), 207–8.

In their petitions the 'Free Congregations' also regularly demanded that they be granted corporate rights.[91] Whereas the old 'tolerated religious societies' were legal entities or 'corporations' who could, for instance, own property, the 'merely tolerated' religious societies were not. They were simply groups of people whose meetings were permitted under certain conditions monitored by the police, with their religious purpose ignored. As a contemporary jurist observed, after 1850 the really important difference between the different 'sects' was whether or not they enjoyed corporate rights.[92] Such categorizations could change. The 'free congregation' in Magdeburg had been granted corporate rights on 13 January 1848 as a tolerated religious society, but the government repealed that concession on 27 August 1853, arguing that religion was serving as a pretence for dangerous political activities.[93] In a similar manner, the German Catholics in the Grand Duchy of Baden had been granted corporate rights on 20 April and 15 May 1848, but these were repealed on 26 February 1852.[94] Like their Protestant counterparts in Magdeburg, they had agitated for democracy in the revolution of 1848–9. After the revolution governments exerted pressure on leaders and members of 'free congregations', several leaders emigrated to America and from 1852 the congregations dwindled and dissolved.[95] Part of their programme was taken up by the National Liberal Party during its ascendancy in Prussian politics from 1867 to 1871.[96]

Of the 'new sects' active in Prussia, only the Baptists gained corporate rights. A law of 7 July 1875 decreed that individual congregations of Baptists could be granted corporate rights by a joint declaration of the three ministers of justice, the interior and religion.[97] They seem to have profited from an intervention by their American co-religionists and their membership in the Evangelical Alliance, but the decisive factor seems to have been the support of the Liberals during their brief period of power. Their parliamentary

---

[91] Compare n. 89 above.
[92] Jacobson, 'Ueber die Arten der Religionsgesellschaften', 424–5.
[93] Ibid. 418, 421–2.
[94] Freisen, *Verfassungsgeschichte*, 193.
[95] Brederlow, *'Lichtfreunde' und 'Freie Gemeinden'*, 112–16.
[96] Evangelisches Zentralarchiv, EZA 7/3543, printed report of parliamentary session, 2 June 1875.
[97] GStA PK I, HA Rep. 76 III, Sekt. 1, Abt. XIIIa, Nr. 17, Bd. 8, fols 69–80, 97, 106, 112–26; *Gesetzessammlung* 1875, 374.

spokesman pointed out that he regarded the question of corporate rights for Baptists as a test case that might open up the way for corporate rights for the free congregations and hopefully for all sects.[98] Officially, it was argued that, except for their views on baptism, Baptists were in conformity with Reformed doctrine, and that they believed in absolute obedience to the higher powers, had declared their readiness to do military service and helped to maintain the social order.[99] The same might have been said of Methodists and Catholic Apostolics, but their attempts at gaining corporate rights in Prussia failed.[100]

On 1 January 1900, a Civil Code (*Bürgerliches Gesetzbuch*) came into force for the whole of Germany. Through it the institution of the 'registered association' (*eingetragener Verein*) was created, which would automatically enjoy corporate rights. Any association could ask a lawyer to draft statutes that fulfilled the required criteria, submit a list of founding members and apply for registration at the regional law court. However, section 61 of the code stated: 'The administrative authority may object to the registration if the association … pursues a political, socio-political or religious purpose'. When the New Apostolic Church, which had come into existence as a result of a schism within the Catholic Apostolic Church in 1863, attempted to achieve the status of a registered association, the Prussian authorities registered an objection.[101]

---

[98] Rudolf Donat, *Das wachsende Werk. Ausbreitung der deutschen Baptistengemeinden durch sechzig Jahre (1849 bis 1909)* (Kassel, 1960), 238–53. Gottfried Wilhelm Lehmann, the Baptist spokesman in negotiations with the Prussian government, had been one of the most ardent proponents of a German branch of the Evangelical Alliance: Nicholas M. Railton, *No North Sea: The Anglo-German Evangelical Network in the Middle of the Nineteenth Century*, Studies in Christian Mission 24 (Leiden, 2000), 53–6, Karl Heinz Voigt, *Die Evangelische Allianz als ökumenische Bewegung* (Stuttgart, 1990), 15. For the arguments advanced by the Liberal spokesperson in the lower house, see *Stenographische Berichte 1875, Abgeordnetenhaus*, vol. 3 (Berlin, 1875), 1980–1. A 'Friend of Light' praised the Baptists in 1847 for democratic elements in their church government (quoted in Railton, *No North Sea*, 173), whereas the established churches were strongly prejudiced against Baptists: Voigt, *Die Evangelische Allianz*, 13–15.

[99] *Stenographische Berichte 1875, Herrenhaus* (Berlin, 1875), Drucksache Nr. 26, 6–7; also in Evangelisches Zentralarchiv, EZA 7/3543.

[100] GStA PK I, HA Rep. 76 III, Sekt. 1, Abt. XIIIa, Nr. 31 adh., fols 44, 73; Nr. 25, vol. 2, fols 39–44, 49–61.

[101] Ibid., Nr. 25 adh. II, fols 21, 22; ibid., vol. 2, fols 306–9; cf. Grass, *Lord's Work*, 76–8, 93.

In Hamburg, the New Apostolic Church had operated under the constitution of 1860 that decreed the separation of church and state. The police had not even collected any information on its activities.[102] Between 1911 and 1913, negotiations took place there to have the New Apostolic Church entered as a registered association. The political police registered an objection based on section 61 because 'the Prussian government' had asked them to do so in order to prevent religious associations from acquiring a secure legal status in a neighbouring German state, from where they could operate in Prussia.[103] Although the constitution of 1860 provided for granting corporate rights, the Baptists were the last society to obtain them, in 1858; subsequent applications by religious communities were rejected.[104] Similarly, one of the first New Apostolic congregations in Thuringia was founded in the small industrial city of Greiz, capital of the tiny *Fürstentum Reuß älterer Linie* ('Principality of the Reuss Elder Line'). Although the prince had permitted Methodist assemblies in 1886 and New Apostolic assemblies in 1891, he refused to grant corporate rights to either of them.[105]

There were just two states where 'sects' became registered associations, the Kingdom of Saxony and the Grand Duchy of Baden. By a law of 6 July 1870, dissenters in Saxony could register their births, marriages and deaths with the local law court. However, religious services could only be held if the ministry of religion granted an organization permission to hold 'a special religious cult' outside the established church.[106] If this was not the case, such religious assemblies were supervised by the police, in accordance with the Law on

---

[102] Hans Georg Bergemann, *Staat und Kirche in Hamburg während des 19. Jahrhunderts* (Hamburg, 1958), 68; Hamburg, Staatsarchiv, Cl. VII Lit. Hf No. 4, vol. 33, fol. 18.

[103] Ibid., fols 7–17, 35, 41.

[104] Ibid., fols 33–4, 101–3.

[105] Christian Espig, 'Die "Soziale Morphologie" als methodischer Zugang einer lokalen Religionswissenschaft am Beispiel des Fürstentums Reuß ä.L.' (doctoral thesis, Universität Leipzig, 2016), 211–17; Greiz, Staatsarchiv, LRA Greiz Nr. 2097, fols 1–2; Nr. 2792, fols 1–9; ibid., n. Rep. A Kap. XII, Nr. 410, Bl. 2–22; ibid., n. Rep. A Kap. XII, Nr. 576; ibid., n. Rep. C Kap. IVb, Nr. 110.

[106] 'Gesetz, die Einführung der Civilstrandsregister für Personen, welche keiner im Königreiche Sachsen anerkannten Religionsgesellschaft angehören, und einige damit zusammenhängende Bestimmungen betreffend': *Gesetz- und Verordnungsblatt für das Königreich Sachsen 1870* (Dresden, 1870), 215–21, at 220 (§21).

Associations and Assemblies of 22 November 1850.[107] Thus the legal situation was similar to Prussia, except that in Saxony the exercise of religious rites was not 'tolerated in fact'. Catholic Apostolic congregations and congregations of the *Bischöfliche Methodistenkirche* (Methodist Episcopal Church) were granted permission for their 'special religious cult' in 1871,[108] but the application of the New Apostolic Church for permission to engage in a separate religious *Kultus* ('form of worship') was at first refused.[109] In one town, the use of prayers and hymns was deemed to render a gathering a religious assembly,[110] whilst in the capital the police only intervened if the sacraments were celebrated.[111]

In Dresden, the local 'apostolic congregation' of the 'new order' was entered in the register of associations on 27 August 1900, but this entry was subsequently deleted ex officio, as it was deemed to have been made in error of law.[112] Apparently there were two objections: Firstly, the congregation had been entered before permission for a 'separate religious cult' had been granted; secondly, there existed another 'apostolic congregation' (of the Catholic Apostolic Church) that had already received official recognition. Two associations with the same name could not be permitted in one place. In June 1901 the applicants were advised by the registrar that they first had to have their 'separate religious cult' approved and then gain registration, but that also failed.[113] Rather surprisingly, a new application made for all New Apostolic congregations in the kingdom in March 1902 was granted without delay.[114]

---

[107] *Gesetz- und Verordnungsblatt für das Königreich Sachsen 1850* (Dresden, 1850), 264–70.

[108] Leipzig, Stadtarchiv, Cap. 42 G No. 1; Dresden, Staatsarchiv, Amtsgericht Königstein Nr. 1032; Rüdiger Minor, *Die Bischöfliche Methodistenkirche in Sachsen. Ihre Geschichte und Gestalt im 19. Jahrhundert in den Beziehungen zur Umwelt* (doctoral thesis, Karl-Marx-Universität Leipzig, privately printed [Leipzig, 1986]), 152–66.

[109] Chemnitz, Staatsarchiv, Kreishauptmannschaft Zwickau Nr. 2091, fols 1–20; ibid., Polizeipräsidium Zwickau Nr. 917, fols 1–4; Leipzig, Stadtarchiv, Cap. 42 H. No. 1, fols 1–23, Dresden, Stadtarchiv, Sect. III Cap. XVII, Nr. 17, fol. 10.

[110] Chemnitz, Staatsarchiv, Kreishauptmannschaft Zwickau Nr. 2093, fols 1–25.

[111] Dresden, Stadtarchiv, Sect. III Cap. XVII, Nr. 17, fol. 61ᵛ.

[112] Dresden, Hauptstaatsarchiv, 11045 Amtsgericht Dresden Nr. 1392, Vereinsregister Nr. 10, 'Apostolische Kirche Dresden, Neuapostolische Gemeinde zu Dresden'.

[113] Leipzig, Stadtarchiv, Cap. 42 H. No. 1, fols 36–49; cf. a similar attempt for Lengenfeld in Chemnitz, Staatsarchiv, Kreishauptmannschaft Zwickau Nr. 2097, fols 1–5.

[114] See, for example, ibid., Polizeipräsidium Zwickau Nr. 917, fols 39–end (erratic pagination, combined from files for several congregations); Leipzig, Stadtarchiv, Cap. 42 H. No. 1, fols 64–74; Dresden, Stadtarchiv, Sect. III Cap. XVII, Nr. 17, fols 73b–74.

Manfred Henke

Apart from Saxony, it was only in the Grand Duchy of Baden that the New Apostolic Church proved able to register its congregations under the provisions of the Civil Code of January 1900. The congregation at Karlsruhe became a registered association on 25 April 1903; Mannheim and Pforzheim followed suit in 1907. Property that the New Apostolic Church had acquired in Hesse and Württemberg was registered as belonging to the congregation in Mannheim.[115]

CONCLUSION

At the end of the eighteenth century, the 'sects', if permitted at all, were subjected to strict control by the authorities of the German territories. This also meant that their legal status was clearly defined in the 'concessions' they had been granted. As a rule, they were restricted to certain regions where they could build up their organizations and maintain meeting places. The more modern 'sects' or 'religious societies' outside the established churches, however, spread wherever people were prepared to accept their teachings. Modern ideas of liberty of conscience prevailed over attempts at restraining people from joining those societies. The monopoly over registration of births, marriages and deaths originally enjoyed by the established churches had been lost where civil registration had been introduced under the influence of enlightened principles spread by the French in their revolutionary wars. That monopoly was eventually removed throughout Germany in 1875.

In order to secure property rights and achieve a permanent legal and economic foundation, the new 'sects' sought to obtain corporate rights. The provisions on 'registered associations' laid down in the *Bürgerliches Gesetzbuch* for the newly united German empire might have given the 'sects' a secure legal status. However, the states could object to that registration through their police, and with very few exceptions they did so. Instead of trying to prevent their subjects from joining 'sects', the civil authorities did what they could to weaken the 'sects' by refusing them legal recognition. In addition, such 'sects' could come under observation by the political police.

[115] Zurich, New Apostolic Church International Archive, AL0106; Karlsruhe, Generallandesarchiv, Bestand 276, Zugang 1994–34, Vereinsregister Amtsgericht Mannheim, vol. 3, 271–2; Bestand 284, Zugang 2014–26, Best. Nr. 2, Amtsgericht Pforzheim, Vereinsregister, vol. 2, 11–12.

They tended to run into difficulties if, as 'free congregations', they propagated democratic ideas. In contrast, loyalty to the existing social and political order, as proclaimed by the German Baptists, might be rewarded.

The monarchical system and the established churches were interconnected. When the monarchs gave way to the Weimar Republic, the established churches, deprived of their monarchical heads, managed to maintain many of their privileges. However, Article 124 of the Constitution of Weimar (1919) removed the possibility of governments objecting to the registration of religious societies, and Article 137 laid out further provisions which aimed at giving religious societies a status similar to that already enjoyed by the 'churches' or 'publicly approved religious societies' of the old kinds. To use Fürstenau's terms quoted at the beginning, a greater degree of religious liberty was achieved by giving the 'sects' the status of 'churches' rather than by denying the 'churches' all state support and turning them into 'sects'.

The Social and Legal Reception of Illegitimate Births in the Gurk Valley, Austria, 1868–1945

Catherine Sumnall*

Sidney Sussex College, Cambridge

This article uses a combination of sources, ranging from statistical material calculated from parish records, through oral history interviews and autobiographies, to letters sent by parish priests to their bishop, to illuminate the spaces between law, marriage and the church in the Gurk valley of southern Austria. It argues that local patterns and trends of illegitimacy were tolerated by the Catholic clergy, and that the relationships concerned were understood both as marriage without ceremonialization, and as stable unions where marriage was impeded by poverty. These attitudes hardened in the state legal practices that formed part of Nazi family policy and reduced rural illegitimacy.

Marriage offers a unique insight into the intersection of the church and the law. It is both a legal contract between consenting adults, witnessed by a community, and (for Catholics) a sacrament celebrated as the foundation of reproduction and family life. This duality imbues the celebration of a marriage with characteristics that are both secular and sacred, individual and communal, as a status-changing event as well as the culmination of a process of courtship.

Marriage occupies a unique space in the legal reach of church and state, and in the moral behaviour both have sought to realize within the realm of population. Different concerns are at play, but marriage is necessarily connected both to the temporal realm, through its relation to inheritance and property ownership, and to the spiritual, in terms of the way it helps individuals to adhere to abjurations relating to fornication and concubinage. The state and church might both have concerns about the size and quality of the population entering into marriage, and about the possible consequences of nuptiality for the number or quality of the couple's resulting children. Indeed, Malthusian ideas of fertility, associated primarily with a couple's ability to support a household, were predicated on married couples, and

* Sidney Sussex College, Cambridge, CB2 3HU. E-mail: cs364@sid.cam.ac.uk.

Studies in Church History 56 (2020), 362–382 © Ecclesiastical History Society 2020
doi: 10.1017/stc.2019.20

saw particular fertility concerns in relation to the destitution of children born to the married poor.[1] It is to marriage, therefore, to which both church and state look, as the 'prudential valve'[2] of both their realms of legal interest, as the necessary sacramentalization and sanction of a sexual relationship between two people, and as the legal context in which (in European history) most births took place.

Beginning in the period immediately after 1868, when the *Ehekonsens*[3] laws were abolished in Austria, and ending in 1945 after the demise of Nazi family policy relating to marriage and illegitimacy, this article explores the connections between marriage as a religious institution, marriage as an important and significant legal state, and the existence of large numbers of illegitimate births in parts of Austria. Focusing especially on the Gurk valley, it considers three aspects in particular: firstly, how illegitimacy was understood and responded to by the Catholic church on a local scale, both by priests working in the Gurk valley and by bishops auditing and collecting statistics about the parishes under their jurisdiction; secondly, how local understandings of the causes of illegitimacy led to specific responses (whether to excuse or to curb it), first by the Catholic church and later by the Nazi state, responses which drew on similar explanations for illegitimacy but were responding to very different fears about its social consequences; thirdly, why rates of illegitimacy changed little over the period from 1868 to 1938, a period when access to marriage for some (especially the landless) became legally easier, and why after 1938 Nazi policy was associated with greater rates of marriage in the Gurk valley.

The article uses a combination of *relatio synodalis* summary statistics produced annually by the diocese of Gurk for its parishes, reports

---

[1] E. A. Wrigley and R. S. Schofield, *The Population History of England 1541–1871: A Reconstruction* (Cambridge, 1989), 457–66.

[2] Malthusian thought on marriage as the key means through which a society limited fertility is often captured as a combination of prudential forethought, in deciding whether to contract a marriage, and a fertility valve, in that there might be lower incidence of marriage in a population when economic circumstances were harder and higher fertility might have difficult consequences for the household. For a brief account of Malthusian thought on marriage and fertility, see E. A. Wrigley, 'Malthus on the Prospects for the Labouring Poor', *HJ* 31 (1988), 813–29, at 817–18.

[3] Legal limitations on marriage, referred to as *politischer Ehekonsens*, restricted the ability of those without property and resources to marry. These were repealed in 1867. See Josef Kytir and Rainer Muenz, 'Illegitimität in Oesterreich', *Demographische Informationen* (1986), 7–21, at 7.

submitted to the bishop of Gurk on themes around marriage, oral history interviews conducted in the Gurk valley, and published autobiographies from the Gurk valley. It also makes use of statistics published in 1941 in Vienna on the impact of the *Anschluss* with Nazi Germany in 1938. The timeframe of the article covers the period from the end of the *Ehekonsens* in 1868, which increased marriage rates in the alpine provinces of Austria-Hungary,[4] through to the end of the Second World War. Consequently, it spans a period of significant social, political and legal change, and it charts changes in the moral and legal framing of illegitimacy, particularly by the Catholic Church. No single source covers this period or these themes in their totality. The *relatio synodalis* statistics offer a quantitative measurement of illegitimacy in parish submissions to the diocese that allows the calculation of illegitimacy rates and shows the continuing relevance of counting illegitimacy within the parish. However, the narratives and explanations surrounding illegitimacy are not discussed annually, nor are they measurable straightforwardly from this source. The article therefore adds qualitative material to the quantitative, illuminating the period with three further sources. Reports submitted to the bishop by his parish priests in the Gurk deanery show the local assumptions, tolerations and concerns of clergy around marriage and sexual morality. The autobiographies and oral histories of Gurk valley residents show how they understood their relationship to marriage, as well as to the church and the state. Finally, publications of the National Socialist state show the impact on illegitimacy of a harsh, intolerant framing in statistical and cartographic terms.

The Gurk valley, in the 'green alps' of southern Austria, was notable for its marginal economic position in the late nineteenth and early twentieth centuries. It was characterized by large farming households with the presence of non-kin acting as servants in husbandry. Impartible inheritance practices[5] and late age at marriage, both exacerbated by economic decline and high rates of farming indebtedness, contributed to a social and economic context in which non-marriage was widespread, and illegitimacy rates in the Gurk valley were among

---

[4] Ibid. 8–10.

[5] Impartible inheritance refers to the practice of not dividing land such as a farm upon its transfer to the next generation. Instead, in a family with multiple heirs, one person (often the eldest son) would take on the property, and pay any siblings their portion of the inheritance, calculated according to the value of the property, through other means.

the highest in Austria and in Europe during this period. The Gurk valley's experience of illegitimacy reveals an adaptation to marriage and courtship processes under economic strain, resulting in significant numbers of couples who could not co-reside but who could and often did bear children together. The local Catholic church regarded some of these couples as married without that marriage being solemnized, but the later Nazi state did not. Through exploring the elision after 1868 of law, marriage and the church, we can not only trace the ways in which local social and ecclesiastical customs understood, and to an extent tolerated, births outside marriage, but also recognize the rapidity of the disappearance of this elision under National Socialist rule.

MARRIAGE AND NON-MARRIAGE IN EUROPE AND AUSTRIA

Illegitimacy has been used as a proxy for a multitude of social trends. One question to have exercised researchers is the Europe-wide rise in illegitimate births after the Napoleonic wars and its relatively sharp decline at the turn of the twentieth century. Such dramatic changes, and their common occurrence over space and time, have led to the equation of illegitimate births with alterations in the wider fabric of society, most regularly with the process of 'modernization'. Some have seen the relationship of illegitimacy to what might be termed 'deviant' sexuality as evidence of movement away from traditional social values, especially those enforced by church customs and marital practices.[6] Others see illegitimate births less as a liberation from restrictive pre-modern institutions and more as revealing a stress fracture in courtship, resulting from new economic opportunities outside a community that nullified the power of that community to govern behaviour.[7] Both theories of modernization see a significantly reduced role for the church, suggesting that it no longer possessed the moral authority over individuals or communities to bring couples to marry where a pregnancy as a result of extra-marital courtship had taken place. Given the significant presence of pre-nuptial pregnancy in some early modern communities, modernization theories such as

---

[6] Edward Shorter, 'Illegitimacy, Sexual Revolution and Social Change in Modern Europe', *Journal of Interdisciplinary History* 2 (1971), 237–72.
[7] W. R. Lee, 'Bastardy and the Socio-Economic Structure of South Germany', *Journal of Interdisciplinary History* 7 (1977), 403–25.

these implicitly suggest the decline of church influence over the long nineteenth century.[8] In rural communities, however, some of these processes of modernization were not felt so keenly or quickly; in the close communities of Alpine villages, the priest's role remained central to communal life and to upholding the moral standards of the parish. Indeed, as Voegler argues, the heavy involvement of clergy as quasi-agents of the state as well as moral leaders in their community made them central to the operation of functions as diverse as poor relief and schooling.[9] Peter Tropper's summary of the reforming aims of the bishop of Gurk, Josef Kahn (1887–1910), highlights the breadth of interest of the Catholic Church in Carinthia in rural life, with commentary in favour of the reform of workers' rights, notably in the limitation of working hours for women and children, and even in support of the building society movement and social security.[10]

Understanding rural illegitimacy, then, requires different theorization. Michael Mitterauer's identification of high illegitimacy in the eastern Alps identified a theoretically sophisticated connection between deeply embedded reproductive responses to the environmental conditions in which a community is located. The pressure of population on the alpine environment was perceived to be hostile to great numerical expansion, thus creating a system in which inheritance was the key to marriage.[11] This finding is similar to those for other mountainous regions of Europe.[12]

In search of additional factors that might account for the difference in the Alps, culture has often been invoked; most persuasive in

[8] E. A. Wrigley, quoted in R. B. Outhwaite, *Clandestine Marriage in England 1580–1850* (Cambridge, 1995), 146.

[9] Max Voegler, 'Religion, Liberalism and the Social Question in the Habsburg Hinterland: The Catholic Church in Upper Austria, 1850–1914' (PhD thesis, Columbia University, New York, 2006), 4.

[10] Peter Tropper, *Das Christentum in Kärnten. Vom 19. Jahrhundert bis zur Gegenwart* (Kehl am Rhein, 2005), 14.

[11] Michael Mitterauer, *Ledige Mütter. Zur Geschichte illegitimer Geburten in Europa* (Munich, 1983); Antoinette Fauve–Chamoux, 'European Illegitimacy Trends in Connection with Domestic Service and Family Systems (1545–2001)', in Ioan Bolovan and Peter Teibenbacher, eds, *Central Europe Population History during the first Demographic Transition: Romanian Journal of Population Studies* special issue 2 (2012), 8–45.

[12] See, for instance, Fauve-Chamoux on France; on Scotland, Andrew Blaikie, *Illegitimacy, Sex, and Society: Northeast Scotland 1750–1900* (Oxford, 1993); and on northern Italy, Pier Paulo Viazzo, *Upland Communities: Environment, Population and Social Structure in the Alps since the 16th Century* (Cambridge, 1989).

exploring its articulation over space and through practice have been Jon Mathieu and Pier Paolo Viazzo.[13] While not centred on illegitimacy per se, Mathieu's analysis of household structure sees more environmental commonalities than differences in the alpine region, especially in the dominant forms of husbandry in each category of environment. This makes use of and refines Mitterauer's ecotype, which sees household structure as deriving ultimately from differences in physical geography and environmentally determined economic activity in Austria, such as pastoral farming in alpine regions and arable farming in the sub-alpine regions.[14] Mathieu opts for sociotype. This recognizes the role of the environment in shaping demographic outcomes, but it also leaves space for considering legal custom and the processes of state formation arising from the structures of local farming households. These factors affected the power relations within households and therefore the form that control of sexuality could take. Mathieu is struck by the number of unmarried servants resident within the households of the Gurktaler Alps in the eighteenth century; such people, who might become long-term residents through ageing or the birth of an illegitimate child, lacked the legal rights of the married couple. Mathieu suggests that impartible transfer of farms amongst a small population entitled to inherit is therefore important in determining which members of the community were best able to access the resources necessary for marriage and household formation. This is also evidence of a certain absolutist tendency reflected in the structures of the household, the ownership of land and the direction taken by the eighteenth-century state.[15]

Much of Mathieu's analysis is interesting, especially in the identification of servants as occupying a highly vulnerable position, in law and in their household of service. The connection between household structure and its influence in 'creating' opportunities for illegitimate conceptions through the presence of unmarried kin, as well as an implicit pathway for such children to be incorporated into an underclass of servants, is of considerable importance. As I have argued

[13] Viazzo, *Upland Communities*; Jon Mathieu, 'From Ecotypes to Sociotypes: Peasant Household and State-building in the Alps, Sixteenth-Nineteenth Centuries', *History of the Family* (hereafter: *HF*) 5 (2000), 55–74.

[14] Michael Mitterauer, 'Peasant and Non-Peasant Family Forms in relation to the Physical Environment and the Local Economy', *Journal of Family History* 17 (1992), 139–59.

[15] Mathieu, 'Ecotypes to Sociotypes'.

elsewhere, illegitimacy in the Gurk valley had a historical grounding in economic rationality that evolved into something approaching a functional requirement of husbandry,[16] as well as one supported by cultural practices of fictive kinship and courtship rituals.[17]

An explicit focus on illegitimacy can easily overlook the fact that births outside marriage were not always that different from births within marriage. The courtship culture that surrounded sexuality outside marriage does not appear to have differed profoundly from the culture which preceded entry into marriage, whether in the Gurk valley or in other rural areas of Carinthia.[18] Therese Meyer describes night-visiting in the parish of Molzbichl, near Villach in the high alps in the west of Carinthia, a custom practised in the Austrian Alps and elsewhere across Europe, according to which young men would visit young women after dark. Women might be gathered as a group to sew, and young men might begin their courtship through a conveniently open window. Molzbichl demonstrates a good deal of resonance with measures taken to observe and regulate relationships and the formation of attachments in the Gurk valley. It was the responsibility of the farmer and his wife to observe and regulate the behaviour of the servants who lived in in their household and thus under their care.[19]

In seeking the ways in which legal frameworks impacted fertility behaviour beyond the regulation of courtship, the entitlement to land and one's prospects of inheritance are key to understanding the Gurk valley experience. As David Sabean notes,[20] the dominant system of passing property in Germany and Austria to a single male heir (usually the eldest) created a hierarchy of power within the farming household. Surviving siblings had to be paid off by the heir once

---

[16] Catherine Sumnall, 'Micro-Geographies of Illegitimacy and Social Change in the Gurk Valley, 1870–1960', in Antoinette Fauve-Chamoux and Ioan Bolovan, eds, *Families in Europe between the 19th and the 21st centuries* (Cluj, 2009), 251–88.

[17] Sandro Guzzi-Heeb, 'Kinship, Ritual Kinship and Political Milieus in an Alpine Valley in the Nineteenth Century', *HF* 14 (2009), 107–23.

[18] Therese Meyer, *Dienstboten in Oberkärnten*, Kärntner Landesarchiv 19 (Klagenfurt, 1993), 228–35.

[19] Franz Eder, 'Sexual Cultures in Germany and Austria, 1700–2000', in idem, Gert Hekma and Lesley Hall, eds, *Sexual Cultures in Europe: National Histories* (Manchester, 1999), 138–72.

[20] David Sabean, 'Aspects of Kinship Behaviour and Property in Rural Western Europe before 1800', in Jack Goody, Joan Thirsk and E. P. Thompson, eds, *Family and Inheritance: Rural Society in Western Europe, 1200 to 1800* (Cambridge, 1976), 96–111.

he came into property; this could represent a source of tension if there was a delay in payment or a dispute over the amount. Not only was the son taking over the farmstead often forced to wait to marry, his siblings too might have to live with him until sufficient resources could be scraped together for them to establish independence and marry. However, in the Gurk valley the absence of marriage did not necessarily preclude a couple's having children.[21] The link between late marriage and illegitimacy, then, was not Malthusian vulnerability but a culturally influenced solution to a system of inheritance in communities with limited and often marginal land. Nor was this unique to the Gurk valley.[22] Fertility testing in rural communities was a means through which late inheritance, a requirement for labour, and a need to produce a viable heir could be reconciled.[23] It is no surprise that in Carinthia, the highest number of retrospective legitimizations per act of marriage occurred.[24] Illegitimacy in the Gurk valley existed on a continuum of fertility, with relationships of various intentions and outcomes partaking in similar courtship activities involving sexual intercourse outside marriage, and doubtless with many more encounters that did not result in a birth (or a marriage) and so remain invisible to us now. The role of the church not only as the recorder and registrar of vital events, through which births were recorded and marriages undertaken, but also as an institution which commented on marriages, relationships and births outside marriage allows us to use its records as a lens into the community. What remains sadly invisible, however, is the intervention of clergy in individual circumstances: we cannot know what was said to the

---

[21] Michael Mitterauer and Reinhard Sieder, *The European Family: Patriarchy to Partnership from the Middle Ages to the Present* (Oxford, 1986), 53–7.

[22] See, for instance, for other parts of Austria, Sigrid Khera, 'Illegitimacy and Mode of Land Inheritance among Austrian Peasants', *Ethnology 20* (1981), 307–23; for Scotland, Alice Reid, Ros Davies, Eilidh Garrett and Andrew Blaikie, 'Vulnerability among Illegitimate Children in Nineteenth-Century Scotland', *Annales de démographie historique* 111 (2006), 89–113.

[23] This has been argued for Scotland by Andrew Blaikie, Eilidh Garrett and Ros Davies, 'Migration, Living Standards and Illegitimate Childbearing: A Comparison of two Scottish Settings, 1871–1881', in Alysa Levene, Thomas Nutt and Samantha Williams, eds, *Illegitimacy in Britain, 1700–1920* (London, 2005), 141–67.

[24] Catherine Sumnall, 'There's no such thing as Sin in the Alps: Some Reflections on the Historical Geography of Illegitimacy in Carinthia after 1868', in Ioan Bolovan et al., eds, *Demographic Changes in the Time of Industrialisation (1750–1918): The Example of the Habsburg Monarchy* (Cluj, 2009), 195–224.

young women and men involved. However, we can glean some sense of toleration of this continuum of fertility, or at least some parts of it where unions were stable but had not been confirmed by a liturgical rite or ceremony, through one of the sources discussed below.

The intersection of the law, the state and the Catholic Church went further than the recording of key life events through the institutional mechanisms of the parish. Marriage, as the gateway to legitimated reproductive behaviour, was a central element of population policy. The framing of marriage by the Austrian state and the Catholic Church in the later decades of the nineteenth century was shaped by a period of significant change during preceding decades. As von Schmädel notes, the shift to liberalization under Joseph II's Toleration Patent (1781) and Marriage Patent (1783) was codified in the Austrian Civil Code in 1811.[25] However, after 1848 there was a resurgence of absolutism and a new concordat between the Catholic Church and the Austrian state in 1855, resulting in the reestablishment of church control over issues related to marriage law.[26] After the *Ausgleich* of 1868 and a period of anti-clericalism, marriage law found itself subject again to the Civil Code and under state jurisdiction.[27]

The response in marriage rates across Austria to the repeal of the restrictions on marriage has been discussed by many authors, none more sensitively than Teibenbacher,[28] who demonstrates a regional diversity across the alpine provinces, with relatively limited change and steadily increasing illegitimacy in Styria, the neighbouring

---

[25] Judith von Schmädel, 'The History of Marriage Law in Austria and Germany: From Sacrament to Civil Contract', *Hitotsubashi Journal of Law and Politics* 37 (2009), 41–7. Von Schmädel's excellent discussion highlights the tension in Austrian law between the sacramental and church-based elements of marriage and the contractual elements gradually claimed by the state during the absolutist period. In highlighting changes in the nineteenth century, she demonstrates that the tension between the absolutist and the liberal state continued, and it is this tension, she suggests, which underpins the changes between 1855 and 1868.

[26] Michael O'Neill Printy, *Enlightenment and the Creation of German Catholicism* (Cambridge, 2009), 101–4.

[27] Von Schmädel, 'Marriage Law', 46.

[28] Peter Teibenbacher, 'Natural Population Movement and Marriage Restrictions and Hindrances in Styria in the Seventeenth to Nineteenth Centuries', *HF* 14 (2009), 292–308; Christine Pelikan, 'Aspekte des Eherechts in Österreich' (PhD thesis, University of Vienna, 1981).

province to Carinthia.[29] The Gurk valley, in its experience of illegitimacy in the period between 1868 and 1945, demonstrates that local practice remained persistent in the face of occasional moral concern from the church and more severe intervention from the Nazi state at the end of the period. It also highlights the ways in which local understandings, sometimes articulated by the attitude of the Catholic clergy of the valley towards marriage and fertility, describe a more resilient socio-economic system than we might infer from nineteenth-century changes in the law surrounding marriage and sanction against single motherhood in the 1930s and 1940s.[30] The parishes of the Gurk valley did not respond to the removal of limitations on marriage amongst the landless by increasing their uptake of the sacrament.[31] Rather, the westerly parishes reached their peak illegitimacy rate of 90 per cent of all recorded births in the 1880s and 1890s. Indeed, between 1870 and 1945 the illegitimacy rate in the Gurk valley rarely dropped below 50 per cent.[32] The ways in which this was counted, recorded and responded to show both the harsher reaction to, or judgement of, illegitimacy by those who measured it from the outside, and the continued importance of long-standing practice in response to illegitimacy.

Nevertheless, there was little sanction against illegitimacy from either church or state until the *Anschluss*, although it was measured, counted and discussed both before and after the Nazi annexation of Austria. The sources used here give an insight into that counting, first through the Catholic Church's *relatio synodalis* and later by means of the statistical mapping and technologies of intervention and impact introduced by the Nazi state.[33] The Catholic Church in the Gurk

---

[29] Peter Teibenbacher, 'The County of Styria in the Eighteenth Century: Socio-Demographic Structures and Processes', in Harald Heppner, Peter Urbanitsch and Renate Zedinger, eds, *Social Change in the Habsburg Monarchy*, The Eighteenth Century and the Habsburg Monarchy International Series 3 (Bochum, 2011), 23–36.

[30] For the nineteenth-century changes in marriage law, see Isabel Hull, *Sexuality, State, and Civil Society in Germany 1700–1815* (London, 1996); for commentary on parochial poor relief, see Blaikie, *Illegitimacy, Sex and Society*; and for a Foucauldian interpretation of the state's increasing legal interest in illegitimacy and marriage, see Gail Reekie, *Measuring Immorality: Social Inquiry and the Problem of Illegitimacy* (Cambridge, 2003).

[31] Teibenbacher, 'Styria in the Eighteenth Century', 26.

[32] Calculated from the *Relatio synodalis* of the Gurk deanery, 1880–1960: Klagenfurt, Archiv der Diözese Gurk, HS.80.

[33] Hartmut Hanouska-Abel, 'Not a Slippery Slope nor a Sudden Subversion: German Medicine and National Socialism in 1933', *British Medical Journal* 313 (1996), 1453–75.

valley, while it recognized the challenges associated with some elements of local culture for the maintenance of morality, maintained consistent patterns of accommodation and tolerance for certain kinds of relationships, solemnized or not, that had been in place for generations and which underpinned practices of courtship, household structure and inheritance, not only there but also elsewhere in Austria. It could not take action against rising illegitimacy rates in the period except through small-scale and occasional initiatives by clergy which were resisted by the local population.

It was in the identification of illegitimacy's association with inheritance, and the action taken around farming household debt reduction, that the Nazi state showed its capacity to act to reduce illegitimacy, at least in the short term. The increase in illegitimacy in the Gurk valley later in the Second World War, however, reminds us that it is not simply to the inheritance of property that we should look to understand illegitimacy, but to cultural values and courtship norms too. These included the local clergy's toleration of the circumstances of illegitimacy, and an understanding of the social and economic pressures which served to hinder marriage. Oral history interviews conducted in the Gurk valley in 2007 and 2008, and the autobiographical publications from the Memoiren Verlag Bauschke, which works with local elderly residents, offer some insight into how individual lives intersected with and experienced these different framings of their courtship behaviours in the mid-twentieth century.

THE COUNTING AND MEANING OF SINS

The Catholic Church and later the Nazi state both encountered and classified illegitimacy using tools of quantification, and these provided the basis for understanding behaviour, or for seeking to change behaviour in response to a perceived problem. For the Catholic Church, the annual deanery submissions of the state of the parish to the bishop in Klagenfurt came in the form of the *relatio synodalis*.[34] Containing counts of population and of the incidence of pastoral

---

[34] The name of the diocese of Gurk reflects its original home in the eponymous town in the Gurk valley. However, the seat of the bishop during this period was in Klagenfurt rather than the cathedral in Gurk; returns from the Gurk valley parishes were thus sent to the bishop of Gurk in Klagenfurt.

offices such as baptisms, marriages, funerals and confessions, these summary statistical sources enabled senior clergy at Klagenfurt to monitor the engagement of parish priests and the morality of their flocks.[35] If it was deemed that too few inhabitants of the parish were taking communion on a regular basis, then a mission was sent out by the bishop to improve sacramental participation. The diocese undertook a number of missions to the Gurk deanery during the late nineteenth and early twentieth century as part of a programme intended to improve the morality of the populace. The Gurktal was not exceptional in this regard; most Austrian parishes received a similar episcopal mission at some point. The deanery was not singled out for special intervention by the responsible bishop; nor was it reprimanded for its high illegitimacy. Given this indifference to the illegitimacy 'problem', we must doubt whether the Catholic Church in Carinthia constructed all forms of extra-marital sexuality as requiring intervention or reform.

Nonetheless, ideas about morality and marriage were of interest to the Catholic Church in Carinthia. In 1891 and 1892, the pastoral conferences held by the bishop in Klagenfurt touched upon sexuality, gender and morality. These conferences were intended to canvass the opinion of all deaconries of the diocese of Gurk on points of theological import. Each deanery was asked to submit a written contribution on a given topic, arranged around key questions, probably set out by the bishop. The theme from 1891 is especially pertinent to determining how far and by which means the clergy felt able to act to improve morality in their parishes: 'Which measures are to be taken to check behaviour which contravenes the sixth commandment? Methods and evidence for the improvement of morality and removal of concubinage.'[36] The clergy of the Gurk deanery divided their thoughts into two sections: standard measures and special measures. The standard measures included the more stringent catechetical examination in the context of religious education, regular communion, making sure children were tidily (and fully) dressed at all times, reminding heads of household of their responsibilities to maintain moral order, and

---

[35] Sumnall, 'No such thing as Sin in the Alps', 197–9.

[36] 'Welche Mittel sind … verzuwenden, um die Verletzungen gegen das VI Gebot hinstanzuhalten … Unser Weisungen zur Hebung der Sittlichkeit u. Behebung der Concubinate': Archiv der Diözese Gurk, HS.80, Gurk deanery submission to the Pastoralkonferenz, 1891.

instructing young men and women not to associate too freely with one another. Indeed, the reference to *solus cum sola* was an indication of the worldly wisdom of the priests, as well as adding a touch of humour to their report.[37] The most important amongst the special measures was the suggestion that girls should be educated separately, in convent schools, due to the better ability of women to understand the needs of girls and girls' responsiveness to a female teacher's maternal side.[38] Illegitimacy, it seems to have appeared to the local clergy, was an inevitable outcome of contact between the sexes. Where this could be controlled and mediated by positive role models of chastity, the vice of fornication could be avoided. The household, then, was key to preventing the pastime of 'night-visiting',[39] and it was therefore to the head of the household that guidance should be given to improve the morality of the unmarried population.

In 1892, the pastoral conference moved on to consider the sanctity of marriage and the encouragement of virginity before marriage. Much ink was spilt in reflection on the indissolubility of marriage, in recognition not only of its sacramental character but also of its nature as the keystone of social and legal order. To this end *Tisch* (table) and *Bett* (bed) were necessarily to be kept together, to prevent both men and women straying and to keep the marriage intact.[40] Perhaps responding to changes in legal responsibility for marriage which were introduced in Austria over the course of the nineteenth century,[41] the priests of the Gurk valley specifically invoked in their commentary a discussion of the validity of clandestine marriages in a papal letter of 1788, which highlighted the sacramental nature of marriage.[42] Clandestine marriages were accordingly deemed to be true and valid marriages, even if they were associated with other faults

---

[37] The complete quotation is: 'solus cum sola non cogitabuntur orare Pater noster' ('When a man and a woman are alone together, they won't be saying the Our Father'): ibid. (my translation).
[38] 'Abälard war nicht glücklich in der Erziehung seiner Heloise' ('Abelard was not successful in educating his Heloise'): ibid.
[39] Meyer, *Dienstboten in Oberkärnten*, 228–35.
[40] Infidelity was recognized as a weakness to which either sex might succumb: Archiv der Diözese Gurk, HS.80, Gurk submission to Pastoralkonferenz, 1892.
[41] Von Schmädel, 'Marriage Law', 44–6.
[42] 'Contractus matrimonialis est vere et proprie unum ex septem Legis evangelicae sacramentis' ('the contracting of marriage is truly and properly one of the seven sacraments of the gospel law'): epistle of Pius VI, *Deessemus nobis*, 16 September 1788, cited in Archiv der Diözese Gurk, HS.80, Gurk submission to Pastoralkonferenz, 1892.

such as disrespect to the church shown by not solemnizing the contract in front of a priest. This view of the nature of marriage might not have chimed with the desires of contemporaries to avoid clandestine marriage, but neither was it separate from a longer practice of marriage without solemnization, dating back to the spousals common in many parts of Europe prior to the Council of Trent.[43] The 'stickiness' of practice over time, and the adaptability of local clergy in accepting stable unions between couples without marriage in church or solemnized by clergy, provides insight into the sensitivity of the clergy to the socio-economic circumstances of the area, and especially into types of sexual relationship outside marriage that were regarded as acceptable and, indeed, effectively marital.

Some parish priests were nevertheless horrified by what they saw in the Gurk valley. Oral history interviews with an elderly resident of Glödnitz parish reported that one early twentieth-century priest insisted upon baptizing all illegitimate babies as Eva or Adam, to make a point about their lack of a father. More drastically, oral history interviews with the priest of one parish revealed the poor example set by one of his predecessors when dealing with illegitimate births. On his arrival in the valley, this priest had been so appalled by the discovery that the majority of children he was called upon to baptize were illegitimate that he simply refused them the sacrament. The townsfolk did not react kindly to what they understood to be the denial of salvation to all those born outside marriage, who made up the majority of births. They attacked the priest, locking him up in a cupboard in his own rectory until he agreed to relent. Soon afterwards, the beleaguered cleric left not only the parish but the country, emigrating to Brazil.[44]

These examples of parish priests taking exception to the behaviour of their flocks, and attempting remedial action of varying degrees of severity with little clear success, are the exception and not the rule. The majority of encounters between local clergy and the population seem not to have regarded illegitimacy as something which might call morality into question. The priest also recounted

---

[43] Richard Smith, 'Marriage Processes in the European Past: Some Continuities', in Lloyd Bonfield, Richard M. Smith and Keith Wrightson, eds, *The World we have Gained: Histories of Population and Social Structure. Essays presented to Peter Laslett on his Seventieth Birthday* (Oxford, 1986), 43–99, includes a discussion of spousal ceremonies across a long period of time and in a range of geographical areas.
[44] Both these stories emerged in oral history interviews I conducted in summer 2007.

the story of a notably pious parishioner, who attended mass conscientiously and was a model of kindness to all, even in times of poverty. That she also brought five illegitimate children into the world was not a reason to doubt her good character, but simply suggested that the opportunity to marry had not been afforded her. Departures by the clergy from the accommodation of illegitimacy appear to have been rare; instead they focused in their statistical returns and their letters to the pastoral conference on the problem of the unstable unions that resulted from night-visiting, fornication and concubinage.[45]

In these large households, labour-intensive techniques were made possible by the continuing patterns of service, which may in turn have been sustained by high rates of illegitimacy. It is, therefore, little surprise that the Gurk valley should have been somewhat slow in adopting more modern, mechanized agricultural practices. Rather than being limited by the difficulty of using machinery on the steep scree slopes found in western Carinthia, it was the deeply-embedded socio-economic structures of the Gurktaler Alps that hindered a progression from subsistence to more market-oriented farming.[46] The level of farming debt was severe. The economic depression of the 1890s had a considerable effect on local farmers because of their low output, and recovery thereafter was slow, and hindered further by the First World War, the Carinthian Civil War and the outbreak of Spanish flu.[47] When the Great Depression hit in 1929, there seemed little prospect of farming in the Gurk valley being viable in the future; rural emigration grew rapidly.

The promise of resolving farming debt was the key means through which the far right gained popular support in the Gurk valley. The westerly parish of Glödnitz in particular was affected by the troubles of the early 1930s; indeed, Klein-Glödnitz was the location of an early

---

[45] Sumnall, 'No such thing as Sin in the Alps', 200–5.

[46] The argument of rural depopulation and limited economic development is made by Peter Cede, *Die ländliche Siedlung in den niederen Gurktaler Alpen* (Klagenfurt, 1994),

[47] The Carinthian Civil War took place after the end of the First World War, and was largely about whether ethnic and linguistic Slovenes resident mainly in the south of the province should belong to Austria or Yugoslavia. To end the conflict, backed by the Paris Peace Conference, a plebiscite of the linguistically mixed regions of Carinthia took place in October 1920; 59 per cent of those voting chose to remain part of Austria. For a detailed discussion of the Austro-Slovene minority in Carinthia, see Thomas Barker, *The Slovene Minority of Carinthia* (Boulder, CO, 1984).

attempt at a *Putsch* by local Nazi sympathizers in 1935.[48] It was quelled by the police, and some of the handful of participants were shot in the resulting scuffle. It stemmed, according to Ferdinand Hochsteiner's autobiography, from mounting anger at the way in which the Catholic Church in particular, and larger (absentee) land-lords and *Bezirk* authorities in general, were dealing with indebted-ness amongst their tenants. Tenants had often been granted a tenancy for many years, or even for life, sometimes in lieu of an inher-itance portion.[49] Increasingly, however, farmers who had insufficient liquidity to pay their creditors were forced off their farms, causing resentment and exacerbating fears amongst the remaining population of uncontrolled rural vagrancy and crime.[50] The relationship between indebted tenants and political dissatisfaction in the 1930s intensified, sowing seeds for political upheaval which benefitted the far right, and in which debt became a political concern.

After the *Anschluss*, one of the first steps taken by the Nazi govern-ment was a policy of *Umschuldung*, or debt rescheduling, intended to alleviate the immediate burden of illiquidity.[51] In this period, illegit-imacy in the Gurk valley also began to decline. However, to see this fall as resulting solely from legislative action on debt would be naïve. Instead it reflects a shifting social context. The mothers of illegitimate children, and the children themselves, were constantly under the observation of the Nazi state.[52] While the monarchy and the First Republic alike had monitored illegitimacy in the alpine provinces, there had been no political or legal action taken to curb it, nor was it regarded as a major threat to the social order, except insofar as it might serve to exacerbate rural pauperization. The Nazi government differed strongly from its predecessors in this respect: it regarded the rural family as the key to Austria's future success, and saw illegitimacy as a direct threat to the family.[53] This threat was understood as arising

---

[48] Ferdinand Hochsteiner, *Es ist nicht alles Gold, was heute glänzt. Erinnerungen einer Bergbauern aus dem Gurktal* (Glödnitz, 2002), 47.
[49] Ibid. 7.
[50] Ibid. 25–6.
[51] The impact of debt rescheduling is discussed by Maria Prieler-Woldan, *Das selbstverständliche Tun. Die Salzburger Bäuerin Maria Etzer und ihr verbotener Einsatz für Fremde im Nationalsozialismus* (Innsbruck, 2018), 106–10.
[52] Stephen Legg, 'Foucault's Population Geographies: Classifications, Biopolitics and Governmental Spaces', *Population, Space and Place* 11 (2005), 137–56, at 145–6. Legg's work on India highlights the process of surveillance through population records.
[53] Lisa Pine, *Nazi Family Policy 1933–45* (London, 1999), 117–46.

Fig. 1. Map of Illegitimate Births in Austria in 1937. Source: Österreich Statistisches Amt für die Alpen- und Donau-Reichsgaue, *Der Umbruch in der Bevölkerungsentwicklung im Gebiete der Ostmark* (Vienna, 1941), 25.[54]

both from the resulting existence of children outside a stable conjugal unit, and from the 'poor quality' of the offspring born of 'mentally unfit' women, that is from women who were evidently unable to make 'rational' decisions about sexuality and fertility. Although illegitimacy was only one area of life among many which came under increased statistical observation, measurement and surveillance in the Nazi state, the intersection of motherhood, and especially single motherhood, with rural poverty is central to understanding both why National Socialism was initially received warmly by those rural Carinthians who benefited from debt reduction. The association between household indebtedness, rural poverty and the lack of marriage is important in understanding why illegitimacy remained high in the nineteenth and early decades of the twentieth century. Marriage, in this period after the repeal of the *Ehekonsens*, was permitted by law but did not take place because of the poverty of tenant farmers. In the reduction of debt, therefore, a barrier to marriage

---

[54] Österreich Statistisches Amt für die Alpen- und Donau-Reichsgaue, *Der Umbruch in der Bevölkerungsentwicklung im Gebiete der Ostmark. Statistische Ergebnisse der natürlichen Bevölkerungsbewegung vor und nach der Wiedervereinigung* (Vienna, 1941), 10–15 (marriage), 21–3 (illegitimate births).

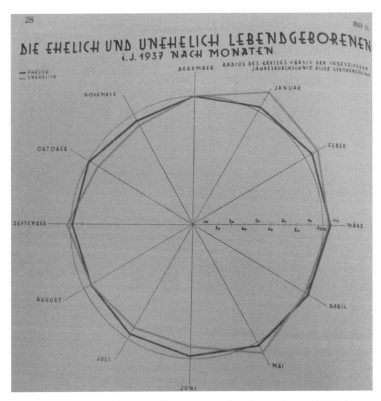

Fig. 2. Radar Graph of Austrian Illegitimacy and its Seasonality in 1937. Source: Österreich Statistisches Amt, *Der Umbruch*, 28.

was removed, and this was accompanied by a discourse of improvement in the 'quality' of the Austrian population.

In 1941 the statistical office in Vienna, recently taken over by National Socialist authorities, emphasized in their publication *Der Umbruch in der Bevölkerungsentwicklung im Gebiete der Ostmark* how the lives and the 'quality' of the Austrian population had improved since 1938. Illegitimacy proved an important axis of this analysis. In this mapping of rural Austria's illegitimacy rates in the early 1930s against the situation in 1941, *Bezirk* St Veit and the Murau belt emerge as notable areas of improvement (Fig. 1). This can be understood in the context not only of Nazi family policy on illegitimacy, which was seen as an expression of weakness in the

Fig. 3. Marriages in 1937/8 compared with 1938/9. Source: Österreich Statistisches Amt, *Der Umbruch*, 17.

mother and as a threat to society when passed onto her children,[55] but also of policies to modernize backward Austrian agriculture in marginal regions such as the Gurk valley. Amongst a wide variety of statistics on life in Austria since 1938, the association of illegitimacy with the state of agriculture (such as the measurement of seasonality in Fig. 2), is interesting for its overt connection of demographic outcomes and socio-economic structures.

The Nazis' desire to understand illegitimacy in scientific, quantifiable terms in order to identify the spaces and peoples most in need of targeted reform was not unique to Austria;[56] nor should it be seen in isolation from the wider interventions in the medico-moral realm that characterized the approaches to morality of the late nineteenth and early twentieth century in general,[57] as well as the Nazi state's intense statistical scrutiny of modernization in its many facets. In seeing

---

[55] Pine, *Nazi Family Policy*, 117–46. For a contrasting view arguing for a pro-natalist stance in all cases, even those of single mothers, see Claudia Koonz, *Mothers in the Fatherland: Women, the Family, and Nazi Politics*, 2nd edn (London, 2013), 197.

[56] J. Adam Tooze, *Statistics and the German State 1900–1945: The Making of Modern Economic Knowledge* (Cambridge, 2001), especially 36–8.

[57] Legg, 'Foucault's Population Geographies', 142.

illegitimacy primarily as a rural phenomenon, associated with agricultural communities, it was perceived as one aspect of Austria's wider need of improvement, to lift the country out of its state of backwardness. In the comparisons of figures before and after the Nazi occupation, it is unsurprising that the areas showing the sharpest decline in illegitimacy and the greatest increase in the number of marriages contracted were precisely those where the most significant problems had been identified: *Bezirk* St Veit and the Murau belt (Fig. 3).

The downward trend in illegitimacy in areas such as the Gurk valley did not last long, however. Illegitimacy rates fell dramatically during the first few years of Nazi rule in Austria. Across the Gurk deanery, these had remained above 50 per cent throughout the period from 1868 to 1938, only some of the smaller parishes showing major variations from year to year. During the First World War, there had also been a brief decline in illegitimacy, while men were away. Such an explanation may also help to account for some of the dip in births outside marriage during the Second World War (there was a peak in births in the spring of 1941, after Austrian troops were allowed home from the front en masse in the summer of 1940), but the fall in the illegitimacy rate after 1938 to levels of 30 per cent for the first time was short-lived.[58]

Conclusion

Illegitimacy and the Catholic Church coexisted in a pattern of toleration and local adaptation seen in communities across Europe. Their coexistence in the Gurk valley shows us that, even when births outside marriage had outnumbered births within marriage for generations, and even when such births became still more prevalent within the community, the socio-legal understanding of marriage as a process rather than an event, and one which might be preceded rather than followed by children, remained highly resilient. Only certain kinds of fertility behaviour were regarded as problematic or transgressive, such as night-visiting, which moved courtship a little beyond the control of the community and its institutions such as the church. These were those in which inheritance, legitimization and the establishment of a conjugal household did not and could not follow,

---

[58] Catherine Sumnall, 'A Historical Geography of Illegitimacy in the Gurk Valley, Austria, *c.*1868 to 1945', (PhD thesis, University of Cambridge, 2011), 73.

because of poverty or moral failing among the parents. The decision of local clergy, by and large, to tolerate such extra-marital fertility stands in sharp relief against the attitude of the Nazi state. While the same kind of fertility behaviour was identified as problematic by both groups, it was in the development not only of measurements but also of penalties and socio-economic rewards for improved behaviour that the Nazi state showed its ability to alter behaviour, at least temporarily, in the Gurk valley.

The religious framing of illegitimacy, and the position of marriage and of illegitimate fertility as a precursor to marriage, existed in the Gurk valley in a space in which these phenomena can be seen as an effect of property law and related local customs. Most particularly, it was impartible inheritance of property that most strongly governed access to marriage, and which therefore mediated illegitimacy, service and relationships within the farming household. The church accommodated illegitimacy, especially illegitimacy which took place prior to marriage amongst those whose unions were stable but for whom access to marriage was delayed by the wait to inherit. Illegitimacy rates therefore increased as the wait to inherit grew longer, over a period characterized by increasing farming indebtedness. It was the Nazi state, which did not accommodate illegitimacy in its family policy, that most actively sought to increase marriage by seeking to act upon its relationship with debt through a process of *Umschuldung*. In casting the legal category of illegitimacy as both a characteristic of rural backwardness and a threat to the race through the 'quality' of illegitimate offspring born into poverty and to 'irrational' mothers, its policy sought to change the structures underpinning births outside marriage in the Gurk valley. However, whilst illegitimacy initially fell, apparently in response to these measures (but perhaps rather because many young men had been called up), its rise after 1941 indicates that births outside wedlock were embedded within structures that were older, more resilient and more complex than inheritance law and debt alone. Although legal changes made a difference to the number of births outside marriage in the short term during the late 1930s and early 1940s, there was no sustained decrease. In the Gurk valley, marriage, and an individual's ability to obtain entry into its contractual and sacramental nature, was a process rather than an event.

Keeping up with the Chinese: Constituting and Reconstituting the Anglican Church in South China, 1897–1951

Tim Yung*

University of Hong Kong

When Anglican missionaries helped to constitute the Chinese Anglican Church (Chung Hua Sheng Kung Hui) in 1912, they had a particular expectation of how the church would one day become self-supporting, self-governing and self-propagating. The first constitution crafted by missionary bishops presupposed an infant church that would require the step-by-step guidance of its parent association. However, the intended trajectory was superseded by the zeal of Chinese Christians and drastic changes in the national government of China. The constitutional basis of the Chinese Anglican Church had to be restructured fundamentally again and again due to political upheaval in republican China, the Japanese occupation and the Communist revolution. This article explores the difficulties of crafting and implementing church constitutions in China in the first half of the turbulent twentieth century. Focusing on the South China diocese, wider questions are posed about the formation of canon law in an age of extremes.

At the end of the nineteenth century, Anglican missionaries in China envisaged the creation of a self-supporting, self-governing and self-propagating church, otherwise known as the 'Three-Self Church'. The establishment of an independent indigenous church had always been hailed as the ultimate goal of missions.[1] Within the Anglican tradition of order and legality, this also meant setting up canons that would clearly define who did what and why within the church and would apply essential principles of the Christian faith in practical, measurable terms.[2] In the South China diocese, three distinct constitutions were issued in 1913, 1929 and 1948 to achieve these ends.

* E-mail: timyung@connect.hku.hk.

[1] Brian Stanley, *The World Missionary Conference, Edinburgh 1910*, SHCM (Grand Rapids, MI, 2009), 132.

[2] Gerald Bray, ed., *The Anglican Canons 1529–1947*, CERS 6 (Woodbridge, 1998), xxix.

Studies in Church History 56 (2020), 383–400   © Ecclesiastical History Society 2020
doi: 10.1017/stc.2019.21

Whilst they appear to show linear development towards the Three-Self Church, the historical context underlying this process of constitutional change reveals a journey of rupture and realignment. Significant changes in both the Chinese political system and world Christendom stalled the steady development imagined by mission organizations and Church of England authorities. Whilst existing historiography has considered how individual missions and churches in China were affected in this age of extremes, the legal aspect remains somewhat neglected.[3]

Up to 1912, the constitutional development of the Anglican missions in China had been a low priority. Since 1845, missionaries had been sent independently from the Church of England, the Protestant Episcopal Church (PEC) in the USA and the Anglican Church in Canada. In the ensuing fifty years, there was sporadic church growth but no concerted legal action across China, since no unifying legislative body existed. Brian Stanley rightly notes that the spirit of the age encouraged a joint effort towards the evangelization of the world, as opposed to the systematic pursuit of inter-church unity.[4] No one contemplated constituting a national Anglican Church in China because so much else was yet to be done.[5]

[3] For politics and the Chinese Anglican Church, see Philip Wickeri, 'The Vicissitudes of Anglicanism in China, 1912–Present', in William Sachs, ed., *OHA*, 5: *Global Anglicanism*, c.*1910–2000* (Oxford, 2017), 148–68. For broader discussions, see Daniel Bays, *A New History of Christianity in China*, Blackwell Guides to Global Christianity (Malden, MA, and Oxford, 2012), Chloë Starr, *Chinese Theology: Text and Context* (New Haven, CT, 2016), Anthony C. Yu, *State and Religion in China: Historical and Textual Perspectives* (Chicago, IL, 2005). For general histories of the CHSKH, see Philip Wickeri, ed., *Christian Encounters with Chinese Culture* (Hong Kong, 2015); G. F. S. Gray, *Anglicans in China: A History of the Zhonghua Shenggong Hui (Chung Hua Sheng Kung Hui)*, ed. Martha Lund Smalley (New Haven, CT, 1996); Gordon Hewitt, *The Problems of Success: A History of the Church Missionary Society, 1910–1942*, 2: *Asia, Overseas Partners* (London, 1977). On South China, see George Endacott and Dorothy She, *The Diocese of Victoria, Hong Kong: A Hundred Years of Church History, 1849–1949* (Hong Kong, 1949); 鍾仁立 [Zhong Renli], 中華聖公會華南教區百年史略 [*Zhonghua Shenggonghui Huanan jiaoqu bainian shilüe / The Centenary History of the CHSKH South China Diocese*] (Hong Kong, 1951).
[4] Stanley, *World Missionary Conference*, 8.
[5] For instance, earlier Lambeth Conferences were occupied with resolving legal problems concerning episcopal jurisdiction (e.g. Lambeth 1878, resolution 11; Lambeth 1888, resolution 19; Lambeth 1897, resolution 24). The question of constituting indigenous churches remained a matter for the future. For details, see 'Lambeth Conference', online at <https://www.anglicancommunion.org/structures/instruments-of-communion/lambeth-conference.aspx>, accessed 12 February 2019.

The first significant act of unity came in 1897, when the six Anglican missionary bishops in China and Korea convened to discuss shared problems, such as Chinese terms for ministers or defining the acceptable limits of Christian marriage in relation to Chinese wedding customs.[6] The more important reason for their meeting, however, as indicated in a letter circulated in their respective dioceses, was a shared commitment 'to manifest the real unity of the Anglican Communion' in light of the need to overcome the self-perceived fragmentation of their mission work.[7] The bishops reconvened in 1899 and again in 1903, when they agreed on a shared structure for divine worship and established a standing committee; this consisted of two bishops together with an external secretary, and decided on similar matters during intervals between meetings.[8] At this point, the bishops had been shaken by the 1900 Boxer uprising and saw the growing need to stand united. So great was the damage that missionary clergy across the dioceses of Victoria (Hong Kong), North China and Shantung (Shandong) issued a joint letter to the bishops' conference, pressing for the formation of an Anglican synod for the whole of China.[9] In their opinion, as a divided force Anglicanism would fail to influence the Chinese nation.[10] Consequently, the 1907 conference resulted in a definite resolution about organizing a general synod to handle common policy more effectively, to provide authoritative decisions and to offer counsel to all.[11] On 26 April 1912, riding on the wave of the Edinburgh World Missionary Conference of 1910, the bishops and diocesan

---

[6] Hong Kong Public Records Office (hereafter: HKPRO), HKMS94/1/5/60, 'Letters and Resolutions of the Conference of the Bishops of the Anglican Communion in China, Hongkong and Corea held at Shanghai', October 1899, 3–6.

[7] Hong Kong Sheng Kung Hui Archive (hereafter: HKSKH), 2183/85, Bishop C. P. Scott, 'The Chung-Hua Sheng Kung Hui', 1918, 1–2.

[8] HKPRO, HKMS94/1/5/60, 'Letters and Resolutions of the Conference of the Bishops of the Anglican Communion in China and Hongkong held at Shanghai', October 1903, 5. The bishops represented the dioceses of Shanghai (established in 1844), Victoria (Hong Kong) (1849), North China (1872), Chekiang (Zhejiang) (1880), Hankow (Hankou) (1901) and Shantung (Shandong) (1903).

[9] HKPRO, HKMS94/1/5/52, 'Letter from Clergy in Dioceses to Anglican Bishops in China about Unity', 1906.

[10] HKPRO, HKMS94/1/6/34, 'Report and Resolutions of the Conference of the Anglican Communion in China and Hongkong held in Shanghai', April 1907, 18.

[11] Ibid. 7–8.

representatives met together in Shanghai to constitute the Chinese Anglican Church (*Chung Hua Sheng Kung Hui*; CHSKH).

Whilst the precise canons of the constitution remained a work in progress, the path for developing the CHSKH was clear. As had been the case in preceding decades, Anglican missionaries generally expected to establish ecclesiastical infrastructure themselves and only then step back from the indigenous church. However, Chinese involvement was slow to develop. In the late nineteenth century, the Church Missionary Society (CMS) exercised great caution in moving towards indigenous church leadership in the light of the memory of the tensions between missionary authority and Bishop Samuel Ajayi Crowther's episcopal authority in the Niger mission, as well as prevalent views about racial hierarchy.[12] The report of the Committee on Foreign Missions at the Lambeth Conference of 1908 adopted the same approach for all Anglican missions worldwide. The bishops recommended that foreign missionaries should be the ones to 'build up an autonomous and native Church' and they should 'retire when the work is done'.[13] In the eyes of Anglican church leaders, indigenous Christians were not yet qualified to govern their own church; important questions ought to be resolved by the missionaries and home authorities. For example, the division of the diocese of Victoria (Hong Kong), which later became the South China diocese, was settled entirely between Prebendary H. E. Fox (honorary secretary of the CMS), the senior clergyman in the field, and Archbishop Randall Davidson (1903–28), without any proper consultation with Chinese church members. The diocese would have been divided along parallels of latitude had it not been for an intervention by Archdeacon Banister, an experienced missionary, whose intimate knowledge of the geographical and linguistic boundaries in the area led him to suggest that the Xi River would be a better line of division.[14] However, it was this very same Banister who wrote to Davidson seven years later, endorsing the view of the CHSKH General Synod's Committee on Church

[12] Gordon Hewitt, *The Problems of Success: A History of the Church Missionary Society, 1910–1942*, 1: *In Tropical Africa, the Middle East, at Home* (London, 1971), 36; Stanley, *World Missionary Conference*, 248–76.
[13] London, LPL, LC100/7, 'Report of the Committee on Foreign Missions', 1908, fol. 7.
[14] LPL, Davidson Papers, vol. 252, fols 2–3, Hoare to Fox, 17 August 1906; fols 9–13, Banister, memorandum on the proposed new diocese, 15 February 1909; fols 26–7, Banister to Fox, 11 May 1909; fol. 57, Fox to Davidson, 8 November 1909.

Extension that 'in regard to a Chinese Bishop, that while setting before the Chinese Church this ideal, we should go slow'.[15]

One of the first acts of the newly established CHSKH General Synod was to organize a missionary district in Shensi (Shaanxi) province in 1915, which up to that point had remained untouched by missionary societies. This was a key step for the Chinese church, for the mission was to be led by Chinese clergy and supported only by Chinese donations. Nonetheless, a certain caution regarding devolution was evident in that Bishop Norris of North China was to play a supervisory and jurisdictional role in Shensi until the time came to consecrate a Chinese bishop.[16] Another example of the desire to 'go slow' was the case of the first Chinese candidate for the episcopate, T. S. Sing (Shen Tsai-sheng), who had been suggested in 1918 by Bishop Molony of Chekiang (Zhejiang). When the proposal was brought to Archbishop Davidson, he thought that a Chinese episcopacy could not yet be realized, 'pending the creation of provincial organization in China for the Anglican Church'. The Chinese church would first need its own creeds, articulation of canonical obedience and method of election in order for indigenous bishops to be integrated systematically into the worldwide Anglican Communion. Whilst Sing was nevertheless consecrated, it was understood to be an extraordinary measure, allowed only because Sing was an outstanding candidate. Davidson, together with many of his contemporaries, reckoned that the church's canonical structure had to be developed over time.[17] The Revd Frederick Baylis, CMS Secretary for Africa and later for the Far East, wrote in a confidential memorandum about 'native episcopates' that, whilst 'native bishops' were the ultimate goal, it was important first to equip candidates to have 'a fairly good understanding of what ... to do, instead of having so very much of it yet to evolve out of the unknown'. Provincial organization and proper doctrine and discipline were yet to be become established. Consequently, Chinese candidates for the episcopacy were at best only 'nearly ready'.[18]

[15] Ibid., vol. 191, fols 120–1, Banister to Davidson, 7 September 1914.
[16] Scott, 'The Chung-Hua Sheng Kung Hui', 4.
[17] LPL, Davidson Papers, vol. 252, fols 85–9, Davidson to Molony, 26 February 1918; fols 93–4, Molony to Davidson, 19 April 1918.
[18] Birmingham, CRL, CMS Archive, CMS/G/AZ4/174, confidential memorandum, Baylis to King, n.d., 2–9.

It is in this light that the approval of the CHSKH Canons and Constitutions of the Diocese of Victoria Hong Kong in December 1913 must be understood. The goal of the constitution was to establish a triennial synod that brought clergy and lay representatives together in order 'to take counsel in matters that concern the welfare and progress of the CHSKH'. With only four canons regulating the basic structure of the new church, the rules and details were to be hammered out over time. The expectation was that further canons would evolve organically over the years to come as missionaries continued to educate indigenous leaders.[19] However, even by 1920, there was a slowness to the whole process. In August that year, Bishop Duppuy of South China (1920–32) wrote to the CMS Parent Committee requesting permission to constitute a Chinese Church Council, citing Resolution 34 of the 1920 Lambeth Conference, which supported the drive towards indigenous church government. He received a firm rebuttal in which Baylis asserted that it was still 'the early days' of the mission and that there was still 'no Church body in existence competent to take over the duties and powers referred to'.[20] At the Lambeth Conference itself, the missionary bishops from China had inquired about the possibility of achieving provincial status for the CHSKH. However, the discussion quickly ground to a halt when major obstacles were highlighted, such as the missionary bishops' also owing allegiance to their home church or the missions' being financially dependent on home societies.[21]

Throughout the previous decade, even leading figures of the CHSKH had preferred to 'go slow', as revealed by their nationwide monthly periodical, *Zhonghua Shenggonghui Bao* (中華聖公會報, *The Chinese Churchman*). In 1914, for instance, Huang Dixin, a church member from Suzhou, published an article about how, although there were thousands of Chinese Christians with some degree of self-support and self-government, the vast majority of Chinese churches were dependent on foreign financial support.[22]

[19] HKSKH, 2755, 'Provisional Constitution and Canons of the Chung Wa Sheng Kung Hui in the Diocese of Victoria Hongkong', 1918, 4.
[20] CRL, CMS Archive, G1/CH/1/L/4/60, Baylis to Duppuy, 23 September 1920.
[21] LPL, LC114, Lambeth Conference 1920, 'Memorandum of a Meeting of Chinese Bishops', 2 August 1920, fols 84–92.
[22] 黃滌新 [Huang Dixin], '中華聖公會自行建堂之芻議' ['Zhonghuashenggonghui Zixingjiantang Zhichuyi' / 'A Modest Proposal on how the CHSKH can be Established as Autonomous'], 中華聖公會報 [*Zhonghuashenggonghui Bao* / *Chinese Churchman*] 7/5 (May 1914), 1.

In sum, the decade before and after the formation of the CHSKH in 1912 saw a general drive towards the Three-Self Church, but it was a hesitant and slow drive. CMS and Church of England authorities thought it best not to rush into creating a new church, since it would take more time and education to equip indigenous leadership adequately. Nonetheless, an intimation of the fiery Chinese zeal of the next two decades came as early as 1913 when Chinese members took the initiative and asked Bishop Lander of South China (1907–20) to establish a diocesan synod, rather than waiting for him to initiate one.[23]

When the Qing empire was overthrown in 1911, China descended into chaos as the newly formed Xinhai republic failed to stop provincial governors fighting amongst each another for dominance. Many supported the nationalist movement as a means of recreating unity and overcoming the confusion across China. In a development exacerbated by the May Fourth Movement and the 1925 Shanghai massacre, foreign imperialism became the scapegoat for China's problems.[24] This sentiment spilled over into parts of the Chinese church. For example, articles in *Shenggonghui Bao* switched from explaining the necessity of foreign support to suggesting how the CHSKH could move beyond it. In 1921, an article by Zhu Zhezhi of Zhejiang diocese called for the CHSKH to develop its own new missionary districts without overdependence on the missionary societies and, in so doing, to instil the Three-Self spirit. Given the changes happening around the world and the founding of the Republic of China, Zhu then explained the goal of autonomy before listing out the necessary steps for the CHSKH to reach independence, such as stronger internal organization and greater unity between the dioceses, which by this time numbered eleven.[25] In 1927, T. Z. Koo (Gu Ziren), secretary of the Young Men's Christian Association

[23] CRL, CMS Archive, G1/CH/1/O/121, Lander to Baylis, 15 August 1913.

[24] For more on the post-Versailles mood in China, see Erez Manela, *The Wilsonian Moment: Self-Determination and the International Origins of Anticolonial Nationalism* (Oxford, 2007).

[25] 朱哲之 [Zhu Zhezhi], '如何使聖公會自養自治自傳' ['Ruheshi Shenggonghui Ziyang Zizhi Zichuan' / 'How the CHSKH can become Self-Supporting, Self-Governing and Self-Propagating'], 中華聖公會報 [*Zhonghuashenggonghui Bao* / *Chinese Churchman*] 14/24 (December 1921), 4–7. After the 1903 conference, four further dioceses were established: Fukien (Fujian) (1906), Kwangsi-Hunan (Guangxi-Hunan) (1909), Honan (Henan) (1909) and Anking (Anqing) (1910).

Student Department, issued a memorandum to foreign church leaders explaining why the Chinese church had to change. In the current political climate, the church was widely perceived as a foreign organization, an instrument of capitalism, opposed to progress and filled with hypocrisy.[26] It was necessary to defend the church against such accusations by demonstrating how the faith was authentically Chinese and how Christian living could make positive contributions to society through healthcare and education. For example, the National Christian Council of China, an interdenominational organization formed in 1922 to coordinate mission work, implemented the Five Year Movement in 1930; this called on churches to reemphasize the benefits of Christian living and deepen knowledge about Christ.[27] Whilst there were many outcomes and initiatives in this inter-war period, two stand out with regard to constituting the CHSKH: granting the CHSKH full autonomy and consecrating Chinese bishops. In both issues, there was tension between what Chinese Christians sought and what home authorities regarded as a deviation from the original plan of gradual constitutional development.

To grant the CHSKH full autonomy in its constitution would demonstrate that it was no crony of imperialism. As early as 1920, the CHSKH bishops had petitioned Archbishop Davidson for full recognition of 'the authoritative Council of an autonomous province of the Anglican Communion'.[28] Not much action was taken in response, and it was not until 1921 that the CHSKH General Synod began to draw up canons to establish its own authority, including metropolitan oversight, a method of electing bishops and a system of clerical discipline.[29] Throughout the 1920s, the Church of Christ in China, a newly formed coalition of churches consisting primarily of Presbyterians and Congregationalists, wrote repeatedly to the Anglican mission in South China about the need for autonomy. In 1925, they emphasized that spiritual sovereignty was essential for the Chinese church, because 'neither the Chinese Christians nor

---

[26] LPL, Davidson Papers, vol. 252, fols 334–44, Memorandum from Tissington Tatlow, 28 February 1927.
[27] Ryan Dunch, *Fuzhou Protestants and the Making of a Modern China, 1857–1927* (New Haven, CT, 2001), is a good case study of the intersection between politics, piety and progress.
[28] LPL, Davidson Papers, vol. 252, fols 132–6, joint letter from the Chinese bishops, 7 August 1920.
[29] LPL, Lang Papers, vol. 100, 'CHSKH General Synod Resolutions', 1921, fols 86–8.

the foreign missionaries can be satisfied with anything less than this'.[30] No direct result came from their request, for they did not possess authority over the CHSKH; nor were the Anglican mission boards particularly interested in their proposal. Bishop Frank Norris of North China wrote to Archbishop Davidson again in 1928 to request formal recognition. Unlike in 1921, there was now greater clarity about the terms and conditions of recognition, namely, the right of the CHSKH General Synod to proceed under its own canons and standing orders, and that CHSKH bishops should no longer be seen as suffragans of Canterbury, North America or Canada, but as bishops of the Chinese province.[31] Davidson, however, was reluctant to take action until the PEC in the USA had moved.[32] Bishop Norris became exasperated when he realized the following month that the PEC was in fact waiting for Canterbury, while Canada was waiting for both.[33]

Ultimately, unilateral arrangements were made through international cooperation and communication as Davidson's successor, Archbishop Cosmo Lang (1928–42), confirmed that CHSKH autonomy would be confirmed by an official resolution at the forthcoming 1930 Lambeth Conference. Lang explained to the bishop of Hankow, Logan H. Roots, that he knew no other way of issuing a formal announcement. He was concerned that using alternative channels would be seen as overstepping his jurisdiction as archbishop of Canterbury. Speaking on behalf of the PEC and the Anglican Church in Canada would imply that he was somehow superior to the presiding bishops in America and Canada. He thought it best not to set up any messy precedents for announcements involving other autonomous provinces.[34] This entire episode reveals that there was no single body that could legally speak for all, and the joint resolution was an unprecedented development in the Anglican Communion. The very process of recognizing the autonomy of the CHSKH reveals the contrasting approaches between the Chinese Christians and the mission boards. The former pushed forcefully for the recognition of autonomy within a politically heated

---

[30] HKSKH, 2183/97, 'Kwangtung Christian Council Notes', 7 November 1925.
[31] LPL, Lang Papers, vol. 100, fols 81–5, Norris to Davidson, 11 June 1928.
[32] Ibid., fols 99–101, Davidson to Norris, July 1928.
[33] Ibid., fols 102–6, Norris to Davidson, 31 August 1928.
[34] Ibid., fols 110–11, 'Memo: Interview with Bishop Roots of Hankow', 13 December 1928.

environment, whereas the latter moved slowly to work out how to establish legality and procedure in uncharted waters.

This tension is even clearer in the question of appointing Chinese bishops. In the South China diocese, discussions began between foreign and Chinese clergy in the late 1920s on the appointment of a Chinese assistant bishop. At the 1928 diocesan synod, the Revd Percy Jenkins, a seasoned missionary based in Canton who was all too aware of how financial constraints hindered idealism, wondered if the assistant bishop could be a foreigner since there was such a drastic shortage of Chinese clergy. The Revd Lee Kau-yan (Li Qiu'en) virtually ignored this point since the unanimous wish within the Chinese church was to see a Chinese assistant bishop as a sign of the times.[35] At the 1929 diocesan standing committee meeting, Chinese representatives reasoned that appointing a Chinese bishop would encourage more young men to study for the ministry, avoid misunderstandings with non-Christians and 'stir up the spirit of a self-supporting Church'.[36] The problem, however, was exactly how to appoint a Chinese bishop, let alone a CHSKH bishop, since historically bishops had been sent as missionary bishops and there was no canonically defined electoral process.

In 1933 a turbulent exchange of correspondence between Bishop Norris and Archbishop Lang sought to clarify the precise procedure. The key question was whether the final election and appointment of bishops should be handled by Canterbury or by the chair of the CHSKH house of bishops.[37] Whilst Archbishop Lang in July 1933 gave consent for future appointments to follow the recently revised self-governing canons of the CHSKH which placed the power to appoint, elect and consecrate bishops with the general synod, just a month later he reversed his stance. This happened after his consultations with the Revd W. Wilson Cash, the CMS general secretary, who thought that the CHSKH was 'not really quite ready for complete autonomy as an independent Province'. Wilson Cash believed that 'a certain section of the Chinese … are more Nationalistic than Christian … and if given a free hand, might act in such a way as to

---

[35] HKSKH, 2930/3, Seventh South China Diocesan Synod Meeting minutes, September 1928, 6–7.
[36] HKSKH, 2486/1, Standing Committee minutes, 30 April 1929, 1–4.
[37] LPL, Lang Papers, vol. 124, fols 191–3, Lang to Mowll, 21 July 1933; fols 194–6, Lang to Norris, 21 July 1933; fols 197–201, Norris to Lang, 24 July 1933; fols 207–9, Cash to Lang, 28 July 1933; fols 211–12, Lang to Cash, 7 August 1933.

sever themselves from the rest of the Anglican Communion'.[38] The long shadow of the fundamentalist controversy of 1922 had caused him to act with caution, for he wished to avoid defining the position of the CMS in a way that would cause schism.[39] After careful consideration, Lang chose to reserve the right to elect and appoint those bishops whose episcopal stipends were provided by the CMS, according to a procedure subsequently adopted by a CHSKH standing order of 1924: this conferred the right of election and appointment of a bishop on the church that provided the bishop's stipend.[40] However, this effectively applied to all CHSKH bishops, for all were funded by mission boards. Norris could do nothing but accept the decision with 'some measure of disappointment'.[41]

The following year, Bishop T. K. Shen (Shen Tzü-kao) was elected as the first Chinese diocesan bishop for Shensi missionary diocese, but only after extensive voluntary fundraising across the other eleven dioceses and from supportive Christian businessmen in Nanking.[42] In South China, Archdeacon Mok Shau-tsang (Mo Shou-tseng) was elected assistant bishop in April 1933, but the requirement for an endowment fund meant that he had to wait until 1935 for his consecration.[43] Although the Chinese sought to establish the Chinese church quickly by appointing Chinese bishops, church authorities in England and America proceeded gingerly, for they saw the legal implications in a more global context and were particularly concerned with the potential risk of indigenous bishops causing schism. The CHSKH missionary bishops continued to sit uneasily between the Chinese clergy and Western church authorities.

The 1920s and 1930s are best summed up by the weary words of Bishop Duppuy at the 1929 diocesan synod. Tired by the confusion and beset with climate-induced health problems, Duppuy began the bishop's charge by quoting the famous last words of Cecil Rhodes: 'So

---

[38] Ibid., fols 194–6, Lang to Norris, 21 July 1933; fols 224–6, Alan Campbell Don, memorandum on China, 18 August 1933.

[39] Hewitt, *Problems of Success*, 1: 465–70. In 1922, a sizeable group chose to break away from the CMS and form the Bible Churchmen's Missionary Society over disagreements on the official stance of the CMS concerning biblical inerrancy.

[40] LPL, Lang Papers, vol. 100, standing order of the CHSKH House of Bishops, 1924, fols 93–4.

[41] Ibid., vol. 124, fol. 252, Norris to Lang, 22 August 1934.

[42] 'Native elected Diocesan Bishop', *South China Morning Post*, 5 May 1934, 3.

[43] 'Assistant Bishop in S. China Diocese', *South China Morning Post*, 5 June 1933, 16; Gray, *Anglicans in China*, ed. Smalley, 50.

little done, so much to do'. As a missionary bishop, he saw both the urgency and vastness of 'shifting the weight of responsibility from the Mission to the Chinese Church'. At the same time, he could appreciate why the CMS and Church of England were restrained in taking steps towards full autonomy.[44] Duppuy tried to wrestle his way to a point somewhere in between through the 1929 constitution, which simultaneously reflected the unanimous desire for change and the muddled relationship of church, mission and metropolitan. The shared drive for change is illustrated in the context of the new canon providing for annual synods, which replaced a previous canon which had established triennial synods. Whilst this measure was first initiated by Chinese clergy through an amendment in 1926, it was the British missionary clergy who suggested going further by incorporating it into a completely new constitution.[45] Equally, the contrast between Chinese and foreign clergy is revealed in their attitudes towards the newly-formed diocesan board of missions, a distinctive feature of the 1929 constitution. To the Chinese, the board was an unprecedented measure in empowering them, since they would receive an opportunity to administer a significant portion of the CMS grants and to direct missionary staff, both Chinese and foreign. Yet to the mother church, the board was a compromise, for its decisions were ultimately subject to the approval of the diocesan standing committee, which was in turn under the ever watchful eye of the CMS Parent Committee in London.[46]

The constitutional stalemate came to an end during the Second World War. The relationship between the CHSKH and Church of England was thrust into a new stage of development as a result of generational change and wartime experience. In 1942, Lang's successor, Archbishop William Temple (1942–4), drafted a memorandum about the CHSKH which acknowledged that the time for change had come: 'It is evident that a stage has been reached when the relations between the Church in China and the Churches in England and USA call for reconsideration'. He suggested that in future CHSKH bishops should not have to make an oath of obedience to Canterbury or the

[44] HKSKH, 2756/1, Minutes of the Eighth Diocesan Synod, 1929, 5–9.
[45] HKSKH, 2930/1, Fifth South China Diocesan Synod Meeting minutes, September 1926, 4; 2930/3, Seventh South China Diocesan Synod Meeting minutes, September 1928, 10.
[46] HKSKH, 2755/36, Constitutions and canons of the CHSKH diocesan synod, 1929, 10–11; 2138/102, CMS resolution on diocesan board of missions, 23 January 1929.

presiding bishop of the PEC, nor should CHSKH bishops be selected by the primates of these jurisdictions. It was time for the church to be 'genuinely Chinese and free from all kind of tutelage'.[47] Temple's memorandum was sent to leading voices in the Church of England, who largely agreed with him. Gurney Barclay, Far East secretary of the CMS, was 'wholehearted in agreement'.[48] Bishop Hall (1932–66), Duppuy's successor in South China, praised the independence and initiative of Chinese Christians he observed while in Central China during the war. For Hall, sections of the church 'had begun to stand on their own feet'.[49] Bishop John Dauglish of the Society for the Propagation of the Gospel, however, still thought the CHSKH was yet to reach this stage although, as a member of the old guard, his view was now the exception rather than the norm.[50] The overall mood and atmosphere were shifting. Max Warren, the CMS general secretary, observed that many of their younger missionaries around the world displayed great willingness to learn the local languages and interact with indigenous cultures, and commented that their view of how the missionary should relate to indigenous cultures was different from earlier generations, who had seen missionaries as slightly more detached.[51]

The more significant reason behind this change was that the CHSKH had proved itself during the war. As Warren put it, it had passed through a time of testing. Despite suffering, evacuation, fighting, famine, disease, death, a dearth of younger clergy, precarious finances and a provincial organization that was slow to develop, they were pressing on.[52] Harry Wittenbach, the CMS East Asia secretary, used the metaphor of a faulty but functioning bus in Canton to describe the CHSKH: 'Travelling over the war-scarred roads they soon become battered and worn. Not an instrument on the dashboard works. The mudguards shake loose. The springs

[47] LPL, William Temple Papers, vol. 10, fols 338–41, draft memorandum on 'Church in China', 26 June 1942.
[48] Ibid., fols 358–61, Barclay to Davidson, 30 July 1942.
[49] LPL, MS 3126, fols 477–8, 'Diocese of Hong Kong Unified Statement 1939–40', 28 October 1938.
[50] LPL, William Temple Papers, vol. 10, fols 349–52, 'Comments on Memorandum on Church in China', 6 July 1942.
[51] CRL, CMS Archive, G/AP3/1, Warren to Wittenbach, 23 October 1946.
[52] LPL, Fisher Papers, vol. 24, fols 251–60, 'Max Warren's Report of Shanghai General Synod', August 1947.

break. They are tied together with bits of string and wire. But they keep going. That is China.'[53] The CHSKH house of bishops had displayed striking resilience in 1943 when it convened without the usual support from missionary organizations, which had been cut off after 1937, following the Japanese occupation. They had at that meeting compiled a memorandum to be taken by Assistant Bishop Andrew Y. Y. Tsu (Zhu You-yu) of South China to America and England in 1944 which explained their revised approach to the mission-church relationship.[54] The document detailed how, although the CHSKH was grateful for the security and fellowship offered by missionary societies in the past, they believed that now 'this great diversity of godfathers and godmothers may prove a source of weakness'.[55] It was unhelpful that different mission boards ran the dioceses (now thirteen in number) differently, creating great inequality in financial support as well as disparity in ministry focus.[56] It would be better to coordinate church work in China through a new non-missionary central authority.[57]

Moreover, there was a growing sense that the missionary enterprise could no longer be the same as before the war, with impending decolonization and a new world order. Following his 1947 trip to the International Missionary Council conference and the CHSKH general synod, Warren shared a report with the CMS executive committee identifying what he considered as fundamental post-war changes that compelled the CMS to change its ways. To Warren, British 'imperium' was no longer operative and colonial law could no longer be relied upon. After the war, the church could not depend on extra-territorial missionary privileges as it had done over the past century. The best way forward was to empower the indigenous churches to confront the two incoming spectres of political communism and American 'big business imperialism' after decolonization, as well as handle the inherited church divisions between 'the

[53] CRL, CMS Archive, CMS/ACC589/O1, Wittenbach's China tour journal, ch. 2, 'Canton', unpaginated.
[54] Ibid., CH/g/O1, Outside Organisations – CHSKH 1937–1950, 'Explanatory Note to Memorandum', 22 May 1943.
[55] Ibid., 'Crises of the CHSKH', May 1943, 1.
[56] The dioceses of Shensi (Shaanxi) and Yunkwei (Yunnan-Guizhou) were established in 1934 and 1947 respectively.
[57] 'Crises of the CHSKH', 2.

Fundamentalist and the Liberal schools'.[58] This unequivocal call to devolve authority to indigenous leaders was echoed at the 1948 Lambeth Conference in which Resolutions 6 to 8 declared that the Anglican Communion was in full agreement with the equality of all people regardless of race and colour.[59]

On behalf of the Church of England, Archbishop Temple assured Bishop Tsu in person that he saw no difficulty in agreeing to the suggested amendments to the constitution of the CHSKH. Tsu invited Temple to visit China in the near future, to which Temple replied that it would be his personal pleasure, a promise which was not fulfilled due to his death in October 1944.[60] Temple's successor, Archbishop Geoffrey Fisher, conveyed a message of Christian fellowship to the 1947 CHSKH general synod, commending them 'to go ever forward in the power of the Holy Spirit'.[61] With the blessings and support of the worldwide Anglican Communion, the general synod swiftly approved the constitutional changes. The constitution of 1948 enabled fully autonomous self-government in financial administration and the election of the episcopate, while new dioceses would be initiated by the general synod without the intervention of external church authorities or mission boards.[62] Missionaries continued to be received warmly as their advice, training and financial support proved indispensable in post-war reconstruction. However, the key difference in legal terms was that the missionaries and home authorities were finally happy to cede their previous role in church government.

For the South China diocese, corresponding shifts took place in the post-war period. The standing committee, which in 1945 was entirely Chinese as the missionaries were yet to return, wrote to the CMS stating that the experience of war had testified to their 'new faith and new courage'. In the same letter, the committee presented its intended 'Ten Year Movement', an action plan that involved the

[58] CRL, CMS Archive, CMS/G/AD1/10, 'Warren's Report to Executive Committee', 14 October 1947, 2–5.
[59] Anglican Communion Office, 'The Lambeth Conference: Resolutions Archive from 1948' (2005), 6, 21, online at: <http://www.anglicancommunion.org/media/127737/1948.pdf>, accessed 12 July 2018.
[60] London, CERC, MC/OV/CHINA/2/1, Tsu-Temple conversation notes, 14 September 1944.
[61] LPL, Fisher Papers, vol. 24, fol. 247, Fisher to Warren, 4 June 1947.
[62] HKSKH, 2755/34, 'Constitution and Canons of the CHSKH', 1948.

extension of evangelism through family prayer meetings and public preaching, which seemed to them the optimal methods of evangelism. It was suggested that the CMS might send returning missionaries to bolster theological training institutions.[63] In this letter, the standing committee was asserting its leadership role by implying that it would define evangelistic strategy and that missionaries should follow their direction. As the missionaries returned, they met in December 1946 to discuss the future development of the diocese along indigenous lines. Speaking for the Chinese synod, Archdeacon Lee Kau-yan (Li Qiu'en) expressed how the war had awakened the church so that the relationship between society and church had had to become closer. A significant outcome of the meeting was the start of the complete transfer of CMS property to the CHSKH.[64] Though the process did not take place as quickly as Archdeacon Lee would have liked, there was undoubtedly a quicker pace of change, as well as consensus on the nature of the redefined relationship.[65] In 1947, Archbishop Fisher formally relinquished to the CHSKH house of bishops his final authority to select the South China bishop.[66] The CHSKH constitution of 1948 thus reflects the complete transfer of property ownership and the emergence of a fully established self-governing church in the wake of the Second World War and its new generation of missionary thinkers.

The realignment was short-lived. The Communist victory in China in 1949 meant that by August 1951, Archbishop Fisher curiously found himself having to reassert his jurisdiction over the diocese of Hong Kong, which was now separate from the rest of South China. Three months earlier, Bishop Hall and Assistant Bishop Nathaniel Moyung (Murong Xian) had agreed on the division of the South China diocese, by which Hong Kong was separated ecclesiastically from the rest of South China. The newly-installed People's Government demanded that religious bodies within China should cut all ties with foreign jurisdiction, which in this case meant separating from Hong Kong, a British colony.[67] Missionaries were forced to

[63] HKSKH, 2737/1, Standing Committee to CMS London, 10 December 1945.
[64] HKSKH, 2737/2, Diocesanization Meeting minutes, 7 December 1946.
[65] HKSKH, 2737/7, Diocesanization Meeting minutes, 6 June 1947.
[66] 'Victoria Diocese: Why the Status of Bishop has been changed', *South China Morning Post*, 8 August 1947, 8.
[67] LPL, Fisher Papers, vol. 84, fols 58–66, Hong Kong Diocesan Synod petition to Canterbury, 21 August 1951.

leave when Premier Zhou Enlai emphasized that the church, in line with the rest of China, had to be cleansed of imperialist connections.[68] Everyone involved considered this a travesty. Bishop Moyung admitted in a private letter that he could not hold back his tears at the separation.[69] Bishop Robin Chen (Chen Jian-zhen), chairman of the house of bishops, delivered a message to Archbishop Fisher, saying that he anticipated hard times and even a time when they would be forced to choose between death and resistance. In spite of the forced denunciations and physical separation, Chen would always view the CHSKH as a part of the worldwide Anglican Communion.[70] In an address to the Hong Kong diocese, Bishop Hall remarked that he knew of no precedent in church history for the constitutional position facing them, whereby a fully participating member of an Anglican province found itself suddenly cut off from the rest. The diocese of Hong Kong chose to continue using the CHSKH canons as an expression of their desire that this would 'not mean any spiritual divorce, but only a bowing to the necessities of the time'. Both Fisher and Hall had every intention of waiting for the reunion of Hong Kong to the CHSKH and the CHSKH to the Anglican Communion. The archbishop of Canterbury affirmed that he would act as metropolitan only on behalf of the chair bishop of the CHSKH.[71] Accordingly, Hall clarified at the 1951 diocesan synod that Fisher was not acting in his former capacity as head of the Chinese church as had been the case before 1947, for he recognized that Hong Kong now belonged to the CHSKH. Rather, Fisher was acting simply as the leading figure in the Anglican Communion.[72]

This unforeseen ending in 1951 is the ultimate illustration of the legal difficulties that beset the CHSKH and South China diocese from the beginning. The CHSKH clergy, CMS authorities and Church of England leaders found themselves having to keep up with volatile political changes in China while coming to terms with an ever-changing understanding of who stood where in global ecumenical fellowship. Each time they adjusted their constitutional structure, the situation altered again. This article has used the

[68] CRL, CMS Archive, CHg/AC1, Purchas to Wittenbach, 12 June 1950, 136–7.
[69] LPL, Fisher Papers, vol. 84, fols 34–6, Moyung to Chung, 13 May 1951.
[70] Ibid., fols 79–83, memorandum on conversation with Purchas, 14 September 1951.
[71] Ibid., fols 40–1, Fisher to Hall, 13 June 1951.
[72] HKSKH, 2463/2, 'The Bishop's Charge', 1951.

constitutional history of the South China diocese and the CHSKH over half a century to demonstrate the enduring difficulties and yet the dynamism involved in constituting a new church during the early twentieth century. This experience was probably not unique to South China; however, to substantiate this claim would require further research into canon law across modern worldwide Christianity in a global, comparative and connective approach.[73] For the South China diocese, developing a stable legal structure was perpetually a work in progress, and this is arguably still the case today.[74]

[73] For more on this method in the history of Christianity, see Joel Cabrita, David Maxwell and Emma Wild-Wood, eds, *Relocating World Christianity: Interdisciplinary Studies in Universal and Local Expressions of the Christian Faith*, Theology and Mission in World Christianity 7 (Leiden, 2017).
[74] The diocese of Hong Kong and Macao became the province of the Hong Kong Sheng Kung Hui in 1998, after Hong Kong and Macau rejoined China with the legal status of 'Special Administrative Region'.

The Church of England and the Legislative Reforms of 1828–32: Revolution or Adjustment?

Nicholas Dixon*

Pembroke College, Cambridge

Since the 1950s, historians of the eighteenth- and nineteenth-century Church of England have generally maintained that the Sacramental Test Act (1828), the Roman Catholic Relief Act (1829) and the Reform Act (1832) amounted to a 'constitutional revolution', in which Anglican political hegemony was decisively displaced. This theory remains the dominant framework for understanding the effect of legislation on the relationship between church and state in pre-Victorian England. This article probes the validity of the theory. It is argued that the legislative reforms of 1828–32 did not drastically alter the religious composition of parliament, which was already multi-denominational, and that they incorporated clauses which preserved the political dominance of the Church of England. Additionally, it is suggested that Anglican apprehensions concerning the reforming measures of those years were derived from an unfounded belief that these reforms would ultimately result in changes to the Church of England's formularies or in disestablishment, rather than from the actual laws enacted. Accordingly, the post-1832 British parliamentary system did not in the short term militate against Anglican interests. In light of this reappraisal, these legislative reforms may be better understood as an exercise in 'constitutional adjustment' as opposed to a 'constitutional revolution'.

Following the Reform Act and the ensuing general election of 1832, the duke of Wellington wrote to the Conservative author John Wilson Croker: 'The revolution is made, that is to say, that power is transferred from one class of society, the gentlemen of England, professing the faith of the Church of England, to another class of society, the shopkeepers, being dissenters from the Church, many

* E-mail: mail@drnicholasdixon.com.

The research upon which this article is based was funded by an Arts and Humanities Research Council Doctoral Training Partnership studentship, grant no. 1653413, supported by Pembroke College, Cambridge. I am most grateful to Andrew Thompson for his comments and suggestions.

Studies in Church History 56 (2020), 401–418   © Ecclesiastical History Society 2020
doi: 10.1017/stc.2019.22

of them Socinians, others atheists.'[1] From 1833 onwards, this stark judgement was reinforced from within the Church of England by the emerging Oxford Movement, whose followers saw the series of reforming laws enacted by the British parliament between 1828 and 1832 as marking a watershed in the relationship between the church and the British state, to the detriment of the former. The Tractarian leader Richard Hurrell Froude wrote in 1833 that the 'joint effect' of the repeal of the Test and Corporation Acts, Catholic emancipation and the Reform Act had been 'to efface in at least one branch of our Civil Legislature, that character which … qualified it to be at the same time our Ecclesiastical Legislature, and thus to cancel the conditions on which it has been allowed to interfere in matters spiritual'. This, in Froude's view, was 'a *downright Revolution*'.[2] Such a framework of understanding became a commonplace of Tractarian and Anglo-Catholic thought.[3] However, the notion of a 'revolution' taking place during the years from 1828 to 1832 was absent from most histories of the period until well into the twentieth century. As James Kirby has argued, nineteenth-century 'constitutionalist historians, Anglican and otherwise', including William Stubbs, J. R. Green and Edward Freeman, treated 'the Revolution of 1688 as the effective terminus of English history'.[4] Correspondingly, in 1848 Thomas Babington Macaulay, contemplating the revolutions then occurring around Europe, declared 1688 to be 'our last revolution'.[5] Later whiggish historians such as

---

[1] Louis J. Jennings, ed., *The Correspondence and Diaries of the late Right Honourable John Wilson Croker, LL.D., F.R.S., Secretary to the Admiralty from 1809 to 1830*, 3 vols (London, 1884), 2: 205–6, Duke of Wellington to John Wilson Croker, 6 March 1833.
[2] Richard Hurrell Froude, *Remains of the late Reverend Richard Hurrell Froude: Part the Second*, 2 vols (Derby, 1839), 1: 185, 192. On Froude's theory and Anglican opposition to it, see Peter Nockles, *The Oxford Movement in Context: Anglican High Churchmanship, 1760–1857* (Cambridge, 1994), 80–7.
[3] See, for example, George Edward Biber, *Bishop Blomfield and his Times: An Historical Sketch* (London, 1857), 219–23; George Anthony Denison, *Notes of my Life, 1805–1878*, 2nd edn (Oxford, 1878), 59–60; R. W. Church, *The Oxford Movement: Twelve Years 1833–1845* (London, 1891), 1–2, 41, 43; S. L. Ollard, *The Anglo-Catholic Revival: Some Persons and Principles* (London, 1925), 19. On the place of 1828–32 in W. E. Gladstone's early thought, see Perry Butler, *Gladstone: Church, State and Tractarianism. A Study of his Religious Ideas and Attitudes* (Oxford, 1982), 79–82.
[4] James Kirby, *Historians and the Church of England: Religion and Historical Scholarship, 1870–1920* (Oxford, 2016), 129.
[5] Thomas Babington Macaulay, *Works*, ed. Lady Trevelyan, 8 vols (London, 1866), 2: 397.

George Macaulay Trevelyan saw the reforming measures of 1828–32 not as having brought about a 'revolution' of any kind, but rather as having helped to avert such an outcome.[6]

The first historical articulation of the idea of an anti-Anglican 'revolution' occurring during these years was given by Geoffrey Best in an article of 1959. Best argued that 'despite the conspiracy of all Whigs and … some Conservatives, to convince the public that nothing so startling as a revolution had happened', the changes of 1828–32 represented a 'constitutional revolution' of the kind posited by Wellington and the Tractarians. The repeal of the Test and Corporation Acts 'abandoned an essential principle, that of the establishment's legal and political superiority over the nonconformists'. Then, '1829 marked another betrayal of old principle', in this case with regard to Roman Catholics. Finally, 'the great change [was] sealed and confirmed by the Reform Act', which left 'the establishment … still afloat and to outward appearances remarkably the same, but bereft of its anchors and rudder, waiting in the sultry calm to see what wind would blow and whether it could safely make any harbour'.[7]

Best's 'constitutional revolution' thesis became the dominant interpretation of the changing relationship between church and state in early nineteenth-century England, and is comprehensively re-examined in this article. The thesis was further expounded by Norman Gash, Scott Bennett, G. I. T. Machin and R. K. Webb.[8] In his history of England in the long eighteenth century, J. C. D.

---

[6] G. M. Trevelyan, *British History in the Nineteenth Century (1782–1901)* (London, 1922), 220, 225; see Gordon Pentland, 'Parliamentary Reform', in David Brown, Gordon Pentland and Robert Crowcroft, eds, *The Oxford Handbook of Modern British Political History* (Oxford, 2018), 383–99, at 385–6.

[7] G. F. A. Best, 'The Constitutional Revolution, 1828–32, and its Consequences for the Established Church', *Theology* 62 (1959), 226–34, at 226, 228, 230–1; see also idem, *Temporal Pillars: Queen Anne's Bounty, the Ecclesiastical Commissioners, and the Church of England* (Cambridge, 1964), 7, 270–1. As Best acknowledged, his arguments were to a certain extent anticipated by Olive Brose, but she did not describe the reforms of 1828–32 as a 'revolution': Olive J. Brose, *Church and Parliament: The Reshaping of the Church of England, 1828–1860* (Stanford, CA, 1959), 7–21.

[8] Norman Gash, *Reaction and Reconstruction in English Politics 1832–1852: The Ford Lectures delivered in the University of Oxford in the Hilary Term 1964* (Oxford, 1965), 61–2; Scott Bennett, 'Catholic Emancipation, the "Quarterly Review", and Britain's Constitutional Revolution', *VS* 12 (1969), 283–304, at 285; G. I. T. Machin, *Politics and the Churches in Great Britain, 1832 to 1868* (Oxford, 1977), 21–2, 26–7; R. K. Webb, *Modern England: From the Eighteenth Century to the Present*, 2nd edn (London, 1980), 186–203.

Clark put forward a variation on the theme. In Clark's schema, before 1828 England was a confessional *ancien régime* defined by an exclusive Anglicanism, but pressure from Catholics and dissenters presented the political elite with a clear-cut choice: 'What mattered most: monarchy or Church? In 1688–9 the political classes ultimately chose the second; in 1828–9 they reversed that choice.'[9] Consequently, the legislative reforms of 1828–32 were (employing another phrase of Wellington's) 'a revolution gradually accomplished', whereby any notion of an Anglican state belonged to a 'lost world' by 1838.[10] Clark differed from previous historians in his shift of emphasis from 1832 to 1829 as the climax of the 'revolution'. Nonetheless, along with a growing body of historians, he upheld the essentials of Best's 'constitutional revolution' thesis.

However, beginning with that of Edward Norman in 1976, a number of relevant studies have used the term 'constitutional adjustments' to refer to the changes of 1828–32. Yet if this signifies a rejection of the 'constitutional revolution' thesis, it is far from being explicitly so, for the thesis is not critiqued in these works.[11] Jonathan Parry and Stephen Taylor have gone a little further in this direction, stating that the legislative measures of 1828–32 were 'not in themselves revolutionary', although they do not explicate the basis of this claim.[12] Perhaps the only historian explicitly to challenge the

[9] J. C. D. Clark, *English Society 1660–1832: Religion, Ideology and Politics during the Ancien Regime*, 2nd edn (Cambridge, 2000), 555.

[10] Ibid. 527, 563; cf. W. H. Conser, *Church and Confession: Conservative Theologians in Germany, England, and America, 1815–1866* (Macon, GA, 1984), 99–111; Richard Brown, *Church and State in Modern Britain 1700–1850* (London, 1991), 203–29; Nockles, *Oxford Movement*, 44; David Hempton, *Religion and Political Culture in Britain and Ireland: From the Glorious Revolution to the Decline of Empire* (Cambridge, 1996), 1, 22.

[11] E. R. Norman, *Church and Society in England 1770–1970: A Historical Study* (Oxford, 1976), 71, 77; Robert Hole, *Pulpits, Politics and Public Order in England 1760–1832* (Cambridge, 1989), 229, 269; Arthur Burns, '"Standing in the Old Ways": Historical Legitimation of Church Reform in the Church of England, c.1825–65', in R. N. Swanson, ed., *The Church Retrospective*, SCH 33 (Woodbridge, 1997), 407–23, at 407; Arthur Burns, 'The Authority of the Church', in Peter Mandler, ed., *Liberty and Authority in Victorian Britain* (Oxford, 2006), 179–202, at 186; M. J. D. Roberts, *Making English Morals: Voluntary Association and Moral Reform in England, 1787–1886* (Cambridge, 2008), 144.

[12] J. P. Parry and Stephen Taylor, 'Introduction: Parliament and the Church of England from the Reformation to the Twentieth Century', in eidem, eds, *Parliament and the Church, 1529–1960* (Edinburgh, 2000), 1–13, at 7.

thesis has been William Gibson. In 2001, Gibson wrote of Clark's iteration of the 'constitutional revolution' thesis that 'ironically for a historian arguing frequently for the continuity of English history, it overstates the effect of the repeal of the Test and Corporation Acts and of Catholic emancipation'. In Gibson's view, the impact of 1828–9 was 'that of a change in the relationship [between church and state] rather than a cessation of it', as '[t]he monarchy, the coronation oath, the exclusion of Catholics from the succession, Church patronage, and the use of Anglicanism as an instrument of the State ensured that the Church of England remained the State religion after 1829.'[13]

Despite Gibson's arguments, the 'constitutional revolution' thesis has remained resilient. Also in 2001, Stewart J. Brown wrote of the legislation of 1828–32: '[t]hese changes had come so suddenly that the description of a "constitutional revolution" is an appropriate one.' Accordingly, 'the balance of power in the parliamentary State seemed to be shifting away from supporters of the established Churches to religious Dissenters'.[14] The enduring dominance of the 'constitutional revolution' thesis is demonstrated by its repeated reiteration in the third volume of the *Oxford History of Anglicanism*, published in 2017. According to editor Rowan Strong, '[t]he constitutional revolution enacted by Parliament in 1828–9 meant Anglicans ceased to be the only enfranchised population in England, Wales, and Ireland, and Parliament was no longer legally solely an Anglican body, though it could still legislate for the Church of England.'[15] Brown writes that 'the "constitutional revolution" of 1828–32 … had largely ended the confessional state in the United Kingdom and weakened the influence and authority of the Established Church of England'.[16] Robert Andrews also endorses the theory, arguing that from 1832 'Parliament, which for centuries

[13] William Gibson, *The Church of England 1688–1832: Unity and Accord* (London, 2001), 18; see also Penelope Corfield's critique of Clark's related notion of England as a 'confessional state': 'Georgian England: One State, Many Faiths', *History Today* 45 (1995), 14–21.

[14] Stewart J. Brown, *The National Churches of England, Ireland, and Scotland 1801–46* (Oxford, 2001), 168; cf. Richard W. Davis, *A Political History of the House of Lords, 1811–1846* (Stanford, CA, 2008), 141.

[15] Rowan Strong, 'Introduction', to idem, ed., *OHA*, 3: *Partisan Anglicanism and its Global Expansion 1829–c.1914* (Oxford, 2017), 1–23, at 1; see also idem, 'Anglicanism and the State in the Nineteenth Century', ibid. 92–115, at 93–4, 105, 111.

[16] Stewart J. Brown, 'Anglicanism in the British Empire, 1829–1910', ibid. 45–68, at 46.

had been a sort of Anglican "lay synod", was now officially a mixed body in terms of religious confessions.'[17]

In its various permutations, the 'constitutional revolution' thesis relies on three basic assumptions: firstly, that prior to 1828 the British parliament was in essence an exclusively Anglican body; secondly, that the legislation of 1828–32 removed the legal underpinnings of the Church of England's political dominance; and, thirdly, that the effect of these laws was to diminish the church's political role. Yet all three of these assumptions are questionable. The purpose of this article is twofold: to re-evaluate the assumptions upon which the 'constitutional revolution' thesis is grounded, and to discuss how contemporary perceptions that a 'revolution' had occurred, such as Wellington's, should be contextualized. Additionally, the article will consider whether the measures of 1828–32 may be better understood as an exercise in 'constitutional adjustment'. While it primarily concerns the legislative evidence bearing upon the 'constitutional revolution' thesis, this article also involves a wider consideration of the political and religious ramifications of the legislation of those years.

The first assumption – that prior to 1828 parliament was essentially an exclusively Anglican body – derives from Froude's interpretation of Richard Hooker's *Laws of Ecclesiastical Polity*. Arguing from Hooker that the realm and church were coterminous, Froude asserted that from the Reformation the English (and later British) parliament had been akin to a 'lay synod', whereby the Church of England had been governed by its members.[18] However, the notion of a parliamentary 'lay synod' was absent from constitutional thought before the 1830s. The only deliberative bodies resembling Anglican synods in England were the convocations of Canterbury and York, which were exclusively clerical and between 1718 and 1852 seldom transacted anything beyond the composition of loyal addresses to the monarch.[19]

---

[17] Robert M. Andrews, 'High Church Anglicanism in the Nineteenth Century', ibid. 141–64, at 145–6, and see also 153, 158, 162; cf. Stewart J. Brown, *Providence and Empire: Religion, Politics and Society in the United Kingdom 1815–1914* (Harlow, 2008), 178; Frances Knight, *The Church in the Nineteenth Century*, I. B. Tauris History of the Christian Church (London, 2008), 14–15.

[18] Froude, *Remains*, 1: 196–207.

[19] Gerald Bray, ed., *Records of Convocation*, 20 vols, CERS (Woodbridge, 2006), vols 11–12, 15.

Indeed, the assertion that the post-Restoration English parliament was, in any meaningful sense, an Anglican 'lay synod' would have represented a blatant denial of reality.[20] From 1660 to 1678, Catholics sat in parliament, and Dissenters (with the exception of Quakers) were never legally barred from being members of parliament.[21] The restrictions that did emerge were of an uneven and ambiguous character. By the Corporation Act of 1661, members of English and Welsh corporations had to receive Anglican communion, but this requirement was not extended to legislators.[22] The Test Act of 1673 stipulated that all holders of civil and military offices in England and Wales had to take oaths of supremacy and allegiance, declare that they did not believe in transubstantiation and receive Anglican communion.[23] By the Test Act of 1678, all peers and members of the House of Commons had to declare that they did not believe in transubstantiation or certain other Roman Catholic doctrines.[24] The 'Glorious Revolution' of 1688 led to the Toleration Act of 1689, allowing freedom of worship to Dissenters in England and Wales on certain conditions, but did not alter the test legislation passed during the reign of Charles II.[25] Occasional conformity, whereby Dissenters communicated in Anglican churches to qualify for civil office but continued to frequent their own places of worship, became widespread, but was banned by an act of the British parliament in 1711.[26] However, this act was repealed in 1719 and, sporadically from 1726 and annually from 1757, indemnity acts

---

[20] Froude was aware of his theory's shortcomings and, according to Peter Nockles, his 'appeal to Hooker had been an essentially rhetorical, tactical device to disarm the "Zs" [non-Tractarian high churchmen]': Nockles, *Oxford Movement*, 80. He even admitted to Newman that the 'facts' employed in support of his case were 'less satisfactory than I could wish – I find that the Test and Corporation Acts applied only indirectly to Members of Parliament': *The Letters and Diaries of John Henry Newman*, 4: *The Oxford Movement, July 1833 to December 1834*, ed. Ian T. Ker and Thomas Gornall (Oxford, 1980), 38, Richard Hurrell Froude to John Henry Newman, [August 1833].

[21] Basil Duke Henning, ed., *The History of Parliament: The House of Commons 1660–1690*, 3 vols (London, 1983), 1: 12. Quakers were effectively excluded from parliament because of the requirement for MPs to take an oath of office, which was repealed in 1833: 3 & 4 Will. IV c.49.

[22] 13 Cha. II c.1.

[23] 25 Cha. II c.2.

[24] 30 Cha. II c.1.

[25] 1 Will. & Mary c.18; James E. Bradley, *Religion, Revolution, and English Radicalism: Nonconformity in Eighteenth-century Politics and Society* (Cambridge, 1990), 51–2.

[26] 10 Anne c.6; Bradley, *Religion, Revolution, and English Radicalism*, 52–3.

were passed, effectively abrogating the requirements of the 1661 and 1673 Test Acts as far as English and Welsh Dissenters were concerned.[27]

Although Anglicans predominated in parliament throughout the long eighteenth century, the Corporation Act and the Test Acts never made it an exclusively Anglican 'lay synod'. This was especially so after the Acts of Union between England and Scotland (1706–7), whereby Scottish MPs and representative peers joined their English and Welsh counterparts in Westminster to legislate for a bi-confessional United Kingdom; Scottish MPs and representative peers were subject to the Test Act of 1678 but were exempted from the Test Act of 1673, which contravened the presbyterian standard of the Church of Scotland that had supplanted episcopalianism in Scotland in 1689–90.[28] However, Scottish presbyterians were not the only non-Anglicans sitting in parliament. At least thirty-nine English and Welsh Dissenters sat in the House of Commons between 1690 and 1715; at least twenty-eight between 1715 and 1754; and at least nineteen between 1754 and 1790.[29] In total, from 1790 to 1820, just under sixty MPs were not members of the established churches of England, Scotland or Ireland.[30]

Of course, there remained a ban on Catholic parliamentarians, perpetuated by the Acts of Union with Ireland (1800) whereby Irish peers and MPs were made subject to the Test Act of 1678.[31] However, even this restriction had come under significant pressure in the later eighteenth century. Between 1754 and 1790, at least

[27] 5 Geo. I c.4; K. R. M. Short, 'The English Indemnity Acts 1726–1867', *ChH* 42 (1973), 366–76; Bradley, *Religion, Revolution and English Radicalism*, 69–84. Also crucial to the equation was the 'Act for Quieting and Establishing Corporations' (1719), which gave members of corporations who held office for six months immunity from prosecution under the Corporation Act: 5 Geo. 1 c.6. Additionally, from 1722 to 1851, Dissenting churches received Treasury funding: K. R. M. Short, 'The English Regium Donum', *EHR* 84 (1969), 59–78.
[28] 6 Anne c.11; 1707 c.7.
[29] D. W. Hayton, E. Cruickshanks and S. Handley, eds, *The History of Parliament: The House of Commons 1690–1715*, 5 vols (Woodbridge, 2002), 1: 311; Romney Sedgwick, ed., *The History of Parliament: The House of Commons 1715–1754*, 2 vols (London, 1970), 1: 139; L. B. Namier and J. Brooke, eds, *The History of Parliament: The House of Commons 1754–1790*, 3 vols (London, 1964, repr. 1985), 1: 115.
[30] R. G. Thorne, ed., *The History of Parliament: The House of Commons 1790–1820*, 5 vols (London, 1986), 1: 294.
[31] 39 & 40 Geo. III c.67; 40 Geo. III c.38. By an act of the Irish parliament that was passed in 1780, Dissenters, although not Catholics, could hold civil office in Ireland: 20 Geo. III c.6.

eight MPs were former Catholics who had renounced their faith in order to sit in parliament.[32] The converts with the highest profile were Sir Thomas Gascoigne and Charles Howard, earl of Surrey, who in 1780 were received into the Church of England by the archbishop of Canterbury at Lambeth Palace.[33] Despite having renounced their former confession, both promoted Catholic interests in parliament, and, in the view of many contemporaries, were not sincere converts. According to Nathaniel Wraxall, the earl of Surrey was known to assert when intoxicated 'that three as good Catholics sate in Lord North's last Parliament as ever existed, namely, Lord Nugent, Sir Thomas Gascoyne, and himself'.[34] As Alexander Lock writes, 'there was seemingly some truth in Surrey's statement'.[35] Tellingly, Lord Nugent, an Irish Catholic who had become Anglican to represent St Mawes and Bristol, reverted to his Catholicism after he left the House of Commons with an Irish peerage.[36] In any case, eighteenth-century parliamentarians were not above concealing their religious allegiance for the sake of political expedience. Frederick North, earl of Guilford, sat as both an MP for Banbury and a peer after his secret conversion to the Greek Orthodox Church while visiting Corfu in 1791. After a parliamentary career of thirty-five years, an Orthodox priest was summoned to his deathbed in 1827.[37]

Having established that parliament was far from exclusively Anglican prior to 1828, it is possible to evaluate the true nature of the reforming legislation enacted from 1828 to 1832. By the Sacramental Test Act of 1828, the Corporation Act of 1661 and the Test Act of 1673 were repealed, removing the requirement for members of corporations and officeholders in England and Wales to take Anglican communion.[38] Some of the strongest opposition to the sacramental test had come from the Anglican clergy, who

---

[32] Alexander Lock, *Catholicism, Identity and Politics in the Age of Enlightenment: The Life and Career of Sir Thomas Gascoigne, 1745–1810* (Woodbridge, 2016), 97.

[33] Ibid. 98–101.

[34] Nathaniel Wraxall, *Posthumous Memoirs of his own Time*, 3 vols (London, 1836), 1: 32.

[35] Lock, *Thomas Gascoigne*, 109.

[36] Ibid.; Namier and Brooke, *House of Commons 1754–1790*, 3: 219, 222.

[37] Kallistos Ware, 'The Fifth Earl of Guilford and his Secret Conversion to the Orthodox Church', in Peter M. Doll, ed., *Anglicanism and Orthodoxy 300 Years after the 'Greek College' in Oxford* (Oxford, 2006), 290–326.

[38] 9 Geo. IV c.17.

viewed it as a profanation of the sacrament.[39] Hence when home secretary Robert Peel proposed replacing sacramental tests with a positive declaration that an officeholder would not harm Anglican interests, the bishops were receptive. Peel's closest confidante on the episcopal bench was his former college tutor, Charles Lloyd, bishop of Oxford, who was of the opinion that 'the best thing for the Church of England would be that it should pass, if that could be managed without a positive surrender of principle on the part of the Bishops'.[40] William Van Mildert, bishop of Durham, told Lloyd that he was not 'anxious to retain the Sacramental Test, if any other, equally efficacious, seemly & respectful, as indicating an acknowledgement of the ascendancy of the Church, can be devised'.[41] Peel ascertained the views of seven prelates, before meeting with six at Lambeth Palace, where, as he reported to Lloyd, '[w]e settled a declaration'.[42]

In its final form, the new declaration required officeholders in England and Wales to assert that they would

> ... never exercise any Power, Authority, or Influence ... to injure or weaken the Protestant Church as it is by Law established in *England*, or to disturb the said Church, or the Bishops and Clergy of the said Church, in the Possession of any Rights or Privileges to which such Church, or the said Bishops and Clergy, are or may be by Law entitled.[43]

Peel considered this a more effective safeguard for Anglican interests than the defunct sacramental test:

> The difference between a declaration and a Test like the present is certainly enormous, if you will bona fide act upon your Test, but 85 years' relaxation of it, and the notorious inability to enforce the Test without absolute confusion, change the nature of the difference, and in my opinion, all in favour of the declaration.[44]

---

[39] London, BL, Add. MS 40343, fol. 189ᵛ, Charles Lloyd to Robert Peel, 2 March 1828; fol. 247ᵛ, Lloyd to Peel, 23 March 1828.
[40] Ibid., fol. 190ᵛ, Lloyd to Peel, 2 March 1828.
[41] Ibid., fol. 203ʳ, William Van Mildert to Lloyd, 3 March 1828.
[42] Ibid., fol. 205, Peel to Lloyd, 4 March 1828; fol. 212ʳ, Peel to Lloyd, 15 March 1828.
[43] 9 Geo. IV c.17.
[44] BL, Add. MS 40343, fol. 252, Peel to Lloyd, 25 March 1828.

The resulting act was, according to Bishop Blomfield of London, 'strictly and literally a measure of the Bishops'.[45] The Sacramental Test Act had no practical effect on dissenting participation either in parliament or in corporations (although participation in the latter was already protected by indemnity acts). Furthermore, it did not bring to an end the use of indemnity acts, which continued to be passed by parliament annually until 1867, although these now suspended the requirement to make the new declaration as opposed to the previous sacramental test.[46] The only significant opposition to the repeal of the Corporation and Test Acts came from Lord Eldon, who believed that 'the Church of England, combined with the state, formed together the constitution of Great Britain, and that the Test and Corporation acts were necessary to the preservation of that Constitution'.[47] Contrary to Richard Davis's assertion, Eldon's view was not one with which '[m]ost ... would have agreed'.[48] As G. I. T. Machin showed in 1979, extra-parliamentary opposition to the repeal of the Corporation and Test Acts was confined to a few petitions, newspaper items and pamphlets, and never gained traction.[49]

The 1828 act was therefore far from revolutionary; if anything, it gave a clearer recognition of the church's constitutional dominance than had existed since the introduction of regular indemnity acts. The Roman Catholic Relief Act of 1829, carried by Wellington and Peel, may be viewed in a similar light. Popular and episcopal opposition and the turbulent political situation in Ireland following the County Clare by-election made the measure much more controversial than the Sacramental Test Act, but the underlying principle of the two acts was very similar.[50] The Roman Catholic Relief Act

---

[45] A. Blomfield, ed., *A Memoir of Charles James Blomfield, D.D., Bishop of London, with Selections from his Correspondence*, 2 vols (London, 1863), 1: 138, Charles Blomfield to James Henry Monk, 22 April 1828. On the bishops' role in securing the act and declaration, see R. A. Gaunt, 'Peel's other Repeal: The Test and Corporation Acts, 1828', *PH* 33 (2014), 243–62, at 253–7.

[46] Short, 'English Indemnity Acts', 376.

[47] HL Deb (2nd series), 21 April 1828 (vol. 18, col. 1576).

[48] Davis, *House of Lords*, 141.

[49] G. I. T. Machin, 'Resistance to Repeal of the Test and Corporation Acts', *HistJ* 22 (1979), 115–39, at 126–32.

[50] On the events which led to the passage of Catholic emancipation, see G. I. T. Machin, *The Catholic Question in English Politics, 1820 to 1830* (Oxford, 1964); Wendy Hinde, *Catholic Emancipation: A Shake to Men's Minds* (Oxford, 1992).

repealed the Test Act of 1678, and stipulated that Catholics entering parliament should take oaths of allegiance and declare that they did 'not believe that the Pope of *Rome*, or any other Foreign Prince, Prelate, Person, State or Potentate, hath or ought to have any Temporal or Civil Jurisdiction, Power, Superiority or Pre-eminence, directly or indirectly, within this Realm'. They were also to 'disclaim, disavow, and solemnly abjure any Intention to subvert the present Church Establishment as settled by Law within this Realm'. Additionally, the act forbade Catholics from holding such high offices as lord chancellor and specified provisions for the 'gradual Suppression and final Prohibition' of the Jesuit order in the United Kingdom.[51] Simultaneously, Irish forty-shilling freeholders, who constituted the majority of the Catholic electorate, were disenfranchised, a provision which led to significant unrest in Ireland.[52]

While to Whigs like Henry Bathurst, bishop of Norwich, the Roman Catholic Relief Act represented a 'triumph of civil and religious liberty', the papacy did not view it in the same light.[53] In a discussion with Peter Baines, the Catholic vicar apostolic of the Western District of England, concerning the declaration imposed by the act, Pope Pius VIII indicated that he could not 'approve a formula so loosely and incautiously worded, containing, moreover, insinuations grossly injurious to the Catholic religion, and to the Holy See in particular', although he would not condemn it either.[54] Yet, with the approval of the vicars apostolic, a small number of Catholics took the oath.[55]

The final element in the supposed 'constitutional revolution' of 1828–32 did not directly concern the religious allegiance of parliamentarians. By the Reform Act of 1832, which was carried under Earl Grey's Whig government, uniform property qualifications for voting were introduced, new county and borough seats were created

[51] 10 Geo. IV c.7.
[52] Ibid., c.8. On this disenfranchisement, see David A. Bateman, *Disenfranchising Democracy: Constructing the Electorate in the United States, the United Kingdom, and France* (Cambridge, 2018), 246–9.
[53] T. Thistlethwayte, *Memoirs and Correspondence of Dr H. Bathurst, Lord Bishop of Norwich* (London, 1853), 352, Henry Bathurst to Thomas William Coke, 16 April 1829.
[54] HL Deb (3rd series), 8 May 1838 (vol. 42, cols 967–8); Owen Chadwick, *The Victorian Church, Part I: 1829–1859*, 3rd edn (London, 1971), 22.
[55] Chadwick, *Victorian Church*, 22–3; John A. Stack, 'Catholic Members of Parliament who represented British Constituencies, 1829–1885: A Prosopographical Analysis', *RH* 24 (1999), 335–63, at 348.

and other seats, mostly the notorious 'rotten boroughs', were abolished.[56] The Church of England at large did not oppose the principle of parliamentary reform, which was supported by a sizeable proportion of Tory politicians and newspapers with the express intention of ensuring that Anglican opinion could not be disregarded, as they perceived it to have been with the passage of Catholic emancipation in 1829.[57] One of the earliest post-1829 schemes for wholesale parliamentary reform, that proposed by the marquis of Blandford in February 1830, included the readmission of Anglican clergymen to the House of Commons, from which they had been barred since 1801.[58] When the second Reform Bill came before the Lords in November 1831, the bishops were divided as to the details of the measure, but, as Lord Ellenborough observed, 'all for Reform'.[59] Indeed, Henry Phillpotts, bishop of Exeter, wished that 'some specific measure were started' on their part.[60] However, the bishops' twenty-one votes against the second Reform Bill helped to block its passage, allowing radicals to lambast them as the inveterate enemies of all reform.[61] This criticism was belied by the willingness of twelve bishops to vote on pragmatic grounds for the third Reform Bill, which became the Reform Act of 1832.[62]

Was the effect of such measures fatally to undermine the political position of the Church of England? Many Anglican clergymen certainly believed so. Yet their despair at the laws of 1828–32 was not so much conditioned by the legislation itself as by an unfounded

[56] 2 & 3 Will. IV c.45. On the Reform Act, see M. G. Brock, *The Great Reform Act* (London, 1973); Jonathan Parry, *The Rise and Fall of Liberal Government in Victorian Britain* (New Haven, CT, 1993), 72–89.
[57] James J. Sack, *From Jacobite to Conservative: Reaction and Orthodoxy in Britain, c.1760–1832* (Cambridge, 1993), 152–5; Clark, *English Society*, 536–7.
[58] HC Deb (2nd series), 18 February 1830 (vol. 22, cols 692–3).
[59] Arthur Aspinall, ed., *Three Early Nineteenth Century Diaries* (London, 1952), 144, diary of Lord Ellenborough, 8 October 1831.
[60] G. C. B. Davies, *Henry Phillpotts, Bishop of Exeter, 1778–1869* (London, 1954), 113, Henry Phillpotts to Ralph Barnes, 8 October 1831. Phillpotts did not, however, offer concrete proposals.
[61] Ibid. 109–10, 114, 139; Chadwick, *Victorian Church*, 26–32; Elizabeth Varley, *The Last of the Prince Bishops: William Van Mildert and the High Church Movement of the Early Nineteenth Century* (Cambridge, 1992), 145–8; J. R. Garrard, *Archbishop Howley, 1828–1848* (Farnham, 2015), 47–8.
[62] HL Deb (3rd series), 13 April 1832 (vol. 12, cols 455–6). On the bishops' attitudes to the Reform Bills, see Davies, *Phillpotts*, 102–4, 109–14, 130–40; Norman, *Church and Society*, 83–9; Varley, *Van Mildert*, 145–7; Garrard, *Howley*, 44–8.

fear that disestablishment or worse was imminent. The measures were perceived as indirectly destructive of the Church of England's formularies and status as a 'national' church. As Thomas Rennell, dean of Winchester, put it in 1829, 'What was begun in the repeal *of the test & Corporation act* [*sic*] continued in the Popish Emancipation, will be consummated in the disfigurement & *exinanition* of our Liturgy & Articles.'[63] George Huntingford, bishop of Hereford, commented: 'How is it possible for me not to dread the arrival of that period, when the Papist Legislators shall feel their strength & degrade the Protestant Church of Ireland? … I am convinced degradation of our own Church will soon follow the spoliation and decadence of the Irish Ecclesiastical Establishment.'[64] In 1832, Henry Handley Norris, perpetual curate of Hackney, wrote that he saw 'an undercurrent of conspiracy ready to rise and sweep all before it, as soon as that which is now upon the surface has done its destruction'.[65] As Robert Saunders has noted, some Anglican preachers responded to the Reform crisis by asserting divine authority over human affairs.[66]

Other Church of England clergy went even further than this in their apprehensions concerning the results of Catholic emancipation in particular. George Lowther, curate of Longford in Derbyshire, placed a letter in a bottle beneath a new pulpit in 1826, prophesying:

> I feel strongly assured that when these papers see the light it will be under the hierarchy of the Roman Catholic Church which will doubtless gain the ascendancy in proportion as ignorance prevails: and I cannot help predicting the downfall of the English nation, as I fancy I behold in it all the signs of a declining state.[67]

John Skinner, rector of Camerton in Somerset, wrote in his journal in 1828:

> Alas! how can our senators know what will be the result of their absurd concessions! Should my papers survive, it will be manifest what was the

---

[63] Oxford, Bodl., MS. Eng. lett. c.789, fol. 203ᵛ, Thomas Rennell to Henry Handley Norris, 15 December 1829.
[64] Bodl., MS. Eng. lett. c.136, fol. 107ʳ, George Isaac Huntingford to Thomas Burgess, 6 May 1829.
[65] London, LPL, MS 2185, fol. 95, Norris to William Howley, 25 October 1832.
[66] Robert Saunders, 'God and the Great Reform Act: Preaching Against Reform, 1831–32', *JBS* 53 (2014), 378–99, at 390–6.
[67] Quoted in Michael Austin, *'A Time of Unhappy Commotion': The Church of England and the People in Central Nottinghamshire 1820–1870* (Chesterfield, 2010), 12.

state of society in the time I wrote, and the determination of one person at least among the millions of Britain to oppose the torrent of iniquity which in all probability will bear him away with it.[68]

Simultaneously, the premillenarian Anglican Henry Drummond, soon to secede and assist in forming what would become the Catholic Apostolic Church, saw the events of 1828–9 as portending the apocalypse.[69]

By contrast, Bishop Bathurst wrote of the church in 1832 that he did 'not think it in any danger at present'.[70] In the short term, this lack of alarm was vindicated. The Dissenting electorate may have increased as a result of the Reform Act, but the number of English Dissenting MPs did not, standing at eight in 1833.[71] The number of English Nonconformists in the Commons increased during the succeeding decades, but its nineteenth-century peak in 1892 was only 117 in a house of 670.[72] Four English Catholic MPs entered the House of Commons in 1830, but by 1837 there were only two. The number rose to six in the 1840s, but from 1852 to 1885 there were never more than three English Catholic MPs, with none sitting between 1874 and 1880.[73] Only two Catholics are known to have served as cabinet ministers between 1829 and 1895, while Queen Victoria displayed a decided reluctance to create any Catholic peers.[74] Among the 105 Irish seats in the Commons, Protestant members predominated until the

[68] John Skinner, *Journal of a Somerset Rector, 1803–1834*, ed. Howard Coombs and Peter Coombs (Bath, 1971), 354.

[69] Boyd Hilton, *A Mad, Bad, and Dangerous People? England 1783–1846* (Oxford, 2006), 405.

[70] Norwich, Norfolk RO, DCN 154/2/117, Henry Bathurst to James Bathurst, 18 June 1832. This was a modification of Bathurst's opinion, expressed the previous year, that '[w]e are told incessantly by the High Church party, that our Ecclesiastical Establishment is in danger, and so it certainly is; but this danger arises from a want of temper and moderation in too many of the clergy, and also from their selfish opposition to a Commutation of Tithes': Bathurst to Coke, 10 September 1831, in Thistlethwayte, *Memoirs*, 384.

[71] S. F. Woolley, 'The Personnel of the Parliament of 1833', *EHR* 53 (1938), 240–62, at 244; Roger Anstey, 'Parliamentary Reform, Methodism and Anti-Slavery Politics, 1829–1833', *Slavery and Abolition* 2 (1981), 209–26, at 220–2.

[72] Simon Skinner, 'Religion', in David Craig and James Thompson, eds, *Languages of Politics in Nineteenth-Century Britain* (Basingstoke, 2013), 93–117, at 110.

[73] Stack, 'Catholic Members of Parliament', 348.

[74] Dennis Grube, *At the Margins of Victorian Britain: Politics, Immorality and Britishness in the Nineteenth Century* (London, 2013), 82–3.

1880s.[75] No Catholic MPs were elected in Scotland until 1885.[76] Hence after 1832 the vast majority of legislators remained Protestant, with Anglicans preponderant.

Furthermore, Whig attempts to dismantle aspects of Anglican hegemony foundered in parliament during the remainder of the 1830s. The Whigs managed to reduce the number of Irish dioceses, increase Dissenting participation in local government through the Municipal Corporations Act (1835), and secure legal recognition of marriages in Dissenting places of worship and commutation of tithe payments.[77] Nevertheless, parliamentary opposition ensured that they failed in attempts to admit Dissenters to full membership of the universities of Oxford and Cambridge, to abolish church rates and to introduce a nondenominational system of state education.[78] During Peel's brief premiership of 1834–5, a moderate and consensual, though not uncontroversial, mode of church reform was inaugurated in the form of the Ecclesiastical Commission.[79] Meanwhile, the Anglican clergy were instrumental in the organization and growth of Peel's Conservative party at a local level, and a major factor in the party's increasingly successful electoral performance.[80] In their election campaigning rhetoric, Conservative candidates presented themselves as defenders of 'Church, Constitution and King', 'your Church and Constitution', the 'Protestant Constitution' and 'our Glorious Constitution in Church and State'.[81] The

---

[75] Kimberly Cowell-Meyers, *Religion and Politics in the Nineteenth Century: The Party Faithful in Ireland and Germany* (Westport, CT, 2002), 80.

[76] Tom Gallagher, *Glasgow, the Uneasy Peace: Religious Tension in Modern Scotland, 1819–1914* (Manchester, 1987), 23.

[77] 3 & 4 Will. IV c.37; 5 & 6 Will. IV c.76; 6 & 7 Will. IV c.71; 6 & 7 Will. IV c.185; 1 & 2 Vict. c.109.

[78] HL Deb (3rd Series), 1 August 1834 (vol. 25, col. 886); J. P. Ellens, 'Lord John Russell and the Church Rate Conflict: The Struggle for a Broad Church, 1834–1868', *JBS* 26 (1987), 232–57, at 238–42; Ian D. C. Newbould, 'The Whigs, the Church, and Education, 1839', *JBS* 26 (1987), 332–46. Before the 1850s, subscription to the Thirty-Nine Articles of the Church of England was required for matriculation and graduation at the University of Oxford; the University of Cambridge did not require subscription for matriculation, but like Oxford enforced it for graduation: Gibson, *Unity and Accord*, 137–8.

[79] Brose, *Church and Parliament*, 120–56; Best, *Temporal Pillars*, 296–347.

[80] Philip Salmon, *Electoral Reform at Work: Local Politics and National Parties 1832–1841* (Woodbridge, 2002), 69–72, 99–101.

[81] See, for example, Cambridge, Cambridgeshire Archives, R89/82/90, 'John Bull', 'Summons to Conservatives', 5 January 1835; *Essex Standard*, 16 January 1835, 2;

non-Tractarian, Conservative-leaning majority of Anglicans evidently believed that there was still an Anglican constitution to defend.

Although it lies beyond the scope of this article to examine events beyond the 1830s in detail, the genuine 'constitutional revolution', if such there was, came in the period from 1854 to 1871. These years saw the abolition of the declarations imposed on Catholics and Dissenters in 1828–9, the excision from the Prayer Book of three services (those which commemorated Charles I's execution, the Restoration and the Gunpowder Plot as well as William III's arrival in England), the abolition of compulsory church rates, the disestablishment of the Church of Ireland and the abolition of religious tests for membership of the universities of Oxford, Cambridge and Durham.[82] Viewed in the light of such transformative measures, the effect of the legislation of 1828–32 on the Church of England appears comparatively insignificant.

What really occurred between 1828 and 1832 was not a 'revolution' but an 'adjustment' of the British constitution, at least so far as the Church of England was concerned. '[S]atisfactory & safe adjustment' was what Peel professed to advocate in 1829, and this, in large measure, was what he, Wellington and Grey achieved.[83] Before 1828, parliament was a multi-confessional body dominated by Anglicans, and it would remain so after 1832. The Sacramental Test Act and the Roman Catholic Relief Act, far from depriving the Church of England of significant privileges, perpetuated Anglican primacy through the declarations they prescribed. Moreover, the Reform Act did not lead, as Wellington had simplistically supposed, to government by Dissenting shopkeepers, even if more Dissenters were enfranchised.[84] Additionally, Anglican apprehensions that reforming

---

Warwick, Warwickshire RO, DR362/133, Evelyn Shirley, 'To the Electors of the Southern Division of the County of Warwick', 17 June 1836; Bolton, Bolton Archives, ZZ/130/3/12, Samuel Scowcroft, 'To the Worthy Electors of the Borough of Bolton', 19 July 1837.

[82] 17 & 18 Vict. c.81; 19 & 20 Vict. c.88; 21 & 22 Vict. c.48; 29 & 30 Vict. c.22; *London Gazette*, 18 January 1859, 161; 31 & 32 Vict. c.109; 32 & 33 Vict. c.42; 34 & 35 Vict. c.26.

[83] BL, Add. MS 40343, fol. 330, Peel to Lloyd, 15 January 1829; cf. Add. MS 40415, fol. 137ᵛ, Peel to Van Mildert, 23 February 1835.

[84] Machin calls Wellington's statement 'wildly exaggerated', but there is reason to think that the statement was not so much an exaggeration as a misrepresentation of the Reform Act's effects: *Politics and the Churches*, 26.

legislation would lead inexorably to disestablishment were quickly demonstrated to be groundless. Hence the framework of 'constitutional adjustment' latent in certain historians' writings should be employed in contradistinction to the notion of a 'constitutional revolution', rather than complementing it. In the light of this reinterpretation, much that has been taken for granted about the relationship between church and state in nineteenth-century England is called into question. For if there was no 'constitutional revolution' in 1828–32, we must consider the possibility that Anglican sociopolitical dominance was both more resilient and more adaptable than historians have previously imagined.

The Decline of the Clerical Magistracy in the Nineteenth-Century English Midlands

John W. B. Tomlinson*
St John's College, Nottingham

A significant proportion of Church of England clergy in the early nineteenth century took up the role of magistrate to help enforce the law in local communities, partly in consequence of the growth of clerical wealth and status which had begun in the previous century. This legal role was perceived by some as contradictory to clerical pastoral duties, and as such detrimental to the church. Some would view it as contributing to a decline of the Church of England, which was seen as too much associated with the established powers in an era of social change. After the peak of the 1830s, the number of clerical magistrates began to fall dramatically, marking the emergence of a more exclusively religious clerical profession uneasy with the antagonisms associated with local law enforcement. This study, focusing on the diverse county of Staffordshire, presents the case that the decline of the clerical magistracy is an early indicator of the withdrawal of the clergy from involvement in secular concerns, and as such provides important evidence for the growth of secularization in British society.

Justices of the Peace, or magistrates as they are commonly known, have been an important part of the English legal system for over six hundred and fifty years. Exclusively a male preserve until the early twentieth century, the magistracy was made up of men of wealth and influence appointed by the Lord Lieutenant of each county in England to enforce the law at the local level. They dealt with a wide range of offences, referring only the most serious to the higher courts, and in addition oversaw many of the functions of local government.[1] For about a century, from the mid-eighteenth century to the mid-nineteenth, the parish clergy of the Church of England became a dominant group within the magistracy, and their engagement in this role created a significant level of debate and controversy within and outside the church. The sharp decline in the numbers of

---

* E-mail: j.tomlinson@stjohns-nottm.ac.uk.

[1] For details of the changing functions of magistrates, see David Taylor, *Crime, Policing and Punishment in England, 1750–1914* (London, 1998), 7–26.

Studies in Church History 56 (2020), 419–433   © Ecclesiastical History Society 2020
doi: 10.1017/stc.2019.23

clerical magistrates at the end of this period has been attributed to several factors, including a growing moral conscience uneasy with the combined roles of pastor and magistrate. However, there is evidence to suggest that the role of the clerical magistrate gave some clergy direct insight into the lives of people beyond their usual congregation, and thus a wider interaction with local society, which was lost when clergy began to concentrate more on ecclesial duties. This study, which focuses on the county of Staffordshire, suggests that the decline of the clerical magistracy was the result of a process of secularization within English society, as the clergy (and thus the church) withdrew from this formal and statutory involvement in local affairs.[2] It provides an early indication of the reduction of the influence of the church in the secular sphere, particularly in urban and industrialized areas at first, but spreading to the rural areas by the end of the period. Staffordshire included a wide spectrum of natural and human environments: heavily industrialized and urban areas, upland moors and rich lowland pastures. It united features from the north and south of England, and as such may be taken as representative for the purpose of this study.

In the mid-eighteenth century, the landed property requirement for Justices of the Peace was lowered to an annual income of £100, which enabled many clergy who held benefices, and therefore freeholds, to become magistrates. In 1760 around 11 per cent of magistrates were clergy, but in the decades that followed, increased wealth from agricultural improvement, reform of the tithe system and widespread parliamentary enclosure raised the income and social status of many beneficed clergy, making them, in the view of those who made the appointments, more suitable as magistrates.[3] About the same time the gentry, the traditional holders of this role, were becoming less inclined to serve as magistrates as they became more detached from the communities associated with their landed estates.[4] There are

[2] Source material to support this forms part of my doctoral research: John W. B. Tomlinson, 'From Parson to Professional: The Changing Ministry of the Anglican Clergy in Staffordshire, 1830–1960' (PhD thesis, University of Birmingham, 2008).
[3] Parliamentary enclosure was a key factor in the rise of the income of landowners: Gordon E. Mingay, *Parliamentary Enclosure in England: An Introduction to its Causes, Incidence, and Impact, 1750–1850* (London, 1997).
[4] For evidence of less involvement in local communities and a more cosmopolitan lifestyle based in London, see James M. Rosenheim, *The Emergence of a Ruling Order: English Landed Society, 1650–1750* (London, 1997).

significant regional differences in these factors, but there was a general trend for beneficed clergy to rise in wealth and social standing until the mid-nineteenth century which is matched by an increase in the size of the clerical magistracy. In England and Wales, the proportion of magistrates who were clergy rose steadily to a peak of over 25 per cent in the 1830s, followed by a sharp decline to around 6 per cent in the 1870s, only two generations or so of clergy later.[5] For Staffordshire, the figures show a similar decline after the 1830s, albeit less precipitous and from a higher peak: 35 per cent in the 1830s, 23 per cent in the 1860s, 12 per cent in the 1890s and 6 per cent in the 1920s.[6] Other county studies show some variation from the national pattern of decline, and the key factors have been identified as the urban or rural character of local communities, the diminishing wealth and social status of clergy, and the presence of other suitable groups to take up the role.[7]

In considering clergy as magistrates, it is important to distinguish between the different types of parish clergy. Those who were freeholders of the wealthier parishes and had landed family connections were much more likely to be appointed as magistrates than clergy serving in poorer parishes or as non-beneficed perpetual curates. A correlation has been found between the number of clerical magistrates in a county and the extent of land that had been granted to clergy in lieu of tithe.[8] In Staffordshire, a clergyman who was a member of one

---

[5] National figures quoted here and later can be found in Carl H. E. Zangrel, 'The Social Composition of the County Magistracy in England and Wales, 1831–1887', *JBS* 11 (1971), 113–25; see also Eric J. Evans, 'Some Reasons for the Growth of English Anti-Clericalism *c.*1750–*c.*1830', *P&P* 66 (1975), 84–109 (based in part on doctoral research on parishes in Staffordshire); Robert Lee, *Rural Society and the Anglican Clergy, 1815–1914* (Woodbridge, 2006), 105.

[6] W. White, ed., *History, Gazetteer and Directory of Staffordshire* (London, editions of 1834 and 1851); E. R. Kelly, ed., *The Post Office Directory of Staffordshire* (London, editions of 1872, 1896, 1912 and 1921); Lichfield RO, Archdeacons Returns 1829–32; *Lichfield Annual Directory* (Lichfield, editions of 1860, 1890 and 1920); see also Roger Swift, 'The English Urban Magistracy and the Administration of Justice during the Early Nineteenth Century: Wolverhampton 1815–1860', *MidH* 17 (1992), 75–92.

[7] Roe M. Wallis, 'The Relationship between Magistrates and their Communities in the Age of Crisis: Social Protest *c.*1790–1834' (PhD thesis, University of the West of England 2016), 89; Lee, *Rural Society*, 105, 107. Some idea of the extent of local variations can be gained from William C. Lubenow, 'Social Recruitment and Social Attitudes: The Buckinghamshire Magistrates 1868–1888', *Huntington Library Quarterly* 4 (1977), 247–68.

[8] Wallis, 'Relationship', 91; Evans, 'Some Reasons', 104; Lubenow, 'Social Recruitment', 264.

Tomlinson

of the influential county families could expect to be presented to a significant parish and be put forward as a magistrate, not least because members of his family made such appointments.[9]

Generally, clergy made up a much smaller percentage of the magistracy in urban and industrial areas, and from this low level declined at a similar rate to the national average. In England and Wales in 1841 the clergy made up less than 1 per cent of magistrates in the urban boroughs, and by 1885 this had fallen to 0.2 per cent.[10] However, local variations from the national figures were significant. For instance, in 1832 clerical magistrates in the urban and industrial town of Wolverhampton (then in Staffordshire), made up over 18 per cent of the total, due in part to the notable reluctance of the Lord Lieutenant to accept candidates from other groups, a prejudice which could not be sustained in the following decade.[11] There was a particular need to increase the number of magistrates after the Chartist disturbances but there were insufficient numbers of suitable clergy to take up the role. At a steady pace, first in the industrial towns and later in the rural areas, the clergy were replaced by others as magistrates, largely those described at the time as 'gentlemen' or 'middle class', or more pejoratively as 'men of trade'.[12]

The decline in clerical magistrates was more profound when active engagement is considered. It was not uncommon for magistrates to be appointed but not serve in the courts, treating the role as symbolic of a particular social status, or in later life to retire from the function but retain the title as a mark of respect. Nationally, the clerical magistrates in the 1880s were, after the gentry, the least active in terms of involvement in court cases, suggesting that many had retained the status

[9] An example in Staffordshire would be the Talbot family, earls of Shrewsbury, who through familial connections controlled both the appointment of magistrates and the patronage some of the wealthier parishes in the county.
[10] Zangrel, 'Social Composition', 115.
[11] Marjorie Jones, 'Justices of the Peace in Wolverhampton: The Clerical Magistrates', *West Midlands Studies* 11 (1978), 19–22.
[12] Zangrel, 'Social Composition', 115. The boundaries of this status are as defined in contemporary records, and largely include businessmen and industrialists. However, these figures need to be treated with some caution because in some areas the clergy were also industrialists, as in the north-east of England where some were substantial coal-mine owners: Christopher J. Frank, '"Constitutional Law versus Justices' Justice": English Trade Unions, Lawyers, and Magistracy, 1842–1862' (PhD thesis, York University, Toronto, ON, 2003).

422

without undertaking the duty, particularly as they grew older.[13] This pattern of younger clergy not choosing to take up the role has been confirmed in Staffordshire, where those ordained after the 1830s were less likely to be appointed as magistrates.[14]

A range of reasons for the steep decline from the mid-nineteenth century has been put forward. Much of the focus is on the turning point of the 1830s. In this period of societal unrest, when the clerical magistracy was at its strongest, magistrates stood on the front line of the violent consequences of social change, imposing laws which were newly enacted or interpreted in the face of established, if informal, custom. Clerical magistrates had the unique and precarious position of combining innovation, such as the new financial model for tithes and the improvements in agriculture with tradition, as both representatives of the church and dependent on patronage. The clerical magistrates claimed ancient rights for modern purposes, exemplified in the tithe disputes, which were prevalent in the first half of the nineteenth century. These changes were resisted by what has been described as a 'robust plebeian culture', expressed in crimes of social protest, such as poaching, arson of hay ricks, animal maiming and illegal gleaning, all in areas of legal enforcement with which clerical magistrates were necessarily heavily involved.[15] Some clergy, and particularly bishops who had direct political influence, were perceived to stand in the way of political reform and as such were targets for acts of violent agitation, to which magistrates had to respond in defence of law and order. Perhaps a reason why clerical magistrates were so widely criticized in this period was their ambiguous position regarding innovation and tradition.[16] This may have weakened the role of

[13] Zangrel, 'Social Composition', 124; see also E. Moir, *The Justices of the Peace* (London, 1969), 106–7.
[14] White, ed., *Directory of Staffordshire*, 1834, 1851; Kelly, ed., *Post Office Directory of Staffordshire*, 1872, 1896; *Lichfield Annual Directory*, 1860, 1890. This is supported in Anthony Russell, *The Clerical Profession* (London, 1980), 165.
[15] The debate about the nature and expression of social crime in this period is covered in Lee, *Rural Society*, 114; see also Andrew Charlesworth, 'An Agenda for Historical Studies of Rural Protest in England, 1750–1850', *Rural History* 2 (1991), 231–40, at 232–3.
[16] Criticism of clergy during the Swing Riots can be found in Carl J. Griffin, *Protest, Politics and Work in Rural England, 1700–1850* (Basingstoke, 2014), 132–43. Clergy are described as exercising repressive force in local society in Mick Reed and Roger Wells, *Class, Conflict and Protest in the English Countryside, 1700–1880* (London, 1990), 91. See also David Jones, *Crime, Protest, Community and Police in Nineteenth-*

John W. B. Tomlinson

clergy as agents of social control, formalized in the position of clerical magistrate, which in turn contributed to their decline.[17]

Furthermore, clerical magistrates were an expression of the shift of local power from patriarchal justice to patrician justice, a process that began in the eighteenth century. It has been suggested that clerical magistrates, as a relatively new group within magistracy replacing (in many cases) the gentry, were more willing to implement the national government agenda than to respond to local sensibilities.[18] However, this was tempered by their personal connections to landed wealth, and to the traditional structures of society upon which they relied.[19] Additionally, by the nineteenth century the practical concept of the parish as a distinct community was under strain, especially in urban areas, and this particularly affected clergy because they were appointed to this geographical unit.[20] In due course, social change would sweep the clerical magistrates away as well, to be replaced by the middle class of industrialists; this change came much earlier in the century in the urban and industrial areas, such as Wolverhampton and Stoke-on-Trent in Staffordshire, than in the rural areas.

Infamous incidents involving clerical magistrates in the 1830s were common, although such accounts did not represent the actions of all such clergy and may have been over-emphasized. One example for Staffordshire is recalled in an account entitled 'The Wolves let loose at Wolverhampton' in 1835.[21] After a particularly contentious parliamentary election a crowd gathered outside the Swan Inn in Wolverhampton, and the Revd John Clare, a long-standing magistrate, stood on a balcony in an attempt to calm the crowd. A missile was thrown that hit him on the shoulder; this convinced him of the

---

Century Britain (London, 1982); John E. Archer, *Social Unrest and Popular Protest in England, 1780–1840* (Cambridge, 2000).

[17] Robert Hole, *Pulpits, Politics and Public Order in England, 1760–1832* (Cambridge, 1989), 252–6.

[18] This argument is put forward in Wallis, 'Relationship', 159.

[19] Ibid. 168, 169. The way clergy enforced the Game Laws was evidence of their commitment to the landed classes: see David Eastwood, *Governing Rural England* (Oxford, 1994), 81-2.

[20] K. D. M. Snell, *Parish and Belonging: Community, Identity and Welfare in England and Wales, 1700–1950* (Cambridge, 2006), 496–504.

[21] A full account is given in David J. Cox, '"The Wolves let loose at Wolverhampton": A Study of the South Staffordshire Election Riots, May 1835', *Law, Crime in History* 2 (2011), 1–31.

need to read the Riot Act and send in the Dragoon Guards. Over the next few hours, sporadic violence filled the surrounding streets, four protestors were wounded by gun fire and several buildings were damaged. Clare, who had a reputation for his harsh response to public disorder, came in for some criticism in the local and national press: 'But who is the author of this outrage? The man who gave the order to fire upon his fellow citizens ... in mere personal vengeful feeling for a slight contempt passed upon him .... was a Clergyman. A Minister of Peace sounded the signal for war.' [22] Also, in the subsequent public enquiry there was strong criticism of Clare: the Dragoon captain complained that the clerical magistrate was keen to send in the troops even before the Riot Act was read, but then declined to lead the troops out into the streets as would be expected.[23] The notoriety of the Wolverhampton incident emphasized the rashness and incompetence of the clerical magistrate. Events such as this, although quite rare, served to reinforce the view that the clergy ought not to accept the role of magistrate, and from this time such a view gathered strength for a variety of reasons.

One important argument at the time was that to be a magistrate was a distraction from parochial duty. This became more of an issue as such duties became more ecclesiastically defined with the development of the clerical profession in the nineteenth century. The expectations that clergy would be resident in their parishes (to avoid pluralism and absenteeism) and adopt a more self-consciously clerical way of life were features of this development. Over the same period, the role of the magistrate became more focused on the judicial function rather than the wider scope of local government administration.[24] Gradually the responsibility for, and oversight of, local gaols and asylums, the licensing of ale houses and the regulation of highways and bridges were taken over by elected councils and other bodies.[25] Thus clerical magistrates found it harder to justify the

---

[22] *Figaro in London*, 6 June 1835, 95.

[23] Clare claimed he was too infirm to do so: Cox, '"Wolves let loose"', 28.

[24] At the same time magistrates were required to be more competent and conversant in the law as they worked with increasingly professionalized lawyers. For a Staffordshire example, see Christopher J. Frank, '"Let but one of them come before me, and I'll commit him": Trade Unions, Magistrates, and the Law in Mid-Nineteenth-Century Staffordshire', *JBS* 44 (2005), 64–91.

[25] The 1835 Municipal Corporations Act and 1888 Local Government Act provided the legislation for these significant changes.

role of magistrate in terms of the general welfare of the parish. The Justice of the Peace returns to parliament specifically asked whether the clerical magistrate had 'the cure of souls, or [was] performing other Clerical duty', implying that this might be an issue.[26] In 1873 a parliamentary bill was presented to disqualify parish clergy from the office of magistrate, which, although unsuccessful, represented a strong body of opinion.[27] Some Lord Lieutenants particularly disapproved of clerical magistrates who had parochial duties and in Shropshire, a county adjacent to Staffordshire, there was an official resistance to such appointments.[28] However, it was recognized that the extent of parochial duties varied greatly between clergy; this allowed some to take up the role, and where they did so the benefits to the local society in maintaining peace and order were tangible to some. The *Church Magazine* observed in 1840:

> A return to the House of Commons has been published, of the names, addresses and residences of the justices of the peace, being ministers of the Established Church, which makes the total number about 2000. In Norfolk there are 102 reverend justices of the peace, and in Suffolk not less than 111. These counties are the best conducted in England.[29]

The view that clergy acting as magistrates provided stability and good governance in the local community was expressed by those who sought to maintain the status quo, but even this viewpoint had to recognize the first call on clerical duty, which was the maintenance of the church. It was natural that, as the clerical role became more professional and specialized as the nineteenth century proceeded, both the availability of, and the inclination for, clergy to be involved in secular legal functions was likely to decline.

Another major reason to oppose clerical magistrates related directly to the special character and role of clergy, which had always been present but became more emphasized in the idea of the cleric as religious

[26] See House of Commons, *Nominal Returns of all Clerks in Holy Orders in the Commission of the Peace in each County in England and Wales* (London, 1863, 1873), as examples.
[27] HC Deb (3rd Series), 18 June 1873 (vol. 216, col. 1150), prompted by the Chipping Norton case, in which two clerical magistrates passed harsh sentences on sixteen women for intimidating blackleg labour.
[28] For example, Viscount Hill in Shropshire: David. J. Cox and Barry S. Godfrey, *Cinderellas and Packhorses: A History of the Shropshire Magistracy* (Logaston, 2005).
[29] *Church Magazine*, September 1840, 287.

professional: it was not fitting for a minster of religion, largely because it involved passing judgment, and in particular passing judgment on others in secular matters. The clergy should not be involved in the business of law enforcement because it was contrary to their vocation. The *Wolverhampton Chronicle*, a few years before the infamous incident outside the Swan Inn, had declared that 'the duties of a Christian pastor are utterly incompatible with those of an active justice in populous towns'.[30] Richard Fryer, MP for Wolverhampton in 1832, who had been turned down for the role of magistrate in his earlier years because he was an industrialist, described the clerical magistrate as having 'the cross in one hand and the gibbet in the other'.[31] Obelkevich, in his classic study of the nineteenth-century clergy in Lincolnshire, suggests that many clergy regarded being a magistrate as inconsistent with their ministry, and Evans gives more examples.[32] Primarily, it was felt that the responsibilities of a magistrate could jeopardize the clergy's pastoral relationships and draw them into disputes that were not just distracting but also damaging to the church. Some clergy, particularly those from the more extreme wings of the church, either evangelical or Oxford Movement, were less likely to aspire to non-ecclesial duties. A recent large-scale study of the Tractarian clergy shows that none of them would have contemplated becoming a magistrate, which is perhaps not surprising, given their attitude to secular authority and their desire for a more distinctively clerical role.[33] Accepting that from the mid-nineteenth century there was a general trend for clergy, whatever their party, to become more ecclesial in their activities, it would be natural for the number of clerical magistrates to fall.[34] Furthermore, this was a consequence of ecclesiastical reform that attempted to make the Church of England more accountable, efficient and focused on religious affairs.[35] However, the opposing view that clergy should take up

---

[30] *Wolverhampton Chronicle*, November 1831, quoted in Swift, 'English Urban Magistracy', 89.

[31] Swift, 'English Urban Magistracy', 81.

[32] James Obelkevich, *Religion and Parish Society: South Lindsey 1825–1875* (Oxford, 1976), 161; Evans, 'Some Reasons', 103.

[33] George Herring, *The Oxford Movement in Practice: The Tractarian Parochial Worlds from the 1830s to the 1870s* (Oxford, 2016).

[34] Russell, *Clerical Profession*, 146–68.

[35] A series of parliamentary acts from *c.*1830 to 1860 was introduced to restrict absenteeism and pluralism, redistribute church funds more equably and make the Church of England more responsive to an urban and pluralistic society.

the magistrate's role so as not to be estranged from society was still being put forward actively at the end of the century. In 1895 an article in *The Spectator* noted that the controversy over clerical magistracy was an issue that was regularly debated and stated that ministers of the established church 'often make admirable Magistrates; and to deny them their right to fulfil that function, when it does not interfere with their other duties, is either a folly, or the outcome of ideas which would in the end change all teachers of Christianity into a secluded and inexperienced priestly caste'.[36]

A third reason given was that the clergy were not fit for the role. The partisan nature of Anglican clerical magistrates was an issue for Nonconformists, both in the urban areas where many of the new industrialists were not part of the established church and in the countryside where the tithe was considered by non-Anglicans as an unfair denominational tax. The impact of the growth of Nonconformity was twofold: it presented a more congregational model of ministry, focused on the worshipping community and less inclined to be involved in local legal functions, and it demanded a more denominationally diverse representation of leaders in the local community. For urban areas like Wolverhampton and Stoke-on-Trent in Staffordshire, Nonconformity, particularly in the form of the various brands of Methodism, attracted the support of a large proportion of the population by the mid-nineteenth century.[37] Comments by some of the clergy at the time betray their establishment leanings. The assize judges came to Stafford in October 1842 to try the Chartist leaders, some of whom were convicted of sedition against the Anglican clergy.[38] The judges attended Salt Church, where the Revd the Hon. Arthur Chetwyn Talbot preached on Psalm 145: 16: 'Thou openest thine hand, and satisfiest the desire of every living thing', a pretext for a sermon on how all in society should be content with what they have. Four years earlier the church had been built at considerable expense as a testimonial to the Earl Talbot, Lord

[36] *The Spectator*, 19 January 1895, 81.
[37] For the statistics from the 1851 Religious Census, see K. D. M. Snell and Paul S. Ell, *Rival Jerusalems: The Geography of Victorian Religion* (Cambridge, 2000), 121–72. In other regions, the effect of the growth of Nonconformity on the magistracy was significant: Rachel Jones, *Crime, Courts and Community in Mid-Victorian Wales* (Cardiff, 2018), 31–51.
[38] This unrest was particularly strong in Staffordshire and magistrates were often a target: Frank, 'Trade Unions, Magistrates and the Law', 72.

Lieutenant of Staffordshire, responsible for the appointment of all magistrates in the county.[39] The close connection between the established church and the magistracy could not have been made more obvious. Other links were more hidden: a correlation between Freemasonry and the clerical magistracy has also been noted in Staffordshire, where the clergy in the wealthier parishes and from the more influential families were often both magistrates and freemasons.[40]

Some clergy were considered unfit because of their supposed party political allegiances. In Staffordshire from 1835 there is evidence of the government policy of attempting to bring a greater balance to the magistracy in response to the predominance of Anglicans and supporters of the Tory party. As a result, the appointment of clerical magistrates became the exception, and such candidates, although put forward by the Lord Lieutenant, were often turned down by the Lord Chancellor.[41] However, the charge of political bias continued through to the 1850s, when the MP for Wolverhampton made a direct intervention to ensure more Liberals were appointed as magistrates.[42] This policy seemed to have had a direct effect on the number of clerical magistrates in Staffordshire.

Some clerical magistrates were criticized for being ineffectual: In Norfolk they were accused of being 'fearful of acting with the promptitude decision and firmness which is required in a Magistrate'.[43] Others, such as Clare in Wolverhampton, were criticized for being too firm or overzealous. As a distinct group within the magistracy, and at this stage fairly numerous, the clergy became an easy target for opposing groups, those who wanted to maintain the status quo and those who wanted change. Some research has shown that clerical magistrates cannot be caricatured in either way, as they were not

---

[39] Stafford, Staffordshire RO, D4327, Baptismal Register, Salt, 1843–78.

[40] As part of my doctoral research, I compared the Staffordshire magistrate lists with the records of the Provincial Grand Lodge of Staffordshire. Further detailed investigation of the familial and associational links between clergy and other significant people in local society would probably reveal a network of influence and control which faced the challenges of social unrest and the rise of the middle class.

[41] David Philips, 'The Black Country Magistracy 1835–1860', *MidH* 3 (1975), 161–90.

[42] Ibid. 174–5.

[43] This was a land agent's view expressed to Lord Melbourne: quoted in Wallis, 'Relationship', 201.

significantly different in their sentencing from other magistrates, and neither more nor less competent.[44]

Beyond these reasons, there has arisen the view, argued by more recent commentators, that clerical magistrates were damaging to the church, creating a poor reputation for the clergy and even a degree of anti-clericalism.[45] Henry Brougham has been quoted in support of this:

> Nothing has a more direct tendency to excite hatred and contempt both towards the men and towards their sacred office. It is also certain that they have not generally shown such discretion, temperance and forbearance in exercising magisterial functions as might either have been expected or desired from men in their station.[46]

It has been suggested that the church was readjusting itself to be less associated with the powerful, and less compromised by involvement in secular affairs.[47] Certainly there is evidence for a strained relationship between the church and some sections of the community because of the actions of clerical magistrates. In 1830 in Norfolk, following some disturbances, the clerical magistrates were described as in 'bad Odour with the People'.[48] Evans argues that clerical magistrates were singled out for attacks in the 1830–1 riots because of their over-enthusiastic strictness in applying the law to maintain the status quo, although often the criticism was that they were ineffectual.[49] Wallis describes how the clerical magistrate drove a wedge between the church and the people.[50] Lee contends that 'whatever the levels of individual culpability, clerical magistrates were seen to operate at the heart of a system that divided, dissembled and discriminated'.[51] Much of the focus has been on tithe disputes, although this issue was

---

[44] Lee, *Rural Society*, 117–18 (examples from Norfolk).
[45] Evans, 'Some Reasons', 101–3; Norma Landau, *Justices of the* Peace (Berkeley, CA, 1984), 141–3; Eastwood, *Governing Rural England*, 31; Frances Knight, 'Did Anticlericalism exist in the English Countryside in the Early Nineteenth Century?', in Nigel Aston and Matthew Cragoe, eds, *Anticlericalism in Britain c.1500–1914* (Stroud, 2000), 159–78.
[46] Brougham, Lord Chancellor in 1843, quoted in Evans, 'Some Reasons', 106.
[47] A classic example of this would be R. A. Soloway, *Prelates and People: Ecclesiastical Social Thought in England, 1783–1952* (Abingdon, 1969).
[48] A land agent's view expressed to Lord Melbourne, quoted in Wallis, 'Relationship', 201.
[49] Evans, 'Some Reasons', 104.
[50] Wallis, 'Relationship', 281.
[51] Lee, *Rural Society*, 114.

only a part of the conflict between church and society in this period and by no means the burden of the clerical magistrates' business. The evidence that this conflict led directly to the decline of clerical magistrates is not conclusive, not least because criticism was levelled at clerical and non-clerical magistrates alike.[52] It does not explain why the decline was general and not directly related to the criticism of particular clergy.

Moreover, it is clear that involvement in the magistracy provided many clergy with first-hand experience of the lives of the poor in a way that their other clerical duties did not. Involvement in the legal system necessarily involved clergy with key issues that affected local communities in a way that enabled them to exercise a positive influence. During the 1832 cholera epidemic in Staffordshire, the Revd William Leigh in Bilston used his role as magistrate to call for medical assistance from the Board of Health in London.[53] Even Clare was noted for standing up for workers unreasonably oppressed by their employers in several cases, and other clerical magistrates in Staffordshire were active in opposing the system of truck, strictly illegal, where employees were paid in tokens to be used only at the factory store.[54] In the coal mining areas of the county, this was in contrast to other magistrates who were often involved in local industry and therefore unable to consider legal action against truck.[55] The approach of the clergy may have been paternalistic but it has been suggested that such experience of involvement in applying the law helped to instil in clergy a social conscience and to encourage them to ask questions about the social reasons for crime and the inherent injustices of society.[56] Rather than damaging the church, therefore, it can be argued that the clerical magistracy strengthened its influence and connections in society. This reassessment, based on a more positive view of the role of some clerical magistrates, runs counter to the dominant narrative of clergy embroiled in legal disputes and always seeking to defend the status quo. As clergy of this period represented that ambiguous combination of innovation and tradition, a more balanced narrative is necessary.

[52] Frank, "'Constitutional Law versus Justices' Justice'", 111.
[53] Swift, 'English Urban Magistracy', 80.
[54] Philips, 'Black Country Magistracy', 181–4.
[55] The law required magistrates in such cases to be unconnected to the industry: Frank, 'Trade Unions, Magistrates and the Law', 81.
[56] Lee, *Rural Society*, 104.

The conflicts of the 1830s over clerical magistracy were symptomatic of social change rather than causes of it. The conflicts may have discouraged some of the younger clergy from taking up the role, but the development of the clerical profession and its focus on a more defined ecclesial role was of more significance. At the same time, other candidates who were rising in social status and power through the development of industry and urban areas were willing and keen to serve as magistrates.[57] In the past, clergy had been appointed because of the perceived lack of other candidates. Thus the marquess of Lansdowne told parliament in 1836: 'in some counties it was absolutely necessary to appoint clergymen on account of the scarcity of persons qualified for the magisterial station'.[58] In 1835 there was prejudice against 'men in trade' in Staffordshire, where the Lord Lieutenant, Earl Talbot, regarded coal and iron masters as unfit for the role.[59] However, this attitude had to give way after the Chartist disturbances increased the need for more justices in the Black Country.[60] Furthermore, these changes were enshrined in law with the introduction of new local government legislation in 1835 which provided for councils in towns to be involved in the selection of magistrates, extended fifty years later to rural areas. By the 1880s, one county, Derbyshire, had no clerical magistrates at all.[61] Nationally, the steady increase of other groups reduced the clergy to less than 5 per cent of all magistrates by the end of the nineteenth century.

The clerical magistracy in England in this period provides a particular example of the church's direct involvement in society, specifically in enforcing the law in a variety of local contexts at a time of considerable social change and unrest. The reasons for the decline of clerical magistracy from the high point of the 1830s relate to contemporary considerations regarding the appropriate roles and character of clergy,

---

[57] In rural areas the role was being taken up by the country doctor: Russell, *Clerical Profession*, 165.

[58] Quoted in Zangrel, 'Social Composition', 118.

[59] Staffordshire RO, Lieutenancy Papers, D649/9/10, Outletter Book 1822–42, 19 September 1835.

[60] Other areas show a similar growing acceptance of 'middle-class' magistrates: see, for instance, D. Foster, 'Class and County Government in Early Nineteenth-Century Lancashire', *NH* 9 (1974), 48–61; Janet Saunders, 'Warwickshire Magistrates and Prison Reform 1840–75', *MidH* 11 (1986), 79–99.

[61] Zangrel, 'Social Composition', 119.

and the fear that it was damaging for the church to be involved so directly in legal enforcement. However, these views were not universally held and there is significant evidence that some clergy, through their work as magistrates, gained a greater awareness of the complexity of society and an appreciation of the societal pressures and injustices that related to crime. It brought clergy into direct contact with people beyond their regular congregations and gave them insight into the lives of the poor and the most disadvantaged. The withdrawal of clergy from the magistracy, particularly amongst men ordained from the 1830s onwards, for a variety of reasons, was a way to avoid conflict and adopt a more distinctively ecclesial role.

The study of the church and the law provides an important insight into the development of secularization in society. The decline of the clerical magistracy that distanced the church from secular authority, requiring clergy to be less formally involved in a key aspect of local society, can be seen as evidence for a process of secularization. Until now the clerical magistracy has not been considered as a measure of secularization in this important period of church history. Such studies have tended to focus on internal features such as church attendance, rather than on the ways in which clergy interacted with people in their communities, perhaps because this is harder to quantify. It has been argued that the clerical magistracy created conflict between clergy and many people, particularly non-Anglicans and the poor, and ultimately damaged the church, adding weight to a process of secularization. However, it is clear that acting as a magistrate brought clergy into a direct relationship with their communities, and in particular with people who were not necessarily members of their congregations. Whether the role was constructive or not, involvement in secular law by clergy gave them a place in secular society beyond the church, a counter-current to any trend of secularization in which clergy were encouraged to be more professional in their outlook and more specialized in their religious duties. Further research into this aspect of the relationship between the church and the law would provide an important indication of how clergy engaged with the local communities beyond their congregations, and thus of how the relationship between church and society developed and changed during the nineteenth century.

Debating the Legal Status of the Ornaments Rubric: Ritualism and Royal Commissions in Late Nineteenth- and Early Twentieth-Century England

Dan D. Cruickshank*

University of Glasgow

This article uses the history of the Ornaments Rubric in the late nineteenth and early twentieth century to explore the emergence of claims to self-governance within the Church of England in this period and the attempts by parliament to examine how independent the legal system of the church was from the secular state. First, it gives an overview of the history of the Ornaments Rubric in the various editions of the Book of Common Prayer and the Acts of Uniformity, presenting the legal uncertainty left by centuries of Prayer Book revision. It then explores how the Royal Commission into Ritualism (1867–70) and the Public Worship Regulation Act (1874) attempted to control Ritualist interpretations of the Ornaments Rubric through secular courts. Examining the failure of these attempts, it looks towards the Royal Commission on Ecclesiastical Discipline (1904–6). Through the evidence given to the commission, it shows how the previous royal commission and the work of parliament and the courts had failed to stop the continuation of Ritualist belief in the church's independence from secular courts. Using the report of the royal commission, it shows how the commissioners attempted to build a via media *between strict spiritual independence and complete parliamentary oversight.*

In the nineteenth century the Ornaments Rubric, a small paragraph in the Book of Common Prayer, became a major point of contention within the Church of England. The debate over the Ornaments Rubric went further than just the material culture of churches, to the questions of what constituted ecclesiastical law in England, who had the right to create such law, and how and by whom it was to be

* Theology and Religious Studies, No. 4 The Square, University of Glasgow, G12 8QQ. Email: d.cruickshank.1@research.gla.ac.uk.
I should like to thank the Anglo-Catholic Historical Society for the award of a bursary that enabled me to present the paper at the Ecclesiastical History Society Summer Conference on which this article is based.

Studies in Church History 56 (2020), 434–454   © Ecclesiastical History Society 2020
doi: 10.1017/stc.2019.24

interpreted. This article will explore how, through the Ornaments Rubric, Ritualists challenged the existing legislative and judicial system of the church, and how parliament reacted to a questioning of its authority.

Recent decades have seen a resurgence in studies of English Christianity in the Victorian era. Nonetheless, in 2010 Jeremy Morris could still assert that 'there remain areas of neglect, including much of the late Victorian and Edwardian history of the Church of England'.[1] This neglect is starting to be ameliorated, for example by Bethany Kilcrease in her study of *The Great Church Crisis and the End of English Erastianism*. Kilcrease's main thesis was that there was a '"Church Crisis," a conflict between the Protestant and Ritualist ... Parties within the Church of England that lasted roughly between 1898 and 1906'.[2] This article places that conflict in context. It consciously begins before the period defined by Kilcrease, starting with the Royal Commission of 1867–70 and ending with that of 1904–6, to show the continuity of this conflict, involving both the church and parliament, as a new Tractarian ecclesiology of the spiritual independence of the church arose, challenging the established right of Parliament to create laws relating to the church, and of secular courts to interpret these laws. It will examine how the Oxford Movement was born as a reaction against key ecclesiastical laws created by parliament, and how the Ritualists took this theoretical opposition to parliamentary supremacy and turned it into practical opposition. It will survey briefly how the Ritualists reimagined the Ornaments Rubric as a legal text, using an interpretative framework that discarded the traditional role of common law in interpreting ecclesiastical legislation in England. It will then examine how parliament responded to the Ritualist challenge through two royal commissions and anti-Ritualist legislation, and how this strengthened Ritualist resolve to ignore the instruments of parliamentary and crown supremacy over the church. Ultimately, it will consider how the report of the Royal Commission on Ecclesiastical Discipline attempted to create a synthesis between traditional parliamentary sovereignty and Tractarian spiritual independence, clearing a path

---

[1] Jeremy Morris, 'George Ridding and the Diocese of Southwell: A Study in the National Church Ideal', *JEH* 61 (2010), 125–43, at 126.
[2] Bethany Kilcrease, *The Great Church Crisis and the End of English Erastianism, 1898–1906* (London and New York, 2017), 1.

which would ultimately lead to the modern constitutional structure of the Church of England.

In the 1830s the Oxford Movement, or Tractarianism, emerged. The movement left an indelible impression on the Church of England, and was a visceral response to a very specific set of circumstances. As Nicholas Dixon has explained, the Tractarians regarded a period of reform legislation from 1828 to 1832 as an anti-Anglican revolution.[3] Writing one of the first histories of the movement in 1843, William Palmer claimed that '[a]t the beginning of the summer of 1833, the Church in England and Ireland seemed destined to immediate desolation and ruin.'[4] Palmer's use of the full title of the church as the 'Church in England *and Ireland*'[5] was more than a formality, for it was the situation regarding the church in Ireland that was the immediate impulse for the birth of the movement. In 1833 the Whig government of Earl Grey passed through parliament the Church Temporalities Act, reducing the number of Irish bishoprics from twenty-two to twelve and moving revenue raising powers from the church to a secular Ecclesiastical Commission.[6] For Palmer, with the passage of this legislation, '[t]he State, so long the guardian of the Church, [was] now becoming its enemy and its tyrant.'[7] What triggered the birth of the Oxford Movement in 1833 was the alarm with which some clergy contemplated a parliament increasingly representative of non-Anglican Britain but having control over the church and acting in ways they thought clashed with the best interests of the church. The movement therefore argued that parliament was no longer the right place to create the laws that governed the Church of England.

Ritualism was inspired by, though not a direct continuation of, the Oxford Movement. The link between the Oxford Movement and Ritualism is contested, although George Herring has thoroughly

---

[3] See, in this volume, Nicholas Dixon, "The Church of England and the Legislative Reforms of 1828–32: Revolution or Adjustment?', 401–18.

[4] William Palmer, *A Narrative of Events connected with the Publication of the Tracts for the Times with Reflections on existing Tendencies to Romanism and on the present Duties and Prospects of Members of the Church*, 2nd edn (Oxford, 1843), 2.

[5] Ibid.; emphasis mine.

[6] Electronic Irish Statute Book (eISB), 'Church Temporalities Act, 1833', online at: <http://www.irishstatutebook.ie/eli/1833/act/37/enacted/en/print.html>, accessed 25 February 2019.

[7] Palmer, *Narrative of Events*, 4.

deconstructed the idea that Ritualism was a natural progression from the Oxford Movement.[8] Herring identifies a dramatic shift in the 1850s through what he calls the 'antecedents of ritualism', specifically the Western Judgment in 1857, which was the first to recognize the legality of certain ornaments in the Church of England, and the publication of John Purchas's *Directorium Anglicanum* in 1858, the first great liturgical manual of Ritualism.[9] These antecedents heralded a dramatic shift in the concerns of high churchmen away from the more theological concerns of the Oxford Movement towards the actual performance of the liturgy and the ornaments required for this. When it came to liturgical changes, the Oxford Movement warned 'against premature developments in ceremonial outrunning the slower pace of doctrinal rediscovery'.[10] Jeremy Morris's research into high churchmen's experiences of continental Roman Catholic liturgy during the first half of the nineteenth century suggests that many proponents of the Oxford Movement were more concerned with liturgy than Herring would suggest.[11] However, Herring's main thesis, that 'the extent of the dissatisfaction with the Prayer Book of 1662 was clearly an issue which marked the Ritualists off from the earlier generation of Tractarians',[12] well describes the relationship between the two movements. The Ritualists would take the theoretical concern the Oxford Movement had identified with parliamentary sovereignty over the church's laws and would push against these boundaries in an attempt to find ways in which the Church of England's legal system supported their belief in the church's self-government. The rest of this article will consider how this occurred, and the reaction it provoked from parliament.

The central text of which the Ritualists claimed to be the true interpreters was the Ornaments Rubric. In the 1662 Book of Common Prayer, the rubric, which appeared at the beginning of

---

[8] George Herring, *The Oxford Movement in Practice: The Tractarian Parochial Worlds from the 1830s to the 1870s* (Oxford, 2016), 191–6.
[9] Ibid. 198–9.
[10] George Herring, 'Devotional and Liturgical Renewal: Ritualism and Protestant Reaction', in Stewart J. Brown, Peter Nockles and James Pereiro, eds, *The Oxford Handbook of the Oxford Movement* (Oxford, 2017), 398–409, at 400.
[11] J. N. Morris, 'British High Churchmen, Continental Church Tourism and the Roman Connection in the Nineteenth Century', *JEH* 66 (2015), 772–91.
[12] Herring, *Oxford Movement*, 209.

the order for Morning Prayer, stated that 'such Ornaments of the Church, and of the Ministers thereof, at all Times in their Ministration, shall be retained, and be in use, as were in this Church of England, by the Authority of Parliament, in the Second Year of the Reign of King Edward the Sixth'.[13] First introduced in the Prayer Book of 1559, this rather vague rubric provided the legal basis for defining the material culture of ministers and churches.[14] Ritualists identified the crux of this rubric in its closing phrase, 'in the Second Year of the Reign of King Edward the Sixth', but what was being referred to by the second year was far from clear. The second year of the reign of Edward VI ran from 28 January 1548 to 27 January 1549. Within that year, on 21 January 1549, the first Act of Uniformity was enacted by parliament, authorizing the first Book of Common Prayer as the only official liturgy of the church, to be used from Whitsunday 1549.[15] It was therefore generally assumed that the rubric had the first Prayer Book in mind; however, as the Ritualists pointed out, this was not clear cut. Although the 1549 Act of Uniformity had passed through parliament in the second year of Edward VI's reign, it did not actually take effect until Whitsunday 1549, in the third year of the king's reign. Thus, the Ritualists argued, the Ornaments Rubric did not seek to impose the material culture envisaged in the 1549 Book of Common Prayer, but rather that of the pre-Prayer Book Church of England. As Percy Dearmer would write in *The Parson's Handbook*, the last great Ritualist manual to appear in the nineteenth century, Ritualists believed that the Ornaments Rubric ordered ministers to 'interpret it [the Prayer Book] in the spirit of a parson of the year 1548, who was conversant with the old ceremonial'.[16] Such a view ignored the Reformation legislation during the first and second year of the reign of Edward VI, including the Royal Injunctions of 1547 and the Sacramental Act of the same year,[17] which marked a

---

[13] *The Book of Common Prayer and Administration of the Sacraments and other Rites and Ceremonies of the Church according to the Use of the Church of England* (London, 1992), 14.
[14] Ironically, it was the prosecution of Ritualists that established in the courts that the Ornament Rubric was legally binding as a result of being part of the Prayer Book attached to the Act of Uniformity of 1662: S. M. Waddams, *Law, Politics and the Church of England: The Career of Stephen Lushington, 1782–1873* (Cambridge, 1992), 296–7.
[15] 2 & 3 Edw. VI c.1.
[16] Percy Dearmer, *The Parson's Handbook* (London, 1899), 32.
[17] 1 Edw. VI c.1.

clear break with, and attack on, the late medieval Catholic tradition. It also ignored the history of the Ornaments Rubric itself.

Between its first appearance in the 1559 Prayer Book and its reappearance in the 1662 Prayer Book, the Ornaments Rubric underwent a major revision. In the Prayer Book of 1559 the rubric had instructed that 'the Minister at the time of the communion, and at all other tymes in his ministration, shall use such ornamentes in the church, as were in use by the authorities of Parliament, in the second yere of the raigne of king Edward the syxt, according to the acte of Parliament set in the beginninge of this boke'.[18] The most important difference here is the legal basis of the rubric. In 1559 the rubric presented itself as being an expression of the law on the matter of ornaments as laid down in 'the acte of Parliament set in the beginning of this boke', that is, the Act of Uniformity (1558). Echoing the Ornaments Rubric, this ordered 'that such ornaments of the church, and of the ministers thereof, shall be retained and be in use, as was in the Church of England, by authority of Parliament, in the second year of the reign of King Edward VI, until other order shall be therein taken by the authority of the queen's majesty'. The similarity of wording highlights the fact that the rubric is a summary of the law as established in the act and not a law itself. The rooting of the rubric in the Act of Uniformity also helps to illuminate what the rubric considered to be the legally binding aspect of the second year of Edward VI. The act referred to the Prayer Book of 1552 as the book 'authorized by Act of Parliament holden in the fifth and sixth years of our said late sovereign lord King Edward VI'. The rubric, and the act, referred to allowing those ornaments that 'were in use by the authorites of Parliament, in the second yere of the raigne of king Edward the syxt'. Given how the act referred to the Prayer Book of 1552, it appears that the appeal to that which was allowed by 'the authorities of Parliament, in the second yere' was a clumsy reference to the ornaments and vestments as defined in the 1549 Prayer Book. This interpretation is further supported by the fact that the 1549 Act of Uniformity was the only legislation to be passed by the parliament that met in the second year of Edward VI which referred to the 'ornaments of the church, and of the ministers thereof'.[19]

[18] See digitized versions online at: <http://justus.anglican.org/resources/bcp/1559/BCP_1559.htm>, accessed 25 February 2019.
[19] 1 Eliz. I c.2.

When in 1661 the Savoy Conference revised the 1559 Prayer Book, it removed the Act of Uniformity and deleted the reference to the act in the Ornaments Rubric. This had a dramatic legal consequence, for it turned the rubric from being an expression of an act of parliament into a law in itself. The alteration also had the effect of turning the law from one of process into an endpoint. The Act of Uniformity of 1559, when discussing ornaments, had stated that they would be as authorised by parliament in the second year of Edward VI 'until other order shall be therein taken by the authority of the queen's majesty, with the advice of her commissioners appointed and authorized, under the great seal of England, for causes ecclesiastical, or of the metropolitan of this realm'.[20] Such changes did take place during Elizabeth I's reign. Thus the 1549 Prayer Book ordered the wearing of 'a white Albe plain, with a vestment or Cope' at communion.[21] However, in 1559 a royal injunction ordered the wearing of the surplice at all services, with the donning of the cope allowed at the communion service.[22] Similarly, in 1566 Matthew Parker, archbishop of Canterbury and thus primate of all England, went further in the *Book of Advertisements*, saying the wearing of the cope at communion was only expected in cathedrals.[23] By the end of 1559, therefore, the Ornaments Rubric as found in the Prayer Book of that year was already a misrepresentation of the law governing vestments; the standard was no longer the Prayer Book of 1549, which envisaged a much wider range of vesture, but that ordered by Elizabeth in 1559. The amendment of 1662, however, failed to recognize this and, by removing the reference to the Act of Uniformity, suggested that the legal standard for ornaments had reverted to either the Prayer Book of 1549 or the preceding Edwardian ceremonial. It was this amendment which would open the door for Ritualist interpretation of the Ornaments Rubric.

For the Ritualists, the only legal text that was needed to interpret the rubric was the rubric itself. Moreover, the only rubric with which the Ritualists were willing to engage was the only one that had legal status in the Church of England, the edited version found in the

---

[20] Ibid.

[21] *The First and Second Prayer Books of Edward VI* (Goring Heath, 1999), 212.

[22] Eamon Duffy, *The Stripping of the Altars: Traditional Religion in England c.1400–c.1580*, 2nd edn (New Haven, CT, and London, 2005), 568.

[23] Calvin Lane, 'Before Hooker: The Material Context of Elizabethan Prayer Book Worship', *Anglican and Episcopal History* 74 (2005), 320–56, at 339–40.

Prayer Book of 1662. This interpretative model stood at odds with much of the English legal tradition. Instead of utilizing common law, considering common usage (and thus the common application of the rubric) and historic interpretations of the rubric, Ritualists argued that the rubric must be understood solely on the basis of the text itself. The Ritualist interpretation rested on an understanding that the rubric of 1662 could only be explained with reference to itself, and so the reference to the second year, even with the clause acknowledging 'the Authority of Parliament' in deciding which ornaments were acceptable left intact, had to be understood as referring to the actual year, not any law enacted in it, and thus to pre-Prayer Book ceremonial. Beyond questions of ornaments and vestments, such thinking had radical implications for how ecclesiastical law was to be interpreted. The Ritualists were, in effect, arguing for the end of the traditional status of common law as an accepted interpretative framework in English ecclesiastical legal matters,[24] in its place proposing a strict interpretation based solely on the text, devoid of legal and historical context. Such a view elevated the rubrics of the liturgy to carry more legal power than acts of parliament, effectively arguing for the supremacy of the rubric of 1662 over the Act of Supremacy of 1558.[25]

With the Ritualists raising such substantial legal questions, it was inevitable that parliament would feel the need to intervene. On 3 June 1867 a royal commission was summoned to investigate 'the Rubrics, Orders, and Directions for Regulating the Course and Conduct of Public Worship'. The twenty-nine commissioners appointed, a mix of clergymen and statesmen,[26] included the archbishop of Canterbury, Charles Longley; the bishop of London, Archibald Tait; Sir Alexander Beresford Hope, co-founder of the Cambridge Camden Society; and John Hubbard, a former governor

---

[24] The role of common law as an integral part of the English ecclesiastical legal system predates the Reformation and even the Norman conquest: see Russell Sandberg, *Law and Religion* (Cambridge, 2011), 18–25.

[25] Elements of the Act of Supremacy of 1558 were repealed during the nineteenth century; it is difficult to ascertain which sections, but it appears those parts relating to ornaments were left intact.

[26] *First Report of the Commissioners appointed to inquire into the Rubrics, Orders, and Directions for regulating the Course and Conduct of Public Worship, &c. according to the Use of the United Church of England and Ireland; with Minutes of Evidence and Appendices*, 3951 (London, 1867), iii.

of the Bank of England and a committed churchman who had clashed with leading Ritualists.[27] They were charged with investigating the Ornaments Rubric and the 'varying interpretations' of it;[28] questions of legal interpretation were thus at the heart of the commission's task.

The work of the commission would stretch over four reports, all of little substance, and all of which avoided tackling the Ornaments Rubric head-on. They were thus of little help in resolving the situation in which the church found itself. Ronald Jasper commented that the fourth report was 'remarkable for its lack of unanimity',[29] but in fact this was true of all four. Not one report received unequivocal support from all the commissioners. The first, delivered on 19 August 1867, was concerned solely with vestments; it concluded: 'it is expedient to restrain … all variations in respect of Vesture from that which has long been the established usage'.[30] Implicitly this criticized the methodology of the Ritualists, by asserting that the guiding rule for interpreting ecclesiastical laws should be common law as expressed through common usage. The commissioners recommended the introduction of a system to allow parishioners to complain about deviations from the established norm, but were 'not yet prepared to recommend' how such a system should function.[31] By the time the second report appeared, on 30 April 1868, the commissioners were ready to propose an outline for such a complaints procedure,[32] but this garnered only qualified support from four commissioners, including the bishop of Oxford, while six commissioners refused to sign the report at all.[33] The second report also condemned the use of candles on the communion table and incense, popular amongst Ritualists, as being 'at variance with the Church's usage for

[27] Hubbard, more of a Puseyite than a Ritualist, had paid for the construction of St Alban's, Holborn, only to clash constantly with its first curate and ritualist pioneer, Alexander Mackonochie: see Nigel Yates, *Anglican Ritualism in Victorian Britain, 1830–1910* (Oxford, 1999), 96–7.
[28] *First Report*, iii.
[29] R. C. D. Jasper, *Prayer Book Revision in England, 1800–1900* (London, 1954), 101.
[30] *First Report*, vii.
[31] Ibid.
[32] *Second Report of the Commissioners appointed to inquire into the Rubrics, Orders, and Directions for regulating the Course and Conduct of Public Worship, &c. according to the Use of the United Church of England and Ireland; with Minutes of Evidence and Appendices*, 4016 (London, 1868), 2.
[33] Ibid. 3–7.

300 years'.[34] The commissioners were here challenging the Ritualist theory of legal interpretation, affirming that common usage was the marker for correct interpretation of the law, although they did not do so explicitly.

As time went by, some commissioners became restless about the failure to tackle the issue of the Ornaments Rubric directly. At the commission's sixty-ninth meeting, on 22 April 1869, now chaired by Archibald Tait after his translation from London to Canterbury following Longley's death on 27 October 1868, several commissioners proposed revisions to the rubric. These varied from Sir Joseph Napier's proposal, supported by the archbishop of Armagh, that the rubric be removed entirely from the Prayer Book, to that put forward by the dean of Ely, Harvey Goodwin, that the rubric be amended to affirm that the canons of the church could overrule it. Both represented drastic ways to try to resolve the Ritualist crisis. Napier's proposal sought to bypass the battle over interpretation of the law by simply revoking the law, whilst Goodwin wished to assert that ultimate legislative power over the Church of England dwelt in the church's law, and that the church could supersede its own legislation through new legislation. Both proposals, however, were defeated.[35] Clearly there remained no agreement amongst the commissioners over the best course of action when it came to the central rubric of Ritualism.

The third report, not released until 12 January 1870, avoided all discussion of the Ornaments Rubric.[36] The fourth report proved to be the most controversial, proposing various alterations to Prayer Book rubrics,[37] but with no change suggested for the Ornaments Rubric. This led twenty of the twenty-nine commissioners to append

[34] Ibid. 1.
[35] *Fourth Report of the Commissioners appointed to inquire into the Rubrics, Orders, and Directions for regulating the Course and Conduct of Public Worship, &c. according to the Use of the United Church of England and Ireland; with Minutes of Evidence and Appendices*, C.218 (London, 1870), 96.
[36] *Third Report of the Commissioners appointed to inquire into the Rubrics, Orders, and Directions for regulating the Course and Conduct of Public Worship, &c. according to the Use of the United Church of England and Ireland; with Minutes of Evidence and Appendices*, C.17 (London, 1870).
[37] The rubric alterations proposed all sought to limit ritual practice, emphasizing the need for services to be audible to the congregation, that there had to be a minimum of two communicants and that wafers were forbidden for use at communion. Arguably none of these were alterations to the rubrics of the Prayer Book of 1662, but merely re-emphasizing what the rubrics left implied: see *Fourth Report*, 17, 20.

only a conditional signature, in protest that 'the obscure and debateable Rubric entitled the Ornaments Rubric is left in its original form, without even proviso, note, or explanation'.[38] Nearly two-thirds of the commissioners had desired the commission to tackle the Ornaments Rubric directly, but they had been unable to agree on the best way of doing this. This tacitly allowed the Ritualist interpretation of the law and the application of their interpretation to continue as it had before the commission, and the commission was in this sense the failure Yates paints it to be.[39] Nonetheless, it had one result: in 1875 the complaints procedure recommended in the Second Report would be set up by parliament; in the closing decades of the nineteenth century this was to become a symbol of parliamentary and state sovereignty over the church and its laws.

In 1874 Tait proposed a draft of the Public Worship Regulation Act; as has been shown in detail by James Bentley, he then approached the newly elected Conservative cabinet to find supporters.[40] There was some suggestion from his fellow bishops that Tait should move the motion through the Church of England's convocations,[41] which had been re-established in the preceding twenty years,[42] but Tait was sympathetic to those who 'believed that Convocation was such a hotbed of ritualism that it ought to be destroyed, not consulted',[43] and, as Peter Marsh has observed, he also thought highly of parliament, regarding it as the 'most important expression of lay opinion'.[44] In seeking to have the worship of the church regulated through a parliamentary act, the archbishop of Canterbury sought to use the power of parliament to legislate for the church in a way he found himself unable to do within the church's internal structures.

Disraeli, newly appointed as prime minister, was initially reluctant to support Tait's measure, having only managed to appoint some members of his cabinet by promising that the new Conservative

---

[38] Ibid. x–xx.

[39] Yates, *Anglican Ritualism*, 234–5.

[40] James Bentley, *Ritualism and Politics in Victorian Britain: The Attempt to Legislate for Belief* (Oxford, 1978), 46–54.

[41] Ibid. 49.

[42] Peter T. Marsh, 'The Primate and the Prime Minister: Archbishop Tait, Gladstone, and the National Church', *VS* 9 (1965), 113–40, at 115.

[43] Bentley, *Ritualism and Politics*, 49.

[44] Marsh, 'The Primate and the Prime Minister', 120.

government 'would not introduce or support any anti-Ritualist measure'.[45] Disraeli, never a supporter of Ritualism, eventually came round to supporting the measure; however, as Allen Warren identified, this was not a result of his religious views but 'a matter of party and parliamentary tactics with Disraeli wanting to win the game, simply in order to put the question at rest'.[46] Faced not only with support for the measure by the majority of the House of Commons but also opposition to the measure from Disraeli's lifelong opponent Gladstone, a man much more sympathetic to Ritualism, Disraeli opted for the winning side of the argument.[47] Appearing before the House of Commons on 15 July 1874 to support the bill, Disraeli demonstrated none of this reticence, instead directly attacking the theological underpinnings of Ritualism:

> [A]s long as those doctrines are held by Roman Catholics, I am prepared to treat them with reverence, but what I object to is, that they should be held by ministers of our Church who, when they enter the church, enter it at the same time with a solemn contract with the nation, that they will oppose those doctrines and utterly resist them. What I do object to is the Mass in masquerade.[48]

Disraeli's speech before the house demonstrated a clear commitment to the traditional post-Reformation ecclesiology of the Church of England. Warren has identified Disraeli's belief in a 'historical national tradition' that united Dissenters and members of the established church in their Protestantism.[49] Disraeli's speech emphasized that, in his view, Ritualists were breaking their 'solemn contract with the nation' by espousing what he regarded as non-Protestant doctrines.[50] These views then justified a parliament of Dissenters and non-Dissenters in legislating to ensure the worship of the church remained within that parliament's view of acceptable Protestant practice. It was this kind of English Erastianism against which the

[45] G. I. T. Machin, *Politics and the Churches in Great Britain, 1869 to 1921* (Oxford, 1987), 71.
[46] Allen Warren, 'Disraeli, the Conservatives and the National Church, 1837–1881', in J. P. Parry and Stephen Taylor, eds, *Parliament and the Church, 1529–1960* (Edinburgh, 2000), 96–117, at 116.
[47] Machin, *Politics and the Churches, 1869 to 1921*, 74–5.
[48] HC Deb (3rd series), 15 July 1874 (vol. 221, col. 80).
[49] Warren, 'Disraeli, the Conservatives and the National Church', 109.
[50] HC Deb (3rd series), 15 July 1874 (vol. 221, col. 80).

Oxford Movement reacted and which it rejected. However, in Disraeli's understanding, that Ritualist belief in the legal independence of the Church of England could be only theoretical; the reality was that parliament was the legislative body for the Church of England.

The Public Worship Regulation Act 1874 came into force on 1 July 1875, legally establishing the kind of complaints procedure envisaged by the second report of the Royal Commission. An archdeacon, a churchwarden or three male parishioners[51] could complain to the bishop if they believed illegal alterations to the fabric of the church had been made by the incumbent, or if the incumbent had used illegal vestments in the twelve months previous to the complaint, or if he had illegally altered or added to the Prayer Book during a service.[52] The bishop would first attempt to resolve the complaint, or exercise a veto over the case.[53] If he were unable to resolve the complaint in twenty-one days, it would be referred to be heard in court, the case to be presided over either by a barrister who had practised for ten years or by a judge; the president of the court was to be selected either by the archbishops or the monarch, with the only ecclesiastical condition being that he must be a member of the Church of England.[54] Any decision could then be legally enforced, with the incumbent being permanently removed if he failed to abide by the judgment. That the final arbitrator was a secular judge rather than an ecclesiastical court was the result of an amendment by the Evangelical leader Lord Shaftesbury.[55] Although the act placed significant decision-making power into the hands of bishops, its use of the secular legal system still clearly conformed to an Erastian view of the Church of England. Parliament had mandated that a secular judge could remove clergy members who broke the laws it had created, and who failed to recognize the authority of these secular courts. The appointment of James Wilde, Lord Penzance, former judge of

---

[51] The act specifically states that parishioner 'means a male person of full age': Public Worship Regulation Act 1874, 37 & 38 Vic. c.85 §6. Women were thus legally excluded from complaining about abuses in the churches they attended.

[52] Ibid., §8.

[53] Ibid., §9.

[54] The judge was to sign a solemn declaration that he was a member of the Church of England: ibid., §7.

[55] Michael Hennell, *Sons of the Prophets: Evangelical Leaders of the Victorian Church* (London, 1979), 66.

the Court of Probate and Divorce, as the judge to oversee prosecutions under the act served only to inflame the anger of those who disagreed that a secular judge should oversee the cases.[56] Prosecutions under the act were much greater in symbolic value than they were in number, creating through the few prosecuted the illustrious 'Ritualist Martyrs'.[57] Indeed, Morris comments that by the time of the infamous trial of Edward King, bishop of Lincoln, for ritual practices in 1888, 'the wave of prosecutions and imprisonments that followed the passage of the Public Worship Regulation Act in 1874 was already spent'.[58] Nonetheless, the act, and the actions of the courts associated with it, provided an embodiment of the secular oversight that Ritualism detested.

The act built on previous practice. In the fifty years leading up to it, a secular court had already established itself as the final arbitrator of church law: the Judicial Committee of the Privy Council. As Frances Knight has demonstrated, this committee was unpopular throughout the emerging Anglican Communion for it was seen as 'the ultimate in Erastian sell-outs'.[59] By contrast Tait valued it 'as an important feature of the intimate connection between Church and State'.[60] Ritualist disdain for this committee had been fuelled by its finding against certain Ritualist practices, such as the use of wafer bread, vestments and the eastward-facing position at the moment of consecration.[61] In *The Parson's Handbook*, Percy Dearmer articulated the problem these decisions created for the Ritualists: 'The object of this Handbook is to help, in however humble a way, toward remedying the lamentable confusion, lawlessness, and vulgarity which are conspicuous in the Church at this time.'[62] Dearmer did not blame this lawlessness on Ritualist practices, even though it was arguably created by the persistent use of rituals deemed illegal, but rather on a system that allowed the legislation of the church to be defined and

---

[56] Bentley, *Ritualism and Politics*, 82–3.

[57] Machin, *Politics and the Churches, 1869 to 1921*, 82–3.

[58] Morris, 'George Ridding', 140.

[59] Frances Knight, '"A Church without Discipline is no Church at all": Discipline and Diversity in Nineteenth- and Twentieth-Century Anglicanism', in Kate Cooper and Jeremy Gregory, eds, *Discipline and Diversity*, SCH 43 (Woodbridge, 2007), 399–418, at 404.

[60] Marsh, 'The Primate and the Prime Minister', 138.

[61] All three were deemed illegal in the Ridsdale case: Bentley, *Ritualism and Politics*, 97–9.

[62] Dearmer, *Parson's Handbook*, 1.

interpreted by a secular court. The fact that at the end of the nineteenth century Dearmer was defending the practices which the Royal Commission, parliament and the Privy Council had tried to tackle, demonstrates both how little these attempts had altered the minds of Ritualists, and how ineffectual these bodies had been in rectifying the state of disorder in the church. For Ritualists, however, parliament and secular courts did not have the right to decide matters of doctrine and ceremony and as such any legal interpretations they provided were illegitimate and could be ignored.[63]

By 1904 many members of parliament had had enough of Ritualist disdain for established legal precedents, and began pushing for new anti-Ritualist legislation or a parliamentary select committee to tackle the Ritualist problem once and for all.[64] Instead, the prime minister, Arthur Balfour, under pressure from the newly appointed archbishop of Canterbury, Randall Davidson, established a Royal Commission on Ecclesiastical Discipline, to try to identify better solutions than the previous Royal Commission had proved able to do.[65] Chaired by Michael Edward Hicks-Beach, a long-serving Conservative MP and former chancellor of the exchequer,[66] the body of commissioners was remarkably similar to that of the commission established in 1867, with a mixture of senior clergy, including Davidson, and political figures. The commission took evidence for nearly a year from a cross-section of society. Protestant organizations, such as the Church Association, engaged enthusiastically with the commission, sending representatives to report on services they had witnessed, which were often portrayed as being of the most extreme nature. William Edward

[63] Charlotte Smith, 'Martin v Machonochie / Machonochie v Penzance: A Crisis of Character and Identity in the Court of Arches?', *JLH* 24/3 (2003), 36–58, at 43–5.

[64] For a thorough overview of the various campaigns inside and outside parliament that led to the formation of the Royal Commission on Ecclesiastical Discipline, see G. I. T. Machin, 'The Last Victorian Anti-Ritualist Campaign, 1895–1906', *VS* 25 (1982), 277–302.

[65] G. K. A. Bell, *Randall Davidson: Archbishop of Canterbury*, 3rd edn (London, 1952), 456–8; R. C. D. Jasper, *The Development of the Anglican Liturgy, 1662–1980* (London, 1989), 75.

[66] MP for East Gloucestershire (made vacant by his father's death) 1874–85, Bristol West 1885–1904; chancellor of the exchequer in the first and third governments of Lord Salisbury 1885–6, 1895–1902: Martin Pugh, 'Beach, Michael Edward Hicks, first Earl St Aldwyn (1837–1916)', *ODNB*, 2010, online at: <http://www.oxforddnb.com/view/10.1093/ref:odnb/9780198614128.001.0001/odnb-9780198614128-e-33859>, accessed 10 March 2019.

Bowen, for example, witnessed at St Columba's, Kingsland Road, in London, a 'Mass of the Presanctified'. 'I followed the service', said Bowen, 'by means of the Roman Missal; a Prayer Book would have been of no use, one could not have followed it.'[67] The wholesale use of a non-Prayer Book liturgy was an unusual example; much more typical of the evidence presented by those linked to Protestant organizations who appeared before the commission was the mixing of non-Prayer Book ceremonial with the Prayer Book liturgy.[68] However, the reply of John A. Le Couter, vicar of St Columba's, to these allegations was typical of responses by Ritualist priests. Writing to the commission, he stated that 'whilst the statement is in the main correct, I must entirely repudiate the colour attempted to be given to the facts. Without pledging myself to all the details, I have to say that the ceremonial used in my Church is that ordered expressly or by implication by the ornaments rubric.'[69]

Whilst the Evangelical wing of the church engaged with the commission with enthusiasm, the Ritualists tried their hardest not to engage at all. Initially the written responses by Ritualist clergy to the charges laid on the evidence of Evangelicals were not only similar, but followed a template. As Le Couter's reply shows, this template stated that they did not disagree with the evidence in the main, but disagreed with the 'colour' given in the reporting of it, and affirmed that their services were not only in line with, but ordered by, the Ornaments Rubric. Most clergy altered this template to suit the particular charges made by the Evangelicals against them; some, however, just sent the template reply itself, resulting in a series of identical responses.[70] This reply not only demonstrated Ritualist adherence to their interpretation of the Ornaments Rubric, but also continued the trend of disregarding bodies that represented the established relationship between church and state, and particularly the power

---

[67] *Royal Commission on Ecclesiastical Discipline: Minutes of Evidence taken before the Royal Commission on Ecclesiastical Discipline: Volume One*, Cd.3069 (London, 1906), 13.

[68] See Dan Cruickshank, *From the Sublime to the Ridiculous: Ritualism and Anglo-Catholicism in the Evidence of the Royal Commission into Ecclesiastical Discipline, 1904–6* (London, 2018).

[69] *Royal Commission on Ecclesiastical Discipline: Volume One*, 13.

[70] Ibid. 13, 22, 23. It is not clear who created the template: Yates claims it was the English Church Union but provides no reference to substantiate this: *Anglican Ritualism*, 327. I would agree with Yates that this is the likely source of the template, although it cannot be certain.

of parliament and the secular courts over the church. This disdain was reinforced when Walter Phillimore, a leading ecclesiastical lawyer, appeared before the commission and lamented the fact that 'the Privy Council does not command the respect of a great number of people who appear before it'.[71] A lack of respect for the established judicial system of the church led to disregard for its decisions, in turn threatening to undermine the very basis of that judicial system. It was becoming increasingly clear, however, that the mood of the Church of England was that consent of churchmen was needed for them to be governed by the secular courts.

After the public giving of evidence, all diocesan bishops were asked to provide responses to various questions linked to ritual irregularities that had been witnessed in their particular diocese.[72] Charles Gore, then bishop of Birmingham and a leading Anglo-Catholic, desired in his reply to bring to the fore the 'principle as to the seat of legislative and judicial authority on matters affecting the doctrine, discipline and worship of the Church' which he believed lay 'behind the controversy about details of ceremonial'. Gore held that Christ had founded the church to have independent authority, but that during the Reformation the distinction between the authority of the church and that of the state had become less clear. Now, Gore argued, this should be corrected, for the Church of England had become 'only one of many religious bodies in the State enjoying practically equal toleration and completeness of civil privilege, and in consequence ... the legislative and judicial authorities of the State have ceased to be in any real sense representative of the church or capable of claiming the allegiance of churchmen in spiritual matters'.[73] This was a more sophisticated ecclesiology than that of many of Gore's fellow Ritualists; it still envisaged the church's independence from parliamentary oversight, but admitted that this had not historically been true of, and was not currently the case in, the Church of England. Instead, Gore advocated this position as a necessary corrective now that the Reformation was over and the state more tolerant of a wider range of confessional groups. Gore was thus admitting that

---

[71] Ibid. 308.
[72] London, LPL, RCED 4, fols 200–9, Charles Gore to the Royal Commission on Ecclesiastical Discipline, [February 1906].
[73] Ibid., fols 201–2.

self-government, which Ritualists desired, was not enshrined in the church's current legal structure, whilst calling for it to become so.

On 21 June 1906, the commission delivered its report. Like the reports of the previous royal commission, this affirmed the nature of the Church of England as the state church. However, instead of framing this relationship in terms of the guardianship of the church by parliament, it described it in terms of oversight by the nation, concluding that 'the nation has right to expect that in the national Church the services shall be conducted according to law'.[74] This was a significant step, as it changed the concept of guardianship from a clear and concrete responsibility of parliament into a more abstract guardianship by the nation. The commission acknowledged that the majority of the English population were not habitual Anglican church-goers, but its report nonetheless affirmed that 'all parishioners', whether members of the established church or not, had the right to expect their local parish church to abide by the law.[75] This distinction between 'parishioners' and 'church-goers' demonstrated a commitment to retaining uniform legal practice across the church, espoused by a parliament that represented the entire nation, and thus all parishioners, Anglican and Nonconformist alike. At the same time, the report recognized that regular churchgoers had desires of their own, and that these could sometimes be in conflict with the law governing the church. It concluded that 'the law of public worship in the Church of England is too narrow for the religious life of the present generation'. The commissioners were also worried that the requirement of legal obedience to the Prayer Book 'needlessly condemns much which a great section of Church people, including many of her most devoted members, value'.[76] The commission was thus attempting to find a middle ground between legal obedience and parliamentary oversight on the one hand, and on the other the desires of some churchgoers to be allowed to worship how they wished.

---

[74] *Report of the Royal Commission on Ecclesiastical Discipline*, Cd.3040 (London, 1906), 2. The question of whether it was through parliament that the nation expressed its idea of right religion would play a central role in the Prayer Book crisis: John G. Maiden, *National Religion and the Prayer Book Controversy, 1927–1928* (Woodbridge, 2009).
[75] *Royal Commission on Ecclesiastical Discipline: Report*, 2.
[76] Ibid. 75.

The report concluded:

In an age which has witnessed an extraordinary revival of spiritual life and activity, the Church has had to work under regulations fitted for a different condition of things without that power of self-adjustment which is inherent in the conception of a living church ... The result has inevitably been that ancient rubrics have been strained in the desire to find in them meanings which it had been judicially held they cannot bear; while, on the other hand, the construction placed on them in accordance with legal rules has sometimes appeared forced and unnatural. With an adequate power of self-adjustment, we might reasonably expect that revision of the strict letter of the law would be undertaken with such due regard for the living mind of the Church, and would secure the obedience of many, now dissatisfied, who desire to be loyal, and would justify the Church as a whole, in insisting on the obedience of all.[77]

In keeping with this call for an 'an adequate power of self-adjustment', the commission concluded that letters of business should be issued to the convocations of the church, to revise the Prayer Book to make it suitable for the twentieth century. This was a significant shift away from Tait's original vision of resolution of the Ritualist conflict through parliamentary imposition of legislation on the church; instead it represented a first step towards self-governance by the church.

Two key themes emerge from the report. Firstly, it affirmed that the Church of England was a national church, a church in which everyone in England had a say, whether they attended on a Sunday or not. As such, they had a right to expect that their church would remain within the bounds of the law and the Protestant establishment. At the same time, the report recognized that the church needed to consider changing the Prayer Book so it could reflect the current state of the church and thus create a new understanding of uniformity. The commissioners also recommended this new uniformity because it would, in their view, make it easier to prosecute those Ritualists whose 'practices lie on the Rome-ward side of a line of deep cleavage between the Church of England and that of Rome'.[78] In terms of ecclesiology, the commission thus sought to

[77] Ibid. 76.
[78] Ibid. 53.

create a *via media* between the traditional ecclesiology of the Church of England and that of the Ritualists. It argued that the nation had a role of oversight of the church and consequently endorsed parliament's attempts to legislate against Ritualism; however, it also recognized that rubrics written in the sixteenth or seventeenth centuries were not universally fit for purpose when it came to the governance of the church of 1906. It therefore recommended giving the church the power of readjustment to fit modern needs. This bypassed the Ritualists' attempts at legislative interpretation, by supporting legislation that had sought to crack down on their interpretation of the Ornaments Rubric, whilst affirming that practices that courts had found to be incompatible with the rubric should be understood as compatible with the essence of the Church of England.[79] The recommendations of the commission were neither strict Erastianism nor Tractarian-style spiritual independence; instead, it presented a halfway house, with the crown being recommended to gift the church the (legal) power to determine its liturgical practice. The Ritualists had lost many ecclesiological battles over the course of the nineteenth century, but with the commission's recommendation of an Erastian-style church independence it seems that they might have been winning the war.

The ecclesiology of the report of 1906 would prove to be the start of a much greater, and much longer, battle over the ecclesiology of the Church of England, which reached a major turning point in the Prayer Book crisis of the late 1920s.[80] The Prayer Book crisis provided a forceful demonstration that parliament was the ultimate legislative body for the church, but in doing so it paradoxically reduced parliament's role in the governance of the Church of England significantly and enhanced the legislative power of internal

---

[79] Ibid. 75–6.

[80] See my study of the Prayer Book crisis: Dan D. Cruickshank, *The Theology and Ecclesiology of the Prayer Book Crisis, 1906–1928* (Cham, 2019). The struggle between church and parliament would not end with the Prayer Book crisis but would continue well into the twentieth century: John Maiden and Peter Webster, 'Parliament, the Church of England and the Last Gasp of Political Protestantism, 1963–4', *PH* 32 (2013), 361–77. In the twentieth-first century the issue rumbles on, with threats to enact legislation to allow women to join the episcopate coming from parliamentarians after it was rejected by the General Synod of the Church of England in 2012: Patrick Wintour, 'Female Bishops Controversy: Government says it will not step in', *The Guardian*, 12 November 2012, online at: <https://www.theguardian.com/world/2012/nov/21/women-bishops-controversy>, accessed 28 January 2019.

church structures. What is clear is that the Ritualist controversy that divided the Church of England in the nineteenth century was focused not only on incense and chasubles, but on questions of who created church laws and how they were to be interpreted. In this regard, the Ritualists ensured that the Oxford Movement lived on by offering a radical embodiment of the idea of spiritual independence and by helping to lay the foundations for an internal church legislature in the Church of England.

'The day of Compromise is past': The Oxford Free Churches and 'Passive Resistance' to the 1902 Education Act

Martin Wellings*
Oxford

Balfour's Education Act of 1902, abolishing directly elected school boards and making rate aid available to denominational schools, provoked a storm of opposition from the Free Churches in England and Wales. One response was to refuse to pay the portion of the rate designated for the support of denominational schools; this led to Free Church representatives appearing in court and facing distraint and even imprisonment for non-payment. This article offers a case study of 'passive resistance' in Oxford, where opposition to the act was co-ordinated by a Citizen's Education League and the Free Church Council. It sets out the case made by the Free Churches, explores the personnel and denominational identities of the resisters, and assesses the impact of the campaign between 1903 and the First World War.

On Tuesday 28 July 1903, the regular sitting of the Oxford City Police Court was enlivened by an exceptionally numerous and unusually respectable body of defendants. Instead of the familiar weekly sprinkling of petty thieves, recalcitrant tramps and habitual drunkards, the magistrates were faced by some thirty prominent citizens, including most of Oxford's leading Free Church ministers. All were answering summonses for failing to pay the district rate.[1] This court appearance was a local manifestation of 'passive resistance' to the Education Act of 1902, part of a nationwide phenomenon which, by the end of 1905, saw 53,863 summonses and the imprisonment of 189 people for steadfast refusal to pay rates for the support of

* 26 Upland Park Rd, Oxford, OX2 7RU. E-mail: martin.wellings@oxfordmethodists.org.uk.
[1] 'Passive Resistance in Oxford: Determined Protest against the Education Act', *Oxford Chronicle* (hereafter: *OC*), 31 July 1903, 8.

Studies in Church History 56 (2020), 455–470   © Ecclesiastical History Society 2020
doi: 10.1017/stc.2019.25

denominational schools.[2] Civil disobedience on such a significant scale took the government by surprise, and although it failed to secure the amendment or repeal of the act, passive resistance contributed to the political changes which brought the Liberals to power in 1906.[3] It also reflected the position and outlook of the Free Churches in the first decade of the twentieth century: a combination of optimism and insecurity, respectability and militancy.[4]

The historiography of the genesis and reception of the act is extensive. As well as brief treatments in general histories of religion and education in the period by Benjamin Sacks, Marjorie Cruickshank and James Murphy,[5] the interplay of political and denominational loyalties in the education debates of the 1890s and early 1900s have been analysed by J. R. Fairhurst in a thesis of 1974,[6] Stephen Koss in *Nonconformity in Modern British Politics* (1975), David Bebbington in *The Nonconformist Conscience: Chapel and Politics 1870–1914* (1982) and Ian Machin in *Politics and the Churches in Great Britain, 1869 to 1921* (1987). D. R. Pugh has explored the debate from the perspectives of Nonconformity, Wesleyan Methodism and those in several denominations who were eager for compromise.[7] James Munson's chapter on 'Passive Resistance and Nonconformist Power' in his *The Nonconformists* (1991) draws on his doctoral thesis of 1973, which gave close attention to the passive resistance campaign. These studies have approached passive resistance from the standpoint of national politics; the present article drills

[2] J. E. B. Munson, 'A Study of Nonconformity in Edwardian England as revealed by the Passive Resistance Movement against the 1902 Education Act' (DPhil dissertation, University of Oxford, 1973), 256. Of those imprisoned, 39 were gaoled for a second time.

[3] Stephen Koss, *Nonconformity in Modern British Politics* (London, 1975), 38–54.

[4] For accounts of Nonconformity in this period, see James Munson, *The Nonconformists. In Search of a Lost Culture* (London, 1991); Michael Watts, *The Dissenters*, 3: *The Crisis and Conscience of Nonconformity* (Oxford, 2015).

[5] Benjamin Sacks, *The Religious Issue in the State Schools of England and Wales, 1902–1914* (Albuquerque, NM, 1961); Marjorie Cruickshank, *Church and State in English Education, 1870 to the Present Day* (London, 1964); James Murphy, *Church, State and Schools in Britain 1800–1970* (London, 1971).

[6] J. R. Fairhurst, 'Some Aspects of the Relationship between Education, Politics, and Religion from 1895 to 1906' (DPhil dissertation, University of Oxford, 1974).

[7] D. R. Pugh, 'The 1902 Education Act: The Search for a Compromise', *BJES* 16 (1968), 164–78; idem, 'Wesleyan Methodism and the Education Crisis of 1902', *BJES* 36 (1988), 232–49; idem, 'English Nonconformity, Education and Passive Resistance, 1903–06', *History of Education* 19 (1990), 355–73.

down into a local context, and offers a textured exploration of Nonconformity in an unlikely setting.

Munson concludes that the majority of cases of passive resistance occurred in smaller towns and cities, with a population of less than one hundred thousand, and there was a correlation between the strength of passive resistance and the strength of Nonconformity.[8] In size, Oxford, a city of some fifty-eight thousand people,[9] was typical of the centres of passive resistance; as a cathedral and university city, and the birthplace of Tractarianism, it was distinctive. This article will argue that Nonconformity was a growing and vocal presence, even in Oxford, and that the Free Churches' ability to muster and articulate significant opposition to the Education Act demonstrated the movement's strength and self-confidence. Going beyond public meetings to passive resistance, although only an option for a minority, carried symbolic weight as an indicator of dissent, recasting the debate over education policy into the rhetoric of martyrdom.

The Education Act of 1902 emerged from more than a decade of debate and failed legislation seeking to address a cluster of issues around primary and secondary education in England and Wales.[10] Before 1870, elementary education was provided by a network of 'voluntary' schools, largely funded and controlled by religious bodies, principally the National Society (Church of England), the British and Foreign Schools Society (non-denominational, but largely Nonconformist in support), the Roman Catholics and the Wesleyan Methodists. W. E. Forster's Education Act of 1870 acknowledged that the voluntary system was failing to keep pace with an increasing population as well as with rising costs and expectations, and so permitted the establishment of local school boards where existing educational provision was deemed inadequate. The boards, elected triennially, were empowered to levy a rate to build and then manage new schools. Consequently the act created a dual system of elementary education, setting the rate-funded board schools alongside the voluntary schools, funded by supporters' subscriptions, pupils' fees and government grants. Most voluntary schools operated on an explicitly denominational basis, but in the board schools

---

[8] Munson, 'Nonconformity in Edwardian England', 277–85.
[9] C. J. Day, 'Modern Oxford', in Alan Crossley and C. R. Elrington, eds, *A History of the County of Oxford*, 4: *The City of Oxford*, VCH (Oxford, 1979), 181–259, at 182.
[10] Fairhurst, 'Education, Politics, and Religion'.

religious education, where offered, was required to be non-denominational, under William Cowper-Temple's amendment to the act.[11]

Forster's act was a compromise, both between the rival advocates
of unashamedly denominational and wholly secular education and
between supporters of voluntary provision and those urging a
state-funded and regulated national system. These debates about fundamental principles continued in the ensuing decades, and were
sharpened by increasing concerns about many aspects of the nation's
educational structure.[12] Under the dual system, voluntary schools
provided the majority of school places and pupil attendances (56
per cent and 52 per cent respectively in 1901)[13] but struggled to
make ends meet. Education department figures for 1900, for
instance, showed that more than half of the voluntary schools were
financially 'under water'; in the same year Randall Davidson warned
Archbishop Temple that legislation was needed to 'avert catastro-
phe'.[14] The board schools had access to rate funding and could pay
better salaries to teachers, but they faced complaints of extravagance
and inefficiency. Anglicans and Roman Catholics denounced the
non-denominational Bible teaching of the board schools as 'godless'
or as 'a new denominationalism' masquerading as tolerance,[15] while
Free Church leaders and Radical MPs lost no opportunity to complain of 'sectarian' teaching and Anglican proselytizing in those sin-
gle-school districts where Nonconformist families had no choice but
to send their children to Church of England schools. The dual system, bedevilled by this 'religious warfare',[16] seemed ill equipped to
deliver consistent and effective elementary education, let alone to
address the need for proper secondary education and professional
teacher training. Through the late 1880s and 1890s, options were
debated in the heavyweight periodicals and explored by royal
commissions. Meanwhile reforms in local government, which
brought the creation of county and county borough councils in 1888,

[11] G. I. T. Machin, *Politics and the Churches in Great Britain, 1869 to 1921* (Oxford, 1987), 31–40.
[12] For the problems with the 1870 compromise, see J. E. B. Munson, 'The Unionist Coalition and Education, 1895–1902', *HistJ* 20 (1977), 607–45, especially 608–13.
[13] Ibid. 608.
[14] Sacks, *Religious Issue*, 16; Fairhurst, 'Education, Politics, and Religion', 205.
[15] R. C. Moberly, *Undenominationalism as a Principle of Primary Education* (London, 1902), 8.
[16] Munson, 'Unionist Coalition', 611.

suggested the possibility of a more comprehensive and less contentious system for managing the nation's schools.[17]

Between 1896 and 1901, the Unionist government brought forward a series of abortive measures to reform education. Finally, towards the end of 1901, A. J. Balfour and the duke of Devonshire took the lead in crafting new and comprehensive legislation. Introduced in the House of Commons on 24 March 1902, the Education Act received the royal assent on 18 December and came into force in England and Wales in March 1903.[18] Balfour's act abolished the school boards, transferring their assets and responsibilities to county and county-borough councils as Local Education Authorities (LEAs). Voluntary schools remained in being, but could opt to be 'maintained' by the LEA. Under this arrangement, the LEA would appoint two of the school's six managers, pay the teachers' salaries and provide textbooks and teaching materials, while the denomination paid for the upkeep of the school building.[19]

From the outset the Education Bill faced strong opposition from the Free Churches. By 1902 the Free Church denominations (the Congregationalists, Baptists and Methodists) felt confident in their numerical strength, financial resources and popular appeal. Statistics suggested that over half the active membership of all non-Roman Catholic churches in England and Wales was Nonconformist; in the wider Anglo-Saxon world, Nonconformists outnumbered Anglicans by six to one.[20] In the National Council of the Evangelical Free Churches, formed in 1896 and co-ordinating a nationwide network of seven hundred local councils and thirty-six federations,[21] the cluster of denominations had a mechanism for joint action, including political lobbying. The gradual repeal of civil disabilities during the nineteenth century had given Nonconformists access to the franchise, to public office and to the universities, but had left memories of battles against injustice and continuing resentment at the privileges of the established church.

---

[17] For a concise description of the problems, see Fairhurst, 'Education, Politics, and Religion', 10–30.
[18] Munson, 'Unionist Coalition', 635–41; Machin, *Politics and the Churches*, 261–5.
[19] Munson, 'Unionist Coalition', 635–6.
[20] Munson, *Nonconformists*, 6–34, with statistics at 9, 10; Koss, *Nonconformity*, 38. For a more cautious appraisal, see Machin, *Politics and the Churches*, 220–1.
[21] E. K. H. Jordan, *Free Church Unity: History of the Free Church Council Movement, 1896–1941* (London, 1956), 53, 55.

This resentment was exacerbated by antipathy and fear as the Church of England seemed to be moving closer to Rome under the influence of Anglo-Catholicism.[22] Free Church confidence and Nonconformist grievances could be mobilized in defence of religious liberty, civil equality and Evangelical Protestantism, and in opposition to privilege and popery. Education, which had been a neuralgic issue between the Church of England and the Nonconformists since the 1830s, was guaranteed to raise Free Church anxieties, reopen old wounds and galvanize opposition. Moreover, after several years of division over the morality of the South African War, the Free Churches needed a cause around which to unite, and education offered an ideal campaign to arouse the Nonconformist conscience.[23] Critical contemporaries were quick to see this, and to level accusations of political opportunism.[24] In their defence, however, it should be said that the Free Churches had consistently supported the school boards and had equally consistently opposed additional state aid to denominational schools. Through the 1890s the annual assemblies of the Baptists, Congregationalists and Primitive Methodists, and the National Council of the Evangelical Free Churches, had called for the establishment of unsectarian Christian schools in every district, demanded the abolition of religious tests for teachers, advocated a national system of teacher training colleges and opposed rate funding for schools giving denominational religious instruction.[25] Balfour's bill cut across all these objectives, and it therefore provoked angry reactions. The exception to this uniformity of Free Church opposition came from the Wesleyan Methodists, because the Wesleyans, with more than four hundred and fifty schools of their own, had a historical commitment to denominational education and also stood to benefit financially from the new system. Wesleyan opinion, therefore, was sharply divided.[26]

Ten days after the introduction of the bill in the House of Commons, Joseph Parker, chairman of the Congregational Union and president-designate of the Free Church Council, wrote to

---

[22] Munson, *Nonconformists*, 228–30.

[23] D. W. Bebbington, *The Nonconformist Conscience: Chapel and Politics 1870–1914* (London, 1982), 142.

[24] Thus *OC*, 18 September 1903, 6, quoting the Marquess of Londonderry; 'Passive Resisters in Court', *Oxford Times* (hereafter: *OT*), 1 August 1903, 7.

[25] Munson, 'Nonconformity in Edwardian England', 68–9.

[26] Pugh, 'Wesleyan Methodism', 232–49.

The Times calling for 'quiet, resolute, and uncompromising resistance' to the proposals.[27] Through the spring and summer of 1902, the regular denominational assemblies and conferences, and specially convened gatherings, focused opposition to the bill. A. M. Fairbairn, principal of Mansfield College, Oxford, led a delegation of church leaders to meet Balfour in June, setting out the Free Churches' objections, and concluding: 'We will not submit.'[28]

Alongside this rallying of opposition and lobbying the government, Free Church spokesmen raised the possibility of 'passive resistance' to the education measure. George White, a Baptist MP, seems to have been the first to suggest that opponents of 'sectarian' schools might refuse to pay the education rate, and the notion was picked up by Robertson Nicoll, the influential editor of the *British Weekly*.[29] Nicoll coined the phrase 'passive resistance', and by the autumn of 1902 the National Free Church Council was asking its local affiliates to consider creating a register of those pledged to refuse the rate. A national Passive Resistance Committee was formed in December 1902, with John Clifford, a doughty veteran of many educational battles, as president.[30] Momentum built up during the first half of 1903, between the passing of the act and the issuing of the first rate demands under the new legislation. Amidst an avalanche of propaganda from the National Council and the press, local Free Church Councils were urged to coordinate resistance directly, or to set up Passive Resistance or Citizens' Education Leagues to do so. The press's resources included a new journal, *The Crusader*, dedicated to the cause. The campaign was pursued with vigour until the Liberal landslide in the general election of 1906. Thereafter, as the Liberal government's attempts to redeem its pledge to amend the 1902 act were frustrated by the House of Lords, passive resistance continued. Most of the active opposition ended with the First World War, but Clifford persisted in refusing the rate until his death in 1923 and a passive resistance case was recorded in Bakewell as late as 1926.[31]

---

[27] *The Times*, 5 April 1902, 8.
[28] W. B. Selbie, *The Life of Andrew Martin Fairbairn* (London, 1914), 272–7; Bebbington, *Nonconformist Conscience*, 143.
[29] Machin, *Politics and the Churches*, 266.
[30] Munson, 'Nonconformity in Edwardian England', 190–1; Charles T. Bateman, *John Clifford, Free Church Leader and Preacher* (London, 1904), 242–86.
[31] Munson, *Nonconformists*, 347.

This, then, was the national backdrop to the court appearance of Oxford Free Church leaders in July 1903. What was the local context for passive resistance? And how did the campaign play out in Oxford?

In 1903 Oxford had a full range of voluntary schools: nineteen Anglican, two Roman Catholic and one Wesleyan;[32] three British or independent schools, two in the city centre and one in East Oxford, had been handed over to the school board in 1898.[33] The city's school board, established in 1871 in the teeth of Anglican opposition, only began to build its own schools in the late 1890s; hitherto, strenuous fundraising by the denominations (mostly Anglicans) met the need for schools in the growing suburbs and kept the board at bay.[34] The board reflected the religious and political complexion of the city, including among its members in 1902 the city's senior Baptist minister, James Dann, and Isaac Alden, one of his deacons, as well as the Conservative Alderman Hugh Hall and Commander W. H. Maunsell, a staunch supporter of the voluntary schools and the National Society.[35] The city council, where the Conservatives enjoyed a comfortable majority over the Liberals,[36] quickly brought forward a scheme to set up an education committee, and the process of implementation rolled forward in the spring of 1903, as managers were nominated for the 'maintained' schools and the additional costs were incorporated into the district rates. At the same time, Free Church leaders signalled their opposition to the act and their determination to resist the rate.

By the beginning of the twentieth century there was a strong Free Church constituency in the city of Oxford and its rural hinterland. A correspondent writing to the Conservative-leaning *Oxford Times* in October 1903 suggested that there were five thousand Nonconformists in the city.[37] Baptists, Congregationalists and three separate Methodist denominations were well represented, and Mansfield College, opened in 1886, brought a distinguished faculty

[32] 'Oxford Education Committee', *OC*, 10 July 1903, 3.
[33] Nesta Selwyn, 'Education', in Crossley and Elrington eds, *History of the County of Oxford*, 4: 442–62, at 442–3.
[34] Malcolm Graham, 'The Suburbs of Victorian Oxford: Growth in a Pre-Industrial City' (PhD thesis, University of Leicester, 1985), 411–19; cf. 'Oxford School Board', *OT*, 4 July 1903, 7, a largely sympathetic account of the board's history.
[35] 'Oxford School Board', *OC*, 9 May 1902, 3.
[36] 'The Local Elections', *OC*, 7 November 1902, 6.
[37] 'Passive Resistance', John W. Embury to the editor, *OT*, 10 October 1903, 3.

and a body of ministerial students to strengthen the Free Church cause.[38] Already linked informally, the denominations came together in the Oxford Nonconformist Council (later the Free Church Council) in 1895. The Free Churches were also active in the commercial life of the city and in municipal politics. Although a minority in a city dominated by a Conservative and Anglican establishment, Oxford's Free Churches celebrated their growing numbers and were alert to perceived infringements of their civil and religious liberties.

Opposition to Balfour's education proposals was to be expected from the Oxford Free Churches. From its inception, education was a regular item on the agenda of the council and its executive committee. Moreover, from 1896 the council's president was John Massie, a tutor at Mansfield College and a member of the Bryce Commission on Secondary Education. Massie was an early and persistent passive resister, a member of the national Passive Resistance Committee and an indefatigable campaigner, to the extent that he resigned from his post at Mansfield in summer 1903 in order to 'devote himself to public work, and more especially to the cause of Religious Equality'. Massie was subsequently elected Liberal MP for the Cricklade division of Wiltshire in 1906.[39]

The Oxford Free Church Council began to coordinate opposition to the bill in the spring of 1902. A 'thoroughly representative' meeting assembled at the Free Methodist chapel on 8 May, and passed a series of resolutions condemning the bill on both educational and Free Church principles.[40] Thereafter the progress of the legislation through parliament was tracked by the *Free Church Magazine*, with its stages punctuated by public meetings, critical resolutions and denunciations from the pulpit. On 27 July 1902, for example, James Robertson told his congregation at George Street

---

[38] Michael Hopkins, *Spires and Meeting Houses: A History of the Origins, Growth and Development of Congregationalism in and around Oxford* (Milton Keynes, 2011), 33–112; Rosie Chadwick, '"Every one of us is called to be a missionary": The New Road Chapel Home Mission, 1882–1916', in eadem, ed., *A Protestant Catholic Church of Christ* (Oxford, 2003), 171–200; Elaine Kaye, *Mansfield College, Oxford: Its Origin, History and Significance* (Oxford, 1996), 69–90.

[39] 'Dr Massie and Mansfield College', *OC*, 1 May 1903, 12; Ian Machin, 'Massie, John (1842–1925)', *ODNB*, 2007, online at: <http://www.oxforddnb.com/view/article/58254>, accessed 25 January 2019.

[40] 'The Government Education Bill: Why it should be opposed', *Oxford and District Free Church Magazine* (hereafter: *ODFCM*), May 1902, 18.

Congregational Church that the bill was 'a contradiction and negation of the very principles which make us Free Churchmen'.[41]
Following the successful passage of the bill, Massie warned the readers
of the *Free Church Magazine* that 'the day of compromise is past'.[42]
Three months later R. W. Perks, the most high-profile lay Wesleyan
of his generation, Liberal MP for Louth, inveterate lobbyist and foun-
der of the Nonconformist Parliamentary Council, was the star speaker
at a public meeting in Oxford, describing the bill, to tumultuous
applause, as 'one of the most reactionary measures which had ever disgraced the Statute Book of this country'.[43]

As well as pulpit and platform rhetoric, letters to the local press and
plans to make the education issue a test question at the municipal
elections,[44] the Free Churches took up the possibility of passive resistance. In September 1902 the National Free Church Council asked
local councils to consider enrolling the names of potential resisters,
and to decide whether to do so before or after the reassembling of
parliament in October. The Oxford Free Church Council voted in
principle for enrolment, opting to wait until parliament gathered.
It also suggested a petition to the king to withhold the royal assent
from the bill, if passed by parliament, pending a general election,
and urged county councils likewise to refuse to implement the legislation. The council argued that the bill was being forced through parliament by undemocratic and unconstitutional means; that the
government, re-elected in 1900 to end the South African War, had
no mandate for such sweeping and contentious domestic legislation;
and that the evidence of by-elections was that the country opposed
the measure.[45]

In March 1903 the council's executive agreed to organize a
meeting to discuss 'the procedure of forming a Citizens' League'.[46]

[41] 'Our Free Churches and the Education Bill', *ODFCM*, August 1902, 34.
[42] John Massie, 'Church v. Education', *ODFCM*, January 1903, 1–2.
[43] 'Mr R. W. Perks, MP, in Oxford', *ODFCM*, May 1903, 23; 'Mr R. W. Perks, MP, in
Oxford', *OC*, 24 April 1903, 7. For Perks, the 'member for nonconformity', see
O. A. Rattenbury, rev. Clive D. Field, 'Perks, Sir Robert William, First Baronet
(1849–1934)', *ODNB*, 2006, online at: <http://www.oxforddnb.com/view/article/
35481>, accessed 24 May 2019.
[44] Oxford, Angus Library, Regent's Park College, Minute Book of the Free Church
Council Executive, 9 October 1902.
[45] 'Oxford and District Free Church Council and the Education Bill', *ODFCM*, October
1902, 41–2.
[46] Free Church Council Executive minutes, 4 March 1903.

At the beginning of May, the Liberal-leaning *Oxford Chronicle* carried 'An Apologia for Passive Resistance', setting out the case for refusing the education rate. The 'Apologia' was unsigned, but Massie's influence was detected in the text.[47] The authors expressed an obligation to explain to their fellow citizens why they were taking the 'unusual course' of refusing the rate. The political and democratic arguments made in October 1902 were repeated and amplified, but the principal reason justifying passive resistance was that the resisters regarded the rate as 'an outrage upon conscience'. Ratepayers of all denominations were being required to fund the teaching of one denomination; citizens were being asked to pay for 'a sectarian teaching in which they do not believe and which they regard besides as, in certain respects, pernicious in itself and injurious to the well-being of the State'; parents were effectively supporting the proselytizing of their own children; and teachers were under pressure to sacrifice their beliefs for the sake of professional advancement. The 'Apologia' continued that the act represented a 'bargain' between the government and the Church of England and so violated the principle that the state should be impartial between denominations, and it broke the principle that publicly funded bodies should be under public management. Quiet resistance to 'an unjust measure, so unjustifiably imposed' was a 'bounden duty', undertaken 'with a solemn and deliberate sense of responsibility' by people who 'have unfailingly honoured and obeyed the law' but who believed that 'there must be limits to civil obedience'.[48]

At the beginning of June twenty ratepayers, headed by Massie, Robertson and Dann, presented a memorial to the city council affirming their intention of 'leaving the law to take its course for the collection of that part of the Education Rate which is levied for the support of sectarian schools'. The signatories emphasized their willingness to pay the rest of the general district and education rate, and expressed 'our sincere regret' that the corporation's collectors had refused to accept part payment, as had happened elsewhere.[49] Two days later the Free Church Council resolved to form a Citizens' Education League in Oxford, comprising 'those who individually

---

[47] 'An Apologia for Passive Resistance', *OC*, 1 May 1903, 7; 'Passive Resistance: The Oxford Apologia', *OC*, 8 May 1903, 7.
[48] 'Apologia for Passive Resistance', 7.
[49] 'The Education Rate: Conscientious Objectors', *OC*, 5 June 1903, 8.

feel constrained to refuse payment of the rate for sectarian schools'
and sympathizers unable to refuse the rate 'for one reason or another'
but nonetheless pledged to support the amendment or repeal of the
act. The officers and committee of the league corresponded closely
with the Free Church Council executive, with the same president
(Massie), secretary (Robertson) and treasurer (James Nix, a
Wesleyan).[50]

By July 1903, when the first resisters appeared in court, the number had grown to twenty-nine, and a further five summonses were
heard in early September. 'Watcher', writing in the *Oxford
Chronicle*, claimed that the authorities wanted to deal with all the
cases together, and that distraints for non-payment would soon follow.[51] On 25 September, the *Chronicle* reported that the city police
had spent two days visiting the homes of thirty resisters, distraining a
range of goods, including a plated spirit kettle and stand and an
omelette dish from Massie's home, a barometer from the Revd
A. S. Welch (Summertown's Congregational minister), a marble
clock from Robertson, two candlesticks from Vernon Bartlet, another
Mansfield tutor, and a brass coal scoop from Mrs Hazel. Clocks,
teapots, candlesticks and cutlery were popular items, carefully
wrapped, labelled and removed by the police in a rubber-tyred
brougham.[52] A week later, when the goods were auctioned at the
town hall, an agent bought the items back on behalf of the original
owners, paying £5 or £6 more than the outstanding rates.

Three themes emerge from the process of summons, distraint and
sale. First, there was a good deal of common ground, sometimes even
collusion, between the resisters and the authorities. This was most
marked in the appearance before the city magistrates at the end of
July. The resisters were not placed in the dock; their solicitor was
given ample opportunity to make a speech against the act; and the
bench overruled the city solicitor's plea that part-payment of the
rate was contrary to administrative practice and perhaps to law.
This 'magisterial compromise' was unsurprising, given the composition of the bench, which included several staunch Free Churchmen,
one of whom, the Liberal alderman Robert Buckell, spoke at a

[50] 'The Free Churches and the Education Act', *OC*, 5 June 1903, 8; compare 'Oxford
and District Free Church Council Annual Meetings', *ODFCM*, June 1903, 29.
[51] 'Out and About', *OC*, 4 September 1903, 6.
[52] 'Passive Resistance: Distraints at Oxford', *OC*, 25 September 1903, 7.

Citizens' League meeting later on the same day. When the authorities came to distrain goods later in the summer, the proceedings were described as 'good-humoured' and 'amicable': the resisters were given notice of the police visit, and had generally identified a suitable and portable item for removal, sometimes leaving it with a maid to hand over to the officers.

Secondly, there was a noticeable concern to avoid public disorder. The police served the warrants for distraint with 'the greatest secrecy' in order 'to prevent any interference or attempts at demonstration on the part of the less considerate of the population'. Evidently this was seen not as depriving the resisters of desirable publicity, but as a courtesy to the respectable citizens whose homes were being raided. In a leading article on 31 July, the *Oxford Chronicle* commented that 'It is not at all likely that [the sales] will be marked in Oxford by the ebullitions of feeling that have broken out in many other towns.' 'Rowdy scenes' would be 'strongly discountenanced by those concerned in the Oxford cases'. In fact the first sale did witness 'noisy demonstrations' and 'lively incidents', but this was attributed to idlers and opponents of the cause.[53]

Thirdly, there was an element of theatricality in the process. Appearing in court in July, Massie attempted to pay the uncontested portion of the rate to the city solicitor, who, pushing the money away, declared: 'I refuse to take it.' Mr Clark, of Polstead Road, initially refused to admit the distraining officers to his house, negotiating with them through the letter-box. Mr Couldrey, of Abbey Road, invited them to stay for tea and a short prayer meeting, suggesting that it 'would do them all a lot of good'.[54]

Theatre of a different kind came into play with the Primitive Methodist minister John Leach. Across the country, Primitive Methodists were among the most determined resisters, and most willing to face imprisonment.[55] Leach, an 'uncompromising Radical' and 'valiant champion of religious equality', was not satisfied with the polite and decorous process of distraint. Like Clifford and other militant resisters, he sought to divest himself of distrainable goods in order to force the authorities to send him to prison. This took

---

[53] 'Passive Resistance: Another Stage', *OC*, 31 July 1903, 6; 'Out and About', *OC*, 4 September 1903, 6; 'Oxford Education Distraints', *OC*, 2 October 1903, 7.
[54] 'Passive Resistance at Oxford', *OC*, 31 July 1903, 8; 25 September 1903, 7.
[55] Munson, 'Nonconformity in Edwardian England', 300.

some time: in September 1903 the police distrained some pictures from his home; in March 1904, when Leach claimed that the contents of the manse belonged either to his wife or to the circuit, the officers politely asked for documentary proof, and left the house with a 'handsome but incomplete Indian tea service' and two vases. By October 1904 Leach was better prepared, and had his documents in place, with the result that he served seven days' imprisonment in Oxford Castle, emerging with the cry 'Hallelujah! I am still a Passive Resister!' The following summer Leach's appointment in the Oxford Circuit ended, but his commitment to passive resistance continued, leading to a further term of imprisonment, this time in Reading.[56] By the time of his death, in May 1912, Leach had been to gaol six times for passive resistance.[57]

John Leach laid the blame for his imprisonment on the archbishop of Canterbury, Cardinal Vaughan and the Wesleyan Conference.[58] This was unfair in all respects, but it did highlight differences between the Free Churches over passive resistance, particularly divisions within the Wesleyan Connexion. When Robert Perks addressed the Free Church Council in April 1903, he praised Oxford's Wesleyans as ahead of their fellows in opposition to the act, and Wesleyan lay leaders such as J. H. Salter and James Nix spoke out strongly against it.[59] Nix was an early passive resister, but he paid the rate before distraint proceedings began, and the same seems to have happened with the small number of Wesleyan resisters in 1904.[60] The Wesleyan ministers, meanwhile, were conspicuously absent from passive resistance gatherings.[61] Compounding the confusion, the Wesleyan Boys' School became a 'maintained' school under the act, and Salter and Nix remained on the governing body; the two managers appointed

---

[56] 'Distraints and Sales', *OC*, 25 March 1904, 7; *OC*, 18 November 1904, 7; 'Rev. John Leach', *Aldersgate Primitive Methodist Magazine* n.s. 8 (1909), 380–1, at 381.

[57] 'John Leach', *Minutes of the Ninety-Third Annual Conference of the Primitive Methodist Connexion* (London, 1912), 26.

[58] 'Passive Resistance in Oxford. Release of the Rev. J. Leach from Prison', *OC*, 18 November 1904, 7.

[59] *OC*, 24 April 1903, 7.

[60] 'Passive Resistance: Distraints at Oxford', 7. The 1904 list included Tom Skinner and Walter Slaughter, both Wesleyan local preachers; both paid before distraint: *OC*, 25 March 1904, 7.

[61] A point noted by Embury, 'Passive Resistance', 3.

by the city council were the sympathetic Nonconformists James Dann and H. S. Kingerlee.[62]

Who, then, were Oxford's passive resisters? In 1903–4, forty-four citizens were involved in passive resistance, as signatories to the memorial to the city council, in answering a rate summons, or as subjects of a distraint.[63] Since ratepayers were householders, and therefore predominantly male, it is not surprising that forty-two of the resisters were men; the two female resisters were Mrs Emma Hazel, of Beechcroft Road, and Miss Emma Barnett, of Park Crescent, both in the affluent northern suburbs. Eleven of the resisters were ministers, or members of staff at Mansfield College, and two others were laymen in church-related employment. Denominational affiliation, where it can be established, indicates a majority of Baptists (13), a significant number of Congregationalists (12) and a smaller number of Methodists (9, across three denominations).[64] The size of the sample makes drawing conclusions difficult, but it may be noted that the Oxford data broadly supports James Munson's analysis that Baptists and Congregationalists were active resisters, but shows a much smaller proportion of Primitive Methodists and a much higher proportion of ministers than across the country as a whole.[65]

The response to the passive resistance campaign largely reflected predictable political and denominational affiliations. The *Oxford Chronicle* supported the resisters, praising their action as 'a question of conscience' and denying any connection between the movement and the Liberal Party.[66] The Conservative-leaning newspapers, the *Oxford Times* and *Jackson's Oxford Journal*, on the other hand, deplored the campaign as 'simply ludicrous' and 'painless martyrdom at the risk of a little personal inconvenience'.[67] For the Conservatives, passive resistance was unjustified and unconstitutional, setting a dangerous example of law-breaking.[68] The controversy played some

[62] 'Oxford Education Committee', *OC*, 10 July 1903, 3.

[63] Lists appeared in *OC*, 5 June 1903, 8; 31 July 1903, 8; 25 September 1903, 7; 25 March 1904, 7.

[64] Using the *ODFCM* and the indexes of Hopkins, *Spires and Meeting Houses*; Chadwick, ed., *Protestant Catholic Church of Christ*.

[65] Munson, 'Nonconformity in Edwardian England', 285–6, 294–5.

[66] 'A Question of Conscience', *OC*, 1 May 1903, 6; 'The Progress of Passive Resistance', *OC*, 18 September 1903, 6.

[67] 'The Farce of Passive Resistance', *OT*, 16 May 1903, 7

[68] 'Free Churchmen and the Education Act', *Jackson's Oxford Journal*, 1 August 1903, 6.

part in the 1903 municipal elections, when Norman Smith, bursar of Mansfield College, was a candidate in the city's North ward. Conservative posters proclaimed that Smith, a resister, stood for 'the destruction of Church Schools', and he was placed at the bottom of the poll.[69] It may be suggested that the education issue strengthened loyalties and inflamed rhetoric on both sides, but therefore did not significantly affect the balance of power in the city.

Passive resistance continued in Oxford at least until the outbreak of the First World War: James Dann was the spokesman for a group of twenty-five resisters, many of them veterans of 1903, who appeared before the magistrates on 13 July 1914 to record a protest against the 'unjust and invidious' Education Act.[70] The city solicitor observed that over 14,000 citizens had paid their rates; he might have added that the great majority of Free Church people had not become passive resisters, that the Liberal government's attempts to amend Balfour's act had proved unavailing, and that both the Liberal party and the Free Churches had turned their attention to other issues. The campaign lent credence to accusations of 'political Nonconformity' from Conservative and Anglican critics of the movement, while there were those within the Free Church ranks who felt that the 'Nonconformist conscience' had been hijacked for militant or party political ends and thereby discredited.[71] For the resisters, however, refusal to pay the education rate was a moral imperative. Even if ineffective in the short term (and the significance of the education debate in rallying support for the Liberals in 1906 and 1910 should not be under-estimated), passive resistance was a declaration of faith in the ultimate triumph of justice and truth. This confidence inspired some of Oxford's most respectable citizens to persevere over more than a decade in quiet defiance of the law.

[69] 'The Municipal Elections', *OT*, 7 November 1903, 3.
[70] 'Oxford Passive Resisters: Continued Protest', *OC*, 17 July 1914, 7.
[71] Munson, 'Nonconformity in Edwardian England', 396–7.

The Chancellors' Dilemma: The Impact of the First World War on Faculty Jurisdiction

Anne C. Brook*

Bradford

The Church of England successfully resisted proposals to bring decisions about alterations to its churches within the provisions of the Ancient Monuments Act (1913). However, the quid pro quo for the continuation of that ecclesiastical exemption was a strengthening of the operation of the faculty jurisdiction of diocesan chancellors. The First World War brought more urgent concerns for dioceses, but what no-one had foreseen was the huge death toll that war would bring, and the consequent pressure for communal and individual memorials to be created in churches and churchyards. In addition to the greatly increased volume of faculty applications, and the problem of some churches going ahead with commemorative projects without seeking the necessary faculties, some war memorial plans involving crucifixes began to raise the spectre of Ritualistic illegality.

It is especially painful to me, and it puts me in a very unfair position, that I should have to give judgment in these matters on application for Confirmatory Faculties. From a very long experience myself during the War in France, the very last thing I would desire to do would be to deliver any judgment which might look [like], or be supposed in any way to be[,] a reflection on a Memorial that is put up to those who have fallen. I would desire (as I hope everybody else would) to do the greatest honour to those who gave their lives for their Country during the War. However, it is a deep mistake, I am certain, to put up as a Memorial to those who have fallen (Memorials which are and which should be intended to be Memorials for all time) some object which is to say the least of it ecclesiastically disputable.[1]

* E-mail: a.c.brook01@members.leeds.ac.uk.

[1] *Wakefield Diocesan Gazette* (hereafter: *WDG*) 26/7 (December 1920), 111–12, reporting the consistory court judgment.

Studies in Church History 56 (2020), 471–486   © Ecclesiastical History Society 2020
doi: 10.1017/stc.2019.26

So spoke Chancellor Ernest Charles, expressing his frustration during a hearing of the Diocese of Wakefield Consistory Court on 27 November 1920, at which he was considering a retrospective application for a faculty from the parish church of St John the Evangelist, Clifton, near Brighouse in the West Riding of Yorkshire.

This article explores issues raised by faculty applications for the creation of memorials commemorating the First World War, particularly those which were open to legal rather than aesthetic objections, focusing on material from the diocese of Wakefield during Charles's period in office. The creation of First World War memorials has been examined from a range of perspectives, from the aesthetic concerns of art and architectural historians to the socio-political motivations of the decision makers. Most attention has been concentrated on the main civic memorials rather than on the multiplicity of other memorials erected by individual communities within villages, towns and cities. Every English parish church had at least one such memorial, but the fact that each one, whether located in the church or the churchyard, required approval at diocesan level has not figured significantly in either national or local studies. Nor has there been any published research on the operation of diocesan chancellors' faculty jurisdiction in the early twentieth century. Parish church memorials are of more than merely denominational interest, as many communities chose to locate their commemorations of all local citizens in the parish church or churchyard rather than in civic space.[2]

A faculty is a legal document issued by a church authority permitting an action. Faculty jurisdiction in the Church of England is of pre-Reformation origin and has as its basis the care and protection of ecclesiastical property. In the mid-nineteenth century, campaigners concerned with the fate of the country's heritage became increasingly critical of the church's record in that respect. Between 1840 and 1875, around 80 per cent of ancient churches had been restored, rebuilt or enlarged. In 1877, disquiet over the restoration of Tewkesbury Abbey prompted the formation of the Society for the Protection of Ancient Buildings. In 1912, a select committee of both houses of parliament recommended an erosion of the

---

[2] An entry point to the extensive literature is Alex King, *Memorials of the Great War in Britain: The Symbolism and Politics of Remembrance* (Oxford, 1998). For the broader context, see Jay M. Winter, *Sites of Memory, Sites of Mourning: The Great War in European Cultural History* (Cambridge, 1995).

jurisdiction of consistory courts, the bodies through which chancellors, the legal officers of dioceses, granted faculties as part of their wider responsibilities. The Church of England resisted these moves successfully and obtained a statutory exemption from state control over its buildings in the Ancient Monuments Consolidation and Amendment Act of 1913, but only after promises that existing faculty procedures would be reviewed. In 1914, Sir Lewis Dibdin, then dean of the Court of Arches (the highest judicial post in the Church of England), presented a report which recommended a general tightening of procedures, as well as the setting up of specialist bodies to advise diocesan chancellors on architectural, archaeological, historical and artistic matters. However, diocesan advisory committees, as they came to be called, did not become a requirement until 1938, and had no decision-making powers of their own.[3]

The timing of the Dibdin report meant that implementation of its recommendations was not the first priority for dioceses struggling to cope with the more urgent problems of wartime. It was early 1921 before the diocese of Wakefield established what was initially called the Ancient Churches Advisory Committee.[4] The diocese included a relatively small number of pre-Reformation churches, and the new framework was regarded as focusing on those, as the committee's name indicated.

The main concern of most dioceses during the war had been the prospect of a plethora of memorials to individual casualties being placed in churches by their families. They did not, however, wish to discourage wealthy parishioners from funding major embellishments to churches, such as new stained glass windows. Public advice was carefully worded. In January 1916, the *Wakefield Diocesan Gazette* urged the clergy to put notices in parish magazines and in the local press assuring readers that 'general and comprehensive memorial[s]' would be created, although memorials to individuals would not be ruled out. Such an initiative, the *Gazette* suggested, would pre-empt the distress which would occur if the desire for individual brasses and tablets overwhelmed church buildings, as it could well do in town churches. It would also be much

---

[3] After 1938 they became statutory bodies but remained advisory in function: Kathryn V. Last, 'The Privileged Position of the Church of England in the Control of Works to Historic Buildings: The Provenance of the Ecclesiastical Exemption from Listed Building Control', *Common Law World Review* 31 (2002), 205–35.
[4] *WDG* 26/9 (February 1921), 136.

valued by those who could not afford 'costly offerings' but could participate in a communal venture.[5] In May 1916, it was considered necessary to reiterate that advice, and to state that Wakefield's chancellor supported it:

> A collective memorial gives a Parish the opportunity of recording its admiration for the services of a man or men, whose parents and friends are probably not in a position from a monetary point of view to erect an individual memorial. It also has a distinct value as associating together in the fellowship of sacrifice names of brave men from every rank and condition of life.[6]

The same article also emphasized that plans for memorials should await the end of the war. That these exhortations were published even before the traumatic events on the Somme that July demonstrates that commemorative pressures were already building up. The *Gazette* is silent about what, if any, discussions took place in Wakefield during the remainder of the war, but by June 1919, the archbishop of York, Cosmo Gordon Lang, was describing the hope that communal memorials would prevail over individual ones as 'very imperfectly fulfilled'. 'Of course, it is very difficult to discipline individual feelings,' he was quoted as saying, 'but I deprecate in the interests of a truer ideal separating individuals from their comrades, when there is to be in the church some adequate and dignified memorial on which the names of all who have fallen are to be inscribed.'[7]

The May 1916 edition of the *Gazette* had also recorded the case of an unnamed church whose application for a faculty had been refused as premature, unsuitable, likely to mislead historically and possibly leading to overcrowded or half-filled tablets. It seems that the church concerned was seeking to commemorate not only those who were losing their lives in the war but also all those who had volunteered to serve. It may be that the latter part of the application had sought to distinguish between those who had joined the armed forces as volunteers and those who, after the introduction of conscription, might be regarded as less worthy of honour. That would explain why the *Gazette* stated that '[a] permanent record of men offering

---

[5] *WDG* 21/19 (January 1916), 159.
[6] *WDG* 22/1 (May 1916), 4–5.
[7] 'Archbishop on War Memorials', *Huddersfield Examiner*, 16 June 1919, 4, quoting from a letter the archbishop had circulated in the diocese of York.

their services for military work ... was felt to be most unsuitable on every ground.'[8] The comment may, however, have reflected a more fundamental worry about commemorating living servicemen and ex-servicemen. In 1921, the chancellor of the diocese of Liverpool was reported as having rejected an application for a faculty for a memorial which included the names of those who had served and returned, as well as those of the dead, because a man named on a similar memorial had gone on to commit a serious offence but still appeared as one whose name should be remembered for ever.[9]

By the spring and summer of 1919, most servicemen had returned home and the numbers of applications for faculties began to rise. The Wakefield diocesan faculty books show the numbers of faculties granted (see Table 1).[10] The peak in 1920 is certainly attributable to war memorial applications but other factors contributed to the overall rising numbers. Many fairly routine alterations to church buildings had been put off during the war because of more urgent pressures on time, money and materials; discussion of possible war memorial projects often triggered suggestions for other alterations which could conveniently be completed at the same time; and the higher profile of the faculty procedures following the Dibdin report probably meant that formal approval was now being sought for decisions which might in the past have been taken locally.

With that background, let us return to what was upsetting Chancellor Charles on that November day in 1920. Ernest Bruce Charles was a forty-nine-year-old barrister and recorder, who had been appointed as chancellor to the diocese of Wakefield in 1912. He was also chancellor of the diocese of Hereford, again from 1912, and would add the chancellorship of the diocese of Chelmsford in 1922. This pluralistic activity was (and is) not unusual.

---

[8] The church concerned has yet to be identified: *WDG* 22/1 (May 1916), 4.

[9] 'The Quick and the Dead: Honour for those who died and those who lived: Church Memorial Point: Interesting Decision by Chancellor Dowdall', *Liverpool Echo*, 3 May 1921, 8; '"In Everlasting Remembrance": Premature Praise in War Memorials', *Huddersfield Examiner*, 4 May 1921, 1. The chancellor did grant a faculty for a memorial naming only the fallen, and suggested that the parish, St Bartholomew, Roby, should seek a separate faculty for a simple list of those who had served, to be displayed in the porch as a permanent record.

[10] Wakefield, West Yorkshire Archive Service (hereafter: WYAS(W)), WD100/109, Diocese of Wakefield, Faculty Books, vols 2 (1908–22), 3 (1922–30); there appears to be no consolidated record of numbers of applications.

Anne C. Brook

Table 1. Numbers of Faculty Applications granted, Diocese of Wakefield, 1913–29

Year	Faculties granted
1913	18
1914	25
1915	11
1916	15
1917	7
1918	22
1919	42
1920	74
1921	54
1922	39
1923	45
1924	46
1925	39
1926	42
1927	57
1928	54
1929	48

Source: WYAS(W), WD100/109, Diocese of Wakefield, Faculty Books, vols 2 (1908–22), 3 (1922–30).

English ecclesiastical law was (and remains) a distinctly niche area of interest and expertise, and diocesan chancellorships were (and are) not lucrative posts. Charles's father had been dean of the Court of Arches, and his son ended his career as chancellor (commissary general) of the diocese of Canterbury. Ernest Charles lived in Kent, and the wide geographic spread of his chancellorships in the 1920s reflected the fact that, provided a diocese had a competent and industrious diocesan registrar, most business could be conducted without the need for particularly frequent visits.[11] He resigned his three chancellorships in 1928, on appointment as a High Court judge. His mention of wartime experience in France, in the quotation which began this article, referred to his service with the Red Cross, initially as an ambulance driver, later as part of the inquiry teams who tried to trace those missing in action,

[11] For the period covered by this article, the Wakefield registrar was William Henry Coles (1877–1963).

and culminating in appointment as director of the Wounded and Missing Inquiry Department, Le Havre.[12]

The 'ecclesiastically disputable' war memorial installed in St John's, Clifton, was a faldstool surrounded by a triptych, with a crucifix in the central panel and, on the two wings, the names of those who had died in the war. The evidence available does not suggest that the church was trying to evade faculty jurisdiction but that it was rather late in making its application, assuming that approval would be granted before the work was completed.[13] However, that was not the case, and the memorial was in place by the time the chancellor came to make his decision. Normally, that would have led to nothing worse than a formal rebuke, before the grant of a confirmatory faculty. However, this case proved an exception. The chancellor had no hesitation in declaring that the element of the triptych depicting the crucifix was illegal. Here he was on familiar ground, having considered the legality of crucifixes ten months previously in the diocese of Hereford, in relation to a war memorial for the parish of Tenbury, Worcestershire. Citing the case of Ridsdale v. Clifton (1877), he had concluded in Hereford that a crucifix without associated figures turning it into a depiction of a historical event was illegal in itself, whether or not there was evidence that the image would be put to a superstitious use. His judgment on that occasion had been reported in *The Times*.[14] In Wakefield, he reiterated the main points of his previous judgment as the basis for his decision on Clifton's application. However, he went on to say that the memorial should remain and should be respected, although if anyone made a formal application for its removal he might have to grant such a request. He urged the parish to consider altering the central element of the triptych to make it a historical depiction, in which case he

[12] *London Gazette*, 8 January 1919, 449; *Who Was Who, s.n.* 'Charles, Sir Ernest Bruce', online at: <https://doi.org/10.1093/ww/9780199540884.013.U223693>, accessed 12 September 2018; obituary, *The Times*, 4 May 1950, 7. He was probably appointed director in 1917, although it has not been possible to verify this. He was mentioned in dispatches in 1917, created a Knight of the Order of St John in April 1918 and appointed CBE in 1919.
[13] WYAS(W), St John's, Clifton, WDP27/34, Charles R. Roberts, 'A Compilation of Historical Facts of the Church of St John the Evangelist, Clifton, Brighouse and of the Church School on the Occasion of the Centenary of the Church, 1860–1960', undated typescript; WDP27/40, faculty papers, August 1920 – October 1922; WDP27/54, PCC minute book, 1920–4.
[14] 'Crucifix as War Shrine: A Faculty refused', *The Times*, 12 January 1920, 15.

would gladly make a retrospective grant of approval. This they did. It is clear that in the months between the two judgments he had become much more conscious of the emotional context of his decisions, or at least more prepared to articulate that pressure. He may also have been aware that there was another application in the diocesan pipeline, which would bring the state of the law concerning depictions of the crucifixion into even sharper relief.

Towards the end of 1920, the parish of St Thomas in Huddersfield requested approval for a rood beam across the chancel arch with a crucifix and figures of the Virgin Mary and St John, commemorating an individual casualty, and a column in the churchyard bearing a lantern head containing a Calvary, as a general memorial. That application was approved a few weeks after the Clifton judgment, following a meeting in Wakefield with representatives of the parish.[15] Nevertheless, the church council of St Thomas was not at all happy. When presented with the bill for the faculty process, it agreed to send a formal resolution to the diocese stating that 'the parochial council regard the whole thing as unnecessary, and a severe tax on the amount subscribed towards the object for which the faculty was obtained'. The council also discussed withholding the architect's fees, feeling that he should have ensured that the application was regarded as routine, not perhaps realizing that his knowledge of the state of the law concerning crucifixion scenes with attendant figures as opposed to a sole crucifix had almost certainly been the reason for the positive outcome.[16]

To the average churchgoer, and indeed to many clergy, the result – that a relatively small image of the crucified Redeemer in front of a prayer desk was illegal, yet an enormous rood beam dominating the interior of the church in pre-Reformation style was legal, as was an outdoor Calvary similar to those found across Catholic Europe – was very difficult to comprehend. There was nothing amiss with Chancellor Charles's understanding of the law. Volume 11 of the first edition of Halsbury's *Laws of England*, which he had no doubt consulted, tracked the less than consistent state of the case law, and advised that crucifixes had normally been held to be illegal, regardless of context, whereas depictions of the crucifixion with associated

[15] WD100/109, Faculty Book, vol. 2, 10 December 1920.
[16] WYAS(W), St Thomas, Huddersfield, WDP115/11, Church Council, 21 January, 11 May 1921. The architect was Sir Charles Nicholson, Wakefield's diocesan architect.

figures had to pass the test of whether or not they were likely to be put to superstitious use.[17] Why an image of Christ on the cross by itself was not considered a depiction of a historical event, whilst adding figures of the Virgin and St John made it into one, was not, to say the least, self-evident. The case law on which all this rested came from the court cases during the height of the nineteenth-century ritualistic controversies. Those Victorian judges who had established the case law were also in a very difficult position. The basis from which they had to start was the Book of Common Prayer of 1662. Like its predecessors, that book was annexed to an act of uniformity, which gave it its statutory authority. A rubric at the beginning of the Orders for Morning and Evening Prayer decreed that the ornaments of the church and of the ministers should be those which were legal in the second year of the reign of Edward VI, repeating the substance of the corresponding Ornaments Rubric in the Prayer Book of 1559. Although usually taken to be a reference to the status quo implemented by the Prayer Book of 1549, the requirement to use that first statutory book did not come into force until a few months into the third year of Edward's reign.[18] The resulting ambiguity, perhaps deliberately retained in 1662 to avoid reopening one of the more contentious issues of the previous century, was never formally resolved.[19] A further complication was that the various documents published during the reigns of Henry VIII, Edward VI and Elizabeth I were written to be interpreted by clerics grounded in the theology of the Reformation era. By the nineteenth century, interpretation was being undertaken by lawyers whose intellectual training had been quite different, and who were required to base their judgments on the words in front of them with very limited regard to the intentions of those who wrote them, even if these intentions could be accurately known or understood.[20] Most of the

---

[17] Earl of Halsbury, *The Laws of England, being a Complete Statement of the Law of England*, 31 vols (London, 1910), 11: §§1330–41.

[18] For a fuller discussion, see, in this volume, Dan D. Cruickshank, 'Debating the Legal Status of the Ornaments Rubric: Ritualism and Royal Commissions in Late Nineteenth- and Early Twentieth-Century England', 434–54.

[19] The rubric is described as a 'puzzling instruction' which '[n]o one has ever satisfactorily explained': Diarmaid MacCulloch, *Thomas Cranmer*, rev. edn (New Haven, CT, 2016), 621; for the texts, see Brian Cummings, ed., *The Book of Common Prayer: The Texts of 1549, 1559, and 1662* (Oxford, 2011).

[20] Until the latter part of the twentieth century, the interpretative tools available to judges when considering the impact of legislation on individual cases were narrowly defined:

Victorian cases were also primarily about the contentious actions of individual clergy during the church's official worship, with questions of church ornaments and decorations being subsidiary matters, some of which could be related to the Ornaments Rubric and others not. It is no wonder that by the time an uneasy truce settled over the Church of England later in the nineteenth century the state of the case law was less than coherent.[21]

The cases of St John, Clifton and St Thomas, Huddersfield were not the end of Chancellor Charles's difficulties. In 1924, he was faced with a fait accompli in Huddersfield's main parish church, where the incumbent had radically reordered the sanctuary to introduce a new freestanding altar with a baldachino and a new east window, displacing in the process various existing memorials, including that of the family of the church's patron. Aspects of the design of the altar and its canopy as finally installed were potentially illegal, and so out of proportion to the chancel as a whole as to be aesthetically questionable too. The parochial church council had not resolved to apply for a faculty until the beginning of October 1923, and the actual application was only made on 15 November, just two days before the dedication ceremony. The formal application represented the whole scheme as a war memorial, although the vicar had made clear his dissatisfaction with the appearance of St Peter's within months of his induction, when discussion of any permanent war memorial was over a year away. The application was vague about the nature of the structure over the new altar, and did not mention the consequential relocation of existing memorials. As the incumbent was rural dean and a canon of Wakefield and former canon of York, and his architect, Ninian Comper, worked almost exclusively on ecclesiastical projects and was noted for his contempt for official process, it is difficult not to conclude that the delay in requesting a faculty was deliberate. Moreover, the incumbent, Albert Darell Tupper-Carey (1866–1943),

Catherine Elliott and Frances Quinn, *The English Legal System*, 17th edn (Harlow, 2016), 55–60, 64–7. My thanks to W. Brian Thompson for advice on this point.

[21] James Bentley, *Ritualism and Politics in Victorian Britain: The Attempt to Legislate for Belief* (Oxford, 1978); Nigel Yates, *Anglican Ritualism in Victorian Britain, 1830–1910* (Oxford, 1999). Martin Wellings, *Evangelicals Embattled: Responses of Evangelicals in the Church of England to Ritualism, Darwinism and Theological Liberalism 1890–1930* (Carlisle, 2003), 9–72, usefully explores the interplay between Ritualism and anti-Catholicism.

was also a personal friend of the archbishop of York, and was shortly to resign the living on medical advice. A faculty was granted, without the *Gazette* making public the fact that the approval was retrospective, and follow-up action concentrated on the unauthorized relocation of the memorials of prominent families. Ironically, the faculty application contained one element which was correctly timed, as the formal decision to commission a stone tablet inscribed with the names of the dead was not taken until the month after the ceremony at which the window and the new altar were dedicated.[22]

Charles was not the only diocesan chancellor to be facing problems. In August 1918, Chancellor the Ven. John Prescott at the Carlisle Consistory Court had considered an application for approval of a new east window at St Paul, Carlisle, in memory of all those who had died in the war from the church and the parish. The design was for a five-light window, with a central panel depicting Christ on the cross. Both the position of the window, in the general view of the congregation at all times, and the nature of the figure, which the chancellor described as 'practically a crucifix', concerned him so much that he reserved judgment. By the time of the next court, changes had been made to the design, which now contained the figures of the Virgin and St John and also extended the arms of Christ into the adjacent lights so as to link all aspects of the crucifixion scene together. However, the chancellor was not persuaded that those alterations met his original objections, nor did he accept arguments that the window was a painted depiction of the crucifixion scene and not a crucifix, that it would enhance the appearance of the church and that it was a very suitable memorial to the war. He refused the application.[23]

In June 1920, in the diocese of Winchester, Chancellor the Rt Hon. George Talbot considered a case involving a crucifix erected

---

[22] The details of the story can be tracked through WYAS(W), St Peter, Huddersfield, WDP32/94, Church Council Minute Book, 1914–24; WDP32/14, parish magazines, 1914–25; WD100/Box 111, Diocese of Wakefield, faculty applications; WD100/109, Faculty Book, vol. 2, 12 January 1924; *WDG* 29/10 (February 1924), 181. Comper's attitude to diocesan advisory committees and to regulation of the architectural profession more generally is noted in John Betjeman, 'A Note on J. N. Comper: Heir to Butterfield and Bodley', *Architectural Review* 85 (1939), 79–82. See also Cosmo Gordon Lang, *Tupper (Canon A. D. Tupper-Carey): A Memoir of the Life and Work of a very human Parish Priest, by his Friend* (London, 1945).

[23] 'A Crucifix in a Window', *Yorkshire Post and Leeds Intelligencer*, 28 August 1918, 8; 'Chancellor Prescott and a Crucifixion Window', ibid., 20 November 1918, 7.

in the consecrated grounds of St Nicholas, Guildford, in memory of an individual casualty. The crucifix had already been dedicated by the bishop of Guildford, on the understanding that a confirmatory faculty would be sought for it. Nevertheless the faculty had been refused, solely on the grounds of its retrospective character. A new application was then made to have the crucifix removed, and a counter-proposal submitted to move it to a disused burial ground adjacent to the church. Arguments were made concerning the illegality of a crucifix per se, and the likelihood of its being the focus of superstitious practices in either location. In his final judgment, permitting the re-erection of the crucifix in its new location, Talbot questioned the contention that a crucifix was always illegal in the Church of England, noting that the Inner Temple accounts showed that there had been one in the Temple Church in 1674. He also dealt robustly with the evidence presented in support of the crucifix's superstitious use: that men had been seen raising their hats as they passed; and men, women and children had been observed making the sign of the cross, bowing, genuflecting or even kneeling in front of it. If the crucifix reminded them of the redeeming passion of our Lord, he said, prompting them to express thankfulness or reverence by outward gestures or public prayer, it was both uncharitable and unreasonable to attribute superstition to them.[24]

A year later in the Exeter diocese, dealing with a very similar case in which a war memorial crucifix had been erected and dedicated without a faculty in the churchyard of St Stephen, Devonport, and its removal requested on the grounds of superstitious actions having been observed by opponents watching responses to the memorial, Chancellor Sir Francis Newbolt came to a very different conclusion. He ruled that superstitious use was very likely and that the crucifix should be removed and replaced by what he called a 'proper war memorial'.[25]

By April 1921, Carlisle had a new chancellor, the Ven. Donald Campbell, whose views appeared rather different from those of his predecessor. It was proposed to erect a large crucifix in the churchyard of Christ Church, Carlisle. Crucifixes as war memorials in church-yards were causing a great deal of difficulty to chancellors, he said,

[24] 'Crucifix as War Memorial: Judgement in Guildford Case: Legality upheld', *The Times*, 7 June 1920, 7.
[25] 'Crucifix as War Memorial: Removal ordered: Parish Action against Vicar', *The Times*, 11 April 1921, 7.

and would continue to do so until there was a Court of Appeal ruling. In most dioceses they had been allowed and many erected, but elsewhere they had been judged illegal. He favoured the view of Lord Phillimore that 'all images in stained glass, painting, or sculpture were lawful unless they were liable to be abused by superstitious devotion', and did not think it possible that a crucifix in a churchyard could be liable to superstitious use.[26]

No new ruling by a higher court on these issues ever materialized. The diversity of judgments by consistory courts arose because, as was the case for the secular courts, chancellors were only required to give respectful attention to the decisions of courts at the same level of seniority as their own. They were bound to follow the decisions of higher courts, unless it could be argued that the essence of the current case could be properly distinguished from the earlier one. The seventh edition of Cripps's *Church and Clergy* (1921) followed a summary of the nineteenth-century rulings on crucifixes with a discreet footnote indicating that unreported consistory court rulings on war memorials were affecting the state of the case law.[27] By 1933, the second edition of Halsbury's *Laws of England* was warning that 'many, if not most, of the things pronounced unlawful by the Judicial Committee of the Privy Council have become of general usage'. One reason given for this was that, as stated in the *Report of the Royal Commission on Ecclesiastical Discipline*, '[a] Court dealing with matters of conscience and religion must, above all others, rest on moral authority if its judgments are to be effective. As thousands of clergy with strong lay support refuse to recognise the jurisdiction of the Judicial Committee, its judgments cannot be practically enforced.'[28] The second edition made no explicit mention of the impact of the commemoration of the war on the changed climate, perhaps feeling that referencing a royal commission placed the volume's stance on safer legal ground.

---

[26] 'Churchyard Crucifixes: Chancellor Campbell's Judgment', *Yorkshire Post and Leeds Intelligencer*, 27 April 1921, 9; Robert Phillimore, *The Ecclesiastical Law of the Church of England*, 2nd edn, 2 vols (London, 1895), 1: 735.
[27] Henry William Cripps, *The Law relating to the Church and Clergy*, 7th edn (London, 1921), 408.
[28] D. G. Hogg, ed., *Halsbury's Laws of England*, 2nd edn, 37 vols (London, 1931–42), 11 (1933): §1442 n. One of the commission's conclusions had been that 'the law of public worship in the Church of England is too narrow for the religious life of the present generation': *Report of the Royal Commission on Ecclesiastical Discipline*, Cd.3040 (London, 1906), §399.

As the statistics in Table 1 indicate, these high-profile cases were occurring in the context of a much greater volume of work generally. Repeated reminders in the *Gazette* that clergy and churchwardens should not enter into contracts for work before receiving faculty approval of their plans indicated that compliance with the faculty procedures was a problem. Over and above the normal uneven implementation of any bureaucratic system, there were particular post-war pressures. Many parishes experienced a substantial change in personnel, as those who would have retired years before had it not been for the war left office and too many pre-war young leaders failed to return. There was also an understandable impatience with traditional decision-making, not only amongst returning servicemen but also amongst men and women who had taken on new responsibilities on the home front. Discussions about the best way to commemorate the war often took place outside formal structures, and were not always underpinned by the necessary official authorizations. To add to the potential for confusion, a major constitutional change took place in 1921, when the long-standing pattern of legal authority resting with the incumbent, the churchwardens and the vestry meetings was replaced by the creation of parochial church councils.[29] In places where voluntary church councils had been established for some years, that change could be almost seamless; in others, the new bodies struggled to understand and carry out their responsibilities; moreover, some clergy and churchwardens were more enthusiastic than others about the changes. The cost of obtaining a faculty was also an issue. Although the standard fee of two guineas (£2 2*s*) appears reasonable, when placed in the context of raising money for a simple wall tablet costing £25, resentment at what seemed like a diocesan tax on honouring the dead is understandable. A contested application could raise the diocesan costs charged to the parish to nearer £15, over and above the additional local expenses.[30]

All these factors contributed to the likelihood that, from a parish perspective, faculty procedures would seem like routine red tape, to be complied with as and when someone remembered the need to do

[29] Parochial Church Councils (Powers) Measure 1921.
[30] The final diocesan bills were £13 15*s* 2*d*: WYAS(W), WDP27/40, St John, Clifton, Faculty: Statement of Fees and Charges; and £13 4*s* 8*d*: WDP115, St Thomas, Huddersfield, Church Council, 21 January 1921. These included the chancellor's travel costs, postage and 'sundries'.

so. Consequently, applications for faculties were often made at a late stage of the creation of a memorial, after its completion or (indeed) not at all. Collation of newspaper reports, parish records and other sources relating to the creation of war memorials for just one borough in the diocese, Huddersfield, suggests that the numbers of faculties granted should have been significantly higher. One church in Huddersfield managed to erect, over a period of five years, a church-yard commemorative cross for the district as a whole, two tablets and a chancel screen for individual casualties, and a stained glass window with an associated tablet for the church's own group of casualties, as well as reordering part of the church to create a memorial chapel, all without even retrospective faculty approval.[31]

Whether the Wakefield diocese found the time and resources to address aesthetic issues arising out of faculty applications for war memorials is not clear. The earliest extant minute book for the diocesan advisory committee dates from 1966, although earlier ones may exist amongst diocesan material not yet catalogued to individual item level. Editions of the *Gazette* to the end of the 1920s noted changes in the committee's membership and title but offered almost no information about its work. The one exception was in November 1924, when, as part of yet another reminder about the need to apply for a faculty before work was commissioned or begun, the *Gazette* stated that diocesan advisory committees 'protect parishioners from unworthy alterations or additions to their churches. The question was nothing to do with the illegality or otherwise of the various proposals.'[32] Earlier that year, the *Gazette* had carried an article publicizing the advice of the Central Committee for the Protection of Churches that the temporary grave markers being returned to relatives from overseas should not be housed in churches. That conclusion was based on the danger of the 'serious disfigurement of churches' as the crosses were 'usually very roughly made of thin, perishable wood for temporary use, and ... quite unsuited for any position of permanency'. The committee had also concluded that '[i]n the majority of cases the names of those

---

[31] WYAS(W), Christ Church, Woodhouse, WDP42/5/1/1, Vestry minute book, 1898–1920; WDP42/5/3/2, Church Council minute book, 1903–20; WDP42/5/4/1/1, PCC minute book, 1920–7; WDP42/9/1/5, Parish magazines, 1918–24. At least two other parish churches in the borough had war memorials for which no approval appears to have been sought: St Paul, Armitage Bridge and St John, Newsome.
[32] *WDG* 30/7 (November 1924), 88.

commemorated are already inscribed in the local War Memorial, very often in the church itself.[33]

Sir Lewis Dibdin could not have foreseen the environment in which his reforms to the system of faculty jurisdiction would unfold. He aimed for greater and more informed scrutiny of the impact of applications on the Church of England's heritage. Whether he achieved that is difficult to assess. At the level of particular dioceses, evidence for the operation of the faculty system is scattered amongst the records of individual parishes, unless diocesan registry files have survived and been catalogued. It would be particularly valuable to locate evidence concerning the extent to which aesthetic considerations influenced war memorial proposals for major pre-Reformation churches. It is also difficult to obtain a national overview of the decisions of consistory courts on applications for faculties involving war memorials which had potentially illegal constituents. Few of the latter cases found their way into the official law reports, so contemporary newspapers are the most accessible source of information.[34] It can, however, be concluded that this is an area where the strict application of case law was increasingly abandoned in the face of a very different climate of opinion from that in which it was first established. Whatever the personal churchmanship of individual chancellors, and the influence of that on their interpretation of the case law, they would also have been affected by the impact of the war on themselves, their families and friends, and the perspective that gave on the emotional context within the parishes applying for faculties. By the end of the First World War, the focus was no longer on errant clergy testing the bounds of the inclusivity of the Church of England but on individual grieving communities who, having come to corporate decisions about the form in which their dead should be remembered and their returned servicemen honoured, saw little reason why bureaucratic procedures and obscure Victorian court cases should conspire to thwart the implementation of those decisions.

[33] *WDG* 30/2 (June 1924), 26.
[34] Now increasingly available through the British Library's digitization project, online at: <http://www.britishnewspaperarchive.co.uk>.

Freedom of Religion and the Legal Status of Churches: A Case Study from the Serbian Constitutional Court

Tijana Surlan*

Belgrade

This article offers a short study of the conjugation of freedom of religion, freedom of association and the legal status of religions and churches. Human rights are elaborated as defined in international human rights law, accentuated by the jurisprudence of the European Court of Human Rights. A compliance case that came before the Constitutional Court of the Republic of Serbia provides a national jurisprudential example useful for the analysis of relations between human rights and the legal status of a church. Analysis of the law is both horizontal and vertical: a description of norms is intertwined with a discussion of principles of identity and equality. The article explores whether the principles of human rights and freedoms and the norms regulating the legal status of a church are consistent with each other; whether these principles are independent and how their mutual relationship influences the application and interpretation of the law; and whether the norms prescribed by international law or in national jurisprudence can be applied independently of canon law, or whether application of the law has to take into account specific religious jurisdictions and relations between churches which are rooted in their autonomous canon law.

The contemporary world can be characterized as traditional and conservative, if we are viewing it superficially from the angle of religions and churches. Whether religions and churches are identified as major, mainstream, traditional or established, both religions and churches have been present for centuries. Religions and churches are deeply rooted in the sociological, political and national identities of nations and states. At the same time, religions and churches form an important aspect of international relations, whether international actors cooperate or (even more importantly) whether they are hostile. Human beings, curious and innovative as ever, tend to form new

* E-mail: tijana.surlan@ustavni.sud.rs.

Studies in Church History 56 (2020), 487–507   © Ecclesiastical History Society 2020
doi: 10.1017/stc.2019.27

beliefs and try to organize new churches. The contemporary world acknowledges in general the possibility, the need and the right to establish a new religion and a new church that will allow such a new belief to be practised and expressed. The law is an important element for defining the position of religions and churches in communities and in states. This article will evaluate the legal issues involved in creating new churches, in terms of the most general principles and aspects of law that deal with these issues.

The moment in central European history when the issue of religions, churches and states reached a turning point, which remains important from the standpoint of modern states and the contemporary world, is the Peace of Westphalia (1648). Marking the end of the European wars of religion, it established *inter alia* the principle of territorial sovereignty and religious tolerance. Since then, legal thinking about religions and churches has been developed in terms of law concerning the legal status of religions and churches within a state and the right of individuals to choose their religion and church. This article is organized according to those two aspects of law, the choice of religion as a human right and the status of a church as subject matter for national law. The aspect of human rights falls under international public law, that is, international human rights. The article will therefore explore human rights as they are prescribed in major international legal acts. The legal status of a church within a state will be elaborated on by means of a case study of Serbian Constitutional Court jurisprudence combined with the criteria developed in the jurisprudence of the European Court of Human Rights (ECtHR).

A case that emerged before the Constitutional Court of the Republic of Serbia, concerning the compliance of the Act on Churches and Religious Communities (2006) with the constitution of the Republic of Serbia, showed how deeply divergent understandings of issues concerning the law and the church could be. The issues elaborated were shown to be far more complex and theoretically challenging than expected, including the conjunction of the law on churches with fundamental principles, freedoms and human rights, as well as important aspects of state organization, such as the separation of state and church.

International law on religions and churches has developed several basic intertwined rights for individuals, states and churches: first, the right of an individual to profess and believe in religion by free choice;

second, the right of an individual or group to establish a new religion, a new church or religious organization; third, the right of a state to prescribe conditions for founding a new religion, church or religious organization; fourth, the right of churches and religious organizations already existing to preserve their legal status at a time when laws and even states are changing; and fifth, the right of churches and religious organizations to organize their internal structure and laws (canon law).[1]

The main legal principles governing these rights are those of equality and identity. The principle of equality, arising from human rights philosophy, has the primary role of allowing individuals equal freedom in choosing their belief and joining the church of their choice. This principle, when elaborated in terms of human rights, is often characterized negatively as the principle of non-discrimination. One of the most important, and oldest, grounds for discrimination was religion. It would be questionable, though, whether the human rights approach could be widened to other fields of law, and specifically to administrative law governing the conditions for registration of religions and churches. It would be even more questionable when it comes to canon law, which has been developed by some churches over hundreds of years. Another aspect of the equality principle is whether churches are equal among themselves, thus presenting individuals with a choice of religions of equal status.

The principle of identity governs whether each and every newly registered church should be considered as a completely new religion, with consequences for its status, even if it is an outgrowth of a traditional church and based on familiar forms of religious thinking. It is doubtful whether the factor of identity influences equality; that is, whether churches can be truly equal if they are considered in terms of 'new as opposed to traditional' and whether if treated differently they can establish their position within a state organization on the same principles and be equal before the law.

The normative frameworks for considering the relevant rights and principles, the activities and contribution of international organizations and the body of court jurisprudence are impressive. For the purpose of this article, their presentation must be simplified and reduced, and the presentation here will focus on the particular case of Serbia. The conclusion will assess the consistency of the law,

---

[1] For further details, see Peter Edge, *Religion and Law: An Introduction* (Aldershot, 2006).

whether individuals are equally protected to believe according to their choice, whether they can organize churches that are equal and whether a state influences the human right to religion by differentiating between churches in their status and identity. In the final analysis, if there is an issue of identity, can there be equality? Who has the final word in judging whether a religion is new: the existing churches or the state?

HUMAN RIGHTS

The human rights approach, as it relates to the main topic of this article, concerns the freedom of religion, the freedom of association and the principle of non-discrimination, that is, the principle of equality.[2] On the level of general international laws, as a beginning, it might be useful to remember that the Covenant of the League of Nations did not include a provision concerning religious liberties; rather, freedom of religion was directly stipulated in bilateral treaties on the rights of minorities.[3] Later on, religious rights emerged as individual human rights, as part of the freedom of conscience.[4]

On the other hand, the principle of non-discrimination, that is, the principle of equality, was based from the very beginning on religious grounds. Through the equality / non-discrimination principle, the protection of religious groups was included in the UN Charter, the Universal Declaration on Human Rights (1948) and important universal conventions such as the International Convention on the Prevention and Punishment of the Crime of Genocide (1948),[5] the International Convention on Elimination of all Forms of Racial Discrimination (1965)[6] and the International Covenant on Civil

[2] Paul M. Taylor, *Freedom of Religion: UN and European Human Rights Law and Practice* (Cambridge, 2005).
[3] Julian Rivers, *The Law of Organised Religions: Between Establishment and Secularism* (Oxford, 2010), 33.
[4] In the human rights instruments produced after the Second World War, these were combined into one article: thought, conscience and religion.
[5] United Nations, Office of the High Commissioner for Human Rights, International Convention on the Prevention and Punishment of the Crime of Genocide, online at: <https://www.ohchr.org/en/professionalinterest/pages/crimeofgenocide.aspx>, accessed 21 August 2019.
[6] International Convention on Elimination of all Forms of Racial Discrimination, online at: <https://www.ohchr.org/en/professionalinterest/pages/cerd.aspx>, accessed 21 August 2019.

and Political Rights (1966). Freedom of religion and freedom of association were prescribed in the Universal Declaration on Human Rights,[7] the International Covenant on Civil and Political Rights,[8] and the European Convention on Protection of Human Rights and Fundamental Freedoms (1950).[9]

Even after all these major measures, legislative activity did not stop. At the level of the United Nations, for example, in 1981 the UN Declaration on Elimination of all Forms of Intolerance and Discrimination based on Religion or Belief was adopted. In 2000 the position of UN Special Rapporteur on Freedom of Religion was established.[10] The Council of Europe also engaged in legal activity regarding freedom of religion. For example, the Venice Commission adopted the Guidelines for Legislative Reviews of Laws affecting Religion or Belief in 2004, revised in 2014, offering its preferred understanding of substantive issues such as religion, belief and the inter-relation of different human rights, and defining the values underlying freedom of religion, and religion and education.[11] In addition, the Organization for Security and Cooperation in Europe (OSCE) adopted several documents and commitments concerning freedom of religion, from the Helsinki Final Act (1975), Principle VII, through the Madrid Principles (1983) and the Vienna Principles (1989),[12] to the Córdoba Declaration

---

[7] Universal Declaration on Human Rights, Articles 18, 20, online at: <https://www.un.org/en/universal-declaration-human-rights/>, accessed 21 August 2019.

[8] International Covenant on Civil and Political Rights, Articles 18, 22, online at: <https://treaties.un.org/doc/publication/unts/volume%20999/volume-999-i-14668-english.pdf>, accessed 21 August 2019.

[9] European Convention on Protection of Human Rights and Fundamental Freedoms, Articles 9, 11, online at: <https://www.echr.coe.int/Documents/Convention_ENG.pdf>, accessed 21 August 2019.

[10] Further to Resolution 1986/20, in 2000 the United Nations Commission on Human Rights appointed a 'Special Rapporteur on Religious Intolerance', whose title was later amended to 'Special Rapporteur on Freedom of Religion or Belief'. The appointment of a Special Rapporteur was endorsed by UN ECOSOC Decision 2000/261 and UN General Assembly Resolution 55/97.

[11] Council of Europe, European Commission for Democracy through Law (Venice Commission), Guidelines for Legislative Reviews of Laws affecting Religion or Belief, Venice, 18–19 June 2004, online at: <https://www.venice.coe.int/webforms/events/>, accessed 21 August 2019. The guidelines were revised by the Venice Commission in 2014.

[12] The commitment, according to §16.3 of the Vienna Document of 1989, is to 'grant upon their request to communities of believers, practising or prepared to practise their faith within the constitutional framework of their States, recognition of the status provided for them in their respective countries'.

(2005), which promoted inter-faith and inter-cultural dialogue.[13] In 2014, the Council of Europe and the OSCE also adopted Joint Guidelines on the Legal Personality of Religious or Belief Communities, intended primarily to 'assist all religious and belief communities in obtaining the status they seek to ensure that everyone can enjoy their freedom of religion or belief fully and with the dignity they deserve as members of the human family'.[14]

The Universal Declaration of Human Rights, the cornerstone of international human rights, provides the main elements of the freedom of religion. Article 18 affirms that every individual has the right to freedom of thought, conscience and religion; this right includes freedom to change religion or belief and also freedom to manifest, cither alone or in community with others and in public or private, a religion or belief through teaching, practice, worship and observance.

The International Covenant on Civil and Political Rights (ICCPR) defines freedom of religion or belief along the lines already recognized in the Universal Declaration, but also imposes limitations on that freedom. It is important to underline that as much as we consider the freedom of religion to be a fundamental right, nevertheless, it is not an absolute right, and as such it is subjected to some limitations. The covenant recognizes limitations in several categories: limitations should be prescribed by law and be necessary to protect public safety, order, health, morals or other fundamental rights and freedoms. Each state can define what is necessary for it, and what measures are to be taken to protect order, morals and safety.

The right to freedom of religion clearly upholds the manifestation of beliefs in a community with others, thus upholding the *ratio* of freedom of association. Nevertheless, religious organizations can also be protected by freedom of association, as prescribed in Article 22 of the covenant. In general, freedom of association is defined in the same fashion as freedom of religion: the general right to the freedom of everyone to associate with others is established, followed

---

[13] OSCE, Córdoba Declaration, adopted on 9 June 2005, online at: <https://www.osce.org/cio/15548?download=true>, accessed 21 August 2019.

[14] Council of Europe, Venice Commission, and OSCE Office for Democratic Institutions and Human Rights, Draft Joint Guidelines on the Legal Personality of Religious or Belief Communities, Opinion no. 673/2012, 21 May 2014, online at: <https://www.venice.coe.int/webforms/documents/default.aspx?pdffile=CDL-AD(2014)023-e>, accessed 21 August 2019.

by a list of possible limitations and restrictions that must be prescribed by law, necessary in a democratic society, in the interest of national security, public safety, public order, public health, morals or protection of the rights and freedoms of others. Freedom of association prescribes the general rule, while expression of belief in community with others represents a specific aspect of the very notion of religion or belief.

In providing full and overall protection for everyone to enjoy their beliefs, the principle of non-discrimination forms an important part of the picture. A state is obliged not only to allow freedom of religion and association, but also 'to respect and to ensure to *all* individuals within its territory and subject to its jurisdiction the rights recognized in the present Covenant, without distinction of any kind, such as race, colour, sex, language, *religion*, political or other opinion, national or social origin, property, birth or other status' (Article 2 §1; emphasis mine). This article, along with others developing the principle of non-discrimination, has been further developed by general comments adopted by the Human Rights Committee,[15] as well as by later UN declarations such as that on the Elimination of all Forms of Intolerance and of Discrimination based on Religion or Belief.[16]

Apart from these provisions of international law, the European Convention on Human Rights and Fundamental Freedoms (ECHR) is of interest.[17] Article 9 reiterates the same rights to freedom of religion as those already elaborated: first, the right for everyone to freedom of thought, conscience and religion; second, freedom to change religion or belief; third, freedom to manifest religion or belief, in worship, teaching, practice and observance, either alone or in community with others and in public or private; and fourth, freedom to manifest religion or beliefs can be limited as prescribed by law and

---

[15] United Nations Digital Library, General Comment no. 22, adopted by the UN Human Rights Committee in 1993. online at: <https://digitallibrary.un.org/record/832961>, accessed 21 August 2019.
[16] UN General Assembly, A/RES/36/55, 25 November 1981. Article 6 of the UNHCR's Declaration on the Elimination of all Forms of Intolerance and of Discrimination based on Religion or Belief, includes as freedoms of religion: the establishment and maintenance of a place where worship can be expressed, the establishment and celebration of holy days specific to the religion, and the organization of ceremonies on a regular basis, as well as the funding of a religious organization, the making of voluntary contributions and the management of funds: online at: <https://www.refworld.org/docid/3b00f02e40.html>, accessed 21 August 2019.
[17] Peter Edge, *Legal Responses to Religious Differences* (The Hague, 2002), 39–40.

when necessary in a democratic society, in the interests of public
safety, for the protection of public order, health or morals, or for
the protection of the rights and freedoms of others. The difference
lies in the specific terms used. One which is immediately apparent
is the formulation 'necessary in democratic society', rather than
merely 'necessary' in general. The convention is founded on democratic values; thus human rights can be limited only by restrictions
that are germane to democratic values. As with Article 18 of the
ICCPR, Article 9 recognizes that the limitations apply only to the
manifestation of religion. The 'right to freedom of thought, conscience and religion' guaranteed by paragraph 1 is absolute, to the
extent that it does not enter the realm of manifestation. This distinction has numerous practical implications. The ECHR also contains
an article on the freedom of association similar to those already
discussed. It stipulates firstly freedom of peaceful assembly and
freedom of association with others, including the right to form and
to join trade unions for the protection of personal interests, and secondly that restrictions can be imposed when prescribed by law and
necessary in a democratic society in the interests of national security
or public safety, for the prevention of disorder or crime, for the
protection of health or morals or for the protection of the rights
and freedoms of others. Together with the freedom of religion and
the principle of non-discrimination, this provision for freedom of
association forms an important aspect of the reasoning of the
ECtHR that will be elaborated further in what follows.

Serbian Constitutional Court Jurisprudence on the Legal Status of Churches

We turn now to the Act on Churches and Religious Communities
adopted in Serbia in 2006. As mentioned in the introduction, this
provoked some controversy regarding the understanding both of
the act in general and of specific parts, which led finally to a process
of determining its compliance with the Serbian Constitution.[18] I shall

---

[18] Danijel Sinani, 'Dawn by Law: Alternativni religijski koncepti i srpski Zakon o
crkvama i verskim zajednicama' ['Dawn by Law: Alternative Religious Concepts and
the Serbian Act on Churches and Religious Communities'], *Antropologija* 3/10 (2010),
121–32; Tanasije Marinković, 'Prilog za javnu raspravu o ustavnosti Zakona o crkvama
i verskim zajednicama' ['Contribution to the Public Debate on the Constitutionality of

focus here on the main points of that case from the aspect of human rights and the associated principles.

The Serbian Constitution maintains 'freedom of thought, conscience, beliefs and religion' and also 'the right to stand by one's belief or religion or change them by choice'. Everyone has the right to manifest religion or belief, and no person should be forced to declare his or her religion or belief. The rights to manifestation of religion or belief are based on standards laid down by international law: the manifestation of religion in worship, observance, practice and teaching, individually or in community with others. Restrictions can be set by national law and 'if necessary in a democratic society to protect the lives and health of people, the morals of democratic society, freedoms and rights guaranteed by the Constitution, public safety and order, or to prevent inciting of religious, national, and racial hatred'.[19]

The act defines freedom of religion in the same manner, including the freedom to have or not to have a religion, to retain or to change one's religion; that is, it establishes the freedom of belief, freedom to profess faith in God; freedom to manifest belief or religious conviction either individually or in community with others, in public or in private, by participating in religious services and performing religious ceremonies, through religious teaching and instruction, and cherishing and developing religious tradition; and freedom to develop and nurture religious education and culture (Article 1).[20] Limitations on freedom of religion may exist only to the extent that such limitations are prescribed by the constitution, the law and ratified international treaties, and which are necessary in a democratic society in the interest of the protection of public safety, public order, morals and the protection of the freedoms and rights of others (Article 3).

---

the Act on Churches and Religious Communities'], *Anali Pravnog fakulteta u Beogradu* 1 (2011), 367–85.
[19] Constitution of the Republic of Serbia, Article 43, online at the website of the Constitutional Court: <http://www.ustavni.sud.rs/page/view/139-100028/ustav-republike-srbije>, accessed 21 August 2019.
[20] 'Zakon o crkvama i religijskim zajednicama' ['Act on Churches and Religious Communities'], *Službeni glasnik Republike Srbije* [*Official Gazette of the Republic of Serbia*], no. 36/06 (2006), online at Legislation Online: <http://www.legislationline.org/documents/id/19516>, accessed 21 August 2019.

The Serbian Constitution defines that churches and religious communities are separate from the state, equal, and free to organize their internal structure and religious matters, to perform religious rites in public and to establish and manage religious schools and social and charitable institutions, in accordance with the law. The Constitutional Court may ban a religious community only if its 'activities infringe on the right to life, the right to mental and physical health, the rights of a child, or the right to personal and family integrity, public safety and order, or if it incites religious, national or racial intolerance' (Article 44).

The Act on Churches and Religious Communities declared freedom of association and assembly (Article 5) as citizens' freedom of association and assembly with the aim of manifesting religious convictions. Restrictions can be defined by the constitution and by law. Churches and religious communities are declared to be autonomous and independent from the state; they are free to determine their religious identities and to arrange and follow their order and structure (Article 6).

These articles are defined according to the highest standards of international law and they do not provoke any debate about compliance with international human rights instruments.[21] The provision that was the starting point for opposing understandings and interpretations of the whole set of norms is the one that defines holders of religious freedom as defined in the Act on Churches and Religious Communities (Article 4): 'Holders of religious freedom according to this Act are traditional churches and religious communities, confessional communities and other religious organisations (hereinafter: Churches and religious communities).'

Two constitutionally challenging elements were identified in this definition, relating to the aspects of freedom of religion, freedom of association, the principle of non-discrimination and the position of a church in a state. The first was apparent in the definition of churches, religious communities, confessional communities and religious organizations. The second relates to the norms governing legal personality and the registration process that should be fulfilled in order to obtain legal personality.

---

[21] See further Nenad Đurđević, *Ostvarivanje slobode veroispovesti i pravni položaj crkava i verskih zajednica u Republici Srbiji* (*The Exercise of Freedom of Religion and the Legal Status of Churches and Religious Communities in the Republic of Serbia*) (Belgrade, 2009).

The definition of 'traditional churches and religious communities' is based on their historic continuity within Serbia for centuries (Article 10). The status of 'traditional church' is held by the Serbian Orthodox Church, the Roman Catholic Church, the Slovak Evangelical Church, the Christian Reformed Church and the Evangelical Christian Church. The traditional religious communities are the Islamic Religious Community and the Jewish Religious Community. All have their status as legal personalities guaranteed. The legal personality of these churches and religious communities is grounded in the law of the earlier Principality of Serbia, dating back to the nineteenth century, and the law of the Kingdom of Serbia and the Kingdom of Yugoslavia from the end of the nineteenth century and the first half of the twentieth century.[22] All these churches and religious communities hold their legal status on the basis of legal continuity.

In contrast, confessional communities are defined as 'all those churches and religious communities whose legal position was regulated on the grounds of notification' as it was regulated in the laws adopted during the period of socialist Yugoslavia.[23] The different legal starting position for these groups provided grounds for severe criticism during the debate of the Act on Churches and Religious Communities prior to its adoption by the parliament. The case was eventually heard before the Constitutional Court. These provisions were held to be unconstitutional on the basis of the principles of freedom of religion and freedom of association, and particularly because they were seen as breaching the non-discrimination principle. In addition, the act was seen as challenging the constitutional provision for the equality of churches and religious communities: the entities were not treated equally, they were accorded a different legal status, and they were subjected to a different registration process. Thus followers and believers in confessional communities had a different legal status, resulting in non-equality between different religions.

These criticisms encountered several challenges. First of all, churches, religious organizations and confessional communities are not identical, but they are equal. This stance was based on the

---

[22] The modern Principality of Serbia came into being in 1804. The Kingdom of Serbia existed from 1882 to 1918 and the Kingdom of Yugoslavia from 1918 to 1941, when Yugoslavia was invaded and partitioned by Germany and other Axis powers.
[23] Socialist Yugoslavia existed from 1945 until 1992.

understanding that in reality it is a historical fact that different churches and religious organizations have existed for quite different lengths of time, that they differ greatly in size, and that their structure and organization varies significantly when we look at their clergy, clerical education and promotion, budgeting and finance, and (probably the most visible) influence in society.

The Constitutional Court therefore did not find the provision on churches, religious organizations and confessional communities to be opposed to the non-discrimination principle, freedom of religion or equality of churches and religious communities as defined in the constitution. The court's reasoning can be summarized as being that not every difference is discrimination, and that difference in definition and style does not necessarily mean a different legal status before the law.[24] In addition, it found that legal status does not depend on designation as traditional or non-traditional, and that the autonomy, possession of assets, financing, and educational and cultural work of all these churches and religious communities, as well as their worship and the rights and responsibilities of their clergy, were all governed by the same corpus of norms and in the same way for all bodies. Moreover, in respect to freedom of religion, the Constitutional Court found that the wording 'traditional church' does not advance freedom of religion in respect to those churches and religious communities defined in this way, and that the lack of the designation 'traditional' does not diminish the freedom to believe as one chooses. The prevailing understanding of the phrase 'traditional church' was that it is accurate in that it expresses the simple historical fact that some churches are older, and in that sense 'traditional', and recognizes that some of them have existed for centuries, that they have been a unifying factor for the nation, that they form part of national identity and that they are older than the state.

Another issue in the procedure before the Constitutional Court concerned the question of differentiation between churches, religious organizations and religious communities through the registration procedure. Traditional churches and religious communities (seven of them, as listed in the act) are subject only to the notification process. Other religious organizations are obliged to submit an application and to undergo an approval procedure. Thus traditional churches

---

[24] Constitutional Court, Case IUz-455/2011, decision of 16 January 2013.

and religious communities are required to provide the name of the church or religious community; the address of the headquarters of the church or religious community; and the full name and capacity of the person authorized to represent and act on behalf of the church or religious community. Applications for registering a new church are required to include the resolution by which the religious organization has been established, with full names, identification document numbers and signatures of founders representing at least 0.001 per cent of adult citizens of the Republic of Serbia; a statute or another document of the religious organization containing a description of its organizational structure, its form of governance, the rights and obligations of members and the procedure for establishing and terminating an organizational unit; a list of organizational units with the capacity of a legal person; any other relevant data concerning the religious organization; a presentation of the key elements of the organization's religious teaching, ceremonies, goals and main activities; and data on its permanent sources of income.

This registration procedure has provoked numerous comments and strong criticism. The first issue that arises from this provision lies more on the level of principle, that is, the principle of the relationship between the church and the state. If the state is to approve or forbid registration, can we conclude that the state is superior to the church? Secondly, a dilemma was expressed concerning the requirement to provide the names, identification numbers and signatures of members: did this conflict with the rules on privacy or the rule that no one should be forced to express their belief? As for the number of signatures, required to exceed 0.001 per cent of adult citizens, what exact number did this represent and who was authorized to decide that number? Why did the act not define an exact number, especially given that the rule for the registration of association requires just three founders?[25]

The Constitutional Court, however, ruled that this norm did not breach the prohibition of discrimination or contravene the principle of freedom of religion or the position of churches within the state. It stated that freedom of association is related to the Act on

---

[25] Whereas two to five founders are often sufficient for associations, for religious organizations ten or more are usually required in order to register. For example, Russia and Kazakhstan require ten members, Poland fifteen, Greece twenty, Hungary one hundred and the Czech Republic three hundred.

Associations, and that freedom of religion is given expression through the Act on Churches and Religious Communities. The understanding of the Constitutional Court was that there is no discrimination between traditional and non-traditional churches in the registration procedure, but that there is an acceptable difference governed by law. Support was also sought in the jurisprudence of the ECtHR, which in general recognizes differences as acceptable. The test was governed by several ECtHR standards, namely, whether the differences in the registration procedure had a legal aim, and whether the request was proportional to the defined legal aim. The justification for a different registration procedure and legal aim was found in the right to freedom of religion, or more specifically in the limitation of that right, in the provision of restrictions such as were necessary in democratic society, for the purposes of order, health, morals and security.

Yet another constitutional compliance issue emerged from the article governing the decision as to the eligibility of a religious organization to be included in the register of the Act on Churches and Religious Communities. The Ministry of Justice is able to reject the application of a religious organization to be included in the register if it finds that the aims, teaching, ceremonies or activities of the organization are contrary to the constitution and public order or if they endanger the life, health, freedom or rights of others, the rights of children, the right to personal and family integrity or the right to property. An especially interesting part of this provision is the requirement set for the ministry to take into account ECtHR decisions, as well as administrative or judicial decisions regarding the registration or activities of pertinent religious organizations in one or more member states of the European Union, when deciding on the application. The ministry is given a task that could be described as quasi-judicial. Deciding on the application in terms of the usual conditions (threat to public order, life, health and so on) is challenging enough. The obligation to take into account ECtHR decisions is a task only for a competent judicial institution, while European Union law is not the part of the Serbian legal regime. An explanation for the legal construction could be found only in the attempt of the legislative body to create a modern law that would guarantee deliberation according to the highest standards, an attempt which did not take into account the inappropriateness of such norms.

EUROPEAN COURT OF HUMAN RIGHTS JURISPRUDENCE ON CRITERIA FOR
THE LEGAL STATUS OF CHURCHES

At this point, it is useful to turn to the main criteria developed in
ECtHR jurisprudence considering the status of churches. In very
general terms, the governing principle for the ECtHR is pluralism
of religion as 'inseparable from a democratic society, and an overall
dependence of democracy on various kinds of differences and diver-
sities'.[26] Over several decades, the ECtHR, while interpreting the
scope of the article governing the freedom of religion, which protects
both religious and non-religious opinions and convictions, studied
churches and enumerated 'major' or 'ancient' churches,[27] new or
relatively new religions,[28] and various philosophical convictions.[29]

The ECtHR has acknowledged that European states recognize
three models of relations between states and religious communities
and each of them is found to be compatible with the ECHR.[30] A
state church, with a special constitutional status, is accepted in the

---

[26] This general attitude has been stated in numerous cases, such as Kokkinakis v. Greece,
§31; Buscarini and Others v. San Marino, §34.
[27] Alevism, a medieval syncretistic form of Islam (Sinan Işık v. Turkey; Cumhuriyetçi
Eğitim ve Kültür Merkezi Vakfi v. Turkey); Buddhism (Jakóbski v. Poland); the different
Christian denominations (for example, Sviato-Mykhaïlivska Parafiya v. Ukraine; Savez
crkava «Riječ života» and Others v. Croatia); Hinduism (Kovaļkovs v. Latvia); Islam
(Hassan and Tchaouch v. Bulgaria; Leyla Şahin v. Turkey); Judaism (Cha'are Shalom
Ve Tsedek v. France; Francesco Sessa v. Italy); Sikhism (Phull v. France; Jasvir Singh
v. France); Taoism (X. v. the United Kingdom).
[28] Aumism of Mandarom (Association des Chevaliers du Lotus d'Or v. France); the
Bhagwan Shree Rajneesh movement, known as Osho (Leela Förderkreis e.V. and
Others v. Germany); the Revd Sun Myung Moon's Unification Church (Nolan and
K. v. Russia; Boychev and Others v. Bulgaria); Mormonism, or the Church of Jesus
Christ of Latter-Day Saints (The Church of Jesus Christ of Latter-day Saints v. the
United Kingdom); the Raëlian Movement (F. L. v. France); Neo-Paganism
(Ásatrúarfélagið v. Iceland); the 'Santo Daime' religion, whose rituals include the use of
a hallucinogenic substance known as *ayahuasca* (Fränklin-Beentjes and CEFLU-Luz da
Floresta v. the Netherlands); Jehovah's Witnesses (Religionsgemeinschaft der Zeugen
Jehovas and Others v. Austria; Jehovah's Witnesses of Moscow and Others v. Russia).
[29] Pacifism (Arrowsmith v. the United Kingdom); principled opposition to military service (Bayatyan v. Armenia); veganism and opposition to the use of products of animal
origin or tested on animals (W. v. the United Kingdom); opposition to abortion
(Knudsen v. Norway; Van Schijndel and Others v. the Netherlands).
[30] Dalibor Djukic, 'Evropski sud za ljudska prava i autonomija crkava i verskih zajednica'
['The European Court of Human Rights and the Autonomy of Churches and Religious
Communities'], *Harmonius: Journal of Legal and Social Studies in South-East Europe* 1
(2013), 30–43.

same manner as a constitution which completely separates state and religious organizations, or the third model which is based on concordat-type relations. The ECtHR has adopted the stance that, in a situation where several religions coexist within the same national population, it may be necessary to place restrictions on freedom of religion in order to reconcile the interests of various groups and ensure that everyone's beliefs are respected.[31] In that case a state must include specific safeguards for individual freedom of religion. In particular, no one may be forced to enter, or be prohibited from leaving, a state church.[32]

Another important standard developed in the jurisprudence of the ECtHR is that mere tolerance by national authorities of the activities of a non-recognized religious organization is not a substitute for recognition, if recognition alone is capable of conferring rights on those concerned.[33] The ECtHR clarified this standard by adding that even where legislation expressly authorizes the operation of unregistered religious groups, that is insufficient if domestic law reserves exclusively for registered organizations with legal personality a whole series of rights essential for conducting religious activities.[34]

Regarding the recognition and registration of religious communities, the ECtHR recognizes the right of a state to verify and register a new religious organization, and to ensure that that entity is not engaged in activities for ostensibly religious purposes which are harmful to the population or endanger public security. In particular, refusal to register a religious organization may be justified by the need to establish whether it presents any danger to a democratic society or to the fundamental interests recognized by Article 9 of the ECHR.[35]

THE IDENTITY OF A CHURCH AS AN ELEMENT OF EQUALITY

Equality among ecclesiastical societies may be challenged by the question of identity. For example, Article 19 of the Serbian Act on Churches and Religious Communities prescribes that a name or

---

[31] Metropolitan Church of Bessarabia and Others v. Moldova, §§115–16.
[32] Ásatrúarfélagið v. Iceland, §27; Darby v. Sweden, §45
[33] Metropolitan Church of Bessarabia and Others v. Moldova, §129.
[34] Sviato-Mykhaïlivska Parafiya v. Ukraine, §122.
[35] Cârmuirea Spirituală a Musulmanilor din Republica Moldova v. Moldova; Church of Scientology of Moscow. v. Russia; Lajda and Others v. the Czech Republic.

part thereof denoting the identity of the church or religious community already listed in the register cannot be registered again.

In the organizational structure of Orthodox churches, it is very important to determine exactly who is the holder of the name and thus of the legal personality. Unlike the Roman Catholic Church, which is a single entity, Orthodox churches are separate and organized in a manner which is rooted in their centuries-long history and internal relations.[36] In the list of churches and religious communities in the Serbian Register, the provision of Article 19 means that the Serbian Orthodox Church is listed but that other entities including the word 'Orthodox' in their names are not found.[37] The Serbian Orthodox Church is the only Orthodox church in Serbia, and is defined as a traditional church in Article 10 of the Act on Churches and Religious Communities, reflecting eight centuries of autocephaly.

Questions of identity are beyond the law of the state, but for some churches they are still very present. This can be illustrated by considering Eastern Europe and questions of the relationship between identity and equality amongst the Orthodox churches. The Serbian Orthodox Church marked eight centuries as an autocephalous body in 2019; throughout that time it was the church for all Orthodox Christian believers in the territory of (what is now) ex-Yugoslavia. Since the break-up of Yugoslavia, nations with a majority of Orthodox Christian believers have tended to establish national Orthodox churches, some of which are struggling for autocephaly, as in Macedonia and Montenegro. These efforts have resulted in several legal cases, including one in Serbia and another before the ECtHR.

In Serbia the process was led by the Montenegrin Orthodox Church (MOC), which has never had autocephalous status. In 2007 the Association of Montenegrins in Serbia 'Krstas', requested the Serbian Ministry to register the MOC as a religious entity, that is, as a church. This application was rejected.[38] The legal process

---

[36] See further Timothy [Kallistos] Ware, *The Orthodox Church*, new edn (Harmondsworth, 1997), 5–8; Tim Grass, *Modern Church History* (London, 2008), 44–57.

[37] In contrast, a number of Christian denominations include 'Jesus' in their name. The reason for this lies in the differences between religions and churches: names of religions can be used in various versions, while the name of a church tends to be unique and recognizable.

[38] Republic of Serbia, Ministry of Religion, decision no. 080-00-45/2007-01, 18 June 2008.

afterwards went through the complete appeal procedure before the courts.[39] One of the key aspects was the name – and thus the identity – of the church. Since Article 19 of the Serbian Act on Churches and Religious Communities unequivocally forbids the inclusion of more than one church with the same name in the register of churches, the outcome of this legal battle was more than predictable. If we look at the legal issue in terms of the formal name, it appears straightforward. However, beyond the provisions of national legislation lies a more fundamental issue: can a non-autocephalous church, which is not recognized by other Orthodox churches, be recognized and registered by state authorities?

Another process involved the Orthodox Ohrid Archdiocese, renamed the Greek Orthodox Ohrid Archdiocese of Pecka Patrijarsija. This has been in a legal battle with the Former Yugoslav Republic of Macedonia (FYRoM) for almost two decades, and the case is at present before the ECtHR.[40] This process considers the legal status and identity of the archdiocese arising from canon law and national law.[41] The legal situation in this case is opposite to the previous one, since the Orthodox Ohrid Archdiocese has evolved from the original Ohrid Archdiocese established in 1018. After several transformations in its status during a period of nearly a millennium, it was finally defined as an autonomous archdiocese within the religious jurisdiction of the Serbian Orthodox Church and recognized as such by other Orthodox churches in 2005. Its legal status was challenged by the refusal of the legal authorities of the FYRoM to register it as a church, a decision which was rooted in the nation's law.[42] The

[39] The Supreme Court of Serbia delivered its judgment on 16 September 2009, ruling on procedural grounds that the complete appeal procedure must be gone through again: case no. U. 5625/2008.
[40] The procedure was formulated according to the Act on Religious Communities and Religious Groups (*Official Gazette*, no. 35/1997), and later the Act on the Legal Status of Churches, Religious Communities and Religious Groups (*Official Gazette*, no. 113/2007); ECtHR, Orthodox Ohrid Archdiocese (Greek Orthodox Ohrid Archdiocese of the Pec Patriarchy [*sic*]) v. The Former Yugoslav Republic of Macedonia, Judgment, 9 April 2018, online at: <https://hudoc.echr.coe.int/eng?i=001-178890>, accessed 21 August 2019.
[41] Dimšo Perić, *Crkveno pravo [Church Law]* (Belgrade, 2006), 23–5.
[42] The basis is in the Constitution of the Republic of Macedonia (1991), Article 19 and Amendment VII, available on the website of the Constitutional Court of the Republic of Macedonia, online at: <http://ustavensud.mk/?page_id=5353&lang=en>, accessed 21 August 2019.

Macedonian authorities maintained that the Orthodox Ohrid Archdiocese should be considered a part of the Macedonian Orthodox Church (MaOC), the main purpose of this being the benefit which the transfer of its autonomy would bring to the new MaOC.[43] The reaction by the Orthodox Ohrid Archdiocese was to amend its name to the Greek Orthodox Ohrid Archdiocese of the Pec Patriarchy [*sic*].[44] This was intended to make more obvious its nature and identity. At the same time, it left the MaOC with no ecclesiastical identity, since that church had never acquired autocephaly. However, an entity under that name does now exist in the eyes of the state, since it was recognized in the 1991 Macedonian Constitution (Article 19). In contrast, the archdiocese has instituted registration proceedings under both its names, and both applications have been rejected. The main arguments were that such an entity is ineligible since it is in canonical union with a foreign church, and that the name cannot be used if already registered. The ECtHR found breaches of freedom of religion (ECHR Article 9) and freedom of association (ECHR Article 11) in the refusal to register applicant associations as religious organizations.[45] According to the ECtHR judgment, Macedonia was therefore obliged to allow registration of the archdiocese. This Macedonian example is opposite to the Montenegrin, but with the same question: can a non-autocephalous church, that is, a church which is not recognized by other Orthodox churches, be recognized and registered by state authorities? Is it a church or an association?

In the Montenegrin example a canonically non-recognized church was denied its canonical and legal status. In the Macedonian example, a canonically recognized church was denied registration by the state institutions, while a constitutionally established church, even though not recognized canonically, has become the leading church in the state.

The right to freedom of thought, conscience and religion encompasses the obligation of the state to stay neutral when it comes to

---

[43] The name 'Macedonian Orthodox Church' was long used as a synonym for the Ohrid Archdiocese, which in canon law fell under the jurisdiction of the Serbian Orthodox Church; thus the MaOC was never autocephalous.

[44] The ECtHR gave the following explanation of the Pec Patriarchy: 'The Pec Patriarchy forms part of the name of the Serbian Orthodox Church and expresses the historical continuity of the Serbian Orthodox Church as canonical heir of the Pec Patriarchy': Orthodox Ohrid Archdiocese v. The Former Yugoslav Republic of Macedonia, Judgment, §30.

[45] Ibid., §121.

legal status of churches, especially those with a long history and complicated inner relations.[46] The *ratio* of such a registration is not in governing the emergence of churches, but rather in ensuring that new religious organizations are not harmful to society in terms of endangering public security, order, health, morals, rights and freedoms of others. Thus registration by state authorities cannot be a substitute for recognition according to canon law. An entity not recognized according to canon law may establish its legal personality on the legal ground of the right to freedom of association, but it is treated as an association, not a church.

From these examples, we may conclude that the identities of already existing religions and churches are complicated and multifaceted, grounded in both canon and state law and with the potential to endanger the absolute scope of the principle of equality. The identity of a church is substantially challenged if a state takes over the power of determining that identity, and so is the equality of believers. New religions and churches pose less complicated issues of identity and thus of equality, for they have no rivalry, no complicated history and are generally not politically motivated.

Both cases show that the question of ecclesial identity strongly affects the legal status of a religious organization, and thus the equality of churches and their believers. In legal terms, the question of identity is defined primarily in terms of canon law, whilst the question of equality is a matter of state law. These two cases show that even when states prescribe equality as the governing principle of the legal status of churches and develop this in legal acts, these external provisions must also be accompanied by provisions in canon law.

Conclusion

At the end of this short study, we may conclude that all the rights mentioned are consistent with one another in general, but that the law has its limitations. Freedoms of religion and association as human rights are prescribed and protected, not as absolute rights, but rather as limited ones. Believers should find their faith in religions

---

[46] The ECtHR has elaborated on the neutrality of the state more than once, for example, Hasan and Chaush v. Bulgaria, Judgment, 26 October 2000; Metropolitan Church of Bessarabia and others v. Moldova, Judgment, 13 December 2001; Mirolubovs and Others v. Latvia, Judgment, 15 September 2009.

and churches that are in compliance with both state law and canon law. Freedom of religion does not in essence support the emergence of new beliefs, and its intent is not the negation of traditional or major religions. States hold the right to prescribe the administrative procedure for the registration of churches, while protecting the freedom of individuals to express themselves through a new religion or church. States hold the right even to opt for a state church, as long as they safeguard the legal status of other churches and the freedom for individuals to choose their church and belief.

The law can address these relations relatively easily, so long as there are no major exceptions. However, the emergence of a new religion or a new church as a local manifestation of an old one can show the limitations of the law and the collision of rights and freedoms. For completely new religions and churches, the state is free to exercise its right to allow it or not, according to the law. A major problem is likely to arise in situations when there is a misunderstanding about whether a religion or a church is theologically new or not. The identity of a church is of utter importance for its legal status, leading to the potential inequality of churches. The inequality of churches leads to a breach of freedom of religion.

Identity as defined by religious thinking and churches, on the other hand, lies beyond the scope of state law. The major religions and churches are far older and more stable than states. Throughout the centuries, states and borders have changed, but religions and churches have been stable, gathering believers and often functioning as pillars of national identity. Law, rules and prescribed legal acts cannot delete centuries of religious tradition but instead must find a balance with it. Only when human rights, administrative law and canon law are in balance can the major governing principles, namely equality and identity, be applied.

History, Sacred History and law at the Intersection of Law, Religion and History

Peter W. Edge*

Oxford Brookes University

Lawyers, both practitioners and academics, engage with legal history in a variety of ways. Increasing attention is being paid to legal regulation of history and memory. This article argues that the interaction of law and history is particularly problematic within the context of a dispute with a religious element. It will use three case studies to illustrate these challenges: (1) The repeal of the Fradulent Mediums Act 1951 by the Consumer Protection from Unfair Trading Regulations 2008; (2) The Babri Masjid / Ram Temple dispute in Ayodhya, India; and (3) The Hindmarsh Island bridge controversy in South Australia. These case studies show the difficulties legal actors face when confronted with incompatible secular and sacred histories and diverse ways of 'knowing history', but also the importance, nonetheless, of understanding history in order to understand the relationship between law and religion.

This brief article argues that interaction between law and history, each with its own distinctive dynamics, is inevitable, and that this interaction has particular, important characteristics in the context of law and religion. Lawyers, both academic and practising, are sometimes keen to avoid engaging in historical debate. In the Indian litigation concerning the Ayodhya dispute, discussed below, Justice Khan noted that, 'having no pretence of knowledge of history, I did not want to be caught in the cross-fire of historians'.[1] Such a separation between law and history is not possible, and indeed Justice Khan himself, as I show below, made a number of findings of historical fact which then shaped his legal reasoning.

Legal actors will face competing, often incompatible, arguments as to historical facts as parties in a dispute seek to advance their present

---

* School of Law, Oxford Brookes University, Oxford, OX3 8EG. E-mail: pwedge@brookes.ac.uk.
[1] High Court of Judicature at Allahabad, Visharad and Ors v. Ahmad and Ors (2010), 277.

Studies in Church History 56 (2020), 508–528   © Ecclesiastical History Society 2020
doi: 10.1017/stc.2019.28

interests. This will require legal actors to engage with historical materials in a way which may be uncomfortable and, in the case of sacred histories, may involve some particularly difficult decisions around what type of historical evidence should be translated into legal evidence. The dynamics of the legal process can mean that determining these historical facts cannot simply be avoided by a state actor, particularly the judiciary. The complexity of historical processes may tempt a legal actor who cannot avoid this to seek to defer it, so that the dispute is resolved by an extra-legal process such as the political process, negotiation between the parties or direct action. Such deferral may itself create significant difficulties.

In exploring these ideas, we draw upon three case studies. All are based in the common-law family of legal systems, which share a common emphasis on particular sources and modes of legal reasoning, and an emphasis on the court as adjudicator between competing arguments put by the different parties. These case studies involve a change to consumer protection in England; the demolition of an ancient sacred site in India leading to national communal violence and at least 1,200 deaths; and an Australian bridge-building project that not only bankrupted the developers but led to a national debate over the rights of indigenous communities.

PROBLEMS IN LAWYERLY USES OF HISTORY

The interaction between law and history is inevitable, at least from a legal perspective. As Cahillane puts it, 'lawyers sometimes feel that history comes naturally to them ... [but] it only comes naturally in a certain way'.[2] While laws are occasionally presented as if their value depends upon their age, or rather lack of age, much of the corpus of materials that lawyers in the United Kingdom work with every day can equally be read as historical documents. A number of technical doctrines actively require lawyers to engage with the historical context of legal materials in order to state accurately their contemporary meaning. For instance, when interpreting an act of parliament, one of the common tools used by lawyers is the purposive approach, sometimes more narrowly stated as the 'mischief rule'. With this

---

[2] Laura Cahillane, 'The Use of History in Law: Avoiding the Pitfalls', in eadem and Jennifer Schweppe, eds, *Legal Research Methods: Principles and Practicalities* (Dublin, 2016), 55–65, at 57.

tool, in order to understand the meaning of a piece of legislation, the lawyer is required to determine what mischief it was intended to address, something hardly possible without some grasp of the context around its passage.[3] As another example, since the landmark decision in Pepper v. Hart the courts have recognized that the parliamentary debates during the passage of legislation can help to determine the meaning the legislation should be held to bear.[4]

Law, and legal materials, may also be seen as inevitable to the study of history. Legal documents can be mined by historians for many more uses than simply the study of the history of ideas in law.[5] Sugarman, for instance, has recently called for increasing dialogue between those working in history, legal history and socio-legal studies.[6] The legal process may also be consciously intended to create a historical record. A recent example of this can be found in work of various bodies set up in response to the civil war in Sierra Leone (1991–2002), which, in the words of the Sierra Leone Truth and Reconciliation Commission Act 2000, included the goal of creating 'an impartial historical record of violations and abuses of human rights and international humanitarian law',[7] as well as that of resolving individual cases.[8] I will leave for elsewhere the extent to which legal processes are particularly suited for determining historical facts. That trials, especially criminal trials, carry some sort of cultural marker of authoritativeness can perhaps be illustrated by the recurrent

[3] See, for example, DPP v. Bull (1995), QB 88.
[4] Elisabeth Laing, 'Pepper v Hart: Where are we, How did we get here, and Where are we going?', *Judicial Review* 11 (2006), 44–56.
[5] Russell Sandberg and Norman Doe, 'Textual and Contextual Legal History', in Norman Doe and Russell Sandberg, eds, *Law and History: Critical Conceptions in Law* (Abingdon, 2017), 1–27.
[6] David Sugarman, 'Promoting Dialogue between History and Socio-Legal Studies: The Contribution of Christopher W. Brookes and the "legal turn" in Early Modern English History', *Journal of Law and Society* 44 (2017), 37–60.
[7] Sierra Leone Truth and Reconciliation Act 2000, Part 3; see further the Sierra Leone Truth and Reconciliation Commission Report (2004), online at: <http://www.sierra-leone.org/TRCDocuments.html>, accessed 26 April 2018.
[8] See Joseph F. Kamara, 'Preserving the Legacy of the Special Court for Sierra Leone: Challenges and Lessons learned in prosecuting Grave Crimes in Sierra Leone', *Leiden Journal of International Law* 22 (2009), 761–77; Tiyanjana Mphepo, 'The Residual Special Court for Sierra Leone. Rationale and Challenges', *International Criminal Law Review* 14 (2014), 177–99; W. A. Schabas, 'A Synergistic Relationship: The Sierra Leone Truth and Reconciliation Commission and the Special Court for Sierra Leone', *Criminal Law Forum* 15 (2004), 3–54.

use of mock trials to 'resolve' historical controversies, for instance the theatrical trial of Richard III in 2018 for multiple murders, presided over by Lady Justice Hallett, who adjudicated in the real dispute over that king's remains,[9] or the various trials of Socrates, Henry VIII and George III.[10]

The interaction between these two disciplines is increasingly subject to critical consideration.[11] Perhaps the highest-profile area of controversy is in relation to Holocaust denial and, to bring in a less commonly discussed example, genocide assertion. The majority of European states now criminalize Holocaust denial, in some instances as part of a broader category of denial of particular historical facts which are treated as criminal.[12] In one case before the European Court of Human Rights, Holocaust denial was distinguished from the assessment of Pétain's role in Vichy France on the basis that it belonged to 'the category of clearly established historical facts ... whose negation or revision would be removed from the protection of the freedom of expression guaranteed under the European Convention on Human Rights.[13] Complex although the legal, historical and human rights issues are around Holocaust denial, these are exacerbated in relation to the mass killings of Armenians in 1915.[14] In 2005, Dogu Perincek was convicted in Switzerland of denying a genocide because of his description of Armenian genocide as 'a great international lie', although the European Court of Human Rights later found that in his particular case the necessary incitement of hatred or violence had not been demonstrated.[15] In 2007, Arat Dink and Serkis Seropyan were given suspended prison sentences

---

[9] See Shakespeare Schools Foundation, 'Trial of Richard III on 29 April 2018', online at: <https://www.shakespeareschools.org/support-us/trial>, accessed 26 April 2018.

[10] Gary Slapper, 'History on Trial', *Journal of Criminal Law* 79 (2015), 375–7.

[11] See Doe and Sandberg, eds, *Law and History*; Uladzislau Belavusau and Aleksandra Gliszczyńska-Grabias, eds, *Law and Memory: Towards Legal Governance of History* (Cambridge, 2017).

[12] Paolo Lobba, 'Holocaust Denial before the European Court of Human Rights: Evolution of an Exceptional Regime', *European Journal of International Law* 26 (2015), 237–53.

[13] Lehideux and Isorni v. France, Grand Chamber, App. 24662/94 (1998), §47.

[14] For an introduction to the legal issues, see V. Avedian, 'State Identity, Continuity, and Responsibility: The Ottoman Empire, the Republic of Turkey and the Armenian Genocide', *European Journal of International Law* 23 (2012), 797–820.

[15] See further his case in the European Court of Human Rights: Perincek v. Switzerland, GC, App. 27510/08 (2015).

under Article 301 of the Turkish Penal Code for printing Hrant Dink's assertion that the killing of Armenians in 1915 was a genocide.[16] So, to gloss over the complexities of criminal liability slightly, asserting the same historical fact may be compulsory in one European country and prohibited in another. Throw in the strategically ill-thought-out libel case brought by David Irving against Deborah Lipstadt and her publisher,[17] whose thirty-two days of trial are available as a complete transcript online,[18] and this area alone provides much food for thought, and has attracted considerable academic attention.[19]

Special Problems at the Intersection of Law, Religion and History

The focus of this article, however, is on particular problems posed by the intersection of law and history around a specific nexus, that of religion. I will seek to bring out these problems through discussion of three case studies, considering each at some length, before concluding by bringing out explicitly the challenges they illustrate.

The Consumer Protection from Unfair Trade Regulations 2008

We start with the surprisingly late demise of the Witchcraft Act 1735, section 4 of which punished specialist offences of pretending to exercise a range of supernatural powers. Although it was possible to bring criminal proceedings for frauds which seemed to fall within the provisions under general fraud law,[20] in the mid-twentieth century the specialist provision was seen as the most appropriate one to use in the historic case of Duncan,[21] discussed at length by Gaskill in his excellent monograph.[22]

---

[16] See the report on Bianet, online at: <https://m.bianet.org/english/media/102745-arat-dink-and-seropyan-sentenced>, accessed 7 September 2018.

[17] Irving v. Penguin Books Limited and Deborah E Lipstadt (2000), EWHC QB 115.

[18] See Emory University, 'Holocaust Denial on Trial: Trial Transcripts' (2000), online at: <https://www.hdot.org/trial-materials/trial-transcripts/>, accessed 26 April 2018.

[19] M. Bazyler, *Holocaust, Genocide and the Law: A Quest for Justice in a Post-Holocaust World* (Oxford, 2017).

[20] See for instance, Lawrence (1876), 36 LTR 404; Davis v. Curry (1918), 1 KB 109; Stonehouse v. Mason (1921), 2 KB 819.

[21] This reached the Court of Appeal as Duncan (1944), 1 KB 773, CA.

[22] Malcolm Gaskill, *Hellish Nell: Last of Britain's Witches* (London, 2001). It is also discussed, with a focus purely on legal issues of proof, in Peter W. Edge, 'Naturalism and

Helen Duncan was a spirit medium operating in war-time Portsmouth. She was initially arrested under the Vagrancy Act 1824 for an offence under section 4, which prohibited, *inter alia*, 'pretending or professing to tell fortunes, or using any subtle craft, means, or device, by palmistry or otherwise, to deceive'. It was decided to proceed with the more serious offence under the Witchcraft Act 1735, section 4 of which punished those who 'pretend to exercise or use any kind of Witchcraft, Sorcery, Inchantment or Conjuration, or undertake to tell Fortunes'.

Her conviction and imprisonment was a key part of the background to law reform. In 1951, following a campaign by the Spiritualists' National Union, the Fraudulent Mediums Act 1951 replaced the Witchcraft and Vagrancy Act provisions in relation to '[acting] as a spiritualistic medium or [exercising] any powers of telepathy, clairvoyance, or other similar powers', similar powers covering all activities within the professed practice of the ability to see beyond what are the normal powers of the human being. According to section 1 of the act, an offence was committed only when the defendant acted for reward, excluded 'anything done solely for the purposes of entertainment', and (crucially) required an intention to deceive.

One of the key features of the Fraudulent Mediums Act was the emphasis it gave to the belief of the defendant in what they were doing. It contrasted rather sharply with the way providers of spiritual services had sometimes been dealt with by the courts. My favourite example is Penny v. Hanson, in which an astrologer prosecuted under general fraud laws received short shrift from Justice Denman:

> It is nonsense to suppose that in these days of advanced knowledge the appellant really did believe he had the power to predict a man's future by knowing at what hour he was born, and the position of the stars at the particular moment of his birth. No person who was not a lunatic could believe he possessed such power.[23]

The Fraudulent Mediums Act survived substantial changes in criminal law, including even a wide-ranging Fraud Act in 2006. It did not, however, survive the Consumer Protection Regulations

---

Neutrality: Trying Miraculous Claims fairly in English Courts', *Journal of Church and State* 44 (2002), 521–37.
[23] Penny v. Hanson (1887), 18 QBD 478, at 480.

2008, which abolished the existing offence, aiming to regulate such activity under the consumer protection regime. Although obviously not a central issue in those regulations, before they came into effect it was confirmed that an important change would be the removal of any intent to deceive requirement in relation to suppliers of services covered by the Fraudulent Mediums Act.[24] Service providers within occulture in particular saw the change as a serious threat to their activities, or sometimes as a threat to their religious freedom. It led directly to the foundation of the Spiritual Workers Association.[25] Why did the founders of this association, and indeed others who lobbied against this change, have cause to be concerned?

The removal of the intent to deceive requirement means false claims are primarily assessed on their truth or otherwise, rather than the sincerity of the person making them. This could lead to statements of religious or non-scientific fact being treated as statements which can be resolved, as any other, by legal actors making findings of fact. To quote Justice Douglas in the US Supreme Court in *Ballard*, 'The miracles of the New Testament, the Divinity of Christ, life after death, the power of prayer are deep in the religious convictions of many. If one could be sent to jail because a jury in a hostile environment found those teachings false, little indeed would be left of religious freedom.'[26] In other words, therefore, when the Consumer Protection Regulations empower a Trading Standards Officer to determine whether a 'fortune teller on Epsom Downs'[27] is acting lawfully, it raises profound issues of the authority of the state over individuals' religious beliefs. Concern about the intersection of fraud, spiritualism and religious freedom had led directly to the Fraudulent Mediums Act 1951, but completely failed to be reflected in the Consumer Protection Regulations. Some historical reflection on the background to the 1951 legislation should have informed the 2008 legislative change.

---

[24] As discussed in David V. Barrett, 'Unintended Consequences', *Fortean Times* 237 (2008), 58–60.
[25] See 'The Law', online at: <http://www.theswa.org.uk/Public/Law.aspx>, accessed 11 July 2011.
[26] US v. Ballard, 322 US 78 (1944) US Supreme Court, at 87.
[27] A phrase used by Theo Mathew, Director of Public Prosecutions in 1952, to indicate unimportant cases of this kind: Gaskill, *Hellish Nell*, 347.

The Babri Masjid / Ram Temple Dispute[28]

The second case study concerns the Babri Masjid / Ram Temple dispute, also referred to as the Ayodhya dispute. Ayodhya is a North Indian town situated in the Faizabad district in the state of Uttar Pradesh. It has some connection with every major religion in India.[29] However, the important affiliations for our purposes are those that Hindus and Muslims have with the place.[30]

For Hindus, Ayodhya existed as a religious centre for many centuries.[31] In particular, Ayodhya is seen by Hindus as the birthplace of the Hindu god Ram, who went on to rule Ayodhya as his kingdom.[32] These events in the age of *Treta*[33] (the distant past) were followed by a period during which Ayodhya disappeared. In the present age, the site was located by King Vikramaditya.[34] In Hindu traditional accounts, although not necessarily archaeological or secular historical accounts, he constructed a huge temple on the birth site of Ram,[35] which was later destroyed by Muslims in order to construct Babri Masjid in

[28] This section draws on work with M. C. Rajan on the Ayodhya dispute, appearing as Peter W. Edge and M. C. Rajan, 'Sacred Sites and State Failures: A Case Study of the Babri Masjid / Ram Temple Dispute in Ayodhya', in M. J. H. Bhuiyan and D. Jensen, eds, *Law and Religion in the Liberal State* (Oxford, forthcoming).
[29] K. N. Panikkar, 'A Historical Overview', in Servapalli Gopal, ed., *Anatomy of a Confrontation: The Babri Masjid – Ram Janmabhumi Issue* (New Delhi, 1991), 22–37, at 25–6; Hans Bakker, *Ayodhya* (Groningen, 1984), 38.
[30] For more information on Ayodhya, see Gopal, ed., *Anatomy of a Confrontation*; for a contrasting view, Koenraad Elst, *Ram Janmabhoomi vs Babri Masjid* (New Delhi, 1990).
[31] Servapalli Gopal et al., 'The Political Abuse of History: Babri Masjid – Ramjanmabhumi Dispute, an Analysis by Twenty-Five Historians', in A. G. Noorani, ed., *The Babri Masjid Question 1528–2003: 'A matter of National Honour'*, 2 vols (New Delhi, 2003), 1: 28–32, at 30.
[32] Peter van der Veer, 'Riots and Rituals: The Construction of Violence and Public Space in Hindu Nationalism', in Paul R. Brass, ed., *Riots and Pogroms* (London, 1996), 154–76, at 160.
[33] In Hindu cosmology, cosmos passes through cycles within cycles for eternity. The basic cycle is the *Kalpa,* formed by a thousand *Mahayugas.* Each *Mahayuga* is divided into four *yugas* or ages, called *Krta, Treta, Dvapara* and *Kali.* Their lengths are respectively 4,800, 3,600, 2,400 and 1,200 'years of the Gods', and each year equals 360 human years. According to Hindu mythology, Rama spent his youth in Ayodhya and was king during the *Treta-yuga,* thousands of years before our present age, the *Kali-yuga.*
[34] Antony Copley, 'Indian Secularism Reconsidered: From Gandhi to Ayodhya', *Contemporary South Asia* 2 (1993), 47–65, at 57.
[35] Roger Friedland and Richard Hecht, 'The Bodies of Nations: A Comparative Study of Religious Violence in Jerusalem and Ayodhya', *History of Religions* 38 (1998), 101–49, at 106.

Peter W. Edge

1528, thus giving Hindu claims over the site temporal priority.[36] From the eighteenth century, Ayodhya was established as a major Hindu pilgrim centre in North India,[37] and by 1991 Bawa estimated there were six thousand Hindu temples in the area, with most of the trade and employment opportunities in serving pilgrims.[38]

The site was also a significant religious centre for Muslim pilgrims. As with the Hindu narrative, the Islamic narrative of the history of Ayodhya stresses the antiquity of the connection between religion and the site, long before conventional history might do so. Muslims argue that their attachment to Ayodhya dates back to the pre-Islamic period, with the burials of Seth and Noah at Ayodhya.[39] Both burial sites continue to attract a substantial number of religious visitors.[40] Ayodhya was ruled by Muslim kingdoms from (it is likely) the eleventh century. The first Mughal emperor defeated the ruler of Ayodhya in battle, and his governor built a mosque in Ayodhya in 1528.[41] Ayodhya is considered a *Khurd Mecca* (small Mecca), because of the large number of Muslim holy persons, including Sufi saints and other revered religious figures, who are believed to be buried there.

The pre-1528 history of the site, then, differs considerably between the two communities. This is reflected in how they see the events of 1528. Hindu groups, particularly *Sangh Parivar*,[42] allege that *Babar*, the first Mughal emperor, destroyed a magnificent and ancient Ram temple in order to build his Babri Masjid. The Muslim view is that the mosque was built on an empty space, and that there is no evidence of the demolition of a Hindu temple.[43] With the beginning of direct rule of the area by the British crown

[36] Peter van der Veer, '"God Must be Liberated!" A Hindu Liberation Movement in Ayodhya', *Modern Asian Studies* 21 (1987), 283–301, at 285–6.
[37] Peter van der Veer, *Gods on Earth: The Management of Religious Experience and Identity in a North Indian Pilgrimage Centre* (London 1988), 36.
[38] M. Bawa, 'Scenes from Ayodhya', *Sunday Times of India*, 3 November 1991, 18.
[39] Mohammad Jamil Akhtar, *Babri Masjid: A Tale Untold* (New Delhi, 1997), 10.
[40] T. Mahmood, 'Ayodhya, Ram and Islam', in Vinay C. Mishra with Parmanand Singh, eds, *Ram Janambhoomi, Babri Masjid: Historical Documents, Legal Opinions and Judgements* (New Delhi, 1991), 13–46, at 24–5.
[41] Akhtar, *Babri Masjid*, 11.
[42] *Sangh Parivar* translates as 'Family of Hindu Nationalist Organizations', an umbrella organization of Hindu nationalist groups.
[43] R. S. Sharma et al., *Ramjanmabhumi – Babri Masjid: A Historians' Report to the Nation* (New Delhi, 1991), 6–7.

in 1856, the stage was set for these and other community differences to begin to be worked out by litigation.[44]

In 1857, a Hindu priest took a part of the Babri Masjid compound and constructed a *chabutra,* a raised platform for idols. This was opposed by local Muslims, and the dispute was initially resolved by agreeing to raise a wall between the mosque and the *chabutra*, which was later called *Janmastan Temple.* The compromise did not suit either party, with Muslims and Hindus litigating over development of the temple.[45] The dispute reached the District Court in 1886. The judge rejected proposals to develop the temple on three grounds. Firstly, whilst it was unfortunate that a Masjid had been built on land specially held sacred by the Hindus, the event had occurred 356 years earlier and it was too late to remedy the grievance. Secondly, any change could produce more harm and derangement of order than benefit. Thirdly, there were no documents to support the claim of the Hindu priest to be the landowner.[46] Both parties were requested to maintain the status quo.[47]

During the final months of 1949, the controversy took an important new turn. A group of Hindu monks occupied a Muslim cemetery near the mosque, and ignited sacred fires to emphasize their claim that the area was originally a Hindu religious site.[48] Some days later, idols of Hindu gods including Ram were discovered inside the mosque. Although there is evidence that these had been placed there by human hands,[49] this was promoted as a miracle. As Gould observes, 'this miracle story created a local sensation. Hindus and Muslims flocked to the *Janmastan*, the former to bear witness to the miracle, the latter to defend the Babri Masjid against desecration and seizure by the Hindus'.[50] As the dispute exacerbated local

---

[44] Panikkar, 'Historical Overview', 31–3.

[45] Mahant Raghubar Das, Mahant of Janmastan, Ayodhya v. The Secretary of State for India in Council, Plaint dated 29 January 1885 (no. 61/280 of 1885); see Akhtar, *Babri Masjid*, 181.

[46] Judgment by F. E. A. Chamier, District Judge, Faizabad, 26 March 1886.

[47] Judgment by Judicial Commissioner W. Young, Oudh, 1 November 1886 (no. 1221 K/1886), in Noorani, ed., *Babri Masjid Question*, 1: 176–215, at 188.

[48] C. Jaffrelot, *The Hindu Nationalist Movement and Politics, 1925 to the 1990s* (London, 1996), 93.

[49] A. G. Noorani, 'Legal Aspects to the Issue', in Gopal, ed., *Anatomy of a Confrontation*, 63–77, at 70–1.

[50] H. A. Gould, *Grass Roots Politics in India: A Century of Political Evolution in Faizabad District* (Oxford, 1994), 181–96.

Peter W. Edge

tensions, the local authorities ordered the gates of Babri Masjid to be locked and prohibited both communities from using it, on the basis that the dispute was likely to lead to a breach of the peace. A receiver was appointed to arrange for the care of the property in dispute, and took charge of the property in January 1950.[51] The dispute was then tied up in suits and counter-suits, decades passing without a hearing of the substantive case.

In the interim, Ayodhya had begun the process of transformation into a national controversy.[52] In 1984, a Hindu nationalist organization initiated a movement to 'liberate' the *Ram Janmabhumi* and rebuild a magnificent Ram temple at Ayodhya. In 1986 a Hindu intervener who was not a party in any of the main suits secured an order allowing him free entry into the building for prayer, which had not been permitted since the interim order of 1950. In his order, Judge Pandey stated:

After having heard the parties it is clear that the members of the other community, namely Muslims, are not going to be affected by any stretch of imagination if the locks of the gates are opened and the idols inside the premises are allowed to be seen and worshipped by pilgrims and devotees. It is an undisputed fact that the premises are presently in the Court's possession and for the last 35 years Hindus have an unrestricted right of worship as a result of the Court orders of 1950 and 1951 (19.1.50 and 3.3.51). The District Magistrate has stated before me today that members of the Muslim community are not allowed to offer any prayer at the disputed site. If this is the state of affairs, then there is no occasion for law and order problem arising as a result of the removal of locks. It is absolutely an affair inside the premises.[53]

In consequence, there was a significant change in the site's status, from one that neither community was able to use as a place of worship to one that could be used by Hindus but not Muslims. This trajectory reached a violent apogee in 1992.

In October 1992 an organization of Hindu priests announced the resumption of religious voluntary work to rebuild Ram Temple from

[51] S. K. Tripati, 'One Hundred Years of Litigation', in Asgharali A. Engineer, ed., *Babri Masjid / Ramjanmabhoomi Controversy* (New Delhi, 1990), 15–42, at 20–1.
[52] Stacy D. Burlet, 'Challenging Ethnic Conflict: Hindu-Muslim Relations in India 1977–1993' (PhD thesis, University of Bradford, 1997), 191.
[53] Umesh Chandra Pandey v. State of UP and Others (1986), Civil Appeal no. 66/1986.

6 December 1992.[54] Although there was some official effort to protect the mosque, this did not translate into security on the ground,
despite a request by the Supreme Court. The Babri Mosque was
demolished by 150,000 volunteers, who proceeded to build an ad
hoc Ram temple on the site. After the demolition, the courts ordered
the relaxation of restrictions on Hindu worship on the site,[55] in part
because Ram was a 'figure constitutionally accepted as the Lord by the
builders of this nation and culture'.[56] The order was challenged
before the Supreme Court, who directed maintenance of the 'status
quo', that is to say, the former balance between Muslims and Hindus,
with the site open to Hindu worship but not Muslim worship.[57]

Although Babri Mosque had now been demolished, proceedings in
the High Court were restarted in January 1996 and continued until
judgment by the Allahabad High Court in September 2010. The protracted hearing resulted in three judgments totalling more than eight
thousand pages.[58]

All three judges noted the undesirability of the very long period
which had passed before the unlocking order of 1986 could be
resolved. Justice Sharma was perhaps the most blunt: 'the disputed
structure is not in existence, it has already been demolished'. There
was a notable willingness to make findings of fact as to the history of
the site: Justice Khan, for instance, found that the constructed portion of the premises under dispute had been built as a mosque under
the orders of Babar,[59] and that no temple had been demolished for its
construction.[60] Justice Sharma, on the other hand, found that such a
temple had existed, that it had been destroyed in order to build a mosque and that, under Islamic law, 'the disputed structure could not be

[54] 'Nothing can stop Kar Seva', *The Hindu*, 1 November 1992, 3.
[55] Judgment delivered on 1 January 1993 by Justices H. N. Tilhari and A. N. Gupta, in
Vishwa Hindu Parishad v. Union of India, in Noorani, ed., *Babri Masjid Question*, 2:
233–65, at 247–8.
[56] Akhtar, *Babri Masjid*, 173.
[57] Sara Ahmad, 'Judicial Complicity with Communal Violence in India', *Northwest
Journal of International Law & Business* 17 (1996), 320–50, at 334.
[58] For a fuller analysis of the decision, see Geetanjali Arcot Srikantan, 'Re-examining
Secularism: The Ayodhya Dispute and the Equal Treatment of Religions', *Journal of
Law, Religion and State* 5 (2017), 117–47, at 117.
[59] *Visharad and Ors v. Ahmad and Ors* (2010), 227.
[60] Ibid. 242.

a mosque as it was raised by force of arms on land belonging to the plaintiff deities'.[61]

The majority of the court (that is, two of the three judges) ruled that the site should be partitioned into three parts, roughly two-thirds Hindu, one-third Muslim. Justice Khan stressed the sharing of the site between Hindu and Muslim worshippers since before 1855, and from this found that both communities were in joint possession of the entire premises in dispute, although for convenience they were using and occupying different portions. The three parties (Muslims, Hindus and a named Hindu sect) were declared joint holders until formal partition. Proposals for partition were required within three months, but some areas were set aside for the non-Muslim parties. Justice Khan was joined by Justice Argawal, who endorsed the tripartite division but was more specific about areas set aside for the Hindus. He also stressed the role of the government of India in making their land available to allow 'separate entry ... of the people without disturbing each other's rights'. The dissenting justice, Sharma, found that the building was not, under shariah, a mosque, and that the land remained owned by the Hindu deities in the (pre-existing) temple. Government attempts to extinguish the sacredness of the place were beyond its competence.

Immediately after the judgment, the Indian prime minister appealed for peace, and suggested that the status quo, under which Hindus could use the site for religious purposes but Muslims could not, would be maintained until the Supreme Court took up the case. In May 2011 the Supreme Court stayed the verdict, describing it as 'strange and surprising'. It noted in particular that the High Court had granted a relief – partition – which had not been sought by any of the parties. Instead, all parties had sought exclusive rights over the entire precinct. The Supreme Court ordered the status quo to continue until the case was resolved by the Supreme Court. Supreme Court hearings began in February 2018, were suspended in March 2019 to attempt a court-ordered mediation, and resumed in August 2019. At the time of writing, proceedings are ongoing.

---

[61] Ibid. 14.

The Hindmarsh Island Bridge Controversy[62]

The final case study comes from Australia. A development company purchased land on Hindmarsh Island, in the Murray River estuary, and sought permission to replace the existing ferry with a bridge. Planning approval was granted, subject to an environmental impact study. That study was completed quickly, and identified the need for an anthropological study. This was carried out by Rod Lucas, who in 1990 reported that existing records did not record mythological sites, but cautioned that consultation with indigenous groups, particularly of the Ngarrindjeri, was needed. Planning permission was granted, but subject to the condition that there be consultation with 'relevant Aboriginal representative bodies', which did not take place. As the project developed, a complex relationship arose between the development company, a state-owned bank and the state government. In 1994 a government-appointed archaeologist, Dr Neil Draper, completed his survey of Hindmarsh Island and the mainland foreshore, identifying a number of significant sites which should be protected under existing legislation.

In 1994, at the request of the Ngarrindjeri, the federal government intervened, with an emergency declaration stopping work until Professor Cheryl Saunders, a lawyer, reported on these sites. One group with whom Saunders consulted was composed of Ngarrindjeri women, who claimed the island was sacred to them as a fertility site and for other reasons that could not be publicly revealed. An anthropologist, Dr Dean Fergie, prepared an assessment of these women's claims which was submitted to Saunders. In the process, some of these cultural secrets were written down and sealed in envelopes marked 'Confidential: to be read by women only'. The (male) minister for Aboriginal affairs received these with the assessment, and placed a twenty-five year ban on the project.

In February 1995 this decision was successfully challenged in the federal court by the development company. In the following month the shadow minister for the environment resigned after he had tabled some of the secret documents in parliament, having misrepresented how he had obtained them, and having not followed the instruction to keep them confidential and read by women only. In May 1995

---

[62] See Margaret Simons, *The Meeting of the Waters: The Hindmarsh Island Affair* (Sydney, 2003).

a number of dissident Aboriginal women stated that the 'secret women's business' must have been fabricated, as they either had no knowledge of it or did not believe it. In June a Royal Commission was appointed, which reported in December. It made no use of the contents of the envelopes, but found that the 'secret women's business' was not authentic. The Royal Commission emphasized that the way the secrets were revealed gradually was suspicious; that the secrets were not documented in the anthropological record; that testimony given by two dissidents supported the allegation of fabrication; that the 'secret women's business' should (to be consistent) have led to objection to earlier barrages, which had not been objected to on that ground; and that one ground for the objection was based on a sacred story about the Seven Sisters constellation which was not part of Ngarrindjeri, as opposed to western Aboriginal, beliefs.

The Ngarrindjeri brought another application for federal heritage protection, and a female senator appointed Jane Matthews, a female judge, as reporter, so that the proponent women would be able to refer to knowledge limited to women. In 1996 there was a change of government, and the new government refused to appoint a woman to receive the report; it also became clear that Australian law would not allow the women to rely on material that was not open to disclosure to other parties. Rather than disclose it, the women withdrew their restricted material from consideration by Matthews. The federal government proceeded to pass specific legislation to ensure the bridge could proceed;[63] this legislation survived constitutional challenge on the basis of racial discrimination.[64]

This was still not the end of the story. In the case of Chapman v. Luminis Pty Ltd (no. 5),[65] the developers, who had entered liquidation, sued a range of parties for financial loss suffered as a result of the delay in the building of the bridge from 1994 to 1999. The judge found against the developers, and in doing made findings critical of the Royal Commission decision. In particular, he considered that late and gradual emergence of sacred knowledge was not indicative of fabrication, that the lack of recording in the anthropological literature was not inconsistent with the material, and that the Seven Sisters

---

[63] Hindmarsh Island Bridge Act 1997.
[64] Kartinyeri v. Commonwealth (1988), HCA 22.
[65] Chapman v. Luminis Pty Ltd (no.5) (2001), FCA 1106.

story was plausible. The court dismissed the claims of fabrication, and found against the developers.

This decision was widely seen as a vindication of the claims to 'secret women's business'. In 2010 a government minister endorsed the finding of 2001 that this was genuine in a ceremony at the foot of the bridge; and Ngarrindjeri elders then led a symbolic walk across the bridge.[66]

SOME LESSONS

The first lesson, which I would draw from the Consumer Protection regulations, is that a lack of interest in history can result in an impoverishment of current law. Russell Sandberg, in his recent consideration of legal history through the lens of the employment status of ministers of religion,[67] argues that the modern law school culture suffers from 'presentism', a privileging of the present, and notes the decline of legal history in law schools over the last century. Legal history, however, has a powerful subversive potential, showing 'that every line drawn in the law and everything the law holds as sacred is arbitrary and that the environment that students are socialised into is a historical construct'.[68] Stewart and Kiyani have made a similar point in their recent critique of the ahistorical nature of analysis of international criminal law, seeing understanding of the legal history of international criminal law as providing an important resource to reduce partiality.[69] The difficulties for lawyers seeking to engage historically with issues of law and religion do not justify their failure to do so. In particular, there are legal structures which may make it crucial to adjudicate between different conceptions of continuity, as well as tactically useful.[70] We see this in particular in the Ayodhya case study, where the question of whether or not a Ram temple had

---

[66] See David Nason, 'Pain eases with Apology over Ngarrindjeri Secret Women's Business', *The Australian*, 7 July 2010, online at: <https://www.theaustralian.com.au/news/nation/pain-eases-with-apology-over-ngarrindjeri-secret-womens-business/news-story/14c6b440265844bda517322686d18925>, accessed 22 May 2018.
[67] Russell Sandberg, 'The Employment Status of Ministers: A Judicial Retcon?', *Religion and Human Rights* 13 (2018), 27–48.
[68] Ibid. 46.
[69] James G. Stewart and Asad Kiyani, 'The Ahistoricism of Legal Pluralism in International Criminal Law', *American Journal of Comparative Law* 65 (2017), 393–449.
[70] Sandberg, 'Employment Status of Ministers', 47.

been destroyed in the sixteenth century was returned to throughout the protracted litigation. As Mehta puts it, '[e]ach of the contending parties, and there are at least four, evokes the status quo to establish the legitimacy of its claims'.[71]

Secondly, the complexity of engaging with issues at the nexus of law, religion and history may tempt a state actor to seek to avoid doing so, in the hope that the dispute will be resolved by extra-legal mechanisms. The Ayodhya dispute shows the drawbacks of deferring engagement. For thirty-five years, from 1950 to 1985, the Ayodhya dispute remained a local dispute between a few members of two religious communities. There was no final legal resolution of the dispute before the 1992 demolition, and indeed the Supreme Court did not begin substantive hearings on the case until 2018. Delay has been described as the 'pathology of the Indian legal system',[72] and has been a long-standing cause of concern. Chodosh has suggested that the adversarial model is poorly designed to meet the needs of a rural population with widespread poverty, illiteracy and unfamiliarity with formal legal procedure, not least since most of it is conducted in the English language,[73] while Deshpande suggests that the legal system creates the opportunity for parties with a weak case to delay resolution against them.[74] Average delays in the civil process have been calculated at between ten and fifteen years,[75] and a similar level of delay can be found in cases before the higher judiciary.[76] However, in the Ayodhya dispute the delay was

---

[71] D. Mehta, 'The Ayodhya Dispute: Law's Imagination and the Functions of the Status Quo', in idem and R. Roy, eds, *Violence and the Quest for Justice in South Asia* (New Delhi, 2018), 291–321, at 293; see also Deepak Mehta, 'The Ayodhya Dispute: The Absent Mosque, State of Emergency, and the Jural Deity', *Journal of Material Culture* 20 (2015), 397–414.

[72] Oliver Mendelsohn, 'The Pathology of the Indian Legal System', *Modern Asian Studies* 15 (1981), 823–63, at 824.

[73] Hiram E. Chodosh et al., 'Indian Civil Justice System Reform: Limitation and Preservation of the Adversarial Process', *New York University Journal of International Law & Politics* 30 (1997–8), 1–78, at 29; see also R. Moog, 'Delays in the Indian Courts: Why the Judges don't take Control', *Justice System Journal* 16 (1992), 19–36, at 19, 22.

[74] V. S. Deshpande, 'Civil Procedure', in Joseph Minattur, ed., *The Indian Legal System* (Bombay, 1978), 177–209, at 201.

[75] Chodosh et al., 'Indian Civil Justice System Reform', 29.

[76] Mamta Kachwaha, *The Judiciary in India: Determinants of its Independence and Impartiality* (Leiden, 1998), 38.

extended to forty-two years, from 1950 to 1992, without even a preliminary hearing.

These issues of continuity and deferring judgment come together
in the seemingly technical issue of interim relief. Interim relief is an
order granted by the court intended to protect the rights of a party
until there has been a final determination of the substantive dispute.
The practical importance of interim relief is considerable, with Bean
suggesting that the English courts grant far more interim injunctions
than permanent ones.[77] In the Ayodhya dispute, interim relief, literally, spanned generations. The interim relief of 1950–1 barred
Muslims and Hindus from Babri Masjid; the 1986 opening of the
locks, a variation of that interim relief, turned the space into a
place of Hindu public worship. The fate of the site has, for generations, been dealt with as interim relief. Given that the purpose of
interim relief is to protect the rights of a party, identifying the status
quo that is in danger of being damaged if there is no interim relief has
been an important part of the work of the courts. One of the significant constitutional issues raised by demolition in 1992 is the flouting
of the authority of the courts in seeking to maintain some form of
status quo before the full hearing.

Thirdly, once a legal actor commits to engaging with history, the
nexus of law, religion and history may raise particular problems
around sacred history. Writing on the Ayodhya dispute in 1990,
Gopal concluded that the historical claims by the Muslim and
Hindu communities 'can find no sanction from history', and stressed
that while appropriation of history is a continual process in any society, 'in a multi-religious society like ours, appropriations which draw
exclusively on communal identities engender endless communal conflicts'.[78] History and archaeology have played a central role in the
framing of the legal dispute over ownership and use of the site.[79]
However, the sort of history which the different religious communities are asserting is particularly challenging. While the claims regarding the burial place of Noah are not easily susceptible to probing by
secular historians, the Muslim arguments are predominantly based on

---

[77] See Andrew Keay, 'Whither American Cyanamid? Interim Injunctions in the 21st
Century', *Civil Justice Quarterly* 23 (2004), 132–51.
[78] Servapalli Gopal et al., 'The Political Abuse of History: Babri Masjid – Rama
Janmabhumi Dispute', *Social Scientist* 18 (1990), 76–81, at 80–1.
[79] See Shereen Ratnagar, 'Archaeology at the Heart of a Political Confrontation: The
Case of Ayodhya', *Current Anthropology* 45 (2004), 239–59, at 239.

a time frame with which such historians may find it comparatively easy to discover common ground. The 'Old Earth Creationism' of the Hindu arguments, with Ram having been born nine million years ago and the Ayodhya Temple having been built in 100 BCE,[80] is more challenging for a court which does not share that religious frame. As Mehta puts it, 'two temporal registers, asymmetric and incommensurate, are entangled with each other – historic time and mythic time. The first is based on rules of evidence drawn from empirical detail, while the second provides a kind of habit within which belief and faith are mobilised'.[81] These different types of history may coexist not only in a case but also in the arguments put forward by a single party. In their discussion of the use of architecture in Ayodhya, Bernbeck and Pollock put it this way:

> Why, in a case such as Ayodhya, in which many Hindu partisans are firmly convinced that a temple did exist under the mosque regardless of any 'proof' and / or that the place is a holy one for Hindus, is archaeological evidence necessary? We suggest that archaeological testimony is primarily a tool to be used to try to convince other, more skeptical audiences (for example, the Indian Supreme Court) because it provides tangible evidence such as the physical remains of a building interpretable as a temple.[82]

The Hindmarsh Island Bridge case shows that, even within a secular frame, different ways of conveying historical knowledge which arise from their religious context can pose real challenges to lawyers who seek to engage with historical information in a particular way.[83] The proponents of the 'secret women's business', and those who opposed them, all framed the debate in historical terms. The key legislation described its purpose as 'the preservation and protection from injury or desecration of ... areas and objects that are of particular significance to Aboriginals in accordance with Aboriginal tradition'.[84] The sociological question of whether an area was of particular significance to Aboriginals was not sufficient: that importance had to be in

---

[80] See the summary in Gyanendra Pandey, 'Modes of History Writing: New Hindu History of Ayodhya', *Economic and Political Weekly* 29 (1994), 1523–8.
[81] Mehta, 'Absent Mosque', 398.
[82] Reinhard Bernbeck and Susan Pollock, 'Ayodhya, Archaeology, and Identity', *Current Archaeology* 37, supplementary issue (1996), S.138–42, at S.141.
[83] See Michael F. Brown, *Who owns Native Culture?* (Cambridge, 2005).
[84] Aboriginal and Torres Strait Islander Heritage Protection Act 1984, Section 4.

accordance with Aboriginal tradition.[85] Accordingly, the key question was whether the 'secret women's business' was a traditional part of the culture of the Ngarrindjeri. The proponents ran straight into two expectations as to how historical knowledge should be accessed.

The Royal Commission was strongly influenced by the absence of any record of the practice in the report by a male anthropologist who had carried out an in-depth study of the group in the 1940s; the rather reasonable comments by Dr Jane Jacobs that a male anthropologist walking into the tribe in the 1940s might not have directed his attention towards women's secrets, and that, even if he had, he would not have got very far, were not taken on board by the commission. The issue of gender-specific knowledge was hotly contested by anthropologists on both sides in the 2001 court case, and evaluating the anthropological evidence was an important part of the judgment.[86] To state it at its simplest, the problem here is that esoteric religious traditions may well be less well documented by outsiders than exoteric ones.

Additionally, women who claimed to have key evidence to resolve this important factual issue would only permit it to be shared with other women. A strong constitutional norm in Australia is that parties should have access to the evidence supporting another party's case; another norm, less historically entrenched, is that decision making should not depend upon the gender of the decision maker. The claims of the proponent women to secret knowledge could not be reconciled with these norms, and attempts to accommodate the women led to significant political, and indeed legal, problems. The decision not to accommodate them, while it can be seen as 'a denial of natural justice',[87] can also be seen as compliant with a broader norm. As Harris puts it, the case shows 'the essential incompatibility of the two systems of law – the emphasis upon disclosure and the law's

[85] See further James F. Weiner, 'Culture in a Sealed Envelope: The Concealment of Australian Aboriginal Heritage and Tradition in the Hindmarsh Island Bridge Affair', *Journal of the Royal Anthropological Institute* 5 (1999), 193–210, at 193.
[86] See Gary Edmond, 'Thick Decisions: Expertise, Advocacy and Reasonableness in the Federal Court of Australia', *Oceania* 74 (2004), 190–230; more broadly, Larissa Vetters and Marie-Claire Foblets, 'Culture all around? Contextualising Anthropological Expertise in European Courtroom Settings', *International Journal of Law in Context* 12 (2016), 272–92.
[87] Marcia Langton, 'The Hindmarsh Island Bridge Affair: How Aboriginal Women's Religion became an Administerable Affair', *Australian Feminist Studies* 11 (1996), 211–17, at 211.

need to know against the essential secret nature of some of the beliefs of Aboriginal peoples'.[88]

To conclude, the nexus of law, religion and history poses some particular challenges for legal actors. These legal actors need to resist the temptation not to engage with historical issues, not least because it is sometimes essential in the light of the internal dynamics of the legal process. A failure to confront the historical dimension also impoverishes the formulation of legal answers to legal problems. For scholars, the existing movement to reinvigorate the understanding of the interaction between law and history needs to take account of the particular challenges of sacred history. Such sacred histories may be mythical, esoteric and gendered in ways which are particularly difficult to slot into lawyerly understandings of history and evidence.

---

[88] Mark Harris, 'The Narrative of Law in the Hindmarsh Island Royal Commission', *Law Context: A Socio-Legal Journal* 14 (1996), 115–39, at 115.